The Routledg... Student's ...

TH. WI...

It is clear that, in the contemporary world, a wide range of practitioners in diverse professional settings, need to study beyond master level. Students across the world are choosing doctorates not only to become career academics, but also to go beyond the academic arena, in order to make a personal and educational, as well as an economic investment, in their workplace careers and their lives. However, for many doctoral students, both full-time and part-time, navigating the literature and key issues surrounding doctoral research can often be a challenge.

Bringing together contributions from key names in the international education arena, *The Routledge Doctoral Student's Companion* is a comprehensive guide to the literature surrounding doctorates, bringing together questions, challenges and solutions normally scattered over a wide range of texts. Accessible and wide-ranging, it covers all doctoral students need to know about:

- What doctoral education means in contemporary practice
- Forming an identity and knowledge as a doctoral student
- The big questions that run throughout doctoral practice
- Becoming a researcher
- The skills needed to conduct research
- Integrating oneself into a scholarly community.

Offering an extensive and rounded guide to undertaking doctoral research in a single volume, this book is essential reading for all full-time and part-time doctoral students in education and related disciplines.

Pat Thomson is Professor of Education at the University of Nottingham, and an Adjunct Professor at the University of South Australia and a Visiting Professor at Deakin University, Victoria, Australia.

Melanie Walker is Professor of Higher Education at the University of Nottingham, and is also Extraordinary Professor at the University of the Western Cape, South Africa.

The Routledge Doctoral Student's Companion

Getting to grips with research
in Education and the Social Sciences

Edited by
Pat Thomson and Melanie Walker

Routledge
Taylor & Francis Group

LONDON AND NEW YORK

This first edition published 2010
by Routledge
2 Park Square, Milton Park, Abingdon, Oxon, OX14 4RN

Simultaneously published in the USA and Canada
by Routledge
270 Madison Avenue, New York, NY 10016

Routledge is an imprint of the Taylor & Francis Group, an informa business

© 2010 Pat Thomson and Melanie Walker for selection and editorial material. Individual chapters, the contributors.

Typeset in Bembo by
Taylor & Francis Books
Printed and bound in Great Britain by
TJ International Ltd, Padstow, Cornwall

British Library Cataloguing in Publication Data
A catalogue record for this book is available from the British Library

Library of Congress Cataloging in Publication Data
The Routledge doctoral student's companion: getting to grips with research in education and the social sciences / edited by Pat Thomson and Melanie Walker. – 1st ed.
    p. cm.
1. Education–Study and teaching (Graduate)–Handbooks, manuals, etc. 2. Education–Research–Handbooks, manuals, etc. 3. Social sciences–Research–Handbooks, manuals, etc. 4. Social sciences–Study and teaching (Secondary)–Handbooks, manuals, etc. 5. Doctoral students–Handbooks, manuals, etc. I. Thomson, Pat, 1948- II. Walker, Melanie. III. Title: Doctoral student's companion.
    LB2372.E3R68 2010
    370.7'2–dc22

                                    2009044881

ISBN10: 0-415-48411-1 (hbk)
ISBN10: 0-415-48412-X (pbk)
ISBN10: 0-203-85224-9 (ebk)

ISBN13: 978-0-415-48411-4 (hbk)
ISBN13: 978-0-415-48412-1 (pbk)
ISBN13: 978-0-203-85224-8 (ebk)

Contents

List of figures

List of tables

Notes on Contributors

Adamson, Bob PhD is Professor of Curriculum Studies at Hong Kong Institute of Education. He publishes in the areas of curriculum, education policy, comparative education and teacher education. His recent publications include *China's English: a history of English in Chinese education* (Hong Kong University Press, 2004) and *Comparative education research approaches and methods* (edited with Bray and Mason), published by CERC and Springer.

Anderson, Gary PhD is Professor of Educational Leadership in the Steinhardt School of Culture, Education, and Human Development. His most recent books are *The Action Research Dissertation* (Sage, 2005, with Kathryn Herr) and *Advocacy Leadership: Toward a Post-Reform Agenda* (Routledge, 2009).

Ball, Stephen PhD is the Karl Mannheim Professor of Sociology of Education in the Department of Educational Foundations and Policy Studies, Institute of Education, London UK. He is currently researching: the relationships between philanthropy and education policy, policy enactments in secondary schools, the educational strategies of the black middle class as well as an international study of the global middle class with colleagues in Spain, Argentina, France, Australia and the USA. His most recent books are: Ball, S.J. (2008) *The education debate: policy and politics in the 21st Century*. Bristol: Policy Press; Ball, S.J. (2007) *Education plc: private sector participation in public sector education*. London: Routledge; Ball, S.J. (2006) *Education Policy and Social Class: Selected Works (World Library of Educationalists)*. London: Routledge; and Ball, S.J. (2004) *The RoutledgeFalmer Reader in Sociology of Education*. London: RoutledgeFalmer.

Barr, Jean PhD is Emeritus Professor of the University of Glasgow, and until 2009 was its Professor of Adult and Continuing Education. Her research interests incorporate popular and higher education. Her most recent book, *The stranger within: on the idea of an educated public*, combines a historical study of the Scottish tradition of the 'democratic intellect' with philosophical analysis, drawing on academic and popular traditions locally and globally.

Bathmaker, Ann–Marie PhD is Professor of Education at the University of the West of England, Bristol. Her research focuses on vocational and postcompulsory education, and new forms of higher education. She is particularly interested in constructions of teaching and learning in changing policy and socio-economic contexts, and the implications for social justice, equity and human agency.

Brown, Andrew PhD is Professor of Education and Dean of the Doctoral School at the Institute of Education, University of London. His research interests include the relationship between every day, professional and academic discourse and practice, the process of research capacity building and research education. His recent publications include *Doing Research/Reading Research: Re-interrogating Education* (with Paul Dowling, 2010, Routledge) and *Working with Qualitative Data* (with Will Gibson, 2009, Sage).

Cole, Peter PhD, is an Associate Professor in Aboriginal & Northern Studies, University College of the North. His research interests include orality, narrativity, First Nations education and self-determination, environmental thought, and Aboriginalising methodology. He is the author of *Coyote and Raven Go Canoeing: Coming Home to the Village* (McGill–Queens University Press, 2006) and co-editor of *Speaking for Ourselves: Environmental Justice in Canada* (UBC Press, 2009).

Colley, Helen PhD is Professor of Lifelong Learning at the Education and Social Research Institute at Manchester Metropolitan University UK. She is also a Fellow of the National Institute of Careers Education and Counselling (NICEC): www.crac. org.uk/nicec Her research interests are in postcompulsory, informal and lifelong learning; professional roles, identities and practices; youth transitions; mentoring; vocational guidance and career development; vocational learning; gender, class, and social justice in education and learning; emotion and learning; critical feminist theory. She is currently working on an ESRC funded project investigating the impact of 14–19 reforms on career guidance. Her most recent book is Colley, H., Boetzelen, P., Hoskins, B., and Parveva, T. (Eds) (2007) *Social inclusion for young people: breaking down the barriers*. Strasbourg: Council of Europe.

Da Silveira Duarte, Joana PhD has recently completed her PhD at the University of Hamburg on the topic of second language learning and bilingual school models. She is now working as a junior lecturer at the University of Cologne, Germany. She is involved in several European projects concerned with the educational achievement of migrants within Europe. She is the Main Convenor of the Postgraduate Network of the European Educational Research Association (EERA).

Garman, Noreen PhD is Professor of Education in Administrative and Policy Studies, School of Education, University of Pittsburgh, USA. Her current research is examining nanotechnology undergraduate education and she also works as a curriculum consultant for the Andy Warhol Museum. Her most recent books are Piantanida, M. and Garman, N. (in press) *The Qualitative Dissertation: A Guide for Students and Faculty*, 2nd edition. Thousand Oaks, CA: Corwin Press; and Garman, N. and Piantanida, M. (2006) *The Authority to Imagine: The Struggle toward Representation in Dissertation Writing*, NY: Peter Lang Publishers.

Gasper, Des PhD is Professor of Human Development, Development Ethics and Public Policy at the Institute of Social Studies (Erasmus University Rotterdam), The Hague. His research interests are in policy discourse and theories of well–being and human development. Publications include *Arguing Development Policy* (Frank Cass, 1996), *The Ethics of Development* (Edinburgh UP, 2004), and *Development Ethics* (Ashgate, 2010).

Gorard, Stephen PhD is Professor of Education Research at the University of Birmingham. He researches in many fields including adult participation, educational choice, school improvement, student perspectives, and policy evaluations. Recent publications include *Equity in Education* (Palgrave, 2010), *Overcoming the barriers to HE* (Trentham, 2007), and 'Serious doubts about school effectiveness' (*British Educational Research Journal*, 2010).

Gorur, Radhika is a doctoral student at the University of Melbourne, Australia. Her research interests include education policy, evidence-based policy making, PISA and actor-network theory. Radhika was the founding student co-ordinator of the Universitas 21 Forum for International Networking in Education (FINE).

Gu, Qing PhD is a senior research fellow at the School of Education, University of Nottingham, UK. Her research interests are teacher professional development, school leadership and improvement and intercultural learning. She is author of *Teacher Development: Knowledge and Context* (Continuum, 2007) and co–author of *Teachers Matter* (Open University Press, 2007), a forthcoming book *New Lives of Teachers* (Routledge) and an original paper on mixed methods research published in *Educational Researcher* in 2008.

Gulson, Kalervo PhD is an Assistant Professor in the Department of Educational Studies, University of British Columbia. His current research examines connections between education markets in K–12 schooling, gentrification, and inequality in inner city areas of London, Sydney and Vancouver. His work has been published in *Race, Ethnicity and Education, Journal of Education Policy* and *Urban Studies*.

Herman, Chaya PhD is a senior lecturer at the department of education policy at the University of Pretoria, South Africa. Her research interest is doctoral education in South Africa. Her most recent publication is 'Political transformation and research methodology in doctoral education' (*Higher Education*, published online 29 July 2009).

Herr, Kathryn PhD is a Professor of Educational Foundations at Montclair State University, Montclair, NJ, USA. Her research interests include equity in education, action/practitioner research, gender issues and youth studies. Recent publications include *The Action Research Dissertation* (2005) (with Gary Anderson).

Kamler, Barbara PhD is emeritus professor at Deakin University, Melbourne, Australia. Her research explores the theory and practice of writing across the life span, from early childhood to old age, in primary, secondary, university and community contexts. Her current work focuses on doctoral education and early career writing and publication. Recent book publications include *Helping Doctoral Students Write: Pedagogies for Supervision* (with Pat Thomson, Routledge, 2006) and *Publishing Pedagogies* *for the Doctorate and Beyond* (co-edited with Claire Aitchison and Alison Lee, Routledge, 2010).

Lingard, Bob PhD is a Professorial Research Fellow in the School of Education at The University of Queensland, Australia. His research interests are education policy and gender and schooling. His most recent books are (with Wayne Martino and Martin Mills) *Educating Boys* (Palgrave, 2009) and (with Fazal Rizvi) *Globalizing Education Policy* (Routledge, 2010). He also has an in-press edited collection (with Trevor Gale) *Research by Association* (Sense).

Lucas, Robert is a PhD student at the Stanford University School of Education. His research interests include online teacher knowledge sharing, history education, digital textbooks, and Open Educational Resources. He is a former middle school teacher and holds a BA and MEd from Harvard University.

McLean, Monica PhD is an Associate Professor and Reader in Higher Education in the School of Education at the University of Nottingham. Her research interests focus broadly on pedagogy, social justice and the applications of critical theory in higher education. Her book *Pedagogy and the University: Critical Theory and Practice* (Continuum, 2008) contains her main ideas.

McWilliam, Erica PhD is Professor of Education in the Centre for Research into Pedagogy and Practice, NIE, Singapore. She is also an Adjunct Professor in the Australian Centre of Excellence in Creative Industries and Innovation. Erica's scholarship covers a wide spectrum, as is evidenced in her numerous publications on creativity, innovative teaching and learning, research methodology and training and educational leadership and management.

Menter, Ian PhD is Chair of Teacher Education at the University of Glasgow in Scotland. He has been President of the Scottish Educational Research Association (2005–7) and is also a member of the Executive Council of the British Educational Research Association. He represents the Scottish Association on the Council of the European Educational Research Association and is currently the Senior Mentor for EERA's Postgraduate Network.

Nixon, Jon PhD has held chairs at four institutions of higher education within the UK. His most recent publications include *Towards the Virtuous University* (Routledge, 2008) and (Ed. with Lingard and Ranson) *Transforming Learning in Schools and Communities* (Continuum, 2008). He is currently working on *Higher Education and the Public Good* (Continuum, 2010).

Noyes, Andy PhD is Associate Professor of Education at the University of Nottingham, England. His research interests are centred in mathematics education, although his research covers a range of concerns. He is currently directing two major mixed-methods studies of 14–19 mathematics education in England.

O'Riley, Pat PhD is an Associate Professor in the Dept. of Equity Studies, York University. Her research interests include research methodology; culturally, socially and environmentally relevant technology discourses in education; and Indigenous thought. She is the author of *Technology, Culture and Socioeconomics: A Rhizoanalysis of Educational Discourses* (Peter Lang, 2003), and co-editor of *Speaking for Ourselves: Environmental Justice in Canada* (UBC Press, 2009).

Paré, Anthony PhD is a professor in the Department of Integrated Studies in Education at McGill University, Montreal, Canada. His research areas include academic and workplace writing, rhetorical genre theory, discourse practices, situated learning, and doctoral education. He teaches courses in literacy, writing theory, discourse theory, and academic writing. He is Editor of the *McGill Journal of Education*.

Parkes, Rob PhD is Deputy Head of School (Teaching and Learning) and Senior Lecturer in Curriculum Theory, History Education, and Media Literacy, in the School of Education, at the University of Newcastle, Australia. His scholarship is built along two axes of concern focusing on 'knowledge, curriculum, and the representation problem', and 'disciplinarity, pedagogy, and self-formation'.

Piantanida, Marie PhD is an adjunct associate professor in the schools of education at Carlow University and the University of Pittsburgh in Pennsylvania. Her academic interests include epistemological and methodological issues of interpretive dissertation research conducted by scholar-practitioners within professional work contexts. Her most recent publication is the 2nd edition of *The Qualitative Dissertation: A Guide for Students and Faculty* (Corwin Press, 2009), co-authored with Dr. Noreen Garman.

Pillow, Wanda PhD is Associate Professor of Educational Policy Studies at the University of Illinois. Her interests include qualitative methodologies and analyses of gender, racialisation, sexuality and class as related to issues of representation, power and access. Author of *Unfit Subjects: Teen mothers and Educational Policy* (Routledge, 2004), she is continuing research on educational access and teen mothers and completing projects on Sacajawea, an iconic American Indian woman.

Pryor, John PhD is a Reader in Education at the University of Sussex. His research focuses on social identity and equity aspects of education and includes formative assessment and pedagogy, the doctorate in the social sciences, international and inter-cultural study. John has directed research projects in both the UK and sub-Saharan Africa, mostly of a broadly micro-sociological nature including collaborative ethnography and action research.

Soudien, Crain PhD of the University of Cape Town has published in the areas of social difference, culture, educational policy, comparative education, educational change, public history and popular culture. He is the co-editor of three books on District Six, Cape Town and the author and/or co-author of two books on the sociology of identity and inclusion.

Su, Feng PhD is a research fellow at Liverpool Hope University. His primary research interest is in cross-cultural learning contexts and the development of the learner within higher education settings. He is currently working on a co-edited text (with Adamson and Nixon), *The Reorientation of Higher Education: compliance and defiance*.

Szkudlarek, Tomasz PhD is Professor at University of Gdansk, where he chairs Department of Philosophy of Education and Cultural Studies in Institute of Education, Faculty of Social Sciences. His interests are contemporary philosophies of education and theories of subjectivity. His publications include 'Empty signifiers, education and politics', *Studies in Philosophy and Education* 26, 2007; and *The Problem of Freedom in Postmodern Education* (Bergin and Garvey, 1993).

Tan, Jennifer Pei-Ling PhD is a Research Fellow at the ARC Centre of Excellence for Creative Industries and Innovation in Queensland University of Technology, Australia. Her research focuses on (i) the adoption and diffusion of contemporary technologies in formal and informal learning environments, and (ii) creativity, multi-literacies and equity issues in educational policy and practice.

Thomson, Pat PhD is Professor of Education in the School of Education, The University of Nottingham and an Editor of the *Educational Action Research Journal*. A former headteacher, her current research focuses on the arts and creativity in school and community change, headteachers' work, and doctoral education. Her recent publications include *Helping doctoral students write: pedagogies for supervision* (with Barbara Kamler, Routledge, 2006); *Doing visual research with children and young people* (Routledge, 2008); and *School leadership-heads on the block?* (Routledge, 2009).

Wagner, Jon PhD is Professor Emeritus in the School of Education at the University of California, Davis. He is a past President of the International Visual Sociology Association and was the founding Image Editor of Contexts, the American Sociological Association's general interest publication. His current research focuses on children's material culture, qualitative and visual research methods, teaching and school change.

Walker, Melanie PhD is Professor of Higher Education in the School of Education, The University of Nottingham. Her research explores the normative purposes of higher education and its potential contribution to more equal societies under contemporary policy and economic conditions, and to poverty reduction. She is co-editor of the *Journal of Human Development and Capabilities*. Her recent publications include: Walker, M. and Unterhalter, E. (Ed.) (2007) *Amartya Sen's Capability Approach and Social Justice in Education*. 1st edn. Palgrave; and Walker, M. (2006). *Higher education pedagogies*. Maidenhead: Open University Press.

Wellington, Jerry PhD is a professor and head of research degrees in the School of Education at the University of Sheffield. He has supervised a large number of PhD and professional doctorate students, and has been external examiner for a wide range of doctoral theses at universities in the UK and overseas. Currently, his main interests are in research methods and in postgraduate education. He has written many journal articles and books on education, methods and methodology, and the role of new technology in education.

Williams, Kevin PhD is a lecturer in the Higher and Adult Education Studies and Development Unit, Centre for Higher Education Development, at the University of Cape Town. With a research background in the sociology of pharmacy, and only recently having moved into higher education research he is pursuing a growing interest in agency and student learning in higher education with particular focus on masters and doctoral learning.

Willinsky, John PhD is Professor of Education at Stanford University and the University of British Columbia, as well as director of the Public Knowledge Project, which is dedicated to doing research and development work that is aimed at improving the public and scholarly quality of academic publishing.

Yates, Lynn PhD is Professor of Curriculum and Pro Vice-Chancellor (Research) at the University of Melbourne, and she is a past President of the Australian Association for Research in Education. Her research interests are in education policy, knowledge, inequality, identities and the changing world. She is actively involved in doctoral education and supervision. Her book *What does good education research look like? Situating a field and its practices* (Open University Press, 2004) is particularly relevant for doctoral students.

Part 1

Introduction

Why *The Doctoral Companions?*

P. Thomson and M. Walker

The Doctoral Companions are designed for doctoral researchers and their supervisors/advisers to read separately and together. The two volumes are neither advice books nor commentaries on the experiences of doctoral research and supervision. Their purpose is to provide complementary and situating commentary about doctoral research and to map key debates that work in and around the burgeoning research methods and doctoral literatures.

Indeed, there are an ever-expanding number of books available to support doctoral research – doing it-guides, toolkits and advice books, methods books, research and evidence-informed policy and practice and how-to-get published. There are countless methodology and methods texts. There is a growing literature on the changing nature of the doctorate, on the doctorate in different parts of the world, on the doctorate and the knowledge economy, on supervision, student experiences and the viva. However, this extensive literature is difficult for doctoral researchers and their supervisors to navigate and will thus not necessarily take students forward in their own doctoral projects. Supervisors are often unaware that their students are consulting advice books and, due to the existence of postgraduate methods training courses, may assume that students understand the nature of the enterprise in which they are involved. Their own intensifying work load also militates against supervisors taking time away from the details of specific supervision projects to engage in more general conversations about the doctorate and the processes of doctoral researchers becoming scholars. Students therefore may well end up confused, with the result that they may follow unproductive methodological and philosophical explorations. Alternatively, they may simply feel inadequate when apparently straightforward advice fails to do the trick. Holbrook and Johnston (1999) explain that such books are unhelpfully decontextualised and fail to acknowledge the messiness of real lives, not amenable to easy control or resolution. They write that, 'Tears and tantrums, frustrations, phobias and personal agendas are missing, so are the supervisors who do have the correct answer or students with unmanageable problems' (1999: 7). Our goal is to support doctoral researchers and their supervisors to interrogate the many catalogues of texts now available for doctoral purchase.

The widely read and highly successful books (Cham 2008a; 2008b; 2008c) and the comic strip titled 'Piled Higher and Deeper' (PhD), developed by graduate student Jorge

1

Cham, offer a humorous take on the life of a graduate student inhabiting a 'world of grant deadlines, employment worries, political correctness and other sources of relentless angst' (Marcus 2009: 1). The most common response to Cham's comic books and the lectures he gives at universities in the USA on the graduate experience is, he says, about students' sense of alienation and isolation so that doctoral students, 'feel like they're the only ones having these difficulties with their advisers or their funding agencies, that they're lost or they don't really know what they're doing with their lives … they see that there are other people out there like them' (Marcus 2009: 2). Cham's books develop comic characters who resonate with readers and take on a life of their own, characters such as 'Mike Slackenerny' and 'Cecilia'. Of academics Cham says, that while being a graduate student is hard going, 'being a professor is even worse' (Marcus 2009: 2). His website is replete with comments from doctoral students at different stages of their endeavour from around the globe (see www.phdcomics.com), suggesting that he has managed to capture, in ways that advice books often do not, the everyday experience of doctoral research.

The reason Cham's cartoons resonate so strongly with doctoral researchers is, we think, because he addresses one of their key challenges. 'Getting' the doctorate is always much more than simply completing the research – in reality it is about becoming and being a scholar. Being scholarly and becoming a scholar are tasks integral to becoming part of, and belonging to, an academic community. Doing a quality doctorate in contemporary times requires more than the technical skills required of a research process; it involves coming to see oneself as a researcher and taking on a confident and articulate researcher identity. This book, therefore, has an integrating theme of exploring how identity and knowledge formation happen together. Producing 'an original contribution to knowledge' is also to construct oneself as a scholar. These two volumes address a set of interlocking and overlapping big questions that run through the practice of knowledge/identity work.

We take the view that becoming a researcher involves engaging with a range of ideas and issues mediated through a particular research project. We believe that our texts will enable students and their supervisors to navigate their way through the vast library of doctoral and research books by bringing together questions that are generally scattered through a range of texts. For example, discussions about the importance of public intellectual work rarely sit alongside questions of getting started on a research project, or discussions about how to choose a research method together with a conversation about the power relationships embedded in scholarship. Yet, in today's internationalised higher education systems and globalised societies, *not* to bring these things together is to create myopic and unnecessarily parochial and partial understandings of the institutionalised enterprise of knowledge production.

Moreover, these are not yet more books on competing paradigms, how to do a piece of doctoral work from beginning to end, a view of the doctorate that comprises 'tips and tricks', approaches to 'writing up' a thesis, or a set of researcher biographies. Rather, *The Doctoral Companions* place at their centre the interwoven questions of what it means to be a doctoral student in the social sciences, and what is involved in becoming and being a researcher. They further ask what 'capabilities' through research are key to confidence, quality and success. We also provide pragmatic and practical thinking about progressing research/scholarly career and identity.

The rationale behind the two volumes is not simply that the concerns of doctoral researchers and their supervisors are both shared and different, rather we hope to promote dialogue. However important it is that students establish and join peer communities amongst whom they exchange and circulate the nascent knowledge they are producing and the joys and tribulations that accompany this process, it is in the interrelationship of student and supervisors that young scholars are produced as confident and successful researchers, or where confidence is as easily diminished. The books, therefore, address the sorts of questions that need to be taken up by developing researchers and which can fruitfully be discussed with supervisors. We suspect from our conversations with doctoral researchers at our own institution, at national and international conferences, and from a variety of reports and research articles, that doctoral candidates want more than conversations about their substantive research. They also want focused 'insider' discussion about 'the rules of the game', what it means to be a scholar, and the purposes and practices of higher education. Much of what appears in the doctoral companions is directed to this end. Authors do not seek to provide answers, but rather to raise issues, which can then be pursued further.

The organisation of *The Doctoral Companions*

Briefly, now, something about the design of each Volume. We have organised both books into large sections, each addressing a key theme associated with becoming and being a doctoral scholar. Volume 1 addresses doctoral students and Volume 2 their supervisors. There is some deliberate repetition of material across the two volumes but we also envisage supervisors finding much of interest in Volume 1, and students locating material of interest in Volume 2.

We begin both volumes by outlining the current global and national policy climate for doctoral education and explain the rapid rise up higher education policy agendas of doctoral students. In Volume 1, Part 2, we take up the theme of becoming a doctoral student and some of the issues students are likely to confront early in their journeys. In Part 3, we address a range of issues around coming to terms with research practice. Chapter authors take up issues and questions; they do not try to address the practical detail of doing a research project but offer ways into thinking about what it means to do a project and be a doctoral student. We then address the question that sits at the heart of the doctorate but is often rather vaguely explained, that of making a contribution to knowledge (although see Yates 2004). Quite what does it mean to make an original contribution? Do different kinds of knowledge count? Who are the students and does their knowledge count at all? We then draw together these interlocking and overlapping themes in our concluding chapter. After the introductory section in Volume 2, we focus on supervision pedagogies, creating productive doctoral education cultures, making contributions to scholarly knowledge and then draw these together in our conclusion. In Volume 2 we also summarise and link as appropriate back to Volume 1.

The brief we gave to the chapter authors was broad and open. We invited specific contributions, sent everybody the outline for both volumes and then trusted authors to decide how they might take up the specifics of their own contribution. We think they have all risen magnificently to this challenge. In many cases there are references to further helpful work by authors, which can be followed up; while their references provide further access to additional helpful resources.

We want to emphasise that these books are not necessarily linear in their workings. Each chapter in and of itself offers a challenge and an invitation to doctoral readers to reflect on their own learning to become and to be, and to provide also resources to support and reflect on this becoming. We imagine readers moving backwards and forwards across the big themes, revisiting early themes and engaging later themes even at an early stage of their studies. We hope that readers will continue to draw on the resources of the book in ways that support their own individually staged doctoral development.

Our understandings, ambitions and acknowledgements

We embarked on this extensive editorial project because of our commitments to the value and process of high quality in doctoral education. We understand the doctorate as a relational and pedagogical project of student/supervisor development and identity formation, grounded in the shared project of addressing significant questions and making knowledge under specific contextual and policy conditions. This sounds serious but we also believe that the doctoral experience ought to be about excitement, engagement and achievement. We know it is also often one of remaking identities, of considerable intellectual challenge, and of emotional bumps and bruises.

Doctoral education and the experience of doing a doctorate ought, we think, to be a period when students develop knowledge, 'capabilities' (Sen 1999) and relationship resources for continuing their 'life-long' professional journeys, including new and unpredictable doctoral study challenges. Experiences of doctoral education – positive and life-enhancing, or narrowing horizons and self-belief – will, we believe, shape life-long learner identities. As supervisors, we hope for the former rather than the latter, while recognizing that each doctoral venture is biographical, complicated and partly unpredictable. As with any pedagogy or educational process, we cannot pin down the one right way – and nor would we want to – but we can develop knowledge resources that help us work towards better practices produced in the interstices of the student, her thesis, her university context, and our supervision interlaced across all three.

Our interests in putting together this extensive edited collection as researchers and doctoral supervisors and examiners ourselves, with personal experience of doctoral education in three different countries and an international network of supervisor colleagues, is the growing significance of doctoral education as a site of practice in universities internationally. The shift in attention to doctoral education over the last 15 years or so has been remarkable: from a kind of cottage industry involving individual students and supervisors with disciplinary expertise, to a deepening focus for policy, research and publications of diverse kinds. Under contemporary conditions of the knowledge economy and the need for professional credentials beyond the masters level, doctorates in education are of increased importance and professional value to practitioners in a variety of professional settings. More and more people are doing doctorates, not only because new forms of work require higher knowledge production capabilities developed through research, but also because of credential inflation. Students are looking to make an economic and educational investment in their own workplace careers; the doctorate is no longer only about becoming a career academic in a university.

We take education in its broadest sense as our field of concern and we hope that the two volumes will be of broad interest in the social sciences. But we think it is not surprising that so much of the work on doctoral education emanates from scholars who see education and pedagogy as the subject of research. We have been informed by a variety of research into doctoral education – for example, signature pedagogies in doctoral education (Golde 2007); a rich and growing field of research on doctoral writing pedagogies from early work by Connell (1985) to recent studies (Bendix Petersen 2007; Kamler and Thomson 2006; Kamler and Thomson 2008; Paltridge and Starfield 2007); supervision practices and pedagogies (Brew and Peseta 2009; Boucher and Smith 2006; Delamont *et al.* 1997; Denholm and Evans 2007; Hasrati 2005; Grant 2003; Green 2005; Holligan 2005; Lamm 2004; Lee 2008; Li and Searle 2007; Manathunga 2005a; 2005b; Murphy *et al.* 2007; Neumann 2007; Sambrook *et al.* 2008); emerging attention to more collective models of supervision and collaborative knowledge sharing environments (Malfroy 2005; Parker 2009); pedagogies of doctoral publishing (Lee and Kamler 2008; Kamler 2008); professional doctorates (Brennan 1998; Evans 1997; Scott *et al.* 2004; Maxwell *et al.* 2008; Wellington and Sikes 2006); supervising professional doctorates (Health 2006); doctoral student development (Gardner 2008); managerialism and supervision processes (Cribb and Gewirtz 2006); and doctoral education and future academic faculty development and recruitment (Ehrenberg and Kuh 2008).

It is particularly noteworthy that this research literature has been generated primarily in the last five years, and although there is much of value to supervisors, it is an expansive terrain to negotiate in busy academic lives. We hope, therefore, in these two volumes to signpost key debates and findings from this emergent corpus of research.

We not only owe an intellectual debt to the community of doctoral education researchers, but we also have had considerable practical assistance in putting *The Doctoral Companions* together and to bed. Producing two edited volumes of this size has been greatly helped by the sterling secretarial support we have had from Uta Feinstein, who developed an effective system to keep track of the large number of contributors and has been the central point of contact for authors. She was also instrumental in the last stages of getting the texts ready for the publishers. Helen Hearn and Tham Nguyen, doctoral students in the School of Education, efficiently undertook some of the early copy-editing support. Martina Daykin also provided secretarial support. We are very grateful for the help we have received from all four of them, and for the support of the School of Education for this project. We must also thank Philip Mudd, our commissioning editor at Routledge, who first raised the possibility of the books with us, who provided feedback on our evolving idea to sharpen our thinking on focus, structure and organisation of the two volumes, and who has been encouraging throughout. Finally, our long-suffering partners, Randy Barber and Ian Phimister, have inevitably lived this project with us and there is little doubt that our efforts here depended on their support. Our dogs, too, have played their part in providing welcome unconditional regard!

In conclusion, we must also thank the following authors and publishers for permission to reprint chapters that have previously appeared elsewhere, although most have been revised and updated for this publication:

(1) Stephen Ball (2006) 'The necessity and violence of theory'. *Discourse* 27(1): 3–10. Reprinted with permission from Taylor & Francis.

(2) Chaya Herman 'Emotions and being a doctoral student'. Adapted from C. Herman (2008) 'Negotiating the emotions of change: Research, restructuring and the doctoral student'. *South African Journal of Higher Education*, 22(1): 100–115. Revised and reprinted with permission from *South African Journal of Higher Education*.

(3) Jon Wagner 'Ignorance in educational research, How not knowing shapes new knowledge'. Adapted from J Wagner (1993) 'Ignorance in educational research or,

How not knowing shapes new knowledge?' *Educational Researcher*, 22(5): 15–23. Revised and reprinted with permission from SAGE.

(4) Kevin Williams '"Guilty knowledge". The (im)possibility of ethical security in social science research'. Adapted from K. Williams (2009) 'Guilty knowledge: ethical aporia emergent in the research, practice of educational development practitioners'. *London Review of Education*, 7(3): 211–221.

References

Bendix Petersen, E. (2007) Negotiating academicity: postgraduate research supervision as category boundary work, *Studies in Higher Education*, 32(4): 475–88.

Boucher, C. and Smith, A. (2006) Up close and personal: reflections on our experience of supervising research candidates who are using personal reflective techniques, *Reflective Practice*, 5(3): 345–56.

Brennan, M. (1998) Struggles over the definition and practice of the Educational Doctorate in Australia, *Australian Educational Researcher*, 25(1): 71–89.

Brew, A. and Peseta, T. (2008) Supervision development and recognition in a reflexive space. In Boud, D. and Lee, A. (Eds). Changing Practices of Doctoral Education. New York and London: Routledge, 126–39.

Cham, J. (2008a) *Piled Higher and Deeper*. Los Angeles, CA: Piled Higher and Deeper LLC.

——(2008b) *Life is Tough and Then You Graduate*. Los Angeles, CA: Piled Higher and Deeper LLC.

——(2008c) *Scooped! the Third Piled Higher and Deeper*. Los Angeles, CA: Piled Higher and Deeper LLC.

Connell, R.W. (1985) How to Supervise a PhD, *Vestes*, 2: 38 (Available at www.ph.unimelb.edu/au/pgss/2520/node33.html. Accessed 5 January 2008.)

Cribb, A. and Gewirtz, S. (2006) Doctoral student supervision in a managerial climate, *International Studies in Sociology of Education*, 16 (3): 223–36.

Delamont, S., Atkinson, P. and Parry, O. (1997) *Supervising the PhD*. Buckingham: SRHE/Open University Press.

Denholm, C. and Evans, T. (Eds) (2007) *Supervising Doctorates Downunder*. Camberwell: ACER Press.

Ehrenberg, R.G. and Kuh, C.V. (Eds) (2008) *Doctoral Education and the Faculty of the Future*. Ithaca, NY: Cornell University Press.

Evans, T. (1997) Flexible doctoral research: emerging issues in professional doctorate programs, *Studies in Continuing Education*, 19(2): 174–82.

Gardner, S. (2008) *The Development of Doctoral Students: Phases of challenge and support: ASHE Higher Education Report, 34*. San Francisco, CA: Jossey Bass.

Golde, C.M. (2007) Signature pedagogies in doctoral education: Are they adaptable for the preparation of education researchers? *Educational Researcher*, 36(6): 344–51.

Grant, B. (2003) Mapping the pleasures and risks of supervision, *Discourse*, 24(2): 175–90.

Green, B. (2005) Unfinished business: subjectivity and supervision, *Higher Education Research and Development*, 24(2): 151–63.

Hasrati, M. (2005) Legitimate peripheral participation and supervising PhD students, *Studies in Higher Education*, 30(5): 557–70.

Health, L. (2006) Supervision of professional doctorates: education doctorates in English universities, *Higher Education Review*, 38(2): 21–41.

Holbrook, A. and Johnston, S. (Eds) (1999) *Supervision of postgraduate research in education*. Coldsteam: AARE.

Holligan, C. (2005) Fact and fiction: a case history of doctoral supervision, *Educational Research*, 47(3); 267–78.

Kamler, B. (2008) Rethinking doctoral publication practices: writing from and beyond the thesis, *Studies in Higher Education*, 33(3); 283–94.

Kamler, B. and Thomson, P. (2004) Driven to abstraction: doctoral supervision and Writing pedagogies, *Teaching in Higher Education*, 9(2); 195–210.

——(2006) *Helping doctoral students write. Pedagogies for supervision.* London: Routledge.

Lamm, R. (2004) *Nurture or challenge in research higher degree supervision.* Paper presented at the annual conference of the Australian Association for Research in Education, Melbourne 28 November to 2 December 2004.

Lee, A. and Kamler, B. (2008) Bringing pedagogy to doctoral publishing, *Teaching in Higher Education*, 13(5): 511.

Lee, A. (2008) How are doctoral students supervised? Concepts of doctoral research supervision, *Studies in Higher Education*, 33(3); 267–81.

Li, S. and Searle, C. (2007) Managing criticism in PhD supervision: a qualitative case study, *Studies in Higher Education*, 32(4): 511–26.

Malfroy, J. (2005) Doctoral supervision, workplace research and changing pedagogic practices, *Higher Education Research and Development*, 24(2): 165–78.

Manathunga, C. (2005a) The development of research supervision: 'turning the light on a private space', *International Journal for Academic Development*, 10(1): 17–30.

——(2005b) Early warning signs in postgraduate research education: a different approach to ensure timely completions, *Teaching in Higher Education*, 10(2): 219–33.

Marcus, G. (2009) Comic-strip hero, *THE*, 12 February 2009 (Available at www.timeshighereducation. co.uk/story.asp?sectioncode=26&storycode=405321. Accessed 9 July 2009.)

Maxwell, T.W., Hickey, C. and Evans, T. (Eds) (2008) *Working doctorates: the impact of Professional Doctorates in the workplace and professions.* Revised papers from the fifth Professional Doctorates conference, Deakin University.

Murphy, N., Bain, J.D. and Conrad, L. (2007) Orientations to research higher degree supervision, *Higher Education*, 53(2): 209–34.

Neumann, R. (2005) Doctoral differences: professional doctorates and PhD compared, *Journal of Higher Education Policy and Management*, 27(2): 173–88.

Paltridge, B. and Starfield, S. (2007) *Thesis and dissertation writing in a second language.* London: Routledge.

Parker, R. (2009) A learning community approach to doctoral education in the social sciences, *Teaching in Higher Education*, 14 (1): 43–54.

Sambrook, S., Stewart, J. and Roberts, C. (2008) Doctoral supervision … a view from above, below and the middle! *Journal of Further and Higher Education*, 32(1): 71–84.

Scott, D., Brown, A., Lunt, I. and Thorne, L. (2004) *Professional doctorates: Integrating academic and professional knowledge.* Maidenhead: SRHE/Open University Press.

Sen, A. (1999) *Development as freedom.* Oxford: Oxford University Press.

Wellington and Sikes (2006) 'A doctorate in a tight compartment': Why do students choose a professional doctorate and what impact does it have on their personal and professional lives? *Studies in Higher Education*, 31 (6): 723–34.

Doctoral education in context

The changing nature of the doctorate and doctoral students

P. Thomson and M. Walker

In June 1996, *The Times Higher Education Supplement* (A. Thomson 1996) reported on a discussion paper called 'Quality and Standards of Postgraduate Research Degrees', produced by the United Kingdom Council for Graduate Education (UKCGE). The article suggested that the postgraduate research sector needed urgent review to secure better quality monitoring, and commented that funding councils had focused little attention on doctoral education because they were more concerned with undergraduate and masters courses. According to the UKCGE report, there was now an urgent need for discussion and clarification of the issues concerning postgraduate research, not least because of a 'dramatic' increase in postgraduates doing research (A. Thomson 1996). Illustrative figures from the Higher Education Funding Council for England showed a 310 per cent increase in postgraduate research (masters and doctoral) between 1979 and 1994 (HEFCE 1996). The report argued for the need to establish effective postgraduate quality assurance policies and procedures, and monitoring and enhancement mechanisms to reassure 'stakeholders', including students.

Earlier that same year *The THES* had published an article by Davies (1996) on 'What is the role of a PhD supervisor?', pointing to the variation in the quality of support students received, and anticipating the debates that were to accelerate over the next decade. Davies reported the, 'by no means exceptional', experiences of one PhD student whose relationship had broken down with his supervisor, pointing to the problematic power relations inherent in the relationship. As a result this student did not expect to complete his doctorate, saying:

> I was taken on as a research assistant without meeting [him], and when I arrived it turned out he didn't have a PhD and hadn't supervised before. ... There has been a breakdown in our relationship. But my funding depends on my supervisor – he's an expert in the area – and the institution doesn't really have anyone to replace him. I'm an outsider and he is an insider – anything I say carries no weight. I do have a second supervisor, but she doesn't have the time to see me. There have been four postgraduates in the past two years in my department, and I'm the only one left. Maybe if I'm lucky I'll get an MPhil here, but I don't have any control over my funding, and I'll need a reference from this institution if I look for a job.
> Davies 1996: 1

In the same article, Davies quotes Tricia Skuse, who was then finishing a psychology PhD; she observed that a wide range of different supervisory problems exist because:

> [O]ne of the fundamental problems with PhDs in Britain is that nothing's standardized. I have friends who start their PhD, see a supervisor a few times and then they're left to fend for themselves. In other universities supervisors will go with you and help you set up your fieldwork, or help you do your analysis and give you a training in research skills.
>
> Davies 1996: 1

The 1996 Chairman's Foreword to the Harris Report on postgraduate education (HEFCE 1996: 1) highlighted 'the central importance of high quality postgraduate education to the creation of the ever more highly skilled workforce which is necessary if the United Kingdom is to flourish in an increasingly complex and competitive world', but also 'the benefits which education at this level, now delivered in a multiplicity of ways, brings to individuals and, through them, to society as a whole'. In the next decade, there was a flurry of policy activity in the UK. By 2006, in the wake of the Harris Report (HEFCE 1996), the HEPI Report (2004) on higher education supply and demand, and the development of UKGCE and the Quality Assurance Agency (QAA) standards for doctoral education, the field and arena of doctoral education had changed considerably, driven at least in part by the fact that postgraduates were by then increasingly seen as the best source for future university income (Leonard *et al.* 2006; Park 2007).

These developments have not been confined to the UK. In Australia, in 1996 Australian universities awarded just fewer than 3,000 PhDs across all subjects. By 2006 the total number was more than 5,500, an 85 per cent increase (Western and Lawson 2008: 1; and see Evans chapters in Volume 2). This expansion was accompanied by intense interest in the process of supervision, with Australian researchers arguably leading the field in investigating the many facets of research supervision in education at a time when there was little empirical research taking place elsewhere. Notably, a pioneering collection edited by Holbrook and Johnston (1999: 6) explored the process and culture of research supervision within the field of education in Australian universities in order to render both less opaque and hence open to improvement. The editors observed that manuals of procedures and lists of suggestions do not successfully address cultures of doctoral education and supervision, because getting a PhD involves more than 'generating a product or perfecting a set of skills'. They pointed instead to the significance of acquiring an academic identity, of belonging to a research culture, and of the work–life pressures that practical self-help books do not address.

In the USA, 52,600 doctorates were awarded in 2004–5, a 14 per cent increase on the figure of 1997–8 (Western and Lawson 2008: 1), while around 1.7 million graduate students study at USA universities (Marcus 2009). Not surprisingly, given these figures, the Carnegie Foundation for the Advancement of University Teaching established an *Initiative on the Doctorate* and commissioned essays edited by Golde and G. Walker (2006) on envisaging its future, including in education (Berliner 2006; Richardson 2006). With a focus on doctoral students as the future 'stewards of the disciplines', the essays express a deep concern with the goals and purposes of doctoral education, and especially with the development of a doctoral scholar as 'someone who will creatively generate new knowledge, critically conserve valuable and useful ideas, and responsibly transform those understandings through writing, teaching, and application' (Golde 2006: 5).

In parts of Europe, doctoral education is similarly expanding and transforming. Considerable changes have taken place over the last decade as doctoral training and education has come under scrutiny as an object of interest to policy makers in the face of global competition for talented 'knowledge worker' doctoral students (Bleiklie and Hostaker 2004; Bitusikova 2009; Kehm 2007; Leonard *et al.* 2006; Szkudlarek – Chapter 29). In 1999, The Bologna Declaration announced the creation of a European Higher Education Area, followed in 2000 by the Lisbon Strategy to create a European Research and Innovation Area. The intention is to produce around 700,000 doctoral researchers in Europe (Park 2007), and to make Europe the most competitive global knowledge economy (Kehm 2007). As with developments elsewhere, the European doctorate is no longer viewed only as a research degree but also as a qualification for other professional fields. In general, there is agreement that high-quality research training and an expanded supply of qualified researchers are both important 'in achieving the vision of a globally competitive Europe of knowledge' (Kehm 2007: 314). Doctoral education in Europe is seen to now require more direction and structure, and not to be solely driven by intellectual curiosity. Rather, new knowledge is a strategic resource and economic factor. The effect, according to Kehm (2007), is that knowledge becomes another commodity and its shape acquires a more instrumental approach.

Not surprisingly, policy makers in Europe have begun to be keenly interested in the state of research training and universities have been requested to develop institutional strategies for training. In addition, research training is deemed so important a resource that it is no longer to be left in the hands of professors and departments but has become an object of policy making and has moved to the institutional, and national, even supra-national level (Kehm 2007: 314). Academics are to be monitored by outside 'agents who have motives, purposes and goals that are not purely academic' (Kehm 2007: 316). Kehm highlights a key tension running through higher education and from which doctoral education is not immune. She puts the problem in this way: 'If a utilitarian concept of relevance becomes so strong that it determines academic notions of quality or excellence and the idea of curiosity-driven research, then we could all end up poorer than we were before' (Kehm 2007: 316).

Diversity of doctoral programmes

Accompanying this accelerating interest in doctoral education, the traditional doctorate in Social Sciences and Education is changing and evolving. In the past it generally involved a period of research by the lone student, supported by a supervisor, culminating in a thesis of around 80,000–100,000 words; this text is required above all to make an original contribution to knowledge (Yates 2004). The PhD is recognised not only as the standard entry qualification for an academic career (although in the past this was not always the case), but also as an important qualification for other professional fields, such as school leadership, educational development roles in higher education, and professional fields such as health and social care. Nowadays, this traditional doctorate model survives, although the student, especially if studying full-time, is likely to participate in a research culture of projects, seminars and conferences, and typically to have more than one supervisor. Unlike in the past, extended time periods for completion are discouraged, and indeed in the UK there is strong pressure for students to complete a full-time doctorate in three to four years and six to eight years for a part-time student. In the USA the PhD period of study is typically longer, at around five or six years for full-time students, and requires two initial years of course work as well as a thesis (Reisz 2008). But these are increasingly more focused and time-bound studies, rather than life-long projects that may have stretched over 10, 11 or more years, as universities bring in rules to limit the period for which a student may be registered for a doctorate.

New forms of doctoral education have also expanded over the last two decades with the professional doctorate growing in popularity, notwithstanding contested views over the value of something described as a 'professional' doctorate (Gill 2009). The thrust of professional doctorates is both to encourage research that contributes to professional practice, but also to open up doctoral education to a wider group of career professionals and a different demographic (Gill 2009). Burgess, founder of UKCGE, explains that the professional doctorate 'opens up opportunities for higher education to talk with professional people who are interested in intellectual problems that arise from their work experience, and that seems to me to be appropriate' (Gill 2009: 32). Others are less certain about the claim of professional doctorates to have parity of esteem with the PhD, given the lack of standardisation and lack of clarity over what a taught doctorate is (Gill 2009), even though it might also be argued that it is not entirely obvious what a PhD is, or that it might not always be fit for diverse purposes. It is, however, certainly the case, that over the last 20 years, the part-time professional doctorate has become widespread in education in the UK and Australia especially (Brennan 1998; Collinson 2005; Costley and Armsby 2007; Evans 2004; Health 2006; Neumann 2007; Sarros et al. 2005; Stephenson 2006; Wellington and Sikes 2006; Taysum 2007a; Taysum 2007b), while already being more established in the USA and Canada. Such professional doctorates are generally comprised of two years of taught coursework and two to four years towards a dissertation, the latter study typically being shorter, more applied and practice-focused than the usual PhD thesis. For most universities, the balance of taught and research elements is over 50 per cent for the research, most often two-thirds. Certainly, in the UK, this is required for the degree to qualify for research funding.

In addition, there are other routes to a PhD. There is a PhD by publication based on the submission of peer-reviewed papers, usually accompanied by an overview linking the papers (see Goode Chapter 3 Volume 2). The new route PhD available at a number of UK universities may contain significant taught elements, usually over one year at masters level, which are examined and must be passed before the student proceeds to doctoral research and thesis, which is usually of the standard length. In other cases, the research project is present from the beginning and runs alongside any taught course in year one (Johnston and Murray 2004; Park 2005; Park 2007 and see www.newroutephd.ac.uk/). There are also practice-based PhDs, with a project report and an exegesis, portfolio and artefact dissertations, and even experiments with group research projects.

Doctoral study can now be face to face, or at a distance using electronic communication technologies, or a blend of both of these (e.g. Butcher and Sieminiski 2006; Crossouard 2008; Sussex 2008). Furthermore, the marketisation of higher education means that doctoral researchers can now enrol in universities far away from their home location and thus may find themselves part of a culturally rich student body, although universities themselves may do little to encourage cross-cultural dialogue and exchange.

More diverse doctoral researchers

Not only is the field of doctoral study far more diverse than it has been in the past, but it also attracts more diverse students with a wide range of reasons for choosing doctoral study, and increasingly it is the focus of academic research. The typical first class honours graduate proceeding directly to doctoral study has arguably never been the norm for education, nursing and social work. In these areas there is no obviously typical doctoral student and ages may range from 24 to 74, in a range of professions, and include white and black candidates, candidates of different ethnicities and religions, men and women, able-bodied and disabled, middle and working class applicants, and international students studying away from their home countries (see, for example, Castellanos *et al.* 2006; Chapman and Pyvis 2006; Gillies and Lucey 2007; Green and Scott 2003; Goode 2007; Leonard 2001; McClure 2005; Mastekaasa 2005; Tubin and Lapidot 2008). In the UK, fear of taking on debt appears to deter many working class students from continuing on to doctoral studies (Rodgers 2006).

Increasingly, not all doctoral graduates will choose professional lives in a university. A recent report published by VITAE (2009) for the UK on first destinations of doctoral graduates by subject for 2003–7 indicates the high value employers place on specialised and doctoral level generic skills. But, significantly for our concern here, only 35 per cent of the total number of doctoral graduates went into a research role across all sectors, only 25 per cent were employed as research staff in higher education, and 14 per cent as lecturers in higher education. Looking more specifically at social science, 42 per cent of the doctoral graduates had studied part-time, 34 per cent went into higher education lecturing and 18 per cent into research roles in higher education (VITAE 2009: 42ff.). All this is to underline that the social science and education doctoral candidate is almost as likely to be studying part-time as full-time, whereas only a minority will enter teaching and research positions in higher education. Many will have come to doctoral studies as professionals from other fields wanting to systematise their professional knowledge, or research policy formation and implementation in their professional fields, or enquire into changing and improving practices in their own contexts. In education, for example, doctoral students include head teachers, teachers in schools, policy researchers, academic administrators, nurse educators, not-for-profit and third-sector professionals, and so on. For the most part, they will continue in this work during their studies and return to it afterwards. They arc in effect knowledge workers in diverse professional fields.

The diversity of doctoral candidates has implications for doctoral student experiences, given that students differently located will have differing opportunities, as Sen (1999) would say, to 'convert' their particular resources into capabilities to be and become doctoral graduates (see Volume 2, Chapter 2). Diversity produces new obligations for institutions and thus for doctoral supervisors. Thus, for example, a disabled doctoral student may need more or different support from an able-bodied student, a working class student may need more or different support from that of a middle class student, and so on. Supervisors now need to be attentive to, and aware of, such differences amongst students, and students themselves also need to attend to, and be sensitive to, diversity in their own peer engagements so that they develop what Nussbaum (1997) describes as a 'narrative imagination', that is the capability to imagine the lives of others and to respond positively.

Doctoral education in globalised times

Golde (2006) points to the changing and changed circumstances of doctoral programmes in the USA, not least shaped by globalisation and the globalisation of knowledge that is effectively borderless in an age of sophisticated information technologies. Under these globalised conditions, doctoral education offers tremendous opportunities to imaginatively contribute to knowledge, to critically systematise valuable ideas, and transform and generate organised knowledge and understanding both through doctoral scholarship and dissemination (Golde and G. Walker 2006). This is, Golde and G. Walker (2006) argue, much more than a technical activity of skills acquisition; as an educational endeavour it is suffused with moral and ethical dimensions that turn on what kind of doctoral education and doctoral scholars are needed by a democratic knowledge society. As Walker writes:

> Today's PhDs have extraordinary new opportunities to lead efforts to extend human knowledge. They already enjoy new possibilities for educating the next generation of scholars and citizens and for doing so in a wide spectrum of institutional settings. They are also called upon to provide expert opinion in a dizzying array of high-profile public areas. They have a special opportunity and responsibility to inform the public about their disciplines and, ultimately, to shape the public's attitudes about the importance of their fields and the attendant habits of mind of an informed, engaged and ethical scholar.
>
> Walker 2006: 427

However, such optimism is insufficient to take account of how developments in the nature and type of doctorates, the increasing numbers of doctoral candidates and shifts in the importance of doctoral students for policy makers, are located in and produced by the macro-discourses that surround globalisation and the idea of knowledge economies.

It is not coincidental that the increase in the numbers of doctoral students has accelerated in the last 15 to 20 years, nor that they have risen significantly up the agenda of most universities as graduate schools and other institutional structures have been put in place to offer training support and to encourage dynamic 'communities of practice' (Lave and Wenger 1998). As global economies are reorganised around knowledge and information as key resources, a view in part produced by scholarship about globalisation, this in turn shapes and reshapes education (Carnoy and Rhoten 2002). Knowledge and skills are now understood as crucial for comparative economic advantage. Although definitions are contested (see Peters 2004), that offered by the OECD (1996: 7) is still helpful when it describes a knowledge-based economy as 'economies which are directly based on the production, distribution and use of knowledge and information'.

The effect is that higher education 'has become the new starship in the policy fleet for governments around the world' (Peters and Besley 2006a: 83). Internationally and nationally, the task of higher education is directed to the creation of intellectual capacity and the construction of knowledge and skills for participation in an increasingly knowledge-based world economy. Castells (2004) argues that if knowledge is the 'electricity' of the new international economies, then higher education institutions are the power sources on which a new development process must rely. New theories of economic growth have conferred on education, on knowledge production and the knowledge society (having replaced the older industrial model) a central role as an essential engine of development (Peters 2004; Peters and Besley 2006; OECD 1996; Coyle and Quah 2002; Stiglitz 1999). But for Nobel Laureate Joseph Stiglitz (1999), knowledge is a global public good; it is not finite in the way that commodities like coal and iron are, and indeed, in and through its use, increases and disperses. Knowledge when used does not become used-up, but can be increased through sharing and further development, so that 'knowledge once discovered and made public operates expansively to defy the law of scarcity' (Peters and Besley 2006: 799).

Not surprisingly, in turn, doctoral education and what purposes it promotes and serves have also been affected by this globalised turn. It must be understood in the context of the tensions between ethical and critical citizenship and human well being, and a focus on economic development and economic life, as Kehm (2007) alludes to in her concern for the possible directions of doctoral education. Kwiek (2003: 81) neatly sums up the shifts that surround, permeate and influence higher education, and for our purposes here doctoral education, when he writes that higher education 'is asked to adapt to new societal needs, to be more responsive to the world around it, to be more market-, performance-, and student oriented, to be more cost-effective, accountable to its stakeholders, as well as competitive with other providers'.

But the effects of globalisation go further than a utilitarian press for employability and labour market-responsive knowledge and skills and the commodification of knowledge. National higher education institutions around the world face declining investment of public funds, and thus there is pressure to diversify institutional sources of income, accompanied by managerial forms of governance, performative and risk avoidance cultures and quality assurance regimes (Kwiek 2003; Peters 2004; Stromquist 2002). International graduate students are sought after for various reasons, but undoubtedly those include the fees premium they command in balancing university budgets.

In recent decades it seems that university education policy (if not academic professionals) has been much more concerned with science and technology and with economic applications of knowledge. The idea of higher education as a public good, enriching both the individual and all of society, has arguably been overtaken by a rhetoric of business models and market relations, together with an audit and accounting regulatory culture. Higher education is as a result increasingly regarded as a private commodity rather than a public good. Pessimists assert the decline or erasure of critical learning in the 'ruins' (Readings 1996) of the university, 'except as the rear-guard protests of an exhausted faculty and a fragment of the largely demobilized student body' (Aronowitz and Giroux 2000: 338).

However, such developments are not uncontested and the pages of *Times Higher Education* in the UK feature regular responses to and critiques of the 'human capital' direction (where the value of educated persons and their knowledge is solely the economic contribution). Giroux and Myriades (2001), for example, offer a robust critique of corporate university cultures and the spread of commercial values in higher education where 'social visions are dismissed as hopelessly out of date' (Giroux 2001: 3). In her book on contemporary life in British universities, Evans (2004) suggests in her title *Killing Thinking* the death of universities under current regimes of funding, regulation and accountability. Evans concludes that universities are in fact unlikely to collapse, but she also suggests that they may 'empty of creative engagement and creativity, as new generations, having experienced the deadly possibilities of the bureaucratized university, refuse to consider further involvement with that world and take their energies and talents elsewhere' (Evans 2004: 152). Those 'taking their talents elsewhere' will, of course, include prospective doctoral students.

That education should equip graduates with the knowledge and skills to participate in the economy is, unsurprisingly, the aspect that most concerns governments. But a problem arises when the meaningfulness of economic opportunities is not debated, and

15

when goals such as intellectual development, equal democratic citizenship and broader social goods are overlooked. Moreover, what Kenway *et al.* (2006) characterise as an older 'gift economy' is rendered fragile by this commodification of knowledge. They argue that an economy cannot simply be defined as a system of exchange. It can also be defined as 'the regulated circulation of values' (Frow 1997: 115; Kenway *et al.* 2006: 2). It is safe to assume that this includes educational values and versions of the ideal doctoral graduate. The cultural competitive thrust of doctoral education may be inimical to the older gift economy of 'knowledge as a non-rival good' (Frow 1997: 65), as shared and circulated, holding 'an obligation to return to the community what one has taken, with interest' (Frow 1997: 72).

For higher education policy makers, it seems that 'serving the economy has become their raison d'être' (Holford 2008: 25). For many higher education policy makers what is valued and promoted is 'acquisitive learning' (Brown 2003) of economic man or woman rather than the 'inquisitive learning' (Brown 2003: 160) of citizen man or woman. Parker (2007: 124), in considering what the humanities have to offer in Europe, warns against 'instrumental assumptions that need to be resisted'. Rather, she emphasises the significance of multi-voiced and complex narratives, of rhythms counter to those of the digital age, and the importance of offering disputed knowledge and allowing learning to thrive in a 'supercomplex' world (Barnett 2000).

Policy and the 'skills' agenda

Peters and Besley helpfully develop the concept of 'knowledge cultures' as a response to neoliberal interpretations of the knowledge economy and education, and provide resources for thinking about the purposes and processes of doctoral education. They describe knowledge cultures as involving 'the cultural preconditions that must be established before economies and societies based on knowledge can operate successfully as genuine democratic cultures' (Peters and Besley 2006: 803). Such knowledge cultures are based on 'shared practices' and 'culturally preferred ways of doing things'. In other words, they ask for thinking about the cultural conditions that enable knowledge to be created, produced and disseminated, and by implication, the cultural arrangements that constrain or cramp such knowledge production. They suggest that such cultural conditions include 'trust, reciprocal rights and responsibilities between different knowledge partners ... The term has the advantage of helping to focus on learning' (Peters and Besley 2006: 803). A focus on knowledge practices and social relations directs us potentially to a richer version of the knowledge economy, they suggest, more focused on public knowledge cultures, less on the neoliberal and bending more towards social democratic interpretations and practices.

Their argument, in turn, points to the broader purposes of doctoral education as developing educated persons for whom 'living life meaningfully' (Higgs 2006: 838) involves more than simply knowledge and skills but rather personal transformation and change and 'a continual becoming'. In his explication of this educated person, Higgs (2006) suggests that education includes 'the outcome of human agency as a matter of personal engagement'. Intersubjective human experiences require social engagement and social relationships in which students are afforded spaces to struggle

> to give form and character and meaning to the experiences of his or her own unique existence ... to develop their own voice ... to become autonomous

persons ... [with a] critical disposition in relation to themselves, others and the world ... [and] whose empowered practice will be directed at a better life for all.

Higgs 2006: 839–40

Thus, doctoral education and the knowledge culture in which it is embedded are rather richer and more expansive than the production only of skills and human capital (and see Walker, Volume 2, Chapter 2).

As we outlined earlier, the current focus on doctoral research skills is an element of, or response to, the dominant human capital and knowledge economy agenda, rather than the notion of becoming and being 'an educated person'. Gilbert (2004) notes a significant shift in doctoral education to reflect a changing emphasis on the PhD – from having one outcome, the thesis; it now foregrounds the actual process of producing the thesis. This has involved a significant shift from an emphasis on a scholarship model to a training model, Gilbert (2004) argues, but we argue that this shift also changes the quality of doctoral students' experiences of undertaking and succeeding in doctoral education by producing critical and innovative work.

We exemplify this argument and the shift by examining events in the UK. From the Harris Report (HEFCE 1996) on, there have been moves in the UK to systematise doctoral education so that what may be expected of students enrolling for a PhD is spelled out clearly, with requirements that doctoral study meets observable and measurable standards. The Harris Report introduced the idea of a Code of Practice for formal adoption by institutions. Such a code, the Report recommended, would require institutions to have in place appropriate facilities and supervisory arrangements.

There may indeed have been serious material concerns about doctoral education that warranted intervention – Coate and Leonard (2002) note the view of the UK Research Councils that the PhD not only lacked the rigour to prepare early career scholars, but was also not an appropriate professional development for those not choosing academic careers. The issue is not whether there were problems in the PhD, but rather how they were understood and acted on, generating in this case a concern for skills development outcomes understood in the context of a specific view of the inevitability of a particular kind of knowledge economy (Gilbert 2004). Gilbert (2004) generates a number of questions to focus any evaluation of the doctoral training curriculum, including asking how doctoral education meets the needs both of students, and 'other interested parties' (Gilbert 2004: 307). Reisz (2008), however, argues that more discipline and rigour in the PhD process is desirable to counter extended completion dates or hopelessly vague or unrealistic proposals. But, he asks how this is to be done without 'dumbing down', given the growing pressure in the UK for timely doctoral completion rates.

Although agreed a few years earlier, the QAA D (doctoral) level descriptors were published in 2008, after consultations with the sector. The QAA had translated these early recommendations into a set of doctoral standards, which remained unchanged. According to the QAA (2008), doctoral degrees are awarded to students who have demonstrated:

- the creation and interpretation of new knowledge, through original research or other advanced scholarship, of a quality to satisfy peer review, extend the forefront of the discipline, and merit publication;
- a systematic acquisition and understanding of a substantial body of knowledge, which is at the forefront of an academic discipline or area of professional practice;

- the general ability to conceptualise, design and implement a project for the generation of new knowledge, applications or understanding at the forefront of the discipline, and to adjust the project design in the light of unforeseen problems;
- a detailed understanding of applicable techniques for research and advanced academic enquiry;
- the QAA goes further to describe specific qualities and 'transferable skills' that the holder of a doctorate might be expected to have – being able to 'make informed judgments on complex issues in specialist fields', being 'able to communicate their ideas and conclusions clearly and effectively', being equipped to continue with research at an advanced level, and embodying qualities and transferable skills 'necessary for employment requiring the exercise of personal responsibility and largely autonomous initiative in complex and unpredictable situations, in professional or equivalent environments'.

Perhaps not surprisingly, critics and supporters of a skills agenda abound. Advocates of a Code of Practice for postgraduate education have included Tim Brown, at the time general secretary of the National Postgraduate Committee, who argued that a code of practice for doctoral education 'will end cronyism in departments. Students will at last be clear about what they can expect in the way of support from their university' (Sanders 2004: 1). Howard Green, onetime Chair of UKCGE, similarly welcomed a Code saying it would 'raise standards and will be something universities can work with – although some will find it challenging' (Sanders 2004: 1).

There are also critiques. We focus here on (admittedly selective) approaches to the issues of codes of practice, doctoral standards and transferable skills, which capture key elements of the oppositional debate. The first is from Rowland (2006), a keen critic of technicist versions of skills; including narrowly instrumental understandings of critical thinking skills (see also Papestephanou and Angeli 2007).

Rowland (2006) opens his critique of the research training agenda by citing a University College, London PhD student as saying of his studies: 'I am currently working on my PhD and am learning a variety of new skills such as self-discipline, time management and developing my own initiative' (Rowland 2006: 45). Rowland's concern is that an undue emphasis on the development of skills to meet the economic growth needs of any society 'may undermine the critical purpose of academic work' (Rowland 2006: 45) and the university's role to 'provide a critical service to society'. Rowland (2006) characterises the tension as that 'between the intellectual, theoretical and critical purposes of higher education on the one hand and the economic, practical and service purposes on the other exemplified in the skills agenda' (Rowland 2006: 45). Exploring the Research Council UK's 2001 joint statement of research skills training requirements for doctoral students, he notes that the lists of skills outlined emphasise performance and demonstration so that, for example, the ability to summarise is not sought but rather the ability to demonstrate this ability. Rowland asks why, if the PhD thesis is itself a demonstration of knowledge and understanding, is any further performance needed? This approach, he argues, shifts the emphasis on the PhD as being judged in its contribution to knowledge (or 'truth') and recasts it in terms of performance. Put another way, there is a move from research knowledge to the person of the knower, the researcher. Increasingly, therefore, PhD students need to market themselves to diverse employers, and to demonstrate that they have generic, core advanced and transferable skills. All this, Rowland says, is to erode a fundamental element of higher education, the nurture of 'criticality' (Barnett 1997).

Turning to a more specific pedagogical issue, critical thinking is arguably the core capability that higher education claims to develop in all its students. Papestephanou and Angeli (2007) point to two different discourses that shape critical thinking. On the one hand, there is the skills paradigm (found in discourses and practices of key skills, generic skills, transferable skills, and some versions of graduate attributes) embedded in what Habermas (1987) would style as purposive rationality, technicism and instrumentality. This, they argue, is 'relevant to the roles of the customer and consumer of services and goods, and not to the active participant in the possible transformation of the public sphere' (Papestephanou and Angeli 2007: 609). Under neoliberalism, they suggest, the dominant policy and the pedagogical vocabulary emphasise skills, performativity and outcomes and purposive rationality (instrumental and strategic), which, in turn, domesticate critique. The idea, they say, is to optimise outcomes, in the case of higher education, human capital outcomes but these are not open to critique. Thus, they write, 'the skills perspective identifies uncritically with the criteriology of the sociopolitical system since it focuses so much on successful performance' (Papestephanou and Angeli 2007: 605–6).

By contrast to this instrumental approach, becoming and being critical and producing 'critical' knowledge means seeing that current policy agendas are subject to contested interpretations. Doctoral students even if embedded in training agendas need to think, with support from their supervisors, about this agenda and how it positions them. They need time and space to consider where their own research is located on a criticality spectrum, ranging from narrow to expansive, from thin to thick, with deep incommensurabilities across this range. If not simply being trained, the question to ask is: how am I critical? And what kind of critical am I?

Different approaches to the doctorate

We have suggested that we understand doctoral education as a process of identity formation. This involves crossing a kind of borderland, transforming an identity as an experienced, highly skilled professional to one of researcher. We have certainly heard our own full-time doctoral students remark, in particular, on not underestimating the difficulties of suddenly no longer being a valued and respected professional, in becoming 'just a student'. What one might have been very good at and very secure about in one's own practice is suddenly of rather less significance. For part-time students the disruptions may work differently, in that students remain grounded in the workplace but are required to scrutinise it in new and often discomforting ways. Yet these disruptions, while difficult, are also productive of the new critically reflexive identity.

We offer two different but related ways of rethinking the work of doctoral education.

1. From professional to researcher-as-professional

In a recent account, Andrews and Edwards (2008: 4) trace their own doctoral trajectory and their 'invention' of themselves as researchers. In both cases they chose to study for an EdD because of the attraction of collaborative, cohort study. Of their doctoral experience they write that: 'It was tempting at first to think of oneself as a deficit model (particularly "not a statistician") but, gradually, we began to move forward with more confidence'. As researchers they became more critical about their own workplace assumptions, but also less uncritically compliant and more creative and confident in

taking risks 'rather than settling for the false security that all ticks have been marked against a list of competencies' (Andrews and Edwards 2008: 5). In becoming researchers they found themselves to be more, rather than less, professional as educators, rediscovering an *educational* identity so that

> [W]e feel able to step back, to theorize to engage with reflexivity rather than letting it leave us baffled and frustrated. ... it has given us greater insight into ourselves as professionals and our ability to articulate what it means to be a professional in postmodernity. It has also given us the courage to stand by the values in education that we feel are important and also to understand how we came to those values.
>
> Andrews and Edwards 2008: 7

Thus, we suggest, the notion of professionalism as involving continuous learning can hold both ends/identities together, albeit in tension.

'Professionalising' doctoral education

The notions of being professional and professionalism are taken up from a slightly different angle by Barnacle and Dall'Alba (2008), who consider the 'professionalising' of the research degree curriculum and the specialised and hence 'professional' knowledge that characterises a doctorate. They ask whether the current concern with generic and transferable skills training might enable a re-engagement with the knowledge that arises through practice (in this case the practice of doctoral education), 'despite the techno-rationality that is evident within the way such skills are often conceived?' (Barnacle and Dall'Alba 2008: 3). They suggest that this goes to the matter of the value of a research degree and how doctoral graduates might contribute to the workplace and society. Increasingly, as we have explained, this contribution is being formed by the demand for knowledge workers with disciplinary knowledge as only one component of the doctoral (Pearson 1996: 307) award. Added to this is a range of skills and dispositions necessary for undertaking such knowledge work and contributing to innovation so that doctoral graduates are able to translate their research skills into economic, social and cultural returns, which are both of private and public benefit. Yet, as they explain, a focus on research training can mean technical skilling, 'rather than the craft or artistry of research required for genuine skilful performance' (Barnacle and Dall'Alba 2008: 5), which is also nevertheless an alternative possible response.

Barnacle and Dall'Alba (2008) concur with those who argue that the artistry of professional practice 'involves a matter of "feel" and judgment, of knowing when to act, of being able to frame problematic situations and fashion new approaches, rather than just applying established routines' (Barnacle and Dall'Alba 2008: 5). But the other side of a focus on 'artistry' is the danger, they suggest, of an over reliance on tacit knowledge, which reinforces individualistic approaches to research practice and supervisory relationships not being open to scrutiny. They summarise the case as one of enhancing the process of doctoral research by identifying and promoting relevant skills on the one hand; or the reverse effect on the other:

> If we are seeking graduates with the ability to work creatively and contribute to innovation, are generic skills really what are required? Skilful practice and

know-how arise within the specificity of particular disciplinary, social and technological practices. If as a society, we want to benefit from the research knowledge and skills of higher degree research graduates, then we need approaches to research education that are neither reductive nor instrumental. An instrumental, reductive view of generic capabilities is necessarily detrimental to efforts to address skilful research practice.

Barnacle and Dall'Alba 2008: 6

They go even further than this. They acknowledge that it is 'reasonable' to expect research education as a preparation for contributions to social, cultural and economic development (broadly, self, others and society, see Booth *et al.* 2009); they raise questions about the feasibility or desirability of assuming any specific match with employment. To do so, they suggest, may ironically produce *less* rather than more skilful graduates.

If, following Barnacle and Dall'Alba (2008), doctoral education can be understood as professional preparation, as much as research preparation, then we need understandings of professionalism that are educational rather than economic. We also need to be aware of both the crisis and promise of professionalism in contemporary society (Sullivan 2005). As Barnacle and Dall'Alba (2008) suggest, we cannot take for granted that the 'professionalising' of the research curriculum will generate rich understandings of doctoral education as intellectual, technical and moral, having a responsibility for influencing public values and public goods, and 'connections to professionalism as a public value' (Sullivan 2005: 11). In our view, doctoral education is both a private benefit to students and a public good in which new and original knowledge and contributions are shared publicly, and professional claims are extended beyond the purely cognitive or technical.

In its own way a skills and training agenda opens up these questions, as Barnacle and Dall'Alba (2008) suggest, and makes available an important debate about doctoral education. The issue is what discourse of professionalism underpins such debates and the extent to which such a discourse is thick or thin. However, opening the debate opens space to assert an approach to doctoral education as embedded in 'thick' professionalism, which includes seeing one's work 'as part of a larger collective project' shaping personal identities and requiring 'considerable individual discernment and capacity for initiative and judgment' (Sullivan 2005: 15). Sullivan argues that a thick discourse of professionalism might address the problems generated by economic development, but also 'takes us beyond the simplistic idea that a market framework can solve the most important issues of social and political life', including 'what constitutes good work, for the society, and for the individual' (Sullivan 2005: 18).

Framed in this way, doctoral education poses significant and exciting challenges for students and their supervisors, and for and to universities. We are challenged to consider what 'good work' means in current times – and to ask how we blend the normative and the technical (skills and training), frame our concern with doctoral standards as concern for 'developing in [doctoral] students the capacity and disposition to perform in accordance with the best standards of a field in a way that serves the larger society' (Sullivan 2005: 30), and strengthen the connections between professionalism and democratic public life. We agree and suggest that doctoral education ought to be suffused with the practical technical competence necessary to do research well, but also be oriented to civic and social purposes and significant questions.

Doctoral education understood as 'thick' professionalism might then be seen as 'a life project' (Sullivan 2005: 22), a source of personal growth and professional renewal for those who undertake and successfully complete doctorates of different kinds, but also 'lived within a larger life' (Haworth 1977; quoted in Sullivan 2005: 22), having civic, ethical and public leadership 'capability' (Sen 1999) dimensions.

2. Life-long learning

Debates about the purposes, practices and outcomes of contemporary doctoral education in higher education institutions can also be productively situated in the context of life-long learning and life-long education (Aspin 2007). Taking this as a starting point means that the doctoral degree ought to be a preparation for learning beyond the award itself, and this, in turn, has implications for what is offered and what is learnt through undertaking doctoral study.

The agendas of life-long learning and doctoral education are remarkably similar. Thus, the European Cologne Charter *Aims and Ambitions for Lifelong Learning*, states that 'Economies and societies are increasingly knowledge-based. Education and [research] skills are indispensable to achieving economic success, civic responsibility and social cohesion' (Aspin 2007: 22). Like research training, the term life-long learning is contested but generally used approvingly, a good and worthwhile enterprise (Aspin 2007). After exploring various contested understandings and definitions of life-long learning, Aspin (2007) offers a metaphor for life-long learning that seems deeply applicable also to the process of doctoral education as a process and contribution to each person's life-long education. Aspin likens life-long learning to a process of coming to comprehend and review:

> [T]he theories with which we are working, to compare them with other theoretical efforts and productions of others faced with similar problems, to subject them to positive criticism, and to attempt to improve them and make them fit for their educational purpose; which is both efficient and excellent and to the good of individuals and societies.
>
> Aspin 2007: 32

According to Aspin (2007), we go on learning in this way, adopting a pragmatic 'evolutionary epistemology' (Bernstein 1983 in Aspin, 2007: 33) to make our own theories, 'meet for application, modification, and repair at every stage of our intellectual journey'. Such a view of life-long learning goes beyond economic purposes to increase, says Aspin (2007), the emancipation and participation of all citizens.

Increasingly, doctoral graduates face discontinuities and 'risk' (Beck 1992) through the life course and these intellectual journeys through which they must make their way. In the context of such uncertainties, a navigational reflexivity is central to doctoral education as a process of life-long learning that involves more than simply passively acquiring generic research skills and qualifications, but rather a form of learning that is 'more consonant with the needs of civic participation and of agents capable of autonomously generating change for themselves' (Edwards *et al.* 2002: 527). Having the kind of reflexivity that enables both self and social questioning develops our agency to shape contexts and conditions. Thus, Edwards *et al.* (2002) suggest that learning of this kind involves:

> [T]he transformation of understanding, identity and agency. ... involving a developing awareness which results in growing understanding of customary practice,

leading to reflexive social and self-questioning and the transformation of "habitus". It is the development of reflexivity, the capacity to develop critical awareness of the assumptions that underlie practices, especially the meta–cognitive, interpretive schema that constitute worlds, which we see as central to an adequate theory of life-long learning … the capacity to develop and sustain reflexivity.

Edwards et al. 2002: 532–3

Such reflexivity and dispositions are learnt in the context of actual practices, activities and learning relationships, including those of doctoral education, and in situated socio-cultural, institutional and historical contexts. Crucially, knowledge is the key to a *critical* reflexivity.

Life-long learning, and indeed doctoral education, is multi-dimensional, embracing economic opportunities, individual development and social goods, rather than a more impoverished neoliberal agenda of education as a private good (see, for example, Rizvi 2007). Although there may be 'no turning back' (Rizvi 2007: 129) from the shifts that have, in turn, influenced doctoral education, it is possible to 'imagine and work with' and create alternative traditions that embrace 'an open dialogue about the new requirements of education' (Rizvi 2007: 129), and promote educated citizens and educated publics (Barr and Griffiths 2007).

Given the world in which doctoral graduates live and work and our human futures, we need to retain knowledge at the centre of doctoral education as has been its traditional role, but also pay attention to being in the world (Barnett 2000). This leads us to ask not only what the knowledge outcomes of doctoral education are, but also what kind of human being we are hoping a doctorate might form through a rich mix of knowledge, skills and dispositions (see Walker Volume 2, Chapter 2).

References

Andrews, D. and Edwards, C. (2008) Consciousness in transition: the experience of doctoral study. In B. Cunningham (Ed.). *Exploring Professionalism*. London: Institute of Education.

Aronowitz, S. and Giroux, H. (2000) The corporate university and the politics of education, *The Educational Forum*, 64: 332–9.

Aspin, D. N. (2007) Introduction. In D.N. Aspin (Ed.). *Philosophical Perspectives on Lifelong Learning*. Dordrecht: Springer.

Barnacle, R. and Dall'Alba, G. (2008) *Professionalising the Research Higher Degrees Curriculum?* Paper presented at the Australian Association for Research in Education annual conference, Brisbane.

Barnett, R. (1997) *Higher Education: A Critical Business*. Buckingham: SRHE/Open University Press.

——(2000) *Realizing the University in an Age of Supercomplexity*. Buckingham: SRHE/Open University Press.

Barr, J. and Griffiths, M. (2007) The Nature of Knowledge and Lifelong Learning. In D.N. Aspin (Ed.). *Philosophical Perspectives on Lifelong Learning*. Dordrecht: Springer.

Beck, U. (1992) *Risk Society: Towards a New Modernity*. London: Sage.

Berliner, D. (2006) Towards a Future as Rich as Our Past. In C.M. Golde and G.E. Walker (Eds). *Envisioning the Future of Doctoral Education*. San Francisco, CA: Jossey Bass.

Bitusikova, A. (2009) Reforming Doctoral Education in Europe, *Academe Online*. (Available at www.aaup.org/AAUP/pubsres/academe/2009/JF/Feat/bitu.htm Accessed 11 February 2009).

Bleiklie, I. and Hostaker, R. (2004) Modernizing research training – education and science policy between profession, discipline and academic institution, *Higher Education Policy*, 17(2): 221–36.

Booth, A., McLean, M. and Walker, M. (2009) Self, others and society: A case study of university integrative learning, *Studies in Higher Education*, 34(8).

Brennan, M. (1998) Struggles over the definition and practice of the Educational Doctorate in Australia, *Australian Educational Researcher*, 25(1): 71–89.

Brown, P. (2003) The Opportunity Trap: education and employment in a global economy, *European Educational Research Journal*, 2(1): 141–79.

Butcher, J. and Sieminiski, S. (2006) The challenge of a distance learning professional doctorate in education, *Open Learning*, 21(1): 59–69.

Carnoy, M. and Rhoten, D. (2002) What Does Globalization Mean for Educational Change? A Comparative Approach, *Comparative Education Review*, 46(1): 1–9.

Castells, M. (2004) *Universities and Cities in a World of Global Networks*, Sir Robert Birley Lecture, City University, London, 17 March 2004.

Castellanos, J., Gloria, A.M. and Kamimura, M. (Eds) (2006) *The Latina/o Pathway to the PhD: Abriendo carninos*. Sterling: Stylus Publishing.

Chapman, A. and Pyvis, D. (2006) Dilemmas in the formation of student identity in offshore higher education: a case study in Hong Kong, *Educational Review*, 58(3): 291–302.

Coate, K. and Leonard, D. (2002) The structure of research training in England, *Australian Educational Researcher*, 29(3): 19–42.

Collinson, J.A. (2005) Artistry and analysis: student experiences of UK practice-based doctorates in art and design, *International Journal of Qualitative Studies in Education*, 18(6): 713–28.

Costley, C. and Armsby, P. (2007) Research influences on a professional doctorate, *Research in Post-Compulsory Education*, (12)3: 343–57.

Coyle, D. and Quah, D. (2002) *Getting the measure of the new economy*. London: The Work Foundation.

Crossouard, B. (2008) Developing alternative models of doctoral supervision with online formative assessment, *Studies in Continuing Education*, 30(1): 51–67.

Davies, J. (1996) *Dangers of no liaisons*, Times Higher Education. Online. (Available at www.timeshigher education.co.uk/storyasp?setioncode=26&storycode=924534 Accessed 6 March 2009).

Edwards, R. Ranson, S. and Strain, M. (2002) Reflexivity: towards a theory of lifelong learning, *International Journal of Lifelong Education*, 21(6): 525–36.

Evans, M. (2004) *Killing Thinking: The Death of the Universities*. London: Continuum Felton 2002.

Frow, J. (1997) *Time and Commodity Culture*. Oxford: Clarendon Press.

Gilbert, R. (2004) A framework for evaluating the doctoral curriculum, *Assessment and Evaluation in Higher Education*, 29(3): 299–309.

Gill, J. (2009) Professional Doctorates, *Times Higher Education*, 26 February 2009: 30–5.

Gillies, V. and Lucey, H. (Eds) (2007) *Power, Knowledge and the Academy*. Hampshire: Palgrave MacMillan.

Giroux, H. (2001) Commodification of Higher Education. In H.Giroux and K. Myrsiades (Eds). *Beyond the Corporate University*. Lanharn, MD: Rowman and Littlefield Publishers.

Giroux, H.A. and Myriades, K. (Eds) (2001) *Beyond the Corporate University*. Lanham, MD: Rowman and Littlefield.

Golde, C.E. (2006) Preparing Stewards of the Discipline. In C.M. Golde and G.E. Walker (Eds). *Envisioning the Future of Doctoral Education*. San Francisco, CA: Jossey Bass.

Golde, C.M and Walker, G.E. (Eds) (2006) *Envisioning the Future of Doctoral Education*. San Francisco, CA: Jossey Bass.

Goode, J. (2007) Empowering or disempowering the international PhD student? Constructions of the dependent and independent learner, *British Journal of Sociology of Education*, 28(5): 589–604.

Green, A. and Scott, L.V. (Eds) (2003) *Journey to the PhD How to Navigate the Process as African Americans*. Sterling: Stylus Publishing.

Habermas, J. (1987). *The theory of communicative action. Volume 2. Lifeworld and system*. Translated by T. McCarthy. Boston, MA: Beacon Press.

Haworth, L. (1977) *Decadence and Objectivity*. Toronto: University of Toronto Press.

Health, L. (2006) Supervision of professional doctorates: education doctorates in English universities, *Higher Education Review*, 38(2): 21–41.

HEFCE (1996) *Review of Postgraduate Education*, Bristol: HEFCE. Online. (Available at www.hefce.ac. uk/pubs/hefce/1996/m14_96.htm Accessed 9 July 2009).

HEPI (2004) *Higher Education Supply and Demand to 2010 – an Update*. Oxford: Higher Education Policy Institute.

Higgs, P. (2006) Higher Education is more than just about the economy, *South African Journal of Higher Education*, 20(6): 838–42.

Holbrook, A. and Johnston, S. (Eds) (1999) *Supervision of Postgraduate Research in Education*. Coldsteam: AARE.

Holford, J. (2008) There is a wider purposes for universities than 'serving the economy', *The Times Higher*, 13 November 2008: 24–5.

Johnston, B. and Murray, R. (2004) New routes to the PhD: cause for concern? *Higher Education Quarterly*, 58(1): 31–42.

Kehm, B. (2007) Quo Vadis Doctoral Education? New European Approaches in the Context of Global Changes, *European Journal of Education*, 42(3): 307–19.

Kenway, J., Bullen, E., Fahey, J. and Robb, S. (2006) *Haunting the Knowledge Economy*. London and New York: Routledge.

Kwiek, M. (2003) The State, the Market and Higher Education, Challenges for the New Century. In M. Kwiek (Ed.). *The University, Globalization and Central Europe*. Frankfurt and New York: Peter Lang.

Lave, J. and Wenger, E. (1998). *Communities of Practice: Learning, Meaning, and Identity*. Cambridge: Cambridge University Press.

Leonard, D. (2001) *A Woman's Guide to Doctoral Studies*. Buckingham: Open University Press.

Leonard, D., Metcalfe, J., Becker, R. and Evans, J. (2006) *Review of literature on the impact of working context and support on the postgraduate research student learning experience*. York: Higher Education Academy.

Marcus, J. (2009) Comic Strip Hero, *Times Higher Education*, 12 February 2009.

Mastekaasa, A. (2005) Gender differences in educational attainment: the case of doctoral degrees in Norway, *British Journal of Sociology of Education*, 26(3): 375–94.

McClure, J. W. (2005) Preparing a laboratory-based thesis: Chinese international research students' experience of supervision, *Teaching in Higher Education*, 10(1): 3–16.

Neumann, R. (2007) Policy and practice in doctoral education, *Studies in Higher Education*, 32(4): 459–74.

Nussbaum, M. (1997) *Cultivating Humanity. A Classical Defence of Reform in Liberal Education*. Cambridge, MA: Harvard University Press.

OECD (1996) *The Knowledge-Based Economy*. Paris: OECD.

Papestephanou, M. and Angeli, C. (2007) Critical Thinking Beyond Skill, *Educational Philosophy and Theory*, 39(6): 604–21.

Park, C. (2005) New variant PhD: the changing nature of the doctorate in the UK, *Journal of Higher Education Policy and Management*, 27(2): 189–207.

——(2007) *Redefining the Doctorate*. York: Higher Education Academy.

Parker, J. (2007) Future Priorities of the Humanities in Europe: What Have the Humanities to Offer? *Arts and Humanities in Higher Education*, 6(1): 123–7.

Pearson, M. (1996) Professionalizing PhD Education to enhance the quality of the student experience, *Higher Education*, 32: 303–20.

Peters, M. (2004) Higher Education, Globalization and the Knowledge Economy. In M. Walker and J. Nixon (Eds). *Reclaiming Universities from a Runaway World*. Maidenhead: SRHE/Open University Press.

Peters, M. and Besley, A. C. (2006) Public Knowledge Cultures, *South African Journal of Higher Education*, 20(6): 792–806.

Peters, M. and Besley, A. C. (2006a) *Building Knowledge Cultures*. Lanham, MD: Rowman and Littlefield.

QAA (2008) *The Framework for higher education qualifications in England, Wales and Northern Ireland*. Online. (Available at www.qaa.ac.uk/academicinfrastructure/fheq/ewnio8/ Accessed 18 March 2009).

Readings, B. (1996) *The University in Ruins*. Cambridge, MA: Harvard University Press.

Reisz, M. (2008) Doctor, doctor, quick, quick, *Times Higher Education*, 4 December 2008: 32–5.

Richardson, V. (2006) Stewards of a Field, Stewards of an Enterprise. The Doctorate in Education. In C.M. Golde and G.E. Walker (Eds). *Envisioning the Future of Doctoral Education*. San Francisco, CA: Jossey Bass.

Rizvi, F. (2007) Lifelong Learning: Beyond Neo-Liberal Imaginary. In D.N. Aspin (Ed.). *Philosophical Perspectives on Lifelong Learning*. Dordrecht: Springer.

Rodgers, M. (2006) *Poor less likely to study for PhD*. Times Higher Education. Online. (Available at www.timeshighereducationco.uk/story.asp?sectioncode=26&storycode-204651 Accessed 6 March 2009).

Rowland, S. (2006) *The Enquiring University*. Maidenhead: SRHE/Open University Press.

Sanders, C. (2004) QAA targets PhD 'cronyism', *Times Higher Education*. Online. (Available at www.timeshighereducation.co.uk/story.asp?sectioncode=26&storycode=183734 Accessed on 6 March 2009).

Sarros, J.C., Willis, R.J. and Palmer, G. (2005) The nature and purpose of the DBA: a case for clarity and quality control, *Education + Training*, 47(1): 40–52.

Sen, A. (1999) *Development as Freedom*. Oxford: Oxford University Press.

Stephenson, J. (2006) Managing their own programme: a case study of the first graduates of a new kind of doctorate in professional practice, *Studies in Continuing Education*, 28(1): 17–32.

Stiglitz, J. (1999) Knowledge as a global public good. In I. Kaul, I. Grunberg and M.A. Stern (Eds). *Global Public Goods: international cooperation in the 21st century*. Oxford: Clarendon Press.

Stromquist, N. (2002) *Education in a Globalized World. The Connectivity of Economic Power, Technology and Knowledge*. Lanham, MD: Rowman and Littlefield Publishers.

Sullivan, W.M. (2005) *Work and Integrity: The Crisis and Promise of Professionalism in America*. 2nd edn. Sanford, CA: Jossey-Bass.

Sussex, R. (2008) Technological options in supervising remote research students, *Higher Education*, 55(1): 121–37.

Taysum, A. (2007a) The distinctiveness of the EdD within the university tradition, *Journal of Higher Educational Administration and History*, 39(2): 323–34.

Taysum, A. (2007b) The distinctiveness of the EdD in Producing and Transforming Knowledge, *Journal of Higher Educational Administration and History*, 39(3): 285–96.

Thomson, A. (1996) Doctoral research in standards limbo. *Times Higher Education Supplement*. Online. (Available at www.timeshighereducation.co.uk/storyasp?sectioncode=26%storycode=94108 Accessed 9 July 2009).

Tubin, D. and Lapidot, O. (2008) Construction of 'glocal' (global–local) identity among Israeli graduate students in the USA, *Higher Education*, 55(2): 203–17.

VITAE (2009) *What do researchers do? First destinations of doctoral graduates by subject*. Online. (Available at voate.ac.uk/CMS/files/upload/Vitae-WDRD-by-subject-Jun-09.pdf Accessed 5 July 2009).

Walker, G. E. (2006) The Questions in the Back of the Book. In C.M. Golde and G.E. Walker (Eds). *Envisioning the Future of Doctoral Education*. San Francisco, CA: Jossey Bass.

Wellington, J. and Sikes, P. (2006) 'A Doctorate in a Tight Compartment': Why Do Students Choose a Professional Doctorate and What Impact Does It Have on Their Personal and Professional Lives?' *Studies in Higher Education*, 31 (6): 723–34.

Western, M. and Lawson, A. (2008) Doctorates ailing on the world stage, *The Australian*. Online. (Available at www.theaustralian.news.com.au/story/0,25197,23319781–27702,00.html Accessed 8 March 2008).

Yates, L. (2004) *What does Good Education Research look like?* Maidenhead: Open University Press.

Part 2

Becoming and being a doctoral student

M. Walker and P. Thomson

i) Producing knowledge

The first cluster of chapters take up the issue of producing and pursuing knowledge. This sits at the heart of doctoral research. We begin with the chapter by Jon Wagner, which we have found useful in working with our own doctoral students. Wagner develops his argument for the counter intuitive notion of ignorance, rather than the pursuit of truth in social science research. He elaborates the idea of blank spots and blind spots. Blank spots are areas waiting to be filled in with empirical description and detail though research, but blind spots are created through looking at one thing but missing another and thus obscuring the truth we are trying to produce through our research. Wagner, therefore, advises a more humble and modest approach to our truth claims, advocating that we see our research as reducing ignorance and that truth is then partial, situated and revisable. Using an extended example from Howard Becker's book on social science writing, Wagner helps to concretise the problem of ignorance over truth. He notes that reducing ignorance is always undertaken in a particular field and that it requires attention to the research process, as well as a more inclusive approach to knowledge, which recognises expertise while also seeing the importance of knowledge communities outside the boundary of the researcher's inner circle. At issue, then, as the chapter by Jean Barr in the next cluster also argues, is the making of new knowledge with and by different knowledge communities.

Erica McWilliam and Jennifer Tan present a story of supervision and being supervised, but here the narrative is framed by cultural difference and conversations about the nature of knowledge. Their chapter enters the conversation about knowledge making and truth advanced by Wagner. McWilliam and Tan hold both threads together in the frame of methodological debates, difference and conversation, thereby making the knowledge project more explicit. They advocate developing 'epistemological agility', in the space between measuring and interpreting. In this doctoral journey both supervisor and student have learned how to lead and how to follow, equal agents in the research and knowledge production and dissemination process.

Des Gasper highlights the limits of discipline-based knowledge in addressing complex social problems. Yet, as the previous chapters attest, disciplinary networks and boundaries are both social and intellectual, and these boundaries exercise control over what can count as knowledge and research in a discipline. Such boundary patrols are not friendly to the eclecticism of interdisciplinarity. Nonetheless, Gasper argues that we need to become interdisciplinary in our approaches to research issues and questions, both as individuals and in research teams, so that we might shed new light on blank spots, which are not evident within disciplinary structures. His chapter provides examples of particularly generative interdisciplinary co-operation, and how these open up fresh connections not evident before for the making of 'humanly useful knowledge'.

ii) Theory and research

The next cluster of chapters takes up the central importance of theories and conceptual framing in the doctoral research process, building on from the earlier chapters on knowledge making. Overall, the writers agree that without attention to theories and concepts, doctoral research comes unstuck at some point in the dissertation process. For Stephen Ball, robust, rigorous attention to theory marks out high-quality work and provides relevance beyond the specific study. Resonating with Wagner's notion of reducing ignorance rather than attaining doctoral truth, Ball underlines the useful work that theory does – problematising, critiquing, challenging and complexifying. Ball shows how theory informs his own research on education and social class enabling him to challenge taken-for-granted orthodoxies, and opening space to understand the social conditions for the production of knowledge. He advocates that, as educational researchers, we ought to appreciate better the work that theory does – for finding concepts to frame the study, for analysis and interpretation and for reflexivity.

Kalervo Gulson and Rob Parkes relate such claims about theory to the specificity of doctoral studies and the 'pleasures and perils' attendant on bringing theory in/to doctoral research. They emphasise that theory is necessary to becoming a scholar, to scholarly identities, and to scholarly practice. Theory forms knowledge and theory enables scholarly argument, by the doctoral scholar. This, they suggest, also enables (rather than disabling, as is sometimes argued) doctoral scholars to find their own voices. The idea is not to be overtaken, overwhelmed or overcome by theory, but to locate oneself with confidence (supported by supervisors) within a theoretical landscape appropriate to the study. Theory works on, and for the doctoral researcher in, productive and expansive ways.

For Feng Su, Jon Nixon and Bob Adamson, conceptual work specifically contributes in interpretive enquiry to the search for understanding. Through concepts we come to know what we are looking for and what we are looking at. Concepts provide signposts without which we cannot know where we are going or how to get there. Thus, the search to understand requires solid conceptual work and conceptual mediation in communicating ideas and understanding to different audiences. But, the authors warn, there is rarely a readymade conceptual apparatus available from theory. Rather, the doctoral researcher must do the work of constructing her own frameworks in the early stages of her study, her own 'theoretical searchlight'. This struggle is integral to producing good research questions and good research. Methodology then grows out of this theory and conceptualisation, and does not precede it or proceed without it. Like Gulson and Parkes, this chapter notes the importance of process in enabling people to find their own voices, with Su recounting his own struggles in the early stages of his doctoral study. Voice, theory, concepts and methodology are then woven together by the Confucian conceptual thread in an intellectually 'joyful endeavour'. This emphasis on joy, hinted at also by Gulson and Parkes reminds us of the enchantment and delight that comes with and from engaging with challenge and ideas and making them one's own.

Jean Barr's chapter demonstrates how different theoretical approaches and related concepts work to generate different, and partial, research narratives about the object under investigation. She illustrates this convincingly by her reflections on three of her own research projects into women's lives carried out at intervals over a 20-year period. Barr further locates this reflexive revisiting of her earlier theoretical assumptions within broader processes of knowledge production, arguing for the need to be more inclusive and attentive to communities outside the academy; allowing activity and knowledge 'from below'. In other words, important though good theory and theorising is, our grappling with ideas needs to be purposeful. For whom, for what is the better knowledge we hope to produce? For truly 'liberating knowledge', she argues, we need to be participants in an ongoing social, and not only an intellectual dialogue. Theoretical deployments are thus intellectual, social and political with the purpose of forming educated publics as much as educated scholars in an ongoing reflexive process.

iii) Becoming and being

Finally, we turn to a cluster of chapters that bring us right into the becoming process of a doctoral scholar.

Anthony Paré's chapter zooms in on a particular aspect of doctoral pedagogy, that of supervisor feedback on draft texts of student writing. Paré addresses this crucial issue of how to receive feedback and how to make sense of what a supervisor means, in order to learn and strengthen a doctoral identity rather than be diminished or lose confidence. He opens out a window into the act and feedback actions of the supervision process; his key purpose is to help students to understand what supervisors mean when they respond to and talk about a piece of doctoral writing. The more students understand this process of writing and feedback, and how it relates to thinking (about their research, about what they are reading, about the discussions in which they take part ...) the better placed they are to locate themselves as agents in scholarly conversations. Thus, Paré seeks to make explicit what is going on in the feedback process.

Using South Africa as a particularly compelling case, Crain Soudien explores doctoral level preparation as a process suffused with marginalisation and exclusion for non-traditional students – women and students of colour. In the South African case, race acts as a strong marker of such marginalisation and is compounded for students who are the first in their families to undertake doctoral study. Although the South African case may be especially stark, universities internationally are stratified and diversified through structures of race gender, social class, nationality and so on, and the challenge of being a doctoral student in South Africa will be familiar and recognisable more widely. Thus, the four 'Universes' that Soudien outlines, which comprise the doctoral research process – of research paradigms, of social context, of knowledge, and of professional development – are familiar and knowable. As Soudien notes, the Universes bring into focus a complex dialectic of structures and agents, which each student negotiates and navigates as she constructs her individual doctoral pathway. Each Universe generates its own challenges (and offers helpful reflexive tools for doctoral students to talk together about their own experiences). Challenges of supervisor capacity, or funding, or prior preparedness for doctoral study resonate well beyond the South African case. Soudien offers valuable stories of being and becoming doctoral students – problems of disorientation, of dissonance and alienation. What emerges is the importance of universities courageous enough to reimagine themselves by exploring the value of difference.

The final chapter in this section works to pull together the disparate strands of supervision, knowledge, theories and methodology and diversity and purposes, while anticipating the chapters still to come, by tracing the multiple elements that comprise the doctoral journey. Jerry Wellington weaves together these threads into an accessible and practical research journey narrative from the outset through to the viva and publication of the research. On the way, he offers helpful advice so that doctoral scholars might successfully complete their journeys and enter into a community of scholars. He also generates questions doctoral scholars might ask of themselves and their own work, and by tracking the various stages of the doctoral process he enables students to understand in which direction they are heading and what they need to arrive at their destination.

2

Ignorance in educational research

How not knowing shapes new knowledge

J. Wagner

The most daunting of doctoral programme challenges is the expectation that graduate students conduct original research that generates new knowledge. This is a formidable ideal for anyone, but especially for people just beginning their acquaintance with the old knowledge.

Few graduate students appreciate, however, that their beginner's ideas about new knowledge are much more grandiose than the ideals their faculty mentors will hold them to. Faculty members won't necessarily tell them that because, in other respects, the asymmetries point the other way. Student ideas about what it means to critically evaluate a line of research, for example, frequently fall short of faculty expectations. But when it comes to the new knowledge ideal, students tend to aim for the stars and fear they'll never get there, whereas faculty members place one foot in front of the other and just move along.

My own experience as a graduate student and mentor suggests that students can benefit greatly from the one foot in front of the other point of view, but only if they have both feet on the ground. That's more likely to happen if students understand the pragmatic contexts in which knowledge can be defined as new – not just by doctoral students, but also by faculty members and other researchers. These contexts usually have something to do with being well informed, industrious, creative, clear thinking and truthful, but they have at least as much or more to do with ignorance.

By ignorance, I mean the role and structure of collective deficits in academic understanding. My argument is that most doctoral students will have an easier go of their dissertation research if they begin by looking for that kind of ignorance than if they begin by looking for new knowledge.

Ignorance and new knowledge

As a point of departure for understanding the kind of ignorance I have in mind, consider the potential of a high school yearbook to help generate new knowledge about education and schooling. At first blush, the prospects are not good. Yearbook accounts provide little or no information about the academic performance of students, the curriculum or financial resources, or about the credentials and careers of teachers, administrators or support staff. As a rule enforced by administrators and faculty who supervise student editors, yearbooks also avoid references to disciplinary issues, drugs, dropouts and other indicators of academic, personal or institutional failure. Yearbook photographs are also a pretty contrived lot. Subjects are carefully posed, their resulting likenesses altered to remove blemishes and flyaway hair. Clubs and groups are everywhere in evidence, but there's not a classroom in sight.

All this suggests that a high school yearbook is untrustworthy, arbitrarily selective, and incomplete, and that it falls far short of providing good data for studying a school. If I have first hand knowledge of the school, the yearbook looks even worse. With direct evidence of distortion and neglect, it would be tempting to define the yearbook in terms of its deficits alone.

But let's say I want to compare this school with another one, or to the same school at another point in time. Could the yearbook contribute to that effort? Perhaps. Yearbook pictures and names might help me identify the ethnic and linguistic heritage of students and teachers or their gender distribution. Or, even if I knew about that from other sources, the yearbook might be the only source of information about how these variables correlate with participation in different school activities.

Let's say I want to report about this school to people who know much less about it than I do. Could the yearbook help with that? What if these people were colleagues of mine from another country, Brazil or China, for example? If I show them the yearbook they might notice that it was written in English. Is that a distortion of the school? They might also note the social organisation of students into four classes, each identified by their graduation year, and note as well the special status of the senior class. In yearbook photographs they might also find evidence of clothing, dancing and sporting activities that differ markedly from the schools they know best in Brazil or China. In helping me communicate all this to them, the yearbook might be a rich source of information indeed, a vehicle for generating what is, to them (and, reciprocally, to me) new knowledge about education and schooling.

As these speculations suggest, in assessing the yearbook's potential to help generate new knowledge, we can begin with what we know about truth or with what we know about ignorance. In the first instance, we ask, how closely does the yearbook approximate a truthful picture of the school? In the second, we ask, compared to what we don't know without it, in what ways can the yearbook help us know more?

Both sets of questions are worth asking, but doctoral students too often beat the second into submission by fealty to the first. It's easy for them to forget what makes a high school yearbook, a fourfold table, an index of statistical correlations, a narrative account of field research or any other document useful to generating new knowledge. These diverse data are not useful to researchers because they are 'true' in some absolute sense, but because they are just 'true enough' to challenge or diminish some form of collective ignorance. The implications of this generalisation for developing a programme of research – doctoral or beyond – become clearer when we consider two different forms this ignorance can take.

Blind spots and blank spots

In constructing new knowledge, researchers use a variety of materials to shape, test, explicate and illustrate propositions about their corner of the world. These materials include data of various forms and types, direct experience, concepts, theories of their own, or those developed by others, and so on. Some of these materials help researchers answer questions they have already considered. Others stimulate them to ask questions they haven't asked before.

These two kinds of questions correspond to two different kinds of ignorance. Questions already familiar to researchers and their colleagues define *blank spots* in emergent theories and conceptions of knowledge. These are matters that scholars know they don't understand. But other kinds of research materials illuminate *blind spots*. These extend outwards from patterned phenomena that existing theories, methods, and perspectives actually keep scholars from seeing, patterns they have not yet noticed.

One way of distinguishing between scientists and non-scientists – or between scientists working in different disciplines or sub-disciplines – is by the characteristic configuration of their blind spots and blank spots, the structure of their collective ignorance. Following the work of Thomas Kuhn (1970), this structure can be represented for a particular tradition of enquiry (e.g. sociology, anthropology, psychology, history, etc.) by a 'disciplinary matrix'. Rows of such a matrix can represent concepts or methods of investigation, the columns phenomena that members of the discipline tend to examine. A matrix of this sort defines sets of related cells, each corresponding to the intersection of a particular concept or method and a particular object of investigation.

Borrowing from different parts of a well-known synthesis by Smelser (1988), a small section of a matrix of this sort for sociology might look something like Table 2.1.

Research contributions of different sociologists could be located within particular cells in a matrix of this sort. Some do work that falls within cells that adjoin along particular rows to examine a concept or theme (e.g. social stratification) across a varied range of phenomena (e.g. jobs and work, education, and so on). Others look at a specific phenomenon (e.g. education) from a range of concepts and perspectives (e.g. social control, stratification, status attainment, and so on).

Social scientists can also construct a more detailed matrix of rows and columns within a single cell of the larger disciplinary matrix. In Table 2.2, for example, I have taken one column from the sociological matrix displayed above – the column called 'sociology of education' – and expanded it into a matrix in its own right.

Table 2.1 One corner of a matrix of sociological inquiry

Themes of Analysis	Phenomena Under Investigation				
	Jobs and Work	Sociology of Education	Sociology of Religion	Medical Sociology	Political Sociology
Social control					
Social stratification					
Status attainment					
Bases of integration and differentiation: class, gender, age, race and ethnicity, etc.					
Social relationships: group, household, community, collectivity					
Social change					

Table 2.2 Sub-matrix for sociology of education

Themes of Analysis	Phenomena Under Investigation				
	Lessons	Classrooms	Schools	School Districts & Communities	The State
Social control					
Social stratification					
Status attainment					
Bases of integration and differentiation: class, gender, age, race and ethnicity, etc.					
Social relationships: group, household, community, collectivity					
Social change					

Blank spot ignorance corresponds to cells of the sub-matrix that are visible, clearly marked, but have not been investigated as adequately as scholars would like. Blind spot ignorance corresponds to matters that don't fit anywhere on the grid. The concepts or phenomena they implicate are not so much missing from cells where we think they should belong, but obscured by the matrix itself. The simplified matrices presented above for sociology and for the sociology of education, for example, obscure attention to individual personalities, technology, and the global economy. An historical example or two may illustrate these distinctions more clearly.

Blind spots in educational research

During the 1970s, Christopher Jencks and his associates conducted a series of ambitious studies about the outcomes of schooling (Jencks *et al.* 1972; 1979). These studies used aggregate data analysis to investigate a row of variable characteristics of schools and a column of schooling effects for different populations of students. The effects in question were educational and occupational achievement subsequent to elementary and secondary schooling. The significance of these studies was linked to increasing concerns about educational equity and the growth in the 1960s of policy interest in alternatives to conventional schools.

The blank spots addressed by the Jencks studies were important, well-established questions, but the framework and aggregate data analysis guiding their enquiries obscured other ways of looking at similar and related phenomena. One set of phenomena obscured in this way involved the achievement and experience of *individual students* in *individual classes*. In a complementary research study, Summers and Wolfe (1975; 1977) took the careers of individual students – not student populations – as a point of reference. They asked some of the same questions about different classrooms that Jencks asked about different schools. In doing so, they came to quite different conclusions.

Jencks and his associates found that organisational differences *between* schools did not generate different schooling outcomes for different groups of students – a conclusion that paralleled the Coleman *et al.* (1966) studies of a decade or so earlier. But Summers and Wolfe found that differences among classrooms *within* schools did generate significantly different outcomes, and did so for members of the same groups examined by Jencks. By aggregating students into groups and classrooms into schools, the Jencks' studies collapsed these differences and made them invisible. By disaggregating school effects by individual students and classrooms, the Summers and Wolfe study made them visible, but it simultaneously concealed the school-wide outcomes documented by Jencks. Each study collected and analysed data to fill in well-defined blank spots, but the framework guiding each approach also created corresponding blind spots.

Matrices true or useful?

Both scientists and lay people have blind spots and blank spots, but scientists have organised their working lives around some of their blank spots. Their reputations and livelihood depend on their ability to use, collect, and create materials to fill these in with additional detail. Given their dedication to avoiding errors in that specialised task, it is understandable that scholars define their investigations as a pursuit of truth. This certainly sets them apart from others who want to fill in blank spots with fantasy and speculation. However, because focusing on particular blank spots always generates some corresponding blind spots, truth seems overly ambitious for judging what they do.

Reducing ignorance seems a better bet, in two respects. First, ignorance provides a pragmatic, rather than merely theoretical, criterion for assessing the value of a research project. Does the research help us fill in a blank spot or reveal a blind spot, or does it not? Second, ignorance is far more likely than truth to invite contextual explication. That is, ignorance claims go hand in hand with attributions to particular groups and individuals, but that's less likely for truth claims. Indeed, within the culture of scholarship, truth claims emphasise timelessness, anonymity, and independence from context and historical moment. Statements about ignorance are more likely to be grounded in particular people, places, times and contexts.

In just these terms, doctoral students who tie their own conception of new knowledge to truth claims can lose their way. Well-defined blind spots or blank spots, however, can provide a map for staying on track. Even when all blind spots are filled in, a map of disciplinary rows and columns can still create opportunities for generating new knowledge. The stimulus required can be as simple as renaming a row or column or merging a pair of cells, or as complex as adding a row or column from the matrix of another discipline. In fact, the borrowed column or row can be far from the cutting edge of a source matrix and still revitalise scholars working within another discipline.

During the late 1980s and 1990s, for example, one of the great new knowledge stories among educational researchers was the importance of social contexts to how and what individuals learned. In some sense this was an unlikely news story. Willard Waller had given life and credence to this perspective in his 1932 book, *The Sociology of Teaching*, and George and Louise Spindler had elaborated it further through their anthropological writings of the 1950s, 1960s and 1970s. But social contexts issues fell to one side among educational researchers themselves, most of whom, for the middle decades of the last century, were trained in psychology.

The emergence of 'social contexts of learning' as new knowledge within the education profession caught some scholars already attuned to these issues quite off guard. At one of two major sessions devoted to this topic during the 1988 national conference of the American Educational Research Association, a panellist remarked:

I have no idea how this change has occurred, but when we held a similar session at the AERA meetings two years ago there were 25 people in the room. Today we have two sessions on the programme and over 1,500 people attending.

The circumstances leading to this shift in emphasis included changes in the national political climate, more than a little policy activity at the state and federal level, a change in the disciplinary affiliations of AERA members, and changes in the schools. The shift itself, however, can be represented by adding a row or column or two from the matrices within which Waller and the Spindlers had worked to the disciplinary matrices of psychologists and other educational researchers. Stated in somewhat too simple terms, the new knowledge of 'social context' was a discovery among psychologists that the categories guiding their research had hidden significant aspects of phenomena they were trying to understand.

This kind of disciplinary annexation is in no way limited to psychology. Discussions about re-incorporating the 'individual' into anthropology (see Wolcott 1991; Trueba 1991; Spindler and Spindler 1991) or sociology point in just the opposite direction. Similar patterns appear among other social science disciplines and among the social sciences, natural sciences and humanities. Members of any discipline can become engaged by new questions that fall outside their old matrix of enquiry and that subsequently appear as added rows or columns. But these questions are not necessarily new to the world. They may be new for researchers doing the borrowing, but they're old for those they are borrowed from.

Because they are less fully socialised into their prospective professions, graduate students are in a somewhat better position to do this kind of borrowing than some of their faculty mentors. That can make for disagreements between graduate students and advisors about methods, concepts and research questions. However, it can also stimulate new kinds of thinking, new applications and new knowledge.

Do these annexations and extensions of disciplinary matrices lead researchers to knowledge that is timeless and independent of context and historical moment? Do they lead scholars closer to the truth? Some might argue that they do, but that description may not fit as well as another, that they reduce the collective ignorance of scientists working in a particular field. A broader and more inclusive perspective, method or theory can help reduce the ignorance stemming from limitations of an existing perspective. But there is no end to what we don't know about our perspectives, methods and theories. As a result, we can frequently determine whether or not a particular approach is useful to reducing ignorance, but we can never confirm that it will generate knowledge that is new to one and all, for all time, everywhere.

Researchers, graduate students and teaching

Thinking about ignorance as the starting point for defining new knowledge has some implications for what veteran researchers do with each other, but probably not too many. Researchers who have exercised their craft for many years work in what Van Maanen and Barley (1984) call 'occupational communities' that have agreed upon ways of doing things. These are as rational as anybody else's, and they are familiar.

Graduate students are in a somewhat different situation. They are just beginning to develop a sense of how disciplinary research works. Where veteran scholars see rows and columns of a matrix, graduate students see largely blank pages dotted with small clusters of studies that lack a unifying order. Indeed, a significant blank spot for graduate students and practitioners is the disciplinary research matrix itself. That's why they can leap so easily from a small node of freshly read reports to generalised questions that over run their warrant. No rows and columns appear to contain or format significant interests. No adjacent cells point to related disciplinary concerns. No columns or rows illuminate or constrain perspectives worth considering in consort with the spot they've chosen to work on.

One way for doctoral students to begin filling in these relatively blank pages is to think less about research, and generating new knowledge, and more about teaching other researchers. For example, if we replace idealised truth claims for research with more modest claims for reducing ignorance, the latter point not only towards a topic but also towards a target group or audience. This articulation of research with teaching alerts us to questions about how research is reported, to whom, and to what effect. As one extension of this perspective, it's important to remember that the people we want to teach have blind spots and blank spots of their own. To teach them effectively, we need to study and consider their own matrices of enquiry, their own rows and columns.

Graduate students rarely notice just how much time veteran researchers spend doing just that for the other scholars to whom they direct lessons from their research, but a well-known genre for summarising these enquiries is the 'literature review'. For many graduate students, the function of this review is to demonstrate how much they have read of what their dissertation advisors recommended. In a thoughtful, professionally mature, publication, however, a literature review (or critique of the literature) provides the introduction to a lesson. It orients other scholars to what the author thinks they ought to know and why this might be important.

Approaching the dissertation literature review from a teaching point of view has two important implications: first, it directs attention to the intended audience for a proposed or completed study. Until that audience is reasonably well defined, it's unclear what kind of introduction will be required or effective. An audience of sociologists could benefit from a different orientation, for example, from an audience of linguists, even if what the intended lesson is about − e.g. peer learning, policy discourse, classroom technology or teaching credential requirements − is the same. These orientations and introductions matter quite a bit, not just for helping different audiences understand a lesson but also in helping them see what might be new about it.

A second implication is that an effective introduction will be attuned to the lesson itself. For graduate students, this is more complicated than it seems, in part because they are frequently encouraged (or even required) to prepare a literature review as part of their dissertation proposal. This encouragement presupposes that the lesson that will be taken away from the dissertation research can be pretty well defined prior to conducting the research. That may be more likely in some kinds of studies than others. For many doctoral students, however, the most notable lessons from their dissertation research will not be clear until their research is well along, or, in some cases, over and done with.

If lessons emerging from a dissertation research project diverge substantially from initial expectations, a literature review based on the dissertation proposal won't work. It might demonstrate that a student has read what faculty advisers recommended at the time, but it will miss the mark of introducing the new lesson. By keeping this prospect in mind, graduate students and their dissertation advisers can avoid potential disconnects between literature review and data analysis. All too often, these two sections of a dissertation can appear as two unrelated columns in the dissertation matrix: one introducing topic X and another reporting observations of topic Y.

Researchers, subjects and practitioners

In addition to giving graduate students a pragmatic framework for guiding their dissertation research, using ignorance as a reference point has implications for how researchers work with research subjects and for boundaries between research communities, practitioners and policy makers. Defined in these terms, ignorance-based research may appear to be more accessible, understandable and productive to non-academics than the more ambitious and abstract ideal of 'pursuing truth'. In recent years, this outcome has been increasingly valued within the professions, particularly those embracing the 'reflective-practitioner' ideal (Schon 1983; 1987; Agyris, Putnam and Smith 1985; Goodlad 1990).

Reflective-practitioner and practitioner-research efforts have met with a fair amount of criticism from members of more traditional academic research communities. This criticism is certainly understandable. The studies teachers conduct of their classrooms – or those that other professionals conduct of their workplace and practice – do not fit well within the traditional enquiry matrix of a single social science discipline. As a parallel challenge, however, investigations that fall entirely within those traditional matrices may miss rows and columns of enduring concerns to schoolteachers and administrators.

The value of teacher research and other forms of practitioner research is more apparent when we apply the ignorance-based standards outlined above. Rather than asking if a research project is likely to generate truth, we can assess its potential to reduce ignorance, about what, and for whom. Will it help researchers, policy makers, teachers or others to fill in blank spots or to illuminate blind spots? If so, it may be quite useful research.

Teaching and collaborative research

The connections noted above between research, teaching and professional practice suggest the potential value of collaborative strategies for conducting and organising educational research, strategies, for example, in which research activities and results are shared with research subjects. Over the past two decades, these strategies have been critically examined and advocated by Lather (1986), by Agyris, Putnam and Smith (1985) and by many others. In terms of the analysis presented here, they represent one way to treat the ignorance of researchers and the ignorance of research subjects with mutual respect.

An intriguing illustration of how iterative this process can become is provided by Howard Becker's book, *Writing for Social Scientists: How to Start and Finish your Thesis, Book or Article* (1986). In the introductory chapter, Becker describes how the book emerged within his own intellectual and professional life: as an alternative to editing the work of graduate students through individual consultations, Becker decided to teach a course on writing in which he and the students could work on these things together. As he stood in front of the class for the first meeting, however, he realised he didn't know how they wrote. When he asked them, he began learning that they didn't know how they wrote either. Through the class, Becker and his students worked on things they were writing and discussed the writing process they experienced as social scientists, and at the end of the class they talked about writing a paper on the subject.

As a first attempt at the paper, Becker wrote a description of the class and some of the ideas he and his students had been discussing. He distributed this to members of the class and to other colleagues, many of whom commented in response and some of whom shared it with other social scientists and graduate students. Becker used these comments to revise the paper and eventually published it in *The Sociological Quarterly* (Becker 1983) where others commented (Hummel and Foster 1984) and Becker responded (1984). Additional readers – probably all of whom were also trying to write social science theses, books and articles – wrote to Becker about the article, some of them sending long notes of their own about how these issues affected them.

Becker revised some more, read some more, wrote some more, and talked some more. As his teaching and research exchanges with other colleagues and students moved forward, he began organising materials for a book and eventually showed it to a publisher.

The publisher sent the manuscript out for review to both social researchers and composition scholars. The composition scholars criticised the book for not taking into account all the work of composition researchers, but social researchers saw Becker's work as a contribution to social science, not composition studies. The column Becker added to the social research matrix about writing was new to social scientists, even if not quite new to composition scholars. And that was enough, because the composition scholars didn't write for social scientists and Becker did. It would be hard for them to do so even if they wanted to because they don't have the same matrices in mind. Composition scholars know how to teach other members of their discipline, but they don't know which blind and blank spots to use in introducing lessons to social researchers.

In *Writing for Social Scientists*, Becker doesn't describe this work as research per se, nor does he include an explicit description of his data sources. However, he does describe the approach he took to writing the book in enough detail to construct a typology of data sources that might look something like Table 2.3.

Displaying Becker's data sources in this form helps clarify the materials he drew upon in generating new knowledge of how social scientists write. He doesn't tell us how many research subjects fell within each cell of this matrix, but we know what the cells are. Some researchers might like to know much more about this; others might not, at least not for the kinds of new knowledge Becker is constructing. In a very favourable review, for example, Cazden (1987) described Becker's book as an 'ethnography of academic writing in which Becker analyzes, as a participant-observer, how social organization [of academia] creates the classic problems of scholarly writing'.

Table 2.3 Categories of research subjects and data sources for *Writing for Social Scientists* (Becker 1986)

Research Subjects	Data Collection Activities			
	Individual interviews	Group interviews	Analysis of written documents	Responses to research reports
Graduate students in first class				
Graduate students in subsequent classes				
Readers responding to draft report of first class				
Readers responding to article in Sociological Quarterly				
Other social science colleagues				
Readers responding to book				

In addition to its trajectory as a research project, Becker's work on this topic is also implicated in a lot of teaching. The data source matrix helps describe that as well, with each row corresponding to a different population of learners. For the bottom row population, the primary medium of instruction was the book itself. For populations defined by the top two rows, Becker's research helped reduce their ignorance, and his own, before the book was written. This teaching occurred as Becker shared what he was learning with research subjects in several iterations over the course of several years. Had those teaching exchanges not occurred, Becker would have learned less than he did about how to introduce lessons of his research to audiences at greater remove who might share similar concerns.

With these considerations in mind, *Writing for Social Scientists* can be regarded as an extended project of *practitioner research* or *teacher research*. Becker's teacher-initiated enquiry was conducted in ways that were of value to his work as a teacher, to the work of his students, and to other teachers working in similar fields. It also appears as a project of *cooperative research*, in which research findings, data-collection strategies and analysis were shared with research subjects, some of whom made their own contributions to the analysis (one chapter of the book is a verbatim account of an analysis prepared by a reader of the first paper Becker wrote). As some reputable scholars have noted, the book also reflects good *social research*.

Is Becker's account the truth about social science writing? I couldn't tell you. Does it help reduce the ignorance of social scientists and those who teach social scientists about writing? Judged by its broad readership and numerous reviews, apparently so (Erikson 1986; Mullins 1987; Platt 1987; Procter 1988; Townsend 1986). Did it therefore generate 'new knowledge'? I think so, at least for social scientists, though I still wonder how and where it sits with the composition scholars.

Knowledge about ignorance

Distinctions between pursuing new knowledge and reducing ignorance are not hard and fast. The same research methods, criteria for evaluating evidence, and logic of argumentation or exposition can apply within either perspective. However, distinctions that seem weak within the formal logic of research can nevertheless generate strong effects within the informal and pragmatic logic that guides the work of individual researchers. That's true for all researchers, but it's especially true for graduate students who are just beginning their careers and for practitioners, policy makers and others who pursue enquiries in non-academic settings.

To summarise these effects, let me refer to three related propositions about the design, conduct and meaning of social research. First, conceptions of epistemology are closely connected to conceptions of pedagogy and method. Ideas about what knowledge looks like necessarily involve ideas about how it is acquired – and can be acquired – by researchers or by other members of society. By helping to define what people don't know and might learn next, ignorance and teaching are central concerns in using research to generate new knowledge.

Second, with ignorance as a reference point, the potential utility of social research by and for research subjects deserves pragmatic, as well as theoretical, attention. Becker's work illustrates the possibility of conducting research in ways that are useful to subjects, other teachers and practitioners, and to professional researchers themselves. Beyond this possibility, research by and for subjects is not only feasible, but also inevitable. It is what subjects do with researchers, whether the researchers want them to or not (Clark 1991; Wagner 1997). But it might be done more gracefully, effectively and humanely if researchers acknowledged it directly.

Third, getting rid of truth as an abstract goal for educational research does not mean abandoning truthfulness in pragmatic efforts to generate new knowledge. We try instead to chart a reasonable course between the foolishness of not caring about truthfulness at all and the distortions of life and work that arise when we care only about truth, and particular truths at that.

Whether anyone regards these propositions as new knowledge will depend on what readers of this chapter already know or don't know. Do the propositions help fill in a blank spot or reveal a blind spot in current theories of doctoral education? That's a test that falls short of truth writ large, but it might still be useful to putting one foot in front of the other.

References

Agyris, C., Putnam, R. and Smith, D. M. (1985) *Action science: Concepts, methods and skills for research and intervention*. San Francisco, CA: Jossey-Bass.

Becker, H. S. (1983) Freshman English for graduate students, *The Sociological Quarterly*, 24(Autumn): 575–88.

——(1984) Rejoinder to 'reflections', *The Sociological Quarterly*, 25(3/Summer): 433–4.

——(1986) *Writing for Social Scientists: How to Start and Finish your Thesis, Book or Article*. Chicago, IL: University of Chicago Press.

Cazden, C. B. (1987) Review of Becker, H.S., Writing for Social Scientists, *Harvard Education Review*, 57(2/May): 220–2.

Clark, C. M. (1991) Real lessons from imaginary teachers, *Journal of Curriculum Studies*, 23(5): 429–33.

Coleman, J. S., Campbell, E. Q., Hobson, C. J., McParland, J., Mood, A. J., Weinfeld, F. F., and York, R. (1966) *Equality of educational opportunity*. Washington, DC: Government Printing Office.

Erikson, K. (1986) The sociologist's hand, *Contemporary Sociology*, 15(6/November): 838–9.

Goodlad, J. (1990) *Teachers for our nation's schools*. San Francisco, CA: Jossey-Bass.

Hummel, R. L., and Foster, G. S. (1984) Reflections on freshman English and Becker's memoirs, *The Sociological Quarterly*, 25(3/Summer): 429–31.

Jencks, C., Bartless, S., Corcoran, M., Crouse, J., Eaglesfield, D., Jackson, G., McCelland, K., Mueser, P., Olneck, M., Schwartz, J., Ward, S. and Williams, J. (1979) *Who Gets Ahead*? New York: Basic Books.

Jencks, C., Smith, M., Acland, H., Band, J.J., Cohen, D., Gintis, H., Heyns, B. and Michelson, S. (1972) *Inequality*. New York: Basic Books.

Kuhn, T. S. (Ed.) (1970) Postscript–1969. In *The Structure of Scientific Revolutions*. Chicago, IL: University of Chicago Press.

Lather, P. (1986) Educational research as praxis, *Harvard Educational Review*, 56(3): 257–77.

Mullins, C. J. (1987) Review of Becker, H.S., Writing for social scientists, *Sociological Inquiry*, 57(1/Winter): 113–15.

Platt, J. (1987) Review of Becker, H. S., Writing for social scientists, *Sociology*, 21(1 February): 135–6.

Procter, D. E. (1988) Review of Becker, H.S., Writing for social scientists, *Communication Education*, 37: 177–9.

Schon, D. (1983) *The reflective practitioner: How professionals think in action*. New York: Basic Books.

——(1987) *Educating the reflective practitioner*. San Francisco, CA: Jossey-Bass.

Smelser, N. (Ed.) (1988) *Handbook of sociology*. Newbury Park, CA: SAGE.

Spindler, G and Spindler, L. (1991) Reactions and worries, *Anthropology and Education Quarterly*, 22(3): 274–8.

Summers, A. A. and Wolfe, B. L. (1975) Schools do make a difference, *Today's Education*, 64 (November): 24–7.

——(1977) Do schools make a difference? *American Economic Review*, 67(4/September): 639–52.

Townsend, B. (1986) Academic writing: Advice on how to do it, *Higher Education*, 15(3–4): 373–8.

Trueba, H. T. (1991) Notes on cultural acquisition and transmission, *Anthropology and Education Quarterly*, 22(3): 279–80.

Van Maanen, J. and Barley, S. R. (1984) Occupational communities: Culture and control in organizations, *Research in Organizational Behaviour*, 6: 287–365.

Wagner, J. (1997) The unavoidable intervention of educational research: a framework for reconsidering researcher–practitioner cooperation, *Educational Researcher*, 26(7): 13–22.

Waller, W. (1932) *The sociology of teaching*. New York: John Wiley & Sons.

Wolcott, H. (1991) Propriospect and the acquisition of culture, *Anthropology and Education Quarterly*, 22(3): 251–73.

3

When qualitative meets quantitative

Conversations about the nature of knowledge

E. McWilliam and J. Tan

We write as supervisor and candidate who have learned much from each other and much together in the years that it has taken to produce the doctoral study: *Digital kids, analogue students: A mixed methods study of students' engagement with a Web 2.0 learning innovation in a high-performing school* (Tan 2009). Our approach to generating this chapter is to present our shared understandings as unboxed text, and to mark our differences by using boxed dialogic texts that are dispersed throughout the chapter. In this way, we both acknowledge and draw on our very different research backgrounds, spanning – as they do – the gamut from meticulous measurement to elusive eroticism.

Box 3.1.

Erica: I already have a problem with what we have written in the second sentence. The idea that erotics and measurement should sit at opposite ends of an epistemological continuum belies the extent to which arithmetic calculation and eros are closely associated historically. In the film The Piano, for instance, the calculation of the size of a hole in the heroine's stocking (the 'size' of the seductiveness) in terms of the number of keys to be 'surrendered' on the piano keyboard, was very important to the erotic unfolding of the pivotal relationship. There are reminders of this in Jane Gallop's (1982) cheeky provocation to educators: 'It does not seem inappropriate that an arithmetic perversion should arise in a discussion of pedagogy…I suppose not all teachers experience as I do a diffuse yet unmistakable pleasure when calculating grades at the end of a term' (p. 128). Of course, it is much easier to expunge eros altogether in educational research – troublesome ethically and impossible to calculate.

Jen: The proposition that erotics and measurement should not sit as binary opposites on a linear continuum is intellectually seductive and compelling, especially when the argument is presented so eloquently by the scholar. While I am enthused by this argument and appreciate its value for challenging taken-for-granted, even 'commonsensical' epistemological assumptions, my primary response is:

'So what does this mean? It is definitely a compelling argument, but is there any empirical evidence to substantiate what would otherwise remain as an unwarranted claim? If evidence is wanting, then how can we best (i) translate the proposition into testable hypotheses, (ii) operationalise key concepts in the hypotheses into measurable constructs, (iii) apply an effective research design (preferably the "quintessential" true experimental design), (iv) develop appropriate sampling and data collection procedures, preferably random and $N>200$, so that we can (v) conduct rigorous statistical analysis of the data, preferably using the "definitive" causal modelling technique to achieve the highest levels of confidence in reliability and validity?'

These thoughts tend to come in quick succession of one another, albeit rather ironically, in a sequential linear fashion. It would not come as a surprise if many doctoral students, particularly those well-schooled in the 'dogmas' of scientific/ empirical research during their undergraduate and postgraduate years, share this almost 'programmed' response – put most crudely, this refuge in the 'rigour of numbers'. While there is little doubt that this intrinsic trust in 'hard' numbers can and has been misplaced and misused, a hasty disregard for the merit of well-conceptualised and well-executed measurement is equally regrettable.

We come from different countries with different pedagogical cultures. Our food preferences are different. Our linguistic capacities are different, although we do have in common the English language.

It is one thing to speak of celebrating all this difference in some flabby romantic way. It is quite another to optimise its usefulness for knowledge production. When the rubber of cultural difference meets the road of doctoral supervision, the journey can be much more demanding than any starry-eyed rendering of an East-meets-West, quant.-meets-qual., young-meets-old, pedagogical narrative might suggest. The potential riches of the cross-cultural meetings can too easily collapse into a push and pull around research trajectory, methodology, and intellectual property, a tug-of-war that the supervisor is most likely to win given her place in the institutional hierarchy. Once this happens, compliance rules, and the value-add that cultural difference could make becomes flattened and meaningless. All this can occur with never a cross or angry word, never a disagreement, never a sign of interpersonal struggle. It may still be that a thesis is written, passes examination, and a doctorate is achieved. So there is no evidence of a problem – nothing seems to be lost.

We would argue that something is lost in such a doctoral journey, and that is the extent to which supervisor and candidate can both develop a capacity for greater epistemological agility as a result of their intellectual, disciplinary and cultural differences.

Box 3.2

Jen: When I embarked on my doctorate candidature, my aspirations were twofold. First, I wanted to capitalise on and refine existing knowledge and skills in my foundational discipline (business) and quantitative research, which were acquired through my undergraduate honours and postgraduate research degrees. Second, I wanted to acquire knowledge in a new discipline (education) and expand my repertoire of research skills to encompass qualitative modes of 'thinking about' and 'doing' research. As a result, I sought out one of the most highly regarded and well-published scholars in the faculty. Erica was then the Assistant Dean Research of the Education Faculty with an exceptional publication record, in terms of both quantity and quality. There was only one small problem. Her expertise lies in social and cultural theory. She was erudite in schools of thought labelled with a 'post' prefix (postmodernism, poststructuralism, among others), a master of well-crafted arguments often supported by qualitative data, if any at all. I was extremely excited when Erica agreed to supervise my doctoral thesis, but was also aware that this was a big risk. Would it be possible to bridge our disciplinary, epistemological and methodological differences, so that we could reap the personal and intellectual fruits of productive diversity?

Erica: Big girls are not supposed to be afraid of numbers. But it was daunting being a supervisor of a doctoral student with advanced skills in quantitative methodology and a capacity to use digital tools in a way that I just could never emulate. I recalled my singularly unpleasant experiences as a Stats 101 student and realised that I had missed an opportunity to round out my understanding of methodology by coming to grips with measurement as a valuable means of enquiry. My scholarly critiques of 'white coat' objectivism had allowed me to step around the judicious use of quantitative enquiry and I came to regret that gap in my knowledge, however much I was able to generate publications about the nature of knowledge and its politicisation. This is not written as a confessional, but a simple acknowledgement that critique is a very useful means for maintaining blind spots in our learning. As a supervisor, I was made aware, through Jen's expertise and ease with statistical calculation, that I lacked some quite precise skills that would have made me a better researcher, and I have been seeking to learn more about quantitative enquiry, at least enough to be able to 'read' its findings intelligently. The work that Jen has done has given me an opportunity to do this new learning.

We note with interest the recent work of John Elliott and Ching-tien Tsai (2008) in exploring and exploiting concepts of education and learning emanating from Confucian scholarship and from recent Western thinking such as that of Lawrence Stenhouse. They argue the importance of 'more dialogue with East Asian educators who are engaged with versions of educational action research that have been shaped by Confucian culture' (p. 569) in the development of new paradigms of educational enquiry.

Although we strongly endorse the move to genuine educational dialogue of this sort, it would be misleading to suggest that the nature of the doctoral research in which we have both been closely involved has been 'cross-cultural' in this sense. In fact, it has been predominantly Western in its conception and its methodology. Yet, in some senses, the space between the imperative to measure and the imperative to interpret can also be understood as a cultural gap, with borders that are not easily negotiated, despite the ease with which the term 'multi-method' rolls off the tongue. It is not a matter of having a bit of 'quant.' and a bit of 'qual.'. For any measurement and interpretation to be mutually informative, scholarly and useful, a great deal of 'thinking about thinking' is involved, and this in turn means ongoing conversations about the nature of knowledge.

Extended and ongoing conversations about the nature of knowledge ought to be commonplace in doctoral programmes. However, it would seem that such dialogic work is less common than we might suppose. Of all the possible reasons for this in the field of social science, three come most readily to mind.

The first is the propensity of the supervisor to direct the study towards a methodological domain with which they are most familiar and feel most expert. This is understandable – after all, doctoral candidates are unlikely to welcome a doctoral experience akin to 'the blind leading the blind', and may be only too willing to be taken by the hand in this way. A new candidate may well see methodology as something akin to snake oil, a mysterious but potent brew of techniques that only the supervisor knows how to apply. It is eminently reasonable that any supervisor should lay claim to at least some methodological expertise, and would therefore be a willing participant in inducting a candidate into that same domain.

Second, in days when doctoral completion is itself calculated in terms of cost to the institution, being in a doctoral programme means getting down to the business of 'doing it' fast. The area of interest must be translated into a do-able research problem, rendered in an appropriate theoretical language. In so doing, one can often find that the aims and parameters of the project are far too ambitious, and a piece of a piece of the original idea is agreed and 'written up' as a bound study. In many doctoral programmes, the administrative requirements for ensuring that this is happening and that the candidate is 'moving forward' can all too readily overwhelm the intellectual requirements of the project, so that the attentional economy of both candidate and the supervisor end up being driven by considerations of what the next 'stage' requirements are: a confirmation document, a report, an evaluation sheet, a seminar presentation, a mandated generic coursework component. Put another way, events can come to matter more than thoughtful engagement.

Box 3.3

Erica: It is an exciting and somewhat daunting time for me as an academic and supervisor of educational research. I am now living and working in the country where Jen was born, grew up and was educated – Singapore. Jen now lives where I was born, grew up and was educated – Brisbane, Australia. This cultural 'crossover' has provided me with more learning opportunities than I expected – or indeed looked for – late in my career. I am experiencing the discomfort of not knowing much that is of local importance, both within a new university and a new country. I need to be 'usefully ignorant' in Charlie Leadbeater's (2000) terms, to be productive in this context; Jen has prepared me for this to some extent by gently seeking to dispel certain cultural myths and stereotypes about Singapore and its people. She also gave me entrée to some of the nuances of Chinese culture when we went to Beijing together in mid-2007. I was there to present an address to the CHITEC Conference, but there she was the teacher and I the learner.

Jen: I experience little discomfort in the Asian context, but I was certainly not prepared for the level of discomfort that came with my opportunity to learn about different epistemologies. In early consultations, I struggled intensely with being supervised. I often left the meetings feeling intensely confused and deeply frustrated

---

that I was not progressing as quickly or 'easily' as I should be, but these came hand in hand with an unmistakable sense of intellectual pleasure and excitement that I was 'onto' something good. Six months into the programme, I made a conscious decision to 'let go' of my existing knowledge and corresponding modes of thinking, at least in the meetings or for a certain period of time before coming back to them with new eyes. I realised that it was my research background and competencies, rather than my lack thereof that were the stumbling blocks of my progress. In Erica's terms, I learnt to unlearn (McWilliam 2005). I also learned to be 'usefully ignorant', that is, to temporarily suspend entrenched epistemological and disciplinary knowledge, so that my mind and the doctoral meetings could become authentic spaces of pedagogical possibilities.

Third, the social sciences seem to be particularly bedevilled by an unseemly rush to the field, in the expectation that 'findings' are sitting neatly out there waiting to be found. Lather (1998) argues that this apparent movement away from scientistic thought in education is an outcome of the growing demand that educational research be 'centred by such concepts as "empathy", "voice" and "authenticity"' (p. 1). The problem that she perceives arising out of this demand is one that has also been identified by Tom Popkewitz (1997) and Deborah Britzman (1997) in recent times – namely, the 'wish for heroism' on the part of the researcher, a wish that is accompanied, problematically, by the presupposition of the researcher as 'a coherent subject ... in charge of their desires and identifications', one who 'speaks for themselves' and is 'capable of knowing others' (Lather 1998: 1). In drawing attention to the 'typical investments and categories of ethnography' that accompany enquiry as a redemptive project, these three authors make trouble for any ethnographic research that responds to 'the demand for voice and situatedness' (Britzman 1997: 31).

The idea that the field itself is constituted in and through the performance of an enquiry is an annoying one because it troubles the 'blissful clarity' that Barthes (1975) speaks of that is so seductive to the knowledge worker. The 'good intentions' of many doctoral candidates in the social sciences adds impetus to this rush to the field – the pleasure of being out there 'really doing it' rather than 'just talking about it'. Of course, this is another binary that we could all do without. We have more powerful supervisor/candidate conversations if it were understood that such conversations constitute what becomes recognisable as 'the field'. It is so easy to 'see' evidence of low self-esteem, for example, or of 'bullying', when one is convinced not only that it is 'out there' but also that it is multiplying at an alarming rate. Steven Ward's paper, 'Filling the World with Self-Esteem: A social history of truth-making' (1986) is a cogent account of the mechanisms at work producing the clarity with which we come to see evidence of a sad lack or a problematic proliferation. It is not that 'positive change' should be off the agenda for educational researchers; it is perhaps that we might well look to Anna Freud's dictum to 'do the least harm' as a moral–ethical standpoint of enquiry.

It needs to be stated quite bluntly here that the blissful clarity of the researcher who already knows 'what is out there' and wants to show it to the world in order to remediate it, is responsible for the sort of research that finds out the educational equivalent of 'men with long legs tend to have longer trousers', for example, that children with high self-esteem tend to have more positive self-talk. Meanwhile, more complex and paradoxical matters, such as the problem of integrating digital technologies into

Box 3.4

Jen: It was indeed tempting to get over the planning stage of the doctoral project quickly, so that I could move on to the implementation stage, to collect, analyse and report on the data. With my background in quantitative research, it would not have been too difficult to plan and execute a research project in my area of interest that was predominantly quantitative or 'hard quant.', complemented by some 'light qual.'. This would ensure that the study would score brownie points of being classified as 'mixed-methods', but not run the risk of being paradigmatically incompatible. Also, I had a good grasp of the existing literature and concepts in the field of innovation diffusion in the business disciplines, and it was tempting to recycle these concepts in the education field. This was further compounded by pressures to perform academically, and, as indicated above, 'speed' in completing the doctorate was definitely a performance indicator. I was, however, not quite prepared to forego the pleasure and pain of learning to 'think about thinking about research' (McWilliam 2006). I wanted to attempt a study that was both 'hard quant.' and 'hard qual.'. I relished the opportunity to engage in a 'serious play' of ideas – to hold large numbers of associations together in the mind, and imagine the interesting possibilities that arise from making novel associations – that is, to be cognitively playful (Tan and McWilliam 2008). I was certain that 'rushing to the field' with a view to achieving 'easy success' would be neither intellectually nor professionally rewarding in the long term. Under Erica's experienced tutelage, we were able to ensure both the timely progress of the candidature, as well as a high quality of scholarly engagement and outcomes from the doctoral dissertation.

    Erica: I have very much enjoyed being part of the theoretical and methodological work done in feminism and poststructuralism, and literary criticism to invite educational researchers to 'trouble clarity' (Lather 1996) by playing seriously with modes of enquiry. I was fortunate to be completing my own doctorate in the early 1990s at a time when methodology was becoming a hotly contested topic in the large professional association conferences, and when there was a momentum emanating from Lather, Britzman, Ellsworth, and other scholars to understand the importance of making educational research more unintelligible to itself. They were heady times, and it is only recently that Alison Lee, Maggie Maclure and I discovered at a British Educational Research Association meeting how much excitement this era gave us in our scholarly formation. It is epistemological excitement that many doctoral candidates miss out on now. The doctoral students who came to our session, called 'The Desire for Discourse Analysis', made this patently clear during and after the symposium.

mainstream schooling in any comprehensive way, continue to be under-researched and under-theorised (see Warschauer 2008). One-shot surveys and/or one-shot interviews cannot of themselves tell us what we need to know when it comes to educational paradoxes. The fact that teachers and students both welcome *and* under use digital technology is a paradox, not amenable to explanation simply by blaming teachers' lack of familiarity with technology as Tan's doctoral research study has found (see Tan 2009; Tan and McWilliam 2009).

Box 3.5

Erica: My first question to a prospective candidate is usually 'What are you curious about?'. I am interested in whether they are positioning themselves first and foremost as advocates or as investigators. Jen was curious about many things, one of which was to understand what was going on with digital tools in schools, and how to find it out without a well-formed conspiracy theory (i.e. teacher deficits) to explain it. She did not think that either measurement or interpretation alone would tell her all that she wanted to know, so began to consider how quantitative and qualitative methods might be brought together in ways that allowed each to inform the other, rather than having one as 'garnish' to the other. Jen was a rarity in doctoral education, as a candidate with strong quantitative credentials who could readily have done a thoroughly number-crunching study but chose to broaden her understanding of how knowledge about enquiry works. My lack of any deep understanding of statistical analysis was no barrier to her, although I certainly felt that I could not provide scholarly feedback on specific matters pertaining to her experimental design. This meant extending the expertise available to her, and she was very proactive in seeking out that expertise. Put simply, she did not need me to know everything about method.

   Jen: What I did need, however, was a supervisor that had not yet retired from learning. I did not need a supervisor who had amassed extensive disciplinary and methodological knowledge over the years and was most comfortable remaining in that zone of expertise. I needed a supervisor who was accomplished in her field of expertise and knowledgeable about the meta-requirements of what constitutes a successful PhD dissertation, but most importantly, possessed a good dose of epistemological agility and methodological generosity. Erica wielded her 'carrot-shaped stick' in our supervisor/student partnership with commendable adroitness. She was keen to share her knowledge but not at all interested in moulding me into 'mini-E'. She was supportive of my exploration, excited when we hit fertile intellectual soil, and always guided me back to higher ground with a firm hand on occasions when I got entrapped in cerebral quicksand. In this regard, she too was a rarity in doctoral supervision.

To think about combining measurement and interpretation is to begin to think about what counts as knowledge production and how it works. It means beginning to question how something comes to go without saying, how one becomes convinced that something is 'out there' or that it does not exist. In trusting in Western tools, we trust their power to let us 'see' what is 'out there', where Buddhist monks might distrust the same tools because they distrust the imperfections of their own senses, and what they perceive using their senses. It is not that we need to engage with Buddhism or any other religion to think deeply about what and how we see as researchers. The point is that radical doubt or scepticism about our tools and what they may or may not deliver is a better start than certainty about their efficacy.

We need to bring that same scepticism to what we can extrapolate about research trends. For example, if there is a 'trend' to larger number of studies focusing on bullying among young people, it is important to imagine that this could arise from (a) more moral panics around bullying, so (b) more funding going to bullying projects and/or (c) more things coming to count as bullying or (d) a self-perpetuating culture of bullying studies, not necessarily that (e) more young people are actually being bullied. Indeed, it could be that there is less deeply troubling peer-to-peer mental and physical cruelty at the same time that we are coming to find it everywhere. This means that we need to think about the limitations of both objective and subjective tools in providing us with the power to 'see' what lay others cannot.

Box 3.6

Jen: The countless conversations about the nature of knowledge that I have had the pleasure of sharing with Erica throughout my doctoral candidature have solidified my desire to interrogate complexity, rather than flatten paradoxes. I am motivated to make ongoing contributions to the field of research and doctoral education by resisting the colonisation of 'findings' that comes with an imperialistic application of particular dominant 'methodologies'. Rather, I aim to build an increasingly eclectic combination of 'quality research tools' – an aromatic blend of epistemological deftness, methodological dexterity and cultural agility that I can bring to any new and worthwhile enquiry. In this way, I hope to press through the replication of old answers to new questions, and uncover some new explanations to old questions yet unanswered.

   Erica: It is clear to me that supervision can be a delight but it is never an unmitigated delight. There is struggle and contestation, and this is not something from which to save a candidate, nor is it something that can be trotted out as an excuse for supervisors to go missing in action. The experience of supervision has been deeply pleasurable for the fact that Jen and I have had an unbroken journey together, and both of us have laughed a lot as well as learning a lot. I have watched while Jen has, in the words of the great Oscar Wilde, spent the morning putting in a comma and the afternoon taking it out again. I have needed patience when tasks that are simple to me are a struggle for her. She has needed patience with me for the same reasons. We have come to work well together as co-authors, able to complement each other's strengths because we now share a platform of understanding and of pleasure in what each of us brings to building and sustaining that platform.

Pursuit of these new ways of seeing has involved us in breaking new research ground and working with colleagues to publish our original research in scholarly collections such as this one, and also in conference papers and refereed journals (see, for example, McWilliam et al. 2008; McWilliam, Dawson and Tan 2009; Tan and McWilliam 2009). Importantly for our shared research future, as supervisor and candidate, we are now sharing first author status and the related responsibility for crafting our shared scholarly work. Simply put, we have both learned how to lead and to follow.

References

Barthes, R. (1975) *The Pleasure of the Text*. New York: Hill and Wang.
Britzman, D. (1997) The tangles of implication, *Qualitative Studies in Education*, 10(1): 31–7.

Elliott, J. and Tsai, C.-T. (2008) What might Confucius have to say about educational research, *Educational Action Research*, 16(4): 569–78.

Gallop, J. (1982) The immoral teachers, the pedagogical imperative: Teaching as a literary genre, *Yale French Studies*, 63: 117–28.

Lather, P. (1996) Troubling Clarity: The Politics of Accessible Language, *Harvard Educational Review*, 66 (3): 525–45.

——(1998) *Against Empathy, Voice and Authenticity*. Paper presented at the Annual American Educational Research Association Conference, San Diego, April.

Leadbeater, C. (2000) *Living on Thin Air: The New Economy*. New York: Viking.

McWilliam, E. (2005) Unlearning Pedagogy, *Journal of Learning Design*, 1(1): 1–11.

——(2006) After Methodolatry: Epistemological challenges for 'risky' educational research. In J. Ozga, T. Seddon, T. Popkewitz (Eds). *World Yearbook of Education – Education research and policy: steering the knowledge-based economy*. London: Routledge, 301–15.

McWilliam, E., Dooley, K., McArdle, F. and Tan, J. P.-L. (2008) Voicing Objections. Invited chapter in A. Jackson and L. Mazzei (Eds). *Voice in Qualitative Inquiry: Challenging Conventional, Interpretive, and Critical Conceptions in Qualitative Research*. New York: Routledge, 63–76.

McWilliam, E., Dawson, S. and Tan, J. P-L. (2009) From Vaporousness to Visibility: What might evidence of creative capacity building actually look like? *UNESCO Observatory*, refereed e-journal on Creativity, policy and practice discourses: projective tensions in the new millennium, 1(3). Online. (Available at www.abp.unimelb.edu.au/unesco/ejournal/vol-one-issue-three.html).

Popkewitz, T. (1997) Educational sciences and the normalizations of the teacher and the child: Some historical notes on current USA pedagogical reforms. In I. Nilsson and L. Lundahl (Eds). *Teachers, curriculum and policy*. Sweden: Umea University, 91–114.

Tan, J. P.-L. (2009) *Digital kids, analogue students: A mixed methods study of students' engagement with a Web 2.0 learning innovation in a high-performing school*. Doctoral dissertation, Queensland University of Technology.

Tan, J. P.-L. and McWilliam, E. (2008) Cognitive playfulness, creative capacity and generation 'C' learners, *Cultural Science*, 1(2). Online. (Available at www.cultural-science.org/journal/index.php/culturalscience).

——(2009) From literacy to multiliteracies: Diverse learners and pedagogical practice. *Pedagogies: An International Journal*, 4(3): 213–25.

Ward, S. (1986) Filling the World with Self-Esteem: A social history of truth-making, *Canadian Journal of Sociology*, 2(1): 1–23.

Warschauer, M. (2008) Technology and Literacy: Introduction to the special issue, *Pedagogies: An International Journal*, 3(1): 1–3.

4

Interdisciplinarity and transdisciplinarity

Diverse purposes of research: theory-oriented, situation-oriented, policy-oriented

D. Gasper

The various disciplines in the social and human sciences have each built up their own worlds of theory, each designed to clarify a selected aspect or aspects of life. But if one wishes to understand a particular person, group, locality or country, a particular situation, one must become 'interdisciplinary': one must attend to diverse aspects and how they inter-relate. This chapter explores the problematique of interdisciplinarity and asks that doctoral researchers give careful thought to how their own research might benefit from an interdisciplinary approach. If, for example, one studies the impacts of education in and on the state of Kerala in India, one cannot sensibly ignore cultural impacts, such that almost no one with a certain amount of schooling will now do heavy manual work: a major economic, as well as educational, fact.

Similar considerations apply when we consider interdisciplinarity in policy-oriented research, including in the field of education. Much policy-oriented research is again situation- and context-focused, although some aspires to widely applicable general-isations. If we find, for example, that in Indonesia private school graduates earn more, and have also learnt more, more cost-effectively, than state school graduates (Bedi and Garg 2000), we cannot directly conclude a need for greater private participation in the education sector, without also giving attention to issues such as future brain-drain, nationbuilding, willingness to work in priority sectors, and possibilities for reforming state schools.

The complexity of policy cases frequently exceeds the grasp of discipline-gained knowledge, even when brought together from various disciplines. Much inter-disciplinarity arises, then, in response to practical and immediate life-problem situations, where we cannot wait for discipline-gained knowledge that is not yet available. Such work oriented to life-problems might not be conventionally scientifically elegant, but it draws on sophisticated craft skills of selection, synthesis and judgement (Rein and Schon 1994; Brewer 1999).

Public administration and urban and regional planning, to take two important exam-ples, are better seen as 'interdisciplinary fields' than as conventional scientific disciplines (Gasper 1990; 2000a; Rutgers 1998). Public administration works at the crossroads of several disciplines and a set of practical demands. Compared to general management it requires stronger involvement from law, history and economics, and it cannot be simply a sub-discipline of management or political science. Whereas disciplines can attain a high degree of enclosure around self-defined concepts, methods and questions, and leave aside matters not convenient for this disciplinary matrix, a practically oriented public-servant enterprise like public administration should never adopt such a prioritisation of tidiness above usefulness. It has to draw on various types of understanding in order to tackle various types of pressing and interconnected real issues; it links material from different fields without unifying them (Gasper 2000a).

Even for theorising, single-disciplinary abstracted theory has serious limits. If we cannot analyse education in Kerala while ignoring the indirect economic impacts of mass aversion to menial work, or analyse the results of economic liberalism while ignoring the impacts of massive concentrations of wealth upon politics and conflict, then neither can we ignore such aspects in a general theory of economic adjustment or human development.

We will see that there are many types and usages of 'interdisciplinarity', ranging from mere juxtaposition of disciplines that do not interact but do acknowledge each other's contribution; through a variety of forms of interaction, giving a range of types of inter-disciplinarity; all the way to 'transdisciplinarity', where disciplines are left in the background and we focus afresh on situations.

Understanding disciplinarity, as a basis for understanding and attempting interdisciplinarity

The terms 'discipline' and 'disciple' are not close purely by coincidence. Similarly, the two meanings of 'discipline' (control, and a socially organised intellectual field) are not accidental namesakes, as Foucault and others have clarified.[1] 'Disciplines' contain social as well as intellectual formations. They are organised groups or networks that discipline members and students – by rewards, punishments and bestowal/withdrawal of identity and recognition – in order to create acceptable disciples. In this sense they are historical successors to the priestly orders. They seduce as well as drill, providing to young researchers a nest, a community, a style and set of habits, a gradual induction to mysteries, and many intellectual rewards from the excitement and tractability of the bounded puzzle. For a variety of reasons, treated by theorists of science such as Kuhn (1970) and Ravetz (1973), an in-depth rather than in-breadth approach is often functional and even necessary. In cases where this is not so, disciplines sometimes discourage exploratory work that crosses borders, in order to maintain their territories.

Sheldon Rotblatt (1998) defends disciplinarity as a system that shields academic freedom against political domination: it asserts the existence of areas of deep and organised knowledge, which are established and are governed by scientific criteria only. Universities are indeed the cradles of disciplinarity, given their roles as a machinery for validating suitability for entry to professional paths and for the socialisation of the next generation of academic teachers; given, too, the incentive structures for academics to play safe after and even during their PhD studies and to publish prolifically by doing detail work (Earl 1983). By basing the organisational structure for research on the structure for training, most universities constrain that research. Co-operation in teaching is sometimes harder still, thanks partly to the defence of turf and of budgets. Academics frequently have little or nothing to do with their colleagues on the same campus from supposedly sister disciplines.

The depth and virulence of disciplinary chauvinism is in many ways surprising, as the current social science divisions only emerged in the late nineteenth and early twentieth centuries, as products of a number of specific features of that era; and they are increasingly under stress as the world changes (see, for example, the report of the Gulbenkian Commission: Wallerstein *et al.* 1996; Wallerstein 1999). Yet consider, for example, the fierce struggles common even within joint sociology–anthropology departments; Giri (1998) cites several such cases that led to partition and one can readily add others. Even after having established their own territories, flags and passports, disciplines continue to often have poor relations with their supposed siblings; to largely ignore and (yet) disparage each other (Salter and Hearn 1996: 157). The indispensable role of generalist-linker is typically accorded low status. Researchers in education often face that risk, and some develop a fierce allegiance to sociology or statistics, philosophy or psychology, in order to avoid this fate.

Why do we mostly find a closed rather than open disciplinarity? Reasons might include an arrogance generated by knowledge; fear of the unknown; single-discipline social science first degrees; the defence of departmental budgets (so that conflicts with one's closest neighbours can be the fiercest); and the delightful convenience of disciplinarity, which like bureaucracy licences its practitioners to believe they can rightfully ignore most details of other people's situations. Professorial designations and professional training often remain weak for building interdisciplinarity. None of this is good for the quality and recognition of social science and educational research.

In addition, we should note three fundamental factors. First, the social science disciplines have historically emerged as, in some respects, competitors rather than partners. Second, disciplines are cultures, and cultures differ; relatedly, they provide 'homes', bases of identity. Third, disciplinary boundary setting is often underpinned by a 'Newtonian' ontology, which declares that the whole is the sum of the parts, which can therefore each be examined purely separately.

First, the social science disciplines and fields did not grow as partners. Aidan Foster-Carter (1998) argues that the social sciences have been competitors for dominance, not a chain of emergent subsets like physics–chemistry–biology. They represent competing perspectives, some of which may consider that they can cover everything or subsume the others as special cases. Also, disciplines are cultures and cross-cultural contact is problem-ridden and demanding (Schoenberger 2001). The different styles of writing between different social sciences and between natural and social sciences form one barrier (Salter and Hearn 1996; McNeill 1999). Economics uses the style of the detective story: characters of restricted depth interact in intricate but standardised ways. For some readers this is a delight, for others a bore. Analysis of these genre differences might improve mutual awareness and communication, including by attention to characteristic root metaphors, illustrations and exemplar cases in different disciplines (see, for example, Apthorpe 1996; Lakoff and Johnson 2003; McCloskey 1994; Roe 1998; 1999).

Second, disciplines often serve as bases of personal identity. Consider two stances. In stance A my discipline/training is my allegiance (a choice comparable to that of Jesuit versus Dominican), my noun-expressed identity ('I am a sociologist'), a caste-mark, for life. In stance B my (original) discipline/affiliation/label/training is one of many relevant adjectives or descriptive clauses about my background ('I trained in sociology 20 years ago'). Stance B is healthier, including for interdisciplinarity; but stance A is common, probably more common. Interdisciplinarity is more achievable when people act as representatives not of disciplines but of themselves, their experiences, values and insights.

Rajni Kothari (1988) argues that the key step in interdisciplinarity is formation of a community of conversers who each seek to cross and perhaps transcend conventional bounds: 'For true interdisciplinarity to develop, it is the individual that has to become interdisciplinary, not the group'. As disciplines can become sources of personal identity, advice to treat interdisciplinarity as a follow-on phase in education, after people have first been immersed overwhelmingly in one discipline, is rather problematic. In addition, the pressures of professional life after doctoral studies make acquisition of adequate grounding in other disciplines less likely at that stage.

Third, several authors argue that disciplinarity reflects dominant premises in modern Western thought, accepted due to their immense success in parts of the physical sciences. Following Norgaard (1994: 62–65), the first two such premises are: (i) Atomism: systems consist of unchanging parts, and a system is the sum of those parts; and (ii) Mechanism: relations between the parts do not change. Given such premises, a disciplinary field of study may treat most things as exogenous, constant, separate, unaffected by those remaining things that the discipline does consider. The other premises are as follows: (iii) Universalism: the same parts and inter-relations apply for all cases, everywhere. (iv) Objectivism: people acting on systems are not parts of the systems they seek to understand and act on. (v) Monism: there is one correct way to understand a system; any plurality of ways will merge into a bigger picture; so the various sciences will fit together without any fundamental difficulties. Each of these premises is adequate in the older parts of physics, but certainly not for complex systems involving people (Norgaard 1994; Wallerstein *et al.* 1996).[2]

Grand visions and feasible proposals

Having identified limitations of disciplinarity, some authors call for ambitious forms of interdisciplinarity. Norgaard (1994) makes a persuasive case for dropping Monism, the premise that there is one correct way to understand a system. Major

> participants in processes of learning and deciding [must]: 1 – be conscious of their own conceptual frameworks, 2 – be conscious of the advantages and disadvantages of the frameworks used by others, and 3 – be tolerant of the use of different frameworks … by others.
>
> Norgaard 1994: 101

Full coherence in the understanding of many issues, e.g. climate change or many aspects of social change, is 'inherently impossible for the knowledges of the scientists from separate disciplines cover different variables, different spatial scales, and different time scales. And multiple incongruent patterns of thinking are being used' (Norgaard 1994: 140), such as the mechanical models of physical scientists versus the evolutionary models of biologists. In Martinez-Alier's view (1999), using terms drawn from Otto Neurath, we can essay 'orchestration of the sciences', bringing them together and inter-relating them, without expecting or desiring to absorb them all into one discipline (old or new). Some areas of consensus are indeed emerging on, for example, climate change, through intensive interaction of disciplines and gradual increase of mutual respect and trust. Integration of the partial, limited perspectives should be through a sort of demo-cratic, multi-cultural politics of science. For: 'The use of a single framework, without

modification for regional differences, facilitates control from a single centre of analysis. Thus, the use of a single framework disenfranchises or disqualifies the majority, facilitates the tyranny of technocrats, and encourages centralization' (Norgaard 1994: 102).

We must take into account the gravitational pull of the disciplines, for reasons good and bad. Resistance to interdisciplinarity comes not only from chauvinism, mis-identification of it with cafeteria-curricula or polymath-ism, or views that it is unnecessary. It reflects also concerns that it typically fails or is too difficult and costly. Lipton (1970) and Berge and Powell (1997) warn, for example, that each new discipline added to a team seriously increases co-ordination costs, so that one must be very selective, deciding according to the case.

Glenn Johnson's (1986) recommendations are based on fuller review of experience from a variety of modes and purposes of research. His book stresses the legitimacy and importance of multidisciplinary work, by which he means not only the side-by-side presence of several disciplines but also an open interdisciplinary interaction in case-focused research and policy research. But as these approaches are demanding, complex and costly, including in management terms, sub-division and specialisation are still sometimes better. Both disciplinarity and interdisciplinarity are legitimate and necessary, separately and in research teams. They are also strongly complementary. Kenneth Boulding observed in his foreword to Johnson's book that intellectual division of labour brings economies of specialisation, which as in other cases of specialisation must be complemented by inter-specialisation trade if benefits are to be reaped (Boulding 1986). Interchange need not lead to consensus, indeed consensus sometimes hinders intellectual progress; but competing views should be formed in awareness of each other, not in mutual ignorance.

Boulding did not ask how, if intellectual specialisation brings narrowness and mercantilist chauvinism, trade will happen. A multidisciplinary team does not automatically lead to interaction. Sometimes people work side-by-side ignoring the content of each other's work. And interdisciplinarity can occur also outside teams, by interaction with those in other disciplines through their writings. Some of the best interdisciplinary work happens within one person – a Jon Elster, Albert Hirschman or Tibor Scitovsky. As Kothari (1988) saw, true interdisciplinarity requires interdisciplinary individuals, whether in teams or not. Giri (1998; 2002) diagnoses the required shift as from a nest of identity as an academic or professional of type T, to a self-conception as pilgrim and seeker. We should expect only a modest rate of progress here. Johnson (1986) himself identified as predisposing factors for effective open inter- (but in his terms, 'multi-') disciplinary work: being 'free enough of disciplinary chauvinism' (p. 204) and 'philosophically flexible' (p. 205). These factors are neither self-nurturing nor non-nurturable. Johnson leaves them as exogenous: some people have them, others don't, so we should pick the first type for certain jobs. We must and can do more than this.

A complex eco-system of enquirers

From the above examination of both disciplinarity and interdisciplinarity, I propose a picture similar in some ways to Johnson's, recognising different valid types of work plus many feasibility constraints on interdisciplinarity. But I draw more on the critique of disciplinarity and thus go beyond him, to look at longer term restructuring of ideas. Before presenting a detailed typology, let us highlight the main themes. We will always need regular communication between a diversity of types and styles of work. In intellectual life just as in other spheres, we need 'bridging capital' to span between communities, as well as 'bonding capital' to bind within them. The bridging and communication involve a variety of networks and roles and require some shared 'languages', mutually accessible frameworks.

(1) By *networks* I refer to organisational and interorganisational linkages and meeting places, as well as to their members and patterns of informal contact. We need interdisciplinary work both in distinct centres, for example on education, international development studies, or urban studies, and also as a leavening factor within the standard disciplinary departments (Klein 1996, gives a wealth of examples). From interdisciplinary centres some members should maintain links to their 'own' (original or later acquired) disciplines, whereas from disciplinary centres some members should link to interdisciplinary work.

(2) Interdisciplinary work cannot flourish merely by interaction of disciplinary specialists. Two sets of *roles* that are sometimes disputed, yet essential, are the methodologist and, especially for action-oriented work, the broker-generalist (Easton 1991). The needed bridgers and synthesisers may be based in a particular discipline (e.g. in the interaction of economics and psychology, Scitovsky in economics and Stephen Lea in psychology); or, unusually, be true masters of more than one discipline (e.g. Amartya Sen in the interaction of economics and ethics); or hybrid intermediaries.

(3) Although 'bridges' and 'bridging capital' are useful metaphors, in many ways a superior image is that of an *eco-system*, within which many species and hybrids co-exist and interact (and sometimes eat others, or get eaten). The scientific eco-system contains a plurality of interconnected research activities and corresponding intellectual communities, as seen in the maps provided by Klein (1996), Wallerstein *et al.* (1996), Wallerstein (1999), Szostak (2003) and others (see Gasper 2004a). To describe and understand a complex eco-system, we require a complex system of concepts and models. The next part of the chapter will elaborate more on types of interconnection, types of interdisciplinarity.

(4) Interaction requires mutually accessible and acceptable *intellectual frameworks*. Sometimes a superior framework is not sufficiently accessible and acceptable to others whose co-operation is needed. Scitovsky's striking work to draw from psychology a more empirically grounded basis for consumer and welfare theory in economics apparently demanded too much adjustment by economists (Scitovsky 1976). It had impact not in economics but in a new cross-disciplinary enclave, economic psychology. Social exclusion theory possibly includes better social analysis than do social capital theory or capabilities theory, yet lies beyond the reach of most economists. Inferior theories might sometimes function better as bridges.

A fuller mapping: interdisciplinary variants defined

'Interdisciplinarity' can be a problematic label. First, it has become a hate-term in the mouths of opponents of cafeteria curricula. Second, 'inter-' connotes between, relations between disciplines, but not all usage of 'interdisciplinarity' respects this. These first two problems might be transcended, but third, even if we respect the connotation, many

Table 4.1 Relationships between disciplines

	UNFRIENDLY	FRIENDLY
NON-RELATIONS	Ignoring the other(s). Planned autarky	Distant well-wishers
LIMITED RELATIONS	Mutual ridicule of the other(s) despite non-trade	Trade (=part of open-disciplinarity)
	Antagonism and ignorance in unhappy partnerships Mercantilism (i.e. seeking only to export, never to import)	Friendly partnership: Multi-disciplinary shared activities
INTENSIVE RELATIONS	Competition	Marriage, and production of hybrid offspring
	Conquest	Merger

forms and outcomes of such relations are possible (Klein 1996). Operating with just one label or with an undifferentiated set of labels often brings inconsistency or reductionism, the equation of interdisciplinarity with just one variant. We need a clear and fuller set of terms.

Table 4.1 suggests some of the possible relationships between disciplines.

All of these relationships sometimes occur. Klein (1996: 22–3) records corresponding terms like 'trading zone', 'pidgin' and 'creole' in the literature. The relationships somewhat mirror those between nations; and just as most nations' history books highlight their victories and pass more quickly over defeats, disciplines tend to downplay their own failings.

Which of these relationships fit the interdisciplinarity label? According to *Webster's* and *Collins'* dictionaries the adjective interdisciplinary means 'involving two or more disciplines'. Universities involve many disciplines, so by this definition they are interdisciplinary, even if the disciplines ignore each other except when they meet in management committees. *The Oxford Dictionary* is more helpful: interdisciplinary means 'of or between more than one branch of learning'. This matches the prefix 'inter-', which means 'between, among (e.g. intercontinental); or mutually, reciprocally (interbreed)' and suggests exchange (see also Karlqvist 1999). Furthermore, we have a better term already, 'multi-disciplinary', to describe constructive relationships that involve separate contributions lacking mutual interaction.

We find the noun, interdisciplinarity, then similarly variously used, to mean: (i) the actual state of relationships between disciplines, even if this is happens to be to ignore each other or fight; more narrowly, (ii) constructive relationships between disciplines, including non-interactive complementarity; (iii) active relationships between disciplines, even if antagonistic; and narrowest, (iv) co-operative relationships in which disciplines learn from each other, to improve themselves or to do new things together, even to build new fields.

Cases (i) and (ii) would be covered by *Webster's* definition, and much American usage includes a weak variant of (ii): any combination of courses, or academics, from more than one discipline. Interdisciplinary Studies programmes in American colleges allow students to combine diverse topics rather than, as traditional academics would prefer, fulfil the prerequisites for further study in a specialised area. 'Between the disciplines' refers in such cases neither to the content of the components nor to interactions between them – the disciplinary courses may not relate to each other and it may be left to the students to try to make the links – but instead merely to their juxtaposition and to the location of the programmes outside the control of the disciplinary departments: in-between. It can mean isolation from, not interaction between, the disciplines. Derogatory usage of the inter-disciplinary label seems to derive from such a picture of North American cafeteria-choice study programmes.

In a more adequate usage, interdisciplinarity means (iii) or (iv), interaction or co-ordination. Thus, Leeson and Minogue, writing about creating a masters in Development Studies at Manchester, recorded that the goal was 'to create from the many separate offerings a genuine interdisciplinary course and not to be content with a mere adding together of a fascinating but uncoordinated menu' (1988: vi).

We can extend and modify the set of labels presented in an oft-cited OECD report (CERI 1972).[3] Let us distinguish the following variants of and successors or partners to disciplinarity.

1. *Multi-disciplinarity*. Although 'multi' implies only the presence of more than one discipline, when contrasted to 'inter-' it suggests that complementary but non-interacting disciplines are drawn on, as happens in a construction project or agriculture project, or in some area studies publications, where each discipline makes its separate input, typically presented in an independently authored chapter. This can also be called pluri-disciplinarity.[4] It involves an uncritical addition of different mono-disciplinarities. It does mean though that the member disciplines are less likely to become imperial in style, claiming to cover and absorb everything else. We must distinguish these non-interacting multi-disciplinary cases from all the variants below, where there is interaction of disciplines, which hence better fit the interdisciplinary label.

2. *Open-disciplinarity*. Here disciplines interact and seek to learn from each other, especially in analysis of a shared issue. Berge and Powell use another term but capture what I refer to: 'researchers identifying and confronting differences in perspectives and approaches; not in order for one to be [judged] "better" ... but for each to learn from, and contribute to others; and hence also become more aware of the merits and limitations of their own' (1997: 5). Van Nieuwenhuijze, too, sometimes espouses this usage: 'In upholding our claim to inter-disciplinarity ... we in fact lay claim to no more than the systematic attempt to give second thoughts, perhaps a bad conscience, to the person who trusts that his own discipline is all he needs to be a student of development ... [to make them] realize the need to look across the fence, to see what colleagues in the other disciplines are trying to do' (1978: 19).

3. Interdisciplinary openness and exchange may lead to:
    (a) *Interdisciplinary fields*, in the sense described earlier, such as public administration, urban and regional planning, and development studies. An inter-disciplinary field can involve all the forms under 1–3 here, and more, as it works at the crossroads of several disciplines and sets of practical demands. Such a field never can, nor indeed should, be integrated by a single agreed definition.
    (b) *New sub-disciplinary fields*, in which a discipline pursues with its existing methods new problems that it has perceived by learning from other disciplines; for example, environmental economics applies conventional economics tools in a new area.
    (c) *Hybrids*. Here new fields arise that have new methods as well as new problems, and with cross-disciplinary participation. Ecological economics, for example, is

not only economics as attempted by ecologists, and by economists who have read some ecology, but by anyone who has absorbed an ecology perspective. It involves real rethinking, not just extension of an existing approach to a new topic. It insists on pervasive and fundamental linkages and complexity, and hence on a broader perspective. Environmental economics in contrast often sticks to mainstream economics' approach of high abstraction, with different aspects of the world treated as largely disconnected so that the *ceteris paribus* condition is assumed to hold (all contextual conditions stay unchanged), often followed by a race to policy conclusions. It has had more money and power behind it than has ecological economics, which is more difficult to execute and more disturbing in its implications (Brasso, in Ravaioli 1995: 121–2).

4. (a) *Imperial-disciplinarity* is where an existing discipline tries to absorb or displace another. Here the eco-system contains predators who wish to eliminate others or at least to colonise them. '"Economic imperialism" is probably a good description of what I do', said Gary Becker (Swedberg 1991: 39). His close colleague George Stigler rode under the same banner (1984). Their associate James Coleman expected instead to absorb economics to sociology, but through reforming sociology by importation in a central role of rational-choice concepts from economics (Swedberg 1991).

   (b) *Mega-disciplinarity:* here a single well-integrated, all-purpose social science discipline is aspired to; as in rational-choice social science, some Marxism, or socio–biology (whose sophisticated versions allow for *co*-evolution of culture and genetic traits; Norgaard 1994). Mega-disciplinarity might be even more dangerous than mono-disciplinarity if it heightens hubris concerning the knowledge claims made and eliminates counter perspectives.

5. (a) *Super-disciplinarity.* 'Super' denotes above, beyond, or over. Here a theory is provided that claims to span, locate and delimit a number of competing disciplines, indicating how they fit different contexts, e.g. as in some more refined Marxism or Mary Douglas' Cultural Theory (CT).[5] Sometimes, though, advocates of such theories move to a mega–mode, seeking to subsume, not merely link.

   (b) *Supra-disciplinarity.* 'Supra' also denotes above, beyond; but, in addition, transcending. Here a framework claims to locate and delimit competing approaches and then guide selection of approach according to not only context but also purpose. Emery Roe (1998) seeks to surpass CT's super-bid, by defining a variety of types of theorising, which one moves between according to purposes as well as context, with CT as only one such type. This stance transcends disciplinarity because selection and definition of problems is no longer determined according to what fits the conventional methods and habits of a discipline; enquiry is driven by externally defined issues and purposes. (Note that both CT and Roe deal with all cases of intellectual approaches, not only with disciplines.)

6. *Transdisciplinarity*: For the International Centre for Transdisciplinary Research (CIRET), a transdisciplinary approach goes across disciplines, brings them together, and goes beyond them. This respects the original sense of trans-: across, on the other side of, beyond.[6] Their approach employs complexity theory and fuzzy logic to understand and interconnect multiple levels of reality (Max-Neef 2005). The aim is to connect fields and transcend barriers, not make a unified super-formulation (see Klein 2004).[7]

One can also speak of *meta-disciplinarity:* 'meta-' denotes after, beyond, with a suggestion of change of type. Here, as in systems analysis and some policy analysis and in various fields of design, we seek case-specific and purpose-specific framing of issues, not a standardised disciplinary framework nor even a wide set of them to choose between (see, for example, Stretton 1969; Rein and Schon 1994). All relevant disciplines are drawn on, as tools, but not granted major independent status; instead they are starting points, that are left behind in the process of dealing with real cases, as we see done in good historiography, good biography, good area studies. This has become a widespread usage of 'transdisciplinary' (see the survey by Wickson, Carew and Russell 2006), different from that of CIRET. It is also the one more accessible and relevant to most researchers in education and social science. This form of transdisciplinarity is necessary because 'there are no "economic", "social", or "psychological" problems, but just problems', which do not respect disciplinary boundaries (Myrdal 1975: 142). Working on real-world problems requires, conclude Wickson, Carew and Russell, a focus on the specific situation in its wholeness; flexibility in methodology (inspired perhaps by 'interpenetration of epistemologies', Wickson, Carew and Russell 2006: 1050), as opposed to adherence to pre-set research designs; and the involvement of or at least communication with a broad range of stakeholders.

Our mapping gives a dozen or so variants, as shown in Table 4.2. They can be grouped into fewer major cases, shown in the right hand column. We could refer to forms 2 through 6, and combinations of these (which are common), as interdisciplinary. In this usage, multi-disciplinarity is not automatically interdisciplinary. However, some people use the term interdisciplinary more loosely to cover that form (1) also; whereas others use it more narrowly than I have done, for only forms 2, 3 and 5.

Why classify, given the inevitable imperfection and incompleteness of any list? Because there is remediable confusion both between and within authors, even some of the best. Wallerstein *et al.* (1996) oscillated between the terms 'multidisciplinarity' and 'interdisciplinarity', and do not provide a clear terminology. The same applies for Easton, Dogan and Pahre, van Nieuwenhuijze, and Johnson, amongst others. Johnson, for example, declared: 'There are people who call themselves interdisciplinarians, implying that they can serve as sources of many different kinds of disciplinary excellence. By and large, interdisciplinarians fail to furnish hard-core excellence from all the disciplines they purport to represent' (1986: 205). But few interdisciplinarians claim poly-disciplinarity, mastery of more than one discipline. Nor need they, as adequacy of grasp for particular work demands is instead the relevant criterion (Klein 1996).[8] More of them are interdisciplinary in the sense of openness, willingness and ability to interact, communicate, learn. Indeed, elsewhere in his book Johnson himself advocated this, but he lacked a term to describe it, for he had made interdisciplinarity a pejorative label.

Usable frames for interdisciplinary co-operation

More widely manageable, for most users, than mega-, supra- or transdisciplinarity as conscious philosophies, may be identifiable interdisciplinary frameworks that link or transcend disciplinary models. In Table 4.2 we called these bridge-formats. Such frameworks can help to fill some of the roles played by a discipline: to provide shared foci, language and morale; to structure training; to mould public discourse. Without these intermediate stepping stones the leap from disciplinarity may be too great; but from such

Table 4.2 Some forms of disciplinarity and interdisciplinarity

Variant	Explanation	Condensed classification
0. Closed disciplines	Islands model	Pure disciplinarity (D)
1. Multi-disciplinarity	Presence of more than one discipline	
1a. Pluri-disciplinarity	Use of more than one discipline: complementary, additive but not influencing each other.	Multi-disciplinarity (MD)
1b. Poly-disciplinarity	Mastery by an individual of more than one discipline	
2a. Open-disciplinarity	Where some disciplines interchange and learn from each other; and co-operate on shared topics and tasks. Without necessarily formalising new sub- or cross- or interdisciplinary fields.	
2b. Bridge-format	Interchange is facilitated by a format to mobilise and relate a variety of inputs	Open-disciplinarity (OD)
3a. Interdisciplinary field	A practical problem-oriented field draws on various disciplines and may devise its own additions; it remains loosely integrated (e.g. public administration).	Interdisciplinary field
3b. Sub-disciplinarity	A discipline expands to deal with a new field—e.g. one that was previously covered only in another discipline—but with no change of its own concepts and methods	Sub-disciplinarity (=Cross-disciplinarity A)
3c. Hybridisation	A new integrated specialised field emerges as a hybrid from interaction of problems, concepts, methods and theories at the intersection of more than one (sub-)discipline	Hybridisation (=Cross-disciplinarity B)
4a. Imperial-disciplinarity	A discipline seeks to displace (some) other disciplines	
4b. Mega-disciplinarity	Goal of a single integrated social science, whether by imperial absorption, fusion or some other route	Mega-disciplinarity
5a. Super-disciplinarity	A theory which purports to show which discipline fits which context; and a practice which draws upon whichever disciplines ('pre-cooked meals') help in the given case	
5b. Supra-disciplinarity	A theory which purports to show which discipline fits which purpose and context	Supra-disciplinarity
6a. Trans-disciplinarity	Understand, connect, and transcend disciplines[1]	
6b. Meta-disciplinarity	One does not proceed by choosing between or combining bits from 'pre-cooked meals'; instead one selects variables and tools more flexibly, according to the situation studied, using post-disciplinary craft skills.	Trans-disciplinarity

Note: [1]Max-Neef (2005) uses 'weak transdisciplinarity' in this sense. He means a complete, conscious coordination of the different disciplines, into an accepted hierarchy of roles.

a basis and training some master craftsmen of supra- or meta-disciplinarity will emerge. And for those who cannot be master craftsmen, worthwhile steps will have been made towards cross-fertilisation and more open-minded thinking. For these purposes we need 'a kind of *cognitive boundary object* (Star and Griesemer 1989) facilitating communication across different cultures' (Jasanoff and Wynne 1998: 37).

Let us take as a possible example or candidate, the 'Cultural Theory' created in the 1960s–70s by the anthropologist Mary Douglas, who influenced the sociologist of education Basil Bernstein and very many others. It has been elaborated and applied by her co-workers Steve Rayner and Michael Thompson (see, for example, Verweij and Thompson 2006 for a streamlined and deepened version), as well as by prominent political scientists Aaron Wildavsky and Christopher Hood (Thompson *et al.* 1990; Hood 1998). It figures strongly in the four volumes (Rayner and Malone 1998) of the Battelle Foundation project on social science approaches to climate change, which drew on large numbers of social and environmental scientists from a range of disciplines. Much of 'Cultural Theory' attempts to provide a super-disciplinary synthesis of many matters, but its simplifying character and (sometimes) grand-theory claims can also become a barrier to interdisciplinary interaction. It could become perceived as a cult with a set of too-ready answers, rather than a forum where analysts of various backgrounds can find help to pursue their questions, not least by talking with each other. Promotion of inter-disciplinarity via a theory that makes strong claims and is mainly propounded by one school from one discipline could be less effective than propagation of a common frame-for-work. The latter is what Hood (1998), for one, provides; he uses Cultural Theory as a 'variety-generator' to spawn ideas and options.

As a second example, the frameworks devised by economist Amartya Sen for explanatory and policy analysis in the areas of human socio-economic development have attracted attention and been fruitful across a number of disciplines and in interdisciplinary discussion (Gasper 1993; 2008). Thus, the 'environmental entitlements' work by a multi-country group drawn from anthropology, human geography and agriculture, and from Ghana, India, South Africa and the UK (Leach, Mearns and Scoones 1997; 1999), reports how Sen's entitlements analysis led them to systematically consider a whole range of connections they would have neglected when following their usual disciplinary habits. Sen's capability approach, adopted as a basis for the UN's Human Development work, has functioned in a similar way (see, for example, Walker and Unterhalter 2007; Pick and Sirkin 2010, for its impacts in education research and community development). By forcefully directing attention to other determinants of quality of life besides commodities, it has contributed to broadening development economics and to much interdisciplinary co-operation (Gasper 2000b; 2008).

This constructive contribution is despite some internal obscurities, misunderstandings about Sen's categories by many users, and even their perhaps rather limited content as social analysis. Sen is indeed an open-minded economist but only strongly cross-disciplinary in respect of philosophy rather than other social sciences (see his interview in Swedberg 1991; Gasper 2000b). Yet capability and entitlements analysis has proven suitable to help economists, geographers, education theorists and others to pose relevant questions that take them beyond their inherited frames. It opens not just conversations within economics, but windows beyond. We should accept the inevitability of having many different lines and styles of conversations; and, although indeed placing each author's work in comparative context, praise anyone who generates sustained interdisciplinary conversation.

Entitlement and capability analysis are two examples of flexible formats that give considerable help in identifying factors to consider. Also important for interdisciplinary work, in helping to avoid a priori exclusions of factors and issues, are formats for analysing and constructing policy arguments (see, for example, Dunn 2007; Gasper 1996; 2000c; 2004b). These can provide both space and specific prompts to bring in issues. They can help us to ask, in the example we saw earlier, about private education's comparative impacts on nationbuilding, the brain-drain, and willingness to work in priority sectors, not only on graduates' earnings. The less pre-emptive and the more exploratory is problem formulation, the more transdisciplinary, creative and fruitful will be the research (see, for example, Brewer 1999).

Conclusion

This chapter has highlighted and tried to respond to needs for sharper concepts, a pluralistic picture of valid relationships, and non-utopianism about interdisciplinarity, and for practicable measures for shorter and longer run progress. We must distinguish multiple modes and purposes of social analysis, and employ a more complex ecology of the social sciences, such as sketched above. This includes being clear on the roles and roots as well as limits of disciplinarity, and observing the variety of types of multi-, inter- and transdisciplinarity. Practicable measures include promotion of 'bridging capital', notably intellectual formats attractive across more than one group, to counteract the 'bonding capital' within disciplines.

In the longer term, multi- and especially, interdisciplinary education are important for better interdisciplinary research and for loosening monogamous bonds of allegiance and identity. Joint degrees, or at least substantial Minors, should be the norm in social sciences, Foster-Carter reasonably suggests. They provide richer intellectual resources, as well as raise the readiness for later interdisciplinary research. In the shorter term, as argued by Johnson and others, interdisciplinary situation analysis and co-operation on policy-related cases are typically more feasible and sometimes more important than interdisciplinary theory building. Recognition of broker and liaison roles, in decisions on posts, training and funding, is required. And, in the present, every doctoral student has an opportunity to explore and think afresh.

We saw that, above all, whatever the organisational structures, we need interdisciplinary individuals, and intellectual frameworks that open and facilitate interdisciplinary conversation and offer attractive concrete activities. Conversation has both intellectual and social dimensions. The 'avenging angel' approach to interdisciplinarity – 'Countering my dear colleague's ignorance and grotesquely crude assumptions about topic X' – may be less effective than the 'Getting to Yes' approach: aiming to jointly generate new activities and insights that transcend and benefit all the starting points. The urgency of issues of education, health and well being, environment and human development provides enormous opportunities for this and for bringing together social, natural and behavioural scientists, and the humanities, to generate humanly useful knowledge.

Acknowledgements

This is a revised, updated and much shortened version of Gasper (2004a), with less historical and theoretical background and fewer examples. Warm thanks to Melanie Walker for her help, and to Thanh-Dam Truong for suggestions.

Notes

1 The *Oxford English Dictionary* traces the term 'discipline' to the Latin *discipulus*, meaning disciple. Salter and Hearn (1996; and sources therein) show how this reflects the history of the European university.
2 Kurien (1996) gives a rich similar characterisation of a Newtonian style adopted by neoclassical economics to study 'the economy'.
3 The CERI report contrasted 'multi-', 'inter-'; 'pluri-' (for juxtaposition of related disciplines) and 'trans-' disciplinarity.
4 The prefixes pluri- and poly- differ only in provenance: the former Latin, the latter Greek. I allocate them in Table 4.2 in light of the familiar concept 'polymath'. Max-Neef uses the term 'pluridisciplinarity' instead to mean 'cooperation between disciplines, without coordination' (2005: 6).
5 'Cultural Theory' claims that we can helpfully understand the range of viewpoints on almost any issue of social organisation in terms of four perspectives, which are permanent contenders, and limitations of which in each case reinforce the other perspectives. One stock viewpoint is 'hierarchist', reflecting acceptance of high group loyalties and high regulation of individual behaviour (high group – high grid); the second is 'individualist' (low group – low grid); the third is 'egalitarian' (high group – low grid); the fourth is 'fatalist' (low group – high grid) (Thompson *et al.* 1990; Hood 1998).
6 The 1972 OECD report in contrast used 'transdisciplinary' to mean mega-disciplinarity: subsumption of more than one discipline by a common set of principles. This usage does not seem to be followed in most recent work (see Wickson *et al.* 2006, for a survey).
7 Klein (2004) surveys much current work on transdisciplinarity, including in education research.
8 Bilingualism is thus a false metaphor for interdisciplinarity: 'Pidgin and creole are the typifying forms of interdisciplinary communication' (Klein 1996: 220). Thus, interdisciplinary PhD research should not face the further barrier, beyond the difficulty of its greater scale and complexity, of subjection to multi-disciplinary assessment by a battery of disciplinary specialists. Their criteria are often inappropriate: demanding maximum elaboration and precision on what are only sub-aspects of an interdisciplinary study, as opposed to a depth sufficient in terms of the whole enquiry. Alternatively, mono-disciplinary theses should be exposed to the critical glare of other disciplines; many will be highly vulnerable.

References

Apthorpe, R. (1996) Reading Development Policy and Policy Analysis, *European Journal of Development Research*, 8(1): 16–35.
Bedi, A. S. and Garg, A. (2000) The Effectiveness of Private versus Public Schools: The Case of Indonesia, *Journal of Development Economics* 61(2): 463–94.
Berge, G. and Powell, N. (1997) *Reflections on Inter-disciplinary Research: A Synthesis of Experiences from Research in Development and Environment*. Working Paper 1997: 4, Centre for Development and the Environment, University of Oslo.
Boulding, K. (1986) Foreword. In G.L. Johnson (1986). *Research Methodology for Economists – Philosophy and Practice*. New York: Macmillan.
Brewer, G. (Ed.) (1999) The Theory and Practice of Interdisciplinary Work, Special issue of *Policy Sciences*, 32(4).
CERI (Centre for Educational Research and Innovation) (1972) *Interdisciplinarity: Problems of Teaching and Research in Universities*. Paris: OECD.
Dogan, M. and Pahre, R. (1990) *Creative Marginality: Innovations at the intersections of social sciences*. Boulder, CO: Westview.
Dunn, W. N. (2007) *Public Policy Analysis*. 4th edn. Upper Saddle River, NJ: Prentice Hall.
Earl, P. (1983) *The Economic Imagination*. Brighton: Wheatsheaf.
Easton, D. (1991) The Division, Integration, and Transfer of Knowledge. In D. Easton and C. Schelling (Eds). *Divided Knowledge: Across Disciplines, Across Cultures,* Newbury Park, CA: Sage, 7–36.

Foster-Carter, A. (1998) Against divisions among the social sciences, *Times Higher Education Supplement*, 9 October.

Gasper, D. (1990) Education for Regional Planning. In A. Helmsing and K. Wekwete (Eds). *Subnational Planning in Southern and Eastern Africa*, Aldershot: Gower, 261–303.

——(1993) Entitlements Analysis: Relating Concepts and Contexts, *Development and Change*, 24(4): 425–66.

——(1996) Analysing Policy Arguments, *European Journal of Development Research*, 8(1): 36–62.

——(2000a) Strengthening 'Public and Development' in the New South Africa. In F. Theron and E. Schwella (Eds). *The State of Public and Development Management in South Africa*, University of Stellenbosch, pp. 165–88.

——(2000b) Development as Freedom: Taking Economics Beyond Commodities – The Cautious Boldness of Amartya Sen, *Journal of International Development*, 12(7): 989–1001.

——(2000c) Structures And Meanings – A Way To Introduce Argumentation Analysis In Policy Studies Education, *Africanus*, 30(1): 49–72.

——(2004a) Interdisciplinarity. In A. K. Giri (Ed.) *Creative Social Research*. Lanham, MD: Lexington Books, and Delhi: Sage, pp. 308–44.

——(2004b) Studying Aid: Some Methods. In J. Gould and H. S. Marcussen (Eds). *Ethnographies of Aid – Exploring development texts and encounters*, Roskilde University, Denmark: International Development Studies, pp. 45–92.

——(2008) From 'Hume's Law' To Policy Analysis For Human Development, *Review of Political Economy*, 20(2): 233–56.

Giri, A. K. (1998) Transcending Disciplinary Boundaries, *Critique of Anthropology*, 18(4): 379–404.

——(2002) The Calling of a Creative Transdisciplinarity, *Futures*, 34(1): 103–15.

Hood, C. (1998) *The Art of the State*. Oxford: Clarendon Press.

Jasanoff, S. and Wynne, B. (1998) Science and Decisionmaking. In S. Rayner and E. Malone (Eds). *Human Choice and Climate Change: The Societal Framework*, Vol. 1, Columbus, OH: Battelle Press, 1–87.

Johnson, G. L. (1986) *Research Methodology for Economists – Philosophy and Practice*. New York: Macmillan.

Karlqvist, A. (1999) Going beyond disciplines – The meanings of interdisciplinarity, *Policy Sciences*, 32: 379–83.

Klein, J. T. (1996) *Crossing Boundaries: Knowledge, Disciplinarities and Interdisciplinarities*. Charlottesville, VA: University Press of Virginia.

——(2004) Prospects for Transdisciplinarity, *Futures*, 36(4): 515–26.

Kothari, R. (1988) *Rethinking Development: In Search of Humane Alternatives*. Delhi: Ajanta.

Kuhn, T. S. (1970) *The Structure of Scientific Revolutions*. 2nd edn. Chicago, IL: University of Chicago Press.

Kurien, C.T. (1996) *Rethinking Economics*. Delhi: Sage.

Lakoff, G. and Johnson, M. (2003) *Metaphors We Live By*. New edn. Chicago, IL: University of Chicago Press.

Leach, M., Mearns, R., and Scoones, I. (1997) Community Based Sustainable Development: Consensus or Conflict? *IDS Bulletin*, 28(4), special issue.

——(1999) Environmental Entitlements: Dynamics and Institutions, *World Development*, 27(2): 225–47.

Leeson, P. and Minogue, M. (1988) Preface. In P. Leeson and M. Minogue (Eds). *Perspectives on Development – Cross-disciplinary themes in development studies*, Manchester: Manchester University Press.

Lipton, M. (1970) Interdisciplinary Studies in Less Developed Countries, *Journal of Development Studies*, 7(1): 5–18.

Martinez-Alier, J. (1999) The Socio-ecological Embeddedness of Economic Activity: The Emergence of a Transdisciplinary Field. In E. Becker and T. Jahn (Eds). *Sustainability and the Social Sciences*. London: Zed, pp. 112–40.

Max-Neef, M. (2005) Foundations of Transdisciplinarity, *Ecological Economics*, 53(2005): 5–16.

McCloskey, D. (1994) *Knowledge and Persuasion in Economics*. Cambridge: Cambridge University Press.

McNeill, D. (1999) On Interdisciplinary Research: with particular reference to the field of environment and development, *Higher Education Quarterly*, 53(4): 312–32.

Myrdal, G. (1975) *Against the Stream: Critical Essays on Economics*. New York: Random House.

Nieuwenhuijze van, C. A. O. (1978) The Study of Development and the Alleged Need for an Interdisciplinary Approach, Occasional Paper 67, Institute of Social Studies, The Hague.

Norgaard, R. (1994) *Development Betrayed – the end of progress and a coevolutionary revisioning of the future.* London: Routledge.

Pick, S. and Sirkin, J. (2010) *Agentic Empowerment: Investing in People for Sustainable Development.* New York: Oxford University Press.

Ravaioli, C. (1995) *Economists and the Environment – What the top economists say about the environment.* London: Zed.

Ravetz, J. R. (1973) *Scientific Knowledge and its Social Problems*. Harmondsworth: Penguin.

Rayner, S. and Malone, E. (Eds) (1998) *Human Choice and Climate Change* (4 vols). Columbus, OH: Battelle Press.

Rein, M. and Schon, D. (1994) *Frame Reflection*. New York: Basic Books.

Roe, E. (1998) *Taking Complexity Seriously*. Boston, MA: Kluwer.

——(1999) *Except-Africa*. New Brunswick, NJ: Transaction Publishers.

Rotblatt, S. (1998) Tug of war for knowledge, *Times Higher Education Supplement*, 4 December.

Rutgers, M. (1998) Paradigm lost: crisis as identity of the study of public administration, *International Review of Administrative Sciences*, 64: 553–64.

Salter, L. and Hearn, A. (1996) *Outside the Lines: Issues in Interdisciplinary Research*. Montreal: McGill-Queen's University Press.

Schoenberger, E. (2001) Interdisciplinarity and social power, *Progress in Human Geography*, 25(3): 365–82.

Scitovsky, T. (1976; 2nd edn 1992) *The Joyless Economy*. New York: Oxford University Press.

Star, S. and Griesemer, J. (1989) Institutional ecology, 'translations' and boundary objects, *Social Studies of Science*, 19: 387–420.

Stigler, G. J. (1984) Economics – the imperial discipline, *Scandinavian Journal of Economics*, 86: 310–13.

Stretton, H. (1969) *The Political Sciences*. London: Routledge & Kegan Paul.

Swedberg, R. (1991) *Economics and Sociology – redefining their boundaries*. Delhi: Oxford University Press.

Szostak, R. (2003) *A schema for unifying human science: interdisciplinary perspectives on culture*. Selinsgrove, PA : Susquehanna University Press.

Thompson, M., Ellis, R. and Wildavsky, A. (1990) *Cultural Theory*. Boulder, CO: Westview.

Verweij, M. and Thompson, M. (Eds) (2006) *Clumsy Solutions for a Complex World*. Basingstoke: Palgrave Macmillan.

Walker, M. and Unterhalter, E. (Eds) (2007) *Sen's Capability Approach and Social Justice in Education*. New York: Palgrave Macmillan.

Wallerstein, I. (1999) *The End of the World as We Know It – Social Science for the 21st Century*. Minneapolis, MN: University of Minnesota Press.

——et al. (1996) *Open The Social Sciences – Report of the Gulbenkian Commission on the Restructuring of the Social Sciences*. Stanford, CA: Stanford University Press.

Wickson, F., Carew, A. and Russell, A. (2006) Transdisciplinary research: characteristics, quandaries and quality, *Futures*, 38(9): 1046–59.

5
The necessity and violence of theory

S. J. Ball

This chapter offers a personal view of the need for and uses of theory in educational research. It draws on the work of two exemplary theorists to point up the epistemological role of theory in making research possible and making it reflexive. The second section of the chapter deploys some recent ideas and research from class theory and class analysis to suggest some of the limitations of the use of social class in current educational research and some ways of thinking differently about class.

Introduction

Perhaps as educational researchers we need to appreciate better the work that theory does. To this end, I want to say something about some general theoretical influences that are important to me in the way I go about research, and then something more specific and substantive about the role of class theory in educational research. I am seeking here to highlight the very practical role of theory in research as a conceptual toolbox and means of analysis and a system of reflexivity.

The two theorists I find most provocative, productive, and 'useful' both deny and avoid having 'a theory' – both are essentially concerned with 'practice', the practice of social science and social research, rather than global abstractions for their own sake. They are both thought of as theorists, but they saw themselves as researchers, indeed they are far more concerned about epistemology and its pitfalls than with theory per se, and with understanding how we think about the social as a starting point for thinking differently about the social world, thinking between existing positions, and thinking against mindless orthodoxies. Both sought to break epistemologically with the scientistic mimicry of the social sciences and find a form of research practice unencumbered by the naturalism of what one called 'spontaneous sociology' (everyday thinking). They were both critically aware of the ways in which sociology constitutes the object of its theorising. That is, the way in which the positions we take and the concepts we use play their part in making up our research objects. That we do not have direct and unencumbered access to a social world waiting patiently and passively to be researched and known. They are also both committed to avoiding closure, their work trades in the possibilities of paradox, and they are against making the social more real, more orderly, more predictable than it is. The world as it is, as one put it, is 'complicated, confused, impure, uncertain' (Bourdieu, Chamboredon and Passeron 1991: 259). And they are both angry and critical, both activists and public intellectuals whose work is a form of 'critical explanation' and a means to 'sap power'. All of which confounds the possibilities of conventional versions of intellectual rigour. And, as it happens, they are both French – they are Michel Foucault and Pierre Bourdieu. Their work is very different, but not as different as is sometimes thought (Foucault was Bourdieu's sponsor to the College de France).

As Foucault explained, his purpose is 'not to formulate the global systematic theory which holds everything in place, but to analyze the specificity of mechanisms of power ... to build little by little a strategic knowledge' (Foucault 1980: 145), and, as Bourdieu often urged, he wanted his readers to read his works as 'exercise books' rather than theories and was keen to 'remind us that "theory" should not be valued for its own sake' (Karakayali 2004: 352). He felt strongly that we need to be reflexively aware of the implications and effects of theory in relation to the social world we conjure up in our work. He was indeed critical of what he called the 'intellectualist bias', which always arises when a researcher is insufficiently critical of the 'presuppositions inscribed in the act of thinking about the world' (Bourdieu and Wacquant 1992: 39) and the failure to grasp 'the logic of practice' that stems from this. Indeed, part of Bourdieu's endeavour was to destabilise and re-invent the sociological habitus, 'a system of dispositions necessary to the constitution of the craft of the sociologist in its universality' (Bourdieu 1993: 271). And, importantly, Bourdieu sought to work between binaries rather than be constrained to make false choices between poles – his social model is articulated between objectivism (construction of a discourse within which to converse with other sociologists about the object) and subjectivism, his epistemology is enacted between scientism and theoreticism, which implies that one can grasp reality without 'touching it' (Karakayali 2004: 365).

Foucault goes further; in his self-awareness and his scepticism about theory and research, he often claimed that his books are fictions, but it is important to understand what he meant by that and how this was part of his own strategic struggle against the traditional disciplines of social science. His books are fictions 'only because the power relations and the disciplinary establishments within which they could be validated don't yet exist' (Foucault 1980: 192–3). In writing outside of the expectations and constraints of intellectualism, his work had no framework of disciplinary evaluation within which it could be judged, and, indeed, Foucault worked constantly to avoid being captured by and within the disciplines of social science, which he saw as limits to the possibilities of thought.

Am I a Foucauldian then? Clearly no! Am I a Bourdieurian? Maybe a failed one! – I do not seek to be anything. I do not want to mimic, or emulate these writers, even if I possibly could. I want to learn from them, I want to be challenged by them and to struggle with the frustrations to certainty that they present. I want to be made uncomfortable and not 'let half-truths and or received ideas steer me along' (Said 1994: 17) – perhaps 'want' is the wrong verb, rather I constantly confront discomforts that I cannot ignore.

But I also want to experience and hold on to those moments when I read a line or a paragraph, and it is like the author stretches a hand out from the page towards my own hand, and I think 'yes, I think that too, that expresses something that I have never been able to quite capture into words'.

Foucault in particular made an art form out of discomforting his readers and would-be emulators. He constantly disavowed and distanced himself from his own work. As noted already, he denied any attempt on his part to construct a theoretical system or holistic account on the social. His work is full of discontinuities, diversions, and evasions. In style as in substance he sought to work outside and against the conventions of 'normal' rigour. Michael Walzer (1988: 193) captures and responds to this in an interesting way when he explains that his own rendition of Foucault's critical stance requires that he 'adopt a "constructivist" position'.

> Since Foucault never presented it [his critical stance] in anything like a systematic fashion, I shall put it together out of the later (and more political) books and interviews, ignoring passages that I don't understand and refusing to live at the heights of his flamboyance.

In other words, quite rightly, Walzer reads Foucault as a 'writerly text', as a text that invites the reader to participate in the making of meaning rather than simply be subject to it. Foucault's elusivity creates spaces for the reader and user of his work to be creative and to be adventurous.

In a different sense, one of the charms of Bourdieu is that it is possible to see the flaws and discontinuities in his work, as well as its clear evolution over time; although the mis-ordering of his French publications when translated into English does not always make this easy. In his efforts to be absolutely clear about the grounds of his work, he reveals, rather than obscures, as is the case in most social scientific writings, its limits, omissions, and inconsistencies. Bourdieu was also very much a pragmatic realist!

All of this is demanding and liberating in equal measure. Bourdieu and Foucault offer a form of social scientific practice and thinking that is not limited to the discursively con-structed boxes, categories and divisions of modernist thinking. But taking them and the way in which they work seriously does not involve giving up what we believe or find useful or productive. It does not mean becoming 'something', swapping new ortho-doxies for old, rather it means struggling against the complacencies and comforts of 'being something', of orthodoxy for its own sake.[1] And all of this in turn requires, as Edward Said (1994) argued, 'both commitment and risk, boldness and vulnerability' (p. 10), and it means accepting that work is always 'unfinished and necessarily imperfect' (p. 17), despite increasingly frenetic demands for definitive statements and firm and conclusive 'findings'.

It also means giving up on spontaneous empiricism, casual epistemologies, theory by numbers, and constantly struggling against the governmentalities of scientism to find a proper rigour, a thoughtful reflexive and practical rigour – a rigour that goes beyond the niceties and safety of technique to find a form of epistemological practice that is not simply self-regarding.

So I will finish with a very brief attempt to illustrate how these fascinations, dis-comforts, and avoidances play upon and within my work. And I will do that in relation to my very modernist preoccupation with social class, a preoccupation that Bourdieu would have little problem with but one that would be anathema to Foucault. I will draw on some of the influences that played their part in the writing of *Class strategies and the education market* (Ball 2003), which both uses and tries to move beyond the existing body of sociological class theory. The book was 'written between rather than against' existing work, it differs from rather than opposes, and certainly does not try 'to reduce others to silence' (Foucault 1974: 17)[2] and it is a strategic, unfinished text.

What do recent developments in class theory, and more generally Bourdieu's writing on class, have to say to and offer to education researchers? Three things perhaps.

1. Certainly in a technical and theoretical sense the class categories used in much educational research seem crude and ineffectual – significant feminist and revisionist critiques of class analysis are ignored, out-moded models of class, and class relations are repeatedly rehearsed, changes in the class structure are unattended to and the complexities of classed families are bracketed away (despite the fact that these have a particular and enduring relevance to educational issues). For the most part, in education research on social class and 'in conventional class analyses' families 'appear like phantoms, clearly implicated in the intergenerational transmission of social and economic advantage, and yet assuming a unitary status lacking in real social content' (Witz 1995: 45). Generally, educational research tends to settle for what is available rather than what is meaningful, often settling for surrogate indicators, such as free school meals, which have little sensible relation to class analysis. The complexities of cross-class, dual-income, and transnational family structures are conveniently avoided, and Rosemary Crompton's warning that 'it is not possible to construct a single measure which could successfully capture all the elements going to make up social class – or even structured social inequality' (Crompton 1998: 114) is constantly ignored. Generally, the nuances and ambiguities of class positionings are set aside, whereas, as Bourdieu (1987: 13) argues, 'In the reality of the social world, there are no more clear-cut boundaries, no more absolute breaks, than there are in the physical world'. Social boundaries, he suggests, can be thought of as 'imaginary planes' or a more appropriate image 'would be that of a flame whose edges are in constant movement, oscillating around a line or surface' (p. 13). Consequently, it is often difficult to read classed individuals as though their experiences were transparent concomitants of the social category they are allocated to. Educational research does this as normal practice. The ontological status of class is not 'ready-made in reality' (Wacquant 1991: 57), but is routinely taken to be so.

2. With notable exceptions, developments in class theory, as in the analysis of class fractions (see Vincent, Ball and Kemp 2004), debates concerning an underclass, and work on class and space – both in local and global terms, are systematically neglected. Educational research can sometimes be read, in class terms, as though it is stuck in the 1950s, whereas almost all of the contributors to the class debate emphasise the need to renew class analysis 'in the context of current social changes' (Butler 1995: 35). Class analysis works, as Crompton (1995: 74) argues, within 'a very fluid and rapidly developing situation', and she goes on to say, 'this does not mean we are witnessing the end of class analysis ... Rather ... the best way forward is to explore a more flexible approach'. In particular, recent work in class theory and class analysis emphasises the interactions of space and social networks in class formation and reproduction. The point is that class is not the same everywhere. It does not mean the same thing in Durham as it does in Cornwall as it does in London or Adelaide. Butler with Robson (2003), for example, explore what they term 'the Metropolitan Habitus' and Savage, Bagnall, and Longhurst (2004) explore four different narratives of middle class life in four different areas of Manchester, which include differences in the involvement of the research families with their children's education (Bagnall, Longhurst and Savage 2003). Class meanings are inflected by culture and place. Class identities are 'located' and 'developed through the networked geography of places articulated together' (Savage, Bagnall and Longhurst 2004: 208). Or in Bourdieu's words, 'Social agents,

and also things insofar as they are appropriated by them and therefore constituted as properties, are situated in a place in social space … ' (Bourdieu 1999: 134). We know ourselves and relate to others from where we belong, or sometimes out of a sense of not belonging, of feeling out of place. The spaces and places of class exist in several senses that have a particular relevance to education. Schools themselves are classed spaces, within which some students feel at home and others can be distinctly uncomfortable. Education is a trajectory through spaces of learning, and our movement through these spaces can be reaffirming of who we are or be part of becoming different, and a process of class disidentification (see Mahony and Zmroczek 1997). What we call social mobility is also typically a form of spatial mobility and exposes those who are mobile to the possibilities of not belonging (see Reay, David and Ball 2005) and a variety of joys and sufferings and renunciations. We may even learn to occupy space and move through it differently as our bodily hexis changes to accommodate to what is 'strict and sober, discreet and severe' (Bourdieu 1986: 338), and as we seek stature and substance, and to display a sense of entitlement. The geography of class and education can also be seen at the present point in time in the interplay of parental choice, school admissions criteria and house prices. Classes use and misuse space differently, sometimes to their advantage, as a resource, and sometimes they are 'trapped' within damaging spatial identities. Spatial resources are unevenly distributed, and some can be deployed to ensure access to schools of a certain kind, that is, to those places where there are others 'like us'. In some circumstances the middle classes are able to colonise schools (Butler with Robson 2003) and concomitantly the process of gentrification is inflected by the availability of particular kinds of school places in particular locations (see Taylor 2002, on the geography of school choice). Indeed, the relations of education and social class do not make much sense without a sense of space and place, but much educational research that deploys social class categories floats free of such material underpinnings.

3. Far too little attention is paid to class practices or given to thinking about the meaning of class – what class is. Bourdieu provides cautions and insights in both respects, and the recent work of Mike Savage, Beverley Skeggs, Diane Reay, Tim Butler and Paul Connolly, all influenced by Bourdieu, to a greater or lesser extent, illustrates what can be done with class by moving beyond the 'theoreticist illusion' (Bourdieu 1987: 7) of 'class on paper' to take seriously how class 'gets done'. Class 'is something that happens (and it can be showed to have happened) in a human relationship' (Thompson 1980: 8–9). Class is an identity and a lifestyle, and a set of perspectives on the social world and relationships in it, marked by varying degrees of reflexivity. Identities, lifestyles, perspectives, and relationships are 'constituted in the course of collective history' and 'acquired in the course of individual history', which 'function in their practical state' (Bourdieu 1986: 467). Class, in this sense, is productive and reactive. It is an identity based on modes of being and becoming and forms of distinction that are realised and reproduced in specific social locations as noted already. We 'think' and are 'thought' by class. It is about being something and not being something else. It is relational. Class is also a trajectory, a path through space and time, a 'history of transactions' (Walzer 1984). We are not always the same, or always able to be the same, as the world around us changes. 'Real world classes are constantly being constructed around us, people are constantly doing class' (Connell 1983: 148). Our current sense of who we are may be

deeply invested in once having been someone different or wanting to be someone else in the future. Similar class positions are held and experienced differently, and have different histories. Class positions and perspectives are produced from and invested with the traces of earlier choices, improvisations, and opportunities, as well as being inflected by chance. Transactions are cumulative: 'aspects of action and interaction are constantly being negotiated, reformulated, modified' (Devine 1997: 9). Each new choice or point of decision making is confronted with particular assets or capitals (economic, social and cultural) in hand, to be exchanged or invested; and for an individual or a family volumes of capital may be 'increasing, decreasing or stationary' (Bourdieu 1986: 120). Advantages in the form of capitals can be stored and accumulated for future use (Lee 1993). In other words, I take class to be dynamic and emergent, as Savage (2000: 69) puts it, 'people now have to achieve their class positions'. As such, reproduction is never guaranteed, and mobility up or down is always possible. Such mobility is both contingently and strategically dependent. Class and class inequalities need to be treated and 'understood dynamically' (Savage 2000: 69), as 'a longitudinal process rather than a cross-sectional one', but without losing a sense of the relative stability of class relations – 'stable' and 'static' are not the same. All this is about how class is achieved and maintained and enacted rather than something that just is! Class is realised and struggled over in the daily lives of families and institutions, in consumption decisions, as much as in the processes of production, and particularly at moments of 'crisis' and contradiction as parents think about the well being and happiness and futures of their offspring. Class is about 'knowing' how to act at these defining moments (see Devine 2004).

Conclusion

In this chapter I have sought to make a case for the urgent necessity for theory in educational research and research training; its crucial role in epistemological decision making; in ensuring the conceptual robustness of conceptual categories; and in providing a method for reflexivity, that is, for understanding the social conditions of the production of knowledge. I also suggested the importance of the violence that theory does, as a reflexive tool within research practice, its role in challenging conservative orthodoxies and closure, parsimony, and simplicity, that is, the role of theory in retaining some sense of the obduracy and complexity of the social. Much of what passes for educational research is hasty, presumptive and immodest. We constantly over estimate our grasp on the social world and under estimate our role in its management. The chapter also offered a short and rather loose example of the useful work that theory can do in relation to categories like social class – categories that otherwise lie moribund and unproblematised within research practice.

Notes

1 As Wright-Mills (1963: 12) put it a long time ago: 'Fresh perception now involves the capacity to continually unmask and smash the stereotypes of vision and intellect which modern communications [i.e. modern systems of representation] swamp us'.

2 Furthermore, no closure is sought or claimed; it is intended to be read as a set of statements to be worked on. It was a book written throughout with the firm idea in mind that it would have to be rewritten, that another book would follow. Part of the exercise of analysis of class in the book is about 'appraising concepts as possibilities for future thinking' (Colebrook 2000: 5) and it is an 'exercise in making things intelligible' Parkin 1979: 115). It seeks, as Bourdieu urges, to develop a set of concepts that are 'polymorphic, supple and adaptable, rather than defined, calibrated and used rigidly' (Bourdieu and Wacquant 1992: 23).

References

Bagnall, G., Longhurst, B. and Savage, M. (2003) Children, belonging and social capital: The PTA and middle class narratives of social involvement in the North-West of England, *Sociological Research Online*, 8(4). Online. (Available at www.socresonline.org.uk/8/4/bagnall.html Retrieved 21 January 2004).

Ball, S. J. (2003) *Class strategies and the education market: The middle class and social advantage*. London: RoutledgeFalmer.

Bourdieu, P. (1986) *Distinction: A social critique of the judgement of taste*. London: Routledge.

——(1987) What makes a social class? On the theoretical and practical existence of Groups, *Berkeley Journal of Sociology*, 23(1): 1–17.

——(1993) *Sociology in question*. London: Sage.

——(1999) *Pascalian meditations*. Cambridge, England: Polity.

Bourdieu, P. and Wacquant, L. J. D. (1992) *An invitation to reflexive sociology*. Chicago, IL: University of Chicago Press.

Bourdieu, P., Chamboredon, J. C. and Passeron, J. C. (1991) *The craft of sociology: Epistemological preliminaries*. Berlin: de Guyer.

Butler, T. (1995) The debate over the middle classes. In T. Butler and M. Savage (Eds) *Social change and the middle classes*. London: UCL Press, 26–40.

Butler, T., with Robson, G. (2003) *London calling: The middle classes and the re-making of Inner London*. Oxford: Berg.

Colebrook, C. (2000) Introduction. In I. Buchanan and C. Colebrook (Eds). *Deleuze and feminist theory*. Edinburgh: University of Edinburgh Press.

Connell, R. W. (1983) *Which way is up? Essays on class, sex and culture*. Sydney, Australia: George Allen and Unwin.

Crompton, R. (1995) Women's employment and the 'middle class'. In T. Butler and M. Savage (Eds). *Social change and the middle classes*. London: UCL Press, pp. 58–75.

——(1998) *Class and stratification: An introduction to current debates*. Oxford: Polity Press.

Devine, F. (1997, April) *Privilege, power and the reproduction of advantage*. Paper presented at the British Sociological Association Annual Conference, University of York.

Devine, F. (2004) *Class practices: How parents help their children get good jobs*. Cambridge: Cambridge University Press.

Foucault, M. (1974) *The archaeology of knowledge*. London: Tavistock

——(1980) *Power/Knowledge: Selected interviews and other writings*. New York: Pantheon.

Karakayali, N. (2004) Reading Bourdieu with Adorno: the limits of critical theory and reflexive sociology, *Sociology*, 38(3): 357–68.

Lee, M. J. (1993) *Consumer culture reborn*. London: Routledge.

Mahony, P. and Zmroczek, C. (Eds) (1997) *Class matters: 'Working-class' women's perspectives on social class*. London: Taylor & Francis.

Parkin, F. (1979) *Marxism and class theory: a bourgeois critique*. London: Tavistock.

Reay, D., David, M. E. and Ball, S. J. (2005) *Degrees of choice: Social class, race and gender in higher education*. Stoke-on-Trent: Trentham.

Said, E. (1994) *Representations of the intellectual*. New York: Vintage Books.

Savage, M. (2000) *Class analysis and social transformation*. Buckingham: Open University Press.

Savage, M., Bagnall, G. and Longhurst, B. (2004) *Globalization and belonging*. London: Sage.

Taylor, C. (2002) *Geography and the 'new' education market: Secondary school choice in England and Wales*. Aldershot: Ashgate.

Thompson, E. P. (1980) *The making of the English working class*. Harmondsworth: Penguin.

Vincent, C., Ball, S. J. and Kemp, S. (2004) The social geography of childcare: Making up a middle class child, *British Journal of Sociology of Education*, 25(2): 229–44.

Wacquant, L. J. D. (1991) Making class(es): The middle classes in social theory and social structure. In S. McNall, R. Levine and R. Fantasia (Eds). *Bringing class back in: Contemporary and historical respectives*. Boulder, CO: Westview Press, pp. 39–64.

Walzer, M. (1984) *Spheres of justice: A defence of pluralism and equality*. Oxford: Martin Robertson.

——(1988) *In the company of critics: Social criticism and political commitment in the twentieth century*. New York: Basic Books.

Witz, A. (1995) Gender and service-class formation. In T. Butler and M. Savage (Eds) *Social change and the middle classes*. London: UCL Press, 41–57.

Wright-Mills, C. (1963) *Power, politics and people: Collected essays* (I. Horowitz, Ed.). New York: Ballantine.

6
Bringing theory to doctoral research

K. N. Gulson and R. J. Parkes

In the USA, the UK and Australia, a combination of credential inflation and attendant instrumentalism has resulted in theory being a disparaged part of educational research, and thus also doctoral research in education. This disparagement comes in part from the conflation of theory with abstract purposelessness, and its connection with soft research as opposed to applied research into, and for, educational policy and practice. In many ways this dichotomy is paradigmatically located, in that it is only some forms of theory that are seen as under attack. In the UK in the mid-1990s, Ball (1995) lamented a-theoretical moves within sociology of education to issues of management, measurement, evaluation, and so forth, and the resultant creation of new fields such as 'school improvement', 'leadership', and so forth. In the early 2000s, qualitative researchers in the USA have felt the veracity of their work is undercut, and inadequately funded due to an emphasis on 'evidence-based' research, coded as large-scale 'scientific research in education', as 'gold standard' quantitative research (see Lather 2006). However, Atkinson and Delamont (2006) argue that this is a very insular viewpoint that conflates shifts in the USA with trends in other countries. They argue that in the UK rigorous qualitative research is not only respected, but also centrally located within research council funding schemes. Nonetheless, Sikes (2006) writes that in the UK the marketisation of education and research has meant that 'research which apparently provides value-free, objective, and quantifiable evidence that can directly inform practice is favoured and funded' (p. 47). Clearly the world of theory and research is a fraught one.

This fraught world also pervades the world of doctoral education, as these debates filter through to the type of doctoral research that gains funding and the type of research that gains clearance by university ethical review boards (Sikes 2006). This can also impact on what gets valorised in doctoral programmes, notably in those countries where doctoral courses are the norm. In reflecting on a conversation she had with her doctoral students about theory in educational research, Pat Sikes comments that:

> the group split into two fundamentally opposing camps. There were those who said that they found theory scary and frightening, the aspect of their work that they approached with the most trepidation and even with fear and loathing. The other,

smaller group, by contrast, said it was theory that excited them, and that theory … 'floated their boat'.

Sikes 2006: 43–4

We are of the latter persuasion, theory floats our boat. The editors of this volume requested that we write to the title or topic of 'bringing theory to doctoral research'. We should be clear that we did not take this title to mean arguing for the need to look at theories *of* doctoral research. Rather, in planning this chapter we wondered whether the proposed title could suggest a paucity of theory that, in fact, needs to be brought, or brought back, to educational research and thus doctoral research, or that this title suggested we offer ways to bring theory *into* doctoral research. We have taken the proposed title as an invitation to touch on both in this chapter. We are convinced of the need for, and subsequent enactment of, theoretically informed doctoral undertakings; that is the ways in which doctoral students can, and should, be cognisant of the pleasures and perils of using theory in educational doctoral work, and that theory is in fact a necessity in order to become a scholar. We work from a similar position to Ball (1995), who argues that 'the absence of theory leaves the researcher prey to unexamined, unreflexive preconceptions and dangerously naive ontological and epistemological *a prioris*' (p. 266). We also recognise that it is difficult to write to any kind of generalised audience about doctoral research due to the differing nature of the doctorate across Europe and North America (though these are becoming increasingly similar), and the arena where we received our doctorates, Australia, let alone across other parts of the world. In Australia there is no doctoral course work, but some understanding that you will undergo a research apprenticeship of some sort. It is certainly not an expectation that doctoral students 'down under' will have developed an understanding of research methodology through a generalist training in the sense that is discussed in the USA and Canada. However, despite these differences, we hope to say something that can be of interest to all doctoral students. We thus attempt to provide a way to articulate theory's place in the process by which doctoral students enter the field of educational research, such that they are versed with theory's role in manifesting one of the aims of this collection, that of 'forming knowledge/forming the scholar'.

Thus, in this short chapter we consider what theory is in educational research, in albeit a limited way, and then reflect on our own doctoral experiences to look at how theory provides a means of finding one's own voice in the field. We conclude by suggesting that theory operates as a form of permission that constitutes the scholar, and that theory is necessary for crafting a scholarly trajectory.

What is theory in educational research?

It is perhaps pertinent to begin with some definition of theory, to put a stake in the ground as it were, so that we have some point from which to launch our arguments.[1] We start with a definition of theory that may resonate with many novice and experienced researchers. According to Berg (1998), theory is usually defined by social scientists as 'a system of logical statements or propositions that explain the relationship between two or more objects, concepts, phenomena, or characteristics of humans − what are sometimes called variables' (p. 16). He goes on to suggest that 'theory might also represent attempts to develop explanations about reality or ways to classify and organize

77

events, or even to predict future occurrences of events' (Berg 1998: 16). It is worth noting that these two definitions share one major feature in common. They both construct theory as explanation, or an explanatory device. Sikes does likewise when she states:

> [m]anaging day-to-day life, let alone engaging in the relatively esoteric pursuit of research, demands some reasonably coherent framework of reference within which to make sense of experiences and perceptions. We need theories – in other words, plausible explanations for what's going on – to live by.
>
> Sikes 2006: 43

Although useful, these definitions represent only the objective end of the theory spectrum, and are likely to arise from the research conducted for the doctoral project in the form of a hypothesis to be tested (such as 'I have a theory about the relationship between comprehension and reading fluency') or as a conclusion the warrant of which comes from its explanatory power (as is the case when multiple hypotheses have been tested against the evidence and only one remains viable).

Anyone who has encountered the work of the French philosopher Paul Ricoeur (1981) will be immediately aware that he makes an important distinction between explanation and understanding, or *erklären* and *verstehen*, respectively, following the German tradition of hermeneutics. Without going into Ricoeur's complicated dialectical 'hermeneutics of suspicion' here, it is worth noting that an argument for such a distinction has been well rehearsed in some scholarly quarters, and that although explanation operates as the act of theorising most closely associated with the natural sciences, understanding or 'interpretation' – violating the complexity of Ricoeur's argument somewhat[2] – operates as an act of theorising most closely associated with the human sciences or more particularly the humanities. Explanation may be conceptualised as a form of theorising that seeks to clarify and explicate a phenomenon, while seeking validation through reference to empirical realties or evidentiary data. Understanding or interpretation, on the other hand, operates as a form of theorising that seeks to articulate the meaning of a phenomenon or communicative event for participants, observers or other interlocutors, and often takes its warrant from reference to pre-existing theories or compelling argument. It sits at the subjective end of the theory spectrum. As the field of education has intellectual roots in both the humanities and social sciences, theory in education may be mobilised for the purpose of, or demonstrate the characteristics of, both explanation and interpretation as defined above.

When we adopt a poststructuralist position, as both of us have done in various ways, theory tends to operate as an interpretive device. As an interpretive device, theory typically acts as a disruptive force, a deconstructive tactic, a denaturalising strategy, or a diffractive lens through which to view afresh a particular set of problems, or to problematise a phenomena, text, or event that is usually taken-for-granted (see the discussion in Baker and Heyning 2004). Ball articulates this work of theory well when he asks:

> What is the point of theory? The point is that theory can separate us from 'the contingency that has made us what we are, the possibilities of no longer, seeing, doing or thinking what we are, do or think? [sic]' (Mahon 1992: 122). Theory is a vehicle for 'thinking otherwise'; it is a platform for 'outrageous hypotheses' and for

'unleashing criticism'. Theory is destructive, disruptive and violent. It offers a language for challenge, and modes of thought, other than those articulated for us by dominant others. It provides a language of rigour and irony rather than contingency. The purposes of such theory is to de-familiarize present practices and categories, to make them seem less self-evident and necessary, and to open up spaces for the invention of new forms of experience.

Ball 1995: 266

There are two points we might draw from Ball. The most obvious point is that theory operates as a tool for defamiliarisation, denaturalisation, diffraction and deconstruction. It becomes a means by which we can challenge the present by bringing a fresh perspective to the object of our concerns. When Noel Gough (1998), following Donna Haraway (1985), uses fiction within his curriculum projects as a diffractive lens 'to reconceptualize or reconstruct some aspect of our work' (p. 107), he is using theory in a similar way to that articulated by Ball. In Gough's work, the figure of the cyborg becomes a means by which to rethink and retheorise the practice of curriculum enquiry. In Haraway, science fiction is used as a means of challenging the limits of scientific discourse. Although we are unlikely to describe the fictional narratives these authors use as theories, they do operate as diffractive devices that perform the disruptive work of theory on the objects of their gaze, allowing acts of retheorisation. We will return to this below.

A second point we might draw from Ball is about theory as a platform from which to launch critique. Ball's articulation of the work of theory relies on a critical insight of poststructural discourse theory: *the impossibility of making statements outside of discourse*. In practice, this means that it is impossible to take a stance on an issue that does not itself situate the speaker in the ambit of a particular theoretical tradition. Thus, within poststructural logic, there can be no statements outside of theory. Or, to place a Foucauldian spin on Derrida's (1976) infamous statement, *'il n'y a pas de hors-texte'*,[3] there is no 'truth' outside of discourse/text, as it is discourse that provides the truth-value of any claim made. Thus, our statements or conclusions only 'make sense' within an academic community when they are situated in a theory that provides them with intelligibility. This feature of theory and theorising is only implicit in Ball's statement. However, it has profound consequences.

If we accept that statements or conclusions will only be intelligible if they sit inside a theoretical frame, then we encounter the problem of epistemic violence first articulated by Spivak (1988) to explore the potential complicity of colonised peoples with the Imperial regime when they attempt to use the language of the Imperial regimes to speak back in a way that will make them understood. The cost of being understood by the colonisers was to be trapped within the forms of colonial discourse. Chakrabarty (1997) made a similar point a decade later when he examined the problem of trying to write a history of India. By definition, such a history would mobilise the artifice of European historiography, and thus rehearse many of its assumptions, even while the Indian scholar might be attempting to escape from such constraints.

We would argue that a similar kind of complicity arises from the use of theory. Although we agree with Ball that theory can be used as a tool to challenge contemporary discourses, it does so by situating us within a parallel discourse. Theory constructs a set of limits that can then be applied as a lens or a tool to new problems. It is productive precisely because it provides a set of epistemological limits, assisting the scholar and the doctoral student to avoid the pitfalls of tripping over themselves, and constructing analysis that can be tested by others against the theory mobilised to produce it. In this way, theory is both empowering and constraining. Disciplining oneself towards consistent application of a selected theory situates one's work in a particular scholarly tradition. Theory thus provides the means for the construction of scholarly argument and the formation of the scholar simultaneously.

Theory and doctoral research: reflections on our journeys

In this section we weave our experiences of using theory in our doctoral studies, with a focus on how theory provides a way of finding one's voice in the field. We see our doctoral experiences as different, but related. Kalervo brought theories in from the outside, specifically theories of space and place from human geography into his work on education policy. His work was in a sense about troubling the boundaries of educational doctoral research. Robert, locating his work in curriculum theory, where a number of different traditions have emerged over the past few decades, was more concerned with developing a scholarly voice by defining his place in a complex theoretical landscape.[4]

Kalervo's doctoral thesis, *Education policy, urban renewal and identity: a spatial analysis of global change* (Gulson 2004), examined relationships between educational policy change and urban renewal in Sydney and London. Two specific policies were investigated through qualitative case studies of schools in disadvantaged areas, employing ethnography and poststructural criticism. Data were generated from census material, relevant policy documents, photographs, field observations and interviews with a range of key stakeholders, including education policy advisers, corporate and public sector employees, school administrators, teachers, students and community workers. The study suggested that educational policy change can be seen as a part of cultural practices, through which global educational policy change is mediated in local contexts. By positioning educational policy change within specific urban change processes and practices, the study pointed to the way in which education is a key, yet often unrecognised, element of urban change in cities. The initial framing for Kalervo's work was within critical policy studies and education policy sociology, which emphasised the centrality of power and discourse in understanding the processes and practices of policy (e.g. Ball 1994; Taylor *et al.* 1997). However, Kalervo realised that existing policy analysis frameworks were not adequate to capture what he felt was significant about relationships between cities, education policy and identity. Ball (2006) suggests 'education policy research lacks a sense of "place"; either in not locating policies in any framework that extends beyond the national level, or in not accounting for or conveying a sense of the locality in the analyses of policy realization' (p. 19). Thus, to undertake the analytical work required in this study Kalervo developed a spatial approach to policy analysis, using cultural concepts of space and place, drawing on work of theorists such as Doreen Massey (Massey 1993a; 1993b; 1994a; 1994b) and Michael Smith (Smith 2001; 2003). However, Kalervo had not undertaken any undergraduate or graduate courses in geography and subsequently read widely across the geography literature, though at times feeling quite adrift in an interdisciplinary wonderland. Nonetheless, bringing in theories of space and place allowed Kalervo to locate his doctoral work in educational policy studies, and attempt to fill the gap of which Ball speaks. It also allowed publications emerging from his thesis to contribute to an emerging part of educational research that looks at the difference space makes to educational policy analyses (e.g. Gulson 2005; 2006; 2007; Gulson and Symes 2007), and the ways education is constitutive of space. The use of theory thus assisted in starting to speak as an educational policy analyst and sociologist to the field of geography (see Thiem 2008).

Robert's doctoral work *Interrupting History: A critical-reconceptualization of History curriculum after 'the end of history'* (Parkes 2006) attempted to challenge the view that if we accept postmodern social theory, historical research and writing will become untenable. His study re-examined the nature of the alleged 'threat' to history posed by post-modernism, and explored the implications of postmodern social theory for history as curriculum. Thus, theory was a significant concern of the study itself. The central pro-blematic at the heart of the study was the (im)possibility of history as curriculum after 'the end of history'. Robert's challenge throughout his doctoral studies was deciding whether his work was educational philosophy, critical pedagogy or something else. After being introduced by a research mentor to the work of the North America Reconcep-tualists (see the excellent discussion in Pinar *et al.* 1995), Robert recognised that his study was best situated within a broadly conceived critical–reconceptualist trend in curriculum enquiry. Locating his study within this 'tradition' of curriculum studies provided Robert with the permission he sought to deploy a form of historically and philosophically oriented 'deconstructive hermeneutics', as the means by which to explore past attempts to mount, and future possibilities for, a curricular response to the problem of historical representation. The study remained philosophical in many ways, opening with an investigation of the many forms of 'end of history' discourse in contemporary theory, particularly the neoliberal form of Francis Fukuyama (1992) that proclaimed we had arrived at a free market liberal democratic capitalist utopia, and the poststructural form that was sceptical of the truth claims of history as a discipline (Barthes 1967/1997; Lyotard 1979), and the teleological claim of history as progress (Baudrillard 1992; Derrida 1994; Foucault 1971/1994). However, the study was empirically grounded through a case study that consisted of a critical exploration of the social meliorist changes to, and cultural politics surrounding, the history curriculum in New South Wales (NSW), Australia, from the Bicentennial to the Millennium (1988–2000), a period that marked curriculum as a site of contestation in a series of highly public 'history wars' over repre-sentations of the nation's past (Macintyre and Clark 2003). It concluded with a strong sense of its place in curriculum theory, discussing the missed opportunities for 'critical practice' within the NSW history curriculum. Mobilising theory by synthesising insights into the 'nature of history' derived from contemporary academic debate (particularly the work of Ankersmit 2001; Ashcroft 2001; LaCapra 2000; White 2001), Robert argued that what remained uncontested in the struggle for 'critical histories' during the period under study was the representational practices of history itself. In particular, Robert operationalised the postcolonial theory of Bill Ashcroft (2001) as a diffractive lens to illuminate which approaches to critical history had been taken up in the curriculum, and which approaches had been neglected. Using this lens as a heuristic device, the study closed with a reassessment of the (im)possibility of history curriculum after 'the end of history', arguing that if history curriculum is to be a critical/transformative enterprise, then it must attend to the problem of historical representation. This aspect of Robert's work, providing a warrant for his identification as curriculum scholar, has since been published in an important international journal in the world of curriculum scholarship, *Curriculum Inquiry* (Parkes 2007).

Conclusion: trajectories, knowledge and being and becoming a scholar

We would like to finish with what we think are two key points about the use of theory, pertaining to the idea of knowledge and permission, and trajectories and the mutual constitution of the scholar and theory.

The first point is that theory operates as permission to make some lines of enquiry legitimate and intelligible, to frame others as illegitimate and unintelligible; recognising this as a form of epistemic violence that produces a scholar who is both constrained and enabled by the theories mobilised in their work. In a sense, this chapter perhaps resonates with Lather's advocacy to teach educational research in the USA:

> in such a way that students develop an ability to locate themselves in the tensions that characterize fields of knowledge. In our particular context of educational research where grand narratives and one-best-way thinking are being reasserted under the banner of SRE (scientific research in education), my major claim is that such efforts need to be situated in a context of historical time marked by multiplicity and competing discourses that do not map tidily onto one another, a time of unevenly legitimized and resourced incommensurabilities regarding the politics of knowing and being known.
>
> Lather 2006: 47

For both of us, albeit from different positions, the theories encountered during our doctoral undertakings, whether they be from human geography or curriculum theory, provided us with the means to find our voices in the field, to locate the place from which we speak, and from which our work, our 'unique contribution to the field', can be evaluated for rigour. This latter point is an interesting one. Once one locates oneself within the theoretical or methodological landscape, rigour may often be determined by the extent to which one's writings embody, and remain consistent with, the principles of the theoretical stance adopted. Thus, theory brings with it the imperative to be careful with language.

The second point is that theory is about being and becoming a subject. We consider theory works on the doctoral student so they become recognisable as a particular sort of scholar, with a particular set of commitments. Theory isn't simply adopted and applied. In the act of mobilising theory we are also adopted by the theory, as another of its conduits into discourse. Thus, the work of theorising, and of adopting a theoretical lens, constructs the scholar as much as it illuminates the data. Theory is not only mutually constitutive of methodology and design (see Lather 2006: 51–2), it is also mutually constitutive of the theorist. Thus, part of the transition from a doctoral student to being a scholar is being recognised and recognising one's own scholarly trajectory. It is a sense of being able to locate not just what you are doing, but also what you have done, and will do. Although completing the doctorate means obtaining a credential as a scholar, you are also always in the process of being and becoming a scholar. We think theory is one way of locating oneself in this process.

Notes

1 In fact, although we use the word theory in this paper, we also acknowledge that some work, such as that of Flyvberg (2001) has argued that in fact the social sciences should not concern themselves

with 'theory' as context-independency, and leave it to the sciences. It is within this contested and fraught arena that we write (and that doctoral students undertake their work).

2 More precisely, Ricoeur (1981) crafts a distinction between explanation and understanding. He argues that both understanding and explanation are particular instances of interpretation. However, in its general usage in educational research, we feel the term 'interpretation' is the analogue of Ricoeur's 'understanding' and so take a little liberty with our use of his work here.

3 This phrase from Derrida's (1976) *On grammatology*, appears thus: '*There is nothing outside the text* [there is no outside-text; *il n'y a pas de hors-texte*]' (p. 158).

4 It is important to note that we both undertook doctoral studies in Australian universities where there are no coursework requirements for doctoral study. In most universities doctoral candidates in education are expected to develop a proposal before moving forward with the study; however, this is more an administrative requirement than an arbiter of quality or a diagnosis of research capacity.

References

Ankersmit, F. R. (2001) *Historical representation*. Stanford, CA: Stanford University Press.

Ashcroft, B. (2001) *Post-Colonial transformation*. London: Routledge.

Atkinson, P. and Delamont, S. (2006) In the roiling smoke: qualitative inquiry and contested fields, *International Journal of Qualitative Studies in Education*, 19(6): 747–55.

Baker, B. and Heyning, K. E. (2004) Introduction: Dangerous coagulations? Research, education, and a travelling Foucault. In B. Baker and K. E. Heyning (Eds). *Dangerous coagulations? The uses of Foucault in the study of education*. New York: Peter Lang, 1–79.

Ball, S. J. (1994) *Education reform: a critical and post-structural approach*. Philadelphia: Open University Press.

——(1995) Intellectuals or technicians? The urgent role of theory in educational studies, *British Journal of Educational Studies*, 43(3): 255–71.

——(2006) *Education policy and social class: the selected works of Stephen J. Ball*. London: Routledge.

Barthes, R. (1967/1997) The discourse of history. In K. Jenkins (Ed.) *The postmodern history reader*. London: Routledge, 120–3.

Baudrillard, J. (1992) *The illusion of the end*. Trans. C. Turner. Cambridge: Polity Press.

Berg, B. (1998) *Qualitative research methods for the social sciences*. 3rd edn. Needham Heights, MA: Allyn and Bacon.

Chakrabarty, D. (1997) Postcoloniality and the artifice of history: Who speaks for 'Indian' pasts? In P. Mongia (Ed.) *Contemporary postcolonial theory: A reader*. London: Arnold, 223–47.

Derrida, J. (1976) *Of grammatology*. Baltimore, MD: John Hopkins University Press.

——(1994) *Specters of Marx: The state of the debt, the work of mourning, & the new international*. Trans. P. Kamuf. New York: Routledge.

Flyvberg, B. (2001) *Making social science matter: why social inquiry fails and how it can succeed again*. Cambridge: Cambridge University Press.

Foucault, M. (1971/1994) Nietzsche, genealogy, history. Trans. D. F. Brouchard and S. Simon. In J. D. Faubion (Ed.). *Essential works of Foucault 1954–1984* (Vol. 2: Aesthetics). London: Penguin Books, pp. 369–91.

Fukuyama, F. (1992) *The end of history and the last man*. New York: Avon Books.

Gough, N. (1998) Reflections and diffractions: Functions of fiction in curriculum inquiry. In W. F. Pinar (Ed.) *Curriculum: Toward new identities*. New York: Garland, 94–127.

Gulson, K. N. (2004) *Education policy, urban renewal and identity: a spatial analysis of global change*. Unpublished thesis, Macquarie University, Sydney.

——(2005) Renovating educational identities: policy, space and urban renewal, *Journal of Education Policy*, 20(2): 147–64.

——(2006) A white veneer: education policy, space and 'race' in the inner city, *Discourse: studies in the cultural politics of education*, 27(2): 251–66.

——(2007) Repositioning schooling in inner Sydney: urban renewal, an education market and the 'absent presence' of the 'middle classes', *Urban Studies*, 44(7): 1377–91.

Gulson, K. N. and Symes, C. (Eds) (2007) *Spatial theories of education: policy and geography matters*. New York: Routledge.

Haraway, D. (1985) A manifesto for cyborgs: Science, technology, and socialist feminism in the 1980s, *Socialist Review*, 80: 65–108.

LaCapra, D. (2000) *History and reading: Tocqueville, Foucault, French studies*. Carlton South: Melbourne University Press.

Lather, P. (2006) Paradigm proliferation as a good thing to think with: teaching research in education as a wild profusion, *International Journal of Qualitative Studies in Education*, 19(1): 35–57.

Lyotard, J. F. (1979) *The postmodern condition: A report on knowledge*. Trans. G. Bennington and B. Massumi. Minneapolis, MN: University of Minnesota.

Macintyre, S. and Clark, A. (2003) *The history wars*. Melbourne: Melbourne University Press.

Massey, D. (1993a) Politics and space/time. In M. Keith and S. Pile (Eds). *Place and the politics of identity*. London: Routledge, 141–61.

——(1993b) Power-geometry and a progressive sense of place. In J. Bird, B. Curtis, T. Putnam, G. Robertson and L. Tickner (Eds). *Mapping the futures: local cultures, global change*. London: Routledge, pp. 59–69.

——(1994a) Double articulation: a place in the world. In A. Bammer (Ed.). *Displacements: cultural identities in question*. Bloomington, IN: Indiana University Press, 110–21.

——(1994b) *Space, place and gender*. Cambridge: Polity.

Parkes, R. J. (2006) *Interrupting History: A critical-reconceptualization of History curriculum after 'the end of history'*. Unpublished thesis submitted in fulfillment of the degree of Doctor of Philosophy, Faculty of Education and Arts, University of Newcastle, New South Wales, Australia.

——(2007) Reading History curriculum as postcolonial text: Towards a curricular response to the history wars in Australia and beyond, *Curriculum Inquiry*, 37(4): 383–400.

Pinar, W. F., Reynolds, W. M., Slattery, P. and Taubman, P. M. (1995) *Understanding curriculum*. New York: Peter Lang Publishing.

Ricoeur, P. (1981) *Hermeneutics and the human sciences: Essays on language, action and interpretation*. Trans. J. B. Thompson. Cambridge: Cambridge University Press.

Sikes, P. (2006) Towards useful and dangerous theories, *Discourse: studies in the cultural politics of education*, 27(1): 43–51.

Smith, M. P. (2001) *Transnational urbanism: locating globalization*. Oxford: Blackwell.

——(2003) Transnationalism, the state, and the extraterritorial citizen, *Politics & Society*, 31(4): 467–502.

Spivak, G. C. (1988) Can the subaltern speak? In C. Nelson and L. Grossberg (Eds). *Marxism and the interpretation of culture*. Urbana, IL: University of Illinois Press.

Taylor, S., Rizvi, F., Lingard, B. and Henry, M. (1997) *Educational policy and the politics of change*. London: Routledge.

Thiem, C. H. (2008) Thinking through education: the geographics of contemporary educational restructuring. *Progress in Human Geography*, preprint online at: http://phg.sagepub.com/cgi/rapidpdf/0309132508093475v1.pdf, pp. 1–20.

White, H. (2001) The historical text as literary artefact. In G. Roberts (Ed.) *The history and narrative reader*. London: Routledge, 221–36.

7

Seeking the single thread

The Conceptual Quest

F. Su, J. Nixon and B. Adamson

'Do you think that I am the kind of man who learns widely and retains what he has learned in his mind?'

'Yes, I do. Is it not so?'

'No. I have a single thread binding it all together.'

Confucius 1893: Book XV, 3

Introduction

This chapter focuses on how research works as a process of interpretive enquiry. It argues that research is necessarily a heuristic endeavour, the outcomes of which cannot be pre-specified. When we ask open questions, we cannot presume to know the answers. The practice of interpretive enquiry requires patience, a waiting mind, a kind of stillness: dispositions that are difficult to acquire. We outline this line of argument in the opening section. The central section is concerned with a specific case: how do we begin to frame questions regarding the experience of students of Chinese origin in an English university that has its own complicated history of institutional development? We build this chapter around that central story of intellectual discovery and conceptualisation. The final section – attempting to weave the various strands into a single thread – returns to the indeterminacy of enquiry. What, under such epistemological circumstances, constitutes a beginning?

The co-authors of this paper are colleagues. Jon and Bob also supervise Feng's doctoral study and together we collaborate on projects that have an international dimension. For example, we are currently working on a comparative study of institutional repositioning within the higher education sector. Recently, we have spent a lot of time thinking and talking about how to conceptualise the learning experiences of Chinese undergraduates studying within the UK higher education system: the subject of Feng's doctoral thesis. We tell the story of this extended conversation in the central section of this chapter, but first we need to reflect on how we understand the relation between conceptualisation and interpretive enquiry. We argue that it is precisely this relation – this process of conceptualisation and mediation – that renders enquiry meaningful.

We stress the notion of interpretive enquiry throughout this chapter to highlight the necessarily hermeneutical aspects of all research and scholarship. Interpretation lies at the heart of all intellectual endeavours. We are not attempting to develop a new approach to research and scholarship, nor are we trying in any way to sideline the contribution that research and scholarship have made to the public good. Our aim is simply to emphasise the formative role of interpretation in all research and scholarship and thereby to gently challenge some of the assumptions that the term 'scientific' – and its associated terminology of 'scientific rigour', 'scientific method', etc. – carries with it. We focus on the nature of interpretive enquiry within the broad traditions of research and scholarship as practised within educational studies and more generally within the social sciences.

Beyond method

Research enquiry is a search for understanding. Understanding involves the construction of ideas in a framework, which, to extend the building metaphor, needs to have strong foundations and to be sufficiently robust to resist all but the most vigorous shaking. These frameworks are the concepts that inform our study and that are also the basis for us to inform others of our study, for concepts have a dual role in the internal process of understanding and the external process of communicating those understandings to our discourse community. The researcher is both a consumer and a purveyor of concepts, with the successful negotiations of transactions being dependent upon the clarity of communication.

Research, scholarship, and the academic writing they give rise to are sometimes sharply criticised, and therefore overlooked, for their over specialisation and their use of mystifying terminology. That criticism comes both from outside and within the research community: from exasperated users of research evidence, from sponsors and funding agents committed to making a difference, and from researchers themselves who are concerned with the impact and accessibility of research. Sometimes such criticisms are misplaced, a failure to engage with the inherent difficulty of a particular research topic or research process. But sometimes the criticisms hit the mark by highlighting instances of obfuscation or lack of clarity. Either way, the role of concepts in the conduct of research and scholarship are crucial to what is at stake.

Concepts have to be mediated. If they are simply adopted unthinkingly, then they fail to do the conceptual work we ask of them (and might rightly, therefore, be termed 'jargon'). They no longer operate as concepts. Research and scholarship are centrally concerned with the process of conceptual mediation. At best, that process is communicative, democratic and in the public interest. It is also necessarily difficult: deliberative, time-consuming, self-questioning. To start on a quest the destination of which is unknown is necessarily anxiety-inducing. The emotional, intellectual and moral labour of research and scholarship is centrally concerned with working on and through, and living with, such anxieties. That is what it means to be, and identify oneself as, a researcher and a thinker.

Polanyi and Prosch (1975: 41) pointed out that if, when riding a bike, we concentrate on the wheels going round, we may well fall off; if, on the other hand, our focal awareness is on where we are going, we are likely to stay upright and on course. The trick is to balance what they called 'focal awareness' (where I'm going) against what they called 'subsidiary awareness' (what my legs are doing). Similarly, if one assumes that imported theory will help, one is again likely to come a cropper:

we cannot learn to keep our balance on a bicycle by trying to follow the explicit rule that, to compensate for an imbalance, we must force our bicycle into a curve – away from the direction of the imbalance – whose radius is proportional to the square of the bicycle's velocity over the angle of imbalance.

Polanyi and Prosch 1975: 41

Such knowledge, they argue 'is totally ineffectual unless it is known tacitly'.

Gaining conceptual focus in any research or scholarly endeavour is not dissimilar, keeping an eye on the road ahead while remaining circumspect. If, continuing this metaphor, we think of concepts as signposts, traffic lights and distinguishable features in the landscape, we might begin to understand how enquiry works; how, that is, it is intrinsically purposeful without necessarily being instrumental (or instrumentalist). This kind of 'tacit knowledge' – feeling one's way – is crucial to all creative enquiry or artistic work. It is a kind of 'connoisseurship' whereby context is itself appreciated as meaningful. The connoisseur understands the provenance and value of a particular work, not because she possesses an 'explicit rule', but because the connoisseur understands the wider context within which that work is located (see also Polanyi 1973: 49–65; Polanyi and Prosch 1975: 22–45).

We may well not know in advance what the conceptual signposts are going to be. At each new crossroads, particularly early on in any study, we have to review the options. We cannot pursue all the available conceptual roadways. Having settled on what feels to be the most appropriate route (in respect of one's particular research interest), then the choices clarify; and, crucially, the reading, thinking and drafting that flow from these choices come more sharply into focus. We are beginning to understand what the study is about, where it could be leading. I begin to answer the inevitable question – 'What's your research about?' – not just with the response 'Kids in playgrounds', but with some fumbling remarks about (for example) 'spatiality', 'place', 'location'. I'm feeling less secure (and more exposed), but I sense that I might be getting there. Living with the insecurity and conceptual uncertainty is an important part of the journey.

This aspect of the process of enquiry plays against received notions of 'rigour' and 'method'. One is supposed to know what one is doing and then get on and do it. However, that is not how understanding works. Understanding is a meeting of minds, an extended and sometimes troubled conversation across sometimes troubled intertextual boundaries. It is deeply deliberative and as such both contributes to and requires the conditions necessary for democratic, civil engagement. Although sometimes involving intensely private activities, it reaches out through its public interest and social engagement. Researchers and scholars are, for much of their time, engaged in the necessarily isolated activities of reading and writing; but those isolated activities are deeply social and necessarily public in their import and intended impact. 'Truth itself', as Arendt (1970: 85) puts it, 'is communicative, it disappears and cannot be conceived outside communication'. That is what locates the researcher, the scholar, the writer, in the tradition of the public intellectual: 'only in communication – between contemporaries as well as between the living and the dead – does truth reveal itself' (Arendt 1970: 85).

This central paradox is crucial to the methodology of interpretive enquiry: to have a generalised sense of direction, but no clear direction; to be purposeful, but be unclear as to the specific outcomes of one's purposes; to have more and more questions, and fewer and fewer answers. To enquire with any degree of seriousness is to dwell in uncertainty. Coping with that uncertainty – living with anxiety – is partly what being a scholar means. One has to learn how to cope with the ineluctable uncertainty of the life of the mind: life lived – enjoyably and at best elegantly – as an unresolved riddle. As scholars, we are always in the middle and the muddle of things; it is the scholar's job to embrace difficulty.

How do we do this? We read and we put together the bits and pieces of our reading in such a way that they raise salient questions, present important themes, define a significant structure of issues. The social sciences generally, and education studies in particular, require a huge effort of lateral thinking and readership. No one can be literate in education studies without having roamed across the relevant literatures in the political and social sciences, the broader humanistic and interpretive disciplines of cultural studies and discourse analysis, the philosophy and sociology of knowledge and human understanding, as well as the specific literatures relating to curriculum, pedagogy and educational policy and practice. To define oneself as an educationist without having attempted to traverse these terrains would be nonsensical.

So, 'we scholars' (Damrosch's 1995 phrase) are travellers. We are on the move, but never quite know where we are going. Scholars are, as Said (2000) reminds us, exilic: at our best we are liminal, marginal, on the edge. Our only homeland, as Williams (1960) puts it, is the 'border country'. We are on our various and interconnected journeys. The following section tracks the early stages of one such journey. Appropriately, some of the conceptual signposts on that journey relate to origins and beginnings, arrivals and departures, transitions and destinations. In starting out on that journey we are intent upon mobilising concepts in such a way that they work with us and are themselves open to mediation. Sometimes the effectiveness of an emergent conceptual framework resides precisely in its fuzziness.

The following section, then, outlines the way in which, through weekly discussions between the co-authors and advice from others, together with some serious and hard reading, a conceptual apparatus was developed to understand and analyse the experience of students of Chinese origin in a particular UK university. There is no readymade theory to hand (there rarely is). We must think without banisters (which may be the only way to think). We are feeling our way both conceptually and methodologically up a difficult staircase without the help of a handrail, or, to switch to a Chinese metaphor, 'crossing a river by groping for stepping stones'. The question 'What are the appropriate concepts?' and the question 'What are the appropriate means of exploring those concepts empirically?' are complicatedly but necessarily related. The following account explores some of those complications.

An unfinished journey

The co-authors of this chapter are colleagues who work together closely. This section, however, comprises my own (Feng Su's) account of our attempt to tease out the conceptual thread of a doctoral study that focuses on: (i) the challenges facing undergraduate students of Chinese origin in a particular UK university, (ii) how Chinese students respond to these challenges, and (iii) what institutional conditions need to be put in place to help that particular group of students face those specific challenges.

I am of Chinese origin myself and have been studying and working in the UK for a number of years before undertaking this doctoral study. Reflecting upon my own learning experience, I feel that undergraduate Chinese students encounter huge difficulties in adapting to a different cultural and educational environment. My experience of being both an 'insider', with regard to the Chinese student community, and an 'outsider', in relation to the academic community within the UK, places me in a good position to conduct this kind of enquiry. Positioning myself in relation to my own study is an important part of the intellectual – and emotional – labour that is involved in teasing out the thread 'binding it all together'.

My study is designed to be empirically grounded, qualitative in methodological orientation, and socio-cultural in its conceptual framing. The latter is important given the potential fuzziness of any study of this kind; any study, that is, that is virtually limitless in its capacity for generating questions. In this first year of my study the development of a framework of analysis that: (i) gathers what I see to be the salient issues and questions, (ii) guides and informs the analysis, and (iii) provides a tentative structure for the thesis as a whole has been of paramount importance. It has also been difficult and demanding, precisely because of the complexity and interdisciplinary nature of the research topic.

I want to try and fill you in on some of my thinking without overwhelming you with the detail of my particular topic. That's a difficult balance to strike. My starting point is the fairly obvious insight that overseas students of Chinese origin who are studying in the UK come to higher education with very different values and approaches to learning and teaching than do their UK counterparts. It is highly likely that the expectations of Chinese students are greatly influenced by their social, cultural and educational contexts of origin, and that these expectations influence the learning approaches and strategies they choose to adopt as students within the UK. Their cognitive and learning styles are shaped, in part, by these contexts of origin. I would like to understand that aspect of transition more fully.

When students of Chinese origin study as undergraduates in the UK, they encounter numerous unpredictabilities over and above the daunting unpredictabilities faced by indigenous students. Not only must they wrap their heads around their chosen discipline or field of study, but also they must do this within an educational and cultural context that differs hugely from their own. They are also managing this transition in a second, or in some cases third, language. Chinese students within the UK are studying in multiple, complicated, overlapping and sometimes contradictory contexts of learning. There is no readymade framework that I can adopt for what I have chosen to study. I must construct that framework for myself – what the textbooks refer to as 'bricolage'.

In the first three months of my doctoral study, I spent at least an hour each week discussing with Jon, my supervisor, how to develop a conceptual framework – or a kind of theoretical searchlight – to sustain and cast light on my study. I was also in regular email contact with Bob on specific aspects of my study. This was a new idea for me, as my previous postgraduate work had not entailed this kind of wide-ranging reading and 'theorising' that is essential for this way of working. In our meetings, different theoretical perspectives were brought to bear on the research topic and gradually a set of research questions emerged. But we had to keep testing and retesting these against the literature and our own understanding of the literature. This was fun – highly disciplined fun – but fun nevertheless. This is a very exciting phase in the development of any intellectual enquiry.

Through our discussions and joint reading a number of key concepts emerged: among them, 'origin', 'destination', and 'multiple-identity'. The work of Said (2004a; 2004b) and Sen (2006) was crucial in helping us identify these core concepts, as was the work of other thinkers and theorists who helped us locate these ideas within the context of contemporary Chinese society and history (see, for example, Chang and Halliday 2007; Hutton 2007; Leonard 2008). Sen's (2006) notion of split identity and multi-culturalism in an international context provided a particularly useful point of reference. Identity, argues Sen (2006), is layered, multi-form, complex, and cannot be reduced to a unitary state of being. This seemed like a useful and highly relevant starting point.

In drawing out this conceptual thread, I found it useful to visualise the conceptual relations and to express these relations in terms of models. My past postgraduate experience had provided me with the technical resources necessary to develop my thinking along these lines. Perhaps if my experience had been different, then I would have worked with these inter-relations in different ways. I have learned that it is important to work with the intellectual resources one has and to make the very best of them. So, I am reasonably good at visualising conceptual relations by drawing models – and I use that capability to push forward my thinking and inform my discussions and presentations.

My first model – my starting point – represents three overlapping contexts that are of relevance to the student experience that I am studying: context/s of origin (Chinese), context/s of destination (UK, more specifically, England), and the institutional context/s (HE) within which the students participating in this enquiry hope to graduate (see Figure 7.1).

I found I needed to explore in greater detail the content of the overlapping circles that comprise Figure 7.1. This exploration involved further reading and discussion. The category of 'Chinese socio-cultural contexts of origin' opened up diverse specialist literatures relating, for example, to geopolitical and geo-economic contexts, Chinese educational values, Chinese traditions and family structures, the Chinese education system, and English language education in China. In exploring these literatures, I found important sub-topics: for example, the literature relating to geopolitical and geo-economic contexts opens up subsidiary literatures on students' education experiences, urban versus rural, north versus south, and coastal area versus inland area. My reading was a constant process of discovery.

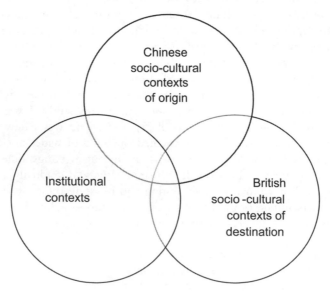

Figure 7.1 Contexts of the study.

I also needed to explore the history of these contexts of origin. The values upon which Chinese education is based have a long history. Education is regarded by many in China as a means not only of personal development, but also of upward social mobility. The present one-child policy in China (whereby each couple is allowed to conceive and rear only one child without incurring penalties) has a major impact on family structure and parents' attitudes toward their child's education. As a result, today's parents in China invest more resources into their only child's educational development and expect her or him to be successful, upwardly mobile and highly productive. The expectations are daunting (see Greenhalgh 2008).

The Chinese education system and English language education within that system are also vital elements within this category of 'socio-cultural contexts of origin'. These are two further frames of reference that have informed my thinking. All this has ideological underpinnings, which I have tried to explore by extending my reading and understanding to include Chinese traditions of thought that impact upon the student experience: Confucianism, Taoism, Buddhism, NeoConfucianism, and Maoism. This circle of understanding is summarised in Figure 7.2.

My next circle of understanding relates to the British socio-cultural contexts of destination for the students of Chinese origin whose experiences provide the focus and the empirical base for my study. Some key factors that may affect Chinese students' experiences in the UK are considered in this micro-frame. I undertook an overview of UK higher education from medieval or 'ancient' universities, through civic or 'redbrick' and the later post-Robins or 'plate glass' universities, to the post-1992 universities or 'new' universities and those institutions more recently recognised as having university status. I have also undertaken a preliminary analysis of some of the market forces operating on overseas recruitment and the overall effects of the massification, marketisation and internationalisation of higher education. Finally, I have found it necessary to look into the literatures relating to the changes and developments in teaching and learning practices within the UK and how these are experienced by overseas students. This aspect of the overall experience of transition is summarised in Figure 7.3 – the second circle of understanding.

The third circle of understanding relates to the institutional contexts of UK higher education within which the overseas students participating in my doctoral research are carrying out their undergraduate studies. My research is located within a single institution

Geopolitical and
geo-economic context;
Chinese education values;
Family structure;
Chinese education system;
English language education
in China;
Chinese traditions.

Figure 7.2 Chinese socio-cultural contexts of origin.

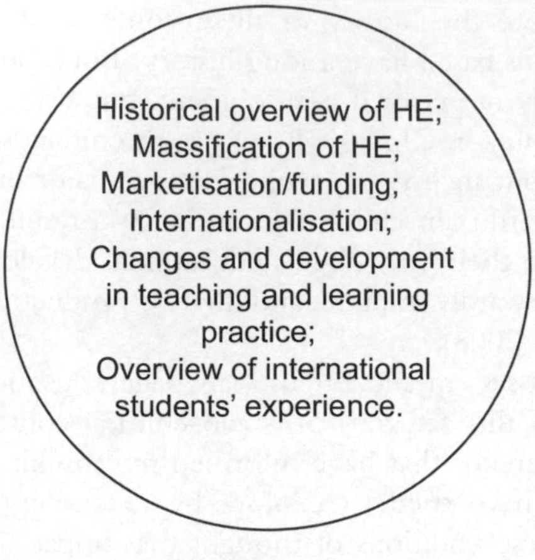

Historical overview of HE;
Massification of HE;
Marketisation/funding;
Internationalisation;
Changes and development
in teaching and learning
practice;
Overview of international
students' experience.

Figure 7.3 British socio-cultural contexts of destination.

of higher education, but that institution experiences all the pressures and contradictions of the higher education sector as a whole. I am particularly interested in how the codes and conventions of British higher education challenge students of Chinese origin. The challenge is both linguistic and cultural. In the UK, for example, institutions of higher education encourage students to become active learners, to be critical and analytical, and to think for themselves. These are not necessarily the pedagogical priorities that have informed previous schooling in China.

Similarly, modes of academic writing and the formalities of academic assessment may differ significantly across continents. Translating concepts from one language system to another is not easy, particularly when those systems differ as radically as they do in shifting between the English language and Chinese. The potential for slippage is enormous. I am interested in these differences and difficulties – these slippages – and in the kinds of institutional support necessary to enable students of Chinese origin – of whom I am one – to cope and excel within the UK. I am interested, in other words, in mapping the institutional conditions for learning onto the overseas student experience of learning (Figure 7.4 summarises this third circle of understanding).

Challenges of academic
conventions of British HE;
International students'
coping strategies;
Institutional formal and non-
formal support for
international students.

Figure 7.4 Institutional contexts.

The mode of conceptual analysis reflects the methodological process. My overseas student interviewees are all from mainland China and have been studying in the UK for at least one academic year. Working with this small group of Chinese students provides me with the opportunity of spending more time with each participant and getting to know each participant as a fellow student. I am bilingual in English and Mandarin and this makes it possible to communicate with participants in their own language, while submitting my thesis in English and contributing to English-speaking conferences across continents. It also makes it possible for me to construct a methodological approach that is sensitive to the voices of those whose student experiences I am seeking to understand.

My sense is that the methodology will have to build on – grow out of – my conceptualisation of what I am trying to understand. How I address my own questions depends upon what those questions are and how I choose to construe them. Method is not technical, but purposeful. It follows the logic of the problem under discussion. My research method and design rolls out from the substantive source of the enquiry; namely, the experience and perceptions of a particular group of overseas undergraduates studying within the UK. There is 'a single thread binding it all together': both the substantive issues to be addressed and the methodological procedures adopted (Confucius 1893: Book XV, 3).

Enquiry as quest

The problem, at both the practical and methodological level, is that of beginnings: getting started, origins and originality, points of departure, authority, the anxiety of influence. It is a twin-pronged problem of finding one's own voice and of understanding something of the conversational context one is entering. Said (1997: xxi) asks:

> What is a beginning? What must one do in order to begin? What is special about beginning as an activity or a moment or a place? Can one begin whenever one pleases? What kind of attitude or frame of mind is necessary for beginning?

These are important questions – not just technical or tactical questions – but questions that lead us to other questions regarding the nature of 'method' within educational studies in particular and the social sciences generally. To make a beginning is both to insert oneself within history and to locate oneself within an increasingly complex global nexus.

The really difficult thing in any intellectual enquiry is not answering questions, but formulating and conceptualising them and appreciating the context within which they have relevance and pertinence. That is the hard and intellectually exciting part of any intellectual endeavour: deciding on its conceptual purposefulness. It requires attention to what others have said and are saying; attention to what others have written; and attentiveness to one's premonitions. All enquiries are a kind of quest; all quests are adventuresome; and all adventures are unpredictable. It is the indeterminacy of all serious research and scholarship that really matters and wherein lies their interpretive potential. Research and scholarship require both courage and circumspection. They require other virtues, but the courage to dwell in uncertainty and the circumspection necessary to pursue the single thread are of paramount importance (see Nixon 2008). The difficulty, as always, lies in knowing what one does not know.

The Confucian 'single thread' is a *conceptual* thread: a means of binding the study into a conceptual whole, giving it conceptual clarity and integrity, ensuring that it has a conceptual focus (Confucius 1893: XV, 3). The crucial questions at the outset of any enquiry are: Where do I start unravelling the thread? How do I find the right loose end, and begin to untwine it? How do I know what I am looking for? How do I know when I have found it? These problems are both methodological (in that they imply a particular epistemological stance in relation to method) and practical (in the sense of requiring deliberation and decision making). Research and scholarship begin and end with the difficult business of thinking. That grounding in the practice of thought is what makes the process of disciplined enquiry both ordinary and extraordinary, a common good.

One last thought: it is conceivable that we only *know* fully what we thoroughly *enjoy*; if so, delight must be sewn in – that single thread again – to our epistemologies, our methodologies, our designs, our plans, our ways of working as researchers and scholars. Delight generates and sustains thought. The intellectual joy of research and scholarship is the conceptual quest, the unfinished journey, the seeking (as well as the finding), the deferments and endless interconnections, the byways and sideways that lead to the big route through. One has to discover enjoyment – delight, well being, happiness – for oneself and others in what one is seeking to understand; otherwise, the thread of understanding cannot unravel. We return to Confucius: 'to be fond of something is better than merely to know it, and to find joy in it is better than merely to be fond of it' (Confucius, 1893: Book VI, 20).

Acknowledgements

The authors acknowledge with thanks financial support from the Hong Kong Institute of Education, in funding an academic exchange that provided some of the time and space necessary to produce this chapter, and Liverpool Hope University in financially supporting the work. Professor Bart McGettrick, in particular, has been influential in ensuring that this venture has come to fruition.

References

Arendt, H. (1970) *Men in Dark Times*. London: Jonathan Cape.

Chang, J. and Halliday, J. (2007) *Mao: the Unknown Story*. London: Vintage Books.

Confucius (1893) *The Analects of Confucius*. Oxford: Clarendon Press.

Damrosch, D. (1995) *We Scholars: Changing the Culture of the University*. Cambridge, MA: Harvard University Press.

Greenhalgh, S. (2008) *Just One Child: Science and Policy in Deng's China*. Berkeley, Los Angeles and London: University of California Press.

Hutton, W. (2007) *The Writing on the Wall: China and the West in the 21st Century*. London: Abacus.

Leonard, M. (2008) *What Does China Think?* London: Fourth Estate.

Nixon, J. (2008) *Towards the Virtuous University: the Moral Bases of Academic Practice*. New York and London: Routledge/Taylor and Francis Group.

Polanyi, M. (1973) *Personal Knowledge: Towards a Post-Critical Philosophy*. London: Routledge and Kegan Paul.

Polanyi, M. and Prosch, H. (1975) *Meaning*. Chicago, IL and London: The University of Chicago Press.

Said, E. (2004a) *Power, Politics and Culture: interviews with Edward W. Said*. G. Viswanathan (Ed.). London: Bloomsbury.

——(2004b) *Humanism and Democratic Criticism*. New York: Columbia University Press.

——(2000) *Reflections on Exile and Other Essays*. Cambridge, MA: Harvard University Press.

——(1997) *Beginnings: Intention and Method*. London: Granta Books.

Sen, A. (2006) *Identity and Violence: the Illusion of Destiny*. London: Allen Lane.

Williams, R. (1960) *Border Country: A Novel*. London: Chatto and Windus.

8
Theory and narrative in the production of knowledge

J. Barr

> The shaping assumptions on which influential knowledge – which is always knowledge-accepted-as-such by a particular group in a particular culture – continues to be based, are influential not despite but because of the fact that most people are unaware of them.
>
> Minnich 1989: 333

The guiding idea of this chapter is that different theories generate different (partial) narratives and explanations, and that educational researchers are wise to cultivate 'reflexivity' and suspicion towards their favourite theories. Often as not, we are not aware of what these are. As a result, they act as filters that frame and shape our perceptions of the world precisely because we do not question them.

A decade ago I wrote a book called *Liberating Knowledge*, which offered a reflexive account of my experiences in adult education, feminist theory and practice, and research in various settings over a period of 15 years. The dual meaning of liberating knowledge is that on the one hand knowledge can be liberating (and what *counts* as knowledge is contestable as well as actually contested), whereas on the other hand, alternative and sometimes subversive ways of knowing can be liberated through teaching, research and other kinds of educational work (Barr 1999).

Underpinning the book is what I called a 'storied epistemology', one that recognises the power of narratives in enhancing understanding; in this case, stories about how knowledge is constructed in different times and places. Adopting an autobiographical approach, I set out to question the abstractions and pretensions of much disciplinary knowledge, whilst recognising, too, that personal experience is not immune from reflection, reinterpretation and critique. In other words, personal experience as a source of knowledge is not a 'trump card of authenticity' (ibid., p. 4). All of our understandings are open to reworking through exposure to other voices and points of view, including theoretical resources. Recognising this is a key to being both critical *and* personal.

I was intent on avoiding a narrow view of 'reflexivity'. This meant that in revisiting three of my earlier research projects in the book I was explicit about wanting to locate this work within a wider social and historical context of knowledge production, shaped by the prevailing discourses, power relations, and material conditions. I described the project of the book in terms of 'healing the breach' between 'words' (discourses) and 'things' (material conditions). And I wanted to suggest how the self (itself) changes over time. That is to say, the reflexive self I assemble in the book, *Liberating Knowledge*, is not quite the same as the selves that undertook each of the research projects (or indeed the self engaged in writing this chapter at a sunny table in Culross, overlooking the Firth of Forth, a cock crowing insistently nearby).

In the book, a central task I set myself was to review my past research for what it masked as well as revealed, for its blind spots as well as its illuminations. In contrast with the original research I inserted myself as researcher into the research process and its products: I put myself 'in the frame'.

The three cases I drew on were all broadly in the field of women's adult education. They were:

1. An evaluation of a pre-school community education project in Glasgow, dubbed 'Headway', as part of a national study conducted between 1979 and 1981 of alternative forms of pre-school provision.
2. A research study in 1989–90 for a masters dissertation in which I explored the influence of different forms of feminism on New Opportunities for Women courses in the North of England.
3. A funded research project from 1991–3 on Women's Perceptions of Science involving various groups of women studying within the adult education curriculum at Warwick University.

Threaded through these accounts as told in my book is a story about the culturally and historically specific forms that feminism took in the UK in the 1970s, 1980s and into the 1990s. In each of my case studies I provide extracts from the original research reports. I then critique these texts for their silences and gaps. Thus, in the case of the pre-school research report (first case study) I re-present my Marxist-feminist theoretical categories as excluding what escapes these categories: women's caring work and the small transgressions and resistances of working class women.

In my second case study of New Opportunities for Women courses, and standing back from my original thesis, I see myself as seduced by theory with a capital 'T' and veering uncomfortably close to a 'banking' view of feminist education where tutors 'deposit' expert knowledge in students' heads (ibid., p. 156). In my third case study, the research project on women's perceptions of science, I allow into the text a more personal and 'reflexive' voice: unlike the two previous research projects, there is no attempt here to fit what the women say into the pre-determined categories of the researchers.

This reappraisal of the three projects is the occasion for an exploration of a number of interlocking themes. These pivot on: the politics of feminism and adult education as played out in each of the case studies under scrutiny; changing fashions in feminist theory and research and in adult education (especially women's adult education) theory and research over the historical period involved; the relationship between autobiography and empirical research; and, finally, the relationship between the relative power of words and things, ideas and structures.

The structure of the book is chronological, a chronology provided by the three case studies of research on adult women's education. Thus, in each case I move between the research reports and present time, reassessing them in companion chapters in the light of current concerns and ideas not available at the time. The changing academic and political context of research is focused on, as is the changing nature of feminism and adult education during the historical period concerned. A central theme is what constitutes 'feminist research'; another is the relationship between theory and practice.

Thus, the book (re)presents my research as *emergent*, subject over time to reformulation and reinterpretation. Its central concern is the evolving relationship between, on the one hand, my work in adult education, women's education and research, and on the other hand, changing social and cultural conditions, adult education policy and practice and feminist theory and practice. In returning to earlier work in the book I make no assumption that what I say here and now (in 1999) is necessarily an advance on what I said then.

Nonetheless, whilst I do not see the development of my work as moving towards *the* right answers, I do think some accounts are better than others. At the same time, I mount a challenge in the book to the notion that the context of knowledge production is *irrelevant* to questions of truth (Assiter 1997). I expand on this below by means of a more extended account of my first case study, Headway.

In my original 'descriptive account' of the area in which Headway was located, my depiction of the area and women's lives highlighted the issue of paid work. I reflect in my book that this focus was undoubtedly conditioned by the categories that were central to feminist theory and practice at the time (and in which I was immersed). In particular, the 'domestic labour debate', which dominated much Marxist-feminist literature in the 1970s (an outgrowth of the Marxist construction of economic relations as the origin of all power relations), lay behind my central motif. In line with that literature I operated with a notion of productive work *as* paid work and as crucial for women's empowerment and economic independence. I regarded childrearing work done by women at home as reproducing labour power, as, that is, functional for the capitalist-patriarchal state.

When I wrote my Headway evaluation report, the state had just become an object of theoretical concern to feminists. In this early theoretical work, Marxist feminists tried to graft an analysis of social reproduction, the family and gender onto a Marxist analysis of the capitalist state (see, for example, Cockburn 1977; Wilson 1977; McIntosh 1978). The focus of this literature on the welfare state was thus on how it reproduces capitalist modes of production and upholds the traditional patriarchal family.

Such prevailing politics, practices and theories had changed by the time I came to do my reappraisal of the Headway research, in *Liberating Knowledge*. Barbara Ehrenreich, the well-known and highly respected socialist-feminist researcher, had recently suggested that the problem with the early Marxist-feminist paradigm was that it was too *deferential* to Marxism. In trying to grant women agency within Marxist politics, the theory, paradoxically, depersonalised women. This is because once the work and investments involved in childrearing have been reduced to 'reproducing labour power', women, within this account, actually lose their autonomy and subjectivity. There is no place in this story for emotion, the body and personal relations, aspects of personal and social life neglected (even repressed) within Marxist categories: 'Trying to fit all of women's experiences into the terms of the market didn't work, and adding on patriarchy as an additional "structure" didn't help' (Ehrenreich 1992: 145).

In my reappraisal of Headway, I maintain that feminist theorising should use forms of argument and critique that take into account aspects of personal and social life that are neglected in Marxist accounts – forms of thinking that can remain receptive to what is most *specific* about female experience (see Felski 1989). I draw on theoretical arguments that were not available (or fashionable) at the time of the original report. Some of these pivoted on notions of power. For example, the Marxist-feminist 'oppressor-oppressed' model of power with which I operated prevented any acknowledgement that power and pleasure do not cancel one another out, as the pleasures of caring for young children testifies.

I confess in the book to having been tied to a restrictive notion of power, power conceived as centrally located in large structures of the economy and the state and as only repressive in its effects. And I express the belief that had I pursued a more open approach, less convinced of the truth of a specific theory of power, the story I told might have been more ambiguous, complex and contradictory, less about 'victimhood' and more, perhaps, about the pleasures and power of mothering. Carolyn Steedman has written with insight about girls' contradictory relations of power and powerlessness with respect to the home and childrearing. She believes in the possibility of using an awareness of this ambiguity and ambivalence to help produce change (Steedman 1980; 1986). By regarding the women in Headway as quite simply power*less*, as not 'having it', I was not in a position to consider this possibility. On the contrary, the position I took up in my research and writing, as spectator and narrator, effectively denied the women's own agency and knowledge, and, paradoxically, my own.

I engaged in a number of rhetorical (and other stylistic) strategies, which actually *masked* my own personal and theoretical standpoint. My chief strategy was to give the appearance of representing the 'natives' point of view': 'giving voice' to the people of the area and those involved in Headway regarding their lives and more specifically, regarding childcare facilities, was a major objective of my evaluation report. Yet this was anything but straightforward. For one thing, we cannot assume any correspondence between a life as lived and a person's narrative about it. Such testimonies do not lie around inside people waiting for someone to come along and ask the right questions. Rather, they are constructs, moments when we reinterpret ourselves and they are structured by unconscious as well as conscious processes (see Linden 1994).

Moreover, the *context* in which such 'stories' are recounted has an influence on them. For example, most of my interviews were one-to-one. Had I made more use of group discussions it is likely that the material derived would have differed, as the kind of experiences, thoughts and feelings expressed (as well as the power dynamics involved) would have been different. As it was, my interviewing, observational and interpreting skills lay, as I saw it, in making coherent sense of the rational and non-contradictory accounts I thought the women were giving me, and in relating these to my own rational account.

Listening to, responding to and interpreting accounts of personal experience are capacities that are *learned*, and of one thing we can be sure: there can be no uniquely true story, nor any uniquely right interpretation (see Code 1989). Related to this, just as listening responsively and responsibly are learned capacities, this is also true of writing. I had learned that a *proper* research account required me to distance myself from the women and their situation, and to bring in academic and other legitimated authorities to interpret and explain. Thus, in writing my text I do not appear as myself anywhere in it. None of it is in the form of conversations or dialogue in which I appear. Instead, parts of my text seem to be a transparent mouthpiece for the women's stories. Thus, I create the illusion of the women 'speaking for themselves' by producing snippets from conversations with them.

Yet my three 'life stories' of Liz, Helen and Pat, important community participants in Headway, are trimmed and edited around my favourite themes. For example, I preface their words with a reference to a written report by project initiators about the 'dependent attitudes' of people in the area. The women's quotations I chose to juxtapose with the report were specifically designed to contradict and falsify that portrayal. Thus, I chose snippets from conversations that demonstrated how Liz coped with a violent husband, a degrading and poverty-inducing social security system and dearth of full-time jobs, but still managed to keep her head above water and care for her children. I show Helen, 'a neglectful mother' according to project leaders, managing against all the odds to pay off debts left by her feckless husband and secure 'independence' for herself. And I portray Pat, caught in an exhausting cycle of caring for her mother and children and a husband who refuses to grant her any autonomy, yearning after the kind of job she once had, where 'there was naebody staundin over the top of ye'.

More obvious strategies that masked my own position included deference to authorities in the critical self-help/community development literature, which backed up my own stance. Another was to make reference to 'community workers in the area' to voice what were, in effect, my own views. And at another point in the text I refer to 'an attempt to introduce a WEA class' into the project, which was stillborn, but omit to mention that I initiated this attempt. Of course, written texts are inevitably crafted and involve selections, editing out and so on. My reappraisal of Headway in the book is not intended as an exercise in self-flagellation, but rather to convey several inter-related points.

The first point is that if we genuinely want to pursue responsive and responsible knowledge-making projects then we should draw attention from time to time to the processes and contingencies of textual production. Good adult education practice similarly draws attention occasionally to processes going on in the group and between the tutor and other participants, which might hinder learning. How we *know* (flexibly, dogmatically, pragmatically), reflects how we *learn*. Similarly, producing research reports (which are closed accounts, with all of the contingencies of their production filtered out), perpetuates a notion of knowledge as certain and fixed, and this is illusory.

Second, when I came to Headway I was immersed in traditions of sociological theory and cultural criticism, which, to the extent that they were interested in working class lives at all, either ignored issues of subjectivity or celebrated a kind of psychological simplicity in working class people that is condescending. I think my account of Headway was to a degree complicit with this refusal of a complex psychology to those living in conditions of material distress.

Third, in the book, I reveal my primary rhetorical strategy of 'allowing' interviewees to speak in their own voices as actually blurring the ways in which meanings emerged from the interviews themselves. This strategy actually obscured whose voice, point of view or interpretation was being represented at any moment – mine, theirs or some theory's – and in fact, much of the time, it was mine or some theory's rather than theirs that was represented on the page.

I was certainly thirled to theory with a capital 'T'. My card index system covering this period of my life offers ample evidence of this. This reflected the state of sociology and British academic feminism at the time, but it also reflected my own privileging of certain ways of seeing and my deference to academic authority. I presented carefully selected snippets of life to exemplify *my* theoretical projects (see Stanley and Wise 1990).

I should clarify that in criticising my earlier research stance in the book my intention was not to support an 'anti-theory' stance. Nevertheless, I had come to believe that it is elitist (and reductive) to think that only highly specialised intellectual work can get behind appearances to the way things really are. Such a position locates all critical thought outside the practices of everyday life. It ignores the complex, contradictory nature of human subjectivity (and the 'good sense' that Gramsci locates in everyday lived experience). Most importantly perhaps, it discounts the differing degrees of dissent, resistance and potential for change that exist in specific social and historical contexts, like Headway (see Hoare and Smith 1971).

Had I regarded the women in Headway as 'co-subjects' of the research, I might have learned an important lesson in how to allow the women's experiences to shape and reshape my own favoured theories. As it was, in the way I conducted the research and wrote my account, it was as if the women's own accounts of their lives and their experiences and my social 'structural' interpretation were two separate stories, moving along in tandem but seldom connecting. When they did connect, I 'read off' their meanings in terms of my macro-sociological account.

To sum up, in writing myself back into the original Headway text, I suggested ways in which it masked my own ideological and emotional investments, as well as my theoretical and epistemological assumptions. Had I been more open (to myself and to my interviewees) about my own theoretical standpoint and political commitments in the processes and writing of the research, participants might have put their finger on my (and my theories') blind spots, denials and contradictions, just as I was keen to do with the project's. Explicit incompleteness and partiality, coupled with greater tentativeness, leaves space for others to enter the conversation. Such a research and writing strategy is more accessible, inviting a response rather than simple acceptance or rejection, the only possible responses to accounts written as if 'from nowhere'.

Nevertheless (and this is to return to the point with which this section began), in returning to the Headway report I maintain in *Liberating Knowledge* that I would still go along with the main thrust of that analysis, overly crude as it then was. The structures of capitalism and patriarchy persist and continue to be reproduced, and they still fundamentally shape the conditions of life of the women involved in Headway. Even now, in 2009, I'd broadly stand by my original critique of the Headway project.

Notwithstanding my reluctance to 'appear in the text', and acknowledging that there is no uniquely right interpretation, some *are* better than others. Just as we cannot absolve ourselves of the responsibility to listen and interpret what people say and do responsively, we cannot absolve ourselves of the need for judgement and choice of political and theoretical perspective. This is so, even as we grant that what we say is never quite what we think we say, and every discourse generates its blind spots. Our particular location in society and history also limits the range of ideological, political and theoretical positions open to us (Moi 1989). And, certainly, it does not do to be too coy about the authority conferred on us by our institutional positions (in this case, as a University-based academic).

With due acknowledgement of its limitations, my evaluation report on Headway was an attempt to define and articulate from a specifically Marxist-feminist standpoint certain needs and interests of women in 'Lochend'. Its often blunt tone and its rhetorical claim to be a true analysis, appear to me now to be a very vulnerable, exposed position to adopt. This is especially so nowadays when so much academic writing, in its excessive self-referential sophistication, refuses to make any truth claims at all, in the mistaken belief, perhaps, that if we give up the search for 'the truth' we cannot claim *any* truth-value for our analyses. Headway, for all its evasions of the self-in-the-enquiry, its uncompromising stance and its blind spots, at least ran the risk of being wrong.

Knowledge is in the end based on acknowledgement. We 'know' as social beings, as members of interpretive communities, and we do not all have access to the 'rhetorical spaces' where *authoritative* interpretations are made (see Code 1995: 231). Beverley Skeggs has commented on her own position as an academic researcher, and on how easy it is to construct those researched as objects of knowledge without agency by slotting them into her own categories. Her suggestion is that: 'It is when different audiences are introduced and respond that challenges over the legitimacy of knowledge are produced. Many theorists do not try to hear or see anything other than from where they are located' (Skeggs 1997: 19).

At the time I wrote my book, vocationalism, accreditation and 'enterprise' were leaving other aspects of adult learning out in the cold. Research indicated that after over 20 years of New Right individualism the notion of social purpose adult education had all but given way among practitioners to notions of 'widening the market'. Students were coming to be viewed as consumers and education was regarded as a commodity. Political critique, traditionally strong in both adult education and feminism, was being lost. My suggestion in the book was that the time had come for more education and research projects that engage with concrete groups and communities struggling towards really useful knowledge to help them live their lives.

This perspective informed the third case study of the book which focused on and deconstructed the 'women's perceptions of science' research. Here, I and my co-researcher, Lynda Birke, did not try to fit what the women said into our pre-determined theoretical categories. Instead, we showed how what they said resonated with other, more academic, voices *and* made it clear that their voices exceeded any efforts on our part to contain and categorise them.

The approach we took to analysing the research data was influenced by the writings of Dorothy Smith, and by her idea of feminist research as requiring acknowledgment by the researcher of being located on the 'same critical plane' as the women being researched (see Smith 1979; 1987). In practice, what this meant was that we did not see our job as involving interpreting the women's testimony in terms of any fixed feminist, sociological or any other given categories or theoretical project. Nonetheless, our understandings and interpretations were clearly deeply influenced by our theoretical beliefs and by our experiences as feminists.

We approached groups, different constituencies of women in different contexts, in an effort not to individualise women or de-contextualise the research too much. This involved us in fairly labour-intensive work to recruit volunteers for interviews. In some cases, this could have been easily achieved via tutors or group leaders, but we always attended class and group meetings to explain what we were about. Black women's groups made it clear that they would in any case have insisted on us meeting them as a group to discuss the nature and possible usefulness of the research. As soon as they were convinced that the research was worthwhile they were happy to participate. Consistent with the views about science that they expressed, the pursuit of knowledge (ours in this case) that would not serve some really useful purpose, was anathema to them. This did not mean it had to be seen as having a direct pay-off for *them*, however.

That social relations of class, gender and race are relevant to the production of knowledge (that they are 'epistemological' factors), was a founding premise of the research. Our own experience as researchers and as adult educators, as well as our reading of feminist theory and the social studies of science, convinced us that this is so. And as we interviewed several women from the same group or course we noticed persistent themes emerging from within each group. There was, for instance, a marked tendency for women from the same group to answer in similar ways. For example, in one institution, one renowned for its emphasis on experiential learning and for its 'women-centred' approach, half of those interviewed shared a distrust of experts, a view that science should 'come out of the closet' and a refusal of the notion of 'scientific facts'.

The aim of our analysis of a number of case studies of different courses and groups was to highlight how narratives as ways of understanding the world are developed in different contexts. In looking at the different groups, our interest was in exploring how they might produce different 'epistemological communities' in their discourses around science. This matters, we thought, because knowledge construction and validation are co-operative, constructive endeavours; they are not the result of the activities of isolated individuals (see Nelson 1993; also Assiter 1997). It mattered to us as feminists because of the feminist insistence on the collective nature of feminist knowing and recognition of the strong relationship between that knowledge and changing social and political relations.

In the research process and our writing up of the research, our aim was to move *between* different standpoints and contexts, between accounts of individual women and different groups of learners and between what was said to us and our own comments (influenced by our own reading of feminist and other theory and our own experiences) in an effort, not to arrive at some privileged account, but to produce a text, which, 'in doing justice to the women's own testimony', went beyond our own understandings (Barr 1999: 139–40). Our strategy in analysing the interviews, questionnaires and group discussions was to seek a balance between identifying persistent themes across the inter-views, charting differences between different groups and treating each woman's narrative as a complete text.

There was, in fact, a remarkable resonance between the women's voices in our research and feminist critiques of science, suggesting potential for the enrichment of these critiques by the inclusion of many more voices to the conversation about science. We believed that if that conversation were to be extended to include many more people, as feminists believe it must be, academic and everyday understanding and knowledge boundaries must be transcended. From this point of view, it matters a great deal who sets the *terms* of the conversation in the first place. Women can only engage in a mutual dialogue, equally, if the cards are not already stacked against some by opaque and esoteric language and by scholarly and culturally specific terminologies.

Thus, we attempted to make the research as interactive and 'power-sensitive' (Haraway 1989) as possible, notwithstanding the constraints of time and the 'academic mode of production' within which the research was located (see Stanley 1990). In the end, of course, we had the pen. It was our job to give form to and interpret the data. The women involved had the right to expect us to do our job. That, after all, was the name of the game (Barr 1999: 140).

The underlying epistemological project of *Liberating Knowledge* could be described in terms of assessing adult education and research programmes in relation to how well they enable the articulation of 'views from below'. This is not because by virtue of being from below they offer truer, more accurate accounts of the world, but because in identifying and making available spaces where alternative ways of thinking and being can be worked up, such practices increase the *possibilities* of knowledge.

As a kind of public dialogue, adult education has this kind of radically democratic development of knowledge at its heart. In its more radical forms it entails the engage-ment of many progressive and excluded 'publics' in the generation of knowledge. Such a way of seeing adult education, that is, in terms of its critical and creative role within the wider culture, does not fit easily with current policy priorities. This is because its emphasis is on the conditions and means through which new meanings and knowledge can be developed, rather than on increasing access to *existing* knowledge.

Nevertheless, as one sympathetic critic of *Liberating Knowledge* pointed out, this aspiration to expand knowledge production to those other than academics is both deeply important *and* deeply problematic whilst we live in unequal social contexts where many do not have access to high-level education. Certainly, whilst I take care in the book to review the experiences and voices of women in my earlier research, and whilst in the third research study I claim to make my own categories porous to those of the research 'subjects', nonetheless, it remains unequivocally *my* story, told for and to an academic audience. How, then, are the excluded 'publics' to be involved in the production of this kind of research and knowledge? (Walker 2001: 283).

Whilst not claiming to answer Melanie Walker's question, I take up her challenge to a degree in a recent publication, *The Stranger Within: On the Idea of an Educated Public* (Barr 2008). The book explores an open-ended, diverse notion of an educated public that is not tied to institutional forms of education (especially higher education). Instead, it draws its inspiration from informal popular education activities, often allied to social and community groups and movements of various kinds. A central argument of the book pivots on the suggestion that social movements (such as, traditionally, the labour, women's, and peace movements and, more recently, networks like the World Social Forum) offer better models for knowledge development than the current compartmentalised arrangements in universities.

The notion of 'knowledge from below' on which the book draws, refers primarily to those independent sources of popular knowledge, groups and social movements that have been traditionally important in the history and practice of adult education. This tradition of adult education, rooted primarily in independent working class education, and reaching back to the Chartists, Owenites and Corresponding Societies of the nineteenth century (bodies which were motors of social change, contesting and sometimes gaining concessions from governments, before creating their own political formations), preceded the idea of adult education as an *institutional* form (Steele 2005).

Today's common sense narrows knowledge and education to the classroom, whether school, college or university. For this reason we need a leap of imagination to appreciate how the production of knowledge became a battleground in Britain in the early to mid-nineteenth century. Eileen Yeo's book, *The Contest for Social Science* (1996), depicts that nineteenth century struggle over ideas, the participants of which were not just individuals, but groups and social movements. Specifically, she seeks to shed light on how various sorts of action-oriented social science developed, as a pre-academic aid to action, which emphasised the condition of the working class as an index of social development. Her concern is to show how some working class people became active producers of knowledge. (Arguably, the current most pressing struggle around ideas is occurring primarily around the global justice movement.)

Yeo explicitly contrasts her way of doing intellectual history with the usual histories of ideas that 'parade great male thinkers … whose notion of contextualization consists in depicting the discussions and quarrels among formally educated men' (ibid. p. 10–11). Her challenge to this sort of intellectual history is summed up when she says:

> If scholars do not seek subaltern groups they do not find them. Without a more spacious idea of context which makes room for less privileged persons, scholars will go on constructing models of a scientific world and of the production

of knowledge which allow no room for activity from below in the past or in the future.

Ibid., p. xi

The Stranger Within proposes that different forms of knowledge need to be granted equal respect. Drawing on recent writing in 'phronetic social science' and 'public sociology' the book proposes an educational research programme in which *praxis* is central, as against current trends in life-long learning that focus almost exclusively on employability and training. It specifies the goal of such a project as being to contribute to society's *practical* (rather than theoretical) rationality (see Flyvbjerg 2001; see also Levine 2005). I suggest, too, that life-long learning/education might be reclaimed as a site for the encouragement, development and validation of this kind of research.

Briefly, phronetic social research aspires to contribute to the ongoing 'social dialogue' in a society, taking up problems that matter to the local, national and global communities in which we live, and communicating research results to citizens *qua* citizens. The assumption here is that the achievement of some kind of educated public in the context of large-scale economies and mass populations differentiated by class, gender, race, age and culture rests on recognising that some of the most important intellectual choices facing us are not about *theories* but our practical dealings with one another.

In conclusion, I want to underline three points. First, by drawing attention in this chapter to how different theories enable different stories and interpretations of the world, I should not be taken to be recommending a 'pick and mix' approach to research and writing. Second, in encouraging 'reflexivity' on the part of educational researchers I am not suggesting that this is a once and for all affair; on the contrary, it is in principle and practice unending. Third, whilst there is never one right story, it is always a useful and fruitful assumption that the experience of people on the downside of societies (or organisations, or whatever) is a resource for enlarging *everyone*'s understanding (see Addams 1964).

References

Addams, J. (1964) *Democracy and Social Ethics*. Cambridge, MA: Harvard University Press.

Assiter, A. (1997) *Enlightened Women: Modernist Feminism in a Postmodern Age*. London and New York: Routledge.

Barr, J. (1999) *Liberating Knowledge: Research, Feminism and Adult Education*. Leicester: NIACE.

——(2008) *The Stranger Within: On the Idea of an Educated Public*. Rotterdam: Sense Publishers.

Cockburn, C. (1977) *The Local State*. London: Pluto.

Code, L. (1989) Experience, knowledge and responsibility. In A. Garry and M. Pearsall (Eds). *Women, Knowledge and Reality*. London: Unwin Hyman, 157–77.

——(1995) *Rhetorical Spaces: Essays on Gendered Locations*. New York and London: Routledge.

Ehrenreich, B. (1992) Life without father: reconsidering socialist feminist theory. In L. McDowell and R. Pringle (Eds). *Defining Women: Social Institutions and Gender Divisions*. Cambridge: Polity Press in association with the Open University.

Felski, R. (1989) *Beyond Feminist Aesthetics*. Cambridge, MA: Harvard University Press.

Flyvbjerg, B. (2001) *Making Social Science Matter*. Cambridge: Cambridge University Press.

Haraway, D. (1989) *Primate Visions*. London: Routledge.

Hoare, Q. and Smith, N. (Eds) (1971) *Gramsci: Selections from the Prison Notebooks*. London: Lawrence and Wishart.

Levine, R. (Ed.) (2005) *Enriching the Sociological Imagination: How Radical Sociology Changed the Discipline.* Boulder and London: Paradigm Publishers.

Linden, R. (1994) *Making Stories, Making Lives.* Columbus, OH: Ohio State University Press.

McIntosh, M. (1978) The state and the oppression of women. In A. Kuhn and A.M. Wolpe (Eds). *Feminism and Materialism.* London: Routledge and Kegan Paul.

Minnich, E. (1989) *Transforming Knowledge.* Philadelphia, PA: Temple University Press.

Moi, T. (1989) Patriarchal thought and the drive for knowledge. In T. Brennan (Ed.) *Between Feminism and Psychoanalysis.* London: Routledge.

Nelson, L. (1993) Epistemological communities. In L. Alcoff and E. Potter (Eds). *Feminist Epistemologies.* London: Routledge, 121–59.

Skeggs, B. (1997) *Formations of Class and Gender.* London: Sage.

Smith, D. (1979) A sociology for women. In J. A. Sherman and E.T. Beck (Eds). *The Prison of Sex: Essays in the Sociology of Knowledge.* Madison, WI: University of Wisconsin Press.

——(1987) *The Everyday World as Problematic: a Feminist Sociology.* Milton Keynes: Open University Press.

Stanley, L. (1990) Feminist praxis and the academic mode of production. Introduction to L. Stanley (Ed.) *Feminist Praxis: Research, Theory and Epistemology in Feminist Sociology.* London: Routledge.

Stanley, L. and Wise, S. (1990) Method, methodology and epistemology in feminist research processes. In L. Stanley (Ed.) *Feminist Praxis: Research, Theory and Epistemology in Feminist Sociology.* London: Routledge, 20–60.

Steedman, C. (1980) The tidy house, *Feminist Review*, No 6.

——(1986) *Landscape for a Good Woman.* London: Virago.

Steele, T. (2005) *Reclaiming Popular Education: Is Lifelong Learning Enough?* Paper presented at The Ends of Education Seminar, Sheffield University, April 25.

Walker, M. (2001) Book Review of *Liberating Knowledge. Teaching in Higher Education*, 6: 2.

Wilson, E. (1977) *Women and the Welfare State.* London: Tavistock.

Yeo, E. (1996) *The Contest for Social Science: Relations and Representations of Gender and Race.* London: River Orams Press.

9

Making sense of supervision

Deciphering feedback

A. Paré

Truth is not born nor is it to be found inside the head of an individual person, it is born *between people* collectively searching for truth, in the process of their dialogic interaction.

Bakhtin 1984: 110

The feedback received during supervisory sessions can be critical to the successful completion of the dissertation. If supervisor commentary is timely, relevant, and articulate, it can allow students to see draft texts in a new light and to revise them. However, if feedback is vague, too critical, or focused on the wrong aspects of the text, students may find supervisory sessions more frustrating than useful. This chapter draws on interviews, focus group discussions, and recorded conversations between doctoral students and their supervisors in order to examine this vital educational relationship. The purpose of the chapter is eminently practical: to help doctoral students take advantage of what their supervisors tell them, even when the comments are obscure. The chapter offers interpretations of supervisors' remarks about content, organisation, strategy, citations, tone, and other aspects of text so that doctoral students can more fully exploit feedback.

Unfortunately, the research informing this chapter indicates that supervisor feedback is often ambiguous, enigmatic, and coded – that is, saturated with meaning, but difficult to understand. The reason for this is clear: really useful advice to writers, the kind that professional editors and critics offer, comes from a deep understanding of how texts work, how they advance arguments effectively, and how they affect readers. Even supervisors who publish frequently may not be capable of conducting the sort of close textual analysis that leads to insightful feedback. Bazerman, a rhetoric scholar, explains:

I have found smart, accomplished colleagues in other disciplines who have little vocabulary for discussing writing beyond the corrective grammar they learned in high school. Although they have learned the genres of their profession and are successful in them, their reflective ability to manipulate them is limited because of a lack of linguistic and rhetorical vocabulary and analytical methods.

Bazerman 2009: 289

In other words, the ability to write well does not confer the ability to teach others to write. In fact, automaticity is a mark of expertise: as we become adept at something, our conscious attention to performance wanes. And some complex behaviours – such as language, and even highly specialised forms of discipline-specific language – are learned tacitly, without much direct instruction, as the by-product of participation in a particular activity. As a result, supervisors can use language to *do* their scholarly work, but might not easily be able to explain why a certain word is wrong, or why a citation is required in a specific location, or why one claim needs no support whereas another needs hard evidence.

Compounding this problem is the scarcity of research into dissertation writing. The development of writing abilities has been a much-studied phenomenon over the past few decades, but the focus of that research has been largely on children (e.g. Emig 1971; Britton *et al.* 1975), undergraduate students (e.g. Freedman 1987; McCarthy 1987), or non-academic writers (e.g. MacKinnon 1993; Paré 1993). The specialised, challenging, and high-stakes writing of the dissertation has been virtually ignored (Aitchison and Lee 2006; Kamler and Thomson 2006; Lee and Aitchison 2008; Parry 1998; Rose and McClafferty 2001).[1] After reviewing the higher education literature, Kamler and Thomson noted that 'doctoral writing was a kind of present absence in the landscape of doctoral education. It was something that everyone worried about, but about which there was too little systematic debate and discussion' (2006: x).

The research reported in this chapter is part of an attempt to inform that debate and animate the discussion. Motivated by a curiosity about what supervisors and doctoral students talk about during sessions devoted to reviews of students' writing, I recorded their conversations and interviewed them, sometimes together, sometimes separately; I also recorded focus group discussions among doctoral students and among faculty members. The data provide a picture of feedback that ranges from the barely articulate to the savvy and even eloquent. At one extreme are the supervisors whose mysterious pronouncements leave students more confused than enlightened, but at the other end are supervisors who have a deep sensitivity to how texts work and how they can be improved, even when they lack the 'linguistic and rhetorical vocabulary' that Bazerman mentions above. In between are supervisors who provide trenchant and usable feedback, but no explanation or rationale; in other words, they make suggestions for change but do not trace their comments back to disciplinary conventions, rhetorical strategy, personal preference, or any other justification. They say, 'do this', but not why it should be done. In the following interview excerpt, a supervisor confesses this failure:

> Supervisor: … it's a very formal exercise, undertaking research for a PhD, in presenting the work in the actual thesis, and so I need to sort of enforce certain conventions.
> Interviewer: Right, and whose conventions are those? Where do those conventions come from?
> Supervisor: Well I … that's an interesting question. I suppose they come to [student] filtered through me, so as a supervisor I suppose at the end of the day it's my view of what is a convention, and I suppose my view is formed partly by seeing other theses. But I'm not sure that's the answer. I'm not really sure where. … I'm not sure I can answer it. I have a view. Obviously it must come from somewhere. But I don't know where. I don't know where we decide how we do this.

Even without knowing the origins of the conventions governing dissertations, however, supervisors often speak with authority about what should and should not be, and much of the advice they dispense comes from a deep, if tacit, knowledge. It is this potentially useful but unelaborated feedback that is the primary focus of this chapter, my purpose is to help students understand what supervisors mean when they talk about texts: why they suggest or demand that something be phrased a certain way, expect a particular tone or style, insist that a specific reference be inserted, or favour one way of organising and presenting data over another. But first, my interpretation of supervisor comments will make more sense if I introduce some ideas from the language and writing theories that shape my perception.

Writing as knowledge-making

There is a common misconception about the relationship between language and thought. Advice to 'choose our words carefully' or 'think before we speak', reflects a view that meaning is first made in the head and then communicated via language, but our day-to-day experience belies that idea. We know that talking is often a way to make sense of things – both in specialised settings, like counselling sessions or graduate seminars, and in ordinary conversation with family or friends. As we struggle to articulate, as we see the effect of our words on others, as we listen and respond, we don't only express ideas, we make them. In this sense, language is heuristic; that is, language supports or makes possible a search for meaning. What is true for speech is equally true for writing, even though our interlocutors are not present; all of us have written our way to greater clarity through drafting and redrafting. Gage offers this description of that phenomenon:

> Writing is thinking made tangible, thinking that can be examined because it is on the page and not in the head, invisible, floating around. Writing is thinking that can be stopped and tinkered with. It is a way of holding thought still long enough to examine its structures, its possibilities, its flaws. The road to a clearer under-standing is travelled on paper. It is through an attempt to find words for ourselves in which to express related ideas that we often discover what we think.
>
> Gage 1986: 24

The same effort after meaning that allows us to generate knowledge in spoken conversation characterises the writing process as well. As we compose, as we search for words, as we anticipate a reader's response, as we link one concept to the next, as we revise for greater clarity or coherence, we are building new ways of thinking and knowing.

This view of writing as an epistemic or knowledge-making activity was central to the process movement that revolutionised writing research and pedagogy in the 1970s and 1980s (e.g. Britton *et al.* 1975; Emig 1977; Flower and Hayes 1980; 1981; Murray 1980). When researchers expanded their focus beyond the individual writer to the contexts and activities within which writing occurs, it became obvious that writing is socially as well as individually epistemic; that is, collectives of various kinds – institutions, companies, disciplines – depend on writing to produce the knowledge they need for their work (e.g. Bazerman 1988; Odell and Goswami 1985). Moreover, such collectives, often called 'discourse communities' (Porter 1992), develop specialised languages and particular discourse practices that are shaped to their purposes. As Berlin puts it, 'Knowledge ... is a matter of mutual agreement appearing as the product of the rhetorical activity, the discussion, of a given discourse community' (1987: 166). Or, in Bakhtin's words, from this chapter's epigram: 'Truth ... is born between people collectively searching for truth, in the process of their dialogic interaction' (1984: 110).

The point is, writing is both individually and socially epistemic: when we write in diaries or journals, and when we draft and revise texts for eventual publication, we employ writing as a tool for making knowledge for ourselves. And when we join a discourse community – such as an academic discipline – we use writing in partnership with others to advance knowledge about the issues and problems we face, and we do that collaborative work in the special forms of 'dialogic interaction' the community has developed.

To make sense of what supervisors are saying, there are two things about the 'dialogic interaction' of disciplines that need to be understood: first, each discipline develops its own discourse practices that are intended to produce particular forms and types of knowledge. Not only are terminologies different, but also the structure and nature of arguments vary across disciplines. What counts as data, how data are collected and analysed, what claims may be made from that analysis, how the researcher is or is not represented in the text, and other discourse features differ from one field to another. Second, that disciplinary conversation isn't always a genteel affair: there are competing theories, historical tensions, opposing ideologies, and other fractures that make the community's discourse a highly contested terrain. The discipline's differences are manifest in words. In discussing possible readers for a student's dissertation, one supervisor put this reality bluntly: 'The thing is, with PhD theses, you've got to be careful about who you choose to be external examiners. ... There's, if you like, a politics to it, right?'

Supervisors' comments begin to make more sense when students see their area of scholarship as a disputed and dynamic field that has developed particular methods of argumentation. Much of what supervisors are saying when they provide feedback is an attempt to help students locate themselves within that ongoing debate. Not all disciplinary discourse is antagonistic, of course. There's a considerable amount of peaceful collaboration, as one scholar builds on the work of others, or provides an alternative perspective. But in every case, the individual contribution is positioned within an historical and conceptual landscape: it follows in some theoretical tradition, it references colleagues past and present, it advances claims that resonate for some and not for others, it constructs particular types of argument, it adds to an account or explanation with which contemporaries agree or disagree. The supervisor's job is to help doctoral students locate themselves in that intellectual and rhetorical territory.

Deconstructing feedback: what supervisors say, and what they mean

Bill Green succinctly captures this key mentorship role: 'the supervisor represents, or stands in for, the Discipline itself, and also the Academy' (2005: 162). In the following excerpts from student–supervisor conversations and focus group discussions, it is sometimes quite clear that supervisors are playing that role; at other times, however, it takes a close reading to see what's going on. Consider this first example, an excerpt from a supervisor–student meeting to discuss a dissertation chapter draft:

> Supervisor: Here you sort of rapidly converge on something, and I don't have
> enough justification for what led you there. And then you need some sort of

conclusion here. So, what does this tell us? Research in this field is frag-mented? Underdeveloped? ... So, you want to give a kind of sum-up. 'Here's where things stand. Here's where I see the strengths and weaknesses of each.'

This brief passage is packed with unexplained significance. Note the first three sentences: is the supervisor asking for greater justification for herself only? Why – that is, for whom and for what purpose – does the student need to insert 'some sort of conclusion'? And who is the 'us' in the third sentence? The supervisor speaks here from an apparent cer-tainty about what is required in the text, although she doesn't elaborate, so we (and the student) can't tell what she's thinking. When shown this excerpt during a focus group discussion, supervisors had this to say:

Interviewer: So who is the reader here? Who is the 'us'?
Supervisor 4: The supervisory committee.
Supervisor 2: The committee.
Supervisor 3: And the external examiner.
Supervisor 1: Well, it's the supervisory committee, but it's potential article readers.
Supervisor 2: ... once it's published.
Supervisor 4: The judges.
Supervisor 1: The potential professional audience.
Supervisor 3: Whoever's going to judge it, assess it.
Supervisor 1: Yeah, but I think it goes beyond that. It's not just, 'Okay, your committee is clueless and is not going to understand this'. It's more, like, in academic writing you have to say this kind of thing in this kind of place.

The final phrase here hints at a profound knowledge of the rhetoric of academic dis-course: 'in academic writing you have to say this kind of thing in this kind of place.' The student's supervisor knows that the many possible readers of the dissertation – from the supervisory committee to members of the student's disciplinary community – will need a certain type of statement here, one that summarises a review of the literature, perhaps, and that offers an assessment. The supervisor's shorthand for that is offered in the final comments of the excerpt, when she speaks to the discourse community in the voice of the student: 'Here's where things stand. Here's where I see the strengths and weaknesses of each.' In the next excerpt, we see the same sort of rhetorical savvy, with somewhat more elaboration. Here the supervisor – again, in a conversation with a student about a chapter draft – articulates the move from the literature review to the student's own research:

Supervisor: So start large: here is a general context; zoom in successively; here is what I'm [i.e. the student is] focusing on. Then look at it from a different angle. What do we know about this problem? What research has been done? That's where your literature review comes in. You say, 'here are all the pieces that are understood well by now'. So obviously we're not going to do those because we know. But here are the gaps, and here is the gap that I'm address-ing. Then it becomes very obvious what your contribution is, to this whole, to the study of this whole problem.

In this short statement, the supervisor offers a neat summary of the main rhetorical strategy of much academic discourse, including the dissertation: a review of previous work identifies an unanswered question or unresolved problem, and the student's contribution fills that gap. In other words, the student's utterance is positioned or located within an ongoing conversation. But this is not a universal move in academic rhetoric; in fact, it replicates or at least imitates a scientific rhetoric, in which contributions to the debate are cumulative, each adding factual evidence to the construction of a community-built account of a particular phenomenon. In that conversation, research questions are indexed to, and justified by, the discipline's literature. In other scholarly traditions, research questions might first arise in the life or professional practice of the researcher herself, or in the day-to-day activities of a non-academic community. So, the supervisor in the previous excerpt is offering the student advice about both location *and* method: how to situate his contribution vis-à-vis other statements, and why such a move is considered appropriate in their disciplinary tradition.

Not all comments are so saturated in disciplinary significance, of course. Some seem motivated by a concern for any reader, not just colleagues from the same field. So, for example, the advice offered by the two supervisors in the following excerpts invokes a more general reader and that reader's need for textual cohesion:

> Supervisor: When you're writing a thesis, one of the things you need are road signs to guide the readers through the thesis [and] prepare them intellectually to expect what's coming. And, if you don't do that, then they get lost, they get confused, and they get pissed off.
>
> Supervisor: First time you introduce a concept, you have to define it. ... the introduction is very important. Right, this is the first thing that people are going to read. They're going to have to understand what problem you're addressing, why is this an important problem ... what don't we know yet about this problem?

Even here, however, there is an assumption of a certain type of academic rhetoric, one following from a Western rationalist tradition that assumes that reason and knowledge can be created through the application of particular forms of observation and representation. The advice above, apparently generic to academic discourse, may be far less helpful to someone attempting to make knowledge through fiction or visual representation, for example, or someone drawing on non-Western traditions of thought. It is these deep assumptions about what constitutes knowledge and knowing that are usually unstated in supervisor feedback, but which are critical for the doctoral student to understand if feedback is to be helpful. Fortunately, much of that commentary is based on assumptions that are more accessible and interpretable than an ambiguous reference to 'road signs'. For example, in the following excerpt, a supervisor makes a comment that isn't too difficult to understand:

> Supervisor: A lot of adult education theory goes back to them [Gramsci and Freire]. So I think what you should do is figure out, when you read this again, just make sure that you've genuflected enough to them.

Again, this statement is about positioning, about the student locating her contribution in some relation to earlier contributions from historical figures in the discipline. Typically, however, the advice is offered without elaboration. The student is told to show some sign of reverence − to genuflect − toward Gramsci and Freire, but not why. Responding to this excerpt, a supervisor in a focus group discussion offered this gloss:

Supervisor 1: ... So maybe it's a kind of sympathetic identification with the writer who just spent an hour telling you why they will not put Gramsci and Freire in there and why they absolutely disagree with them and why they are totally irrelevant, and you say, 'look, you gotta bow to the gods, and just do it'. ... I think that's disciplinary. It's like socializing people into the rules of the discipline, like who can you criticize, who it's cool to criticize now, who it's not. Then sort of the tribal elders that you can disagree with and you can build on, but you're not allowed to totally dis them. ... You have to acknowledge them. I think every discipline will have its people like that.

This brief explanation is already an improvement over the original imperative; it situates the reverence for elders in the context of a disciplinary culture and history and provides justification for a certain type of citation: the paying of tribute. But there is also a blunt statement here about a key purpose of supervision: 'It's like socializing people into the rules of the discipline.' This recognition and acknowledgement would make the whole process of supervision more transparent. Doctoral students are apprentices preparing for a certain kind of work in a certain kind of community, and supervisors are meant to help ease the transition from novice to practitioner. In the following excerpt from a supervisory session, the student – who has already published some of her dissertation research – is being told to include a footnote that will establish her postapprenticeship status as a participating member of the disciplinary community:

Supervisor: I think maybe what you should say is – have a footnote to say in that chapter – that some of this work has already been published in an international journal, or whatever, because that's gone through a peer review process, it's been published and [that] tells people that you've already got the seal of approval from your academic peers in an international journal.

The fact that the student's work has passed the test of blind review marks her as having authority, as having already made a contribution (and an 'international' one, at that), and therefore as having located herself in the disciplinary conversation.

Conclusion

Knowing that supervisory sessions are part of an enculturation process might help students understand what their supervisor is saying and doing, but it also gives them a new task: to learn more about the community they are joining, its past, its current debates, its cultural and discourse practices. The supervisor is a member of that community, and a chief resource to students in their transition to life as scholars. She or he might not make explicit reference to the rules of rhetorical engagement in the discipline, and might not even be able to articulate those rules, but students should still not accept unjustified directives. If a supervisor asks for changes in a draft, students should ask for explanations; if the supervisor says the student must cite Foucault (or anyone else) in the midst of a particular passage, without explanation, the student should ask 'why here?' and 'why Foucault?'

There are two benefits to a more open and explicit conversation with supervisors. First, as I have argued here, students will be engaging in a kind of meta-analysis that asks not only about the value or relevance of their texts but also about the disciplinary culture within which those judgements of quality are made. That knowledge will make students better scholars and better writers. Second, that meta-analysis will make students better teachers if and when they supervise doctoral students. In closing, I offer a final excerpt, this one from a focus group discussion with doctoral students. The student quoted is explaining what has made his relationship with his supervisor so positive and so productive. His comments about 'apprenticeship' and becoming 'a member of the guild' perfectly capture what I have argued in this chapter:

> … what I have with my supervisor, and what I hear other people have, is there is a shared passion and engagement for the craft, for the process and the product and the unknown future. There is this kind of thrust towards the future and being valued for what you are now but also valued for what you could produce, what you can be. That for me is a part of a good apprenticeship where it is kind of like you join a guild because you want to do this thing that other people are doing in the best possible way. And I don't know how you gain that experience if you are with someone who is not valuing you as someone who is a potential colleague, a member of the guild. That's really tough. I need that affirmation.

Notes

1 A notable exception, and profitable reading for both supervisors and doctoral students, is Kamler and Thomson's 2006 book, *Helping Doctoral Students Write: Pedagogies for Supervision*.

References

Aitchison, C. and Lee, A. (2006) Research writing: Problems and pedagogies, *Teaching in Higher Education*, 11(3): 265–78.

Bakhtin, M. (1984) *Problems of Dostoevsky's Poetics*. Trans. C. Emerson, Minneapolis, MN: University of Minnesota Press.

Bazerman, C. (1988) *Shaping Written Knowledge: The Genre and Activity of the Experimental Article in Science*. Madison, WI: University of Wisconsin Press.

——(2009). Genre and cognitive development: beyond writing to learn. In C. Bazerman, A. Bonini, and D. Figueiredo (Eds). *Genre in a changing world*. Fort Collins, Colorado: The WAC Clearinghouse and Parlor Press, 279–94. Available at wac.colostate.edu/books/genre/

Berlin, J. A. (1987) *Rhetoric and reality: Writing instruction in American colleges 1900–1985*. Carbondale, IL: Southern Illinois University Press.

Britton, J., Burgess, T., Martin, N., McLeod, A. and Rosen, H. (1975) *The Development of Writing Abilities, 11–18*. London: Macmillan Education.

Emig, J. (1971) *The Composing Process of Twelfth Graders*. Urbana, IL: NCTE.

——(1977) Writing as a mode of learning. *College Composition and Communication,* 28(2): 122–8.

Flower, L. S. and Hayes, J. R. (1980) The cognition of discovery: Defining a rhetorical problem, *College Composition and Communication*, 31(1): 21–32.

——(1981) A cognitive process theory of writing, *College English*, 44: 765–77.

Freedman, A. (1987) Learning to write again: Discipline-specific writing at university, *Carleton Papers in Applied Language Studies*, 4: 95–115.

Gage, J. (1986) Why write? In A. Petrosky and D. Bartholomae (Eds). *The teaching of writing*. Chicago, IL: National Society for the Study of Education, 8–29.

Green, B. (2005) Unfinished business: subjectivity and supervision, *Higher Education Research and Development,* 24(2): 151–63.

Kamler, B. and Thomson, P. (2006) *Helping Doctoral Students Write: Pedagogies for Supervision.* London: Routledge.

Lee, A. and Aitchison, C. (2008) Writing for the doctorate and beyond In D. Boud and A. Lee (Eds). *Changing Practices of Doctoral Education.* London: Routledge, 147–64.

MacKinnon, J. (1993) Becoming a rhetor: Developing writing ability in a mature, writing-intensive organization. In R. Spilka (Ed.). *Writing in the Workplace: New Research Perspectives.* Carbondale, IL: Southern Illinois University Press, 41–55.

McCarthy, L. P. (1987) A stranger in strange lands: A college student writing across the curriculum, *Research in the Teaching of English,* 21: 233–65.

Murray, D. (1980) Writing as process: How writing finds its own meaning. In T. R. Donovan and B. McClelland (Eds). *Eight Approaches to Teaching Composition.* Urbana, IL: National Council of Teachers of English, pp. 3–20.

Odell, L. and Goswami, D. (Eds) (1985) *Writing in Nonacademic Settings.* New York: Guilford Press.

Paré, A. (1993) Discourse regulations and the production of knowledge. In R. Spilka (Ed.). *Writing in the Workplace: New Research Perspectives.* Carbondale, IL: Southern Illinois University Press, 111–23.

Parry, S. (1998) Disciplinary discourse in doctoral theses, *Higher Education,* 36: 273–99.

Porter, J. (1992) *Audience and Rhetoric: An Archaeological Composition of the Discourse Community.* Englewood Cliffs, NJ: Prentice Hall.

Rose, M. and McClafferty, K. A. (2001) A call for the teaching of writing in graduate education, *Educational Researcher,* 30(2): 27–33.

10

Entering the gates of the elect

Obtaining the doctorate in education in South Africa

C. Soudien

The acquisition of a PhD in South Africa is as big an achievement as it is elsewhere in the world. It is an event that has deep significance for the questions of self and other, especially as these are refracted through the vectors of race, class and gender. It constitutes a moment where individual identity is profoundly reconfigured and where the social hierarchies that order status positions of subordinate-ness and superiority are, if not turned upside down, then certainly, recomposed and rearranged. What I do in this chapter is lift out for consideration the sociological issues that present themselves in the course of doing a PhD in South Africa. In identifying these issues I draw essentially on my experience as a participant in the development of a number of doctoral initiatives in South Africa, a convenor of PhD programmes and, most pertinently, a supervisor/adviser of more than a dozen doctoral students in the last 14 years. My experience during this period has essentially been with students from historically disadvantaged backgrounds, namely, students of colour and women. Although I have had the opportunity of advising socio-economically advantaged students – those who come to the PhD with the economic, cultural and social backgrounds to manage the progression into the PhD with relative ease,[1] it is my work and relationship with many economically and socially disadvantaged students, and particularly female students of colour, that is of consequence here. The approach I take is not empirical, in the sense that I have systematically documented the experience of my students. Instead, I reflect on the issues that they have deliberately and consciously raised with me, and also many that they have not but of which I have become aware. It is for this reason that I present this chapter as an exploratory analysis.

I look particularly at the experience of what it means to do a PhD from a social and cultural perspective as opposed to the procedural mechanics of doing so. I am not concerned with the questions of supervisor–relationship per se, or the kinds of questions that relate to how one conducts these. I do not look at the question of how one might do a PhD. What kinds of challenges arise in this experience and how these experiences reflect the specific dynamics and nature of the South African higher education environment are essentially what I am interested in.

The context of higher education in South Africa

The question of the PhD, particularly that of how to do it, has become the subject of some interest in South Africa. Although there isn't the welter of texts that one might see in countries with long-established traditions of doing the doctorate, such as the USA, a small corpus of work is emerging in the country in the form of monographs (see, for example, Hofstee 2006; Mouton 2001) and unpublished PhD manuals that can be found in schools and faculties of education in virtually every university in the country. There is also some analytic work on the state of PhD programmes in South Africa and elsewhere on the continent (Bailey 2001; Szanton and Manyika 2002). Predictably, the focus of much of this work, both that which is interested in how to do the PhD and that which looks at the state of programmes, has been around how the doctorate should be approached, what a good research question might look like, what kinds of research methodologies one might develop with respect to different kinds of data, the research frameworks for managing data and so on. One effect of this preoccupation has been the emergence of a debate about whether South Africa should introduce a course-based PhD.[2] Although proposals to this effect have not found general acceptance, there remains a concern about the efficacy of current approaches to doctoral training. These concerns emanate largely, on the one hand, from statistics in the Department of Education that show unsatisfactory completion and time-to-degree rates in South Africa, and, on the other, from persistent critiques about the quality of the training provided by higher education.[3]

Legitimate as the focus is, and indeed must remain, on how to improve the structure, content and format of the doctorate, there is a case to be made for bringing into perspective the question of higher education's exclusionary history. That higher education in South Africa has historically discriminated against people of colour, and even white women, is a matter of not inconsiderable significance. I want to make the argument in this chapter that there is a need to bring into much clearer view the realities of privilege and marginalisation in understanding how doctoral-level preparation is and can be conducted in South Africa. Taking this approach by no means suggests that I am asking for a displacement of the issues raised above, but I want to emphasise how important it is for concerns with marginalisation and exclusion to be incorporated into them. In terms of this, a number of enduring features of the South African higher education landscape are relevant.

The first is coming to terms with the variegated nature of South Africa's higher education landscape. There continues to exist in the postapartheid era universities that are largely white and those that are largely black. Why is this pertinent? The nature of the two kinds of institutions is shaped by histories and practices that have made them quite different institutions. Although the South African government has made extensive efforts to flatten out this landscape, a bifurcated world continues to manifest itself in the ways in which institutions are resourced, managed, the kinds of academic and social cultures that operate inside of them, and the goals and objectives they set for themselves. Although there are historically black institutions that have challenged the historical divide between white and black, the University of the Western Cape, for example, has sought to challenge the presumptive alignment of 'white' with the conceit of quality and 'black' with inferiority; by and large, understandings of what constitutes 'first tier' and 'second tier' are closely tied up with institutions' apartheid legacy positions.

The second feature of this bifurcated environment, one which was avoided when the National Commission for Higher Education considered how the sector should be

117

reformed, is that a particular economy of programme and qualification delivery has come to exist. Historically, white institutions, most tellingly, have assumed for themselves the untouchable mantle of 'world-class-ness', whereas historically black institutions have effectively, for political reasons that are beyond the scope of this chapter, been treated as 'sites of crisis'. Despite this, and the repeated placing of institutions such as the Durban University of Technology and the Universities of Limpopo and Venda under the direct administration of the national Department of Education is a testament to this reality, the government has struggled to work out how it should structurally and formally deal with this racial legacy. The immediate upshot of this history – belying a story of complex racialisation and re-racialisation – is that quality has been appropriated unproblematically as a 'white' preserve. The impact of this on who does what and what counts for anything in the system is complex. For many operating in the system, the consequent effect is to confirm the association of historically privileged institutions in the country as places of 'serious' work. By contrast, a PhD emanating from the historically black institution is almost *ipso facto* a cause for concern. What has happened in the system following these developments is that not a great deal of PhD work has taken place in historically black institutions. Academics in historically black institutions without PhDs have not registered in their home institutions, but have gone to the historically white and advantaged universities. The discussion about doing a PhD and how it might be managed, as a result, has largely been a discussion for the historically advantaged universities. The only historically disadvantaged universities to feature with any kind of presence in these national dialogues have been the Universities of Durban-Westville and the Western Cape.[4] In the former, for example, an influential Dean of Education played a major role in promoting doctoral-level work and quickly raising the level of awareness amongst his members of staff, and in the whole university, of the importance of high-level research and the doctorate. He himself had been a product of a doctoral programme at a premier American research university.

Making the point about the racialised nature of the PhD, consequently and strikingly, the less visible and more sociological dimensions of doctoral study have attracted almost no attention in the South African literature. Apart from the work of Wickham (1999), we know, for example, little about the subject of *graduateness*, and even less about the politics of becoming a graduate in South Africa. Even Wickham's work, it needs to be said, does not broach the question of graduateness as a sociological process.

The specific context of the PhD in education in South Africa

In countries such as the USA it is not uncommon to hear the PhD being described as a 'rite of passage' or as a stepping-off point for those seeking to enter the academy. 'There is no need to see your PhD as your definitive contribution', many advisers tell their students. It is essentially a credential to show that you broadly understand the nature of the debates in your field, know how to frame a research question and can execute a research plan. It is upon this platform, particularly in the social sciences, that they are told that they will build and go on to make their mark in the field. By contrast, not unlike many other countries in the British Commonwealth higher education environment, becoming an academic in Education, especially in the English-speaking South African university, did not routinely require a PhD. Many academics in Education became professors on the strength of a good masters degree. The masters degree, moreover, especially in the English-speaking environment, was regularly a work of a scope and gravity not unlike many doctoral dissertations produced in the current era. As a result, it was not unusual that a professor, as the most senior academic in the department, would have a masters degree only. The achievement of this masters degree and its intellectual weight would have been a major achievement. To illustrate the point, there was a time in the early 1990s in my own School of Education where we had five professors. Three of these professors did not have PhD degrees.[5] Amongst the ranks of the associate professors, of whom there were four, only one had a PhD. That many of these professors were without PhDs did not mean that the academics concerned were lesser scholars. It happened to be the case that they produced work of the best quality.

But there was a sub-text to this situation. As recently as the late 1980s, in contrast to the USA, where the PhD was a requirement – a kind of licence – in the South African setting, the PhD *did*, possibly not explicitly so, constitute a pinnacle moment, a major achievement in one's academic career. One might carry on to produce further work, but having done the PhD was more than just receiving one's licence to enter the ranks of the academic world. It was a marking-off event and denoted the achievement of a very special social status. It is the nature of this status in relation to the particular social dynamics of South Africa that is relevant for this discussion. Why is this so? It is so because often the PhD so acquired would be used as the basis for one's major publication. One's reputation was built on it. But it is also so because getting a PhD in South Africa tended to be a largely white and male preserve. There were very few people of colour, and to a lesser degree, women, who were able to achieve this feat.

A decade and a half later the situation has changed. It is now almost inconceivable that one might ascend to the ranks of the professorship, and in many universities now even that of senior lecturer, without a PhD.[6] The modes of progression in the academic hierarchy at the South African university have changed dramatically. It is the case, as it is now virtually everywhere in higher education, that the North American experience has profoundly reconfigured the image and the ideal of what it means to be an academic. In the field of Education this change has probably lagged behind those of other fields, but the qualification profile of the professoriate is now substantially more top-heavy. PhDs not only abound, but are now also universally expected. Promotion requirements, moreover, have hardened around the PhD. The history of this development, in reshaping the South African university, still needs to be written. Behind it lies a story, there are many, of the entry of South African higher education into a world constituted differently, made up of modes of intellectual deportment and scholarly dispositions that were very different to those from which it traditionally drew its valorisation, credibility and referents for social status. The significance of this moment can be over exaggerated, bringing as it does a switch in the English-speaking South African university from a British allegiance – whether it is in the loaded cachet of an Oxbridge label or, relatively speaking, the new postwar, postclass British pride of a nouveau redbrick Sussex, Warwick or Birmingham T-shirt – to one that now has to accommodate the much more variegated, uneven and even unpredictable valence of an American qualification. Hyperbolise this moment as some might, it takes place sociologically as the entire edifice of whiteness in South Africa begins to be undone (at least legally) with the rapid process of deconstructing racial hegemony, which starts, surprisingly for some, under the aegis of the apartheid government. The point about this is that a kind of democratisation of the PhD takes place at the same time as South African society begins to loosen up. The apartheid government begins the process of relaxing what is called petty-apartheid.

119

It abolishes corner-stone laws, such as the Group Areas Act, the Mixed Marriages Act and a number of other pieces of legislation that prescribed the separation of people of different 'racial' backgrounds. When the African National Congress-led government comes into power in 1994 this legislative apparatus of race is finally abolished. From approximately 1985 universities and schools gradually become more and more open, black people move into white suburbs, and a process of loosening the grip of racial intolerance is set in motion.

The developments that take place during the late 1980s and early 1990s are profound. Over a period of something like 10 years, beginning in 1985 and coming to a climax in 1994, the entire country – formally – moves from being an exclusionary social state to becoming one where inclusion now matters. Critical about this process, however, I argue, is that it is managed as a largely legal process. The administrative rules of governance change. And it is true that these changes have consequences. They bring into spheres of interaction people from significantly different backgrounds. But as these changes happen, strikingly, people receive very little help in how to manage them. Schools are largely left to themselves. Leaders in various sectors of public and private organisations have to work out how they might manage themselves and their spaces of work and engagement. The university is no exception. From being a closed institution, it becomes, not quite over night, but rapidly, a remade space. In the context of this, a number of difficulties arise. In the remainder of this chapter, I look at some of these and focus particularly on those that relate to being a student.

Challenges of being a doctoral student in South Africa

The challenges that South African universities confront, and students experience, are no different in general to those experienced at even the most advantaged institutions in the world. A Task Force set up by the Chicago-based Spencer Foundation in 2007 to look at what a good, rigorous and relevant doctoral programme might look like has suggested that an aspirant doctoral-level researcher will encounter four universes.[7] These universes are presented as an attempt to reorientate the discussion of doctoral work away from the language of competences and skills towards a recognition that doctoral training is not a linear and additive process, but one in which a new identity is forged. This process is rich in challenges and opportunities. The four universes the Task Force has identified are the following: the Universe of Research Frameworks or Paradigms, which consists of social science theories and conceptual frameworks and research methodologies; the Social Universe, consisting of the context in which students will work and which typically is made up of the actual programmes the students attend; the Universe of Educational and Related Substantive Knowledge and Research that the student will encounter in the course of his or her study; and finally the Universe of Professional Development, where the student will encounter scholarly associations, conferences, journal publishing and so on.

The approach taken by the Task Force is that the student has to manage his or her movement through these universes. By bringing the universes into focus, what one is doing is highlighting the complex dialectic of structure and agency that frames the student's passage through his or her studies. Institutions provide opportunities such as courses, internships, research-assistantships and project-work, which seek to model for the student the kind of deportment and disposition that an ideal graduate student ought to develop. It is the responsibility of the student, on the other hand, to navigate and chart a path for him or herself. In this, the student is expected to be alert to opportunities and to make decisions that will optimise his or her experience.

The Universes of Paradigms, Substantive Knowledge and Professional Practice

The Universes of the Framework and Paradigm, Substantive Knowledge and the Professional have come, it can be suggested, to constitute the foci of higher education. It is in these universes that universities in South Africa have tended to operate. They have, as a result, made the challenges of quality the major areas of their engagement. Amongst these challenges the following have been central:

1. Institutional challenges such as the capacity of staff members to supervise and advise students. When institutions began to admit doctoral students in large numbers they first of all had to make sure that their staff members could oversee high-level student research. Two problems presented themselves with respect to this. First, the situation continued to exist that significant numbers of staff-members did not themselves have PhDs. Although some institutions overlooked this matter and allowed staff members with only masters degrees to supervise doctoral students, in a number of institutions, such as the Universities of Cape Town and the Western Cape, this was permitted only by exception. At institutions such as the University of Cape Town, to supervise, the rule was introduced, one had to have completed and been awarded a doctorate. This is now largely the practice in most institutions. The second problem related to experience. Not many members of staff, even those with PhDs, had supervised at this level. Universities such as the Universities of Durban-Westville, the Witwatersrand, Cape Town and KwaZulu-Natal put in place a number of mechanisms to deal with this. In some, such as the University of Cape Town, inexperienced staff members were placed on US-style doctoral committees where they assumed secondary responsibilities for the supervision process. A similar arrangement was made by pairing them with a mentor. In a number of institutions around the country supervision workshops were instituted. These were also promoted by large funding bodies such as the National Research Foundation.

2. Funding challenges that inhibited the capacity of an institution to enrol students on a full-time basis. Many institutions did not have earmarked funds for supporting doctoral work. At the national level, this situation was attended to in two ways. First, organisations such as the NRF began making available sizeable sums of money to supervisors who had research grants to distribute as bursaries to their students. Institutions themselves have undertaken fund-raising initiatives from which have come extremely generous streams of funding. Major examples have been the Mellon, Spencer and Rockefeller Foundations. The Spencer Foundation has been especially important for education. In 1999 it included a consortium of South African universities, including the Universities of Cape Town, Durban-Westville, Natal, Western Cape and the Witwatersrand, in its Research Training Grant (RTG) programme – the only non-US-based programmes. The RTG programme was immensely important. It not only kick-started large-scale doctoral level work, but also brought the South African universities into a 10-year long conversation with their US-based counterparts about the doctoral process. The

121

highlight of this relationship was a large colloquium at the University of Cape Town in 2001 around the doctoral degree. Participants in the colloquium included all the RTG partner universities and students from the South African universities. Since then, South African doctoral students and their supervisors have participated in regular Spencer Foundation sponsored forums such as special workshops at the American Educational Research Association annual meeting. The National Research Foundation has since developed similar initiatives. It has since 2007 held a regular doctoral conference. Important gains have developed out of these relationships. It still is true, however, that large numbers of students drop-out because of financial difficulties.

3. The under preparation of students for doing doctoral-level work. Many institutions found that the students either did not have the required research-training or the disciplinary background to be able to carry out the level of research that was required. The students, as a result, struggled through the process of developing a proposal and continued to carry particular kinds of shortcomings into their fieldwork and then finally the writing up of their empirical results. Responses of institutions to this situation have been varied, but have broadly sought to explore how they might address the students through the demands posed by working in the three Universes of the Paradigm, Substantive Knowledge and Professional Development. With respect to students' disciplinary knowledge, extensive efforts have been made to build students' capacities. The RTG institutions in South Africa introduced an annual Spencer Research Colloquium. This colloquium gave students the opportunity to present their work and to get extensive feedback from a wide range of faculty members and also from their fellow-students. Against the recognition that many students enter doctoral-level programmes without the appropriate sociological, psychological and educational theory backgrounds, students were offered high-level input from specialists. Over the course of many years, a number of American professors regularly visited South Africa to teach. In addition to the structured initiatives of the Doctoral Consortium, a number of institutions, where their students are insufficiently prepared, have required they register for masters level courses in those areas. On occasion, they have also been required to do undergraduate courses in the areas where they have manifested particular needs. Less satisfactorily, many have placed their students on reading programmes. Although these have provided students with an introduction to the languages and concepts of the issues they are looking at, it has often been the case that the students continue to struggle.

The situation with respect to research methodologies has seen similar initiatives being undertaken. In some institutions students were required to obtain a masters level research methods credit, whereas in others, a wide variety of tailormade courses (not for credit) were developed for them. These courses were presented by visiting foreign-based lecturers or were developed by groups of experienced academics in the country. In a number of institutions, such as the Universities of the Witwatersrand, Cape Town and Pretoria, a doctoral seminar was instituted where students both received and made inputs. They received support from technical experts on how to write literature reviews, how to develop conceptual frameworks, how to conduct observations, how to design questionnaires, how to manage databases, how to run statistical analyses and so on. They themselves often presented work-in-progress in seminars attended by their peers and lecturers. In a few places students were included in large research projects and given the opportunity of participating in the design, establishment and operationalisation of a particular line of enquiry.

The significance of outlining these challenges and the initiatives undertaken to deal with them is to make clear that South African supervisors have had, and continue, to deal with the challenge of working out how best to meet the needs of their individual students. In the process they have learnt a great deal. Although it would be difficult to state unambiguously that the quality of PhD programmes has improved as a result of the work of higher education institutions over the last 10–15 years, it is true that some institutions are now much more conscious of what the character and nature of a good doctoral programme ought to be.

The Social Universe

In working with the notion of Universes, the Spencer Task Force came to understand that the experiences defined in each were not self-contained. Working in the realm of paradigms and frameworks, for example, raised questions for students and faculty that became relevant in the Substantive and the Professional Universes. The Universes, therefore, overlapped each other. In their totality they constituted a whole social experience. Students, as a consequence, were being acculturated and socialised into the world of the advanced researcher. They saw and imbibed how their supervisors and mentors carried themselves, how they managed the demands of initiating, establishing and bringing to a conclusion a research problem. They were, as a result, made aware of the social, cultural and regulatory modes of the research world. But the rules of the academic game with all its hidden codes, its disciplinary conventions and the overlay of the country's racial and class political economy were never explicitly explained. Problems, as a result, continued to arise, especially for students of colour. What constituted appropriate behaviour and what made it likely that one would be accepted as an insider were never issues that were openly addressed. The example is extreme, but it was likely that these kinds of ambivalences and uncertainties were present in the tragic attack by a recent black doctoral graduate in mathematics on his white professor at the University of Cape Town. A recent stint of duty I had as Chairperson of a Ministerial Committee for the Minister of Education on Transformation in Higher Education also revealed a pervasive sense of dissatisfaction amongst both graduate and undergraduate students of colour about their status in historically advantaged universities.

In terms of the discussion above it is clear that discomfort continues amongst students of colour. This discomfort manifests itself in the following ways:

- disorientation
- dissonance, and, most critically
- alienation.

Disorientation: Many students of colour, especially if they have not had previous experience of the former advantaged higher education institution, struggle to navigate their way through the physical, emotional and administrative space of the university. They arrive on campuses and generally do not have access to the kinds of orientation programmes that are lain on for undergraduate students. Occasionally, such as the University of Cape Town, graduate students associations arrange meetings where graduate

issues are discussed but a systematic orientation to the university is not routinely provided. The experience is for the most part an extremely difficult one for many students. One of my students spoke of being in a state of trauma for several weeks when she first arrived at the University of Cape Town from a neighbouring southern African country. She had not been sufficiently prepared for the difference of the city and the university. Unlike her previous university, the University was decentralised with campuses and administrative facilities located in several different parts of the University. Not only did she find herself being shunted from one office to the next, but she also had to deal with the difficulty of finding accommodation, seeing her financial resources drain away and depending completely on random people for providing her with the kind of information she needed.

The first encounter of students such as these with the physical space of the university is an unnerving one. For many, fear and anxiety accompany their learning of the routeways into the university. Strangers in an environment they don't yet perceive as their own, they begin their lives as doctoral candidates struggling to find their balance.

Dissonance: A sense of dissonance is experienced by many students coming to the historically advantaged university, even those who come with the kind of cultural capital that the university recognises. At the heart of this sense of dissonance is a clash of cultures. For students who come from socially and economically disadvantaged backgrounds this dissonance, which can often be productive in the sense that it forces them to deal with the issues, becomes attached to them. They become aware of how little their own social and cultural universes, in which they might have even held positions of high status, count in the new space of the university. How to carry oneself, how to approach people in authority, when to speak, the modes of discourse, and many more, are all experienced in terms of subordination. Problems arise when this dissonance fails to convert or translate into productive self-reflection. When it is productive, the student consciously appraises his or her situation and begins to recognise that the dissonance between what is brought into the context and what is found there need not position him or her in a state of fixed subordination. In this context, dissonance is an opportunity for important new insights into how the intellectual space of the university works and can be analysed. The productive engagement produces an awareness of identity as being legitimately multiple. A student can feel a sense of belonging in more than one space without having to abjure or deny any part of it. Optimally, it produces the ability inside of the student to look critically on all the social and cultural spaces he or she inhabits. In these terms dissonance is embraced. Relevant are the issues raised in Soudien (2008) and Jacobs (2005; 2007). Although Jacobs (2007: 21), for example, is talking about black lecturers in a largely white environment, her observations apply to doctoral students, too:

> lecturers needed to work within their disciplinary discourse communities, while simultaneously having a critical overview of this 'insider' role, from outside of it. The study found that it was through engaging with academic development practitioners, who were 'outsiders' to their disciplinary discourses, that lecturers found themselves at the margins of their own fields, and were able to view themselves as insiders from the outside, as it were.

Often, however, a student experiencing dissonance is unable to convert it into an intellectually and cognitively productive process. Students in this situation are unable to assimilate the contraries they see and experience, and so only experience the university as a space that is intolerant of them and their ways of managing their lives. Students in this situation become resentful. In a recent meeting with students at a prominent historically advantaged English-speaking university, students told me that they felt proud to have been admitted into the university but even prouder that they had survived it. The university is for them a lost opportunity.

Alienation: Those students who find themselves in the group described above go through their entire university experience never feeling 'at home'. The point has been made by scholars such as Thaver (2006) that the institutional culture of the historically advantaged institution is of such a nature that many students never reach the point where they are able to identify with the university and what it stands for. They resent what is taught, how it is taught and by whom it is taught. In these contexts the entire process is experienced as a deep racial assault. The conflation of colour with worth and value seems to be a lesson that is hard to evade. Students such as these might survive the process of study to which they have committed themselves, but they feel no loyalty to the institution. Although this experience is not that through which the majority go, it certainly is prevalent. A number of students made direct complaints to me about the persistent sense of discrimination they felt at the university. In making sense of this, it is clear that this experience presents itself as a distinctly South African one given the particular dynamics of the South African university. In the American university black students have found the kind of voice in many institutions that allows them to engage with it. In the South African situation, interestingly, this voice has not arisen and a process of dialogue around it has failed to materialise. This is the case, I suggest, because the academy continues to present itself as a race-blind space when in fact all its codes, whether they are presented in the register of the academic, the social or the cultural, take their legitimacy and currency from the country's racial-class history. Its socio-cultural referents are closely tied up with wider experiences of privilege and marginalisation in society. These never became the objects of inspection with the consequence that how inclusion and exclusion actually work are never made the subject of any kind of scrutiny. Alienation from the institution results. The kind of doctoral experience that students such as these have is marked by resentment.

Conclusion

Many universities in South Africa have clearly made major strides in developing their capacity to deliver the PhD. This is evident in the increasing number of students who are registering and earning doctorates. But the quality of their experience is weakened precisely because the major legacy issues of race have been inadequately addressed. The capacity of many students grows. They learn, despite the circumstances in which they find themselves, and many have become adept in the world of knowledge production and in the market of ideas. Hesitancies remain with many, however, not developing a sense of ease and at-homeness because the university is inhospitable to them. The consequences for the higher education enterprise in the country are tragic. They are tragic because the university continues to define itself, by and large and essentially, in terms of an unproblematised and a taken-for-granted symbolic order. Central to this symbolic order are uninspected assumptions around whiteness and blackness. What is lost, I suggest, is the opportunity for the university to reimagine itself. In failing to provide a space for students who are not traditionally associated with the university, the opportunity is

125

foregone for exploring how the value of difference that the new students constitute can catalyse and lead to new ways of working with even old questions.

Notes

1 'Ease' can be misunderstood here given the extent to which the cognitive dissonance of high-level intellectual work by its very nature involves questions of power and authority and the redistribution of these in contexts such as the academy. The point is, of course, that it is rare for the process of studentship to be without its transitional/adaptational dynamics. Even the most socially, economically and culturally advantaged students go through intense moments and even periods of alienation, loss of self-confidence and even feelings of worthlessness. In comparison to people from historically and experientially disadvantaged backgrounds it is their social location, however, that is important to emphasise here, given the different kinds of capitals on which they can draw to mitigate the most disempowering elements of the adviser/advisee relationship.

2 The backwash effects of these developments have been profound on schools and faculties of education in South Africa. The effects have been most pronounced in the debates about the relationship between theory and practice and what, if PhD training is to enter the range of teaching that staff members do, the academic emphasis and orientation of the School of Education ought to be.

3 These have been articulated at both formal and informal forums of South African academics. The South African National Research Foundation (NRF), for example, has instituted an annual doctoral conference. This conference was first held in 2007. At the same time, key institutions in the country, such as the University of Pretoria, and a consortium of Western Cape-based universities, have established annual graduate conferences particularly to provide doctoral candidates an opportunity to expose their work to a wider critical audience. In this chapter, I base much of my discussion on the experience of working in the Spencer Foundation Doctoral Consortium, in which I played a leading role.

4 I am very aware, of course, of the contentious nature of what I am saying. The problem, however, is that these issues, like many dealing with advantage and disadvantage, have not been systematically considered in the South African setting.

5 When I became tenured at my university, after serving a period of probation of three years, my Dean enquired where I intended taking my research and upon hearing that I wished to complete a PhD said to me that that was not entirely necessary for my career.

6 The rank of senior lecturer is the median status for an academic member of staff in higher education in South Africa.

7 This Task Force will report in the course of 2009. The report is, for the meanwhile, not available for referencing.

References

Bailey, T. (2001) *The PhD Degree: An Investigation into Doctoral Education in South Africa and International PhD Reform Initiatives*. Unpublished PhD. Pretoria: University of South Africa.

Hofstee, E. (2006) *Constructing a Good Dissertation: A Practical Guide to Finishing a Masters, MB or PhD on Schedule*. Sandton, Johannesburg: EPE Publishers.

Jacobs, C. (2005) On Being an Insider on the Outside: New Spaces for Integrating Academic Literacies, *Teaching in Higher Education*, 10(4): 475–87.

——(2007) Teaching Explicitly That Which is Tacit – The Challenge of Disciplinary Discourses, *For Engineering and Science Educators*, 11: 21–5.

Mouton, J. (2001) *How To Succeed in Your Masters and Doctoral Studies. A South African Resource and Guide Book*. Pretoria: Van Schaik Publishers.

Soudien, C. (2008) The Intersection of Race and Class in the South African University: Student Experiences, *South African Journal of Higher Education*, 22(3): 662–78.

Szanton, D and Manyika, S. (2002) *PhD Programmes in African Universities: Current Status and Future Prospects.* Berkeley, CA: University of California Press.

Thaver, L. (2006) 'At home': Institutional Culture and Higher Education: Some Methodological Considerations, *Perspectives in Education*, 24(1): 15–26.

Wickham, S. (1999) *Towards a Postgraduate Identity: Guidelines for M and PhD Supervisors and their Students. Workbook.* Unpublished paper of the Research and Academic Development Unit, South Africa.

11

Weaving the threads of doctoral research journeys

J. Wellington

This chapter takes a holistic view of the entire process of a student's journey through his/her research study, written from the perspective and observations of an experienced supervisor and doctoral examiner. The chapter argues that it is not a clean, seamless process but a cyclical, sometimes messy business – and that this is inevitable. I look at the traditional structure for a dissertation, which suggests that the research pathway is a straightforward one. In reality, creating and presenting a coherent story of research is more about weaving the threads of the different aspects of the research, rather than pretending that the process was a smooth linear one. These various threads need to be recognised and linked together at different stages of the journey, from proposal to viva, and, perhaps in future, publishing.

Threads? What threads?

Practical and personal threads

Some of the threads in any research project are very practical in nature. For example:

- Time constraints: every person doing research has a finite amount of time to complete their work
- Gaining access to the people the doctoral researcher needs or to the documents they require; we would all like to gain access to the ideal research participants or the 'key informants' (Wellington 2000) in our field of research. In the real world, this is never possible. Compromise is nearly always necessary
- Sampling: similarly, we would all like to base our findings and discussion on the 'perfect sample'. For the two reasons above (time and access), with the additional issue of money to collect data, this is never possible.

Some of the threads in any research project are about the people involved in it:

- The first key thread is the doctoral researcher – the key factor in any research study. It is vital to reflect on one's own position as far as it influences what was done, how it was done and how data are to be interpreted. This reflection on oneself as a key 'thread' is known as refleXivity (I have capitalised the X to highlight that the X in this aspect is the doctoral research designer, creator and executioner)

- Reflectivity: this is broader than reflexivity because it involves reflection on the entire process. It is the essential activity of reflecting on all threads of the research and trying to weave them together. This is the cornerstone of research in education and the social sciences, and most of this chapter is about being reflective. This includes the next thread: ethics

- Ethical issues: these occur with any research project involving people as participants, whether as objects or subjects of research. It is also important if documents such as letters, reports or minutes of meetings are being studied – people wrote these so they need to be analysed, discussed and written about in an ethical way. Ethics comes in at every stage: planning, doing and writing up research.

The three '-ologies'

As well as some of the practical threads above, perhaps the three main threads or pillars in any research project are what I call the three '-ologies': epistemology, ontology and methodology. All three are closely linked. The main questions they raise are: What is the researcher claiming and on what basis is he/she making that claim? In other words, 'how does one know?' And what methods were used to come to this position?

In simple terms, the three pillars can be summed up as:

- Epistemology: this is literally the study of knowledge. Broadly, epistemology as a field of study involves huge philosophical questions about what knowledge is and how we can know anything. For the purposes of a specific research study it involves such questions as: What does the doctoral researcher claim to 'know' or to have found out? What is their contribution to knowledge in this field? (which I discuss more fully later). How do they 'know' this?

- Ontology: this is related to both the other -ologies, but in general it concerns the nature of reality and existence: What does the researcher believe exists? Is there such a thing as an external reality? In the context of educational research it might involve questions about, for example, 'race' or racism, disability, social class or causality. Is there such a thing as 'race' or racism? Can we attribute cause and effect to certain situations?

- Methodology: this is very much the study of methods: what did the researcher do? Why did they do what they did? Why this approach? Why these methods and not others? This third pillar is so important to any individual research project that we now elaborate further (a helpful discussion of the E and O words is given in Thomas 2009: 83–5).

Methodology: a constant thread

Methodology is defined by the *Shorter Oxford English Dictionary* as the 'science of method' or more historically as 'treatise on method'. My own interpretation of methodology is: the activity or business of choosing, reflecting upon, evaluating and justifying the methods you use. Indeed, the latter is an essential feature of any written report or research thesis, i.e. justifying the decisions we have made on methods. This process of reflection and justification needs to happen before, during and after their research – and during their viva.

No one can assess or judge the value of a piece of research without knowing its methodology. Table 11.1 summarises some of the key aspects of methodology in educational research.

Matching methods to questions

Framing research questions should always be the first step in the doctoral research process. Unfortunately, one of the hardest things to do is to formulate questions that make sense and are actually, in some sense, answerable.

It should always be a case of questions first, methods later. For example, it makes no sense to decide: 'I am going to use questionnaires/interviews/observations' before clarifying the questions that you wish to address or shed light upon. They may be what, which, where, how or why questions. The former may imply a straightforward collection of information, perhaps a survey approach. But the latter, i.e. the how and why questions that seek *explanations*, will demand more in-depth exploratory approaches, e.g. a detailed case study.

I suggest (for the early, planning stages of research) a 'horses for courses' matrix. This is shown in Table 11.2.

Once the research questions have been formulated down the left of the matrix, the appropriate methods can be decided upon along the right. Some research questions might demand several methods, others only one. These are decisions that need to be made in the planning stages, but, given the complexity of educational research, will need to be reviewed and revised in the light of other difficult decisions, e.g. gaining access, as mentioned earlier.

Table 11.1 Key aspects of methodology

Thinking about methods, reflecting on them, evaluating them, assessing data…
Why did the researcher use these methods?
What was the quality of the data they gave the researcher?
Can one learn lessons, or perhaps 'generalise' from the data?
How could a sample have been better?
Could, or should, other methods have been used? Why?
How did the researcher affect the data collected?

Table 11.2 A questions-methods matrix (horses for courses)

Research methods	Questionnaire	Interview	Observation	Follow-up interviews	Document analysis	etc…
Research questions						
1						
2						
3						

In summary: threads to be woven by the doctoral researcher

Another way of portraying what really happens in educational research is shown in Figure 11.1. This shows the difficult decisions that have to be made in real research. They cannot always be made in the ideal order. For example, we may plan to interview a certain sample of people, e.g. teachers, students, only to find that we cannot gain access to them, they are unwilling, too busy, too sensitive or just fed up with 'being researched'. This may, in turn, force us back to reconsider our methods and even our original research questions. All the decisions are intertwined and connected by arrows going both ways. Even constraints on the way the research must be presented, e.g. in the form of a book or thesis that is written *and* in the public domain, can impinge on decisions about who to involve in the research and which methods to use.

A rather messy Figure 11.1 is an attempt to represent the difficult and interconnected threads that go into the *actual* design of an educational research project, as opposed to the idealised version.

The hardest part? Choosing and refining the research topic

Choosing a doctoral topic – what does each researcher want to do and why?

Deciding on exactly what one wants a doctoral dissertation to be about is never an easy task; the subsequent activity of refining that topic to make it do-able is equally hard.

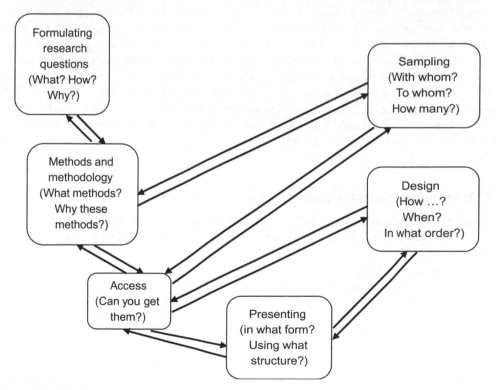

Figure 11.1 Difficult and interconnected decisions in educational research.

(And part of that process will be developing clear research questions as discussed above.) In the arts, humanities and social sciences it is probably true that a student has more of a free rein than in engineering or science. A student will often choose a topic that is related to their own individual or professional interests (especially for a professional doctorate), perhaps an area that interested them as an undergraduate or even one that is 'dear to their heart' for more personal, life history or emotional reasons. So, to some extent, they have greater freedom of choice than, for example, a science student who will have to work within one of the research paradigms of the department and within the constraints of the department's resources and equipment. In other situations, in any discipline, students may be sponsored by a research council or funded by an employer, their own institution or their government and such sponsors will undoubtedly require a say or a larger stake in what goes on. Thus, few students will have complete freedom of choice; they will also be dependent on the expertise and interests of the staff who are likely to supervise them and this will involve a lot of important, mutual discussion from both supervisor and student about how the area of study is to be shaped and focused.

Deciding on a research plan and writing a research proposal

One of the earliest, but unfortunately the hardest, tasks is to make plans and to write a clear research proposal. To a large extent, students have to do this at a very early stage in order to apply for and be accepted onto a research degree programme. This is especially true for the MPhil/PhD; whereas, in contrast, for many professional doctorates the job of writing a research proposal may be the final written assignment in the 'taught' element. It would be unfair to make one of the admission criteria for a PhD the production of a perfectly formed research proposal, with clearly formulated research questions, stating exactly what is to be done and when, how data are to be collected and analysed, which ethical issues will arise, what the literature base will be, and how the study will make a contribution to knowledge in the field. Those may well be the criteria for a finished dissertation, but real world research is far too unpredictable and 'messy' for the perfectly polished proposal to be an admission requirement. My view is that the research proposal at the admission stage should show potential or 'mileage' and admit that certain aspects of the study, e.g. gaining access to informants, deciding on the sample, will have to be determined as part of the process.

What should a research plan or proposal contain?

I suggest that the initial proposal should address, at least, the following 12 questions; many of these relate to the questions often posed during a viva, which I discuss later.

1.   What is the provisional title?
2.   What area/field am I investigating or working in?
3.   Why is this topic or area important? Why have I decided to study this?
4.   What are my main research questions? Where do or did these 'come' from?
5.   What has been done in this area already? (an outline, at least, of the likely literatures)
6.   What is the context for the study? (global, national, institutional, personal)
7.   What theory/theories/theoretical framework can I draw upon?
8.   What is the proposed methodology? Why? And which specific methods are likely to be used? Why these and not others?

9. For an empirical study, how will the sample be determined?
10. What issues are likely to emerge around: (a) access, and (b) ethics, in the course of the research?
11. How will data be analysed (whether primary or secondary data)?
12. What timescale, approximately, will I try to follow – and is it humanly possible?

And finally, one needs to ask: How many doctorates am I writing? The answer to this question should be one!

Criteria for reflecting on doctoral research plans or dissertation proposal

The criteria below are based on my own experiences of looking at thesis proposals, and also comments made by staff at different universities. The criteria have been grouped fairly arbitrarily into categories. Clearly these categories link and overlap. The criteria are biased towards empirical studies, i.e. where the student is going to do some fieldwork.

My experience is that proposals are often said to be 'good' or strong if they have most of the characteristics shown as 'strong' under the five aspects or threads; or as 'needing more work' if they have the features listed in the third column in Table 11.3.

Focusing the research, making it do-able

No research proposal can be perfectly polished or focused at the outset. Indeed, the main purpose of the early stages of supervision is for the student to work with her supervisor on achieving more focus, improving the research design, and not least, making it do-able.

Table 11.3 Criteria for reflecting on research plans

Aspect or thread	Strong proposals	Needing more work...
1. Research questions (RQs)	Clearly spelt out and focused; the terms are defined; they are answerable; the project is 'do-able'	RQs are too general; they just cannot be answered; the terms are not clearly defined; they are too ambitious, wide ranging or over optimistic
2. Methodology	Appropriate for the RQs; access and ethics have been considered; there is some idea of how the data are to be analysed	It is not clear what will be done or why; plans are not clear; not clear how the planned methods relate to the RQs or are appropriate for them
3. Summary of the literature base	Proposed study is set in its historical and methodological context; comprehensive coverage; critical review	Too descriptive (not critical); the social, geographical or historical context for this study is not clear
4. Theoretical framework/ conceptual base	Shows theoretical clarity; the RQS are located in a theoretical framework	No or little theoretical framework; key terms are not defined or discussed (see 1 above)
5. General issues	Has the potential to make a contribution to the field; has potential 'mileage', currency or scope	Not clear how it would add or contribute (either through its methods/process or product)

This is a large job and will take time – in many cases, a clearer focus may not even emerge until after the student has started empirical work and begun to see what can or cannot be done in 'the field'. It is a constant process of thinking, refining, going back, checking and sometimes guessing. As the Nobel Prize-winning scientist, Sir Peter Medawar, described it, scientific method is a 'mixture of guesswork and checkwork' (Medawar 1963; 1976).

In short, the research process is not linear, but cyclical or iterative.

Producing the written dissertation: weaving the threads and creating coherence, articulation and linkage

When one reads a completed dissertation, its presentation makes the research journey look remarkably clear. In reality, as I have suggested, appearances are deceptive. Doing a coherent research study is more like piecing together a patchwork quilt than forming a neatly woven fabric. In producing a written dissertation, the researcher's task is to create coherence, articulation and linkage.

The traditional structure for a dissertation

The traditional structure for a dissertation makes the process look more like a flow chart than perhaps a truer portrayal such as a spider's web. As Medawar (1963) might have said, the traditional dissertation is a fraud.

There is no fixed or set way in which a dissertation should be structured. Presentation, ordering of contents and chapter headings can vary enormously, depending on all sorts of factors. However, I do find from experience that many written theses do follow some kind of pattern. This is shown in the Table 11.4, which often goes as far as being translated into chapter headings along these lines.

There are ways of deviating from this 'norm' and of presenting a dissertation in a totally different format, many of which will be acceptable. These are always interesting and often creative, but I still feel that it is important to have a conventional framework in mind that one can deviate from! Again, these are issues that will need to be discussed with a supervisor(s), bearing in mind who the examiners are likely to be and how they will receive a dissertation that does not follow a traditional framework. For a much fuller discussion of these important decisions on how to present and structure your thesis, see Wellington *et al.* (2005).

What makes a good thesis?

My informal discussions with colleagues, examiners and supervisors over a long period have shaped my own, personal views. In general, my perception of a good dissertation is that it should have the following characteristics:

- It should be clear what the thesis is about and what its contribution is
- It should not be over ambitious, either in making exaggerated claims for its contribution or raising the reader's expectations too highly and unrealistically, i.e. it does what it says it is going to do (in modern advertising parlance, one could say 'it does what it says on the tin')

Table 11.4 The traditional structure for a dissertation

Abstract	e.g. What you did; Why it is important; How you did it
	Key findings
Introduction	e.g. Main aims; Key research questions
	Scene-setting/the context of the study
	A 'map' for the reader
Literature review	e.g. Main areas covered: why these, why not others
	Links with other parts of the dissertation
	Theoretical frameworks used and why these
Methodology and methods	Research design and approach
	Which methods? Why these?
	The sample; gaining access (if an empirical study)
	Ethical issues
Results/findings/analysis	Analysis approach and technique
	Theoretical frameworks used
Discussion and evaluation	Reflection on both findings and methods
	Relation to existing literature
Conclusions and recommendations	Contributions
	Limitations
	What are the implications of the work?
	Ideas for further research
Appendices	e.g. Interview schedule; Detailed tables of data
	Ethical procedures
References/bibliography	Full list of all sources cited above

- A wide range of relevant literature is critically discussed
- It is well structured, signposted and clear to follow; the different parts of the thesis link together and 'knit well' to make a coherent whole
- The researcher has managed to link his/her work to the work of others
- Methods and methodology (including ethical issues) are deliberated upon before discussion of the researcher's own empirical work
- The researcher is honest and open about the methods used, and why, and reflects on methods and methodology after presenting and discussing her/his own work
- Some attempt is made to draw out implications; lessons that can be learned are made explicit, i.e. implications for policy makers or practitioners, or both, are drawn out
- Limitations of the study are discussed (without being too apologetic) and areas for further research are suggested.

Perhaps the main criteria for me are to do with *linkage and articulation* of the various parts. In other words, the data collection is linked to the research questions, the theoretical discussions and the literature review, i.e. the empirical work is closely linked to the theoretical work; the data are fully used and connected to the rest of the dissertation (the student has not been guilty of 'over collecting and under analysing' or not fully discussing her or his data).

Weaving the threads towards the ultimate goal: 'doctorateness'

'Doctorateness' is sometimes seen as the Holy Grail; it is occasionally left largely undefined and tacit. My view is that this attitude is not helpful to the student. We can and should look at the tangible products of the doctorate: the written dissertation and the viva. We should unpack and discuss the key notions of coherence, clarity, criticality, contribution and 'originality'.

What is the purpose of a doctorate?

Personal goals

One way of looking at doctorateness and what it means is to take a teleological approach, i.e. to consider what it is for – what is its purpose? My own research with a colleague (Wellington and Sikes 2006) has revealed that students have a vast range of motivations for undertaking a doctorate. Some reasons may be *intrinsic* and very personal, for example: 'I wanted to prove to myself that I could reach the highest level'. Intrinsic motivations can also relate to personal curiosity and interest or the challenge that doctoral work poses. Equally, motivations can be *extrinsic* and related to factors outside of the student's intrinsic desires and goals. For example, some see it as a 'ticket' to either a job or to promotion if they are already employed; some see it as a means to improving their kudos and standing, perhaps in their own work setting or even their home context.

Process versus product

Another useful distinction when considering the nature of a doctorate is to ask: Is it largely about *process*, i.e. personal development, preparing a person for a career, giving personal satisfaction and pride? Or is the doctorate mainly concerned with its *product*, i.e. a body of knowledge, adding to existing work? This could be seen as a tension – between process and product. In reality, many doctorates are concerned with both.

These issues are particularly relevant during the examination process, i.e. the written dissertation and the viva voce. In the viva (which I consider later), there really should be questions about both areas: to what extent was the doctoral journey a vehicle for personal development, learning and growth; and to what extent is it a contribution to the body of knowledge in an area of study?

'Doctorateness': what do written regulations say?

One important way in which we can explore how people perceive and articulate doctorateness is by looking at written regulations. All universities that offer, and therefore examine, research degrees will have documents with titles such as: 'Guidelines for examiners of candidates for ...', or 'Notes for the guidance of research students, supervisors and examiners ...'. Having been external examiner for research degrees at a number of these institutions, I have collected an extensive sample of such documents. It is a valuable exercise to pick out some of the key terms, criteria and descriptors that are written in them.

Here is a sample from my collection of key phrases and expressions relating to doctorateness:

- Addition to knowledge
- Shows evidence of systematic study and the ability to relate the results of the such study to the general body of knowledge in the subject

- The thesis should be a demonstrably coherent body of work
- Shows evidence of adequate industry and application
- Understands the relationship of the special theme of the thesis to a wider field of knowledge
- Represents a significant contribution to learning, for example, through the discovery of new knowledge, the connection of previously unrelated facts, the development of new theory or the revision of older views
- Competence in appropriate methods of performance and recording of research
- The dissertation is clearly written
- Original work.

This difficult word: originality

The word 'originality', like many words including 'criticality', is one that is widely used in this context, but (again like many) has a range of meanings, few of which are shared perhaps. The key question is: What forms can an 'original contribution' take in a doctoral thesis? A range of authors have written on this – I attempt below to provide my own summary of the different meanings given to the term 'originality' in regulations, handbooks, documents, discussions and vivas. I have grouped them, arbitrarily, into eight categories:

1. Building New Knowledge: wall metaphors abound here, for example, building on or extending previous work, putting a new brick in the wall, plugging a perceived gap in the wall
2. Using Original Processes or Approaches: for example, new methods or techniques applied to an existing area of study or to a new area ...
3. Making New Syntheses: for example, of methods or methodologies; connecting previous studies connecting/linking/juxtaposing existing theories; linking two or more previous thinkers
4. Charting or Mapping New Territory: opening up new areas (e.g. that were taboo) or neglected areas; clearing the conceptual undergrowth to make way for further thinking or empirical work
5. Drawing Out New Implications: for practice and practitioners, policy and policy makers, or theory and theorists
6. Revisiting a Recurrent Issue or Debate: bringing either new evidence, new thinking or new theory to bear on an 'old chestnut' or a recurring issue
7. Replicating or Reproducing Existing Work: for example, replicating work from elsewhere in a new geographical context; replicating in a new time context; reproducing or replicating existing work with a different sample
8. New Presentation: new ways of writing, presenting, disseminating.

The key factor is how the qualities of a thesis are judged in reality, i.e. how the examiners judge whether they are present in the written and oral parts of the examination. By their deeds they shall be known – not by the written regulations of the university they are examining in, either as externals or internals. How do they interpret these criteria and judge their presence or absence?

My personal view is that the key word is 'contribution', without the complication of the adjective 'original' or even publishable. The key criteria would then be: Does the doctoral project have a thesis in the sense of a position and an argument? Has the study made a contribution to the field? Has it built on previous arguments and research literature and pushed the issue forward a little or added to it? Does it provide another brick in the wall? Will this contribution potentially make an impact – or bring about a change – on thinking and theory, policy or practice?

The viva voce – 'live voice'

All of the above questions should be considered in the crucial event: viva voce. In other words, a good viva should discuss all the threads and how they come together. Many of the questions asked are remarkably similar to the elements presented above in considering a research proposal.

Below, I present a list based on my own experience of conducting vivas either as an internal or external examiner, of the questions that are most likely to be asked. I offer no guarantees that they will be asked of course! (Most vivas have their unpredictable moments.)

Questions that might be asked in a viva for a doctorate

General

Motivation: What made you do this piece of research? Why did you choose this topic? Why do you think it is important?

Position

What is your own position (professional or personal) in relation to this field and these research questions? What prior conceptions and/or experiences did you bring to this study? How did your own position/background/bias affect your data analysis and your data collection?

Contribution

Please could you summarise your thesis. What are the main findings of your research? What would somebody from this field learn from reading your thesis that they didn't know before? What did you learn from doing it? What original contribution to knowledge do you feel that you have made?

Publication

Which elements of your work do you feel are worthy of publication and/or presentation at a conference? What plans do you have for publication and dissemination?

Research questions

What are the main research questions that you were trying to address in your work? What was the origin of these questions?

Theories and theoretical frameworks

What theories/theoretical frameworks have you drawn upon in your research? Which theories did your study illuminate, if any?

Literature Review

What shaped or guided your literature review? Why did it cover the areas that it did? (And not others?)

On methodology and analysis of data

Why did you employ the methods you used? Why not others, e.g. X? What informed your choice of methods? What would you do differently, with hindsight? What ethical issues did your study raise? How did you deal with them?

The Sample: Why did you select this sample? Can you see any problems with it? If it is a small-scale study, can you justify why so few were involved? (Note that these questions would only apply with certain types of research.)

Data analysis: Did anything surprise you in the data ('hit you in the face')? Any anomalies? How did you analyse your data? How did you categorise/filter the data? Did themes emerge from your data (a posteriori) or did you 'bring them to the data' (a priori)? Why did you analyse it in this way? Could it have been done in another way?

Further work: Which aspects of the work could be taken further? How?

Generalisability and key messages

How far do think you can generalise from your work? What lessons can be learnt from it by practitioners/policy makers/other researchers? What are its key messages and implications?

Reflection

Reflections on the thesis: What are its strengths? And its limitations or weaknesses? Is there anything else you would like to say or discuss that we have not asked you about?

Please note that all these questions relate to the points presented above on 'what makes a good thesis'.

The final step – publishing and spreading the word

I have heard it said that if research is worth doing then it is worth disseminating; I have also heard this expressed in stronger terms: it is unethical to do research, especially if it involves the time and effort of participants, and not disseminate their 'voices' and your findings to a wider audience (who may be practitioners, policy makers, theorists, or even all three).

What should a researcher do with her thesis after a successful viva? For many students, there can be a feeling of anti-climax after finishing the dissertation and submitting it. This can be felt even more deeply after the viva is over and any necessary rewriting has been completed. One possible antidote to this is to consider producing either one or more conference papers or journal articles from it, or possibly a book with a commercial publisher – after all, two of the key criteria for the award of a doctorate are that it should make a contribution to knowledge in an area, and that at least some of it should be publishable.

Why publish ... and what puts people off?

One of the first things to discuss, with both peers and supervisor, is the question: why publish? This is the starting point because it will determine not only which parts to disseminate more widely but also which targets one should aim for (e.g. journal or book? Which types of journal? Book chapters?).

Over a number of years I have been asked to run seminars for students and new lecturers on publishing. I always begin with the question of: What are your motives for wanting to publish? The responses are many and varied (several have been recorded in more detail in Wellington 2003: 2–11). Quite commonly, the motivations are extrinsic: to improve my CV, to get a job, to gain promotion, to join the research community, to earn respect and credibility, to enhance my standing, to become known and so on. But equally commonly, the motivation for publishing is more an intrinsic one: to clarify my own thinking, to share my ideas more widely, personal satisfaction, contributing to change and improvement, to make a difference, to set up a dialogue, and so on.

On the other side of the coin, I also explore with students and new lecturers some of the factors that prevent them from publishing or even attempting to do so. Responses are again many and varied, but include such feelings as: lack of self-belief, fear of criticism or rejection, not knowing where to begin, wondering 'am I good enough?', not having a track record, lack of time and energy, not knowing the right targets and so on.

All of the above motivating *and* de-motivating factors are important in considering how to disseminate your work. For example, if one's aim is to gain a job or promotion within academia, then consult the supervisor about which targets for publications – probably academic journals – are most appropriate. On the other hand, if the work relates to a particular profession (most likely for a professional doctorate) then the motivation for publishing and the most productive 'outlet' for it will be different (see Wellington and Szczerbinski 2008, for a summary of types of publication).

Converting thesis to 'publication' ... or more

For many students, the last thing they feel like doing after the examination process is complete is to return to their thesis and start to 'chop it up' and 'mould' it into some other form or forms. But this is exactly what is required. Perhaps the best tactic is to ignore it for several weeks, and then to return to it with the explicit aim of disseminating and 'getting published'. Some may wish to be the sole author, which is fine, but the act of getting started is best done in collaboration with someone else, preferably the supervisor or a colleague who has experience of writing for journals or book publishers.

The first task is to set some goals. The thesis may contain different papers for different audiences: for example, there may be an important article to be written from the thesis on the methodology or even the specific methods used; or if a thesis has a very strong, critical, perhaps systematic review of the literature in one area then this may form the basis of a publishable article. These might be targeted (see later) on one journal. Another article might be written on the findings and their implications for practice – this might be geared at a more 'professional' journal, aimed at practitioners such as teachers or lecturers. Third, within the thesis there might be an article that can contribute to thinking and theory within an area; and finally, between the two poles of practice and theory, there might be important messages for policy makers and planners, and this might be targeted at a refereed journal on policy or a more 'professional' journal for policy makers. It may be that the external or internal examiner has been particularly complimentary about one or more sections of the thesis and these may be singled out for 'converting' into a publication for a journal.

If the goal is to be a book, then it might contain a combination of all the above. However, commercial book publishers will want a clear statement of the potential market for the book (see Wellington 2003, for fuller discussion).

Entering the community of scholars

This section has discussed the important business of deciding what to do after the viva: the final thread. Should students continue to work with their supervisor and consider the pros and cons of publishing some or most of their thesis in the form of articles, book chapters or even a book?

My suggestion is to go for it. For many established authors, their first academic book or journal article was a by-product of their doctoral thesis; many theses have the potential to be transformed into one publication or more. The article or book is unlikely to have the extensive data presentation, tables of results, comprehensive literature review, methodology discussion, appendices and plethora of references that would be expected in a doctoral thesis – but its central themes, its contribution to knowledge and its innovative ideas and discussion are all likely to interest a book publisher or a journal editor. Everyone starts somewhere. The viva and the written thesis are the first steps to getting known and entering the 'community of scholars' that newcomers often find difficult to locate and become a part of. Conference presentations and posters, papers, journal articles and books all play a part in feeling part of that community.

Concluding comments

This chapter has considered the wide range of threads that need to be woven together into a coherent whole in any research project. Some are very practical – others are more philosophical.

Weaving the threads of a research project is not an easy task. I would not advise trying to do this (or writing a journal article or book) alone. In my view, autonomy, in the sense of working totally independently, is highly over rated. But for most of us, help is at hand: friends, peers, colleagues, supervisors or mentors. We can all make use of the networks that we have, principally:

- one's supervisor, in cajoling, feeding back and helping achieve the focus
- critical friends, peers, networks and conferences.

And finally, never underestimate the value of one's own writing – treat this as a form of thinking (Richardson 2000) and the writing process becomes one of the most effective ways of weaving the threads of the doctoral research journey.

References

Medawar, P. (1963) Is the scientific paper a fraud? *The Listener*, September 1963.

——(1976) *Advice to a young scientist*. London: Harper and Row.

Richardson, L. (2000) Writing: A Method of Inquiry. In N. Denzin, and Y. Lincoln, (Eds). *The Handbook of Qualitative Research*. 2nd edn. Thousand Oaks, CA: Sage.

Thomas, G. (2009) *How to do your research project*. London: Sage.

Wellington, J. (2000) *Educational Research: contemporary issues and practical approaches*. London and New York: Continuum.

Wellington, J (2003) *Getting Published*. London: RoutledgeFalmer.

Wellington, J., Bathmaker, A., Hunt, C., McCulloch, G. and Sikes, P. (2005) *Succeeding with your Doctorate*. London: Sage.

Wellington, J. and Sikes, P. (2006) A 'doctorate in a tight compartment': why do students choose a professional doctorate and what impact does it have on their personal and professional lives? *Studies in Higher Education*, 31(6): 723–34.

Wellington, J. and Szczerbinski, M. (2008) *Research methods for the social sciences*. London: Continuum.

Part 3

Coming to terms with research practice

P. Thomson and M. Walker

This section addresses the processes of coming to terms with research practice. Like the previous sections we see this as part of the formation of a doctoral identity rather than only a matter of acquiring discrete, albeit useful, research skills. It is not that the techniques and skills of research do not matter; it is that in themselves they do constitute a scholarly identity. Rather than tell students 'how to do it', these chapters are intended to provoke thinking and reflection about the doing of research, about what matters and why. Although the chapter titles might bear a resemblance to chapter headings in methodology textbooks, they do different work in raising questions and issues that we anticipate will provide resources – not only for students individually, but also for peer groups working and studying together – which support coming to terms with doctoral research practice. The chapters need to be seen as an integrated whole – the issues addressed overlap and relate to each other and they build on and are nested within the issues and chapters in Parts 1 and 2. We hope that this section in particular might be used as a resource for student–supervisor conversations and more generally to enhance research environments in departments and schools.

i) Engaging with literatures

This section foregrounds the process of writing because writing is so central to the process of researching, the production and defence of a doctoral dissertation and for communicating research to diverse audiences. It is important for students to understand this from the earliest stage of their work. Concern for pedagogical process is further woven implicitly through both these chapters in this section.

Pat Thomson and Barbara Kamler argue that to disassociate the writing process ('writing up the thesis') from the production process is problematic and unhelpful for student development. They frame writing as 'writing the research and writing the researcher'; in putting one's writing into a public domain, both the text displayed and the researcher's capabilities are on view and both may be enhanced or diminished. Through their writing, doctoral students become known to their peers, to their department, to academics and to stakeholders. With this in mind, Thomson and Kamler consider what it means to work with literatures (rather than the literature), eschewing the more traditional notion of doing 'a literature review'. New scholars are required to do more than read selected books, articles and papers in their research field; they must enter 'occupied territory', gain control and position themselves in the debates. Thomson and Kamler illustrate what they mean by looking closely at students grappling with producing authoritative evaluations of a field of study, learning how to perform as expert scholars. They show that 'doing the literature review' is not a mechanistic step to be completed early in the doctoral process before moving on to doing the actual research, but a key site for the production of a confident (or if not supported and scaffolded, an unconfident) scholarly identity – both text and scholar are formed at the same time.

ii) Asking good research questions

Posing good research questions, like 'the literature review' is a lot harder to do than it may at first appear. In addition, we think there is an issue about what is worth asking and why. Both the chapters in this section take up this challenge.

John Pryor starts with the point that identifying a good research question is not just a technical matter but a complex task that demands thinking about the substantive issues of the field, the knowledge the project will produce and how the research is to be done. Research questions work to capture just what the project is about; they provide focus and set boundaries for research, which is about this and not about that. They sharpen what it is a researcher wants to look at, and get them to think about why. They will determine methodology, but may even shift as a study unfolds – as Pryor suggests there is nothing that says you must stick with your original questions. Pryor puts forward ideas and practical ways for asking good research questions, moving from research focus to research questions. He characterises this as a process, rather than event, as cyclical and recursive, as structuring and being structured by the research, as integral to theorisation and structuring the field under study, and as always worth spending time on composing and refining.

Andrew Brown first addresses the contemporary context influencing doctoral education before considering the matter of research questions and their location within broader processes of doctoral education, examination and communication. He suggests that research questions are personal, practical and situated. Because research questions are located in a field of doctoral practice, writing and refining them is beyond the technical. Like Pryor, Brown acknowledges that research questions may change as a study progresses, even if a researcher has committed to a clear question at the outset. But avoiding the 'tyranny' of research questions also does not mean that any old research question will do to get the work started! Research questions help to identify what literatures need to be selected and how to read purposefully with a question or questions in mind. To pose questions that can be considered worthwhile requires positioning oneself (taking up a stance for Thomson and Kamler) in the substantive field – as Brown makes clear there is an iterative relationship between the literatures and posing and refining research questions. But examiners and others working in the field also need to be convinced of the worthwhileness of the research questions, the field may be contested, what for some is worthwhile for others might be less so, or even worse, trivial. And, of course, the questions must be do-able within doctoral timeframes. In short, what's worth asking and why is, Brown argues, a function of the current field of study – what is currently known, where are the blank spots, what would be an interesting study in relation to other work in the field, how the question might generate an original contribution to the field? Thus, asking research questions means being able to identify a recognisable community of researchers with common interests and approaches who will recognise the value of the research being done, who will constitute a readership for the research and judge its quality. But what is worth asking also needs to resonate personally with the researcher – if he or she does not care much about the question under scrutiny it is unlikely that the study will be completed or that anyone else will particularly care.

iii) Data analysis

The next section of chapters looks at the process of data analysis, often strangely neglected in many methodology textbooks. However, we do not propose a practical guide to analysis but have invited researchers to consider their own approaches and struggles with data analysis in coming to terms with research.

We open with the chapter by Helen Colley, drawing on the experience of doing her own doctorate. Rather like the literature review and research questions, there is no magic way to analyze data, no infallible set of guidelines that can be followed, no simple and transparent technique of extraction and coding. Instead the issue is to know that there is 'no golden key' and not to be too alarmed if data analysis all turns out to be harder, more slippery and more tricky than anticipated. Moreover, as Colley explains, she found that questions, values, theorising, methods, analysis and reflexivity are inextricably related. Like others, she emphasises that data analysis does not happen once all the data have been generated but begins during the process of data production, sometimes requiring adjustments to data methods. In her own work, despite having the data corpus and having done a code-based analysis, Colley ran into some data that did not 'fit'. Having found 'proper' methods of analysis wanting and indeed limiting, Colley turned to a narrative approach to transforming her data, and to synthesis rather than taking apart. She works with some of her data to show what she was attempting in producing a creative storied approach, to show how she made a new contribution to knowledge about forms of mentoring that was open to cultural resources beyond the research community and beyond an admissible narrow set of methods.

Ann-Marie Bathmaker considers what can be learned from data analysis by looking closely at examples of published research, rather as Colley has done. In this case she does not scrutinise her own research but that of others (including that of Helen Colley), trying to understand what can be learnt from each study about the process of data analysis. She describes a range of textual resources offering guidance on data analysis, suggesting that this rapid increase in the guidance on offer occurs at a time when qualitative research is under attack for its lack of rigour. She outlines what might constitute the analytic process: close engagement with 'raw data', interpretation of data (relating data-interpretation-theory), and theorising. Bathmaker's exploration of research through reading research exemplifies a valuable way for doctoral researchers to become more skilled at analysis – by looking at research texts (their own and that of others), rather than by only reading material on how to do analysis. For Bathmaker, data analysis is understood also as involving more than technique. It includes being able to see some things and not others (as Wagner argues in Part 2); it involves the researcher's own worldview, it involves interpretation and theorisation and it involves complex interpretational relationships between data-explanation-theory. Because the decisions and dilemmas with regard to data analysis rarely find their way into published texts she advocates more time and space for critical discussion of the analytic process (which doctoral researchers might do in peer groups and networks, and with supervisors).

While Colley and Bathmaker focus primarily on dealing with qualitative data, Andy Noyes recounts his own experiences of researching with large datasets. He problematises what he describes as a new statistical language – the current discourse of power – in English schools, which is freely used and probably poorly understood. His concern is that statistical analyses might obscure the individuals in education, and thus he prefers to search for ways to hold large numbers and individuals, the macro and micro, in tension together so that large- and small-scale together generate insight and impact. This involves a mixed methods approach, but his is not technique driven. Rather, for Noyes the power of mixed methods lies in its attention to the generation of different perspectives in addressing theoretical framing, in being able to draw on existing datasets and in expanding the range of methodological expertise. He draws on his own learning from experience in ways that will reassure doctoral researchers. Like other contributors to this volume, he holds truths to be partial and a critical stance towards findings as essential.

Stephen Gorard argues the case for doctoral researchers making use of large secondary datasets, rather than expending time and expense to generate their own. He helpfully suggests a number of sites and sources for such datasets and further proposes that researchers consider combining two or more datasets in an original way. Gorard provides concrete examples of ways to think about and interrogate available data and suggests that looking anew at secondary data might address gaps (Wagner's 'blank spots'). Gorard further provides advice on analysis, with selected examples of how this might be done. He argues that doctoral researchers ought not to fear working with numbers and statistics. Rather, engagement with large secondary datasets might expand not only their repertoire of research skills but also the questions they can ask and answer.

iv) Argumentation and writing research

The two chapters in this section return to the specific site of writing addressed in the first section of chapters, with different perspectives. Monica McLean focuses in particular on the process of argumentation and strongly advocates that all doctoral students need to develop the capability to develop good arguments based on critical reasoning and oriented to communication of the ideas. Argumentation capability, she claims, is crucial to scholars being able to tackle the problems of the contemporary world. In other words, she ties argumentation capability to the cultural and humanistic purposes and social responsibility of universities and the doctoral graduates they produce.

For McLean, a doctoral dissertation ought to contribute to scholarly arguments (as was argued in the section of chapters on reviewing literatures). Argument is presented as the key strategy for a doctoral researcher being able to locate herself, her stance and her own voice in relation to the knowledge community or communities of which she seeks to be part and to which she hopes to contribute scholarship. McLean provides guidelines to think about the features of scholarly argument, which she says, demands more than a one-off writing process. She sets out examples of students developing and improving abstracts of their studies as a way to sharpen the argument and focus, and further provides an example from the work of one of her own doctoral students developing the line of argument in her study. Finally (using examples on the way), she relates making good arguments to good doctoral writing – the one requires the other, while learning to write in a scholarly and interesting way is key to quality in doctoral work, and this means learning to make good arguments. For doctoral researchers this requires that they write and rewrite their arguments. McLean concludes with an exercise to help students improve and develop their critical argumentation capability.

The chapter by Maria Piantanida and Noreen Garman further argues that the process of writing is central to the production of a doctoral dissertation. Piantanida and Garman add a new dimension to earlier chapters by arguing that doctoral study can be transformative and that writing is the vehicle for such change. They point to the agentic and creative elements of writing; mimicry and diffidence will not suffice. Writing is the means to make available one's thinking to oneself and to others. Writing research, they suggest, requires attention to the ontological fit between the researcher's worldview and way of being, and between thinking, research and narrative. For example, being drawn to storied accounts of experience needs to have some kind of fit with the researcher's worldview and intellectual traditions within which she is working. To illustrate the need for congruence, they draw on examples from the work of their own doctoral students, each using a language, a voice and stance consistent with the genre within which each is working. The implication of their argument is that each doctoral researcher needs to ask themselves: What is the research genre within which I am working and what are its conventions with regard to language and structures? At stake is the production of well-written and elegant arguments and insightful research, and the interplay between what is being said and how it is being said.

v) Ethics and reflexivity

The chapters in this section address issues central to any doctoral project and to the doing of good research.

Kevin Williams takes up the matter of ethics and doing research. For all doctoral students, attention to the ethical issues that may arise in their research is both a moral and a formal university requirement, with most or all universities having ethical codes to which prospective researchers are expected to adhere. Doctoral researchers are expected to obtain ethical clearance for their research and will generally adhere to core principles of informed consent, confidentiality and doing no harm. But, argues Williams, the ethics of research ought also to be an ongoing reflexive process. Researchers need to develop and exercise a capacity for moral judgement that formal procedures cannot anticipate. Williams' chapter outlines some ethical challenges that might arise for doctoral researchers, problematising the ethical procedures we take for granted. As he notes, formal ethical procedures and codes should not be conflated with research ethics and may even work to 'imperil' ethical values. Although his specific focus is on qualitative research, the arguments hold for any doctoral researcher. Williams illustrates his argument through interviews with five higher education researchers and the moral decisions they confront, and for which codes may indeed be necessary. The implication of his analysis is that ethical codes do not resolve or absolve the doctoral students' moral judgement or reflexivity. Williams makes a plea for ethics committees to be more educative and less performative in their approach to research ethics.

Developing and deepening the process of reflexivity in doing research, Wanda Pillow's chapter takes up the problems and 'dangers' of reflexivity from a feminist perspective, and considers what it might mean to practise reflexivity with rigour and responsibility. Having traced how reflexivity has come to be a priority in social science research, she moves on to consider what the purpose is 'of all this reflexivity talk'. She takes reflexivity to involve a critical examination of the research process, doing research differently (for example, research with and not on), attention to how knowledge is produced and represented, and how voice and power are addressed. 'Reflexivity talk' surfaces the problematic of doing research. How then does one do reflexivity? Pillow's advice is that new researchers need to read widely, deeply and critically, to understand the history and debates in qualitative research, paradigms and stances. Reflexivity emerges out of deep dialogue between the researcher and the knowledge she is producing. To assist in the process of becoming reflexive, Pillow suggests some practical help. But she also warns against turning reflexivity into another research method for acquiring more data. Pillow argues that what is 'dangerous' about reflexivity is that researchers have not gone far enough in questioning 'what is most hegemonic in our lives'. There is no escaping the need for reflexivity, however, because researchers are ultimately responsible for the knowledge they produce, and how they produce it and reflexivity contributes to making better knowledge and better research practice.

vi) Emotions and the research process

The chapter in this section of the book addresses the emotional aspects involved in coming to terms with research practice and in the formation of a scholarly identity. This is not much written about and even less spoken about for fear of being labelled negatively by a supervisor or peers, yet is deeply embedded in being a successful doctoral student. Emotions are fundamental to the process of reasoning that characterises doctoral study; emotions properly understood and managed are resources, not burdens, for thinking and writing.

Chaya Herman explores the personal and intellectual dimensions of doing a doctorate as the source of the deep awareness and the ethical judgement that Kevin Williams highlighted. For Herman, the person and the researcher, the emotional and the rational, cannot be separated but work together to problematise assumptions and strengthen self-understandings. Herman contextualises her argument against her own doctoral study into the restructuring of Jewish community schools in one South African city. As an insider to the community and an outsider researcher, she both struggled emotionally with the complexity of the research process and with clarifying the boundaries of her community role. Such emotions resurfaced at the stage of data analysis and in writing and completing her dissertation, and through to its publication as a book. But she also writes that the emotional, investment she had in her study motivated her and kept her going. Yet she had not anticipated the 'vortex of emotions' that engulfed her; she argues that doctoral students ought to be aware of the emotional dimensions of their work and be supported in managing them.

12

It's been said before and we'll say it again – research *is* writing

P. Thomson and B. Kamler

Doctoral writing is often seen as a technical matter, simply a question of skills. Problems in writing can be readily addressed through the provision of a set of guidelines and handy hints. Writing is simply the means by which the real work of doctoral research is finally 'written up'.

Nowhere is this better demonstrated than in the catalogues of academic publishers who specialise in research methods books. After pages devoted to general research methods, philosophy of research, research skills and design, there are then more pages of offerings about specific methods – quantitative, mixed methods, and various kinds of qualitative approaches. There are small collections of research in specific areas – psychology, geography, business, politics – and then a series of expensive and comprehensive handbooks designed for library purchase. At the very back of the catalogues are a set of texts called projects, dissertations and study skills. Here are books that offer guidance on project design, conducting literature reviews, writing the thesis, managing the viva, publishing and presenting research and coping with the postgraduate experience (see Kamler and Thomson 2008). It is highly likely that this volume is listed in just such a section of a catalogue.

We do not have hard evidence about who buys such texts. However, judging by our own universities, we suspect that one of the most important things about project, dissertation and study skills books is that they are *less* likely to be used in research education courses than methods texts, and *more* likely to be bought by universities for individual use, or by students for their own libraries. And in the university library shelves we see exactly the same kind of cataloguing organisation – writing is separated from other aspects of research.

The discursive dissociation of writing from the central concerns of research may make one kind of sense, but it is also problematic. In this chapter, we argue that writing is central to research and we consider the 'work' that it does. We then show how research and scholarly identities are co-constructed in and as writing, using examples of doctoral researchers' struggles with literatures, chapter conclusions and journal articles. We conclude by returning to the problem of disconnecting writing from thinking, doing, arguing and representing research.

No research without writing

Social scientists recognise that human beings make sense of their experiences, observations, relationships and everyday worlds through language (Saussure 1959; Wittgenstein 1976).[1] Because language is a cultural artefact, it follows that what can be seen, known and said is not 'objective', but is rooted in socially constructed subjectivities (Rosaldo 1989). Research can thus be said to be situated (that is, it exists in a particular time–space), partial (that is, because of the limitations of time–space, there are things that cannot not be seen and understood) and particular (that is, what can be seen, said and understood is limited by what is available for observation and documentation) (Harding 1993; Lather 1991). The ways in which such understandings are communicated and recorded are through languages – movement, images and writing. As a human activity, research is thus inextricably saturated in language because this is how we make meaning (Hall 1997). However, in the social sciences, writing is privileged as a means of recording and communicating, although images do have an increasingly important role in social science research (Chaplin 1994).

Researchers continually work through various forms of writing (Richardson 1994) – notes, journals, records of reading, jottings, conference papers, draft chapters and eventually the dissertation and published papers and books. We refer to these as research texts. One of the benefits of texts is that they are not fixed, they can be rewritten over and over again and indeed researchers do this as a means of refining insights and analyses. In research, some of the writing is 'writing along the way' – writing that is intended to sort out what we think, why, and what the implications of a line of thought might be. Only some research writing is intended to be a final, albeit temporary, text.

All of these writings are, of course, representations. Language is an approximate medium and there is no direct correspondence between words (or numbers) and the material phenomena they are meant to describe. Readers always bring their own interpretations to what is written, mentally rewriting the text in order to make their own meanings of the words that researchers have laboured over (Barthes 1986; Game and Metcalfe 1996). Researchers also undertake this same rewriting process as they read what others have written and interpret what informants tell them. We therefore think of words as being like clay: they can be moulded and shaped in various ways to suit various purposes. Just as researchers make selections from the phenomena they observe, research writing is also always a selection from a possible lexicon – and each selection attempts to steer the reader/rewriter in one direction rather than another.

Researchers can make it difficult or comparatively easy for readers to follow what they have written, and in the social sciences there are well-established textual conventions intended to provide meaning-making scaffolding for the reader. Dissertations, for example, conventionally use signposting for what is coming up, summaries of key points and careful use of headings to summarise the major point(s) to be made.

But research writing does more than make meaning of phenomena.

Research writing as text work/identity work

Research writings come to stand for both the scholar and their scholarship (Kamler and Thomson 2006).

Researchers are engaged in a process that aims to make a contribution to knowledge. Research writing is the major means of communicating what we claim to have 'found'. This endeavour is situated within a given community of scholars, a discipline, an institutional and policy context, all of which place constraints on what can be done. Researchers want their work to be taken seriously within the field and by key stakeholders. They also have careers to forge, and a desire to make stimulating, critical and supportive connections with others who work in the same field. In each of these areas — specifying contribution, influencing action, networking and becoming known within the field — writing is the primary means of accomplishment. Within the field, researchers thus become known by and through their writings.

Reading scholarly texts is, therefore, not a neutral activity, but always involves evaluation about the kind of contribution that is made: whether its claims are sound, whether it has been generated through trustworthy means, whether it is appropriately connected to other relevant literatures, and whether it is elegantly and engagingly expressed. Doctoral researchers come to know other scholars via reading their texts and this, of course, includes those who are no longer physically alive but whose ideas and work have been 'fixed' via the written word. At the same time, their own writings become the ways in which their supervisors/advisers come to know what they think — and can do.

This doubled activity — writing the research and writing the researcher — accounts for much of the anxiety that doctoral researchers experience. Writing the kinds of texts that are intended to communicate the research to critical and evaluative readers is not simply a matter of taking 'findings' into public arenas. It is also to put on view scholarly competencies, claims and contributions. It is literally taking the textualised scholarly self out of the closet and exposing it to others so that they might appreciate and admire (best case scenario), engage with (desirable result) as well as judge, critique and assess (high-risk activity carrying significant fears of being found wanting).

Thus, doctoral writing can be seen to be both text work and identity work (Kamler and Thomson 2007). Identity work, of course, is not a simple process. Holland *et al.* (1998) argue that identity formation is always formed in social settings and is continually under construction, going through four 'authoring' stages:

- Identity devaluation, in which a new understanding of self develops at the expense of an old one — the scholarly identity begins to take precedence over other professional identities. For experienced professionals who are increasingly taking up part- and full-time doctorates, this process can be highly emotional and give rise to feelings of anger, fear, resentment as they experience moving from being an 'expert' in one field to being a 'beginner' in the academy.
- Personalisation of the identity, through identification with key figures — including their supervisor/adviser, another member of the faculty, and/or a key researcher whose work and writings are ones to which they might aspire.
- Emotional attachment to the new identity, through the processes of researching, writing and performing the identity of scholar — doctoral researchers gradually come to see themselves as scholars and value this identity as an important part of 'who I am'. The alignment of identity with text brings vulnerabilities when judgements affirm (emotionally pleasing) or critique (wounding) their work.
- Identity reconstitution, through exorcising negative practices (e.g. fears about writing or speaking in public) — doctoral researchers learn to resolve tensions between their scholarly identity and other aspects of their self/ves.

We find this authoring heuristic useful for making explicit the idea that scholarly identity formation is a continuous cycle, always closely aligned with text formation. This identity formation process appears in many doctoral texts and will look different at different stages of candidature and beyond, but too often these textual/identity struggles are mistaken for technical incompetence. Nowhere can this be more clearly seen than in the work that doctoral researchers do with literatures.

Working with the literatures

One of the key tasks that doctoral researchers must undertake is commonly called 'the literature review', a misleading term as it implies that there is a single set of homogenous texts, rather than a diverse mix that may include books, articles, policy documents, media reports, images, professional writings and so on. Further, the notion of 'review' suggests that all researchers need to do is see what is out there and then summarise 'it' to see what 'it' says. In reality, the task of engaging with what we call 'the field of knowledge production' is a much more complex task of reading, summarising, comparing and contrasting, synthesising and mapping in order to:

1. sketch out the nature of the field or fields relevant to the enquiry, possibly indicating something of their historical development and
2. identify major debates and define contentious terms, in order to
3. establish which studies, ideas and/or methods are most pertinent to the study and
4. locate gaps in the field, in order to
5. create the warrant or mandate for the study in question, and
6. identify the contribution the study will make.

There is no correct way to accomplish these tasks, and there are many possible interpretations of them. Indeed, although a 'literature chapter' is often recommended as an essential part of a dissertation, many researchers work with literatures all the way through, rather than confining them to the beginning and end of the thesis narrative. Reading programmes at the outset of doctoral research play a crucial role in this regard, in assisting researchers to focus their question and identify what they will add to the body of extant work in the field.

Because doctoral researchers have an emerging relationship with their chosen field, engaging with literatures is not only a daunting intellectual task, but also a site of intensive text/identity work. Fragile scholarly identities in the early stage of formation are required to not only enter occupied territory, but also to evaluate, assess and pass judgement on key figures, debates, alliances, accommodations and feuds. The processes of exclusion, inclusion, categorisation and discussion of the field or fields are time-consuming as well as risky. The doctoral researcher may well stumble in the process of traversing an unfamiliar terrain, and it is the fear of giving offence, getting it wrong and simply not gaining control that makes it such a difficult task.

We want to illustrate some of the ways in which the struggle to be authoritative and take a stand in the field – running up a flag to say 'I am here' – appears in doctoral texts, as well as the texts that are published from the doctorate.

Grappling with writing about literatures

In this section we discuss three extracts from one review of literature. It is difficult to select segments from what is a long piece of writing and readers will have to take it on trust that the snippets we have chosen are reflective of patterns that appear throughout the text. They are intended to be illustrative, 'pithy' and typical examples of identity/writing problems that appear not only in this dissertation text, but also in many others. It is important to recognise that even successful dissertations that 'pass' may well have aspects that are of lesser quality than other parts. It is equally important to understand that this is not 'bad' or wrong' writing, but writing about literatures that could be 'better', that is better able to do what had to be done.

Mahomet was an experienced educator whose research investigated the ways in which school principals influenced teachers' professional behaviours and students' learning. It was located within the school improvement field where there are a number of key debates and a well-documented history of development. This was indeed very much occupied territory. Mahomet's task in his literature chapter was to show that he understood the history of the field, to take up and justify his position within the debates, and to signal clearly what his research might contribute. This required him to identify areas where more work was needed and/or gaps in knowledge and/or a debate that might be resolved.

Extract One is taken from an early section in the chapter where Mahomet is attempting to show the differences between a school effectiveness and school improvement approach and the ways in which they have been combined, a position he took up in the design of his field work.

Extract One

There are significant differences in opinion on how to define school improvement. Gray *et al.* (1999) point out that school improvement secures year–on–year improvement in the outcomes of successive cohorts of similar pupils. Improvement is measured in terms of raising attainment of all students over time (Chapman 2002). In other words it increases the school's effectiveness over time. In contrast, Mortimore (1998) describes school improvement as the process of improving the way a school is organized, its aims, expectations, ways of learning, methods of teaching and organizational culture. For Gray *et al.* (1999) student outcomes are preeminent, whereas for Mortimore (1998) it is the process that is vital. Hopkins (2001) combines these two ideas i.e. school improvement and school's capacity by describing school improvement as a 'distinct approach to educational change that aims to enhance students' outcomes as well as strengthening the school's capacity for managing change' (p. 23). He is concerned with raising students' achievement through focusing on the teaching-learning process and the conditions that support it. According to Hopkins, 'authentic' school improvement focuses on enhancing students' learning and achievement, in a broader sense than mere examination results or test scores and it provides those involved in the change process with the skills of learning and 'change agents' who will raise levels of expectation and confidence throughout the educational community.

What Mahomet is attempting to do here is to identify a key debate within the field, namely whether change can be measured by looking at the end points or the process. He wants to argue that both are important, and that it isn't possible to do one without the other and he needs therefore to show why and how they are inter-related. However, he has not discussed the field per se, but tries to exemplify the debate by citing a few key figures. The reader does not know whether these are the only texts he has read, or whether he has picked these writers because they are leading exponents of each position. The text reads as 'he said, she said'. Almost every sentence begins with a named researcher followed by a neutral verb (*point out, describes, are, combines, is concerned* …). The syntax of these sentences reads like a list because Mahomet has piled one study upon another, without putting them in the broader context of a significant difference of opinion within the field. We are not clear of his views, although we might surmise that he is allowing Hopkins to stand in for his own position.

Later on, Mahomet attempts to signal another debate within the field and the position he holds.

Extract Two

Some researchers in the field of school leadership posit that principals can affect achievement indirectly by establishing a mission or set of goals and building school capacity (Heck *et al.* 1990; Leithwood 1994; Silins 1994). Although Bush (2002) states that 'vision is increasingly regarded as an important component of leadership' (p. 3), he argues as to whether it is an essential aspect of school leadership or, rather, a feature which distinguishes successful from less successful leaders. Kouzes and Posner (1996) point out, 'Inspiring a shared vision into the leadership practice with which heads felt most uncomfortable' (p. 24) and more critically, Fullan (1992) postulates that visionary leaders may damage rather than improve their schools.

Here, again, we have an emphasis on researchers rather than the ideas that are at issue. Clearly, there is a debate about vision and mission and the efficacy of leaders having one or both. Mahomet introduces a troublesome proposition, the importance of mission/vision, but does not stake a claim. He stands aside and allows other researchers, the established scholars in the field – Bush, Kouzes and Pousner and Fullan – to introduce the idea of critique. His position is obliquely produced through this discussion rather than being stated authoritatively. He stands behind the words of others and uses their authority to support his position. This gives an impression of criticality that does not stand up to close syntactic scrutiny.

In both Extracts One and Two, the literatures are neither used to locate the study nor to advance an argument about the state of the field in order to make the case for Mahomet's own work. This is characteristic of diffident scholars who have not been encouraged to take a stand, and who have been allowed to be literally overshadowed by the textual presence of leading figures in the field. In these extracts Mahomet does not show that he can take a 'hands on hips' stance, critically surveying and categorising texts and the field itself.

However, this tentativeness is not consistent throughout the literature chapter. Extract Three is illustrative of places in the text where Mahomet *is* able to take a more evaluative stance.

Extract Three

Central to effective working together is the development of organizational culture (Schein 1985; Hoy and Miskel 2005). Culture can be defined as the product of the shared values, beliefs, priorities, expectations and norms that serve to inform the way in which an organization manifests itself to the world (West Burnham 1992). According to Hoy and Miskel (2005) 'organizational culture is a system of shared orientations that hold the unit together and give it a distinctive identity' (p. 165). School culture however is complex because it is largely implicit and we only see surface aspects, for instance staff who work in isolation, in collaboration (Stoll 1999) or in balkanized groups (Hargreaves 1994).

The paragraph is not about researchers, it is about the topic of school culture and this is the subject of three of the four sentences. Here, Mahomet offers a proposition in his own words, followed by a definition. He then moves to researchers who support the proposition and follows with a counter proposition in his own words, supported by relevant citations. This is Mahomet in charge of the discussion. He makes an evaluative judgement – school culture is complex – and a gentle critique, flagged through his use of 'however', of the two venerable researchers he has made visible in the text. Readers do get a sense of the debate in the field and something of Mahomet's own views.

However, the text could be much more authoritative than it is. Mahomet's writing does not really give us a strong sense of a researcher who is confidently surveying the field, its various camps and the knowledge that has been produced, in order to locate his work and situate his original contribution.

Writing with authority about the field of knowledge production

Mahomet's writing can be contrasted with doctoral texts that present more authoritative evaluations of a field of study.

Dierdre is also an experienced professional. Her action research study involved working with teenagers to better understand their experiences of, and views about, school attendance. She did not have a single literature chapter in her dissertation, but one chapter that discussed truancy and another that discussed the rights of the child. These two chapters thus addressed the two specific fields of knowledge production that she was drawing together. Extract Four is taken from the penultimate draft of her dissertation.

Extract Four

This chapter presents a brief review of truancy research which can largely be seen as an historical debate between proponents of either psychological or sociological reasoning. In recent years, however, truancy has increasingly become a contest between the sociological and the school effectiveness approaches, neither of which deny the existence of an influential causal range of factors outside of the school. I argue that while each of these three lines of inquiry has interesting and important insights, they also have deficiencies and that therefore 'solutions' rooted in each 'camp' have shortcomings.

Right at the outset of this chapter Dierdre clearly signposts not only the content of the chapter, but also the position that has informed her research. She frames her discussion as a debate, a set of ideas in competition with one another. She locates the field of truancy research as having a historical bifurcation, followed by a significant difference within one of the two strands. Through this economical statement about the field, the reader is

155

given to understand that Dierdre has read widely and is able to succinctly analyse and evaluate a corpus of texts in order to locate her own work, that is to *argue for* the position she takes. The evaluative discussion of the field that is mandated through this signposting can be clearly seen in Extract Five.

Extract Five

Research into school attendance, its causes and possible solutions, started to become a significant field of study in the 1950s. In the late 1950s and 60s research focused on the personality and social background of the child and made links between absenteeism and delinquency. But as early as 1925 Burt had claimed an association between delinquency and truancy (Galloway 1982) that assumed that pupils were wholly the problem, rather than the schooling they received. Several studies found a correlation between absenteeism and children of families with parents who were manual workers or unemployed, having only one parent living at home, and socio-economic deprivation and poverty (e.g. Tyerman 1968; Fogelman, Tibbenham *et al.* 1980; Hersov and Berg 1980; Galloway 1982). There was an assumed deviancy on the part of the child with delinquency and truancy as symptoms. Truants were lazy, lacked concentration, were restless, were difficult to discipline, did not care about being a credit to their parents and were not clean or tidy on their arrival at school (Farrington 1980: 11). Early solutions to truancy were to be therefore found in treatment of the child (Reynolds and Murgatroyd 1977). Although there were slight suggestions that schools could be influential in causing truancy, these were not given credence.

Dierdre has made ideas central to her discussion, rather than other researchers, and she takes the lead in guiding the reader through developments in the field. She uses evaluative language to sort and clarify (*... had claimed ... an assumed deviancy ... there were slight suggestions ... the response was ... the conclusion being ...*) She is not, however, disrespectful in her judgements. She is not dominated by the literatures, but firmly in charge.

Most importantly, because Dierdre is able to understand the field in which she is researching, she is able to clearly identify where her own research fits in and what traditions it draws on. She can, therefore, also delineate with precision in her writing the contribution she makes.

Forging a textual scholarly identity as an ongoing process

Our analysis shows Dierdre as a doctoral researcher whose identity formation is more firmly textualised than Mahomet. Although both are going through the process of scholarly identity formation that we outlined earlier, Dierdre has a much stronger grasp of how to be and perform like an expert scholar. This is not to deny that she may still feel uncertain and unsure about her place in the academy. She has, however, already learnt to adopt a confident position in her dissertation text, and this will be more convincing to her examiners than the less assured writing offered by Mahomet.

This process of forging a confident scholarly identity, however, does not simply end when the dissertation is examined and successfully lodged in real and virtual library spaces. Literature work, in particular, often remains a site of struggle when doctoral graduates write for research journals. It is here where they continue to work out an authoritative position vis-à-vis the community of experts they have finally been author-ised to join. Years of writing as a novice researcher can take its toll textually: fostering a deferential stance to experts and/or a felt need to parade knowledge in order to appear 'expert enough' in their respective fields.

Calvin, an experienced educator with a recent tenured university position, continued to struggle to write with authority two years after candidature. He was not a diffident scholar, but was under great pressure to publish from his thesis and journal articles were a new genre for him. His doctoral research examined his own teaching of first- and second-generation Chinese American middle years students and the ways they engaged with multi-modal and web-based literacies. Extract Six is taken from the introduction to an article he submitted to a high-profile literacy journal.

Extract Six

Changing social conditions brought about by globalization and shifts in com-munication technologies have elicited new, inventive pedagogical responses. They include multiliteracies (NLG 1996; Cope and Kalantzis 2000; Albright, Purohit and Walsh 2006a; Walsh 2006), multimodality (Jewit 2008; Kress, Jewit, Ogborn and Tsatsarelis 2001; Kress and van Leeuwen 2001) and design (NLG 1996; Kress 2000, 2003; Janks 2000). These pedagogies build on a range of traditions from critical literacy studies (Lankshear and McLaren 1993; Lankshear 1998; A. Luke 1996; C. Luke 1992). The New London Group (1996) introduced the term multi-literacies and called for a literacy pedagogy that moved beyond the constraints of linguistic texts to provide students improved social futures. Multimodality, like multiliteracies has also emerged in response to the changing social and semiotic landscape (Jewit 2008). In terms of literacy education, multimodality is about making meaning through a variety of modes (linguistic, image, audio, gestural, gaze and spatial), where no one mode is necessarily privileged. The theory of multi-modality (Kress and van Leeuwen 2001) focuses on all modes of communication and what it is possible to express and represent in particular contexts. Teachers who enact multiliteracies pedagogies apply the theory of multimodality to explicitly instruct students to analyze all modes in any text (linguistic, audio, visual and so on) or communicative event (talk, gesture, movement and gaze) …

Notable here is the way Calvin cites and brackets a wide array of prominent researchers in the field of multi-literacies and multi-modal textual practices to situate his own work in the field. This piling up of scholars bears some resemblance to Mahomet's tendency to stand aside and let the experts do the talking, but Calvin is not selective. He compiles an excess of six pages to recount the history of a field, but does not take up a position within it or signal where his work might fit. There are no evaluations made or debates highlighted, and some traces of the 'he said, she said' pattern are evident. Most significantly, there is no relationship forged between previous research and his own. The textual incapacity to insert himself amongst expert scholars echoes a continuing identity struggle, and is similar to a doctoral researcher parading knowledge for examiners.

Clearly the journal reviewers were not impressed by this tactic, although they found the article of sufficient quality to request Calvin to revise and resubmit. One wrote:

The paper sets out to connect with the key theories in the first section of the paper. The author tries to use the literature to frame the case study but I don't

think it adds very much to the empirical data and the theoretical ground it covers will be well trodden for the readers of *X Journal*. The writing suggests the author is much more at home with the study than the literature review aspect of the paper and I would suggest that much of this first section be deleted and/or substantially condensed ...

This is in fact what Calvin did. He reduced six pages of literature work to one, to better highlight the ideas from the literature needed to showcase his study. Extract Seven comes from the revision where Calvin drastically changes his stance to the work that precedes him.

Extract Seven

This article describes practitioner-research where I enacted a multiliteracies curriculum (The New London Group, 1996; Walsh, 2006) that required students to engage in a discourse analysis of school and media texts (Albright, Purohit and Walsh 2006a; Walsh 2007, 2008). As a teacher practitioner working in the new media age (Kress 2003), I integrated Internet communication technologies with my literacy instruction (Albright, Purohit and Walsh 2002, 2006b; Kamler and Comber 2005; Lankshear, Snyder and Green 2000; Marsh 2005; Snyder and Beavis 2004) and asked students to re-represent their literacy learning through multimodal digital design. The paper first outlines the multiliteracies curriculum that provided a new critical framework, helping me cope with the complexity of digital texts and their access, production and distribution. It then illustrates how digital technologies were incorporated into the curriculum, through a school-museum partnership. I argue that this partnership provided spaces where students could interact, socialize and learn in both the real and virtual world (Beavis and Charles 2007; Lam 2006; Marsh 2003; Sefton-Green 2006). Importantly they were also able develop a new set of multimodal literacy practices to talk back to and challenge racist and exclusionary discourses they find problematic.

Here Calvin is no longer simply reporting or informing the reader, he is interacting with the literature to make an argument for his contribution. A confident scholarly identity is performed: he represents himself as an informed teacher–researcher interacting with the new media age and its literatures to make a difference to his students. He *uses* multi-modal theory (rather than parades it) to argue and illustrate the effects of the new multi-modal practices he designed.

It was difficult for Calvin to perform this expert scholar stance – it took many drafts and further critical readings from colleague mentors to achieve it. But his article was accepted and it became a pivotal moment in his identity reconstitution, where he felt more confident and textually skilled to take his place alongside scholar peers competing for academic journal publication.

In sum: the problem of disconnection

At the beginning of this chapter we pointed out that it is common for commercial publishers to separate out books about research methods from books about the dissertation and books about writing. The same separation occurs through library cataloguing. It may make good 'market' sense to have particular aspects of research as the focus, the lens through which the holistic enterprise of inquiry can be seen. It may also make sense to offer in-depth treatments of particular aspects of research, but these linguistic bifurcations also work discursively. One unfortunate result is that the centrality of language and writing to every aspect of the doctoral scholarly endeavour becomes invisible and is only worthy of comment when students demonstrate apparent technical difficulties in writing.

We have argued against the back-grounding of the mutually constructed tasks of making meaning and making scholars, and shown how one of the most central tasks of doctoral research, working with literatures, is integral to the text work/identity work of scholarship. The texts we have examined demonstrate the complexities of taking up an expert scholarly stance and how the process of ongoing identity formation will always surface in text, whether as awkward, overly deferential or confidently expert doctoral text.

We are grateful to Mahomet, Dierdre and Calvin for allowing us to use their writing to exemplify and illustrate what textwork/identity work might look like on the page, both during and after candidature. Too often the struggle to become authoritative is misread as 'poor writing' and no pedagogic assistance is available to help students take a 'hands on hips' stance. We argue that the process of scholarly identity formation is positively shaped by contexts where doctoral scholars are encouraged to textually justify their positions and advance an argument. Clearly, literature work is a rich site for students and supervisors/advisers to engage in this work together to foster the dual process of scholarly text formation and identity formation.

Notes

1 It is argued that feelings can be prior to their articulation (Lacan 1968): our emphasis here is on sense-making and hence the prioritising of language.

References

Barthes, R. (1986) *The rustle of language*. Trans. R. Howard, Oxford: Basil Blackwell.

Chaplin, E. (1994) *Sociology and visual representation*. London and New York: Routledge.

Game, A. and Metcalfe, A. (1996) *Passionate sociology*. London: Sage Publications.

Hall, S. (Ed.) (1997) *Representation. Cultural representations and signifying practices*. London: Sage.

Harding, S. (1993) Rethinking standpoint epistemology: What is 'strong objectivity'? In L. Alcoff and E. Potter (Eds). *Feminist epistemologies*. New York: Routledge, 49–82.

Holland, D., Lachicotte, W., Skinner, D. and Cain, C. (1998) *Identity and agency in cultural worlds*. Cambridge, MA: Harvard University Press.

Kamler, B. and Thomson, P. (2006) *Helping doctoral students write: Pedagogies for supervision*. London: Routledge.

——(2007) Rethinking doctoral work as text work and identity work. In B. Somekh and T. Schwandt (Eds). *Knowledge production: Research in interesting times*. London: Routledge.

——(2008) The failure of dissertation advice books: towards alternative pedagogies for doctoral writing, *Educational Researcher*, 37(8): 507–18.

Lacan, J. (1968) *The language of the self. The function of language in psycholanalysis*. Baltimore, MD: John Hopkins University Press.

Lather, P. (1991) *Feminist research: with/against*. Geelong: Deakin University Press.

Richardson, L. (1994) Writing. A method of inquiry. In N. Denzin and Y. Lincoln (Eds). *The handbook of qualitative research*. Thousand Oaks, CA: Sage Publications, pp. 516–29.

Rosaldo, R. (1989) *Culture and truth. The remaking of social analysis*. 1993 edn. Boston, MA: Beacon Press.

Saussure, F. D. (1959) *Course in general linguistics*. Trans. W. Baskin. New York: McGraw Hill.

Wittgenstein, L. (1976) *Philosophical investigations*. Trans. G. E. M. Anscombe. Oxford: Basil Blackwell.

13

Constructing research questions

Focus, methodology and theorisation

J. Pryor

Introduction

As a supervisor, doctoral convenor and book reviews editor for an educational research journal, a large number of books on doing social research find their way into my hands during the course of a year. Although I cannot claim to have read them all, I often scan through them for specific issues and topics. In particular, I am always on the lookout for a good reading on research questions to accompany a course I convene on research design, but am never very satisfied. Virtually all the books mention research questions as being very important and many stress that not having good ones can seriously weaken the research project. Wilkinson (2000: 16) even goes as far as to claim that many research projects fail because of poor decisions over research questions. However, having issued the warning this book, like most of the rest goes immediately on to other matters without further discussion about what would constitute suitable research questions to avoid failure. Perhaps this is because as Bryman (2004: 31) suggests, 'the process of formulating and assessing research questions is difficult to spell out'. My suspicion is, however, that in many cases the reason so little space is devoted to the subject is because the process is assumed by many to be a technical one; the way that research questions relate to the wider methodology of research is under estimated. In this chapter I shall argue that selecting research questions is not just a straightforward technical matter. On the contrary, it is a complex task, which brings together a great deal of thinking about the fundamental issues that underpin the project, the way the research is practised and the knowledge that it will hope to produce. However, it is this complexity that gives meaning and importance to social research and what makes its practice so exciting. Moreover, the chapter will also contain practical suggestions as to how to generate research questions where this complexity can be turned to advantage in finding a methodological fit with the intentions of the researcher and others involved in the research.

Research questions are important – but for whom?

For qualitative researchers the research process seems to be full of questions.[1] It is launched with a proposal containing questions; a dataset is created usually through using research methods such as interviews or questionnaires, which depend on questions; and even when the thesis is written, it will need to be defended in an oral examination or defence, which is structured by the questions of the examiners. However, of all these, the research questions are arguably the most important. Research question(s) – for there may only be a single main one – are a device to encapsulate what your research is about. They summarise and sit at the top of a hierarchy of all the other questions that make up the research. They are the super-ordinate, the big questions that both generate and are generated by all the smaller questions.

The most frequently identified way in which research questions work is as a heuristic device for the researcher. They provide focus by defining what the project is about and, equally importantly, they provide boundaries about what the research is not about. Bryman (2004: 31), for example, suggests that they therefore 'stop you from going off in unnecessary directions and tangents' throughout the research process. He continues that they guide your literature search, your decisions about research design and about what data you should 'collect' and from whom; they shape the way that you will analyse the data and the way that you write up the research.

Whilst I generally concur with this and will later explore its implications, the research questions are not just a device for the researcher, but also for the other people involved in your research. For example, research questions may be a way of explaining to collaborators and informants what the research is about. Although the notion of obtaining informed consent is not as straightforward either practically or conceptually across all contexts as it may appear, it does form a useful basis for thinking about the implications and consequences of other people's involvement. If the fundamental questions the research is addressing have not been broached, it may be difficult to make a case for informed consent having been negotiated. Even where, as in my own doctoral research, the researcher decides against giving the research questions to participants, their formulation can be important in thinking about what to say to them, what to withhold and in making a case as to why.

If the research questions are essential to the researcher and the researched, they are also important to the readers and users of the research. Amongst this group, those most salient are the examiners appointed by the university to decide whether you get your doctorate or not. The criteria for a doctoral degree are slightly different at different universities, some specifying more in terms of the process and the acquisition of expected competencies. However, agreement throughout the English-speaking world converges on a criterion of knowledge. Taking three out of many possible examples, a candidate's thesis or dissertation is expected to demonstrate, in the UK: 'the creation and interpretation of new knowledge' (Quality Assurance Agency for Higher Education 2008); in Australia: 'value of original contribution to knowledge in the field' (Australian Council of Deans and Directors of Graduate Studies 2005); and in the USA: 'a genuine contribution to knowledge' (University of Alabama 2008). It is often useful to think of a doctoral thesis as being pyramid-shaped: the different elements of the research, all the steady building of the conceptualisation, the fieldwork, the telling of the story, the analysis and the creation of an argument culminates in the apex of this contribution to knowledge. A way of thinking of this, the point of the research, is as the response to the research questions. Indeed, in the now considerable numbers of doctoral defences I have attended, I can think of several where, when the examiners were not clear about the project's original contribution to knowledge, they asked for it to be reformulated in terms of the research questions.

Important as they are, examiners are only one part of the audience for doctoral research. Increasingly, people undertake a doctorate as part of a commitment to a professional field rather than as an entry into an academic job. The purpose of the research is then to have some influence on the field in which they work, in which case, even if the thesis is not the actual text that will be used to communicate with the professional audience, the research questions will have to address their concerns. Looming even larger for many people are the sponsors of the research, the employers, governments or foundations who provide time and money for the project in the expectation that it will engage with the issues that occupy them and meet their criteria for useful research.

Robinson-Pant (2005: 1) finds that this presents such an important dilemma for international students studying in universities in the UK that she begins her book on cross-cultural perspectives in education research with the question asked by one of her students: 'Should I write two theses or one? My employer might not like the kind of thesis my supervisor encourages to me to write'. She then devotes almost the whole of her chapter on defining the research question to the ramifications of this dilemma.

To summarise, the importance of research questions lies not only in their function as a guide to the researcher, but also in their ability to encapsulate and give meaning to the research for all the people involved with it. The implications of this are that when formulating research questions, we should be thinking not just about the way they may define and focus our own abstract conceptualisation of the area to be researched, but also how other people and discourses are involved. Thus, they are laden with theory in the sense that they derive their meaning from what both the researcher and their potential audience may consider to be important. Research questions are, therefore, far from a technical matter, and any process of creating them will involve both cultural and social engagement.

Research questions and methodology

We can extend this thinking by considering research questions and methodology. Methodology is a slippery term. The addition of the 'ology' widens its meaning beyond that of method, so that it is concerned with thinking about method and the way that research is done. However, within this many people give it a restricted meaning, for example by following Burrell and Morgan (1979) who see methodology as something separate from issues about the nature of knowledge (epistemology), of reality (ontology) and of human nature. Yet your position as a researcher on these issues inevitably shapes the research that you will do and the way you go about it. Therefore, it seems helpful to think of methodology as encompassing all these different dimensions.

In a previous work I have suggested that we might identify six different sets of issues that make up the methodological (Pryor and Ampiah 2004; Dunne et al. 2005).[2] These are the epistemological, ontological, practical, micropolitical, macropolitical, ethical. This is shown in Figure 13.1 by arranging the sets of issues around methodology and connecting them to it by double-headed arrows.

The sets of issues are separate but also paired. It is difficult to speak of epistemology without invoking ontology. Stating an epistemological position, for example, that it is possible to discover knowledge of the world that can be reliably substantiated or disproved, requires particular ontological premises, in this case that there is an objective reality separate from the knower. Similarly, it is very difficult to talk of one's political

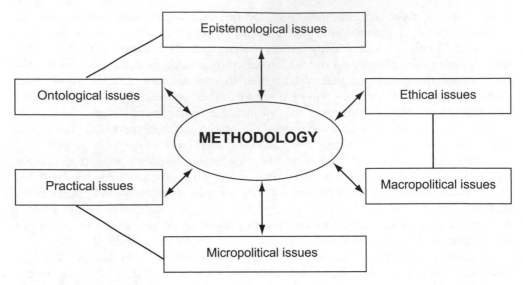

Figure 13.1 Methodology.

views without reference to ethical issues: both tend to relate to generalised positions outside the particular situation in which one is operating and people often have recourse to the one to justify the other. Finally, both practical issues and micropolitics depend on local conditions: which method or instrument is suitable to use and how, will be determined not just by what is physically possibly or convenient but also by the micropolitics of the situation. For example, a busy, powerful head teacher as respondent will call for different techniques from working with a 'captive' group of students; enquiring about institutional strength may need to be approached in a different way from asking about perceived weakness.

Following the arrows on the diagram inward together, the sets of issues constitute the methodology of a research project. Methodology here is concerned with ideology and also with context, both of which cut across the different six sets of issues. The diagram thus offers researchers a kind of checklist for describing and explaining their approach. However, arrows can also be followed outwards to suggest a more dynamic way in which the shape of the methodology results from 'pulls' from the six different dimensions. These methodological pulls take place throughout the research process, not least when one is formulating research questions.

In considering what is worth asking and why, all of the issues exert some influence. For example, a doctoral research student I am currently supervising is involved in a study of second chance education in Sudan. He is interested in the students' perspective, but is constrained by a micropolitical need to work mainly with the teachers. In formulating a research question about students' values, he is therefore concerned to focus the question in the teacher's realities. 'How do the teachers perceive the processes and structures in Adult Education Centres influence the development of the students' values?' What is less apparent is his ontological position, whereby he accepts that values are real and can be developed, and an epistemological one that it is possible, though difficult, to capture and represent the teachers' perceptions. Nevertheless, working at this and his other two questions has entailed a process of thinking through these issues. It is, therefore, not only the research questions, but also the process of having worked on them, that has generated the provisional positions that are proving helpful to him as he does his fieldwork.

Considering research questions within methodology is also important in considering what might constitute good ones. Bryman (2004) suggests that good research questions should be clear, researchable, linked and neither too broad nor too narrow; they should connect with established theory and show potential for new knowledge. This is an uncontroversial list; it is echoed elsewhere and is consonant with many of the things said in this chapter. However, thinking about how research questions relate to a wider notion of methodology, suggests the limits of this list to specify what may be good. Being stretched to cover many different contexts and methodological purposes, the meanings of the terms become elusive. What is the meaning of researchable? A realist researcher may be posing questions in the hope of finding clear answers to research questions, whereas for a poststructuralist finding an answer in this way would be seen as closing down a problem, when their intention is to 'open up' (Stronach and MacLure 1997). Goodness is then more a question of thinking about whether the questions have a methodological fit, both with the project in hand and with the identity as a researcher that you are embracing (Dunne *et al.* 2005). Ultimately, a good research question is one that works in the interests of the research. This performative judgement may include another common idea about what makes a good research question – that it addresses a topic in which the researcher is interested (see, for example, Andrews 2003) – but it goes well beyond individual preferences and emphasises research as social endeavour.

In this section I have suggested that the formulation of research questions is at the heart of methodology. As well as seeing research questions as guiding the research and its methodology, they are themselves guided by the positions that the researcher takes up. Research questions, therefore, have a reflexive or recursive nature: they are both constituted by the different aspects of methodology and in themselves constitute the methodology of an enquiry. Bearing this in mind will be helpful when formulating them.

Useful typologies?

Another common feature of the sections of guidebooks devoted to research questions is systems of categorising them. These are usually allocated most importance by those who take a fairly technical approach to research questions or whose research is more quantitative than qualitative. At their simplest they usually have three categories, such as Drew's (1980) *Descriptive, Relationship and Difference* (often called *comparison* in other schemes). A much more detailed typology is presented by Flick (1998), derived from the work of John Lofland and colleagues (latest edition, Lofland *et al.* 2006). Here, you can locate your questions in the cells of a matrix. Along one axis there are seven types of question, where 'it' is the phenomenon under investigation:

- What type is it?
- What is its structure?
- How frequent is it?
- What are the causes?
- What are its processes?
- What are its consequences?
- What are people's strategies?

165

Table 13.1 Focusing questions (original focusing questions are adapted from De Vaus 2001:17–18)

Focusing question	Expansion
What is the scope of the core concepts?	*What am I referring to?* *What do I mean by…?* *Does that include…?* *Either or both?*
What is the timeframe?	*Am I aiming for a snapshot or a dynamic description or a longitudinal study?* *How far back do I need to go?* *Over what period of time do I need to investigate the phenomenon?*
What is the geographical location?	*How do I define the place in which I am interested?* *How does this relate to the choice of sites or sampling of the research?*
How general is the focus?	*Am I interested in differentiating sub-groups?* *At what level of detail?*
What is the unit of analysis?	*What is the thing about which I hope to draw conclusions: Meanings, Practices, Episodes, Encounters, Roles, Relationships, Groups, Individuals Organisations, Settlements, Worlds, Lifestyles?* (Lofland *et al.* 2006)
How abstract is my interest?	*How central are the phenomena I am exploring to my main interest?* *Am I seeking conclusions on a micro- meso- or macro-level?*

Overarching question:
How can I balance the desirable with the practicable?

On the other axis of the matrix are suggestions for units of analysis, or what kind of 'it' is referred to in the questions (see Table 13.1, in which they are listed).

Despite their ubiquity, I am not certain as to how useful they actually are for doctoral students planning their project. Often they are more useful for locating, describing and analysing a readymade research question than for generating a new one, though even this is problematic. One of my own doctoral thesis questions – 'What strategies can teachers adopt to promote equity in group work in this gender-sensitive area?' – fits very neatly with the last category above. However, the other – 'What gender issues emerge when children are working in groups with computers?' – is more difficult to place. I think it is of the first variety – *what type?* – though this is debatable. But whichever category it fitted made little difference to the research. In practice, people do not begin from the position of thinking that they wish to ask research questions in the form of a particular category, but rather start from thinking of the substantive issues of the field.

Where the different categories may be most useful is in offering another checklist of possibilities when formulating or reformulating a question. Here, the longer lists are possibly more useful, though perhaps less so than looking at actual examples of research questions.[3]

Generating and refining research questions

Creating focus

The notion that research questions define and provide boundaries for a research project provides the rationale for this first activity in formulating them. It also addresses the problem of conceptual scope, which people often encounter in trying to manage their research projects. Very occasionally, the ideas are too narrow and they are left with something that seems to make little sense without taking in a broader picture; however, mostly the boundaries are set too wide, leading to what Kvale (1996: 176) calls the '1000 page question'. In order to develop research questions that work for your project, you need to focus both conceptually and practically and it is the analogy of focus that is exploited here.

The diagram in Figure 13.2, modelled on the viewfinder of a camera, represents your research project. The circle in the middle is the focus of your research, the significant original knowledge that you wish to create. The rectangle around the circle denotes the concepts and ideas that are also in the picture in your research, but which lie outside the central focus. The area outside this rectangle represents things that are obviously part of the field in which the research is situated, but are outside the scope of your prospective investigation. If you copy the diagram out onto a large sheet of paper, you can then write words and phrases and move them around it as you decide what is important in the research. Sometimes writing the ideas on pieces of paper is helpful so that they can be physically moved.

For some people, this activity is enough to produce a map of significance for their prospective research. Others find it useful to have a more structured approach, which is provided by the focusing questions in Table 13.1, adapted and extended from an original model by De Vaus (2001: 17–18). As an analytic framework the table is far from perfect as it contains overlap, but as we have already noted this does not necessarily go hand-in-hand with practicality. Indeed, here the overlap adds to its usefulness as a thinking tool by offering different paths into similar issues. The activity is fairly concrete but it is also intellectually demanding, because as well as encouraging thinking about the logistics of the research, it includes engagement at a theoretical level. Indeed, the more the kind of deconstructive move that questions premises and taken-for-granted assumptions, the more satisfying and creative the exercise is likely to be. During the process the various sets of methodological issues represented in Figure 13.1 will bear on your thinking. Although some issues will arise spontaneously, it is worthwhile looking through them again to check that you have taken them into consideration.

At the end of this process you will have a somewhat messy diagram, which, like a photograph, represents a moving situation in a provisionally concrete form, allowing you to take a more critical look. At this stage the diagram can be a useful artefact to bring to

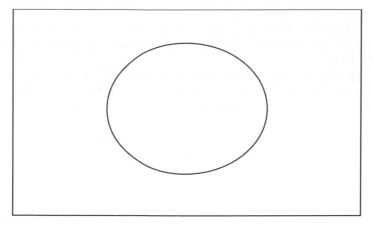

Figure 13.2 Focus diagram.

a supervision session or for discussion with a colleague whilst you clarify. Following discussion, you may decide to change the diagram to make a more advanced working document.

From focus to questions

Doing the focus activity provides ideas that then can be turned into questions by constructing the words produced into question form. What comes forward at this stage may be research questions that you feel are conceptualised, focused and expressed well enough for you to feel happy to work with them. However, it is often useful to go through a further stage of refinement, and here again it is worth holding in mind the issues of methodology outlined in Figure 13.1.

Starting with what is in the circle of your focus diagram, try to formulate a question that encapsulates the whole research. At this stage it does not have to be well formed, nor does it matter if its level of generality makes it somewhat banal. The next stage is to interrogate this question so as to expand it into the series of smaller, though still fairly wide, questions that seem to underlie and proceed from it. The questions within this expansion can then be worked on to produce a second, wider expansion. The notion of deconstruction is often useful here – looking to subvert the assumptions that are behind the original questions, seeking to question binary oppositions and destabilising the obvious. This process will certainly generate a long list of questions. The next stage is to group these together. Then for each group of questions you should seek a super-ordinate question that brings together and covers the ideas in the group. These are potential research questions and the final stage is to go through them adopting them as they are, combining them or ruling them out as your focus has shifted.

To summarise the process:

- Formulate a single overarching question
- Expand into a small group of questions
- Expand each of these through interrogation and deconstruction
- Regroup the resulting questions
- Summarise each group by a new question
- Adopt, combine or reject.

To illustrate this process, Table 13.2 contains an actual example from a doctoral student who was planning a collaborative action research within her context as a teacher trainer in the Middle East.

Further work may still be needed on the questions, for example by checking back against your previous thinking and discussion, and it may be worthwhile doing another iteration of the expansion and contraction. Essentially, this should lead to some research questions that you can work with.

The example ended up with two research questions, and I have already said that my own doctoral project had two questions. However, there is nothing special about this number and again what is a right number will depend on contextual issues. However, as research questions are, by definition, big overarching questions, there are inevitably not too many of them, and if there were they would defeat their purpose of summarising the research. Most doctoral research in my experience ends up with between one and four main questions.

Table 13.2 Example of expansion and contraction of research questions

Initial research question:
Why do trainee teachers go about assessing pupils in the way that they do?
First expansion:
What do they understand by assessment?
Why are they not influenced by my college course on assessment?
What are they influenced by?
Second expansion:
What do they claim as assessment goals?
What assessment methods are they using?
What do they say they are doing?
How do they use assessment in their classrooms?
What do the other people they come into contact with think of as assessment?
What are the supervisors' conceptions of assessment (goals, methods, etc.)?
What are the supervisors' and schools' official requirements and the unofficial expectations of the pre-service teachers in assessing their students?
How are the pre-service teachers made aware of these requirements and expectations?
What are the official requirements of the supervisors in assessing their students, including administrative aspects and educational criteria?
How do supervisors actually assess their students?
How are the pre-service students assessed in the college disciplinary courses?
Recontraction:
1. What are pre-service teacher's conceptions of assessment?
2. What factors might contribute to their conceptions of assessment?

The expanded questions, of course, are not thrown away, but again possibly after some combination and reformulation can be arranged under the main questions as subsidiary questions.

Secrets

Having brought the process of formulating the questions to a neat conclusion it is now time to return to a few more complications.

Within an administration known for the gaffes and inanities of its leader, the US Secretary for Defense made a statement that attracted a lot of ridicule at the time, which on closer examination may not be justified. At a news briefing in February 2002 he said:

> As we know there are 'known knowns'. There are things we know we know. We also know there are 'known unknowns'. That is to say, we know there are some things we do not know. But there are also 'unknown unknowns', the ones we don't know we don't know.
>
> Donald Rumsfeld, Department of Defense, cited in BBC News 2007

Social research can be seen as pursuing knowledge in Rumsfeld's three categories. Replication studies that might fit into the first category are not common in social research at doctoral level, and risk not meeting the criterion of new or original knowledge. If the research is only concerned with known unknowns, then the research questions that are identified at the outset may be still as useful and relevant at the end. However, once you embark on a project those unknown unknowns often start to creep in. Social research is not practised in an idealised environment, but takes place in and investigates specific and changing contexts. In seeking for coherence, you may attempt to be consistent and to hold onto the original research questions. However, contextual flux at all stages of the research process means that it is subject to methodological pulling from the different directions identified in Figure 13.1.

If we extend the idea of the research questions as a guide, we can, of course, treat them as a protection against distractions and diversions. However, while receiving the direction from the guide, we can decide that a diversion is, in fact, more inviting than the original route. But, as we discussed earlier, research questions are not just a guide for a researcher, but also for the reader of the final thesis. So, here, I shall let out the big secret about research questions not widely known by doctoral students at the start of their studies: once you have chosen your research questions there is nothing to stop you from abandoning them completely and making up others that fit better with what you have done. Indeed, if you do change course, to keep the same research questions would actually be counter productive and even confusing for your reader, as their guide will have pointed them in the wrong direction. Unlike projects that are commissioned – though this may be the case for some students – there is nothing to hold you to the same research questions in doctoral research.

As Lather (2007: 29) asserts, decisions about whether you choose to foreground or background your manipulation are up to the researcher and the methodological tradition they are working with. If you choose to foreground it, you may make a virtue out of your changes of direction to demonstrate your reflexivity. I have read more than one thesis where the twists and turns in research questions are a useful analytic narrative device.

With the secret about the mutability of research questions comes another one that has been hinted at before: the significant original knowledge that is the point of the thesis comes through addressing, but not necessarily answering, the research questions. Although it is helpful to think of questions that might be answerable when preparing them, the knowledge produced by many good theses is too contingent, too contextualised and too provocative to be an answer. Indeed, many would claim that this is so for all knowledge in the social sciences – but here we are back to competing epistemological positions.

To summarise, what emerges from this discussion is that formulating research questions is not so much an event as a process. It tends to be cyclical and recursive rather than being linear, and, although it may most obviously happen at the planning stage, it is well worthwhile going again through the thinking that underlies it throughout the project. Research questions both structure, and are structured by, the research, so time spent in composing, reviewing and refining them is time well spent, and offers considerable rewards in thinking about and making meaning from the project. Far from being a simple job to be completed in complying with the technical requirements of a proposal, developing research questions is an important part of structuring the field under study (Flick 1998). To decide on research questions is, thus, to begin the process of theorisation.

Notes

1 For quantitative researchers this may not be quite so true. In research that relies on statistical analysis, research questions are often replaced by hypotheses. Although this chapter may be of some interest to those embarking on a quantitative study, it is mainly addressed at qualitative and mixed methods researchers.

2 This section of the current chapter draws heavily on the argument contained in chapter 11 of Dunne *et al.* (2005).

3 The internet provides a source of many research questions that can be focused towards your particular field by using suitable search terms.

References

Andrews, R. (2003) *Research Questions.* London: Continuum.

Australian Council of Deans and Directors of Graduate Studies (2005) *Framework for best practice in doctoral examination in Australia.* Online. (Available at www.ddogs.edu.au/download/85503575 Accessed 21 March 2009).

BBC News (2007) *What we know about 'unknown unknowns'.* Online. (Available at news.bbc.co.uk/1/hi/magazine/7121136.stm Accessed 21 March 2009).

Bryman, A. (2004) *Social Research Methods.* 2nd edn. Oxford: Oxford University Press.

Burrell, G. and Morgan, G. (1979) *Sociological Paradigms and Organizational Analysis.* London: Heinemann.

De Vaus, D. (2001) *Research Design in Social Research.* London: Sage.

Drew, C. (1980) *Designing and Conducting Research: Inquiry in Education and Social Science.* St Louis, MO: Mosby College.

Dunne, M., Pryor, J. and Yates, P. (2005) *Becoming a Researcher: A Companion to the Research Process.* Maidenhead: Open University Press.

Flick, U. (1998) *An introduction to qualitative research.* London: Sage.

Kvale, S. (1996) *InterViews: An introduction to qualitative research interviewing.* London: Sage.

Lather, P. (2007) *Getting Lost: Feminist efforts toward a double (d) science.* Albany, NY: State University of New York Press.

Lofland, J., Snow, D., Anderson, L. and Lofland, L. (2006) *Analyzing social settings: A guide to qualitative observation and analysis.* 4th edn. Belmont, CA: Wadsworth.

Pryor J. and Ampiah J. G. (2004) Listening to voices in the village: collaborating through data chains. In E. Swadener and K. Mutua (Eds). *Decolonizing Research in Cross-Cultural Contexts: Critical Personal Narratives.* Albany, NY: State University of New York Press.

Quality Assurance Agency for Higher Education (2008) *The Framework for Higher Education Qualifications in England, Wales and Northern Ireland,* London: QAA. Online. (Available at www.qaa.ac.uk/academic infrastructure/FHEQ/EWNI08/default.asp Accessed 21 March 2009).

Robinson-Pant, A. (2005) *Cross Cultural Perspectives in Educational Research.* Maidenhead: Open University Press.

Stronach, I. and MacLure, M. (1997) *Educational Research Undone: The Postmodern Embrace.* Buckingham: Open University Press.

University of Alabama (2008) *Graduate Catalog 2008–2010.* Online. (Available at main.uab.edu/show.asp?durki=95303 Accessed 21 March 2009).

Wilkinson, D. (2000) Planning the Research. In D. Wilkinson (Ed.). *The Researcher's Toolkit.* London: RoutledgeFalmer.

14
Research questions

What's worth asking and why?

A. Brown

'What's worth asking and why?' is without doubt a key question for all researchers. Behind it lies a complex array of issues, some specific to the particular field of research and others more general. The question is of particular pertinence to postgraduate researchers embarking on or working towards a doctorate. The doctorate not only constitutes the highest level of earned academic award, but also arguably involves the highest level of personal investment and greatest level of risk, particularly in the light of high levels of non-completion across the disciplines and apparently increasing time to completion for those who persist (see Halse 2007, for discussion of contemporary concerns about the doctorate and the rhetoric of crisis, and McWilliam 2009, for consideration of the impact of risk consciousness on doctoral education). At every point in the journey, from application for a university place to embarking on the research to completion and award of the doctorate, the issue of whether or not the question you are answering, the problem you are addressing, or the hypothesis you are testing is worthwhile will continue to be a concern (and maybe, even, for a good time after the journey to the award of a doctorate is brought to a successful conclusion).

In this chapter I am going to consider a range of factors underpinning or influencing judgement of 'what's worth asking?' with a particular focus on doctoral research projects. It is clearly going to be difficult to address the issue of the 'worthwhileness' of a specific question in a manner that encompasses the specialised knowledge of the full range of disciplines, subjects and fields of research covered in the modern university (let alone the late- or postmodern university, with its complex offer of interdisciplinary, hybrid and practice-oriented regions of knowledge and research). Indeed, the question of 'field' is of central concern in determining whether or not a research question is worth asking, an issue to which I will return later in this chapter when considering what it means to make an original contribution to knowledge (a common requirement for the award of a doctorate), and the imperative to be able to identify the field to which you are aiming to make a contribution.

The task is further complicated by institutional, national and regional differences in the form and content of doctoral programmes and the criteria for the award. An additional level of complexity is added by the increasing diversity of types of doctorates within any given system of awards, with many institutions offering a range of professional doctorates, as well as doctorates by publication and performance and practice-based awards, alongside more established PhD programmes. These awards, such as the EdD in education, DBA in business, the DEng in engineering and the DClinPsy in clinical psychology, can embody very different expectations about research and the relationship between research and practice (both academic and professional). Consequently, they attract postgraduate researchers with very different backgrounds and aspirations, and offer very different opportunities for research and development (see Scott *et al.* 2004, for an exploration of the professional doctorates in a range of areas of professional practice). My strategy, in the face of this diversity, is to address the more generic issues, and when straying into more specialised concerns to stick, at least initially, to the social sciences, and in particular to my own quasi-discipline of education, and broadening out to consider other disciplines and regions of research as appropriate. My approach will also clearly be coloured by my own sociological and educational interests. In following this path, I aim to be able to say something that is of genuine general interest, and, I hope, utility to postgraduate researchers from diverse disciplines, programmes and contexts.

The research question

It is common for higher education institutions to require a clearly defined research question at the point of application to study for a research degree. In most cases this question is crafted by the applicant, based on previous studies at first degree or masters levels, other academic work they have done, professional and personal interests and experience, or some combination of these. How these influences are weighted may vary according to the form of doctorate (with, for instance, professional concerns coming more to the fore in identifying potential research questions for a professional doctorate such as the EdD or DEng). In some cases, for instance for a scholarship related to a larger funded research project, the research question might already be defined.

There are obvious benefits to having a clearly defined question at the outset of a piece of research, particularly where time and resources for the conduct and completion of the research are limited, as they are for the vast majority of postgraduate researchers. It is vital, however, to acknowledge that, in the course of conducting the research, this question is likely to change. This change might involve anything, from the refinement and clarification of the question as the researcher becomes more familiar with the literature in the field of enquiry, to the outright rejection of initial focus of the research in favour of a completely different question. The degree of latitude available in precision of definition of the initial question and in the degree to which the research can depart from this question will vary between disciplines and with the particular circumstances of the researcher (for instance, the condition of the funding of the research or supervision of the project). The key issue here is that although postgraduate researchers are commonly required by institutions, for understandable reasons, to appear to commit themselves at the very outset of the research to a tightly defined question, in practice it is likely that in the course of the research the question will change. Researchers and their supervisors have to be prepared for interests to shift, and indeed it can be argued that dynamism and flux in 'the research question' are fundamental features of the research process. This does not mean that the definition of an initial research questions serves no useful purpose. It does, for instance, set a direction for the research and place useful limits on the reading to be done in the initial stages of the project. It also enables supervision arrangements to be made that are appropriate to the specialised nature of a doctorate.

Institutional and personal demands for a research question continue throughout the life-course of the research project. Shaping your concerns and interests into a question helps you to gauge your progress according to the extent to which you are moving towards providing an answer to the question. A commonly given piece of advice to postgraduate researchers is to write your research question on a card, which you pin close to your computer screen or other prominent place in your work space. Periodically you should look at the card and consider whether or not what you are currently writing addresses the question written on the card. If it does not, then either adjust what you are doing to address the question, or flip the card over and write on it a question that you are addressing. Although this is crude advice, it makes sense to have some way of assessing the extent to which your activity at any given time is advancing your research. Having a defined research question to which to refer your activity is one way of doing this.

A clearly defined research question also helps in communicating what it is that you are doing to others: from fellow researchers working in the same or a related field, to interested friends and family with no detailed knowledge of your work. Suppose you meet someone in an informal setting, such as a party, who asks what you do. On hearing that you are studying for a doctorate, they ask what your research is about. The challenge here is to provide a succinct description of your research for a non-specialist audience. A clear research question helps provide a way in to understanding what it is you are doing and should give a clear sense of direction to the activity that can be grasped by a non-specialist, though they may not, of course, appreciate the finer details of the research, nor indeed see the importance or fascination of your research endeavour at all. Here, the research question is a device for codifying and communicating what you are doing to a range of different audiences.

The point here is that the formulation of a research question can, and should, have utility to you as a researcher, as well as meeting more formal, institutional and other requirements. It is, though, dynamic, and in many cases will, and should, change, to a greater or lesser extent, as the research develops, and as your knowledge of the field in which you are working (which itself will be in a state of flux) increases. Brown and Dowling (1998; see also Dowling and Brown 2010) present the development of a research project as a dialogue between the theoretical field (where the research question, or problem, is formulated as a relationship between a number of concepts) on the one hand and the empirical field (where research strategies are operationalised and outcomes produced) on the other. Neither side necessarily has the upper hand, with developments on one side warranting adjustments on the other, in a dialogue that continues throughout the process of research.

Question form might not be the best way of encapsulating the focus of your research. In some disciplines, the formulation of a hypothesis to be tested is more appropriate. In other areas of work it might be more appropriate to identify a problem to be addressed, or an issue to be explored, which will be broken down into more specific questions that are formulated as the research progresses. In some cases, the production of the question being addressed, in its final form, might not be possible until a relatively late stage in the research, as it is formulated and reformulated in an iterative process in dialogue with a progressive programme of empirical and/or analytic work. The latter is clearly a high-risk strategy if you want to be confident that the question you are addressing is worthwhile.

What must be avoided at all costs is tyranny of the research question. Here, researchers, under pressure to capture their work as a clearly defined question, formulate it in a way that misrepresents or is tangential to their interests. Subsequently, attempts to answer the question lead them away from their interests, or even expertise, and begin to dictate a particular approach or form of work with which they feel uncomfortable, uninterested and unprepared. The research question should guide, but not dictate.

Contribution to the field

One common feature of doctorates, certainly in the UK at the time of writing, is that they should make an original contribution to knowledge in their field. *The Framework for Higher Education Qualifications in England, Wales and Northern Ireland* (Quality Assurance Agency for Higher Education 2008: 23), for instance, states that

> doctorates are awarded to students who have demonstrated: the creation and interpretation of new knowledge, through original research or other advanced scholarship, of a quality to satisfy peer review, extend the forefront of the discipline, and merit publication.

This means that, whatever the discipline or area of research, to begin to get a sense of what is worth asking entails engagement with what constitutes original research and new knowledge within your field of work, and getting a sense of the principles of evaluation of the quality of research. Clarity regarding the field in which you are working is essential, not least because your supervisor, colleagues and examiners will be members and representatives of that field, and will have particular expectations about the manner in which research is conducted, the kinds of knowledge produced and the manner in which the process and outcomes of research are presented in the thesis. For some researchers, identifying the field in which they are working is straightforward. They might, for instance, be working in a highly specialised and well-established area of work that is strongly institutionalised with clear boundaries, a well-defined academic community and a strong sense of disciplinary identity. Their project could, for instance, be a part of the work of an established research team, which has a clear sense of what constitutes legitimate research in the field and where the limitations in the current state of knowledge lie. This form of 'lab culture', in which postgraduate researchers are inducted into the academic culture of the field in which they are working, is more common in the natural sciences than in the social sciences and humanities. Although this has the advantage of presenting a strong sense of field membership and the security, often, of an already specified research question, it does place constraints on the extent to which postgraduate researchers can take control of or influence the direction their research takes.

As Bernstein (1975) has observed, in his discussion of forms of knowledge in the field of sociology in the 1970s, some disciplines comprise a number of distinct, and sometimes competing, sub-groups. These groups can differ not only in the form that research takes, but more fundamentally in how the social and/or physical world is conceived, what constitutes a legitimate question and how the outcomes of research are mediated and evaluated. A worthwhile question or research focus for one of these sub-groups may not be recognised as worthy of any attention at all by another. The growth of inter-disciplinary research and increasing interest in practice-oriented research complicates the situation further by bringing together disciplines and areas of professional practice in a multiplicity of ways, which makes it impossible to provide straightforward explicit guidance on how to identify your field. It also makes it more likely that your research can be positioned in not one but a number of fields. The relative maturity of a field of research can have an impact on the consensus on and stability of the principles of evaluation of research in the field. The bringing together of fields or disciplines in new configurations of inter-disciplinary or interprofessional work also entails the need to resolve diverse and possibly conflicting criteria for evaluation of research. In making decisions about questions to address and approaches to take, postgraduate researchers need to be aware of possible areas of instability, uncertainty and contestation, and the associated opportunities and risks.

In order to gain a sense of what constitutes a worthwhile question, we, as researchers, have to position ourselves and our work in relation to what has already been done and is currently in progress. This means that we have to engage with existing research and other writing, encompassing our theoretical, empirical and practical academic, personal and professional interests. What is commonly referred to blandly as a 'literature review' in the social sciences is, more accurately, a form of active engagement with writing and other academic and professional artefacts in order to gain a sense of the landscape in which we are working, and figure out where we stand in this landscape, and, import-antly, a clear sense of the other individuals and groups standing alongside us. That said, fields are dynamic, with differing degrees of coherence and stability, making it more or less easy to gain a sense of where one stands. As both the field and our own research develop, where we stand and who stands alongside us may change, and we need to have a clear sense of when and how these changes take place and what the consequences are of any given shift. Thus, although an initial identification of and engagement with our field of research and sharpening of our sense of its dynamics and limits are necessary to provide an initial orientation, this engagement has to continue throughout the life-span of the project, and, in the development of an academic career, beyond the project. Working at the outer edges of current knowledge in the field is, by definition, unstable and risky. Continuing engagement with work in the field is necessary in managing this uncertainty and maximising confidence that a worthwhile contribution is likely to be made to the field, in a way that is recognised as original and rigorous by other researchers.

No matter how pertinent and interesting the question being addressed in the research, not knowing the field in which you are working and not knowing it sufficiently well to be able to position your work and establish its originality and rigour, clearly constitutes a major threat to the perceived value of the project. There are clearly ways of mitigating this risk. A field is sustained by a community of researchers, and so interaction with members of the community and participation in its activities, for instance, help to ensure the relevance and value of the research, and help, in turn, to shape the field. The char-acteristics of this community might, indeed, influence the decision to conduct research in a particular area.

Ultimately, the examiners of the thesis, as representatives of the field of research, have to make a judgement about the extent to which your thesis makes a legitimate and ori-ginal contribution to knowledge in the (that is, their and your) field. In cases where the research spans more than one academic field, or combines professional and academic interests, the examiners, if they represent different disciplines, fields or interests, may come with very different expectations. In research of this sort, it pays from the outset to be clear about the extent to which these expectations are likely to be compatible. In the social sciences, for instance, it is common for a thesis to address a particular specialised area of practice from a particular theoretical perspective or from a specific methodologi-cal position. A thesis that examines the processes and practices of inclusion of children with specific special education needs in primary schools from a sociological perspective may lend itself to examination by experts in both the substantive area of special needs education and in the sociology of education (or a more specialised sub-group or either or both these fields). The combination of examiners (as representatives of the fields and legitimate evaluators of the thesis) will be very different if the topic is approached from, say, a psychological, historical or philosophical perspective. Bringing together a set of substantive professional interests with a particular disciplinary perspective requires mutual recognition of the value of the accounts produced by the other. For a postgraduate researcher deciding on whether a question or topic is worth asking, it is necessary to be confident that such areas of mutual recognition exist, or can be created, or that potential differences can be resolved with respect to the project and the approach adopted.

The key issue here is knowing the audience, or audiences, for our research, and being clear about who can, and ultimately will, evaluate the work. A major threat to successful completion of a doctoral project is, in relation to this, not having an audience, or having an audience that is not in a position, in the eyes of the accrediting institution, to evaluate the work. A postgraduate researcher who is convinced that her or his work is so innovative that there is no one who is in a position to evaluate it, is clearly going to have trouble bringing her or his doctorate to a successful conclusion. Similarly, there are projects that are seen as being of vital importance to a community, but where members of that community are not in a position, with respect to the criteria for examination held by an academic institution, to evaluate the research. This is not an argument for a conservative orientation. Academic fields, like fields of practice, have differing appetites for risk, challenge and change, and clearly change does take place. It is, however, an argument for recognition that the doctorate is an academic award and that academic fields are regulated and institutionalised, albeit to differing degrees. In attempting to assess whether or not a research question is worth asking, it is important to bear this in mind. We have to assess our own appetite for, or tolerance of, risk and be aware of strategies that are available to mitigate this risk.

Processes and products

Though the feature that distinguishes the doctorate from other earned academic awards is making an original contribution to knowledge, how that contribution is achieved and how it is presented in the thesis is also important. The criteria for the award of a PhD at my own institution, for instance, include a formidable list of other requirements: that the thesis consist of the candidate's own work, that it 'be an integrated whole and present a coherent argument', that it includes a full list of references, that it is written in English, that it demonstrates the capacity for autonomous research, that it provides a critical assessment of relevant literature, that it demonstrates a deep understanding of the field, that it demonstrates relevant research skills and that it is 'of a standard to merit publication in whole or in part or in revised form', and more. And all in 80,000 words, and taking just the equivalent of three years full-time study, and presented in print with specified line spacing and page margins, and so on.

The issue here is that although the question being addressed must be of current interest in the field of study, and hold the potential to give rise to an original contribution to knowledge, this is not necessarily sufficient for it to be worth asking. For a postgraduate researcher working towards a doctorate, the question must also be 'do-able' within the constraints and expectations of a doctoral thesis. It must also be do-able given the institutional context and the skills, interests, circumstances and dispositions of the researcher and his/her supervisor, who has a key role in supporting and enriching the process of research. Furthermore, it has to have the potential to give rise to a process through which specialised knowledge and research skills can be developed and deployed alongside generic, transportable and employment-related knowledge, dispositions and skills. Finally, the question must engage you as a researcher, and the process of research must have the potential to meet your immediate and longer term aspirations. Here, we are focusing on the process of research, and addressing the extent to which the research question will give rise to a process that delivers more than just a completed thesis.

Working towards a doctorate should be an educational experience. Your supervisor plays a key role in supporting you in the development of your project and in providing guidance and feedback on progress towards successful completion. Your supervisor also has a more general educative role to play, in helping you to explore and understand the field in which you are working and in enabling you to acquire both the specialist and generic skills and knowledge you require not only to complete the thesis successfully, but also to become an active participant in the relevant research community or communities and to meet your own academic and/or professional career aspirations.

Clearly, it is important that your supervisor has the expertise and experience to be able to assess the value of your project and advise you on how it might be developed. With less experienced supervisors, or with experienced supervisors who are supervising on the edges or outside their immediate field of expertise, it is important that some kind of additional expert support is provided, in the form of either joint supervision, a supervisory panel or supervisor mentoring. It is, in any case, advisable to have people in addition to your principal supervisor involved in support of your project, or at least involved in the monitoring of progress. This is commonly achieved by appointing a second supervisor to work in a supporting role, or the appointment of a supervisory panel to support the supervisor.

As research into the process of supervision has consistently demonstrated (see, for instance, Delamont, Atkinson and Parry 2000), the strategies used by supervisors, and the level and quality of support provided, is highly variable. Institutions also vary in the form and quality of support provided for postgraduate researchers, both in terms of the facilities offered and the scope and quality of the research training provided. For a postgraduate researcher, the lack of suitable institutional and/or supervisory support for a project can render a potential worthwhile project highly problematic. The context has to be right to realise the full potential of a project.

The form of support provided by the supervisor constitutes one part of the institutional environment that facilitates the 'do-ability' of the project (and therefore the 'answerability' of the question). As the project develops, other factors come into play that influence the extent to which a project is do-able, both generally and more specifically within the confines of the journey to completion of a doctoral thesis.

Ethical considerations, for instance, clearly impact on whether or not a project is do-able, and, if it is, whether or not the conduct of the project is advisable or desirable. An investigation of, say, the educational progress of children identified as having a particular kind of learning difficulties, which requires access to data collected routinely and confidentially by schools for purposes other than research, is going to confront a number of difficult ethical issues relating to access to and use of data. Likewise, a study by a senior manager in an organisation, which involves interviews with members of staff about their aspirations and perceptions of decision making in the organisation, is going to involve difficult conversations in which interviewees may feel they are compromising their position in the organisation and endangering their prospects by revealing aspects of their lives and selves that would normally have been kept private. It also opens up the possibility that this unease will lead to partial accounts that compromise the quality of the data collected. In both these cases, the research questions being addressed may be, from the perspectives of researchers and/or practitioners in the field, well worth asking. The means by which they have to be, or are being, addressed may render the research questions, from an ethical and practical perspective, 'not worth asking'.

As studying for a doctorate is likely to span a number of years, it is important that the initial enthusiasm that you have for your project can be sustained (and that the interest of others in your field can also be assured over the period of research). Is the topic of research sufficiently engaging? Is the approach you are adopting one with which you feel comfortable? Does the mode of data collection lead you to engage in forms of activity that you enjoy, and thus are more likely to be able to sustain (for instance, a project in which data is collected through interviews is more likely to be sustainable and successful if the researcher particularly enjoys talking to people). Sustainability also has to be considered with respect to issues such as access to empirical settings over the period of research and meeting the costs of the research. Whatever the potential of the question to give rise to a contribution to knowledge in the field, it has to be possible to complete the project itself with the time, resources, expertise and support available to you, as the researcher, bearing in mind the circumstances you are in, your own particular skills, interests and dispositions and so on. And, ideally, the process should be enjoyable and fulfilling.

'What's worth asking' is also influenced by what you hope to gain from the process of working towards a doctorate, and from the eventual award of the doctorate. Analysis of UK first destination occupational data (UK Grad Programme 2008) shows that graduates from doctoral programmes take up a wide range of forms of employment across diverse sectors. Although a significant proportion of graduates do take up research-related employment, it can no longer be assumed that a doctorate is principally preparation for a research or academic career. This has fuelled a greater emphasis on generic and transferable employment related skills in PhD programmes. It has also led to an acknowledgement that people enter PhD programmes with a broad range of aspirations and follow diverse occupational trajectories on graduation. Diversification in the types of doctorate offered, for instance the growth of professional doctorates that act as either initial training or a form of further professional development for particular professional groups, has also increased awareness that what postgraduate researchers hope to gain from a programme is increasingly varied. This diversity of aspirations is catered for in the structure and content of programmes, with professional doctorates, such as the Doctor of Engineering (DEng), offering a range of taught courses, which combine specialised skills and knowledge relating directly to the area of research, with more explicitly employment-related components, such as input on business practice, production processes, research management and knowledge transfer.

Career, and other personal aspirations, should also be taken into account in ascertaining whether or not a research question is worthwhile, for you personally, to address. This involves a balancing of academic field-related and professional concerns with personal dispositions, skills and circumstances. Particular questions offer specific opportunities, for skills development and new experiences in the short term, and for work and life opportunities in the longer term. Analysis of particular forms of data may, for instance,

179

provide opportunities to use and develop expertise with certain forms of analysis software, which, in turn, may place you in an advantageous position with respect to future occupational choices. This also holds for the substantive focus of the research. Knowledge and expertise developed through your research may have greater or lesser utility to you in future career development.

Current circumstances also influence the selection of a question to research. Your personal and professional commitments determine the time you have available to study and how this time is distributed. For postgraduate researchers studying part-time, professional commitments and conditions can both create opportunities, for instance to carry out a study focusing on the setting in which you work, and render some lines of enquiry impossible, for instance research that requires an extended period of time in another setting. From the possible array of potentially worthwhile research questions in your field, there are going to be some that are not, through personal and professional circumstances, possible to take up, and others, through the opportunities that they afford in relation to interests and aspirations, which would be particularly worth addressing.

This is not to sanction or encourage a purely instrumental view of selection of a topic to research, but rather to emphasise that 'what's worth asking' is not just a function of the field of research, but also relates to who you, the researcher, are, and how your circumstances and aspirations position you in relation to the processes and outcomes of doing research.

Conclusion

Formally, 'what's worth asking and why?' could be seen as a function of the current state of the field of study – what is the current state of knowledge, where are the gaps, what constitutes an interesting and productive study in relation to other work in the field? So, to answer the question 'what's worth asking?', we could say 'a question is worth asking if it makes an original contribution to knowledge in the field'. Fields are not always quite so simple to identify, and exploration of the field, in order to position one's own work, constitutes a major part of the project of completion of a doctorate. Fields are not discrete, nor are they defined by or limited to academic disciplines, but incorporate, relate to, overlap with, influence and are influenced by each other and domains of professional practice. You have to know the field in order to be confident that the question you are intending to address will give rise to knowledge that is considered within the field to be new, original and interesting. Although this does not enable us, here, to make a positive, non-contingent statement about what is worth asking, it does carry a very important message with respect to doctoral projects. You must be able to identify a field, in the sense of a recognisable community of researchers with common interests and approaches, in which to locate your work. It is from this community that representatives will be drawn (as examiners) in order to evaluate the extent to which your work advances knowledge in the field, and does so in a way that demonstrates a good understanding of the field (substantively and methodologically) and adopts a form of research that is recognised as appropriate and legitimate by other members of the field of research.

A topic or question might appear to a researcher to be worthwhile in itself, but without a field or community, its value cannot be recognised. Although doctoral theses can, should and do play an important part in the development of new fields of study and new approaches to research, it is unlikely that a new field will be initiated, though it can be signalled, in a doctoral thesis. The nature of, and risks associated with, the examination of a doctoral thesis place limits on novelty. The 'attack on the taken for granted world of their audience' that Davis (1971: 311) associates with 'interesting' social theories (and, for Davis, all 'great' social theories are considered as such because they are seen within the field as 'interesting', not because they are seen to be 'true') carries a huge risk for a postgraduate researcher. So, although originality is essential in a worthwhile doctoral research project, there are distinct dangers in being, or at least seeing oneself as being, so far ahead of the cutting edge of contemporary research that no one is in a position to judge its value or quality. For originality to be established, someone has to be in a position, other than the researcher her- or himself, to make that judgement. There has to be a readership that is knowledgeable and respected in the field.

For a question to be worth asking, it also has to be answerable, and answerable within the limits imposed by a doctoral programme and thesis. These relate, as we have seen, to the resources available to do the research (in terms of time, money and equipment, for instance), the institutional setting (in terms of supervisory expertise, training to do the research and access to sites of research, for instance) and the form and format of the thesis (in terms of both how the research has to be physically presented in thesis form, and the requirements of the thesis to demonstrate broader competence, expertise and knowledge than may be strictly required for completion of the project and answering the question, exploring the problem or testing the hypothesis). As the foundation for a doctoral project, to be worth asking the question has to be answerable within the confines and affordances of a doctoral programme. This is in addition to other 'do-ability' issues that concern all research, for instance relating to ethical research practice.

A worthwhile project must not only be do-able in relation to the doctoral programme and the support it provides, it must be personally engaging and sustainable for you, as the postgraduate researcher, in your particular circumstances. This personal dimension should not be under estimated. A worthwhile question that is not personally engaging, or that requires expertise and attributes that you do not have, is unlikely to give rise to a process of research that can be brought to a successful conclusion. Losing motivation, either through loss of interest in your work, or through the trials of meeting constant personal and academic challenges, can be fatal for a doctoral research project. Making a judgement of 'what's worth asking' must thus take into consideration the researcher her- or himself and her or his circumstances. It is not just 'the field' that renders a project worthwhile; who is asking and in what circumstances is equally important in figuring out 'what's worth asking?', and 'why?' is as much an issue of the extent to which it is answerable in personal, practical and situated terms, as it is a matter of the state of knowledge of the field of research.

References

Bernstein, B. (1975) *Towards a Theory of Educational Transmissions* (Class, Codes and Control, Vol. 3). London: Routledge and Kegan Paul.

Brown, A. J. and Dowling, P. C. (1998) *Doing Research/Reading Research: a mode of interrogation for education*. London: RoutledgeFalmer.

Davis, M. S. (1971) That's Interesting!: Towards a phenomenology of sociology and a sociology of phenomenology, *Philosophy of the Social Sciences*, 1(2): 309–44.

Delamont, S., Atkinson, P. and Parry, O. (2000) *The doctoral experience: success and failure in graduate school*. London: Falmer Press.

Dowling, P. C. and Brown, A. J. (2010) *Doing Research/Reading Research: re-interrogating education*. London: Routledge.

Halse, C. (2007) Is the Doctorate in Crisis? *Nagoya Journal of Higher Education*, 34: 321–37.

McWilliam, E. (2009) Doctoral education in risky times In D. Boud and A. Lee (Eds). *Changing Practices of Doctoral Education*. London: Routledge, 189–99.

Quality Assurance Agency for Higher Education (2008) *The Framework for Higher Education Qualifications in England, Wales and Northern Ireland*. Gloucester: The Quality Assurance Agency for Higher Education.

Scott, D., Brown, A., Lunt, I. and Thorne, L. (2004) *Professional doctorates: integrating professional and academic knowledge*. Buckingham: Open University Press.

UK Grad Programme (2008) *What do PhDs do?–trends*. London: Careers Research and Advisory Centre.

15

'There is no golden key'

Overcoming problems with data analysis in qualitative research

H. Colley

Introduction

This chapter draws on experiences from my own doctoral research project, conducted from 1998 to 2001, to explore problems I encountered with data analysis, and to describe a variety of techniques that (eventually) helped me transform the data successfully. In short, it is a story about how data analysis *was* the problem; how (in this case) data *synthesis* proved a more suitable method for transforming data; and how I learned through this that there is no 'golden key', no 'proper' method that will unlock our data for us. It is our research enquiry that must drive the methods we adopt, otherwise the risk is that the methods will drive our enquiry – possibly entirely off course.

My PhD project focused on the experiences of two sets of learners involved in mentoring – young 'disaffected' people, and university undergraduates who acted as mentors for them – and the meanings they brought to and developed through mentoring. Therefore, I begin by explaining the type of mentoring involved, and the research concerns that this practice posed for me. This includes the identification of particular gaps in existing knowledge about mentoring that I wished to address.

After briefly indicating the nature of the research project and the critical interpretive approach I took, I go on to explore the particular difficulties of making sense of the interview data I had generated with mentors and mentees, giving illustrative examples of different techniques of analysis I applied, and their results. I evaluate the texts I produced at different stages of the research from the perspective of how I presented issues of cultural capital (Bourdieu and Wacquant 1992) through them. A case study of one particular mentoring relationship is discussed to show how I finally developed a theoretical framework for understanding mentoring as a process of emotional labour to produce specific and gendered forms of cultural capital in both mentor and mentee.

However, the struggle to make sense of my data also revealed how I, as the researcher, needed to be aware of my own power to construct the cultural resources of respondents as cultural capital or as culturally redundant within the educational research field, and the tendency of inappropriate use of research methods both to reinforce and to obscure that power. By the end of this journey, I realised that research questions, researcher values, theoretical understandings, research methods, and a need for sociological reflexivity in research are all far more inextricably inter-related than I had anticipated at its start. I conclude here by considering the place of methods in qualitative research in this light, especially in the current context of debate about the future of educational research and the dangers of imposed consensus in the field. I turn first to an explanation of the context of my research, starting with a definition of the practice of engagement mentoring that I studied.

What is 'engagement mentoring'?

Engagement mentoring is a term I have used to designate a particular form of mentoring for socially excluded youth that emerged in the USA in the early 1990s, and in Britain in the latter half of that decade. I have given a fuller account elsewhere of this model of mentoring and the socio-economic context for its development (see Colley 2001a; 2003a; 2003b). Examples include a range of projects funded by the European Youthstart Initiative (Employment Support Unit 2000; Ford 1999) and of local projects funded through the voluntary sector (e.g. Benioff 1997; see also Skinner and Fleming 1999 for a review of over 40 similar projects). Since the election of the Labour government in Britain in 1997, engagement mentoring has also become a central feature of initiatives addressing youth offending and health education, and of school-to-work transition systems such as the Learning Gateway, New Deal for Young People, and the Connexions service.

In brief, engagement mentoring has a number of defining characteristics. First, its nature is planned and formalised within institutional contexts and agendas. This contrasts with the informal mentoring relationships that many young people seek out for themselves, in which agendas are negotiated without external third-party intrusion. Second, it is targeted at socially excluded young people, and its aim is to re-engage those young people with the labour market and structured routes thereto. The underpinning assumption is that paid employment is the prime condition for social integration, and legal or financial compulsion to participate is sometimes a factor. Third, the role of mentors in this process is to transform young people's attitudes, values, behaviours and beliefs so that they acquire 'employability'. Employability itself is frequently defined as a requirement for young people to engage their personal commitment to the needs of employers and the economy (e.g. Industry in Education 1996), although this requirement has been criticised as having 'more to do with shaping subjectivity, deference and demeanour, than with skill development and citizenship' (Gleeson 1996: 97). There is, of course, nothing strikingly new in this concept of employability shaping various education and training frameworks as instrumental (cf. Bathmaker 2001), but its influence on the practice of mentoring has barely been questioned or investigated until now.

A fourth characteristic concerns the subjectivity and disposition of mentors themselves. A particular construct can be identified in the discourse of mentoring that includes the specific context of engagement mentoring, but also extends into other fields of professional development. Mentors are expected to go 'beyond the call of duty' on behalf of their mentees, and they are often portrayed as saintly or god-like characters (Ford 1999: 13; see also Megginson and Clutterbuck 1995; Shea 1992; Standing 1999). In engagement mentoring, their role has been compared to that of a parent, exhibiting selfless devotion to the needs of the mentee. They must embody the ideal of both rational control and self-sacrificing care, in order to rectify the deficits or deviancies of their mentee and render them employable. Compounded by the fact that the vast majority of mentors for socially excluded young people are women, this is redolent of the gender stereotype of female nurture that is a central aspect of women's oppression (for a fuller critique of this construction of mentors' role, see Colley 2001b; 2003a; 2003b). Furthermore, this is connected with a view that mentoring will also enhance the employability of those who act as mentors, whether they are already in employment (Skinner and Fleming 1999), or whether they are students preparing to enter the graduate labour market themselves (Goodlad 1995).

Researching mentoring through the perceptions of participants

In reviewing the literature on mentoring socially excluded young people, it appears that a considerable research agenda remains unexplored. Most mentoring research takes an individualistic approach to the subject, and much of it is conducted through the discipline of psychology. It consists predominantly of quantitative surveys that measure standardised 'before and after' indicators of outcomes for mentees such as criminal offending, educational grades and attendance, violent behaviour or substance misuse, or aspects of individual interactions between mentoring partners (e.g. Alleman 1986; DuBois and Neville 1997; Golden and Sims 1997; Grossman and Tierney 1998; McPartland and Nettles 1991; Ringwalt *et al.* 1996). Such literature has been criticised for bias in favour of mentoring, for failing to substantiate its claims for the benefits of mentoring, and for ignoring the 'dark side' of mentoring and its possible harmful effects (Long 1997; Merriam 1983; Scandura 1998). A few critical studies have challenged the ideological basis of engagement mentoring for young people, and the way the practice is usually disembedded from its broader socio–economic and political context (Gulam and Zulfiqar 1998; Piper and Piper 1999; 2000).

There are no in-depth studies of the progress of engagement mentoring relationships between the 'before and after' measurements, so existing research gives us little insight into how such relationships develop through the perceptions of those involved. The generation of such data seemed to be a valuable contribution to this field of knowledge. I have also argued that the power dynamics of engagement mentoring need to be considered beyond the one-dimensional view of mentor–mentee relations, to take into account the operation of power at institutional and structural levels (Colley 2003a; 2003b; 2007). In particular, as the data were generated, it allowed me to address three neglected questions about engagement mentoring:

- Do young people exercise agentic power, and if so, how?
- Are mentors subject to external sources of power through control and surveillance, including self-surveillance?
- How are mentoring dyads situated in relation to wider power relations, through their overt institutional setting as well as more covert aspects of power such as dominant discourse and structural forms of oppression?

In the empirical study, funded by the Manchester Metropolitan University through a three-year PhD student bursary, I used qualitative methods to investigate a small number of mentoring relationships between two groups of learners. The mentees were 16–18-year-olds on a pre-vocational training scheme I shall call 'New Beginnings'. It was run by a local Training and Enterprise Council (TEC) for young people it classed as 'disaffected'. Mentoring was an optional part of the package for the young people, which also included in-house basic and pre-vocational skills training and intensively supported work experience placements. The mentors were all volunteers, and were undergraduate students from the local university. Most were either student teachers or students of applied social sciences, and were aged between 20 and 48. The goal of the scheme was to achieve outcomes of employment or Youth Training for the young people, and the mentors' training course and handbook made it clear that their primary task was to promote this goal in their discussions with their mentee.

The fieldwork consisted primarily of semi-structured individual interviews with mentors and mentees in established relationships. These were followed up when the relationship ended, or up to a year later in the case of ongoing relationships. The opportunity sample used (all the willing respondents during my period of access to the scheme) resulted in data about nine relationships. I also interviewed New Beginnings' staff, related professionals, and was a participant observer in the mentors' training course and the scheme management committee. All interviews were taped and fully transcribed.

In contrast to the dominant approaches to research on mentoring, I used a tripartite analysis to explore the connections between micro-level interactions, identities dispositions, cultural backgrounds and discursive constructs that mentors and mentees brought to their relationships; meso-level influences on mentoring relationships through their local and institutional context within a particular scheme; and the macro-level influences of national policy, dominant discourse and wider socio-economic structures. I wanted to make sense of the way the young people and their student mentors experienced mentoring and the meanings it had for them, with a recognition that such experiences and meanings are inevitably mediated by contextual factors beyond the purely individual.

Accordingly, the research approach I adopted was a critical interpretive one (Anderson 1989), informed by my socialist-feminist perspective and my own disposition as a white woman from a poor working class background. At the same time, I wanted to avoid that perspective becoming a rigid mould for the data (Lather 1986). I had to be constantly aware that my biases could easily lead me to be partisan towards the young people and to blame the mentors for any difficulties in the relationships. This would have framed my interpretations within the same individualistic interpretations by which most mentoring research constructs an opposition between the powerful mentor and the powerless or disempowered mentee.

My original research proposal posed just three key questions, which informed my interview schedule:

1. How do mentors' and mentees' self-perceptions and interperceptions influence their mentoring relationships?
2. To what extent is the process of mentoring perceived to be empowering by/for 'disaffected' young people and students in their transitions to adulthood and work?
3. How do social, economic and political contexts impact on the effectiveness of mentoring in addressing young people's disaffection and in preparing students for graduate employment?

Paradigmatic analysis of data

In one sense, it is of course artificial to separate out entirely any one stage of research from another. We talk about data generation and analysis as separate tasks, yet in reality I was making spider diagrams of each interview after I had carried it out, listening to the tapes, jotting notes and partial transcripts of what seemed to be significant passages, continuing to read the literature and make connections with that, cross-referencing different interviews with margin notes in the full transcripts, and so on. At the same time, issues I had expected to explore were becoming redundant, whereas unexpected themes emerged.

Two of my early assumptions, reinforced by the literature, were quickly challenged. First, it became evident that young people did not only assert their own agency through a 'take it or leave it' approach to the experience of mentoring, but also engaged in active struggle within their relationships to pursue their own agendas rather than the institutional agenda mentors were expected to convey. Second, I had assumed that the students, possessing greater cultural capital than disaffected young people, would be able to accumulate relatively more through their experience of mentoring, and to obtain greater benefits than the young people from the process. In our interviews, however, the students seemed to have lost confidence the longer they had been mentoring. A number also described a strong sense of surveillance and even fear about their experiences, as they located themselves in relation to the New Beginnings scheme and its staff.

As these concerns emerged, I adjusted my interview schedule to explore them in further interviews. In this way, ongoing analysis and generation of data came together in an iterative process where each fed into the other. Nevertheless, by the time I had completed my first round of data generation, I needed to focus on the analysis in a more concentrated way, and so – despite the cautions of my director of studies – I turned to research method textbooks for advice.

Both qualitative and quantitative research are dominated by a paradigmatic approach to data analysis and to cognition itself (Polkinghorne 1995). This suggests that the basic technique is to identify key categories or classifications that emerge from the data in relation to the research questions; to code the data according to these categories, with the use of the 'cut-and-paste' word-processing facility often recommended as an alternative way to extract and classify data (Mason 1996; Ritchie and Spencer 1994). Software programs such as NUD*IST allow similar but more sophisticated facilities writ large. Fundamentally, however, the process is one of identifying similarities and differences (Dey 1993; May 1997). The process then moves on to the elaboration of more abstract concepts, and the interconnections that can be drawn between categories, with recommendations for the drawing up of matrices, typologies and spectra. Huberman and Miles (1998) advocate that this should be pursued with an 'audit trail' approach that would allow other researchers to trace each step in the process. Such transparency is supposed to provide a further methodological guarantee of validity through the application of ever-more-perfect technique.

Some of these techniques were pragmatically impossible for me to pursue, given my limited IT competence and facilities, and constraints of time. However, I did set about constructing my categories, using mind-maps for all of the interview transcripts. I knew I was not genuinely using grounded data theory, because the relationship between my analysis and data generation was not premised on the evolving alternation of the formation of hypotheses and their verification in the field (Strauss and Corbin 1998), but like many other researchers I drew on its ethos, trying to ensure that the analysis emerged from the data, that I had 'saturated' all my categories and that I had not glossed over relevant data (Bryman and Burgess 1994a; 1994b). I hoped that I would be able to discern relationships of similarity and difference, both within each group of interviewees, and between them, and I worked extremely hard at the laborious task of trawling what was already a huge amount of data to produce the following categories:

- Self-description
- Motivation for involvement with mentoring
- Perception of partner
- Perception of disaffection
- Understanding of the mentoring process
- Impact of mentoring
- Surveillance
- Future prospects and wider social/economic/political factors.

I felt confident in these categories, because they seemed rooted in the data and the iterative process of ongoing analysis. I was pleased I had had some surprises, and this reassured me that, despite the impossibility of eliminating my subjective values and disposition, I was keeping a sufficiently open mind in the face of some very rich data. I then began to code the data in order to produce a written account of the early findings.

It was during this process that I began to encounter a number of problems. First, no matter how hard I tried to concentrate as I cut-and-pasted passages from the interviews into the various categories, and despite the assurances of the textbook authors that with care this would not happen, I found myself constantly drifting into an automatic mode. My very familiarity with the data was decontextualising it – an error that was particularly disappointing given the way I wanted to locate mentoring through my research. Later discussions in research student workshops helped me see the myopia induced by this process had obscured the significance of some of the data. On a number of occasions, young people with learning disabilities had told me long and rather rambling stories that seemed irrelevant during the coding process, but these appeared valuable when placed back in the context of the whole interview.

For example, when I asked one young person, Neil, who else he could talk to in the same way as his mentor Keith, he mentioned his granddad, aunts and uncles, brothers. He then launched into what my coding had dismissed as a long 'shaggy-dog' story about his washing getting stolen off the line in his garden, and the police coming round when his mum reported it. I came to see that Neil was offering me some really important data about his mentor: he was telling me that Keith belonged to a whole class of people in Neil's world who were 'good-to-talk-to'. They listened to your troubles and wanted to help, gave you advice about avoiding problems in the future, but could not really do much about what had already happened.

Second, the difficulty of the coding process led me into an unintentional prioritisation of the data generated with the student mentors over that generated with the young people. This relates to the greater degree of cultural capital the students possessed. They were highly articulate and talkative. One mentor, in reply to my first question about 'how things were going', spoke solidly for about six minutes, barely drawing breath. Although some of the young people also talked quite freely and at times eloquently in the interviews, the data generated by those with learning difficulties or who were severely shy was naturally much thinner. Moreover, most of the students were doing education or social science degrees, and had undergone a mentor training programme equivalent to the input of a unit on a degree, whereas the young people had no induction to the mentoring process per se at all. Some of the young people knew about issues of social exclusion from the media or had discussions with parents who were mature students, and had some remarkably sharp critiques of government policy. However, the mentors tended to have much more theoretically constructed accounts, and often linked their experiences to their studies.

Unconsciously, I had allowed this imbalance of cultural capital between the two groups to influence my use of the data. It was easier to begin with the data from the mentors, and to feel that I was making some substantial progress in creating a textual product from our interviews. The volume and richness of the mentors' data came to overwhelm the voices of the young people. The students provided so much more to cut-and-paste, whereas some of the transcripts from the young people reflected the difficulty in getting them to talk about their experiences, with one- or two-word answers, silences, and 'don't know' replies. Although I felt the interviews as a whole gave a strong sense of young people's feelings about their mentors, and the meanings they brought to the process of mentoring, the data were not easily coded to reveal their constructions. So much of their practical knowledge of relationships was tacit, and was therefore difficult for them to put into words. At one point, I even considered abandoning my ambition of foregrounding the young people's views altogether, to focus my thesis on the experiences of the mentors, and I am grateful to my supervisors for encouraging me to see that this was not the only solution.

This taught me how easy it is for researchers to interpret young people's puzzlement at some of our questions as not-knowing, as we overlook the deeply integrated and internalised nature of tacit understanding – which is not consciously remembered or articulated precisely because it *is* so thoroughly known (Altheide and Johnson 1998; Edmondson 2001). In this way, we risk under estimating and misrepresenting the cultural resources that young people possess. As we construct the field of educational research, we use our more powerful position within that field to dictate which resources count as capital, and which do not count and therefore cannot be brought into play (cf. Bourdieu and Wacquant 1992; Hodkinson 1998; Reay 1998).

Third, as I wrote up the results of my analysis, I found myself increasingly embarrassed by the text I was producing. Here is one brief extract where I was discussing the mentors' understanding of mentoring:

> There is universal agreement among the mentors that mentoring is about listening to young people, but this is construed in different ways along a spectrum of judgementalism, including acceptance or mistrust of what the young people have to say. For Patricia, Sian, Jane and Yvonne, listening also includes 'filtering out rubbish', taking things with a pinch of salt, going along with initial pretence, wondering about the other side of the story. Along with Aileen also, they talk about their efforts not to appear shocked or to react judgementally when young people talk about their lives. Aileen was the exception in another regard, however, as all of the others explicitly saw their role as to empathize with the young people, whereas she clearly stated that it was not about saying 'I know what you're going through'.
>
> Paper written for supervisors, November 1999

This category had been particularly difficult to try to analyse, as the above extract shows, despite subjecting it to a whole battery of sub-coding and matrices in the hope of coming up with a typology or a spectrum. I have even managed to work one in with my 'spectrum of judgementalism'. What can one make of similarities or differences when there are only differences? And what sense does this approach make anyway, when the data come from only nine people? This extract apes quantitative methods in a non-sensical way, as if I could declare that '$n=9$ ... 100 per cent of the sample felt that listening was a key aspect of mentoring, although 40 per cent dismissed some of the young people's talk as "rubbish"'. It clearly misses the point of small-scale case study research, which is not primarily to engage in comparison, and certainly not to provide any statistically generalisable findings, but to consider each case as singular, and to learn as much as one possibly can from it in the hope of generating deeper insights (Wolcott 1994).

Finally, as the examples above reflect, the technique of 'slicing' the data according to categories resulted in my representation of the relationships themselves becoming fragmented, although providing insights into their development was a key objective of my research. Categorisation of the data led more easily to a consideration of the respondents in groups – mentors, mentees and scheme staff – rather than of the mentoring dyads. Such grouping can be extremely valuable in analysing certain kinds of research. Ainley and Bailey's (1996) presentation of FE tutors', managers' and students' responses to the incorporation of FE colleges from 1992 is a case in point. Wolcott (1994), using the example of his own writing on US volunteers doing aid work in a Malay village, argues that this technique can be highly revelatory in researching processes of change. However, it seemed inappropriate for providing insights into the progress of dyadic mentoring relationships over time. My efforts seemed to be propelling me away from the very ambitions I had for my research, and my director of studies was finally able to say 'I told you so'.

These false starts brought me to a realisation that, unless the qualitative enquiry drives the methods, the methods will drive the enquiry. By 'enquiry' I do not mean the linear pursuit of textbook-style research questions and hypotheses, but enquiry as grounded in my own deeply held interests, values and beliefs, which are themselves partly tacit and partly emotive as well as intellectual. There is no neutral space in which one can diligently apply positivist or postpositivist methods, while pursuing critical and interpretive insights. Techniques and procedures can never be the guarantors of knowledge production in qualitative research (Gallagher 1995). At the same time, I do not believe the false starts had been a complete waste of time, not least of all because they had helped me get to know my data so well, even if I needed to step back from it and gain a more holistic perspective. I had also learned some lessons the hard but effective way – through confronting the consequences of my mistakes. I abandoned paradigmatic analysis, turned to my supervisors' suggestions for guidance, and began to study some literature on life history and narrative analysis.

Narrative synthesis of data

> Finally, the heuristic researcher develops a *creative synthesis*, and original integration of the material that reflects the researcher's intuition, imagination, and personal knowledge of meaning and essences of the experience ... In this way the experience as a whole is presented, and, unlike most research studies, the individual persons remain intact.
>
> Moustakas, 1990: 50–1, original emphasis

In a sense, a narrative approach to transforming research data is not properly analysis at all, although, like others, I shall continue to refer to it as such. It is more appropriately thought of as a process of synthesis (Polkinghorne 1995). The etymological roots of analysis mean 'taking apart', whereas those of synthesis mean 'putting together', so that the two would appear to be polar opposites. However, analysis in research can be defined as a reductive process, an essentially conservative narrowing of the data to issues relating to the research questions, and to a systematic description of what it is possible to know from the data with relative certainty (Wolcott 1994). Narrative can fulfil this role, albeit in a very different way from standard research methods.

One of the major shifts that distinguishes narrative analysis from paradigmatic analysis is in its abandonment of the quest to catalogue similarities and differences (Polkinghorne 1995; Wolcott 1994). Instead, it looks for patterns of connections between *diverse* phenomena, and seeks to reflect both the richness of context surrounding the data, and its complexity. 'The search is for data that will reveal uniqueness of the individual case or bounded system and provide an understanding of its idiosyncrasy and particular complexity' (Polkinghorne 1995: 15).

As such, narrative is particularly appropriate for the analysis of data that does not fall into a neat catalogue (Josselson 1995). This method overtly acknowledges that the story produced cannot be a neutral representation of reality, and that theory built from it never just 'emerges' from data, but arises through the work of the researcher as the main instrument of the research, as she brings her own standpoint, efforts and interests to the process. It also helps to produce explanations. The construction of a narrative not only presents a story of what happened (rather than a series of topics), but also helps synthesise answers to questions about how and why things came about in a certain way (Zeller 1995). As Richardson (1998: 345) argues 'writing is not just a mopping-up activity at the end of a research project. Writing is also a way of "knowing" – a method of discovery and analysis … Form and content are inseparable'.

Multiple sources of data and layers of context can be woven into a story and its interpretation, and this seemed to fit the aims of my research much better. It also seemed to offer a way to allow my own intuition and hard intellectual work to balance the data from the mentors and the young people in a more adequate way, allowing the young people's experiences to share centre stage, and locating all the players, including the mentors and New Beginnings' staff, within fields of wider power dynamics. Above all, it promised a way of writing about my research findings that might arouse meaning and interest for the readers, and evoke in them the same fascination as I felt for what I was discovering (cf. Fine and Deegan 1996).

I used this approach to carry out my final analysis of the data, beginning with the three mentoring relationships that were still continuing a year after the first round of inter-views, which I have treated as the core of my data from which to work outwards in recurrent hermeneutic episodes. I used the method of 'emplotment' (Polkinghorne 1995), and working backwards chronologically, framed the outcome of each mentoring relationship, then selected data, including contextual material, according to its contribu-tion to the plot. I made a point of always beginning with the data from the young person at each stage of the 'plot', rather than with that from the mentor. The process of returning to the data revealed any weaknesses in the plot, and allowed its readjustment to present a more faithful construction of the whole. It also mitigates the tendency to focus only on 'spicy' data, or to revel in the dysfunctional and lose sight of the importance of the mundane and routine that is often crucial to meaning (Fine and Weiss 1998). I was able to write about two of the mentoring relationships I had studied, with far more satisfactory results than my previous attempts. I felt I had found my 'golden key', the methodological tool to unlock my data. I was confident that the third major case study I wanted to write up, that of Lisa (the mentee) and Yvonne (her mentor), would be quickly produced. I found myself once again frustrated, however, and the difficulties I encountered taught me even more about the nature of qualitative research.

Lisa and Yvonne's case study: the problem

Yvonne, a 21-year-old Applied Social Sciences student, had worked full- and part-time for several years in a respite home for severely handicapped children, as well as helping her mother care for her learning disabled brother. Yvonne intended to continue working with disabled children after her degree. Yvonne had already been mentoring 17-year-old Lisa for almost a year when I first interviewed them in June 1999, and they were still meeting together nine months later. (Their relationship is described in detail in Colley 2001a; 2003a; 2003b.) Yvonne and Lisa perhaps represented the opposite extremes of response in generating data through our interviews. Lisa was extremely shy and had difficulty communicating with others. Yvonne would respond at length to every question I posed.

Lisa had repeated a pattern in several work experience placements of starting well for a few weeks, then failing and withdrawing from the placement. As the placements started, Yvonne would lessen the frequency of their mentoring sessions, hoping the need for them would lessen and the relationship could be brought to an end. As the placements broke down, Yvonne felt obliged to return to weekly mentoring, and New Beginnings' staff would have to renew their efforts to try and find a suitable alternative placement for Lisa. Yvonne found this increasingly frustrating and disappointing as her mentor. She would tell Lisa to 'pull her socks up' and 'stick with it', but felt that Lisa was just acquiescing verbally without any intention of following her mentor's advice. At the time of our final interviews, both admitted to me that they wanted to stop mentoring together, but neither felt able to say this to their partner. Of all the relationships I studied, the story of this one seemed the most obvious to me: here were two people going round in circles, failing to make progress, but unable to draw conclusions or to draw their relationship to a conclusion.

However, as I tried to use the linear method of emplotment to create a narrative from the data, I found myself going round in circles. The repetitious nature of the story – Lisa's placement successes turning into failures, Yvonne's exhortations collapsing into demoralisation – presented a number of problems. The first and most obvious was that of writing in an interesting way about something – repetition – which is generally regarded as inherently *un*interesting. Second, how could I represent circular experiences in a narrative style that tends inherently to the linear? Third, how could I avoid a reductive diminishment of a story that is far more complex than can be represented in the remit of this chapter?

Coding of Lisa and Yvonne's responses about their experiences and meanings of engagement mentoring had led me to a fairly definite interpretation of their relationship. It appeared thus as a tale in which Yvonne bullied Lisa, did not reflect sufficiently on her own practice, and was therefore unable to break the cycle of repeated failure for Lisa's placement and for her own role as mentor. It offered evidence of the counter productive nature of directive approaches to mentoring disaffected youth, and revealed the harsh and unpleasant realities of the engagement mentoring model. It would have fitted well with some of the psychological research about dysfunctional mentoring relationships. For example, following Scandura's (1998: 454) typology of mentoring behaviour that can result in psychological damage for participants, Yvonne could have been presented as a tyrannical mentor, whereas Lisa's responses could be seen as sabotage of Yvonne's efforts and of the employment goals of the scheme.

There would undoubtedly have been some element of truth in such an explanation, but a major problem for me was that it reduced the question of power to the micro-level of individual interactions, and to the issue of the mentor's abuse of her superior power over the mentee as a passive victim. It also distorted their story by imposing a diachronic form in addition to this relational opposition, whereas I needed to find a way to express the *synchronic* nature of the repetitive cycle of their relationship. What might be the similarities and parallels in the two women's experiences, including the subjection of both to the operation of wider and more covert dynamics of power?

A creative approach to transforming data: 'radial' narration

Discussions with supervisors and colleagues led me to follow the advice of Nelson (1993) to overcome writer's block by being creative and playful with my writing. I spent an invaluable hour with Ian Stronach, one of the professors then at MMU, talking over metaphors I might use to engage with Lisa and Yvonne's story, which led to the notion of the relationship slowly 'freezing up'. He also gave me a copy of an article about radial narration by the science fiction writer, Ursula K. Le Guin (1981). In that article, she argues that linear, logical narratives derive from Aristotelean tradition, whereas contrasting traditions, such as the Celtic, do not follow that dominant cultural norm of 'beginning, middle and end'. Instead, '[its] normal structure is "radial", circling about, repeating and elaborating the central theme. It is all "middle"' (Clancy 1970, cited in Le Guin 1981: 190). In a metaphorical sense, such narratives are more like a hologram, or a crystal (Richardson 1998), than a storyboard, allowing us to approach a story from a myriad tangents, and at the same time to see into the centre of it in a way that linear or plane representations cannot allow. This is a radically different kind of transparency than that of Huberman and Miles' (1998) 'audit trails'.

Using some of these insights, I recast the writing of Lisa and Yvonne's story in a creative framework, not fictionalising it as such (see Campbell 2000 and Campbell and Kane 1998 for an account of 'telling tales' hybridised from a number of respondents; and Sparkes 1995, for a defence of the use of fiction in research), but presenting the data in a more ludic way, by interweaving it with the fable of 'Good King Wenceslas', presented in a visual way, with large amounts of blank space on the white pages to evoke some sense of the growing emptiness, frustration and disoriented unhappiness that seemed to characterise the later stage of Lisa and Yvonne's relationship. Although I engaged in free writing, with no object other than creatively expressing the data before me, the result confronted me with a radically different interpretation of that data. Instead of focusing on the opposition between the two women, and the tussle between them in the relationship, something else emerged much more clearly from the 'impressionist tale' (Van Maanen 1988) I had constructed. Here is one illustrative extract:

> Lisa was on New Beginnings. New Beginnings was about getting into training and work. Yvonne's Dream Line says that mentoring helps young people get problems off their chest so they can get on with training and work. Problems are burdens,

like heavy stones. Unless they get help to off-load this burden, young people may end up going round in circles. Lisa wanted help carrying her stones.

Helen: Tell me what it's like in general, having a mentor, from your point of view?
Lisa: Someone to talk to. Because I take on my family's problems and my friends' problems as well as my own.

Someone-To-Talk-To should help with the stones.

Lisa knew what the stones were made of:

One of the stones was Her Dead Mother.

One of the stones was her Little Brother who was Really Really Bad and Naughty, and whom she Does Not Get On With. And that stone carried its own sack of stones, which were the Dead Mother, Emotional and Behavioural Difficulties, Swearing at Adults, Being Excluded from School, Refusing to Help with the Housework, Smashing Windows, Hitting Lisa's Friends, Needing Bereavement Counselling, and Refusing To Go For Counselling.

One of the stones was her Big Sister. And that stone carried its own sack of stones, which included the Dead Mother, Lisa, the Little Brother, Giving Up her Job to Look After the Family, Being Mother-Auntie-Cleaner, Arguing with her Boyfriend, Crying, and Needing Lisa's Shoulder to Cry On.

One of the stones was her Father. And that stone carried its own sack of stones, which included the Dead Mother, Lisa, the Little Brother, the Big Sister, and Working Nightshifts to Earn Enough Money to Support the Family.

One of the stones was her Best Friend Who Is 12 Years Old. And that stone carried its own sack of stones, which included Learning Difficulties, Being Bullied Because She's Fat, Not Being Listened To by Teachers Who Say She Is Lying About Being Bullied, and Something That Happened When She Was Young.

Some of Lisa's other stones were: Sexual Abuse by Her Uncle When She Was Five, Missing School in Year 10 to Be With Her Dying Mother, Being Bullied at School About Her Dead Mother, Refusing to Go Back to School, Not Doing Her Exams, Wishing She Had Done Her Exams (Especially History), Needing Counselling, Refusing To Go For Counselling, and Being the Spitting Image of Her Dead Mother.

It was a very heavy sack. It held a lot of stones. Maybe Someone-To-Talk-To would help.

Maybe Yvonne would help. Yvonne had quite a few stones to carry herself. Some of Yvonne's stones were:

A Brother with Learning Disabilities, Getting Burnt Out by Exams, Hating Sixth Form College, Hating College Courses (Especially Sociology), Giving Up a Good Job to Come to University Because Her Mother Wanted Her To and Tuition Fees Were Being Introduced the Following Year, and Studying a Social Sciences Degree Even Though She Hated Sociology Which Is a Load of Waffle Just Strange Theories Ranting On About Life Why Bother?

The last one was getting heavier all the time.

These had given her lots of practice at carrying stones. Plus her mother had taught her how.

I came to see that a gendered concept of care was a central aspect of both women's dispositions. As I have discussed in relation to discourses of mentoring (Colley 2003a; 2003b; 2007), feminine stereotypes of care serve to oppress women through deeply internalised roles that serve the interests of dominant groupings (Gaskell 1992; Gilligan 1995; Walkerdine 1992). They obstruct rather than enhance the possibility of communication and relationship between individuals through their demand for self-sacrifice and the repression of powerful emotions. This profoundly ideological construction of care was produced and reproduced in both Lisa and Yvonne through the process of mentoring, as each learned more thoroughly from her partner that caring involved the attempt to absorb and neutralise the other's difficulties and pain. Yet the longer their mentoring went on, the less able they were to escape the idealised images each brought to the process, or to admit that truth to each other. Mentoring had become – to borrow Walkerdine's (1992) phrase – 'an impossible fiction'. No wonder, then, that the relationship descended into immobility and silence.

In this respect, the course and outcome of this particular mentoring relationship was inextricably bound up with power dynamics that have defined patriarchal class society for millennia. This aspect of the operation of power in Lisa and Yvonne's relationship reveals another layer of complexity in their experiences of mentoring, going beyond the individualised explanation I had traced through Scandura's (1998) psychological model. It highlights the contradiction in feminist models of mentoring that advocate a basis of nurture rather than control. For Yvonne and for Lisa, nurture through engagement mentoring inevitably involved control: over others, and over oneself. Both were positioned as twin objects of the project of forming employable dispositions that are also structurally gendered. In hermeneutic fashion, I then went back to all the data, and reconsidered it in the light of this interpretation. The insight I had gained from Lisa and Yvonne's case study became a pivotal experience around which the entire thesis was eventually constructed and theorised.

In considering the researcher–researched relationship and my stance towards the data, the issue of cultural capital had been transformed. In my initial analysis, the focus has been Lisa's lack and Yvonne's wealth of cultural capital as represented in the different volume and character of their responses within our interviews. In the later analysis, I became concerned with the way in which mentoring appeared as a process of emotional labour worked upon both women's dispositions or, to use Bourdieu's (1986) term, their *habitus*, to produce a gendered form of cultural capital or employability.

The place of method in qualitative enquiry

Many qualitative researchers advocate the rigorous use of 'proper' research methods, although they may differ radically in what they judge such proper methods or rigour in their use to be (see, for example, Delamont 1999). I tried the 'proper' methods of paradigmatic analysis recommended in many textbooks, and found these wanting. In applying emplotment to synthesise my case studies, I thought I had found a 'proper' method, a 'golden key' that did indeed work for some of the data. Even this did not prove effective in analysing and interpreting a different kind of relationship between Yvonne and Lisa.

The lesson I have drawn from this experience is that there are *no* techniques, whether conventional or radically non-conventional, to which we can turn with certainty that they will resolve our problems in making sense of qualitative data. If deployed unthinkingly, research techniques may drive our enquiry off course rather than help us gain in understanding. The use of radial narration is no more a guarantee of success than any other method. But this is not a pessimistic lesson, and it should not dishearten anyone struggling to transform their data. With all data, we have to be able to think through the *most appropriate* methods of making sense of it. This may of course entail an assumption that all research is value-laden, rather than the positivist/postpositivist declaration that research ought to be value-free (Hammersley 1992). How we transform our data is determined by the way we intend to use it.

In my case, I had the critical aim of revealing covert aspects of the operation of various echelons of power, and revealing the misrecognition (Bourdieu and Passeron 1990) that the practice of engagement mentoring can entail. My initial errors placed me, as researcher, in the power position within the educational research field. Unwittingly, I arbitrated through my early analysis, interpretation and writing the degree to which different responses, mediated through differing types of cultural resources, would count as cultural capital in the academic text produced. The unthinking use of dominant research techniques resulted in reinforcing my power as researcher to rule different respondents' cultural resources in or out of the educational research 'game', and to dictate what from the data would appear as cultural capital in the research text. At the same time, it obscured the power I was wielding through its claimed status as a rigorous and value-neutral guarantor of truth. Paradoxically, it was through allowing my less conscious but deeply held values and beliefs to play on the data through free creative writing that I was able to accept both mentors' and mentees' cultural resources as valid, to foreground both, and to arrive at a very different view of how issues of cultural capital were posed for them within the fields of engagement mentoring and of gendered social relations.

I would conclude by arguing that such questions are of vital importance in the UK research community today, given cautions about the growing threat of imposed universal criteria and standardised methods for research (Hodkinson 2001; Stronach 2001). Critical research has shown that positivist methods in mentoring research have limited our understanding of mentoring relationships for over two decades (Merriam 1983; Piper and Piper 2000; Roberts 2000). Despite the volume of academic literature it remains poorly conceptualised and under theorised. Diversity in research purposes and methods, and the ability of researchers to adopt and adapt research techniques flexibly as appropriate to their data, are essential to enabling new contributions to our knowledge about new forms of mentoring, such as engagement mentoring, as they emerge. If practice is genuinely to be based on evidence that expands our understanding, it is unwise to restrict the cultural resources of the research community to rule only a narrow set of methods admissible as cultural capital in the educational research field.

Acknowledgements

I remain always in debt to my PhD supervisors, Phil Hodkinson, Jane Artess and Mary Issitt, for their support. I am grateful to Ian Stronach for his challenging conversations in times of stuck-ness, and to numerous colleagues and research students with whom I have discussed earlier versions of this chapter. My profound thanks are also due to the young people and their mentors who so generously gave of their time and experiences in the research project.

References

Ainley, P. and Bailey, B. (1996) *The Business of Learning: Staff and Student Experiences of Further Education in the 1990s*. London: Cassell.

Alleman, E. (1986) Measuring mentoring – frequency, quality, impact. In W. A. Gray and M. M. Gray (Eds). *Mentoring: Aid to Excellence in Career Development, Business and the Professions Vol. II.* Vancouver: International Association for Mentoring.

Altheide, D. L. and Johnson, J. M. (1998) Criteria for assessing interpretive validity in qualitative research. In N. K. Denzin and Y. S. Lincoln (Eds). *Collecting and Interpreting Qualitative Materials.* Thousand Oaks, CA: Sage.

Anderson, G. (1989) Critical ethnography in education: origins, current status and new directions, *Review of Educational Research*, 59: 249–70.

Bathmaker, A.-M. (2001) 'It's the Perfect Education': lifelong learning and the experience of Foundation-level GNVQ students, *Journal of Education and Training*, 53: 81–100.

Benioff, S. (1997) *A Second Chance: Developing mentoring and education projects for young people.* London: Commission for Racial Equality/Crime Concern.

Bourdieu, P. (1986) *Distinction: A Social Critique of the Judgement of Taste.* London: Routledge.

Bourdieu, P. and Passeron, J.-C. (1990) *Reproduction in Education, Society and Culture.* 2nd edn. London: Sage.

Bourdieu, P. and Wacquant, L. J. D. (1992) *An Invitation to Reflexive Sociology.* Cambridge: Polity Press.

Bryman, A. and Burgess, R. G. (1994a) Developments in qualitative data analysis: an introduction. In A. Bryman and R. G. Burgess (Eds). *Analyzing Qualitative Data.* London: Routledge.

——(1994b) Reflections on qualitative data analysis. In A. Bryman and R. G. Burgess (Eds). *Analyzing Qualitative Data.* London: Routledge.

Campbell, A. (2000) Fictionalising research data as a way of increasing teachers' access to school–focused research, *Research in Education*, 63: 81–8.

Campbell, A. and Kane, I. (1998) *School-Based Teacher Education: Telling Tales from a Fictional Primary School.* London: David Fulton.

Clancy, J. P. (1970) *The Earliest Welsh Poetry.* London: Macmillan.

Colley, H. (2001a) *Unravelling Myths of Mentor: power dynamics of mentoring relationships with 'disaffected' young people.* Unpublished PhD thesis, the Manchester Metropolitan University.

——(2001b) Righting re-writings of the myth of Mentor: a critical perspective on career guidance mentoring, *British Journal of Guidance and Counselling*, 29: 177–98.

——(2003a) *Mentoring for Social Inclusion: a critical approach to nurturing mentor relationships.* London: RoutledgeFalmer.

——(2003b) Engagement mentoring for 'disaffected' youth: a new model of mentoring for social inclusion, *British Educational Research Journal*, 29: 505–26.

——(2007) Myths of mentoring: developing a Marxist-feminist critique. In A. Green, G. Rikowski and H. Raduntz (Eds). *Renewing Dialogues in Marxism and Education: Openings.* Basingstoke: Palgrave Macmillan.

Delamont, S. (1999) Confessions of a ragpicker. In H. Hodkinson (Ed.). *Feminism and Educational Research Methodologies.* Manchester: the Manchester Metropolitan University.

Dey, I. (1993) *Qualitative Data Analysis.* London: Routledge.

DuBois, D. L. and Neville, H. A. (1997) Youth mentoring: investigation of relationship characteristics and perceived benefits, *Journal of Community Psychology*, 24: 227–34.

Edmondson, R. (2001) *Time and Memory in Rural Connemara.* Paper presented at ESRC/BERA research training event on 'Memory and Research', the Manchester Metropolitan University, May 2001.

Employment Support Unit (ESU) (2000) *Mentoring Young People: Lessons from Youthstart.* Birmingham: ESU.

Fine, G. A. and Deegan, J. G. (1996) Three principles of Serendip: insight, chance and discovery in qualitative research, *Qualitative Studies in Education*, 9: 434–47.

Fine, M. and Weiss, L. (1998) Writing the 'wrongs' of fieldwork: confronting our own research/writing dilemmas in urban ethnographies. In G. Shacklock and J. Smyth (Eds). *Being Reflexive in Critical Education and Social Research.* London: Falmer.

Ford, G. (1999) *Youthstart Mentoring Action Project: Project Evaluation and Report Part II.* Stourbridge: Institute of Careers Guidance.

Gallagher, D. J. (1995) In search of the rightful role of method: reflections on conducting a qualitative dissertation. In T. Tiller, A. Sparkes, S. Karhus, and F. Dowling Naess (Eds). *The Qualitative Challenge: Reflections on Educational Research.* Norway: Caspar Forlag A/S.

Gaskell, J. (1992) *Gender Matters from School to Work*. Milton Keynes: Open University Press.

Gilligan, C. (1995) Hearing the difference: theorizing connection, *Hypatia*, 10: 120–7.

Gleeson, D. (1996) Post-compulsory education in a post-industrial and post-modern age. In J. Avis, M. Bloomer, G. Esland, D. Gleeson, and P. Hodkinson. *Knowledge and Nationhood: Education, Politics and Work*. London: Cassell.

Golden, S. and Sims, D. (1997) *Review of Industrial Mentoring in Schools*. Slough: NFER.

Goodlad, S. (Ed.) (1995) *Students as Tutors and Mentors*. London: Kogan Page.

Grossman, J. B. and Tierney, J. P. (1998) Does mentoring work? An impact study of the Big Brothers Big Sisters Program, *Evaluation Review*, 22: 403–26.

Gulam, W. and Zulfiqar, M. (1998) Mentoring – Dr. Plum's elixir and the Alchemist's Stone, *Mentoring and Tutoring*, 5: 46–56.

Hammersley, M. (1992) *What's Wrong With Ethnography?* London: Routledge.

Hodkinson, P. (1998) Career decision making and the transition from school to work. In M. Grenfell and D. James (Eds). *Bourdieu and Education: Acts of Practical Theory*. London: Falmer Press.

——(2001) *The contested field of educational research: hegemony, policing and dissent*. Paper given at British Educational Research Association Annual Conference, University of Leeds, September 2001.

Huberman, A. M. and Miles, M. B. (1998) Data management and analysis methods. In N. K. Denzin and Y. S. Lincoln (Eds). *Collecting and Interpreting Qualitative Materials*. Thousand Oaks: Sage.

Industry in Education (1996) *Towards Employability: Addressing the Gap Between Young People's Qualities and Employers' Recruitment Needs*. London: Industry in Education.

Josselson, R. (1995) Imagining the real: empathy, narrative and the dialogic self. In R. Josselson and A. Lieblich (Eds). *Interpreting Experience: The Narrative Study of Lives Vol. 3*. Thousand Oaks, CA: Sage.

Lather, P. (1986) Research as praxis, *Harvard Educational Review*, 56: 257–77.

Le Guin, U. K. (1981) It was a dark and stormy night; or, why are we huddling about the campfire? In W. Mitchell (Ed.). *On Narrative*. Chicago, IL: University of Chicago Press.

Long, J. (1997) The dark side of mentoring, *Australian Educational Researcher*, 24: 115–33.

Mason, J. (1996) *Qualitative Researching*. London: Sage.

May, T. (1997) *Social Research: Issues, Methods, Processes*. Buckingham: Open University Press.

McPartland, J. M. and Nettles, S. M. (1991) Using community adults as advocates or mentors for at-risk middle school students: a 2-year evaluation of Project RAISE, *American Journal of Education*, 99: 568–86.

Megginson, D. and Clutterbuck, D. (1995) Mentoring in action. In D. Megginson and D. Clutterbuck (Eds). *Mentoring in Action: A Practical Guide for Managers*. London: Kogan Page.

Merriam, S. (1983) Mentors and protégés: a critical review of the literature, *Adult Education Quarterly*, 33: 161–73.

Moustakas, C. (1990) *Heuristic Research: Design, Methodology, and Applications*. Newbury Park, CA: Sage.

Nelson, V. (1993) *On Writers' Block: A New Approach to Creativity*. Boston, MA: Houghton Mifflin.

Piper, H. and Piper, J. (1999) 'Disaffected' young people: problems for mentoring, *Mentoring and Tutoring*, 7: 121–30.

——(2000) Disaffected young people as the problem. Mentoring as the solution. Education and work as the goal, *Journal of Education and Work*, 13: 77–94.

Polkinghorne, D. E. (1995) Narrative configuration in qualitative analysis. In J. Hatch and R. Wisniewski (Eds). *Life History and Narrative*. London: Falmer.

Reay, D. (1998) Cultural reproduction: mothers' involvement in their children's primary schooling In M. Grenfell and D. James (Eds). *Bourdieu and Education: Acts of Practical Theory*. London: Falmer Press.

Richardson, L. (1998) Writing: a method of inquiry. In N. K. Denzin and Y. S. Lincoln (Eds). *Collecting and Interpreting Qualitative Materials*. Thousand Oaks, CA: Sage.

Ringwalt, C. L., Graham, L. A., Paschall, M. J., Flewelling, R. L. and Browne, D. C. (1996) Supporting Adolescents with Guidance and Employment (SAGE), *American Journal of Preventive Medicine*, 12: 31–8.

Ritchie, J. and Spencer, L. (1994) Qualitative data analysis for applied policy research. In A. Bryman and R. G. Burgess (Eds). *Analyzing Qualitative Data*. London: Routledge.

Roberts, A. (2000) Mentoring revisited: a phenomenological reading of the literature, *Mentoring and Tutoring*, 8: 145–70.

Scandura, T. A. (1998) Dysfunctional mentoring relationships and outcomes, *Journal of Management*, 24: 449–67.

Shea, G. F. (1992) *Mentoring: A Guide to the Basics*. London: Kogan Page.

Skinner, A. and Fleming, J. (1999) *Mentoring Socially Excluded Young People: Lessons from Practice*. Manchester: National Mentoring Network.

Sparkes, A. C. (1995) Writing people: reflections on the dual crises of representation and legitimation in qualitative enquiry, *QUEST*, 47: 158–95.

Standing, M. (1999) Developing a supportive/challenging and reflective/competency education (SCARCE) mentoring model and discussing its relevance to nurse education, *Mentoring and Tutoring*, 6: 3–17.

Strauss, A. and Corbin, J. (1998) Grounded theory methodology: an overview. In N. K. Denzin and Y. S. Lincoln (Eds). *Strategies of Qualitative Enquiry*. Thousand Oaks, CA: Sage.

Stronach, I. (2001) NERF strategy proposals: not national, not educational, not research-based, not a forum: otherwise a good idea, *Research Intelligence*, 74: 22–3.

Van Maanen, J. (1988) *Tales of the Field: On Writing Ethnography*. Chicago, IL: University of Chicago Press.

Walkerdine, V. (1992) Progressive pedagogy and political struggle. In C. Luke and J. Gore (Eds). *Feminisms and Critical Pedagogy*. London: Routledge, p. 27.

Wolcott, H. F. (1994) *Transforming Qualitative Data: Description, Analysis and Interpretation*. Thousand Oaks, CA: Sage.

Zeller, N. (1995) Narrative strategies for case reports. In J. Hatch and R. Wisniewski (Eds). *Life History and Narrative*. London: Falmer.

16
Dealing with data analysis

A.-M. Bathmaker

> You have defined the focus for the research. You have worked at the research questions. You have planned the methods for conducting the enquiry. The analysis and interpretation. ...

It is here that the research plan often starts to become vague and short on detail. Despite all the advice that appears in guides to research methods, that analysis should start early and go on throughout research, rather than be left until after all the fieldwork is completed, work on analysis and interpretation appear as something that occurs after any data collection phase, at least a year away, in some almost unimaginable territory.

One of the difficulties facing qualitative researchers is that the processes involved tend not to be visible in published research work. Some miracle seems to have happened between the mass of data that must have been gathered, and the printed page. As Ball (1994: 107) has observed, in addition to the mysteries of how the data were reduced through analysis, 'Most analysts leave the interpretational relationships between data and analysis heavily implicit.'

In this chapter I consider what can be learned about data analysis from looking closely at two examples of published research. The chapter starts with a brief overview of literature that offers guidance on data analysis. The second section of the chapter looks in detail at the two examples, in relation to what the reader can learn about the analytic processes that were involved. The final section offers a summary of key issues that arise in the chapter for carrying out data analysis.

Resources for data analysis

The literature on data analysis in qualitative research appears to grow daily, and it would be impossible in this brief introduction to offer a comprehensive overview of all the literature that is now available. The range of publications indicates the increasing diversity of approaches to qualitative research, including the collection and analysis of data. Although most books cover all aspects of the research process, some are dedicated specifically to data analysis (e.g. Bryman and Burgess 1994; Coffey and Atkinson 1996;

Miles and Huberman 1994; Silverman 2001; Wolcott 1994). Some address data analysis in the context of qualitative research in general (e.g. Ely *et al.* 1997; Lofland *et al.* 2006), whereas others consider data analysis in the context of particular sorts of enquiry, for example case study (Stake 1995; Yin 2009) or narrative research (Atkinson and Delamont 2006; Clandinin and Connelly 2000; Czarniawska 2004; Riessman 2008). A further area of growing interest is computer-aided qualitative data analysis (Fielding and Lee 1998; Lewins and Silver 2007), often linked to particular software programs. Although more recent publications may address new thinking and ideas about data analysis, earlier texts are an important and rich resource (see Price 1999 for a useful review of some of the earlier qualitative research texts).

There are also growing numbers of large edited volumes, such as Sarantakos (2007), Given (2008) and Denzin and Lincoln (2005). Whereas the first two offer detailed descriptions of techniques, Denzin and Lincoln have a somewhat different purpose, and engage with the histories, controversies and current practices in a range of different methods and paradigms. In addition to this range of published materials, research training workshops on data analysis are offered through organisations such as the UK's Economic and Social Research Council (ESRC) (www.ncrm.ac.uk/).

On the one hand, this richness of information and opportunities appears very helpful. On the other, it could be seen as confusing fragmentation (Atkinson and Delamont 2005). However, there are reasons for the fragmentation that Atkinson and Delamont refer to, which are to do with very differing worldviews amongst different qualitative researchers about how they know what they know. These personal worldviews influence and shape the differing methodological approaches they advocate. As Price (1999: 2) explains:

> [A researcher's] personal stance may range from a rationalist, empiricist search for truth and underlying law to a postmodern, deconstructionist view of the world as complex, chaotic, and unknowable; from a highly structured process of inquiry to a more individualized perception and interpretation.

Works about qualitative methods illustrate this wide span, and each author is a firm believer at some point along this spectrum.

To understand better the differences between approaches in this increasingly diverse literature, Denzin and Lincoln's (2005) edited collection and Alvesson and Sköldberg (2000) are useful sources, which consider different traditions and perspectives within qualitative research.

At the present time, these differences form part of heated debate about the quality of social research, referred to as the 'science wars' (Lather 2004).[1] The increase and diversity in detailed guidance coincide with criticisms of qualitative social research as lacking rigour. Discussions and advice about how researchers should go about analysis, how closely qualitative research should emulate what are described as 'scientific' methods, and whether analysis is an art or a science, are reflected in the literature on data analysis. These debates about what constitutes disciplined inquiry, involving considerable differences in conceptualising the research process, mean that different ways of analysing qualitative data cannot be conflated as though they all reflect the same way of thinking about the world. At the same time, analysis for many researchers combines creative, as well as rigorous, systematic processes.

In search of the analytic process

What is meant by data analysis? In this chapter, I do not attempt to offer a detailed description of methods for data analysis and interpretation. This sort of information can be found in a range of texts, such as those referred to above. I do, however, need to briefly explain how I use the term analysis here.

Qualitative data analysis embraces a number of different processes. There is general agreement that the first stage involves close engagement with raw data, or 'exploring systematically what the data are saying' (Delamont 2002: 177). Coffey and Atkinson (1996) suggest that this part of the process is about data handling and management. It may mean coding and categorising, though this is not what all qualitative researchers do.

Although analysis may start with the processes of data handling, engaging with data very quickly moves into developing interpretations. Ely *et al.* (1997) define analysis as involving close engagement with the data, and interpretation as taking a step back from the immediacy of the field and the data, and separating ourselves from them. For LeCompte and Schensul (1999), (writing specifically about ethnography), analysis involves bringing order to the data that have been collected, summarising, and looking for patterns and themes. Interpretation means 'going beyond results [...] attaching meaning and significance to the patterns, themes, and connections that the researcher identified during analysis' (1999: 5).

In addition to the overlap between analysis and interpretation, the analytic process also involves theory and theorising. Ely *et al.* (1997: 205) take the view that although 'sense-making' occurs during analysis, at some point making sense of data needs to be done against 'some specific theoretical frames'. They define interpretation as 'thinking within theoretical frames and holding conversations with theory and with the findings of other research in "the literature"'.

In the rest of this chapter, analysis is understood as a combination of close engagement with data, interpretation of data, and theorising. While working on a research project, it is clearly, at times, useful to think about these aspects of analysis separately. However, in the final account of the research, it is the interaction of data-analysis-theory that is important, and here I look at the ways in which all three aspects are apparent and interact in published work.

Using two examples, I consider both what the authors say about their work on analysis and how analysis shapes the written text. I also look at how analysis is informed by particular concepts and ideas, drawn from previous research or a particular theoretical perspective. These might be described as 'heuristic tools' (Coffey and Atkinson 1996: 157), or interpretational resources (Ball 1994). I consider how these resources are engaged with critically in the context of the particular study, to create a form of dialogue between data and theory. As Coffey and Atkinson (1996: 157) emphasise, what is important is the ways in which authors '*use* concepts, theories, and ideas constructively and creatively', rather than simply describe them. The overall aim is to consider whether 'the problems and processes of interpretation (the relation between data-explanation-theory)' (Ball 1994: 119) are visible in the two examples, and how the relation between data-explanation-theory shapes the final account.

The examples I use are from my own broad field of interest. The first is Kathryn Ecclestone's (2002) book entitled *Learning Autonomy in Post-16 Education: the Politics and Practice of Formative Assessment*. The second is Helen Colley's (2003) *Mentoring for Social Inclusion: a critical approach to nurturing mentoring relationships*. When I first read these books,

I was more interested in finding out what the authors had to say about young people's experience of postschool transitions, than in examining how they came to say what they had to say. Looking for discussion of the analytic process provided a different lens for reading the texts. Each example is introduced by outlining the focus of the study, before going on to explore what can be learned about analysis by looking closely at each text.

Writing analytically: Kathryn Ecclestone

Kathryn Ecclestone's study of formative assessment focuses on the introduction of new forms of assessment in post-16 vocational education in England in the 1990s. The policy aims of motivating young people who might otherwise leave education, and making them more independent or autonomous learners, are explored in detail through two related but distinct case studies of the introduction of Advanced General National Vocational Qualifications (GNVQs), a vocational qualification offered in England during the 1990s. The first is at the macro-level of national policy design and implementation. The second is a micro-level case study of the implementation of GNVQ assessment in two further education (FE) colleges. Overall, the research explores the impact of assessment, particularly formative assessment, on students' autonomy and motivation.

Constructing the interpretive 'story'

The chapter titles (see Figure 16.1) provide a picture of the interpretive 'story' that is presented in the book. The structure builds on the analytical framework that Ecclestone discusses in chapter 2. This is particularly clear in the three chapters, which are based on fieldwork data from the two case study colleges (chapters 5, 6 and 7). Each of these chapters analyses the data in relation to one of the key areas discussed in chapter 2. The chapter headings provide not only an organisational structure to the text, but also a picture of the interpretational storyline, highlighting, for example, the theme of risk in the first and final chapters.

Introduction

Ch 1 Learning in a risk society: empowerment, care or control?
Ch 2 Theorizing autonomy, motivation and formative assessment
Ch 3 Constructing GNVQ assessment policy
Ch 4 Changing FE colleges
Ch 5 Getting through: motivation in GNVQs
Ch 6 Doing it their way: autonomy in GNVQs
Ch 7 Biting the bullets: formative assessment in GNVQs
Ch 8 Risking motivation and autonomy in lifelong learning

Figure 16.1 Chapters in Ecclestone (2002).

Discussion of the analytic process

Turning to what is said about the analytic process, Ecclestone discusses this (though only very briefly) in the introductory chapter. She describes her approach as combining 'structural, interactionist and discourse analyses', which allow her to 'make sense of

203

policies and their effects in different ways.' (p. 7). These multiple perspectives are intended to help make connections between the structural context of policy, and the effects
on individuals and organisations.

She goes on to explain how she analysed her data as follows:

> Analysis was based on intensive, systematic 'open', 'selective' and 'axial' coding
> (Strauss 1987; Strauss and Corbin 1990). This grounds some ideas in the data and
> seeks discrepancies, rich detail and lateral connections.[2] It also enables *in vivo* codes
> to arise from language used by participants, for local meanings to be connected
> with broader concerns and for categories to be distilled into central themes for
> follow-up sampling. Additional ways of not taking the apparent 'reality' of tran-
> scripts and fieldwork notes at face value were to quantify themes or ideas, to look
> for silence or absence of issues or, conversely, to see if a particularly strong emphasis
> given by participants might really signify the opposite case.
>
> Ecclestone 2002: 8–9

She then briefly outlines the theoretical typology used to analyse her data, which leads
her to the notions of 'assessment regimes' and 'assessment careers' (p. 12) to conceptualise
the impact of policy and practice on post-16 vocational education.

As readers, we are provided, then, with a summary overview of the analytic process.
We learn that she coded the data, although the codes that were used do not appear in
the book. She then developed themes, which combined coding categories. Although
the process of combining codes into broader themes is not discussed in detail, the
resulting themes are apparent in the presentation of data, where responses from different
interviewees are reported thematically, using key themes as headings.

Ecclestone's theoretical typology is explained further in Chapter 2. Here, she discusses
previous research and theory, which she draws on to develop a typology, connecting
types of motivation and autonomy with theories and practices of formative assessment.
She explains at the end of the chapter:

> The typology offers a basis for exploring constructions of autonomy, motivation
> and formative assessment within the 'black boxes' of policy processes, college
> classrooms and relationships between teachers and students and amongst students.
>
> Ecclestone 2002: 44

Dialogue between data and theory

The following extract provides one example of how she then uses the typology with her
data. The extract is taken from chapter 6, which explores students' and teachers' constructions of autonomy in GNVQs. In the typology, autonomy is defined in terms of
procedural, personal and critical autonomy, and here she presents data, where images of
autonomy are described. She starts by presenting examples of how autonomy tends to be
understood as procedural autonomy amongst the participants in her study:

> Throughout the fieldwork, students and teachers conflated autonomy with 'being
> on your own' or 'doing everything yourself'. From a group interview with Year 1
> students at Bridgeview, for example:

It [independence] means going off yourself and find out more yourself and getting it checked and then carry on; you like to do things on your own, you don't
need any help, you don't rely on anybody else to do your work for you, you go
and you do your research.

Ecclestone 2002: 132

She goes on to discuss the absence of critical autonomy in the data:

Although procedural autonomy, ipsative targets and criteria for personal autonomy
were evident, indicators of critical autonomy were much less apparent. [Examples
from the data are then used to explore this claim further.]

Ecclestone 2002: 138

At the end of the chapter, she makes interpretive comments about why she found these
patterns in her data:

At one level, students seemed to bear out my initial proposition that procedural
autonomy may be both a necessary pre- or co-requisite for other forms of autonomy. [...] In the light of the typology, some developed aspects of personal autonomy and occasional, fleeting aspects of critical autonomy. [...] Although procedural
and personal forms of autonomy were important, there were more barriers to critical autonomy than robust indicators of it. This arose both from the specifications
themselves and from students' responses to them.

Ecclestone 2002: 147

From analysis to interpretive conclusions

Based on her analysis, Ecclestone draws conclusions in the final chapter, which include
proposing a refinement to her theorisation, encapsulated in the notion of 'assessment
career'. She argues that a combination of policy making in GNVQs, and the ways in
which teachers, awarding bodies and students in colleges interpreted policy, created an
'assessment regime' that was complex and contradictory, but which encouraged subtle,
self-regulating acceptance of its purposes, practices and effects. She links this to the idea
of 'assessment careers', whereby students are socialised into an assessment regime, which
influences their orientations to and actions during learning. The close connection
that Ecclestone maintains between data, explanation and theory throughout the book
provides a firm basis for offering these interpretations and conclusions in the final
chapter.

Ecclestone discusses in considerable detail her interpretive resources, and how they
relate to analysis. However, she talks only briefly about how she went about working
with the data. The messiness and the dilemmas that arise in dealing with data analysis are
smoothed out in the final account. A reader seeking to understand the more detailed
aspects of the process needs to be alert to brief comments made at various points in the
book to gain any insight into the complexity involved. In the second example, Helen
Colley does provide some commentary on the choices that she made in relation to data
analysis. Nevertheless, as in this first example, what the reader sees is the outcomes of
these choices, rather than how the process evolved through various stages of data analysis.

205

Writing analytically: Helen Colley

Helen Colley's study of mentoring examines the policies and practices of mentoring young people for social inclusion, intended to re-engage young people with the formal labour market. She focuses on one mentoring scheme, and sets this case study within the history of youth mentoring and within the context of economic, social and political developments of the time. Her aim is to explore mentoring at the micro-level of personal interaction between mentors and mentees, the meso-level of institutional context, and the macro-level of political and economic conditions, social structures and inequalities.

Constructing the interpretive 'story'

The book is organised into three parts (Figure 16.2). The first section offers a policy analysis, which sets the context for the 'case stories' from the research in part 2, and it is not until part 3 that Colley discusses her theoretical resources.

Colley explains her reasons for the structure of the book as follows:

> The first is to ensure that the reader does not view mentor relationships in a purely individualized way, but understands them in terms of their local and global settings. The second is to ground a new theoretical framework for mentoring in the data. This has the added virtue of allowing the readers to interpret the case stories for themselves, rather than imposing a preconceived theorization.
>
> Colley 2003: 6

Nevertheless, the titles of chapters 4, 5 and 6 (see Figure 16.2) all represent themes and issues that come from her theoretical analysis. These chapters foreshadow the theory discussed later, and indicate, as Colley herself admits, that she already offers 'an initial interpretation of the data' (p. 7). And, as with Ecclestone's book, the chapter titles as a whole provide an overview of the interpretive 'story' that Colley puts forward.

Introduction

Part I. The rise of the mentoring movement
Ch 1 The emergence of engagement mentoring
Ch 2 Unravelling myths of Mentor

Part II. The mentor relationship
Ch 3 New Beginnings: an engagement mentoring scheme
Ch 4 'I know I'm only young, but I know what I want': resistance and agency on
        the part of mentees
Ch 5 'To suffer and be still': surveillance, self-surveillance, and the transformation
        of mentors' dispositions
Ch 6 Love's labour lost? Mentoring as an impossible fiction

Part III. A new analysis of mentoring
Ch 7 Mentoring for social inclusion: empowerment or control?
Ch 8 Mentoring for social inclusion: issues for policy, practice and research

---

Figure 16.2 Chapters in Colley (2003).

Discussion of the analytic process

In the first two chapters of the book, there is some commentary on the analytic process. Colley describes how she analysed the data as follows:

> Narratives of each mentor relationship were synthesized through repeated listening to the tapes and reading of transcripts, starting with the accounts of the young people to ensure these were not submerged by the data of more articulate adults.
>
> Colley 2003: 45

She explains that this raised issues for the analysis:

> Conventional methods of analysing the data – coding and grouping it according to key categories – thus presented two main problems. Not only would this fragment the holistic view of mentor relationships that I wanted to convey, 'slicing' the data across a number of stories; it would also risk submerging the voices of the young people. There was so much more to code from other respondents, and the coding was much more easily done. The only way to balance their perspectives was to transform the data through a process of *creative synthesis* rather than traditional methods of analysis (Moustakas 1990), to put the stories together rather than take their elements apart. These are my stories in a fundamental sense, so I refer to the accounts of individual mentor relationships as 'case stories' rather than 'case studies'.
>
> Colley 2003: 6

We learn, therefore, that she listened to the interview recordings and read through transcripts repeatedly. She tells us that she chose not to break the data down into themes, or report separately the stories from different types of participant (mentors, mentees and managers) in her study. Instead, she created 'case stories', each focused on one mentoring relationship. She also explains that, as a further part of the analytic process, she reviewed her interpretations of the data through discussion with others:

> These stories were subjected to challenge and reinterpretation through discussion with my doctoral supervision team, and public presentation of interim findings to practitioners and academics at seminars and conferences.
>
> Colley 2003: 45

She problematises further the moves from data collection to analysis and interpretation and then to representation of data in the book, by emphasising that the case stories do not represent some form of objective reality. They are narratives that she has constructed, and they are derived from narratives that were constructed by the interviewees:

> [T]hey are not objective representations of 'what happened' in mentoring. Such perfect representations are impossible (Smith 1993). As some of the stories illustrate very well, there were often different versions of what happened, from the young person, their mentor and the staff at the scheme. Each of their accounts is true, in the sense that it reflects the perceptions, intentions and beliefs of the speaker. In this respect, the differences between their stories are far more illuminating than the pursuit of some factual resolution.

[...] I have then reconstructed these narratives, by selecting, interpreting and ordering small portions of lengthy interview transcripts.

Colley 2003: 6

Her interpretation of the data is based on three theoretical resources, which she discusses in chapter 7 of her book: first, poststructural analyses, linked to the work of Foucault; second, Bourdieu's concepts of habitus and field, and third, Hochschild's concept of emotional labour. All three are used to explore questions of power and empowerment in relation to her study.

Dialogue between data and theory

Although these theoretical resources are not discussed until part 3 of the book, the beginnings of a dialogue between data and theory can be found in earlier chapters. One of the key arguments that Colley puts forward in her theoretical analysis is that empowerment through engagement mentoring is an 'impossible fiction' (p. 141). She proposes that 'Engagement mentoring seeks to reform young mentees' dispositions in line with employers' demands for "employability"', and that 'engagement mentoring seeks to engender devotion and self-sacrificing dispositions in mentors through its dis-course of feminine nurture' (p. 152). In the following example taken from Chapter 6, Colley develops the idea that mentoring is an impossible fiction through the case story of Lisa (a mentee) and Yvonne (a mentor). The story centres around how both young women have a vision of the mentoring scheme that is impossible to fulfil in practice.

For Lisa, mentoring meant finding someone else to take responsibility for her problems:

[O]ne of Lisa's hopes was that mentoring would help her cope with her own emotional problems in a quasi-therapeutic way, allowing her to offload the burden of caring for others. [...] [Lisa] thought that her mentor could help her by 'telling her what to do', and chiding her if she did not follow this advice.

Colley 2003: 123–4

Yvonne expected to support her mentee, imagining that her support would lead to a positive employment outcome:

Yvonne had her own dream of how mentoring should work. As she explained it to me when we first met, her understanding was that the young people would go to New Beginnings for a while. They could talk to their mentor about any problems they had, and this would give them a chance to 'air off' and 'get it off their chests', so that things would start to 'clear in their heads'. They could then concentrate on what the TEC wanted them to do, and settle into their work experience, hopefully progressing to a job.

Colley 2003: 124

In practice, though both young women persevered, their story is one of 'going round in circles, getting stuck' (p. 128). Colley quotes Yvonne's comment when the mentoring seemed to be leading nowhere:

'I just sit there and I think, "Why did I do this?" I put it on my CV, and then I dread anybody asking me about it in an interview.'

Colley 2003: 128

Lisa, meanwhile, not only failed to pursue any of her job placements, but also had sorted out some of her home problems, and no longer needed her mentor for this purpose. She explained:

'Lately, we haven't got anything to talk about, so we talk about watching TV. [...] So it's quite. [...] There isn't that much to talk about any more.'

Colley 2003: 131

Colley observes that 'It would be easy to offer an interpretation of this mentor relationship that fits well with some of the research about dysfunctional mentor relationships reviewed in Chapter 2' (p. 132). However, she continues by arguing that 'The stories from this research allow us to revisit the meanings of mentoring in a new light' (p. 135), and she uses her theoretical resources to develop an alternative analysis.

From analysis to interpretive conclusions

As the above extract shows, Colley's case stories are not uninformed by her subsequent theoretical analysis. Rather, the structure of the book acts as a presentational device. It represents a way of suggesting an interaction between data and theory, where theorisation is influenced by the data, as much as data analysis is influenced by theory. In Chapter 7, Colley does not, therefore, simply describe her theoretical resources, but discusses what interpretations of the data they allow, and the implications of such an analysis. She concludes that:

This theoretical analysis suggests major flaws in policies to develop engagement mentoring as a key intervention for social inclusion, and calls into question the practices these policies promote.

Colley 2003: 159

As with the previous example from Kathryn Ecclestone, Helen Colley provides considerable detail about the construction of her interpretation, and creates strong links between data and her analytic framework. Here, too, however, the reader can learn more about the creation of a final text, than about the complex processes of analysis that lie behind what appears on the printed page.

Conclusions: issues for carrying out data analysis

There is now a wealth of resources available on qualitative data analysis, so that doctoral students and novice researchers have plenty of sources to choose from. But this also means that choices have to be made and justified. As Colley's (2003) explanation of why she did not break her data down into themes indicates, different ways of dealing with data analysis have an effect on the interpretive re-presentation of the data, on the story that can be told.

In addition, the choice of an analytic perspective provides a particular lens on a research issue, which may make it possible to see some things, but not others. Ecclestone (2002) says that she tried to overcome this by using multiple analytic approaches to understand the construction of assessment policy by policy makers, and the relationship between policy as intended and policy as experienced on the ground.

It is also important to be aware, when selecting an approach to qualitative data analysis, not just of the methods advocated by a particular author, but the personal worldview (the author's ontology and epistemology if you like), that influences how individual authors understand data analysis. Colley's critical observations on the narrative constructions that are created both by her interviewees and subsequently by herself are a good example of this. As she explains, she did not interview different participants in each mentoring relationship in order to find an objective, 'true' story, but views each account as true, 'in the sense that it reflects the perceptions, intentions and beliefs of the speaker' (Colley 2003: 6).

This chapter has also aimed to show, that although data analysis may be narrowly defined as working closely with raw data, it is also inextricably bound up with processes of interpretation and theorisation. Although there are times during a research project when it is useful to separate these aspects out, inevitably they have to be brought together as an interaction between data-explanation-theory. The two studies discussed here provide good examples of how interpretational relationships between data and analysis may be constructed. Although Ecclestone introduces her theoretical framework before discussing her data, and Colley does the reverse, a dialogue between data and theory – whereby concepts are used creatively, and where the data are used to think with and to adapt theory – is clearly visible in both studies. The two authors offer different examples of what theorising involves. Where Ecclestone constructs her theoretical typology of motivation and autonomy out of a critical review of previous literature and research in her field, Colley draws on the work of social theorists (Foucault and Bourdieu), which she links to the concept of emotional labour taken from Hochschild. Both, drawing on different types of resources, are using and developing 'theory' as part of the analytic process.

Perhaps the greatest value in examining closely examples of published work lies in seeing how interpretational relationships between data-explanation-theory are constructed. However, as is apparent in both the examples discussed in this chapter, very little detail is provided about the moves from data gathering to initial analysis, and about how the authors reduced large amounts of raw data to what appears on the printed page. They indicate just how difficult it is to give the reader any meaningful insight into what the process involved, without the sort of detail that, as here, tends not to be included in published accounts of research.

It is to research methods texts that researchers must turn to find more extensive information about the practices involved in data analysis. Books on research methods not only provide a wealth of advice, but may also include material that rarely appears in published form. Ely *et al.*'s (1997) book is just one example, where the authors present and discuss extracts from fieldnotes, research diaries and analytic memos, which give insights into how researchers think about their data, begin to identify themes, construct codes, and use theory to move towards interpretation. What normally appears in print as the published accounts of completed research is rather different and may only hint at the analytic processes that have led to what is presented to the reader.

My final point, therefore, concerns writing about the analytic process. In both the examples presented here, chapters detailing methods and methodology do not feature.

However, although this may be common practice in published research, the expectations for a doctoral thesis are that much more space will be given to discussion of the methodological approach (whether that takes the form of a designated chapter or not). Yet even here, rarely is much attention given to analysis, and the decisions, dilemmas and moves that take place. I would suggest that it is not only worth heeding the advice that thinking about analysis should begin when you start a research project, but that there is also a bigger place for critical discussion of the analytic process. Not only will such discussion help to explain how the research was conducted, but it will help to clarify for you as a researcher, as well as for your readers, the moves that are made from close engagement with your data, to developing interpretational relationships between data and analysis.

Notes

1 For those interested in the 'science wars' see Blunkett (2000) and Tooley and Darby (1998) for criticisms of social and educational research in the UK, and Denzin (2008), Hodkinson (2008), and Lather (2004) who challenge the narrow direction of the evidence-based practice movement in the UK and the USA.

2 However, Ecclestone notes later that 'the study did not aim for a "grounded" ethnographic approach' (p. 9) so is not strictly following a 'grounded theory' approach.

References

Alvesson, M. and Sköldberg, K. (2000) *Reflexive Methodology. New Vistas for Qualitative Research*. London: Sage.

Atkinson, P. and Delamont, S. (2005) Analytic Perspectives. In N. K. Denzin and Y. S. Lincoln (Eds) *The Sage Handbook of Qualitative Research*, 3rd edn. London: Sage, 821–40.

——(Eds) (2006) *Narrative Methods*. London: Sage.

Ball, S. (1994) Researching inside the state: issues in the interpretation of elite interviews. In D. Halpin and B. Troyna (Eds). *Researching Education Policy: Ethical and Methodological Issues*. London: Falmer.

Blunkett, D. (2000) *Influence or Irrelevance: Can Social Science Improve Government?* Secretary of State's ESRC Lecture Speech, 2 February 2000, London: DfEE and ESRC.

Bryman, A. and Burgess, R. G. (Eds) (1994) *Analysing Qualitative Data*. London: Sage.

Clandinin, D. J. and Connelly, F. M. (Eds) (2000) *Narrative Inquiry: Experience and Story in Qualitative Research*. San Francisco, CA: Jossey-Bass.

Coffey, A. and Atkinson, P. (1996) Making Sense of Qualitative Data: Complementary Research Strategies. Thousand Oaks, CA and London: Sage.

Colley, H. (2003) *Mentoring for Social Inclusion: a critical approach to nurturing mentoring relationships*. London: RoutledgeFalmer.

Czarniawska, B. (2004) *Narratives in Social Science Research*. London: Sage.

Delamont, S. (2002) *Fieldwork in Educational Settings. Methods, pitfalls and perspectives*. 2nd edn. London: Routledge.

Denzin, N. K. (2008) The Elephant in the Living Room: or extending the conversation about the politics of evidence. In J. Satherthwaite, M. Watts and H. Piper (Eds). *Talking Truth, Confronting Power*. Stoke on Trent: Trentham, 1–16.

Denzin, N. and Lincoln, Y. S. (Eds) (2005) *The Sage Handbook of Qualitative Research*. 3rd edn. Thousand Oaks, Ca and London: Sage.

Ecclestone, K. (2002) *Learning Autonomy in Post-16 Education: the Politics and Practice of Formative Assessment*. London: Routledge/Falmer.

Ely, M., Vinz, R., Downing, M. and Anzul, M. (1997) *On Writing Qualitative Research. Living by Words.* London and Washington, DC: Falmer Press.

Fielding, N. and Lee, R. M. (1998) *Computer Analysis and Qualitative Research.* London: Sage.

Given, L. M. (2008) *The SAGE Encyclopedia of Qualitative Research Methods.* London: Sage.

Hodkinson, P. (2008) *'What works' does not work! Researching lifelong learning in the culture of audit.* Valedictory lecture at the University of Leeds, 23 June 2008. Online. (Available at www.education.leeds.ac.uk/research/lifelong/pdf/Phil_Hodkinson_valediction.pdf Accessed January 2009).

Lather, P. (2004) This is Your Father's Paradigm: Government Intrusion and the Case of Qualitative Research in Education, *Qualitative Inquiry*, 10(1): 15–34.

LeCompte, M. and Schensul, J. J. (1999) *Analyzing and Interpreting Ethnographic Data.* Walnut Creek, CA and London: Altamira Press/Sage.

Lewins, A. and Silver, C. (2007) *Using Software in Qualitative Research: A Step-by-Step Guide.* London: Sage.

Lofland, J., Lofland, L. H., Snow, D. and Anderson, L. (2006) *Analyzing Social Settings: A Guide to Qualitative Observation and Analysis.* 4th edn. Belmont, CA: Wadsworth/Thomson Learning.

Miles, M. and Huberman, A. M. (1994) *Qualitative Data Analysis. An Expanded Sourcebook.* 2nd edn. London and Thousand Oaks, CA: Sage.

Price, J. (1999) In Acknowledgement: A Review and Critique of Qualitative Research Texts. In R. Josselson and A. Lieblich (Eds). *Making Meaning of Narratives* (The Narrative Study of Lives Volume 6). Thousand Oaks, CA and London: Sage, 1–24.

Riessman, C. K. (2008) *Narrative Methods for the Human Sciences.* Los Angeles, CA: Sage.

Sarantakos, S. (2007) *Data Analysis* (Four-Volume Set). London: Sage.

Silverman, D. (2001) *Interpreting Qualitative Data: Methods for Analysing Talk, Text and Interaction.* 2nd edn. London: Sage.

Stake, R. E. (1995) *The Art of Case Study Research.* London and Thousand Oaks, CA: Sage.

Strauss, A. (1987) *Qualitative Analysis for Social Scientists.* Cambridge: Cambridge University Press.

Strauss, A. and Corbin, J. (1990) *Basics of Qualitative Research Techniques and Procedures for Developing Grounded Theory.* London: Sage.

Tooley, J and Darby, D. (1998) *Education research: an OfSTED critique.* London: OfSTED.

Wolcott, H. F. (1994). *Transforming qualitative data: Description, analysis, and interpretation.* Thousand Oaks, CA: Sage.

Yin, R. K. (2009) *Case Study Research: Design and Methods.* 4th edn. London: Sage.

17

Researching with large datasets

Learning to *think big* when *small is beautiful*

A. Noyes

Introduction

I began my research career in 2001, following 10 years as a classroom teacher in a comprehensive secondary school in England. During the 1990s schools were changing fast. Following the introduction of the National Curriculum in the late 1980s, national tests for 7-, 11- and 14-year-olds were introduced. This was part of the establishment of quasi-markets in education engineered through the inculcation of a new education culture characterised by managerialism and performativity (Ball 2008). One of the principal technologies of this new culture in schools was the performance or 'league' table of results. Such league tables were being made possible by the rapidly expanding capacity to gather, store, manipulate and present data electronically. So statistics, 'the language of politics and persuasion' (Dorling and Simpson 1999: 1), became an increasingly powerful tool for reforming education. My attention as a new teacher was now not only on the individual learner in my classes, but also on the contribution that each would make to the group results and therefore my performance management. This period marked a shift in the politics of schools, in which economic imperatives were increasingly at the heart of a new Standards agenda. A key ingredient in this shift was the increased use of data.

Anyone familiar with education in England in 2009 will be all too aware of the tide of data that flows into and out of schools. Engagement with this data is unavoidable. The work of teachers and pupils and the choices of parents in this education market are now framed by the use (and abuse) of data (Goldstein 2001). My research tries to embrace the tensions of researching both the texture of learners' daily experiences and the depersonalised bigger pictures that get painted with statistical data. Here, I will be talking in particular about the Department for Children, Schools and Families' (DCSF) National Pupil Database (NPD). This database includes the records of attainment, schools attended and social data for all students in England. The database will soon have grown sufficiently large to enable the tracing of an individual student's educational trajectory from pre-school through to 18 years of age and will, in the future, also be linked to higher education data. Needless to say, this is a vast dataset. You might be working with other types of large datasets (e.g. questionnaires) and many of the issues raised here will be the same.

My current research explores the attainment and participation of learners in 14–19 mathematics education in England. The project design utilises a mixed methodology and does so because I want to hold in tension the macro- and micro-dimensions. This is motivated by the theoretical framework that I first used in my doctoral work and continues to inform much of my thinking (Bourdieu's 1977 *Theory of Practice*). Both macrothinking 'big' and 'small is beautiful' are phrases that have their origins in divergent economic philosophies.

English schools are now constantly compared, and the whole education system is held to account through the use of 'big' statistics. Value-added measures (and more recently, contextual valued-added) for schools are now well embedded into school attainment discourses. In a recent interview with a head of department, I was told that the department had 'a positive residual' for attainment in the GCSE (General Certificate of Secondary Education). Beyond the assumption that this is a good thing, I suspect that this statement, and similar statistical phrases which are increasingly common in schools, are not well understood, and perhaps more worryingly are misunderstood and misinterpreted. The problem with this new statistical language is that the individual student becomes obscured – they simply contribute to this global figure. Such discourse, part of the political economy of education, is deeply embedded in modern schooling and needs to be understood and critiqued. Schumacher's (1973) challenge to big thinking economic perspectives of his day (i.e. the 1970s, but still pertinent today) was titled *Small is beautiful: a study of economics as if people mattered*. In a similar way, I am convinced that statistical analyses of the education system need to aim to be similarly subtitled: 'a study of education/schools as if people mattered'. Researchers are right to be concerned about the potential for statistical analyses to obscure the individual. In my mind this leads to two alternatives: (i) don't engage with, or produce statistical research, or (ii) look for ways to view, analyse and understand the large and small scale together. I am currently having a go at option (ii).

Recently, whilst in a well-attended seminar at the annual conference of the American Education Research Association, several senior US academics were urging for new studies of social class that bridged the traditional paradigm divide of qualitative and quantitative researchers. That is what I am arguing for here too – holding the macro and micro in tension. Not that this is easy, or a new problem for academics. In C. P. Snow's famous lecture 'The Two Cultures and the Scientific Revolution' in 1959 he argued that:

> [T]he intellectual life of the whole of western society is increasingly being split into two polar groups. Literary intellectuals at one pole; at the other scientists, and as the most representative, the physical scientists. Between the two a gulf of mutual incomprehension.
>
> Quoted in Schumacher 1973: 61

I suspect that this sense of 'mutual incomprehension' often inhibits necessary dialogue between researchers in education and across the social sciences.

There is a commonly held view that all research is autobiographical. That is, although we like to feel that we have chosen our researcher trajectories those choices are constrained by life history, experience, locations, the interests of those around us, and so on. For many conducting education research, their studies are practitioner-focused enquiries into aspects of their own work. This sense of autobiography is as much in the context of the research and the questions posed as it is in the particular theories and methods adopted. What I want to focus on here is methodology. Why, when one has a natural inclination towards rich, thickly descriptive case study, might one consider using quantitative methods to analyse national datasets? My reasons for using such datasets include the following:

- They helped to give me a *different perspective* on my particular research questions – exploring patterns of participation, which also allows me to map these patterns across the region
- My *theoretical framework* led me to consider how the patterns derived from large-scale statistical analyses and accounts of daily experience (as well as some layers in between) are part of a slice though a complex web of social structures and agents
- *The datasets exist* and are already being used to tell particular stories. Therefore, being interested in issues of social justice I should explore whether alternative stories can be told
- I come from *a mathematics background* and so assumed that I could handle the statistics, although I am still not sure how much this has helped
- I had a sense that, given the concerns about shortage of quantitative researchers in the social sciences, *funding* might be more easily forthcoming for a mixed methods study
- I was trying to create a *breadth in my research methodology expertise*, which would be helpful in my career as an academic.

Other researchers will have different reasons for making this decision. Of course, the principal concern should be how using such data will enable one to answer the particular research questions of interest. I am not trying to explain the application of a particular statistical method here. Rather, my aim is to reflect on some of the challenges I have faced in the first two years of working with these datasets. Hopefully, this will give a sense of the challenges faced at each stage: data acquisition, cleaning, analysis and reporting. Some of the issues raised are peculiar to working with a national dataset owned by a national government, but I also consider more general aspects of beginning to work with large datasets.

Working with national datasets

Although the National Pupil Database is available for researchers to use, there are strict guidelines for its use. Formal requests need to be made to the DCSF in which a business case is made for getting access to data. When this case has been accepted, the researcher needs to sign a confidentiality declaration. Included in this contractual agreement are commitments to maintaining data confidentiality, destroying data at the end of the research, not using the data to identify schools for further research (without DCSF agreement) and not publishing results from analyses without prior permission. These constraints seem considerable, but in view of the nature of the data, recent legislation on data protection, and the well-reported lapses of security resulting in the loss of large, potentially sensitive data by government officials and public sector workers, the need for secure storage of data is clear.

Before getting to that stage the researcher needs to decide what it is they should request. This process began by my trying to read and understand a document of several dozen pages outlining all of the fields available in the various datasets. The whole data-base is sub-divided into smaller parts, but can be joined up through the use of unique pupil identification numbers. For each 18-year-old there are hundreds of datafields, many of which are not required for any particular study. Making these choices without an in-depth knowledge of the data was extremely challenging, and I ended up requesting all of the data for particular cohorts of students across a large region of England. This region included over 120,000 16-year-olds and the matched datasets for their education back to primary school and, where relevant, through to 18 years of age. Moreover, I was interested in looking at trends over time so wanted to use the data for four successive cohorts. So I have hundreds of bits of data for around half a million students. It is all too easy to collect too much data.

If the selection of data to request was bewildering, this was nothing compared to the first experiences of working with the datasets, particularly as a newcomer to quantitative research methods. It took several months of work to become comfortable handling these large datasets and to develop the technical skills (usually with SPSS) to manipulate the data. Due to the nature of the project, I was unable to commit continuous periods of time to the work and so was further delayed. This data is really something in which a researcher needs to be immersed for some length of time, which is no different from working with any complex and extensive dataset. Another thing I had to learn was how to keep track of my progress with careful records of decisions made and filing of adapted files.

Beyond the practical skills of manipulating the data, the researcher needs to develop some methodological sensitivity to the process of data cleaning, organisation and selection for analysis. As a newcomer to this type of work, I continue to be struck by the similarity with managing large sets of qualitative data. Decisions need to be made about how to select, organise and analyse the data. In both circumstances the process is more of an art than a science, although clearly any decision making needs to be defendable. In each case there is also the challenge that comes from often being the only person who really knows that data well; including the untidiness of it which often gets swept under the carpet in the process of academic writing. It took me many months until I felt confident to write about the analysis that I had been doing on this data. Even then, I felt compelled to spend considerable time explaining the decisions made in the analysis.

Gorard's (2008) recent statistical analysis of widening participation in higher education in England draws attention to the need for making the analytical decision making process transparent.

> [E]very analysis concerning patterns of participation must make, even by default, a bewildering number of decisions … and every analyst might quite reasonably make a different set of decisions. Unless these analytical compromises are clearly reported, there is a danger that debates about what is happening in Widening Participation will be misinterpreted by commentators as being about issues of substance, whereas they are, in reality, merely about differences in making these analytical decisions.
>
> Gorard 2008: 423

This point does not only apply to analyses of widening participation, but also to any analysis using large datasets. Appreciating how the process of making multiple decisions, each of which has a small but cumulatively significant effect on results, is very important. In my own work I needed to decide who to include in my analyses of Advanced level participation. Should it be all students with a higher GCSE grade (i.e. C and above) in mathematics, or those who have achieved 5 A*–C GCSE grades including English and mathematics (i.e. the standard entry requirement for Advanced level study), or one of these categories but then only those who had proceeded to an A level (rather than vocational) programme? But this is made more complicated as students from independent schools, although included in the dataset, do not have the same range of recorded social characteristics (e.g. ethnicity) that I wanted to use in some of my analyses. At each of these junctions the researcher needs to decide how best to proceed in order to adequately explore their particular research question. All such decisions need to be defendable and recorded. This reminds me of the Greek myth of Theseus of Athens who found his way into and out of the Cretan labyrinth using a ball of string by which he could retrace his steps. In some sense working through these large datasets has a similar feel, that of feeling your way though a labyrinth of data, including taking many wrong turns. However, being careful in recording one's 'analytical compromises' and reporting them allows the researcher, and peer referees, to trace the route taken and this seems preferable to leaving one's analysis shrouded in mystery and inaccessible to validation.

After becoming familiar with the datasets, and of how to organise and manipulate, clean and reduce them, there is the need to start to explore the particular research questions for which one acquired the data in the first place. There is the temptation of getting distracted by all kinds of other interesting issues now made possible due to the range of data available. Again, in my experience this is no different from any other research activity that I have been involved in; there are always other research questions that seem to be as interesting as the ones on which you are supposed to be focused. Although my work is considering engagement with mathematics in the 14–19 age range, the possible research questions that could be explored are limitless. Many of these are quite closely related to the particular research questions of my project. I have had to learn to be quite ruthless in my data reduction activity. This process is determined not only by the particular research questions, but also by the kind of analysis that you are planning to undertake. My work began with descriptive analyses (e.g. cross-tabular analyses of participation by gender), but has moved on to use multi-level modelling techniques to explore the between-school variation in attainment and post-16 participation in mathematics.

For many embarking on this kind of analysis for the first time, there will be a need for some specialist training. Appropriate courses might be available in one's own institution but the particular expertise for any one study might need to be accessed through courses elsewhere. One of my personal reasons for using such quantitative methodologies was for personal and professional development, particularly given the well-documented shortage of quantitative researchers in the social sciences in England. It might be that there are few researchers who are able to offer local support with these methodologies. Indeed, given the broad and expanding range of statistical techniques available, accessing such expertise might not be straightforward. That said, there are many support networks available online, although these serve a different purpose from the critical friend in the next office. The absence of local support can result in a lack of reassurance that comes from not having regular discussion of the research process and conclusions with like-minded colleagues. For me, the process of working on these datasets has felt quite isolating, even though it can be utterly absorbing.

Reporting your analysis

Given what might be called the 'gulf of incomprehension' between different paradigms in education research, and social science more generally, anyone working with such datasets will need to consider carefully how to communicate their analyses. How can statistical reports be accessible to the general academic reader and to the serious statistician or quantitative methodologist? Surely good statistics should lead to clear interpretations that can be communicated to a wide audience – that is, if the researcher really understands what their statistics are telling them. Despite my background in mathematics I have generally shied away from reading quantitative research reports, often because I feel threatened by the mystifying statistical terms and methods, and because many such papers seem to have lost sight of the people being researched; they say a lot about everyone but little about anyone. As an education researcher trying to 'see' the individual and the group together in the research process this is demotivating. Moreover, there can sometimes be a tendency towards positivistic over confidence in the results and a lack of subjectivity, as in Gorard's (2008) warning mentioned earlier. The quantitative researcher must remember 'that there is always an *interpretative gap* between objects in the world and our representations of them' (Parker 1999: 84). Holding results loosely is important, statistical findings are not proofs and should always remain open to critique.

So how should these analyses be reported? Of course, the answer depends upon one's notion of audience and ultimately where one wants to be positioned in the field of education research (although we do not articulate such strategic professional decisions very often). For example, do I want to communicate the results of my multi-level models to education researchers and policy makers and/or to statisticians and quantitative methodologists? Some might be interested in the headline findings and not in the methods, and so I will omit methodological detail that will make the reporting insufficiently rigorous to the expert. On the other hand, I can include the full complexity of the method and risk losing the broader readership who might be interested in the implication of the key findings. For me the answer is that the full range of audiences needs to be appropriately addressed. This presents me with a challenge as the norms for writing statistical papers are quite different from policy or qualitative research reports, for example. Learning to write for an academic audience is challenging enough, but to write for a range of quite different audiences presents new challenges, and of course opportunities. Whomever I am writing for, it is essential to hold onto the idea that statistical analyses are generally not trying to prove anything, although the strength of my claims no doubt varies depending on the audience. Rather, I am trying to show that a particular hypothesis is, or is not, untenable due to its having a very large or small probability of happening.

Much academic writing comes in pretty well-defined lengths and formats. A PhD might be 60–80,000 words and have a great deal of flexibility. However, my writing seeks to communicate to a wide audience in the form of conference papers and peer-refereed journal articles, and there are typically only 6,000 words to play with. This presents researchers with a critical question: What should I include and what can I omit? When I learnt to write qualitative research for publication, I quickly developed a sense of how much could go into a typical paper and how that might best be structured; it was a rather formulaic process but it seemed to work. This process is similar to the quantitative work in which I am now engaged, but I do need to leave a lot more out. This is due in part to the scale of dataset with which I am working. So, what should be omitted?

Gorard's (2008) plea to make analytic decisions clear seems sensible but this can take up quite a lot of the paper. Although this might be regrettable if one wants to impress with results and statistical wizardry, this advice, if adopted more widely, might actually have the effect of making some of the mysterious processes of quantitative analysis more transparent, so offering a way across the 'gulf of incomprehension'. Developing a more reflexive and critical stance on my own statistical findings might also help to placate those aligned with that famous nineteenth century adage: 'There are three kinds of lies: lies, damned lies, and statistics'.

Although the best way to develop one's writing in a particular genre of research might well be to immerse oneself in work of a similar style, I need to bear in mind that this style might not be the ideal for the particular audience with whom I am trying to communicate in any one piece of writing. All of this requires careful thought when embarking on a programme of research dissemination.

Final comment

Having worked on projects using a range of methodologies I have found that the problems around reliability and validity are as challenging when working with observational and interview data as they are when analysing a large dataset. The hard numbers of quantitative research can be beguiling, but a critical stance enables one to maintain a healthy scepticism of any results. Statistics is an art in a not dissimilar way to qualitative analysis. The datasets used in qualitative and quantitative research are clearly only a highly selective and subjective view of the social objects that they are seeking to understand. Moreover, one cannot easily be exhaustive in analysing any dataset and so findings are always, to a greater or lesser degree, partial. In both instances the *interpretive gap* remains, and ignoring this in quantitative analysis and reporting merely exacerbates the space between research paradigms and inhibits the potential for researchers to work across and between methodologies to ensure better social outcomes from their research.

In my own work I have faced considerable challenges in accessing, cleaning and analysing large datasets, but as part of a mixed methodology this work has been invaluable in understanding school policies, classroom practices and individual dispositions. I under estimated just how much time it would take to work with the data and how messy the whole process would be. The art of analysing large datasets is much closer to that of working with qualitative data than I had previously imagined, although admittedly the analytical tools can be quite different.

So, why bother with large datasets? For a start, they are a readymade resource, albeit not perfect, for researchers. As I am interested in issues of social justice and educational policy and come from a mathematics background, I feel compelled to try and engage with such data. But whether I do or do not, I can guarantee that a range of influential, high-level reports, many of which never enter the mainstream of published educational research, will be using these datasets and be influencing policy decisions. So, in one sense, I am engaging with statistics as part of the discourse of power in the current political climate, whilst at the same time aiming to critique that power through my own analysis. Second, it seems to me that perpetuating a research culture in which sub-groups with allegiances to various paradigms will not, or cannot, engage with one another's work, even when it is trying to explore the same research questions, is detrimental to our collective aims of better understanding and making a positive difference in society. And if, through the development of mixed methods approaches in my own work, the large and small scale become mutually indispensable in developing both research insight and impact, I will have made a small contribution to bridging the *gulf*.

References

Ball, S. (2008) *The Education Debate*. Bristol: The Policy Press.

Bourdieu, P. (1977) *Outline of a Theory of Practice*. Cambridge: Cambridge University Press.

Dorling, D., and Simpson, S. (1999) Introduction to statistics in society. In D. Dorling and S. Simpson (Eds). *Statistics in Society: the arithmetic of politics*. London: Arnold.

Goldstein, H. (2001) Using Pupil Performance Data for Judging Schools and Teachers: scope and limitations, *British Educational Research Journal*, 27(4): 433–42.

Gorard, S. (2008) Who is missing from higher education? *Cambridge Journal of Education*, 38(3): 421–37.

Parker, I. (1999) Quantitative data and the subjectivity of 'objective' facts. In D. Dorling and S. Simpson (Eds). *Statistics in Society: the arithmetic of politics*. London: Arnold.

Schumacher, E. F. (1973) *Small is Beautiful; a study of economics as if people mattered*. London: Vintage.

18

Doing data analysis

S. Gorard

Introduction: four kinds of evidence

Research is about more than empirical evidence, but evidence is at the heart of finding out more about the social and education world. One way of marshalling evidence on a topic, or to answer a research question, is to use the findings of others as published in the literature. This use of evidence at third hand is common – in the notorious literature review for a PhD, for example. I say 'third hand' because the analyst does not have access to the primary evidence, nor are they re-presenting an analysis of the data. They are presenting a summary of what a previous author presented about an analysis of data. Done well, with a clear focus, such a review of literature can be useful, at least in establishing what others think, how a topic is usually researched, and why the topic might be important to research further. Some of the inherent weaknesses of using the accounts of others might be overcome by ensuring that all of the relevant literature was used, even accounts of unsuccessful studies and evidence from unpublished studies, and then conducting a full meta-analysis of the results (I recommend using a Bayesian approach, see appendix to Gorard *et al.* 2004, which allows the relatively simple combination of different kinds of evidence). But such systematic reviews of evidence are rare, very difficult to do properly, and both expensive and time-consuming. And, anyway, this second approach does not overcome the chief drawbacks of the literature, which are that we have no direct access to the evidence of others, and often face a very partial view of the assumptions made and the analyses conducted.

Much better, in many ways, is the approach of collecting primary data yourself and con-ducting the cleaning, coding and analysis yourself. This third kind of evidence overcomes many of the drawbacks you will encounter in trying to understand what other people have done from their own accounts (but try to remember to make your own accounts suitably clear about the assumptions, short cuts and compromises you have made). It is prob-ably true to say that most education researchers use primary evidence at some stage, just as most of them conduct reviews of literature. The drawbacks of generating primary evidence include the time and cost involved, and so the likely small scale of your own study.

A compromise, used by only a minority of social science researchers at present, lies in the reanalysis of secondary data. Secondary data has been generated by others, but is available directly to new researchers to conduct their own analyses. Many of the techniques, craft tips, and issues covered in this chapter may have applications beyond the use of secondary data, but secondary data is the focus of what follows. I consider, in turn, some of the likely sources of this fourth kind of evidence, why all of us should perhaps be using secondary evidence more, and how such data might be analysed.

Where do we find secondary data?

Much of the existing data that might be useful for education and social science researchers is available for download from websites, or can be requested from official bodies via their websites. I suggest some likely sources here for illustration, predominantly from the UK, but the details of internet resources are likely to date rapidly, and to vary between countries.

The (Office for) National Statistics (2001) is a one-stop shop for evidence on almost anything. It includes evidence at small area level on all 10-yearly national censuses of the population, most recently from 2001, and next run in 2011. Here, you can find such things as the highest educational qualification of everyone in the population aged 16–74, broken down by sex, age, area of residence, type of accommodation, health, religion, occupation, marital status and so on. You can also request bespoke tables and specific analyses.

The UK Data Archive (2009) is a repository of all datasets generated through research paid for by the taxpayer-funded Research Councils (such as the Economic and Social Research Council), and from a number of other sources. It includes historical archives, policy and other documents, and transcripts of interviews undertaken as part of previous research projects. Some of it is relevant to education studies. You can register for access to these resources, and then reanalyse the evidence for your own purposes.

The National Digital Archive of Datasets (2009) similarly contains a wide range of data – including a database of the annual schools census for all schools in England, undertaken in January each year, collecting data at school level on pupil intake characteristics (poverty, special needs, ethnicity, sex, first language), and on the teaching and support staff. The Department for Children, Schools and Families (2009) has a website full of data on all aspects of school and childhood, including an archive of examination and key stage results for each school up to the current year. Linking school and pupil characteristic data from the annual census to the corresponding records of school examination entry and attainment is a common but influential approach to secondary data analysis.

Edubase (2009) is a set of data about every educational institution in England, summarising their intake, management, whether they are in special measures (for schools) and even including information on the population density of the locale. The publicly available component can be accessed at www.edubase.gov.uk/home.xhtml More complex, but even more detailed, are two related databases held by central government and made available to researchers on request. These databases are not more generally available as they might identify individual students, and researchers can only request them for a specific study that meets ethical and data protection approval, and they must return or destroy the figures after completion. The Pupil Level Annual Schools Census (PLASC, also now increasingly just called ASC) contains a record for every pupil in maintained schools in England. It details their background characteristics, including periods in-care, special needs status and first language. It also has some attainment data. The National Pupil Database (NPD) holds individual records on every pupil in maintained schools in England. It details their examination and assessment entry and attainment, and also has some background data. An application for both datasets would be via the DCSF. There are some equivalent datasets for other home countries (see, for example, National Pupil Database – Wales 2009).

The PLASC/NPD combination, perhaps with Edubase as well, is very powerful. The individual records for schools and pupils can be matched across datasets. You could find out whether pupils eligible for free school meals in villages enter more GCSEs than equivalent pupils in cities – if you wanted to. Even more importantly, the records can be matched across years, so that individual pupils can be tracked annually from the moment they enter the system. This means that you could relate subsequent patterns of post–16 participation for each ethnic group to their earliest primary school qualification, for instance. These datasets are widely used in policy and practice, perhaps most notably in calculation of contextualised value-added scores, which are meant to provide measures of school standards and effectiveness, and so inform a range of processes from OFSTED inspections to parental choice (Gorard 2006a; 2008a; 2010a).

Many other official and government websites include downloadable data. One of these is the Higher Education Statistics Agency (2009). Here, you can find an archive of applications and admissions to higher education, and discover changes over time or regional variations in what kind of students study what kinds of subjects at university, for example. Or what happens to patterns of application for HE following a new policy, such as the introduction of student loans (Gorard *et al.* 2007).

Beyond the UK, the OECD website has a collection of international educational evidence, including the annual Education at a Glance, which has sections on work-based and tertiary education as well as schooling. It also contains the results of successive rounds of the international PISA study. The most recent PISA study at the time of writing was in 2006, and the database includes the views of teachers and students, student test results in a range of subjects, and school-level data. It can be downloaded from the website, giving records for individuals within schools, in around 80 countries. If you want comparative data about schools, teachers or education systems, or to place your evidence in an international context, then there is unlikely to be a better source of readymade evidence. An example of reuse of PISA data appears in Gorard and Smith (2004).

For more on where to find data, and how to analyse it, see Gorard (2003) and Smith (2008). The examples here only touch the surface of the local, national and international datasets made available specifically so that you and I can use them for our own purposes. Whatever you want to know about education, it is very likely that someone has already collected the evidence you need on a larger scale and with higher quality than your resources would allow. Perhaps the most original new use of these existing datasets lies in combining evidence from two or more in a way that has not been done before. Can you imagine linking the schools data with the HESA data – who is qualified for but missing out on university? You could use the resident population census data with the schools intake data. Do the pupils in different kinds of schools represent their local residents, or do faith-based schools 'select' by socio-economic background as well as religion? You might try to decide whether pupil views on citizenship (from PISA 2006) are related to the type of school they attend (Annual Schools Census). One of the many interesting projects I conducted involved comparing present day stories of adult learning with those in the taped oral archive of families living in the South Wales coalfields in the 1890s

(Gorard and Rees 2002). There are many such possibilities, but they are often ignored by scholars.

Why might we use secondary data?

Where you are able to gain direct access to the evidence collected by others this allows you a larger scale and range of data than you could collect yourself, but still with many of the advantages of primary data in terms of knowledge and control. A range of existing evidence is available on almost all social science topics. Such secondary evidence has the disadvantages, for you, that it was usually collected for another purpose and so may not be ideal, that you may have little idea of the conditions under which the data was collected, and you may therefore be misled about its completeness and accuracy. Nevertheless, when considering an education issue, secondary evidence is usually about as useful as primary evidence, immediately available, larger in range and scale, and much cheaper to get hold of.

Most simply perhaps, secondary data might be used to help select the sample for a further in–depth study. For example, Gorard and Rees (2002) used the electoral register in each region to select cases for their door-to-door household study of patterns of life-long learning. The 10-yearly census of population can be a useful way of characterising the population of different regions, and so selecting an area sample (Gorard and Selwyn 2005, Selwyn *et al.* 2006). The Annual Schools Census in England can be used to select schools to represent the range of pupil intakes (Gorard *et al.* 2003). In all of these ways, the large–scale dataset can be argued to yield cases for more detailed study that represent the larger picture. This approach overcomes some of the deficiencies of both kinds of data, providing an audit trail of generalisability for in-depth case studies perhaps (Gorard and Taylor 2004).

Secondary data can also provide the evidence for a stand-alone initial analysis. For example, if you wish to find out whether the number of applicants to study under-graduate science at universities in the UK has been going up or down in the last 10 years it is difficult to imagine that you could collect better data on this than the Higher Education Statistics Agency (HESA) already has (or via UCAS 2009). However, it is possible to conduct a new analysis of these data and produce original publishable research that could be important in terms of policy and practice (e.g. Gorard 2008b).

As a snapshot consider Table 18.1, showing four years of new entrants to undergraduate higher education in the UK, broken down by social class.

This pattern changes very little over the time period shown, despite a concurrent policy emphasis on widening participation for less-elevated occupational groups. There is a small decline in the proportion of students from the most-elevated occupational back-grounds, but this is matched by an increase in students whose background we do not know. Does this mean that widening participation had failed during that period? Perhaps students from more prosperous families became less likely to complete sections of the application form that might be deemed relevant to income, and thought, mistakenly, to affect their student grants and loans. On the other hand, the proportion of each class in the population from which these students come also changes over time. How much of any difference is due to that? To answer the first question, we might want to conduct interviews or observations of form-filling to help decide what is going on. To answer the second question, we might want to combine the simple analysis here with consideration

Table 18.1 Percentage of all HE students by occupational class, UK, 2002–5

Occupation	2002	2003	2004	2005
Higher managerial	19	18	18	17
Lower managerial	25	25	25	24
Intermediate	13	12	12	12
Small employers	6	6	6	6
Lower supervisory	4	4	4	4
Semi-routine	10	11	11	11
Routine	5	5	5	4
Don't know	18	20	20	23

Source: UCAS.

Note: Don't know includes never worked, long-term unemployed (and unknown or invalid response).

of another dataset, such as the census of population. Neither question can be answered with the kind of data in Table 18.1 by itself. Table 18.1 raises the issues for investigation. Secondary analysis, like most research, leads naturally to further questions and study. Use of a large-scale dataset is frequently the start of further investigation, not an end in itself.

Secondary data might also be used to try and ensure that you understand the problem or pattern you are investigating with in-depth data. In the late 1990s in the UK, there was considerable concern about the apparent under-achievement of boys. A lot of research focused on why boys were failing, and why girls were, for the first time, ahead of boys in terms of examination and assessment. But this research appears to have been looking at the wrong research questions in a number of ways (Gorard *et al.* 2001). The difference between boys and girls, where it appears, is not in terms of failing. It is, or at least was, at the highest levels of attainment, such as grade A at A-level (Table 18.2). In subjects like maths and sciences, there is actually very little difference between the results of boys and girls. There used to be a gap in favour of boys at the highest grades, despite a higher proportion of boys taking these subjects. This gap has now disappeared. So, the follow-up questions include why the gaps appear only at high levels of achievement, and why they differ over time and between subjects? Is it changes in subject entry, the nature of the teaching, or the form of assessment? Once again, we need more evidence, more data. The initial secondary analysis helps us onto the most appropriate track, but it represents a starting point only.

A recent study involving the PLASC/NPD combination of datasets (see above) related to a purported decline in the number of students selecting courses in the traditional sciences (Gorard and See 2008; 2009). Where does this decline start, and who is it that

Table 18.2 Achievement gap in favour of girls at each grade, A level mathematics, Wales, 1992–7

	A	B	C	D	E	F
1992	−7	−4	−2	−1	1	1
1993	−15	−9	−5	−3	−1	−1
1994	−5	−2	0	0	0	0
1995	−3	−2	−2	0	0	0
1996	−5	2	−2	0	0	0
1997	0	1	0	0	0	0

Note: The achievement gap for any grade is calculated as the number of girls attaining that grade, minus the number of boys attaining that grade, divided by the total attaining that grade. This is a very simple analytical procedure.

drops out of science? It is certainly evident after GCSE in England, and may be related to prior attainment at GCSE/Key Stage 4 (Table 18.3). There are clear differences in overall attainment in sciences at Key Stage 4 between students of differing backgrounds. However, these differences are no larger than, and often much smaller than, the differences for all subjects. Whatever the problem is, leading to the differential attainment of social, ethnic and economic groups, it is certainly not one that is specific to science. The general patterns are the same as for science. The large gap between students identified by their schools as 'Gifted and Talented' (G&T) and the others is expected if the identification of G&T has been even moderately successful. It is what G&T means, after all. So what is interesting here is the relatively small gap in science. Therefore, perhaps the most worrying gap in all these subjects is between students eligible and not eligible for free school meals (a measure of poverty). This useful preliminary analysis involved matching and counting millions of records. But it is simple. Using software to count a million cases is no more complex than counting 100.

How are large-datasets analysed?

I focus in this section on the analysis of numeric datasets of the kind illustrated so far. The 'good' news for would-be analysts is that most of the secondary datasets discussed in this chapter are not based on random samples; in fact most are not samples at all but data from entire populations such as all of the pupils in maintained schools in England in 2009. This means that none of the statistical techniques based on sampling theory can or should be used with these data. No significance tests are needed or possible; no confidence intervals and no standard errors. If female pupils attain a higher average GCSE points score than males in England in 2009 that is the end of the matter. We can calculate and present that difference, and we can comment on it. We cannot and should not ask if that difference is statistically significant, or whether there really is a difference (Gorard 2010b). Our commentary might consider how large the difference is compared to other years, other phases, other countries, or how large it is in relation to what we know about missing data and errors in the measurement process. Again, none of these issues relates to random sampling and so no statistics, as traditionally conceived, are involved.

Here is a simple example, involving only the production of a graph, created from figures provided by a DCSF Statistical First Release (Figure 18.1). At the beginning of

Table 18.3 Mean capped points scores (all subjects and sciences) and percentage attaining grade C or above (maths and English), all students, KS4, England, 2005–6

	All subjects	Science subjects
Male	338	33
Female	378	34
'Gifted and Talented'	501	46
Not 'Gifted and Talented'	308	33
Non-FSM	373	35
FSM	266	25
Overall	359	34

Source: NPD/PLASC.

the twenty-first century, commentators in England were alarmed by an apparent shortage of teachers, especially for secondary education and in some subject areas. Newspapers, politicians and some academics talked of a 'crisis'. This 'crisis' is, presumably, represented by the rise from 1999 to 2001, when advertised jobs for teachers (vacancies) were at their highest since 1990. What caused this growth in vacancies or, looked at another way, why were vacancies so low between 1992 and 1999? Figure 18.1 is useful because it leads us to search for an explanation(s) that covers the two abrupt changes over time and the relatively flat picture otherwise (Gorard *et al.* 2006). Again, having some data leads to a desire for more. Was it a sudden surge or drop in demand caused by the birth rate of pupils? Is it a consequence of the economy, with teaching more attractive during a downturn? Was it just the consequence of increased funding – with schools advertising posts because they have the money? Was it because teachers were moving more or less between sectors such as primary, secondary, further, and extended education?

It is also not necessary to consider generic issues of epistemology or ontology when presenting an analysis of numbers like these. If you are writing a chapter based on your own interview data trying to explain why female pupils have higher average GCSE points scores than males, and you start the chapter with a table of analysis in which you summarise GCSE points scores by sex and by subject, then the two parts are synthetic. You do not enter some different paradigm of research when presenting the table of frequencies to when you present the results of your interviews. The interviews explain and illustrate (or not) the patterns in the larger data. The common analytical themes are clarity of presentation and judgement in selecting what to present and what to omit (Gorard 2006b).

Of course, large datasets of population figures also can be modelled using regression techniques and similar, and the results can be fascinating. But such modelling is not essential and does not represent any kind of definitive test. Mostly, large datasets can be analysed as simple frequencies and/or percentages, broken down into categories such as year, sex of student or geographical region (see Gorard 2006c for suitable approaches). It

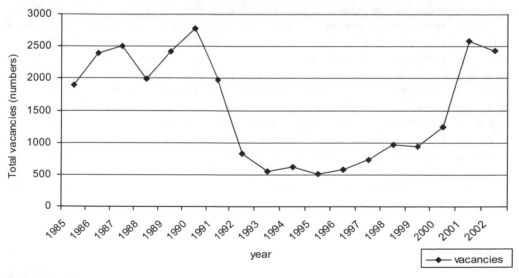

Figure 18.1 Teacher vacancies in maintained secondary schools, England, 1985–2002. Source: See *et al.* (2004).

Table 18.4 Percentage of pupils in school eligible for FSM, 2002 cohort of academies, 1997–2007

	1998	1999	2000	2001	2002	2003	2004	2005	2006	2007
Business	49	52	50	49	46	42	37	38	39	39
Greig	56	42	43	31	39	43	47	44	38	39
Unity	62	51	46	57	47	49	50	49	44	45

Source: ASC.
Note: The figures in italics are from the predecessor schools before the academies.

Table 18.5 Level 2 percentages for 2002 cohort of academies 1997–2007

	1998	1999	2000	2001	2002	2003	2004	2005	2006	2007
Business	24	14	10	17	–	21	34	29	32	31
Greig	11	15	25	30	–	35	26	54	59	65
Unity	2	13	4	17	–	16	17	16	34	45

Source: DCSF website.
Note: The figures in italics are from before the academies. Results are not publicly available for the first year of each academy.

is slightly more complicated when cross-analysing two or more large datasets, but even here the complication relates to the organisation of the datasets rather than the analysis as such.

Here is a simple example of cross-pollination of two sets of figures. Academies are a relatively new kind of maintained independent school in England, the first three of which opened in 2002 (Gorard 2005). They were, at least initially, intended to improve local education in areas of high disadvantage. How have they done so far? Table 18.4 shows that all of these first three academies have an increasingly different intake in terms of pupils considered to be living in poverty (and so eligible for free school meals). This change in intake should lead to higher levels of public examination attainment, as there is a well-known correlation at an aggregate level between poverty and low attainment.

This is what we find (Table 18.5): the Bexley Business Academy had the smallest decline in free school meals pupils, and shows the smallest gain in the percentage of pupils attaining level 2 (GCSE or equivalent) qualifications at the age of 16. The other two 2002 academies had considerable increases in level 2 results – Unity from 17 per cent in 2001 to 45 per cent in 2007 and Greig City from 30 per cent to 65 per cent. This is associated negatively with a shift in free school meals for both schools. Even so, these more recent gains look impressive. However, some commentators have suggested that these schools have merely changed their examination entry policies, targeting easier exams and courses. Perhaps we should test this by looking at level 2 qualifications including English and maths, the new DCSF standard threshold. And so we need to refer to more data, and the cycle of research continues. The key point to note for this chapter is that the analysis lies in cross-comparison of relatively simple tables of percentages, and yet can lead to findings of national interest (Gorard 2009).

Conclusion

Whatever you wish to research relevant to education, life-long and society wide, it is very likely that large datasets already exist that are relevant to your topic. These datasets are likely to be larger in scope and scale, and higher quality in terms of completeness and validity, than anything you could generate through primary fieldwork. They can be accessed directly, combined, cleaned, sorted and analysed by you, making them much preferable to the third hand accounts of evidence usually found in literature reviews.

You might use a large dataset on its own, to present a new analysis of an educational phenomenon in terms of place, time, the standard social sciences categories (such as class, sex, ethnicity, or age), or indeed any classification available from the data. You might use a large dataset at the outset of a more in-depth study – to select cases or areas, or to establish the pattern, trend or problem to be researched. More creatively, you might use one or more datasets in a synthesis with your own in-depth evidence.

It is arguably more important for you to examine the actual evidence available from previous research on your topic than it is to consider the accounts by others of that evidence in the literature. Of course, existing data, however generated and for whatever purpose, will have deficiencies. Cases will be missing, data will be missing from existing cases, measurements taken will be imprecise, some items will be miscoded, and transcription and representation may introduce further errors. The 'construction' of the entire enterprise may be biased, perhaps due to the underlying purpose for which the data was originally collected. But this is true of all datasets, including your own. Looking at the evidence itself gives you a good idea of these deficiencies, and therefore of the substantive importance of any patterns. This is preferable to reading about the evidence in the sanitised form provided by the literature. And, of course, the limitations of any dataset can themselves be a fascinating and controversial topic for secondary research (e.g. Gorard 2008c; 2010a).

Analysing large datasets is easy, mostly because the intimidating and flawed panoply of traditional statistics is irrelevant. You do not even have to use specialist software like SPSS – Excel will do. Many large datasets are available immediately, and free for use by researchers. What possible reason could you have, except fear of the unknown, for not pursuing this? Research is, at least partly, about discovery of the new. Fear of the unknown is, therefore, not something that a researcher can allow themselves to be inhibited by.

References

Department for Children, Schools and Families (2009) *Performance Tables*. Online. (Available at www. dcsf.gov.uk/performancetables Accessed 12 February 2009).

Edubase (2009) Online. (Available at www.edubase.gov.uk/home.xhtml Accessed 12 February 2009).

Gorard, S. (2003) *Quantitative methods in social science: the role of numbers made easy*. London: Continuum.

—— (2005) Academies as the 'future of schooling': is this an evidence-based policy? *Journal of Education Policy*, 20(3): 369–77.

—— (2006a) Value-added is of little value, *Journal of Educational Policy*, 21(2): 233–41.

—— (2006b) Towards a judgement-based statistical analysis, *British Journal of Sociology of Education*, 27 (1): 67–80

—— (2006c) *Using everyday numbers effectively in research:* Not *a book about statistics*. London: Continuum.

—— (2008a) The value-added of primary schools: what is it really measuring? *Educational Review*, 60(2): 179–85.

—— (2008b) Who is missing from higher education? *Cambridge Journal of Education*, 38(3): 421–37.

—— (2008c) Research impact is not always a good thing: a re-consideration of rates of 'social mobility' in Britain, *British Journal of Sociology of Education*, 29(3): 317–24.

—— (2009) What are Academies the answer to? *Journal of Education Policy*, 24(1): 1–13.

—— (2010a) Serious doubts about school effectiveness, *British Educational Research Journal*. Online. (Available at www.informaworld.com/openurl?genre=article&issn=0141-1926&issue=preprint&spage=1&doi=10.1080/01411920903144251&date=2009&atitle=Seriousdoubtsaboutschooleffectiveness&aulast=Gorard&aufirst=Stephen Accessed 7 September 2009).

—— (2010b) All evidence is equal: the flaw in statistical reasoning, *Oxford Review of Education*.

Gorard, S. and Rees, G. (2002) *Creating a learning society?* Bristol: Policy Press.

Gorard, S. and See, B. H. (2008) Is science a middle-class phenomenon? The SES determinants of 16–19 participation, *Research in Post-Compulsory Education*, 13(2): 217–26.

—— (2009) The impact of SES on participation and attainment in science, *Studies in Science Education*, 45(1): 93–129.

Gorard, S. and Selwyn, N. (2005) What makes a lifelong learner? *Teachers College Record*, 107(6): 1193–216.

Gorard, S. and Smith, E. (2004) An international comparison of equity in education systems? *Comparative Education*, 40(1): 16–28.

Gorard, S., and Taylor, C. (2004) *Combining methods in educational and social research*. London: Open University Press

Gorard, S., and Taylor, C. and Fitz, J. (2003) *Schools, markets and choice policies*. London: RoutledgeFalmer

Gorard, S., Rees, G. and Salisbury, J. (2001) The differential attainment of boys and girls at school: investigating the patterns and their determinants, *British Educational Research Journal*, 27(2): 125–39.

Gorard, S., Roberts, K. and Taylor, C. (2004) What kind of creature is a design experiment? *British Educational Research Journal*, 30(4): 575–90.

Gorard, S., See, B. H., Smith, E. and White, P. (2006) *Teacher supply: the key issues*. London: Continuum.

Gorard, S., Adnett, N., May, H., Slack, K., Smith, E. and Thomas, L. (2007) *Overcoming barriers to HE*. Stoke-on-Trent: Trentham Books.

Higher Education Statistics Agency (HESA) (2009) Online. (Available at www.hesa.ac.uk Accessed 12 February 2009).

National Pupil Database – Wales (2009) Online. (Available at www.npd-wales.gov.uk Accessed 12 February 2009).

(Office for) National Statistics (2001) Online. (Available at www.statistics.gov.uk/census2001/topics.asp Accessed 12 February 2009).

PISA (2006) *OECD Programme for International Student Assessment*. Online. (Available at pisa2006.acer. edu.au Accessed 12 February 2009).

See, B. H., Gorard, S. and White, P. (2004) Teacher demand: crisis, what crisis? *Cambridge Journal of Education*, 34(1): 103–23.

Selwyn, N., Gorard, S. and Furlong, J. (2006) *Adult learning in the digital age*. London: RoutledgeFalmer.

Smith, E. (2008) *Using secondary data in educational and social research*. Maidenhead: Open University Press.

The National Digital Archive of Datasets (2009). Online. (Available at www.ndad.nationalarchives.gov.uk/ Accessed 12 February 2009).

UCAS (2009). Online. (Available at www.ucas.ac.uk/about_us/stat_services/ Accessed 12 February 2009).

UK Data Archive (2009). Online. (Available at www.data-archive.ac.uk/ Accessed 12 February 2009).

19

Argumentation and the doctoral thesis

Theory and practice

M. McLean

We use the term *argumentation* for that type of speech in which participants thematize contested validity claims and attempt to vindicate or criticize them through arguments. An *argument* contains reasons or grounds that are connected in a systematic way with the *validity claim* of a problematic expression. The 'strength' of an argument is measured in a given context by the soundness of the reasons; that can be seen in, among other things, whether or not an argument is able to convince the participants in a discourse.

Habermas 1984: 18, italics in the original

Introduction

I want to make the strongest possible case for nurturing PhD students' capacity for argumentation. To do so, I turn to Jurgen Habermas, the influential social theorist for whom hope for modern society lies in argumentation. Making arguments is central to his theory of communicative action: where there is a possibility of influencing the public political sphere, citizens' capacity to make arguments and to accept 'the persuasive force of the better argument' (1990: 159) provide grounds for hoping that right and just decisions will be made in accordance with the general will (1984; 1987). Many have argued that Habermas' vision of communication free from the constraints of power relations is utopian. Yet, if there is an everyday model of reasoned argument and open, reciprocal communication surely we would find it in a university. Indeed, Habermas (1989) argues that universities and modern democratic societies are connected by a shared necessity for the processes of critical argumentation to ensure their health. So, from this perspective, it is not far-fetched to propose that doctoral education is the acme of the human capacity to 'raise claims to validity that we are prepared to defend against criticism' (Habermas 1990: 56) as a form of participation in the direction society takes.

The doctoral thesis is a part of the discourse of a field or discipline, in which a community of enquirers operates relatively coherent modes of argumentation. A doctoral thesis is written to contribute to scholarly arguments that are already under way. Watson (1987: 24) emphasises the importance of argumentative communicative in research: the topic 'is a response to the climate of opinion one lives in; and that it necessarily [...]

depends on some acquired sense of other minds–their puzzles, preoccupations and fears.' For this reason, the place of argument in doctoral work is to convince others – who are part of the relevant arguments – of an interesting, new and worthwhile point of view.

The intention of this chapter is to take a practical approach to what convincing arguments might look like. Its structure is:

1. An outline of general features of doctoral argument
2. A discussion, with illustrations, of the central importance of sequencing in making an argument at all textual levels: sections within chapters, chapters and the whole thesis
3. Some comments on what distinguishes good and bad arguments
4. A discussion of argumentative writing conventions and styles
5. Suggestions of some comparatively simple practical exercises towards writing the thesis as an argument; and
6. A conclusion that summarises the main points as a basic check-list and repeats the claim for the importance of doctoral argument for society.

This chapter is *not* a comprehensive account of the nature of argument, the many forms it can take and the many possible fallacies. On the whole, it does not use the specialised language of logic and rhetoric. Books that usefully do this are: Toulmin's (2003) seminal *The Uses of Argument*; Phelan and Reynold's (1996) *Argument and Evidence: critical analysis for the social sciences*; and Weston's (2000) succinct and lucid *A Rulebook for Argument*.

General features of scholarly argument

Arguing is an act of rational persuasion, distinct from appeals to emotion: an argument offers reasons and evidence to justify taking a position or coming to a conclusion. Scholarly argument is a means of enquiry requiring processes of critical assessment (Kamler and Thomson 2006; Weston 2000). Argumentation is not the only type of writing that appears in a doctorate. There are descriptions or accounts (e.g. of how research was conducted or historical information); and there are summaries, which are economic and accurate representation of events, actions, ideas, texts, speech (e.g. 'syntheses' of literature and reports of what people have said). The argument is, however, the main organiser of the doctoral thesis.

A scholarly argument must be forged. Research involves discovery and it might take some time for a line of argument to begin to emerge; nevertheless, it will not arise naturally or easily from deciding on research questions, selecting an appropriate conceptual frame-work, and collecting and analysing evidence. 'Writing up' does not adequately or accurately express the difficult work of writing the doctoral thesis as an argument. Writing argument demands reorganising, editing, cutting, adding, clarifying and refining.

The components of an argument

Kamler and Thomson (2006) use the metaphor of 'choreography' to convey the work that needs to be done to pattern a thesis as an argument. Arguments take the form of a series of 'moves' within and across chapters in a scholarly dance.

When the thread of an argument is evident and embedded, the essential components are: a series of points (i) arranged in logical order, (ii) supported by evidence and examples, and (iii) linked together by connections that reveal persuasive/rhetorical 'moves'. Anything that does not contribute to the argument should not be included. A typical structure for a piece of scholarly, argumentative prose is:

- *Delineation* of the problem (for example, issue, event, question)
- A *statement* of position on the problem. This is the main argument written succinctly and is referred to as the 'thesis statement'
- A brief *account* of how the position will be justified (of what reasons and evidence will provide a 'warrant')
- An *evaluative synthesis* of relevant literature emphasising how it supports and does not support the claims being made and creating a warrant for the research questions
- A justification for the *research question* generated from an evaluation of literature
- An *account* of collecting and analysing empirical data. The weight of evidence must be sufficient for the claims that are being made. In other words, the evidence must *warrant* the claims
- An *evaluative summary* of findings from the empirical data
- *Making the case* based on an interpretation of, and examples from, empirical data in the light of the literature. The writer is making claims about what is true and/or just. The reasoning will take the form of a series of assertions or denials. Claims are elaborated and justified in logical order: to convince the reader that what the writer claims is trustworthy
- A *conclusion* in which the argument is reasserted
- An *explanation* of how new light has been shed on the topic and why this is important (What contribution is being made to the field?).

Clarifying an argument

Much academic writing does not contain strong or clear enough arguments. The worst is a collection of unfocused observations deriving from the investigation; or, more commonly, the argument is hidden from view. I illustrate the latter with reference to the abstracts of two published papers about aspects of doctoral education. Abstracts can be thought of as small arguments and the rewritten abstracts below demonstrate how an argument can be revealed (I have, of course, had the advantage of reading the complete papers).

Paper 1 about research cultures: abstract

The article explores how different kinds of social science students from two universities, Woodside and Hillside, access and experience a variety of research cultures in those universities [...] The research involved interviews with 26 home and international students, studying both full- and part-time. [...] The data suggest that international students and part-time students have the most difficulty in accessing peer cultures and academic cultures. However, international students are much more favourably disposed towards research training cultures than other students. Some evidence of gender differences affecting student experiences was found but was not as widespread as other differences. The article ends by suggesting some practical changes that could be made in universities to provide more equal access to research cultures by all research students.

233

Abstract rewritten as a small argument

A small–scale study demonstrates that there are diverse and overlapping reasons why international, part–time and women PhD students might find it more difficult than others to enter the range of 'cultures' necessary to progress through a PhD. These are research training, student and academic cultures. Difficulties in accessing research culture should be understood and taken seriously by supervisors and institutions.

Paper 2 about overseas students' experience: abstract

There is in higher education a powerful discourse of 'independent learning'. While there may be pedagogical rationales to support the desirability of increased independence at the tertiary stage, it may also serve other institutional agendas, such as functioning as a way for academic staff to 'manage' the frustrations experienced by teachers as a result of pressures to prioritize research. However, the individualization of learning constituted by this discourse under-emphasizes the collaborative nature of learning. Academic success and failure are neither the property of individual students nor the instruction they receive, but lie rather in the relationships between students and the practices in which they and their teachers engage during the course of their on-going interaction. The learning experiences of international doctoral students are used here to illustrate ways in which discourses of dependence and independence can operate to disempower students.

Abstract rewritten as a small argument

The trope of the independent learner is over valorised in Western higher education, individualising learning, which, even at doctoral level, is more productively seen as social and dialogic. Generally, doctoral students who appear not to take active responsibility for their own learning are considered deficient; and overseas students specifically are disadvantaged because their attempts to make cultural adjustments are perceived as either a lack of autonomy or over demanding. Supervisors are both insufficiently sensitive to cultural difference and adjustment, and insufficiently aware of the social nature of learning.

In both cases, the second version is both more economical and clarifies a line of argument. Chapter 4 of Phelan and Reynolds' (1996) book *Argument and Evidence* presents a useful general method for perceiving arguments in texts.

Structuring an argument

Probably the most important element of a good argument is sequence because:

An argument is an ordering principle, like a story; and like a story, it needs to be in the right order to be followed at all. Each part of the argument, as it evolves, can be seen to relate to the contention challengingly thrown down at the start.

Watson 1987: 70–1

The importance of right order can be illustrated by Weston's (2000) example of a small argument of Bertrand Russell's (1935: 127):

> The evils of the world are due to moral defects quite as much as to lack of intelligence. But the human race has not hitherto discovered any method of eradicating moral defects. ... Intelligence, on the contrary, is easily improved by methods known to every competence educator. Therefore, until some method of teaching virtue has been discovered, progress will have to be sought by improvement of intelligence rather than of morals.
>
> Weston 2000: 3

Each move comes naturally after the one before. In the first sentence, Russell (1935: 127) begins with a (reasonably convincing) premise; from which, in the second sentence, two more premises arise. The 'therefore' in the final sentence signals his conclusion. Weston (2000) points out that the sentences could have been in the wrong order, like this:

> The evils of the world are due to moral defects quite as much as to lack of intelligence. Until some method of teaching virtue has been discovered, progress will have to be sought by improvement of intelligence rather than of morals. Intelligence is easily improved by methods known to every competent educator. But the human race has not hitherto discovered any means of eradicating moral defects.
>
> Weston 2000: 3

The premises and conclusion are the same, but it is a great deal harder to follow the argument because the order obscures it.

An excellent piece of general advice about organising a thesis comes from Dunleavy (2003: 274), who proposes the 'say it once, say it right' principle. The principle is to gather similar material together and deliver it in a 'single compelling bloc' (ibid.). This approach guards against repetition and a sense of fragmentation, in my experience both common problems in the arrangement of theses.

Structuring the overall argument

As I write this chapter, my PhD student Lillian (this is a pseudonym) is writing and rewriting her thesis for submission in five months time. This process is difficult. It is not one of straightforward, if tedious, 'writing up' of an investigation, nor is it involving much new reading, rather it is one of structuring chapters as sub-arguments that contribute to the overall argument. She is after a convincing sequence of sub-arguments within and across chapters. To support this effort, she is writing her whole thesis as a small argument or abstract. I have reproduced two efforts.

Lillian's first try

> This research takes the form of a case study of a well-established and developed programme of assessed, student-led seminars in a university history department. Still regarded as innovative practice, the case study seminars have three distinctive

features. They are assessed, they contain a range of different types of dialogue and they are student-led. The research considers how these dimensions impact on the students' learning experience.

Through interviews with staff and students and observations, it creates a holistic picture, which takes account of the participants' perspectives, as well as the socio-ideological context of the seminars and socio-linguistic structures, which constitute the actual interaction. The study adopts an ethnographic methodology drawing on a Bakhtinian theoretical framework to offer fresh insights on aspects of assessment, dialogue and classroom dynamics.

Assessment is shown to be a powerful director of student effort amplifying the students' learning experience. Different types of dialogue ensure that students actively engage with the issues in ways that allow them to assimilate new ideas. Peer facilitation and leadership of the seminars, along with other structuring devices ensure that the power dynamics of the classes remain open and fluid and prevent the tutor from unwittingly suppressing active student involvement. It is when these three conditions are in place that the potential for dialogic learning is maximised. When this occurs, students are able to engage with the material in-hand in an open manner and a rich learning experience ensues.

The case study shows that assessment, dialogue and student-centred learning are not an unproblematic panacea for student learning, nor are they the only factors that support student learning, but in these seminars they appear to be influential factors. The case study also sheds light on other related aspects of policy and practice and the wider concept of dialogic learning.

This attempt starts with a description of the case, when it should start with the central argument. The third paragraph contains the crux of the matter, but it can be taken as description, the reader is left wondering if this is, indeed, the main point.

Lillian's second try

A Bakhtinian theoretical framework is used to argue how university assessment, dialogue and classroom dynamics might combine to enable students to experience open and rich learning.

The case study is a well-established university history department programme of assessed, student-led seminars. These seminars have three distinctive features: they are assessed; they are designed to elicit a range of different types of dialogue; and, they are student-led. Through interviews and observations, a holistic picture has been created, which takes account of the participants' perspectives, as well as the socio-ideological context of the seminars and socio-linguistic structures, which constitute the actual interaction.

Empirical data was filtered through the lens of Bakhtinian concepts revealing that it is when three conditions are in place that the potential for dialogic learning is maximised. First, when the learning is assessed; second, when different types of dialogue are used students actively engage with the issues in ways that allow them to assimilate new ideas; and, third, when peer facilitation and leadership of the seminars and other structuring devices ensure that the power dynamics of the classes remain open and fluid.

The second attempt, which might yet need tweaking, is shorter and crisper and we are challengingly informed of the overall argument at the start. And now it is evident how each part of the thesis will be a sub-argument contributing to the overall argument. The arrangement of chapters might look like this:

- A chapter on current literature about university assessment, arguing that it does not adequately explain the effects on students' learning of assessing oral work.
- A chapter setting out Bakhtin's theory, arguing that it will illuminate research questions about student engagement in dialogic academic work in seminar rooms.
- A chapter arguing that the selection of the case study department and the methods of data collection used are congruent with the theoretical lens and will address the research question.
- Three chapters using Bakhtin to analyse and interpret empirical data: (i) to argue that assessment motivates students, (ii) to argue that when students are required to use different types of dialogue learning is enhanced, and (iii) to argue that the organisation of seminars can structure power relations between students and between students and tutor.
- A chapter arguing that combined assessment, engagement in a range of dialogues and the impositions of specific roles in seminar rooms enriches student learning and that Bakhtin's theory explains why this is so.

Of course, all these chapters will contain description and explanation, but, finally, these modes of writing are in the service of the overall argument.

Within chapters

Within the thesis, then, each chapter contains a sub-argument that relates to the overall argument. Within each chapter, each section needs to move logically to the next. The list of section headings and sub-headings should reflect a logical and lucid arrangement of steps towards an argument. Often, overviews at the beginning of sections and summaries at the end are necessary to clarify the detail that comes between and to remind readers periodically of the major claims.

By way of illustration of how a chapter might work as a contributing argument, I take one chapter from another student's thesis, which is historical and focuses on a wide-ranging educational initiative of 20 years ago to argue that it illustrates a qualitative change in conceptions of school teachers' work. First, here is part of her abstract:

The organising concept 'the colonisation of the life-world', supplied by Jurgen Habermas, refers to the state's invasions of human realms of life with subsystems of money and power. Using the case of TVEI between 1988 and 1993, it is argued and demonstrated that state policy interventions are always mediated by teachers' life-worlds, which contain options and constraints, capacity and incapacity in the pursuit of communicative competence. I conclude that the teachers' collective and individual life-world is being distorted by current state intervention and that a renewed professionalism would restore to teachers options for autonomy and intellectual engagement with their work.

In chapter 8 she argues that a team of advisory teachers supporting the initiative provide evidence of the distortions of colonisation of the life-world.

Chapter title: 'The advisory support team: 'new' managers?

The overall argument is that the advisory support team acted as collusive colonising agents for the state. They peddled the 'new vocational' ideology and lost their own sense of authenticity. The main symptom of colonisation is the distorted communications of the team with researchers and schools: they block open, un-coerced, reasoned discussion about teaching. The team's dealings with schools elicited 'image management' and education was dealt with as if questions of moral and political value are irrelevant.

Each sub-section intends to contribute to the argument as a whole, sub-headings are:

Introduction: Argues that the advisory support team can be seen as a 'state agent' mediating between policy directives and schools.

The support team's role in a categorically funded initiative: Argues that, even though many of the members started by genuinely wanting to improve education for disadvantaged children, they became drawn into acting as messengers and monitors in relation to schools, exhorting them to keep to a mythical 'contract' with the agency dispensing funding.

The support team as 'new entrepreneurs': Argues that the team left behind an attitude of 'old professionalism' associated with a concern for social justice in schools for a commitment to career advancement in a 'brave new entrepreneurial world'. They became believers in a new creed, in which they could not afford to lose faith. (For emphasis an individual who is an exception to the generalisation is discussed.)

The support team as evangelists and managers: Argues that the team coped with the resistances they experienced from schools by convincing themselves they were right and behaving with missionary zeal. As it became clear that preaching was not going to convert non-compliant schools, the team turned to the tenets of 'management of change' to persuade the reluctant. This move involved alien, impoverished 'management-speak', which did not connect to the everyday life of schools. The workings of the team become increasingly *dirigiste*. (The section includes extended illustrations.)

The reality: limitations and spaces in the support team's work: Argues that, despite efforts to appear in control by way of much paperwork, the reality was messy. As aspects of the initiative proved unworkable, the team had to absorb constant changes in the policy texts from central government. Some members also felt 'colluded', they had surrendered collaborative ways of working with schools and by the end of the initiative, spent most of their time writing mendacious reports to satisfy state agencies.

Conclusion: Finally, the hollow nature of their work de-skilled the advisory support team. They came to measure success by what was appearing to happen and spent time collecting trivial data. They also became de-moralised by compromising important values. Whereas this chapter tells a story of colonisation and lack of hope, the next presents a story of resistance to colonisation (counter evidence).

Bad and good arguments

An overall argument, then, should dictate the shape of the thesis. However, some arguments are better than others and the thesis should be a *good* argument, although, as

Watson (1987), insists any argument is better than none (and will probably contain some truth).

Perhaps the most straightforward way to characterise a good argument is to point out the features of a bad argument. Weston (2000: 71) identifies 'two great fallacies' or errors. The first is to draw conclusions from too little evidence. Examiners of theses will want to be confident that relatively general conclusions can be drawn from the evidence presented. They will be wary of over generalisation, especially if the evidential base is not large or deep enough or if it has not been analysed critically and subtly enough (e.g. taking what people say at face value: people make mistakes, lie and forget). The second common error is to 'overlook alternatives'. For an argument to appear sound it is necessary to present counter arguments, competing theories, alternative sides in controversies and different possible interpretations of empirical data. I would add a third serious error. Assumptions or premises are taken for granted and not declared; and, sometimes, in addition, such undeclared assumptions are not plausible and reliable (Weston, 2000).

A good social science thesis handles the complexities of human motives, intentions, interests and convictions and explains why it is important to do so. And a good argument in these disciplines is kept open, social matters cannot be settled once and for all.

Writing style

Although the essential structure of the argument might be settled, there is still the matter of how it is expressed. Unfortunately, many theses are marred by deadening and hard-to-understand prose. Undoubtedly, like felicitous structure, a clear, elegant, compelling, lively writing style is the result of hard work in the form of many revisions and much editing. The tone of writing is important. Watson (1987: 68) suggests that in writing the doctoral thesis the one to strive for is 'cool, explanatory and varied, but not neutral'. Taking a different approach, Kamler and Thomson (2006: 15) tie writing style to the 'identity work' of becoming a scholar and propose an 'authoritative' stance, (Kamler and Thomson 2006: 100). Yet, such a stance will not entirely solve the problem of tone and style. For example, as part of a scholarly argument, the doctoral student must convey what has gone before, especially in relation to 'giants', but simultaneously not be obsequious. It takes time and adherence to a number of principles and conventions to achieve a quiet authority. It would be as well to read about style in the effort to grasp such principles: two classics are Strunk and White's (2000) *The Elements of Style* and Gower *et al.*'s (2004) *The Complete Plain Words*. Also, Kamler and Thomson's (2006) *Helping Doctoral Students To Write* is a valuable discussion laced with much useful advice.

Here, I select the principles that strike me as the most powerful. 'Clarify, clarify, clarify' is Weston's (2000) mantra for those embarking on an argumentative piece of writing. The overarching principle for clarity is pursued in many ways (starting, of course, with a logical, clear structure), four of which are discussed below: the use of 'signposting'; clarification of specialist terms; grasping academic conventions; and, making writing interesting.

One of the most often repeated pieces of advice given in books about writing academic prose is to use textual signals – known as 'signposts' – to reveal to the reader the 'moves' of arguments. For example, using such words and phrases as 'therefore', 'on the contrary', 'if it can be accepted that', 'as demonstrated earlier' and so on. Graff (2003) suggests that an effective argumentative essay consists of two texts: in the first the argument is made and the second is a 'meta-text', which tells readers how and how not to read it. The 'meta-text' uses reflexive phrases such as 'I do not mean to suggest', and 'in summary the main points to keep in mind are … ', to keep the reader informed about how the writer is thinking about the claims and counter claims being made. It *is* necessary to be explicit about the role of statements in the argument as a whole. However, the use of signposts does not compensate for a poorly ordered argument, nor does littering a text with signposts signal a well-ordered argument.

Although it is necessary to engage with the specialist language of the relevant field, it is important not to fall into using taken-for-granted, obfuscating jargon. Connected to this error, is the problem of misdefinition of terms or of not explaining key concepts or theories or justifying use in the argument (examples I have come across are 'epistemology' and 'ontology'; Bourdieu's (1985) concepts of 'habitus' and 'field'; 'positivism'; and, Lave and Wenger's (1998) 'communities of practice' – all insufficiently explained and justified, sometimes used as if the terms are self-evident, sometimes misused). It is essential that specialist terms are introduced, explained and defined in a concrete, accurate and precise manner; and, that terms are used consistently, adhering to one meaning for each term.

In all academic writing, including argumentation, there are linguistic conventions intended to prioritise reason and analysis rather than description and feelings. Gerald Graff (2003) calls the cluster of conventions 'Academicspeak' and gives some sound advice:

> Be bilingual. It is not necessary to avoid 'Academicspeak' – you sometimes need the stuff to say what you want to say. But whenever you do have to say something in, try also to say it in conversational English as well. You'll be surprised to discover that when you restate an academic point in your nonacademic voice, the point will either sound fresher or you'll see how shallow it is and remove it. Don't kid yourself. If you couldn't explain it to your parents the chances are you don't understand it yourself.
>
> Graff 2003: 277

I have found that many students do not possess the language of grammar. And the following paragraph might be difficult to follow without it because it contains comments about 'nouns', 'verbs', 'person' and 'voice'. Notwithstanding controversy about the usefulness of understanding grammar, I am inclined to suggest that students who want to write well search the internet for palatable ways of understanding some of the terms.

Formal, academic language differs from informal ways of speaking and writing, and, as Graff implies, doctoral students need it to use it. However, there are no hard and fast rules: it is always necessary to exercise judgement. For example, traditionally, academic prose was associated with the third person and passive voice; these days advice books variously assert that the use of the first/third person and the active/passive voice should be avoided. Yet, both for clarity and to enliven text, the writer should make considered decisions about which person and tense to use. Similarly, the practice of 'nominalisation', which is converting verbs into nouns (that is emphasising things rather than processes) can have the effect of making the prose sound more scholarly.[1] The example in the footnote comes from Kamler and Thomson's (2006) *Helping Doctoral Students to Write*, which contains an invaluable discussion about avoiding either under or over use of academic conventions: the former results in lack of authority; and the latter deadens prose and misleads by obscuring humans as agents of their own actions.

It is as well to keep examiners interested and stimulated as they read 100,000-word theses. Reading dull theses in which the argument is unclear is most dispiriting. Clarity goes a long way towards keeping the spirits up. And there is other helpful advice for those practising to write in a scholarly and interesting manner: for example, dissect and emulate the style of admired writers; vary the length of sentences, purposeful use of short sentences can keep the reader awake by changing pace; punctuation can be used to powerful effect (for extended discussion of these ideas and more see Carey 1983; Kamler and Thomson, 2006; Strunk and White 2000; Truss 2003; Watson 1987; Weston 2000).

Finally, writing style is about finding an individual 'voice', which can be an exciting discovery, as Strunk and White (2000: 67) put it: 'Writing ... is the self escaping into the open'.

Two useful exercises

I want to suggest two activities that, in my experience, are particularly efficacious supports for doctoral students learning to write argument.

The first is to evaluate the arguments of others. This exercise can be approached systematically by interrogating at least two academic texts with questions such as:

- What is/are the research question(s) being addressed?
- How does/do the author(s) locate the significance of their work?
- What 'conversation' is/are the author(s) in? Where do they stand in relation to the problem?
- What is the balance of the different elements (location in a scholarly discourse; report of empirical research; commentary)?
- What is being argued? How is the reader being persuaded? How is the argument set up, staged and substantiated to make claim convincing? Are the 'moves' evident?
- What are the signposts or guidance given to the reader? Headings, sub-headings, paragraph beginnings and endings can be highlighted to ascertain whether the basic argument can be grasped from the highlighted parts.

Once this has been done, the answers to the questions for each text can be compared to assess which carries the better argument and to give reasons why.

The second exercise involves the writing of small arguments and there are variations relating to the stages of thesis preparation: rewrite the argument of published texts to reveal the argument; writing arguments of chapters (the first will probably be the literature search, which should be written as an argument rather than a survey); and, most important, writing the argument of the thesis as a whole. I want to stress the arduous and long-term nature of writing and rewriting abstracts as arguments. I usually start asking students swamped by reading or by empirical data to begin the iterative work of forging small arguments early on, this helps constrain the tendency to simply report.

241

Conclusion

The list below summarises and clarifies the main points in this chapter as a check-list:

- Work towards giving the thesis a structure and shape by making 'moves' and by playing with the moves (that is, shuffle chunks around, foregrounding and de-emphasising, to see what works best).
- Ensure that the thesis makes critical connections to a community of published scholars, clarifying what is the wider debate of which the argument of the thesis is part, and where it is positioned within it.
- Make a claim or claims early on in the thesis and reassert the claim(s) from time to time as the thesis proceeds.
- Elaborate fully, logically and clearly the reasons and/or (well-supported) evidence for claims.
- Ensure that every point made plays a part in building a convincing or valid argumentative conclusion.
- Summarise the objections to the argument that might be anticipated and consider alternative explanations.
- Use signals that tell the reader *how* to read the argument (reveal how the moves are woven together).
- Learn about style, tone and voice; and practise writing in an engaging manner.
- Indicate what is important, useful and/or interesting about the argument.

My intention has been to convince the reader that the thesis *is* an argument and that it should be thought of as such from the beginning of the doctoral process. This does not mean that the argument should be clear from the start, it will not be. Rather that the assessment and writing of arguments should become a natural part of the doctoral process.

The emphasis here has been on the practical nuts and bolts of writing scholarly argument, which should pay dividends in the form of thesis worth defending. But this is not all that is at stake. To return to Habermas (1984: 22), learning argumentation is to engage in 'learning processes [through which] we acquire theoretical knowledge and moral insight, extend and review our evaluative language, and overcome self-deceptions and difficulties in comprehension'. The potential of developing the capacity of critical argumentation is the production of scholars and citizens needed to solve the problems of the contemporary world.

Notes

1 An example is 'If you revise each chapter carefully before you submit the thesis, then you're likely to get a good result' (spoken) and the nominalised, written version 'Careful revision of each chapter prior to thesis submission will increase the likelihood of a good result' (Kamler and Thomson 2006: 105).

References

Bourdieu, P. (1985) The genesis of the concepts of habitus and field, *Sociocriticism* 2(2): 11–24.
Carey, G. V. (1983) *Mind the stop*. Harmondsworth: Penguin.

Dunleavy, P. (2003) *Authoring a PhD*. Basingstoke: Palgrave Macmillan.

Gowers, E., Greenbaum, S. and Whitcut, J. (2004) *The Complete Plain Words*. 3rd edn. Harmondsworth: Penguin.

Graff, G. (2003) *Clueless in Academe: How Schooling Obscures the Life of the Mind*. New Haven, CT and London: Yale University Press.

Habermas J. (1984) *The Theory of Communicative Action, Volume One: Reason and the Rationalisation of Society*. Trans. T. McCarthy. Boston, MA: Beacon Press.

——(1987) *The Theory of Communicative Action, Volume Two, Lifeworld and System: A Critique of Functionalist Reason*. Trans. T. McCarthy. Boston, MA: Beacon Press.

——(1989) The Idea of the University: Learning Processes. In J. Habermas, *The New Conservatism: Cultural Criticism and the Historians' Debate*. Trans. S. Weber Nicholson. Cambridge: Polity Press.

——(1990) *Moral Consciousness and Communicative Action*. Trans. C. Lenhardt and S. Nicholsen. Cambridge: Polity Press in association with Basil Blackwell.

Kamler, B. and Thomson, P. (2006) *Helping Doctoral Students to Write: Pedagogies for supervision*. London: Routledge.

Lave, J. and Wenger, E. (1998). *Communities of Practice: Learning, Meaning, and Identity*. Cambridge: Cambridge University Press.

Phelan, P. and Reynolds, P. (1996) *Argument and Evidence: critical analysis for the social sciences*. London: Routledge.

Russell, B. (1935; reprint 1977) *Skeptical Essays*. London: Allen and Unwin.

Strunk, W. and White, E. (2000) *The Elements of Style*. Needham Heights, MA: Allyn and Bacon.

Toulmin, S. E. (2003) *The Uses of Argument*. Cambridge: Cambridge University Press.

Truss, L. (2003) *Eats Shoots and Leaves*. London: Profile Books.

Watson, G. (1987) *Writing a thesis: a guide to long essays and dissertations*. London: Longman.

Weston, A. (2000) *A Rulebook for Argument*. Indianapolis, IN and Cambridge: Hacket Publishing Company.

20
Writing research

M. Piantanida and N. B. Garman

Introduction

In this chapter we explore the question, 'What does *writing research* mean in relation to writing a doctoral dissertation?'[1] The views expressed in the chapter have evolved over more than 25 years as we have worked with doctoral students, primarily in the field of education. During that time, the paradigms of educational research (as well as research in other fields) proliferated (Donmoyer 1996), affording doctoral students great latitude in the rhetorical form and style of the dissertation. With this freedom came a responsibility to understand the epistemological and ontological assumptions that were guiding one's research (Kilbourn 1999; Piantanida and Garman 2009; Schwandt 2007), and, in turn, the representation of that research (Tierney and Lincoln 1997). Thus, the task of authoring a dissertation became more complicated, as did the task of guiding students' writing. What may be relevant for one student in one context could be completely misleading for other students in other contexts. Therefore, to avoid the risks associated with offering categorical advice, we have chosen to explicate a series of premises that underpin our thinking about writing research in the form of a dissertation. Hopefully, calling attention to these premises will help doctoral students think more carefully about themselves as writers, about advice they may encounter, and about 'writerly decisions' they must make.

Premise one: writing one's thesis can be transformative

Within the context of revisioning the purpose of doctoral education, The Carnegie Foundation for the Advancement of Teaching put forward the following position:

> We propose that the purpose of doctoral education, taken broadly, is to educate and prepare those to whom we can entrust the vigor, quality, and integrity of the field. This person is a scholar first and foremost, in the fullest sense of the term – someone who will creatively generate new knowledge, critically conserve valuable

and useful ideas, and responsibly transform those understandings through writing, teaching, and application. We call such a person a 'steward of the discipline'.

Golde 2006: 5

When undertaken conscientiously, doctoral study can serve as a crucible for one's transformation from student to scholar–steward. In our experience, it is often through the process of writing the dissertation that this transformation comes to fruition. To explain this perspective, let us turn to *The Oxford English Dictionary*, which describes an author as a 'person who originates or gives existence to anything' as well as a 'person on whose authority a statement is made; an authority'. By extension, then, 'to author' is defined as 'to be the author of an action; to originate, cause, occasion'. These definitions point to the creative nature of scholarship embodied in the process of writing a dissertation. In short, writing dissertation research entails more than plugging information into a prescribed format. It requires constructing a conceptual argument – a thesis – that is well reasoned, well warranted and well articulated.[2] This process of creative scholarly writing holds the transformative possibility of the dissertation, and it is this possibility that underpins all of the premises that follow.

Premise two: writing dissertation research supports a deliberative process in which reading, writing, and thinking are inextricably connected

Not surprisingly, many doctoral students enter the dissertation process assuming that any document they share with their adviser[3] or other committee members is a 'finished product.' This may be an unfortunate carryover from learning within faculty-structured courses, where a final grade often rests upon a demonstration of one's best thinking. Furthermore, the structure of academic semesters encourages a compartmentalisation of writing where term papers are submitted, graded, and then filed or discarded as students move on to meet new expectations in new courses. The process of working on a complex research project for a prolonged time is often a new and unsettling experience. Especially disquieting is the recursive and deliberative nature of the process in which ideas are drafted, shared, critiqued, reworked and rewritten. In short, *writing dissertation research* is not a discrete task to be completed at the end of a study, but rather an integral part of the enquiry in the service of deliberation. This deliberation takes multiple forms – between student and adviser, between student and scholarly discourses, among student and committee members, and ultimately between dissertation author and broader communities of discourse.

Writing, then, becomes a way of making one's thinking manifest so that ideas can be examined, challenged, contested, refined, expanded, discarded, reworked, etc. Sometimes this testing of ideas takes place in private as students read literature in order to push beyond their current understandings in light of what scholars have written. Sometimes the testing is more public as the student shares his or her own thinking/writing with others. Creating a generative balance between private and public deliberation necessitates a willingness to share ideas that are in formation, an openness to multiple perspectives about one's thinking, and a capacity to use these multiple perspectives to advance one's enquiry.

Premise three: writing research is not an act of generic composition; it is an endeavour grounded in one's ontological relationship with language

Ontology, as Crotty (2003) explains, 'is the study of being. It is concerned with "what is", with the nature of existence, with the structure of reality as such' (Crotty 2003: 10). When we say 'ontological relationship with language', we are referring to the ways in which individuals come to understand the world and themselves as beings in the world. To illustrate what we mean, let us begin with a comment made by playwright Edward Albee in a 2008 interview on National Public Radio. When asked where his ideas come from, he responded:

> Everybody's brain is differently wired. Some people are playwrights. Some people are axe-murderers. Now, that is because of certain twists in the cortex. That's where creativity comes from. That's it. We are not 'inspired'; if we are a playwright, our brain takes the experience that everybody else has and turns it into a play.
>
> Albee 2008: 2

Our colleague, Patricia McMahon (2000: 134), expresses a variation of this point, saying, 'I typically render experience in the form of story because it is my proclivity to apprehend experience by storying it'. Another colleague commented, 'Whenever I hear about an educational policy, my immediate reaction is to ask who loses as a result of this. I see everything as a conflict between those with power and those without it'. Not surprisingly, his scholarly writing takes the form of social and policy critique. Another colleague, Wendy Milne (2006), is an art teacher who thinks in visual images, sometimes only swirling patterns of colour. When she divorces her writing from her 'seeing', she struggles to express ideas. When she uses words to explain her visual images, her ideas take on greater clarity and power. As this last example suggests, an ontological relationship with language refers not merely to words, but also to the multiple ways in which individuals make meaning of their experiences. Indeed, the Reggio Emilia philosophy of education holds that there are 100 languages that might be nurtured in children (Edwards *et al.* 1998; Guidici *et al.* 2001). Yet, for much of the twentieth century, this multiplicity of languages was obscured by the privileging of scientific research with its emphasis on quantification. Thus, students often found themselves cut off from their deepest proclivities for shaping questions to study, modes of enquiry, and forms of expression and representation. Even now, when the hegemonic grip of postpositivist science has been successfully broken, its residue lingers in federal policy for funding of educational research, guidelines of institutional review boards on the ethical conduct of research, and numerous books on how to write a dissertation. As pernicious as such documents can be, even more debilitating can be a student's own unexamined assumptions about how one 'must' write research. Premise three is meant to challenge such tacit assumptions and urges students to pay careful attention to the ontological fit between their way of thinking and their way of engaging in and writing research.

In offering this premise, we recognise that even the advent of electronic dissertations (with the capacity to accommodate audio and visual images) has not eliminated reliance on verbal language to report one's study. Furthermore, we acknowledge that each university has its own specific requirements for the dissertation document per se, and obviously, students must attend to such requirements. So, inevitably students must consider their relationship with linguistic forms of representation. One gauge of this relationship is the visceral reaction evoked by the mere thought of writing the dissertation. For some, this represents an exciting challenge. In all likelihood, such individuals have a natural proclivity for writing as well as a firm grasp of the technical aspects of writing, e.g. correct grammar, appropriate syntax, nuanced vocabulary. For others, it may engender stark terror, precipitating flashbacks to the trauma of high-school English classes and, as one student put it, harsh criticism by the grammar police.[4] Occasionally, students who are daunted by the prospect of writing will tell us they are planning to hire an editor. Although this has a certain pragmatic appeal, we want to raise two cautionary notes. First, we have seen students pay considerable sums of money for editing preliminary drafts of their dissertation, which in the end, were never circulated, even to their committee. In other words, before the student had really sorted through what he or she wanted to say – the major messages of the dissertation – someone with no understanding of the topic under study or research method was tinkering with the technical details. Correct punctuation and grammar are fairly pointless when the conceptual content of the document is still quite muddled. Second, hiring an editor may give a false sense of security by diverting attention from the issue we have been raising with Premise three, i.e. the importance of owning one's language(s) for understanding the phenomenon under study and for representing those understandings in the dissertation. We suggest that students who may be considering the use of a technical editor work closely with their adviser to determine when or if such assistance might be of benefit. We also urge students who have a weak grasp of the technical aspects of writing to begin early in their doctoral work to seek out resources such as university writing centres where they can begin to develop greater proficiency. Beyond such technicalities, however, we encourage all students to find resources that will strengthen their sense of self as dissertation author, that is, the author – of a thesis that makes a meaningful contribution to one or more communities of discourse.

Premise four: authoring a thesis is accomplished within a particular worldview

Worldview encompasses the totality of one's beliefs about one's self and the world. For purposes of research, it is most useful to focus on assumptions related to ontology, epistemology and axiology. As mentioned above, ontology refers to the study of being and one's assumptions about the nature and structure of reality. In educational research, ontological assumptions relate to a host of beliefs, such as those about the nature of learning and teaching, relationships among teachers, learners and subject matter, the purpose of education, and the structure of education as a social institution. Those who ascribe to a behaviourist theory of learning, for example, embody a different ontology than those who ascribe to a constructivist theory. What one takes to be the reality of education shapes the types of questions one is drawn to ask, as well as the methods one uses to seek answers. In this way, ontology intersects with epistemology, which refers to assumptions about what it means to know something, what counts as knowledge (truth), and the methods by which knowledge is generated. Axiology refers to assumptions about what one values as both legitimate and worthwhile knowledge. Taken together, these assumptions comprise the researcher's worldview, and either implicitly or explicitly serve as the intellectual context for *writing research*.

247

Since the Enlightenment in seventeenth century Western Europe, the epistemological assumptions of positivism served as the intellectual context for conceptualising, conducting and reporting legitimate research, initially in the natural sciences, and subsequently in the human or social sciences. As Polkinghorne (1997) points out, during the heyday of positivism,

> [A] true knowledge statement has logical certitude because it was the product of a formal process. As was the case with mathematical solutions, the validity of research conclusions were understood to be independent of both the person making the claim and the audience to whom the claim was presented.
>
> Polkinghorne 1997: 7

This intellectual tradition gave rise to many of the rhetorical conventions that have dominated the way in which doctoral students have been expected to write research. One such convention is the five chapter format of the dissertation, i.e. introduction, review of literature, methodology, findings, conclusion. This rhetorical structure is an economical, even elegant, format for reporting research that posits an insightful hypothesis, lays out procedures for testing the hypothesis, and reports the outcomes of the procedures. Because the research conclusions are considered context- and researcher-independent, the convention of writing from a detached, depersonalised stance in a third person voice makes sense. Many guides to writing dissertation research still promulgate these conventions, which can be helpful *if* one is writing within the intellectual legacy of positivism.

By the middle of the twentieth century, however, the ontological and epistemological foundations of positivism had been shaken, giving rise to alternative conceptions of knowledge and the processes through which legitimate knowledge might be generated. Although it goes beyond the scope of this chapter to detail variations in worldview that now co-exist within the field of educational research,[5] two crucial ontological and epistemological differences are worth mentioning here. First is the assumption that knowledge of human affairs is context-specific and value-dependent. Second is the assumption that knowledge is constructed by researchers who are situated within particular socio-political, historical and cultural contexts, and who make meaning of educational phenomena from particular positions within those contexts. Given these assumptions, the five chapter dissertation format is often too confining for the representation of the context and the complexities of the phenomena under study. The format of a scholarly book may be more conducive to laying out the intricately connected lines of reasoning that are necessary to warrant an interpretive thesis. Furthermore, writing in the third person would be incongruous, because it obscures the contextual, positional and perspectival nature of the knowledge claims being offered. So, within constructivist or interpretivist traditions, writing in the first person has become an accepted convention.

Hopefully, this brief discussion of worldview underscores the point of Premise three that *writing research* is not an act of generic composition. Rather, research is written within an intellectual tradition and is shaped by the author's worldview. Without understanding these points, students risk making writerly decisions that undermine the conceptual coherence of their document and call into question the credibility of their thesis.

By 'writerly' we are not referring to individuals who have an innate flair for writing (although that is certainly helpful). Rather, crafting a document encompasses a multitude of technical and stylistic decisions from the placement of commas, to the choice of words, to the crafting of sentences, to the ordering of paragraphs, to the flow of ideas. Individually and collectively such decisions either contribute to or undermine the coherence of the thesis – the conceptual argument – being offered in the dissertation.

Premise five: writerly decisions are best made within the conventions of a particular research genre

Each intellectual tradition encompasses a variety of approaches for conducting research. Typically, these are referred to as research methods or methodology. We prefer the concept of research genre, however, because of an important distinction offered by Smith and Heshusius (1986):

> Method can be characterized in at least two ways. The most commonly encountered meaning is method as procedures or techniques. In this case the term invokes the kinds of 'how-to-do-it' discussions long found in introductory textbooks on quantitative inquiry and, more recently, in a number of basic textbooks on qualitative inquiry … The second characterization of method is as 'logic of justification.' In a sense common to continental European social philosophy, the focus here is not on techniques but on the elaboration of logical issues and, ultimately, on the justifications that inform practice. This conceptualization involves such basic questions as, What is the nature of social and educational reality? What is the relationship of the investigator to what is investigated? And how is truth to be defined?
>
> Smith and Heshusius 1986: 8

When the epistemological and ontological assumptions of positivism (and later post-positivism) comprised the prevailing paradigm of educational research, students were not necessarily challenged to explain the logics behind their techniques for data collection and analysis. This changed as students began to work in ways that seemed to violate principles (e.g. statistical sampling, objective measurement) considered to be the *sine qua non* of reliable and valid research. Indeed, reliability and validity (along with replicability and generalisability) were seen as essential hallmarks of legitimate and supportable knowledge claims. The question arose, 'Were methodological deviations from these accepted principles indicative of poorly designed research and researcher incompetence or were they manifestations of a different paradigm of research which yielded different sorts of knowledge claims?'. In essence, each doctoral committee must make a determination about this question, and it is incumbent upon the dissertation author to offer a logic-of-justification for major decisions they have made in conceptualising and conducting the research project. Only in making these logics explicit can the merits of the thesis be fairly judged. For us, the concept of research genre conveys the totality of conventions that support the dissertation author's decisions. In short, each research genre has its own language, encompasses its own techniques, and is represented in its own rhetorical form and style.

Elsewhere (Piantanida and Garman 2009), we have used sports and literature analogies to give a sense of what we mean by research genre. Just as baseball differs from football and novels differ from poetry, experimental research differs from narrative research, and survey research differs from case study, ethnography or grounded theory. An athlete who decides to play football or rugby follows through by learning a very different set of conventions and skills than one who commits to playing baseball or basketball or golf. An author who decides to write novels commits to learning a set of conventions that differ markedly from one who decides to write poetry. Similarly, a doctoral student who decides to engage in experimental or survey research follows through by learning a set of conventions that differ from the conventions to be mastered by those who choose to author a narrative, a case study, an ethnography, a grounded theory, or a polemic. Two types of literature can help to support the learning process. One type encompasses examples of research within the genre including dissertations, books and articles. The other type of literature offers theoretical and methodological explications of the genre.

In both cases, it is important not to rely on only one or two sources. Dissertations and articles written within a given genre can vary dramatically from one academic discipline to another. They can also vary widely in the quality of thinking and writing exemplified. Although students reading about various genres within a postpositivist, scientific tradition may find a great deal of consensus about the 'rules of the game,' those looking for guidance in constructivist or interpretive genre are likely to encounter variations in approach. Just as novels take many different forms (e.g. romance, mystery, science fiction), so, too, can dissertations take different forms within a given genre. For example, Richardson (1990), writing from a sociological perspective, characterises five types of narrative (everyday life, autobiography, biography, cultural story, collective story). Taking a more literary view, Barone (1995) refers to weakly fictive narrative, and McMahon (2000) distinguishes between mildly and wildly fictive narrative. Stake (1995) differentiates among intrinsic, instrumental and collective case studies. Since the formulation of grounded theory by Glaser and Strauss (1967), heated debates have been raging on the conventions of this genre (see, for example, Charmaz 2000; Rennie 2006; Strauss and Corbin 1990; Glaser 1992). The point to keep in mind is that the conventions of any research genre may encompass many variations. Students who read only a small sample of work in and about a genre risk making simplistic and naïve writerly decisions.

To give a sense of variations in structure and language used to craft a dissertation, we offer thumbnail sketches of several dissertations authored by members of our dissertation study group. It is difficult to capture the intricacies of these dissertations within the confines of a short chapter, but the students' own accounts of their struggle to conceptualise and represent their interpretive studies can be found in Garman and Piantanida (2006). Patricia McMahon, Pamela Krakowski and Lynn Richards all worked within the genre of personal narrative to study an aspect of their teaching practice. Patricia's study of reflection in a college level composition course was organised into a six chapter dissertation: (1) Introduction; (2) Selected Review of Literature; (3) My Story of the Educational Encounter: A Teacher Reflects on Her Practice; (4) Facing Sixty-Five Portfolios: Reflection Relating Theory to Practice; (5) A Conceptual Framework by which to Consider Portfolio Reflection and Teacher–Student Discourse; and (6) Lessons Learned. Lynn also organised her dissertation of creative dramatics in a second grade classroom into six chapters: (1) Introduction; (2) Drama Definitions: A Selected Review of the Literature; (3) Drama Data: The Study Process; (4) Drama Depictions: The Narratives of Our Classroom; (5) Drama Disclosures: Drama as Analogy; and (6) Drama as Pedagogy: Observations for the Elementary Educator. Pamela, an art teacher, used the metaphor of a mobile, as an organising principle to portray her study of narrative pedagogy: (1) Introduction to the Study; (2) A Call for Balance: A Selected Review of Literature; (3) A

Search for Balance: Narrative Enquiry as Research Genre; (4) Understanding the Narrative and Normative and Their Relationship in Five Art Classroom Contexts; (5) A Delicate Balance: Cultivating Aesthetic Sensibilities. In some ways, these structures mirror traditional dissertations, beginning with an introduction and followed by a review of literature. It is in the portrayal of context, data, and results where the authors struggled to conceptualise a meaningful and manageable structure. The sections of Pamela's fourth chapter help to illustrate this point. The 100-page chapter is divided into five sections (Art Classroom as Museum Gallery, as Studio, as Haven, and Stage, and as Laboratory). Each section presents one or two vignettes followed by a reflection on the vignette, and concludes with a sub-section entitled 'balancing the lessons' learned about normative and narrative pedagogy within each art classroom context. This is a far more intricate representation of data than is typically found in a quantitative study.

Although the writing in Marjorie Logsdon's dissertation on pedagogical authority has a strongly narrative quality, she claims her genre as speculative essay and organised her document into seven chapters, each of which comprised an essay: (1) Preliminary Musings on Enquiry; (2) Memory Texts; (3) The Lanyard and the Whistle: Being an Authority; (4) Turning toward Portfolios and Writing: Sharing Authority; (5) The Crucible: Authority and the Matter of Time; (6) The Crucible: Authority and the Matter of Texts; and (7) Pedagogy of Authority: A Matter of Meaning. Marjorie's chapter on memory texts offers an extended logic-of-justification for memories and dreams as 'data'. Marilyn Llewellyn also drew upon memories as a rich source of materials for her dissertation on spirituality as pedagogy. Unlike Marjorie who drew upon the conventions of essay as a genre, Marilyn turned to the conventions of spiritual enquiry to shape her five chapter dissertation: (1) Coming to the Study; (2) Memoir; (3) A New Window; (4) Meditative Writings; and (5) Spirituality as Pedagogy: An Exegesis. Marilyn's second chapter is a series of recollective vignettes and her fourth chapter is a collection of six meditations, which illuminate the pedagogical meanings embedded in those vignettes.

Wendy Milne, whom we mentioned above, used the metaphor of an art exhibit to structure her nine chapter dissertation on reflective artmaking: (1) Welcoming the Audience; (2) Rationale for the Study: Preparing for a One Woman Exhibit; (3) Procedures of the Study: A Portrayal of Reflective Artmaking; (4) Portraits of Teacher as Reflective Artmaker; (5) Portraits of Teacher as Subject-Centred; (6) Portraits of Teacher as Artmaker; (7) Portraits of Teacher as Listener; (8) Critiquing the Calls for Reflection and Artmaking; (9) Reflective Artmaking in Perspective. In Chapters 4 through 7, Wendy includes a series of visual portraits, which she follows with a section titled 'Educational Insights' where she explicates what she has learned by creating and reflecting on the portraits.

Kathleen Ceroni situated her study of a teacher leadership programme within a genre of literary theory and criticism. She deliberately adopts a different stance and voice for each of the six chapters in her dissertation as a way of warranting the various types of knowledge claims she is making: (1) The Promise and the Caution: Teacher Leadership as Resource; (2) The Promise in Perspective: A View of Teacher Leadership Incentive Plans; (3) The Promise Made: The Official Story of the Pennsylvania Lead Teacher Initiative; (4) Teachers' 'Inner Views' of the Pennsylvania Lead Teacher Initiative; (5) The Promise Revisited: An Interpretation of the Contradictions Embedded in the 'Inner Views Storied' of the Pennsylvania Lead Teacher Experience; and (6) The Promise Abandoned: The Illusory Nature of Teacher Leadership Reform. A final example is

Preface

Section 1. Educational Inclusion: From Problem to Problematic
(1) Professional Unrest
(2) Responding to Complexity: Problem-Solving and Problematizing

Section II. Problematizing Educational Inclusion
(3) Politically-Oriented Images of Education Inclusion
(4) Community-Oriented Images of Educational Inclusion
(5) Culturally-Oriented Images of Educational Inclusion
(6) 'Practically'-Oriented Images of Educational Inclusion
(7) Moral/Ethical Images of Educational Inclusion: 'The Bottom Line'

Section III. Imagining Educational Inclusion
(8) Understanding Educational Inclusion: From the Language of Technique to a Discourse of Ethics
(9) Understanding Educational: The Call of Imagination

Figure 20.1 A call to conscience: problematising educational inclusion.

drawn from Micheline Stabile's heuristic study of educational inclusion. Because the structure of Micheline's dissertation is complex, it is outlined in Figure 20.1. In Chapters 3 through 7 Micheline portrays a particular perspective or gaze on educational inclusion and then concludes by repositioning the gaze to offer different ways of thinking about inclusion.

Hopefully, these few exemplars help to illustrate what we mean by the conventions of a genre. Each dissertation author uses language, a voice and a stance consistent with the genre within which she is working to construct and represent knowledge claims. Woven throughout the dissertation are the logics that justify both what she is saying and how she is saying it. In some cases the logics are drawn directly from literature about the genre; in other instances, the dissertation author has drawn from collateral sources (e.g. dream theory, literary theory) and related these sources to the study at hand. In creating these logics-of-justification, dissertation authors are in a position of adding to the conventions of a genre, thereby contributing not only to the discourses on the topic under study but also the nature of interpretive enquiry.

Conclusion

Throughout this chapter, we have stressed the importance of each dissertation author claiming a rhetorical form and style for *writing research* that fits their own ontology, epistemology and axiology. In doing so, students must be cognisant of the ontological, epistemological and axiological traditions of their field of study and mode of enquiry. By drawing insightfully from the conventions within particular traditions, dissertation authors can provide the logics by which the merits of their scholarly work can be judged. Thus, students working within postpositivist traditions of scientific research are well advised to attend to issues of reliability, validity, replicability and generalisability. Those working within interpretive traditions grounded in the arts and humanities face a more difficult challenge of meeting criteria that are still very much in flux and are likely to remain so. For our purposes, we have found nine criteria to be particularly useful. In brief, these include:

- *Self-conscious method:* Does the author provide explicit rationales for conceptual and methodological decisions within the conventions of his/her research genre? Is one's process for thinking through the interconnected facets of the enquiry visible? Does the author demonstrate an understanding of the epistemological and onto-logical implications of his/her decisions? Is there a persuasive logic-of-justification?
- *Verisimilitude:* Is the description of the experiential context of the study richly textured and nuanced, exhibiting vibrancy? Is it evocative, inviting readers to enter vicariously into the experiential context? Does the description raise in the readers' mind the question, 'How might I have reacted in such a situation?' Are the events/contexts as portrayed conceivable and believable?
- *Verité:* Does the work ring true? Is it consistent with accepted knowledge in the field? Or, if it departs, does it address why? Does it fit within the discourse in the appropriate literature? Is it intellectually honest and authentic?
- *Integrity (as in architecture):* Is the work structurally sound? Does it hang together? Is the research rationale logical, appropriate and identifiable within an enquiry tradition? Is the proper persona (or voice) used for the author(s) and other participants?
- *Vitality:* Is the enquiry important, meaningful and non-trivial? Does it have a sense of vibrancy, intensity and excitement of discovery? Do metaphors and images communicate powerfully?
- *Rigour:* Is there sufficient depth of intellect, rather than superficial or simplistic reasoning? Are the conclusions carefully crafted from sufficiently thick and rich data? Does the researcher avoid solipsistic reasoning? Was reflection done in a careful and systematic rather than haphazard fashion? Has the analysis/interpretation of data been thorough/exhaustive?
- *Ethical sensibility:* Has the researcher attended to requirements of all relevant internal review boards? Does the language of the dissertation adhere to the principles of non-discrimination? Does the description of research procedures demonstrate an ethical sensibility?
- *Aesthetics:* Is it enriching and pleasing to anticipate and experience? Does it give me insight into some universal part of my educational self? Are connections between the particular and the universal revealed in powerful, provocative, evoca-tive and moving ways? Does the work challenge, disturb or unsettle? Does it touch the spirit?
- *Utility:* Is the enquiry useful and professionally relevant to an identifiable discourse community? Does it make a contribution to a recognised field of study or estab-lished bodies of discourse? Does the piece have a clearly recognised professional and/or scholarly audience? Is it educative?

Elsewhere (Piantanida and Garman 2009), we elaborate on these criteria. Hopefully, however, even these brief descriptions underscore the point that well-written research is an elegant interplay between what is being said and how it is being said. No generic formula can substitute for the thoughtfulness and insightfulness of the researcher's unique construction and expression of meaning. In the end, *writing research* is a creative act in which knowledge claims – a thesis – are persuasively put forward and warranted.

Notes

1 In the USA, the term 'dissertation' refers to doctoral level research, whereas thesis refers to research at the masters level. In the UK, Australia, and Canada, doctoral-level research is typically referred to as a thesis. For the purposes of this chapter, we use the term 'dissertation' to refer to the document itself and the term 'thesis' to refer to the conceptual argument being put forward.

2 Among the many books on dissertation research, several that tend to emphasise the relationship between writing and thinking include Ely *et al.* (1997), Holly (1989), Meloy (2002), Schram (2003) and Wolcott (2001). Richardson (1990; 2003), although not focusing specifically on dissertation research, is also useful.

3 In the USA, the faculty member who chairs a student's dissertation committee is usually the person who works most closely with the student and is referred to as the student's adviser. In the UK, Australia, and other countries this faculty person may be called the thesis supervisor.

4 In the USA, many of the traditional methods for teaching English composition are coming under criticism. Students who have internalised a dysfunctional template of the five paragraph essay may find it freeing to read how published authors think about the process of writing. Some students with whom we have worked valued the liberating perspectives on writing offered by Dillard (1990), Lamott (1995) and Ueland (1987).

5 Those who want to explore these different traditions might find the following references to be useful: Crotty (2003), Paul (2005), deMarrais and LeCompte (1999) and Schwandt (2003).

References

Albee, E. (2008) *Albee at 80: Still Asking the Big Questions.* An Interview by Jeff Lunden. Online. (Available at www.npr.org/templates/story/story.php?storyId=88141908 Accessed 11 March 2009).

Barone, T. (1995) The purposes of arts-based educational research, *International Journal of Educational Research,* 23(2): 169–80.

Charmaz, K. (2000) Grounded theory: Objectivist and constructivist methods. In N. K. Denzin and Y. S. Lincoln (Eds). *Handbook of qualitative research,* 2nd edn. Thousand Oaks, CA: Sage.

Crotty, M. (2003) *The foundations of social research: Meaning and perspective in the research process.* Thousand Oaks, CA: Sage.

deMarrais, K. and LeCompte, M. D. (1999) *The way school works: A sociological analysis of education.* 3rd edn. New York: Addison Wesley Longman.

Dillard, A. (1990) *The writing life.* New York: Harper Perennial.

Donmoyer, R. (1996) Educational research in an era of paradigm proliferation: What's a journal editor to do? *Educational Researcher,* 25(2): 19–25.

Edwards, C., Gandini, L. and Forman, G. (Eds) (1998) *The hundred languages of children: The Reggio Emilia approach—advanced reflections,* 2nd edn. Norwood, NJ: Ablex.

Ely, M., Vinz, R., Downing, M. and Anzul, M. (1997) *On writing qualitative research: Living by words.* Philadelphia, PA: Falmer Press.

Garman, N. B. and Piantanida, M. (Eds) (2006) *The authority to imagine: The struggle toward representation in dissertation writing.* New York: Peter Lang.

Glaser, B. G. (1992) *Basics of grounded theory analysis: Emergence vs. forcing.* Mill Valley, CA: The Sociology Press.

Glaser, B. G. and Strauss, A. L. (1967) *The discovery of grounded theory. Strategies for qualitative research.* Hawthorne, NY: Aldine.

Golde, C. M. (2006) Preparing stewards of the discipline. In C. M. Golde and G. E. Walker (Eds). *Envisioning the Future of Doctoral Education: Preparing Stewards of the Discipline.* San Francisco, CA: Jossey-Bass.

Guidici, C., Krechevsky, M. and Renaldi, C. (Eds) (2001) *Making learning visible: Children as individual and group learners.* Reggio Emilia, Italy: Reggio Children.

Holly, M. L. (1989) *Writing to grow: Keeping a personal-professional journal.* Portsmouth, NH: Heinemann.

Kilbourn, B. (1999) Fictional thesis, *Educational Researcher,* 28(12): 27–32.

Lamott, A. (1995) *Bird by bird: Some instructions on writing and life*. New York: Anchor Books.

McMahon, P. L. (2000) From angst to story to research text: The role of arts-based educational research in teacher inquiry, *Journal of Curriculum Theorizing*, 16(1): 125–45.

——(2006) Narrative yearnings: Reflecting in time through the art of fictive story. In N. B. Garman and M. Piantanida (Eds). *The authority to imagine: The struggle toward representation in dissertation writing*. New York: Peter Lang.

Meloy, J. M. (2002) *Writing the qualitative dissertation: Understanding by doing*. 2nd edn. Mahwah, NJ: Lawrence Erlbaum.

Milne, W. M. (2006) Imagining reflective artmaking: Claiming self as artist-teacher-researcher. In N. B. Garman and M. Piantanida (Eds). *The authority to imagine: The struggle toward representation in dissertation writing*. New York: Peter Lang.

Paul, J. L. (2005) *Introduction to the philosophies of research and criticism in education and the social sciences*. Upper Saddle River, NJ: Pearson.

Piantanida, M. and Garman, N. B. (2009) *The qualitative dissertation: A guide for students and faculty*. 2nd edn. Thousand Oaks, CA: Corwin.

Polkinghorne, D. E. (1997) Reporting qualitative research as practice. In W. G. Tierney and Y. S. Lincoln (Eds). *Representation and the text: Reframing the narrative voice*. Albany, NY: State University of New York Press.

Rennie, D. L. (2006) The grounded theory method: Application of a variant of its procedure on constant comparative analysis to psychotherapy research. In C. T. Fischer (Ed.). *Qualitative research methods for psychologists: Introduction through empirical studies*. Boston, MA: Elsevier.

Richardson, L. (1990) *Writing strategies: Reaching diverse audiences*, Newbury Park, NJ: Sage.

——(2003) Writing: A method of inquiry. In N. K. Denzin and Y. S. Lincoln (Eds). *Collecting and interpreting qualitative materials*. 2nd edn. Thousand Oaks, CA: Sage.

Schram, T. H. (2003) *Conceptualizing qualitative inquiry: Mindwork for fieldwork in education and the social sciences*. Upper Saddle River, NJ: Pearson Education.

Schwandt, T. A. (2003) Three epistemological stances for qualitative research: Interpretivism, hermeneutics, and social constructivism. In N. K. Denzin and Y. S. Lincoln (Eds). *Landscape of qualitative research: Theories and issues,* 2nd edn. Thousand Oaks, CA: Sage.

——(2007) *The Sage dictionary of qualitative inquiry*, 3rd edn. Los Angeles, CA: Sage.

Smith, J. K. and Heshusius, L. (1986) Closing down the conversation: The end of the quantitative-qualitative debate among educational inquirers, *Educational Researcher*, 15(1): 4–12.

Stake, R. E. (1995) *The art of case study research*. Thousand Oaks, CA: Sage.

Strauss, A. L. and Corbin, J. (1990) *Basics of qualitative research: Grounded theory procedures and techniques*. Newbury Park, CA: Sage.

Tierney, W. G. and Lincoln, Y. S. (Eds) (1997) *Representation and the text: Reframing the narrative voice*. Albany, NY: SUNY Press.

Ueland, B. (1987) *If you want to write: A book about art, independence and spirit*. Saint Paul, MN: Graywolf Press.

Wolcott, H. F. (2001) *Writing up qualitative research*. Thousand Oaks, CA: Sage.

21

'Guilty knowledge'

The (im)possibility of ethical security in social science research

K. Williams

Qualitative research: ethics in the swamplands

> I tried to just make ethics [an] inevitable ... and quite ordinary part of the [research] in thinking about it and then I felt ok ... but as soon as ... the ... *subject* of ethics ... comes into the centre ... I find it quite intimidating and ... loaded ... and so I tried to think ok I'm going to be talking to [you] about my research project ... and then it felt fine ... but when I think about this as about ethics it, it reframes it.
>
> Respondent 2, senior lecturer and PhD student

Schon's (1987) metaphorical distinction between the high ground of research *versus* the swamplands of practice has evidenced considerable heuristic utility. When looking at the practice of research itself, however, the clarity of the high ground rapidly blurs into the messiness of the swamplands. Ironically, the swamplands are nowhere more obvious than when the focus is on research ethics.

Recognition of ethical risk in social science research is not new, and research texts are replete with guidelines on ethics; this chapter does not attempt to add to that literature. Indeed, the chapter may raise more questions than recommend solutions. Using excerpts from interviews with five higher education development researchers, I consider five often unthought-of ethical challenges that emerged from their reflections on their experiences. These challenges involve the problematic nature of anonymity and confidentiality, representation, role conflict and the risk of instrumentalism. Such challenges, I suggest, originate from the essence of social science research in general, and qualitative social science research in particular.

Qualitative research *sui generis* invokes ethical complexity as it 'probes the very personal, subjective truths of people's lives', which in turn exposes 'our own frailties, concerns, and questions as interpretive researchers' (Clark and Sharf 2007: 399). Added to which, research is not only about something or someone, but *for* someone, and this renders it morally vulnerable. Current pressures to increase research outputs may serve to emphasise this dimension of the instrumentality of academic research (Payne 2000). Well-meant advice 'to proceed ethically and without threatening the validity of the research endeavour in so far as it is possible to do so' provides no talisman against ethical dilemmas (Cohen *et al.* 2000: 49).

Advice to resort to criteria for well-designed research methodology also fails to offer protection from ethical complexity – indeed such design may well cloak unintended ethical risk (Ramcharan and Cutcliffe 2001). Not far beneath the surface of such advice lies a reef of instrumentalist risk–benefit ethics. Even reversion to ethical codes offers cold comfort, serving to surface the ethical impasse of the imposition of the general onto the particular. It may well be that, as Homan (1991) suggests, the apparent conflation of ethics with codes of conduct may serve to imperil the very values such codes were intended to protect. Codes provide principles, but principles rest on moral bases and require moral judgement to apply in the particular circumstances of each research event (Pring 2000). Moral judgement brings educational researchers face to face with the character, the 'moral virtues' (Pring 2001: 418), the '*disposition* to act appropriately in a particular situation' (Pring 2000: 143, italics original) of the researcher.

In reflecting on the responses of colleagues whose research practice I have chosen (perhaps expediently) to surface, I am confronted with the very concerns about which I write. For example, my research project referred to in this chapter arose originally out of a question posed during a faculty research ethics week: How do faculty-based researchers experience ethical dilemmas in their research? As a member of the faculty research ethics committee, I justified the research on the long-established principle of the 'right to know'. Pring (2000) argues that such a right is conditional on, for example, at least three other principles: the right to respect held by research subjects; commitments to confidentiality; the provisional nature of truth claims. My research project has resulted in a conference paper, a faculty seminar, a journal article and a book chapter. These 'outcomes' pose uncomfortable questions: What is the relationship between means and ends? Who was this research 'for', at whose expense, and what right had I to undertake it and publish the results – irrespective of 'informed consent' and 'ethics permission'? As one of the HED practitioner project respondents remarked with respect to his research: 'the ethical issues are very large, and … even though … [his] … project … has reached a kind of an end point, the consequences … continue all the time' (Respondent 1, senior lecturer). This going beyond ethical codes and admitting the moral into consideration of research ethics leads to potential impasse: '[I]n beginning to spell out the virtues, I came to recognise my own vices. But that is why I am not a researcher. But perhaps many others should not be either' (Pring 2001: 421).

In order to further interrogate the business as *un*usual nature of ethical challenges emergent from qualitative research, what follows offers a brief discussion of the usage of 'ethics' in research literature. I then consider the application of two particular lenses not traditionally found in research ethics literature to an exploration of the ways in which the five HED practitioners reflected on their experience of researching in their own backyards. The two lenses are those of:

- the understanding of aporia attributed to Heidegger (1945), and
- evetts (2003: 400) usage of 'guilty knowledge' as part of the professional burden.

The inclusion of the HED researchers' experience is more than illustrative. It is through the qualitative examination of the mundane practices of academics that we can better understand the impact of policy (such as research assessment policies and ethical codes) on practice (Clegg 2005).

Coming to terms with research 'ethics'

Etymologically 'ethics' derives from the Greek *ethos*, offering two translations into English: custom or character (Booth *et al.* 2003: 285–6). For Booth *et al.* (2003), this distinction is broadly between, respectively, the *don'ts* and the *do's* of social science research. They recognise that custom does not adequately serve the complexity of qualitative research. They argue for character, the *do's*, developed through 'ethical choices ... [that serve to] ... build ethical communities' (Booth *et al.* 2003: 287). Through the practice (and practise) of ethical decision making within situations that are most often not of our own making, these ethical choices form our 'ethical dispositions' (Sayer 2004: 99).

Often, however, the emphasis in research ethics discussion seems to fall on *custom*, the 'concern for the appropriateness of the researcher's behaviour in relation to the subjects of the research or those affected by it' (Gray 2004: 58). Gray (2004), although acknowledging that ethical research action lies in a 'grey area' where clear demarcation of right and wrong is not possible (ibid.), proceeds to focus on custom, beginning with the importance of guidelines and '*informed* consent' (Gray 2004: 58, italics original). Gray (2004: 58) does not explicitly reflect the moral and ethical uncertainty that saturates 'informed consent' – not the least of which is that the signature on the form potentially compromises confidentiality and does compromise anonymity (Price 1996. See also Homan 1991, Chapter 4; Fisher 2006).

The recognition of the central role of character suggested by Booth *et al.* (2003) surfaces the 'attendant *moral* issues implicit in the work of social science researchers' (Cohen *et al.* 2000: 49, italics added). Cautioning against ethical principles being seen as absolute, Cohen *et al.* (2000: 56) argue that 'there can be no rigid rules ... It will be a case of formulating and abiding by one's own situation ethics'. 'Situation ethics', however, needs to be treated with caution, in part because of its association with a specific faith-based approach to ethics (Fletcher 1976). In addition, situation ethics reflects the risks of 'virtue ethics', and similarly shares the risks not only of relativism and relying on tacit knowledge thereby becoming un-examinable, but also of perpetuating gender and other stereotypes in research ethics (Eriksson *et al.* 2007: 213).

Pring (2001) locates research ethics squarely in the character of the researcher as 'trustworthy' and possessing the moral virtues of courage, honesty, concern for the well being of the other, modesty about the intrinsic worth of research, and 'humility in the face of justified criticism' (Pring 2001: 418). Such virtues, he argues, can only emerge and be sustained in a research community that is marked by the same characteristics. It is small wonder that Pring (2001) appears relieved at not being a researcher!

For Costley and Gibbs (2006: 96), too, it is the ontological emphasis of character rather than the methodological emphasis of custom that is foremost. They propose an understanding of qualitative research ethics rooted in Heidegger's (1945) '*aboding* in the world'. They, too, reject the reduction of ethics to 'a process of competence' (Costley and Gibbs 2006: 96). Their 'ethic of care' requires context sensitivity and is rooted in Heidegger's (1945) understanding of ethics as a 'process of being' (Costley and Gibbs 2006: 96). The ethic of care is an ontological realisation of ethics rather than an epistemological or methodological process. The core of this approach lies in the reflexive awareness of the researcher 'whose singular care is the advancement of the whole of humanity and the totality of being as such' (Costley and Gibbs 2006: 96). As with Pring (2001) and Eriksson *et al.* (2007), Costley and Gibbs (2006: 96) regard the research community as central, but as a 'community of learners'.

Addressing educational research specifically, Small (2001) argues that codes of conduct and the like are minimally necessary, but inadequate instruments in highly complex education research contexts. Codes of ethics, Small notes, tend to lead to complacency and a focus on enforcement and juridical discipline. Quoting Homan (1991), Small (2001: 391) notes 'Statements of ethics invite the individual to surrender moral conscience to a professional consensus'. Small (2001) argues that, although they retain a place in the research community, codes of ethics cannot adequately meet the unpredictability of individual research instances. What should supplement the code of ethics, argues Small (2001), is a focus 'on procedures and strategies' for making *ethical decisions* not simply for conducting ethical research (Small 2001: 403). Such an educative approach seeks to equip both the individual researcher and relevant research committees to look beyond custom and methodology. Small concludes:

[T]here is no substitute for the individual's development of the capacity to make ethical decisions about the design and conduct of his or her project. In the end, it is everyone's responsibility to ensure that educational research is ethical research, and the better prepared we are to address this task; the better our research will be.

Small 2001: 405

The position that I adopt supports the core of the argument that the high degree of complexity emergent from qualitative research practice is not adequately served by codes, compliance or custom alone but foregrounds 'character' – the personal identity of the researcher as social actor formed through attention to the reflexivity of the researcher. My use of 'reflexivity' here

[R]efers to the practice of the *internal dialogue* through and in which we go about formulating a thought, 'questioning ourselves, clarifying our beliefs and inclinations, diagnosing our situations, deliberating about our concerns and defining our own projects'.

Archer 2003: 103, italics original

This foregrounding of the researchers' character through reflexivity and the backgrounding (not eliminating) of codes and ethical guidelines, even given the emphasis on the role of the research community, appears to reinforce Pring's (2001) dilemma. Research ethics cannot be reduced to custom, but must be enlarged to include character, a matter of ontology not methodology, a matter of being: can we *be* ethical researchers rather than a methodological can we *do* ethical research?

'Guilty knowledge' and aporias: working with research ethics super-complexity

Writing from within the philosophy of higher education, Barnett (2000) defines the late twentieth century, early twenty-first century age as one of 'super-complexity', an age marked by

[C]ontestability, changeability, uncertainty and unpredictability ... These four concepts are surrounded by others such as change, turbulence, risk and chaos.

259

Together, this set of concepts mark out the conceptual geography of our super-complex age as an age of fragility ... It is an age in which nothing can be taken for granted. In short, all bets are off. It is an age of conceptual and, thereby, emotional, insecurity.

Barnett 2000: 415–16

In such an age it is inevitable that research will be similarly characterised by an inability to take anything for granted. Central to research involving human subjects are a range of competing rights such as the right of the public to know, versus the rights to privacy and not to be harmed (Pring 2000). Rather obviously, however, '[w]e learn things through our inquiries, and there are times when what we learn can have consequences for our informants. Is the truth always beneficial? No. Can it be harmful? Yes' (Clark and Sharf 2007: 400). In this juxtaposition of the twin imperatives of qualitative research to understand the world better and yet to do no harm to our informants, one of the most pressing burdens of the research professional emerges: we acquire what Evetts (2003: 400) terms 'guilty knowledge'.

Evetts (2003: 400) regards the acquisition of 'guilty knowledge' as a burden of professional practice. The term 'guilty knowledge' is usually associated with forensic contexts, specifically with *mens rea* (Verschuere *et al.* 2004; *Oxford Dictionary of Law* 2006). In the context of professional activity it may have wider reference to any knowledge about a person that has the potential for harm. It may, for example, include information the professional significance of which the research respondent and even the researcher may not have been explicitly aware, and which does not necessarily carry any connotation of moral wrong-doing. Exposure in the outputs from the research may, however, prove to be an embarrassment to the respondent. This is a particular concern in research into the practice of educators by researchers from the same institution, and is tied to the complex dilemmas of core ethical concerns such as anonymity and informed consent (Zeni 2001; Yu 2008).

This experience of researchers in an age of super-complexity appears well described by Heidegger's (1945) usage of aporia. Heidegger (1945: 41) described an aporia as 'a lack of resource ... a specific kind of lack or want, a perplexity achieved by an encounter with the previously unthought, an uncertainty about where to go next driven by a desire to progress'. Heidegger's (1945) description rings true with Josselson's (1996: 70) reflection on narrative research as 'an ethically complex undertaking' that she would not advise against because of that complexity, but argues that 'it is work we must do in anguish'.

It is this experience of impasse that I seek to highlight in the five researcher accounts below as these accounts may provide an idea for extending the role of the ethics committees beyond that of gatekeeper and watchdog, to guide and educator. Considering these aporias may also serve to remind researchers that 'we are responsible because it is a delicate kind of research, we are holding the meaning of people's lives in our hands. Our successes will be gratifying, but our failures may become irreversible' (Bar-On 1996: 20).

Surfacing the ethically complex

With respect to the research project that informs this chapter, five aporias emerged through the analysis of respondents' interview transcripts. These are by no means exhaustive, but illustrative of the moral decisions demanded of the researchers for which conventional custom proves to be necessary but not sufficient. In these instances the researchers relied on their own reflexivity – their own moral dispositions.

1. The aporia of the agency of subjects – the fragility of anonymity

This aporia reflects the unexpected way in which research subjects could, and did, compromise the protection of their own identity. In one project involving the assessment practices of academics, Respondent 1 (R1) was concerned to avoid breaches of confidentiality that may arise through his own actions. He was caught off guard, however, by participants' lack of concern about confidentiality. One dimension of this lack of concern revealed itself months after the research when he bumped into one of his respondents in a meeting, and the respondent publicly reintroduced herself saying '"Oh yes, no, you interviewed me for your study", openly, publicly to everybody present' (R1). Reflecting back on the incident, R1 commented:

> I never said to my, my interviewees 'you cannot discuss this study' … What I said to my interviewees was that *I* will not be talking about this study to anybody else in your department, they will not know that I have interviewed you. … I recognised that I couldn't stop people going around and saying, ah I had this interview and etcetera, etcetera. So the actual control I had, or I have, over the level of anonymity is very little … because all the interviewees are free to talk about it, whatever they wish … *however*, they compromise their colleagues when they do so.
>
> R1

The actions of his research participants in publically discussing their participation in the project with himself and others left him feeling that:

> I felt I lost control, and I didn't know how else to do it. I could not insist that people not talk about the research … I felt that that was a complete violation … of their rights … so I never insisted that people not talk about although I realised that I was compromising other people's level of confidentiality.
>
> R1

The risk at which R1's subjects placed themselves is illustrated in the following section. Although this next extract is still an example of the exercise of the agency of subjects, it has its own nuance.

2. The aporia of the agency of subjects – the sequestrated research space

As researchers we construct the research space as 'ours' ('my research project' or the objectivist, un-owned 'this research'). This has the tendency to blind us to the agency of our participants and expose us to their 'previously unthought' (on the part of the researcher) actions. R1 recalls a participant in his assessment research project describing prejudice he had experienced in the workplace:

> *He* chose to use my research space, as an opportunity to reveal these issues and to discuss these issues 'cos … he has no other space to do it … and in a sense to get me

on board in order to *do* something about it, so … my understanding of his expectation, even though I made it very clear that I wouldn't be doing anything … is that … he would in a sense get an ally … in helping to deal with address some of the stuff.

R1

Facing this sequestration of the research space by the respondent, the researcher had to choose between obscuring important evidence, or surfacing an issue about which he feels very strongly (racial prejudice) with the consequential risk that may arise from these comments making the respondent identifiable. The researcher argued that

> I had to say, I'm sorry … I'm constructing myself here in a way where I'm not going to explicitly be able to help you in this way, there might be other avenues, but in particular [this] research avenue is not going to be … one of them … because of the way in which I had to construct anonymity and confidentiality, I can't take this to, *anywhere* in this institution, and say … *this* is what your institution is like … I can't say that. I can't go to anybody and say, *look* at what your institution *does* to people … so he has to find his own ways to say that, he's not going to be able to say it through me.

R1

Asked how this choice left him feeling, R1 replied:

> I find it makes me feel terrible, because, … I mean … my *role* … is to support this individual, an' I have to in a sense find other mechanisms to support this individual and others like him … so, I have to look for opportunities to do that, in my ordinary working day. But … I cannot use the kind of insight that he gave me … *anywhere* in that work.

R1

The researcher found himself without resource to manage the moral challenges posed in part by his own dual role as education developer and as researcher, but in part by the exercise of subject agency. Certainly, ethical procedures permitted action: but the residue of guilty knowledge remains. The dilemma is unresolved. This experience also reflects a second aporia that arises from the experience of HED practitioners engaging in research 'in their own backyard':

> [T]he other thing that this, this particular incident highlighted is my, my role as researcher and my role as developer. … In my journal I wrote lots of times about how, particularly in the first few interviews, is how do I not answer the questions that I'm so used to answering.

R1

3. The aporia of multiple practitioner roles

The peculiarity of '[r]esearch involving friends, work colleagues and other professionals' (Costley and Gibbs 2006: 89) poses particular dilemmas for HED researchers. One example is evident in the comments of Respondent 3 (R3), a senior academic with an extensive research background.

262

R3 is conscious that at one level the HED research space is 'a relatively small back-yard'. Frequently, the same academics become the research subjects for a range of projects of benefit to the HED researcher and/or the institution. A sense of weariness (and wariness) is evident as she describes the moral dilemma inherent in her awareness of the utilitarian 'use' of people for the purposes of publication or qualification, while at the same time she is conscious of the need for HED research:

> I really increasingly struggle to, justify the research to myself and therefore to them as something that's in their interest as well ... so sometimes I think y'know *stop* researching in your own backyard ... it's just wearying, maybe, for the individual that you're researching.
>
> R3

It would be easy to reduce this dilemma to a simple concern to seek out 'better subjects', but that would miss the underlying concern about the moral dangers inherent in opportunism and instrumentalism. The word 'justify' elevates this beyond conduct, and signals the underlying moral concern: once we are aware that our research subjects may feel this way, can we claim to be doing no harm when we approach them?

Respondent 5 (R5) provided another example of the aporia that may arise through role conflict inherent in practitioner research. As a HED practitioner with research interests in both policy and knowledge and the curriculum, the respondent has been involved in assisting with academic reviews. This role is primarily intended to support departments in preparing for and responding to review. However, on at least one occasion the respondent was also placed on a review panel. Together, these roles created a significant ethical problem as one such department is also part of the respondent's HED research project on knowledge and the curriculum. Arising from this role conflict, R5 notes that

> [F]unny things happen in the interviews like I have been asked to switch off the tape, somebody else kind've bared ... [their] ... soul, then said 'oh my goodness I've said far too much, I *must* see the transcript and I'm probably going to delete ask you to delete some of it. ... I've also been asked what other people have said ... which is quite difficult, they haven't asked me to give the names of course ... but they have sort've said well what did others say [indistinct], and ... I've just given extremely evasive answers, then I thought that perhaps I should say 'I don't think that's an appropriate question' ... So I'm almost becoming a bit've a 'go-between'.
>
> R5

The reported request to 'see the transcript' bears added weight when Josselson's (1996) caution is considered:

> I worry about the intrusiveness of the experience of being 'writ down', fixed in print, formulated, summed up, encapsulated in language, reduced in some way to what the words contain. Language can never contain a whole person, so every act of writing a person's life is inevitably a violation.
>
> Josselson 1996: 62

263

Each of these researchers (Respondents 1, 3 and 5) find themselves caught in an aporia that appears to emerge from the combination of the agency of their research subjects, and the HED role that demands both a professional developmental relationship, and an intrusive research relationship. Proceed they must, but they lack the resources (of ready-to-hand codes and procedures) to do so, and are left with a sense of holding guilty knowledge and compromised values.

4. The aporia of identity and representation

Right at the outset of the research process an aporia emerged for Respondent 2 (R2), in part because 'solutions' implicit within established ethical procedures gave her an ulti-mately false sense of security. In her research she had decided to use video as a way of capturing the research contexts she had identified (specific activities during lectures). She 'knew there would be challenges about how I would identify the people ... I was going to have to *blur* my images or something like that' (R2), but:

> I think what I hadn't thought of was the vulnerability it would [cause because of] the particular *layer* of ... one's working with bodies and embodiment. It's so much about what people give off ... y'know in addition to, say the content and the subject matter ... I hadn't really thought about all of those issues.
>
> R2

Although R2 had identified strategies to at least in part deal with the conventional (confidentiality), the aporia becomes evident to her when R2 realises 'the vulnerability' of the respondents that emerged when seeing themselves on video, and experiencing that video excerpt being analysed. It is a moral concern for the being of the respondents that surfaces the aporia, which may otherwise have been submerged as an ethical dilemma of identifiability that could be reduced with a technical fix. As it stands, the more funda-mental concern for *representation* and its impact on the being of the research participants emerges as a thoroughgoing concern in her research process:

> I think the challenge of representation is something that I've absolutely battled with throughout here, and that remains a sticky issue. [It] has become for me almost a central issue ... when you're looking at people's writing it's not there. ... But I think, something about the complexities of research as representation ... is, like a *shadow* for me ... throughout this whole process, and I think a major, major learning ... which has ... ethical implications ... every inch of the way.
>
> R2

Identity and representation meet in consideration of confidentiality, as an aporia for Respondent 4 (R4). Her qualification-related research involved the interface between teaching and social responsiveness. R4 had committed herself to confidentiality with regards to the names of academic staff and students, although she realised that given the cases under consideration the identity of the academics could easily be established. Unexpectedly, however, when approached about confidentiality, her research partici-pants from the community felt they would benefit from having their identity evident in the research. Towards the final stages of the research, R4 suddenly became aware of the moral disjunction in the way she was treating the identity of the academics over against the identity of the community. Discussion with a colleague served to emphasise the disjunction.

> [Participant identity is] … a complex issue to try and unpack, I've had one post-study informal interview with one of the community members and, y'know as a colleague pointed out to me 'but they told you exactly what you wanted to know you're white, you're the researcher, you've got power … they're not going to, sort've necessarily tell the "truth" in that sense' … but I didn't know to … reapproach the community members and say look this is the issue, and so I thought well I've got to anonymise everything.
>
> R4

In the following excerpt her supervisor's response to R4, concerns appears to mistake her aporia for a conventional dilemma for which there appeared to be an established strategy. For the researcher, the problem lay precisely in the moral lack within the established conventions. The understanding of the burden of ethics that appears in the extract underlines Small's (2001) insistence that 'what is required is to extend our existing abilities, not to return to first principles' (Small 2001: Abstract):

> [O]ne of my colleagues said that we always presume that the anonymity has to happen on the university side … so what are we talking about when … we don't seem to have that same level of anxiety [about the community] … and I … was really caught, I … thought I've always gone into research, I've done quite a bit with communities, with a lot of integrity … and here I was shown up, to myself, I got quite a fright [laughs] … as a researcher, I just suddenly thought y'know it *is* the degree of formality, … it *is* the power of the institution, that ultimately … showed up … that contradiction … which I then had to resolve myself, and I think I even spoke to my supervisor about it and, and I think his thought was … find out from everyone concerned then make a decision … *the decision was still mine.*
>
> R4, italics added

5. The aporia of the confessional space

R5's experiences of respondents asking her to turn off the tape or wanting to retract what they had said and requesting deletions are not unusual requests in qualitative research. They reflect examples of the burden of guilty knowledge arising from the respondent being 'seduced by the caring interview' (Clark and Sharf 2007: 405), rather than simply a sequestrated research space. The role conflict between HED practitioner and HED researcher creates particular opportunities for such exposure as was noted earlier. R3 recalled what she experiences as a peculiar characteristic of academics that:

> [T]here were a lot of kind … of confessional data in a way, I mean it's actually the lovely thing about academics is that they are often quite happy to air their dirty laundry … maybe because my topic is assessment and so there is quite lot've dirty laundry … to be aired … but I have … more often than not been surprised by people's candid and frank responses rather than a sense that they're covering things.
>
> R3

For R3, the 'dirty laundry' poses a number of ethical problems, one of which is:

> [H]ow do I represent this data in a way that doesn't come across [indistinct] an indictment of the institution, ... sympathetic marking equals lowering of standards equals, y'know, reputation of this department etc. etc. ... Now those issues are *always* lurking in the kind of research we do.
>
> R3

Asked how she managed this ethical dilemma, R3 replied:

> I remember very consciously phrasing the analysis so that it did ... what I thought did justice to the speakers ... because I mean that I am aware that very same data, could be *used* in a very indicting way of those individuals, I mean whether you know who they are or not doesn't matter the point is you're saying. 'There's some *really* bad practice going on here' ... and ... I was determined that it not be perceived as bad practice in the way I wrote it up. ... to actually remove the analysis from individuals but locate the discourse in bigger discourses that are actually constructing that. Which would, I would hope, in the mind of the reader of the publication, create a kind've 'we understand this' ... not we *damn* it, we condemn it: we actually understand it.
>
> R3

These experiences bear resemblance to that noted in narrative research by Lieblich (1996: 176), 'that people liked to tell their stories and tended to forget the possible price of their exposure'.

The fundamental aporia

Although the forgoing examples are all from the particular context of higher education practitioner research, the fundamental aporia with which they confront us are not unique to this context.

- *Within academe in general we cannot avoid engaging in research* for our own development (including gaining qualifications), for our survival within the economic system of 'publish or perish', and to grow our discipline. With rare exceptions, such research has at least an element of selfishness, and yet we are charged with doing no harm. Can we act selfishly and claim no harm?
- *The nature of qualitative inquiry involves guilty knowledge* – 'holding the meaning of people's lives in our hands' (Bar-On 1996 in Clark and Sharf 2007: 402–3) and the consequent knowing exposure of people to potential for harm.

The examples above remind us that reverting to ethical codes or the imagined comfort of 'common practice' in research – the kind of justification alluded to by Sayer (2004: 93) as ethics understood as 'simply "what we do around here"' – fails to provide a moral basis for qualitative research. For, as Sayer (2004: 93) argues in another context, such explanations 'will always be unconvincing, producing an alienated view of actors as mere dupes that misses what they care about and why'. In qualitative research there is always more than one social actor present, and social actors will exercise their agency in ways that may not be confined to the imagined possibilities of informed consent, anonymity or con-fidentiality. Ethical codes do not rescue the researcher from the aporia of moral judgement, which *is what we "always already" exercise in virtue of being immersed in a network of human relations that constitute life together'* (Benhabib 1992 in Sayer 2004: 94, italics original).

Where to from here?

Although we must progress then, we have no resources to do so. I have argued that the complexity of qualitative research is inadequately served by codes, compliance or custom, but, as noted earlier, should foreground *character:* the personal identity of the researcher-as-social-agent formed through the reflexivity of the researcher. Such a proposal recog-nises and perhaps maintains the aporia – but leaves us with an unsatisfying: so what? Cautioned by Pring's (2001) conclusion that attempts to close off the aporia in a list of ethical researcher virtues ends in more questions than answers, I would risk the following three proposals for working within the aporia: not denying it, or resolving it, but proceeding because we must.

Surface and examine reflexivity

At the core of our way ahead lies reflexivity. As Archer (2003) argues reflexivity has causal powers ('we can modify ourselves by reflecting upon what we most care about') (Archer 2003: 41), even if these powers do not operate free from constraints, nor 'under the circumstances of our own choosing' (Archer 2003:104).

'Reflexivity' is thus not to be confused with a cognitive reflective practice. It is active and causal, and reflects our commentaries on the relations between our projects and the world (Archer 2003). This understanding of reflexivity and its role in mediating between our subjective powers and 'the role objective structural or cultural powers play in influ-encing social action' (Archer 2007: 5) is congruent with the emphasis placed by Clark and Sharf (2007), Costley and Gibbs (2006), Pring (2000; 2001) and Small (2001) on the role of the individual researcher in making ethical choices. In keeping with Archer (2003; 2007), reflexivity is a matter of ontology, not epistemology. This resonates with Costley and Gibbs' (2006: 96) 'ethics of care' as an ontological, not epistemological, process.

Articulate the values underpinning research.

Practically, this may be encouraged by expecting researchers to make explicit *the values* that underpin their research, and not merely the strategies they intend to employ. In addition, researchers could be expected to identify the ethical concerns that they expect may arise through the project. This would be in keeping with Pring's (2001) call for an unavoidable 'moral deliberation in considering the ethical dimension of research. Such deliberation does inevitably call upon or embody certain principles, but can by no means be simply the application of those principles. ... There is *judgement* required ... ' (Pring 2001: 411).

Refocus the roles of ethics committees.

Small (2001: 405) argues that although codes and committees might well have a con-tribution, 'there is no substitute for the individual's development of the capacity to make ethical decisions about design and conduct of his or her project'. Ethics committees need to shift from a reactive emphasis on the performative and procedural, to an educative focus. This may focus on developing research ethics awareness by creating opportunities for the research community to engage experientially ('engaging personally, thinking reflexively') and epistemically ('developing meta-cognition, thinking epistemically, contextually and systematically') (Luckett 2001: 55) in discussions around the moral bases for research. Backgrounding the policing roles, ethics committees need to focus on developing and sustaining the researcher's 'capacity to make ethical decisions about design and conduct of his or her project' (Small 2001: 405). One way of contributing to this may be through public sharing of 'stories and narratives of research ethics to help fashion our research lives' (Plummer 2001 in Clark and Sharf 2007: 412) within our research communities.

I am cognisant that these remain broad proposals in need of flesh, but such fleshing out must be done in context. These will not overcome aporia but they may serve to surface them, thus reducing the levels of risk to both researcher and researched.

References

Archer, M. S. (2003) *Structure, Agency and the Internal Conversation*. Cambridge: Cambridge University Press.

——(2007) *Making our way through the world. Human reflexivity and social mobility*. Cambridge: Cambridge University Press.

Barnett, R. (2000) University knowledge in an age of supercomplexity, *Higher Education*, 40: 409–22.

Bar-On, D. (1996) Ethical issues in biographical interviews and analysis. In R. Josselson (Ed.). *Ethics and process in the narrative study of lives*, Vol. 4. Thousand Oaks, CA: Sage.

Booth, W. C., Colomb, G. C. and Williams, J. M. (2003) *The Craft of Research*. 2nd edn. Chicago, IL: University of Chicago Press.

Clark, M. C. and Sharf, B. F. (2007) The dark side of truth(s). Ethical dilemmas in researching the personal, *Qualitative Inquiry*, 13(3): 319–416.

Clegg, S. (2005) Theorising the mundane: the significance of agency, *International Studies in Sociology of Education*, 15(2): 149–63.

Cohen, L., Manion, L. and Morrison, K. (2000) *Research methods in education*. 5th edn. London: RoutledgeFalmer.

Costley, C. and Gibbs, P. (2006) Researching others: care as an ethic for practitioner researchers, *Studies in Higher Education*, 31(1): 89–98.

Eriksson, S., Helgesson, G. and Höglund, A. T. (2007) Being, doing, and knowing: developing ethical competence in health care, *Journal of Academic Ethics*, 5: 207–16.

Evetts, J. (2003) The sociological analysis of professionalism. Occupational change in the modern world, *International Sociology*, 18(2): 395–415.

Fisher, J. (2006). Procedural misconceptions and informed consent: Insights from empirical research on the clinical trials industry. *Kennedy Institute of Ethics Journal*, 16(3): 251–68.

Fletcher, J. (1976) *Situation ethics: The new morality*. Louisville, KY: Westminster John Knox Press.

Gray, D. E. (2004). *Doing research in the real world*. London: Sage Publications

Heidegger, M. (1945) Heidegger on the art of teaching. Excerpts of the transcript of the deposition of Professor Dr. Martin Heidegger, submitted before the Committee on de-Nazification of the Albert Ludwig University, Freiburg im Breisgau, July 23, 1945. Trans. V. Allen, and A. D. Axiotis. In M. A. Peters (2002) (Ed.). *Heidegger, Education, and Modernity*. Lanham, MD: Rowman & Littlefield Publishers, Inc., 27–46.

Homan, R. (1991). *The ethics of social research*. New York: Longman.

Josselson, R. (1996) On writing other people's lives. In R. Josselson (Ed.). *Ethics and process in the narrative study of lives*, Vol. 4. Thousand Oaks, CA: Sage.

Lieblich, A. (1996) Some unforseen outcomes of conducting narrative research with people of one's own culture. In R. Josselson (Ed.). *Ethics and process in the narrative study of lives*, Vol. 4. Thousand Oaks, CA: Sage.

Luckett, K. (2001) A proposal for an epistemically diverse curriculum for South African higher education in the 21st Century, *South African Journal of Higher Education*, 49–61.

Martin, E. A. and Law, M. (Eds) (2006) Oxford Dictionary of Law. *Oxford Reference Online*. Oxford University Press. Online. (Available at www.oxfordreference.com/views/ENTRY.html?subview= Main&entry=t49.e1745 Accessed 5 November 2007).

Payne, S. L. (2000) Challenges for research ethics and moral knowledge construction in the applied social sciences, *Journal of Business Ethics*, 26: 307–18.

Price, J. (1996) Snakes in the swamp. Ethical issues in qualitative research. In R. Josselson (Ed.). *Ethics and process in the narrative study of lives*, Vol. 4. Thousand Oaks, CA: Sage.

Pring, R. (2000) *Philosophy of Educational Research*. London: Continuum.

Pring, R. (2001) The virtues and vices of an educational researcher, *The Journal of the Philosophy of Education Society of Great Britain*, 35(3): 407–21.

Ramcharan, P. and Cutcliffe, J. R. (2001) Judging the ethics of qualitative research: considering the 'ethics as process' model, *Health and Social Care in the Community*, 9(6): 358–66.

Sayer, A. (2004) Restoring the moral dimension in social scientific accounts. A qualified ethical naturalist approach. In Archer, M. S. and Outhwaite, W. (Eds). *Defending objectivity. Essays in honour of Andrew Collier*. London: Routledge.

Schon, D. A. (1987) *Educating the reflective practitioner: toward a new design for teaching and learning in the professions*. San Francisco, CA: Jossey-Bass.

Small, R. (2001) Codes are not enough: What philosophy can contribute to the ethics of educational research, *The Journal of the Philosophy of Education Society of Great Britain*, 35(3): 378–406.

Verschuere, B., Crombez, G. and Koster, E. (2004) Orienting to guilty knowledge, *Cognition and Emotion*, 18(2): 265–79.

Yu, K. (2008) Confidentiality revisited, *Journal of Academic Ethics*, 6: 161–72.

Zeni, J. (2001). The IRB, the HSR – and the Ethics of Insider Research. *Networks: An On-Line Journal for Teacher Research*, 14(1). (Available at journals.library.wisc.edu/index.php/networks/article/view/ 147/146 Accessed 1 September 2009).

22

'Dangerous reflexivity'

Rigour, responsibility and reflexivity in qualitative research

W. S. Pillow

All ethnography is part philosophy and a good deal of the rest is confession.

Geertz 1973

The primary purpose is ... to provide guidance for what constitutes rigorous scientific research in education.

NRC 2002

Specifically, the article highlights the extent to which the paradigm of feminist research methods has come to influence the conduct of qualitative research, carrying with it a potentially high cost for the health and well-being of researchers.

Sampson *et al.* 2008

Dangerous introductions

It would appear from the above quotes that qualitative researchers find themselves in a quandary, if not indeed at risk, when practising research. We run the risk of not being confessional enough, to being too confessional and thus not rigorous enough. After coming across the 2008 article by Sampson *et al.*, which squarely lays blame for all this worry on feminist methodologies, I began to wonder: Is qualitative research dangerous? Bad for my health? Bad for my mental well being? And are feminists to blame?

Although these questions can be read as playful, I am interested in how as a field, we have moved from Clifford Geertz noting in 1973 that a major component of ethnography is 'confessional,' to a 2002 call in the USA for 'rigorous scientific research', to a 2008 indictment against feminist research methods for exponentially raising the stakes because, according to the authors, 'the particular concern of feminist researchers with reflexivity, with research relationships and with the interests of research participants may make them especially vulnerable to emotional harm' (p. 920). It is unclear who the 'them' in this sentence refers to – perhaps not only the researcher but also the research participants – but the dangers and costs of reflexivity, specifically feminist reflexivity are made clear.

As a feminist researcher and methodologist who has written on reflexivity (Pillow 2003), I am probably, from the above authors' point of view, part of the problem. Here then, I want to take up what the problems, the dangers, of reflexivity are and for whom? Is reflexivity dangerous and if so how and why? And what does this mean for current and future practices of reflexivity?

Before beginning, I want to raise another critique of feminist reflexivity, one that I have addressed previously but continues to have currency. That is whether continued conversations and debates about reflexivity actually accomplish anything? Some have described the proliferation of reflexivity talk as, at best, self-indulgent, narcissistic and tiresome, and, at worst, undermining emancipatory research (Patai 1994; Kemmis 1995). Daphne Patai was particularly critical in the 1990s of what she saw as 'academic fads' in the face of the 'crisis of representation', stating that 'notwithstanding, babies still have to be cared for, shelter sought, meals prepared and eaten' (p. 64). Patai situated those scholars 'who stay up nights worrying about representation' (p. 64) as privileged academics engaged in the thrill of language games and also challenged: 'Does all this self-reflexivity produce better research?' (p. 69).

Does self-reflexivity produce better research? In response to this question, I have suggested that not talking about our positions and positionalities will not fix the problems of reflexivity (nor the many social ills and inequities that many of us are concerned with changing), but that rather we need to move beyond reflexivity as simply a validity method, to something more uncomfortable (Pillow 2003). Here, I extend this previous conversation about reflexivity, working out of the multiple challenges of the so-called dangers of feminist reflexivity, with present calls for rigour in educational research, and the lingering hesitation over Patai's question. After an overview of reflexivity in qualitative research and common reflexive practices, I consider what it means now to do reflexivity, to practice reflexivity with rigour, responsibility and yes – dangerously.

Reflexive beginnings

Reflexivity is discussed, or at least mentioned, in nearly every qualitative research book or article and has been accepted as a method qualitative researchers can and should use to represent difference better (Wasserfall 1997) and establish 'ethnographic authority' (Britzman 1995: 229). Reflexivity is used by a wide range of scholars in a wide arena of fields including anthropology, dance, education, health, medicine, psychology, sociology and social work, and is also employed by those utilising a range of paradigmatic approaches including hermeneutics, critical theory, feminism, race-theory and/or poststructuralism. Whether using reflexivity as a methodological tool to better represent, legitimise, or call into question data, most researchers state they are using reflexivity without defining why or how they are using it.

It is useful at this point to differentiate practices of reflexivity as methodological practice in the social sciences from reflection as a form of professional practice or intervention. For instance, when doing a search on reflexivity, research that utilises reflective practice to promote better leadership skills or as a tool for intervention with 'at-risk' youth will also show up (Cunliffe 2009; Threadgold and Nilan 2009). This latter form of reflection as a form of practice to know ourselves and improve ourselves has a long intellectual history growing out of the Enlightenment. Although reflexivity is linked to and historically tied to philosophical forms of reflection and reflective practice, it is necessary to differentiate this form of reflection and its use in the philosophical sciences from the use of reflexivity and self-reflexivity as methods in social science research (see Pillow 2003, for further detail). In this chapter, the emphasis is upon reflexivity as a methodological tool and practice in ethnographic and qualitative research in the social sciences.

Discussions of the use of reflexive methods in anthropology, generally beginning in the 1970s, were a response to critiques of ethnocentrism endemic to ethnographic and qualitative research methods and initially emphasised the role of reflexivity in situating the researcher in a neutral but compassionate relationship toward the research subjects (Rabinow 1977; Clifford and Marcus 1986). The researcher's role was to understand as fully as possible, without judgement or insertion of the researcher's own values, the subjects' ways of knowing and being. In order to do this, the researcher would need to be reflexive about his assumptions and biases and thus control for those when analysing and writing. Just how this was supposed to happen was never made very clear; reflexivity at this point seemed like something the researcher/author would do, say he was doing and perhaps write about it.

However, as Denzin and Lincoln (2005) note, the field of ethnographic and qualitative research continued to be questioned and scrutinised by those internal to the field. Denzin and Lincoln identify eight 'moments', key shifts in thinking that impacted the doing of qualitative research. Feminist theory according to them arose during a time of 'blurred genres' and gained in importance through a 'crisis of representation', and continued into 'postmodernism' and 'postexperimental' periods. These moments/shifts corresponded with a change in who were becoming researchers, and who were being researched, when, where and how. As the credentialing of all women through higher education increased and women began studying women and women's issues, on the ground, in the field, in the homes of women, methodological discussions expanded and changed (Oakley 1981). A similar shift and expansion of discussions and methodologies occurred as racialised researchers and lesbian/gay researchers entered the research arena not only as subjects of, but also as researchers/authors of research (Villenas 1996; Johnson–Bailey 1999; Parker et al. 1999). The importance of this is significant: What happens when those who typically were the objects of the gaze become the gazers? Does research change, do researcher responsibility and relations change, when we research ourselves?

These questions altered qualitative research and methods. Whereas previously, objectivity and neutrality were seen as clearly linked and vital to the doing of valid research projects and findings, now the objectivity of research was brought under question and issues of power in research relations begin to be acknowledged and challenged. No longer could researchers claim a fly on the wall approach, a neutral view from everywhere and nowhere. When objectivity became open to question, the researcher's subjectivity also became open to scrutiny and questions of how research relations and researcher subjectivity impact the doing of research became equally important.

Feminist theory and feminist researchers significantly contributed to these methodological discussions and shifts. Indeed, feminist contributions to methodology, although initially ignored (Behar and Gordon 1995), are now widely acknowledged, for example: 'Evolving primarily from feminist research, reflexivity has become a priority on the research agenda, focusing on the construction of knowledge and power as an inherently social process' (Riach 2009: 359). The key concerns of feminist methodologists in the 1970s – relationships with research subjects, politics of representation, power and reflexivity – remain key topics today (Pillow and Mayo 2006). As Taylor and Rupp

(2005) note, 'what is distinctive about feminist methodology is not the use of particular techniques but rather an epistemological understanding of how knowledge is generated, how it is reported, and how it is used' (p. 2116). Reflexivity as a form of feminist methodology arose as key to the process of knowing and confronting knowledge production. Fonow and Cook (2005), revisiting their key publication on feminist methodology, *Feminist Methodology*, note 'we defined reflexivity as the tendency of feminists to reflect on, examine critically, and explore analytically the nature of the research process' (p. 2218).

Feminist attention to the whole research process – from forming research questions, gaining access and entrée, conducting interviews and observations, research relations, to analysing data and writing up results – is central to feminist methodology. Reflexivity under feminism is not only about investigating the power embedded in one's research, but is also about doing research differently at each step of the research process. To be reflexive, then, not only contributes to producing knowledge that aids in understanding and gaining insight into the workings of our social world but also provides insight on how this knowledge is produced at each stage of the research process (Clough 1992). Thus, reflexivity, as Rosanna Hertz (1997) notes, is focused upon 'what I know' and 'how I know it', and entails 'an ongoing conversation about experience while simultaneously living in the moment' (viii).

A review of reflexivity in qualitative research reveals that authors may be reflexive about the research process, the subjects or issue they are researching, and the world through which they are researching and creating knowledge. Most common is self-reflexivity – critical consciousness through a personal accounting of how the researcher's self-location (e.g. across gender, race, class, sexuality, ethnicity, nationality), position and interests influence all stages of the research process. Self-reflexivity is most identified with self-disclosure. Self-reflexivity acknowledges the researcher's role(s) in the construction of the research problem, the research setting and research findings, and highlights the importance of the researcher becoming consciously aware of these factors and thinking through the implications of these factors for her/his research. Van Maanen (1989) characterises such work as the 'confessional tale' and notes that confessions may take place around oneself, others, the field or the data. In this way, the choices involved in doing fieldwork and representation are no longer viewed as incidental but can become objects of study themselves. As Gray writes:

> Reflexivity here involves a turning back of inquiry on the formative conditions of its production by variously addressing questions of the researcher's biographical relationship to the topic, the multiple voices in the text, different potential readings and the instability between the research text and the object of the study or representation.
>
> Gray 2008: 936

One of the most noticeable trends to come out of a use of reflexivity is increased attention to researcher subjectivity in the research process – a focus on how does who I am, who I have been, who I think I am, and how I feel, affect data collection and analysis? – that is, an acceptance and acknowledgment that 'how knowledge is acquired, organized, and interpreted is relevant to what the claims are' (Altheide and Johnson 1998). Such thinking, influenced by feminism and poststructural theory, has yielded further questions about a researcher's ability to represent, to know another and questions the construction of research texts. Can we truly represent another? Should this even be a goal of research? Whose story is it – the researcher or the researched? How do I do representation knowing that I can never quite get it right? Discussion of these questions is now often a part of the qualitative research project and researchers who engage in asking these questions cite a need to foreground the politics of representation by making visible, through reflexivity, how we do the work of representation (Britzman 1995; Fine 1994; Lather 1993; 1995).

Yet, what is the purpose of all of this reflexivity talk? In addition to altering how we think about the research process and altering how we conduct research, one result of all the attention to reflexivity is to produce research that questions its owns interpretations and is reflexive about its own knowledge production towards the goal of producing better, less distorted research accounts (Hertz 1997). Thus, reflexivity is often understood as involving an ongoing self-awareness during the research process, which aids in making visible the practice and construction of knowledge within research in order to produce more accurate analyses of our research. Reflexivity challenges the common sense; it promises to help us see what is unthought by helping us to see what at other times is invisible. As Kleinsasser sums up:

> Researcher reflexivity represents a methodical process of learning about self as researcher, which, in turn, illuminates deeper, richer meanings about personal, theoretical, ethical, and epistemological aspects of the research question. Qualitative researchers engage in reflexivity because they have reason to believe that good data will result.
>
> Kleinsasser 2000: 155

Perhaps because of its multiple uses, reflexivity has also became associated with or used as a measure of legitimacy and validity in qualitative research. Listening and writing with reflexivity are often described as tools to help unravel the ways personal history can influence the research process and thus yield more 'accurate', more 'valid' research (Altheide and Johnson 1998). Although discussions of validity have been troubled in qualitative research (Kvale 1989; Lather 1986; 1993; Maxwell 1992), these debates have if anything situated self-reflexivity as even more important to the doing of qualitative research. If traditional measures of validity are not useful to qualitative researchers, then what are we left with to discuss and determine whether our data and analyses are 'accurate'?

Over time and in response to shifting moments in qualitative research, reflexivity has become an important tool to demonstrate one's awareness of the problematics of doing research – issues of power, voice, researcher and researched subjectivity – and is often used to potentially validate and legitimise research precisely by raising questions about the research process. How reflexivity is discussed and performed in the research process and text varies according to what purpose(s) the researcher is putting reflexivity to work and is explored further below.

Doing reflexivity

'What is reflexivity, really?' 'How do I do it?' 'How do I know I am doing it?' 'How do I know if I am doing it right?' These are questions students ask each semester in qualitative research courses and each semester I face the challenge of what it means to teach reflexivity. Is reflexivity a skill, a set of methods that can be taught? If so, what are the methods of reflexivity – is it keeping a research journal or the inclusion of a questioning researcher voice in the text? What should we be reflexive about? The other? Ourselves? The place? Who gets to be reflexive? How does one write reflexively? How or should the reader judge whether the researcher was too reflexive or not reflexive enough? And if ethnography is confessional, can we avoid narcissistic tales?

Although I tend to trouble these questions, I do understand the need of the novice researcher to attempt to define what reflexivity is and the desire to 'get reflexivity right'. Part of what makes reflexivity so obtuse is that although we can form definitions of what it is, the distinctions between the differing roles of reflexivity are rarely made and although 'reflexivity is a term which is widely used in social constructionist writing … (it) is not necessarily used in the same way by different writers' (Burr 1995: 160).

We can, however, consider trends within the field and initially these trends are helpful to understanding and later extending reflexivity for one's own usage. Several writers have attempted to identify varying types of reflexivity and identify where reflexivity occurs. According to Anderson (1989), reflexivity involves a dialectical process consisting of:

The researcher's constructs
The informants' common sense constructs
The research data
The researcher's ideological biases; and
The structural and historical forces that shaped the social construction under study.

Denzin (1997) identifies five differing types of reflexivity in use in qualitative research: methodological, intertextual, standpoint, queer and feminist reflexivity (p. 218–23), and Marcus (1998) similarly describes 'four styles of reflexivity' (p. 394).

Whether using Anderson's or Denzin's taxonomy, or another comprehensive listing of where reflexivity occurs and how, I find what matters most is that the new doctoral researcher reads widely, deeply and critically. That is, doctoral researchers engage with and understand the history of qualitative research, key moments of change and shifts and what characterised such fissures; understand what is meant by humanism, subject, subjectivity, data, power and method, voice, representation, and text; understand a range of paradigmatic approaches to qualitative research; and taking the above typologies of reflexivity, can apply this knowledge specifically to reflexivity in order to understand why, for example, 'data' would be questioned and how that questioning might change from a standpoint, queer or postmodern stance.

What I am suggesting is that the doing of reflexivity is linked with and only as deep as our methodological and epistemological knowledges. Reflexivity can only be as strong, as rigorous, as our own knowledge base and our abilities to continually and critically interrogate our knowledges and constructions. If we accept and understand that reflexivity is the task of analysing one's own experiences in the process of fieldwork, that 'understanding emerges out of interaction between me as a researcher and the situation within which I find myself – out of the questions that emerge from my response to the situation' (Williams 1990: 254), then these 'responses', reflections, do not come out of thin air; they are also dependent on our understandings and constructions.

In addition to reading widely and deeply as a way to become critically reflexive doctoral researchers and writers, there are several mechanisms and practices of doing qualitative research that are useful to the researcher. These practices are necessary for engaged, rigorous research. These include keeping a:

- Researcher log
- Researcher field notes
- Researcher journal.

Whether one is doing a case study, document analysis, ethnography, observation and interviews, surveys, or focus groups from several months to several years, it is the responsibility of the researcher to keep an explicit and detailed log, field notes, and journal of the research. The log will include specific details such as date, time, place – the who, what, when, where, how – of, for example, an observation or interview. The field notes correspondingly provide a thick description of everything that was said, done and observed during the research event, whereas the researcher journal is the place for the researcher's thoughts, emotions, questions and notes to self (Emerson *et al.* 1995).

The style and format of how these three are kept is not important – they may be typed together on one computer file, written in three separate notebooks, audio recorded on a drive or walk when leaving a research site; they may be colour coded or scribbled messages on scraps of papers or sticky-notes – what is important is that these logs and journals are consistently kept. The combination of the log, notes and journal provide a working history of the unfolding process of the research and provide the researcher with initial text to work from and respond to. Again, each researcher style and mode of keeping the log, notes and journals will vary; some might include personal shorthand, long narratives, short notes, prose, questions, venting or quotes. These jottings may or may not end up in final writing; but the process of coming to know, the process of recording the constructions of the research will greatly enrich the final product.

The notes and journals also provide an initial mapping of researcher reflexivity, what the researcher was thinking and how at the beginning, middle and end of the research project, and later distance from the notes and journal will provide further opportunity for reflexivity. As Akom (2008), who uses 'critical reflexivity to decenter whiteness' (p. 259), notes,

> Researchers might use several options for incorporating this reflexivity into a narrative account. They may create a separate section on the 'role of the researcher,' provide an epilogue, use interpretive commentary throughout the discussion of the findings, or bracket themselves out by describing personal experiences as used in phenomenological methods.
>
> Akom 2008: 249

Burr (1995) states that the most common usage of reflexivity is researchers 'analyzing their own writing, reflexively discussing how their own accounts have been constructed' (p. 160). One example is a focus on developing reciprocity with research subjects – hearing, listening and equalising the research relationship – doing research 'with' instead of 'on'. In this way, reflexivity is also used to deconstruct the author's authority in the research and/or writing process. Interest in this practice has led to 'multi-vocal' texts and explorations of attempts to let the data, the subjects, speak for themselves. Researchers have tried differing writing and representation styles to accomplish this, including writing data as a play, as a literary story or as a split multi-voiced text (Eisner 1997; Lather and Smithies 1997; Richardson 1994; Sanders 1999). They have developed metaphors such as 'cultural intuition' (Delgado Bernal 1998), 'fictions' (Visweswaran 1994), 'performing theories of the flesh' (Villenas 2000), 'white noise' (McCoy 2000), 'exposed methodology' (Pillow 2000), 'skirting a pleated text' (Richardson 2000), and 'methodology in the fold' (St. Pierre 1997) to not only explain but also expand and speak to the complexities of qualitative research methodology.

Yet although I have encouraged practices of responsible and rigorous reflexivity through in-depth reading and diligent keeping of a researcher log, notes and journal, it is also important to understand that none of these practices is a panacea. In other words, reflexivity cannot solve all the problems of voice, power and representation in qualitative research nor should it be used as such a method. Unfortunately, some doctoral researcher/writers pick up and use reflexivity as if it were a legitimation tool. I have identified four commonly used 'validated reflexive strategies' (Pillow 2003: 181):

- Reflexivity as recognition of self
- Reflexivity as recognition of other
- Reflexivity as truth; and
- Reflexivity as transcendence.

I argue that these four validated strategies, that is, ways of proving reflexivity, although arising out of critical attention to the politics of the gaze, can often collapse into usages of reflexivity simply as a method to get more 'valid' data. The four strategies then simply become a research tool, a method, presented as confessions that provide catharsis for the researcher and seem to cure what ails us in the doing of representation. In this way, reflexivity becomes another trope with accepted story lines and phrases that are commonly recognised and expected.

Given the continued usage of reflexivity as 'validated reflexive strategies', I return then to a question I previously asked:

If, as I suggest, we are currently taking comfort in common usages of reflexivity in the postmodern – relying upon reflexivity as methodological power and listening to and desiring only certain kinds of reflexive stories – how can we interrupt these common practices?

Pillow 2003: 187

Or as Varadharajan (1995: xi) asks: How can we engage in a 'possibility of critique beyond a certain kind of paralyzed reflexivity'?

Practising responsible reflexivity: dangerously

According to Britzman:

Recent educational ethnographies and writing about this genre are pushing at normative disciplinary boundaries in terms of what is it that structures methodological imperatives, the ethnographer's stances, and the ethnographic voice; the kinds of theoretical traditions through which data are constructed, represented, and narrated; what are taken to be problems suitable for ethnographic research; and the problems of how one might read against the ethnographic grain.

Britzman 2000: 29

Reflexivity has and continues to play a major role in the 'difficult questions' surrounding ethnographic and qualitative research. Reflexivity is the interplay between theory and data; between researchers and researched, between field and text. Although we can attempt to create working definitions of reflexivity and define where it occurs and how; although we can require that all researchers keep logs, field notes and journals; although we can suggest that the way into critical reflexivity is by reading deeply and widely, reflexivity will necessarily remain fluid, forever changing and questioning.

What is 'dangerous' about reflexivity is not that we have gone too far as the quote at the beginning of this chapter suggests, but that we have not gone far enough. Once reflexivity becomes a static tool, a bounded method, to increase the legitimacy or validity of our research, we have lost the intent of reflexivity.

Doing reflexivity rigorously takes time and interaction. Consider, for example, reading your reflexive journal notes aloud or sharing your reflections with a peer research group – how do these interactions change your reflections on your reflexivity? But how much reflexivity is enough or too much? Some consider this yet another 'danger' of reflexivity; not knowing when enough is enough. As Gewirtz and Cribb write:

There is no obvious limit to how far researchers can unpack, reflect upon, analyze and defend the value judgements implicit in their work; and, if this process of reflection were taken to extremes, it seems that all research would collapse into a process of value analysis at the expense of the substantive issues that are the focus of the research.

Gewirtz and Cribb 2006: 149

Gewirtz and Cribb would like to see 'ethical reflexivity as a mode of rigour' (p. 150), but note 'The problem is how researchers can both let their value commitments fuel their research and, at the same time, be scrupulous about not simply discovering what it is they would like to find out' (p. 150–1).

Can we do this work? Can we really find out what we do not know or cannot imagine? Some researchers return to critically reflect on earlier analyses, sometimes after a period of years, reading differently what they had previously assumed. Gordon performs such a reflection on earlier research findings, a process that she states reveals:

Within this perspective, reflexivity holds the potential to undermine the notion that 'reality has been captured' by situating the account within the partial and positioned perspective of a particular researcher. Reflexivity offers an invitation to readers to challenge the accounts offered to them, and reminds both readers and researchers alike that these accounts, as textual creations, are, at best, insightful.

Gordon 2005: 281

Reflexivity, rigorous and dangerous reflexivity, pushes us to question and deconstruct what is most hegemonic in our lives. As Adkins (2003) states: 'reflexivity must therefore be understood to involve reflection on the unthought and unconscious categories of thought, that is, the uncovering of unthought categories of habit which are themselves *corporealized* preconditions of our more self-conscious practices' (p. 25). However, entrenched, hegemonic social categories, such as gender and race, may remain untransformed by reflexivity. We each reach the limits of our own reflexivities, our own reflexive abilities and understandings; we can push these limits by reading, by sharing and talking with others, but reflexivity does not fix the dangers of qualitative research.

So why do reflexivity? Why spend so much time keeping a researcher journal, unpacking assumptions, reading widely and deeply in methodological and theoretical arenas, and talking to a peer research group if reflexivity cannot 'fix' my project? The specific response to this question lies within each individual, but in general the short response is 'because we must write':

> On the one hand, the ethnographer must make her way into new worlds and new relationships. On the other hand, she must learn how to represent in written form what she has come to see and understand as the result of these experiences.
>
> Visweswaran 1994: 15

Whether writing in traditional text form or including additional forms of text and media, the researcher's role and job continues to be to represent (in whatever form, fashion, or take on representation the author takes or refuses). Researchers are responsible not only for what they write and produce, but also *how* we write and produce. 'Writing is therefore first and foremost an act of self-witnessing and self-knowledge' (Colyar 2009: 429).

Research, writing and representation have been changed and impacted by what we have questioned about the role of research, politics of the gaze and what it means to do representation. To do research and writing now, is always to research and write with this knowledge and critique, and rigour requires a continued critical internal self-reflection on the field of qualitative research (Moss 2005). Reflexivity, although not a fix to the challenges and questions facing qualitative researchers, is a methodological practice that can enable us to continue to unpack and trouble the doing of our research, while at the same time allowing us to get doctoral research work done.

Here, I think there is something to be learned from continued applications of feminist theory and methodology across a range of issues, people and places. For example, what does feminist methodology look like when applied to women interviewing men who have committed violent sexual crimes against women? (Presser 2005) Such research operates within and against the limits of law, criminal law, sociology, psychology and feminist research. Presser states that her research in this area calls for 'strong reflexivity' due to the challenge of being a woman listening to stories narrated by men who are re-relating and remaking sense of their violent sexual acts against women as they are talking to a female researcher. Likewise, but in a very different project, Taylor and Rupp discuss the need for, but also challenges to, 'strong' feminist methodology in their research on drag queens. Self-identified lesbian, female, feminists studying self-identified queer drag queens creates unique and complex intersections of power, gender and sexuality. As what we research, who we research, and how we research become more complex and sophisticated, our methodologies and practices of reflexivity will also need to become more complex. Rice (2009) suggests that such examples of 'strong reflexivity' are best described as an 'embodied engagement' (p. 257), reflexivity that fully engages ourselves in relation to others.

The above examples confront the challenge of continuing to ask how reflexivity can act not simply as a tool of methodological power but also as a methodological tool

[I]nterruptive of practices of gathering data as 'truths' into existing 'folds of the known'. … and to what I suggest are unfamiliar – and likely uncomfortable – tellings. Such uses of reflexivity acknowledge the critiques … [of reflexivity] without shrugging off reflexivity, while at the same time interrogating reflexivity's complicit relationship with ethnocentric power and knowledge in qualitative research.

Pillow 2003: 192

Although the discomfort of the unfamiliar may to some seem too dangerous, unruly and not rigorous enough, I have argued for continued deeper critical engagement with reflexivity as methodological practice in qualitative research. Reading, re-reading; writing, rewriting; sharing and discussing our work; diligently keeping and reviewing field notes and a researcher journal; and giving time and more time to reflexivity can work to counter comfortable research practices of reflexivity and interrupt too easy and neat usages of reflexivity. This work will be rigorous, responsible and dangerous.

References

Adkins, L. (2003) Reflexivity: freedom or habit of gender? *Theory, Culture and Society*, 20(6): 21–42.

Akom, A. A. (2008) Black metropolis and mental life: 'beyond the "burden of "acting white"'" toward a third wave of critical racial studies, *Anthropology & Education Quarterly*, 39(3): 247–65.

Altheide, D. and Johnson, J. (1998) Criteria for assessing interpretive validity in qualitative research. In N. Denzin and Y. Lincoln (Eds). *Collecting and interpreting qualitative materials*. Thousand Oaks, CA: Sage, pp. 283–312.

Anderson, G. (1989) Critical ethnography in education: Origins, current status, and new directions, *Review of Educational Research*, 59(3): 249–70.

Behar, R. and Gordon, D. (1995) *Women Writing Culture*. Berkeley, CA: University of California Press.

Britzman, D. (1995) 'The question of belief': writing poststructural ethnography, *International Journal of Qualitative Studies in Education*, 8(3): 229–38.

——(2000) 'The question of belief': writing poststructural ethnography. In E. St. Pierre and W. Pillow (Eds). *Working the ruins/feminist poststructural theory and methods in education*. New York: Routledge, 27–40.

Burr, V. (1995) *An Introduction to Social Constructionism*. London: Routledge.

Clifford, J. and Marcus, G. (Eds) (1986) *Writing Culture: The Poetics and Politics of Ethnography*. Berkeley, CA: University of California Press.

Clough, P. T. (1992) *The End(s) of Ethnography: From Realism to Social Criticism*. Newbury Park, CA: Sage.

Colyar, J. (2009) Becoming writing, becoming writers, *Qualitative Inquiry*, 15(2): 421–36.

Cunliffe, A. L. (2009) The philosopher leader: on relationalism, ethics and reflexivity – A critical perspective to teaching leadership. *Management Learning*, 40(1): 87–101.

Delgado Bernal, D. (1998) Using a Chicana feminist epistemology in educational research, *Harvard Educational Review*, 68(4): 555–79.

Denzin, N. (1997) *Interpretive ethnography: Ethnographic practices for the 21st century*. Thousand Oaks, CA: Sage.

Denzin, N. and Lincoln, Y. (2005) *The Sage handbook of qualitative research*. Thousand Oaks, CA: Sage.

Eisner, E. (1997) The promise and perils of alternative forms of data representation, *Educational Researcher*, 26(6): 4–10.

Emerson, R. M., Fretz, R. I. and Shaw, L. L. (1995) *Writing ethnographic field notes*. Chicago, IL: The University of Chicago Press.

Fine, M. (1994) Dis-tance and other stances: Negotiations of power inside feminist research. In A. Gitlen (Ed.). *Power and method*. New York: Routledge, 13–35.

Fonow, M. M. and Cook, J. A. (2005) Feminist Methodology: New Applications in the academy and public policy, *Signs: Journal of Women in Culture and Society*, 30(4): 2211–36.

Geertz, C. (1973) *The interpretation of cultures*. New York: Basic Books.

Gewirtz, S. and Cribb, A. (2006) What to do about values in social research: the case for ethical reflexivity in the sociology of education, *British Journal of Sociology of Education*, 27(2): 141–55.

Gordon, J. (2005) White on White: Researcher Reflexivity and the Logics of Privilege in White Schools Undertaking Reform, *The Urban Review*, 37(4): 279–302.

Gray, B. (2008) Putting Emotion and Reflexivity to Work in Researching Migration, *Sociology*, 42(5): 935–52.

Hertz, R. (1997) Introduction: Reflexivity and Voice. In R. Hertz (Ed.). *Reflexivity and voice*. Thousand Oaks, CA: Sage, xii-xviii.

Johnson-Bailey, J. (1999) The ties that bind and the shackles that separate: race, gender, class, and colour in a research process, *Qualitative Studies in Education*, 12(6): 659–70.

Kemmis, S. (1995) Emancipatory aspirations in a postmodern era, *Curriculum Studies,* 3(2): 133–68.

Kleinsasser, A. M. (2000) Researchers, Reflexivity, and Good Data: Writing to Unlearn, *Theory into Practice*, 39(3): 155–62.

Kvale, S. (1989) To validate is to question. In S. Kvale (Ed.). *Issues of validity in qualitative research*. Sweden: Student Literature.

Lather, P. (1986) Issues of validity in openly ideological research: Between a rock and a soft place, *Interchange*, 17(4): 63–84.

——(1993) Fertile obsession: Validity after poststructuralism, *Sociological Quarterly*, 34(4): 673–93.

——(1995) The validity of angels: Interpretive and textual strategies in researching the lives of women with HIV/AIDS, *Qualitative Inquiry*, 1(1): 41–68.

Lather, P. and Smithies, C. (1997) *Troubling the angels: Women living with HIV/AIDS*. Boulder, CO: Westview Press.

Marcus, G. (1998) What comes (just) after 'post'? The case of ethnography. In N. Denzin and Y. Lincoln (Eds). *The landscape of qualitative research: Theories and issues*. Thousand Oaks, CA: Sage, 383–406.

Maxwell, J. (1992) Understanding and validity in qualitative research, *Harvard Educational Review*, 62(3): 279–300.

McCoy, K. (2000) White noise—the sound of epidemic: Reading/writing a climate of intelligibility around the 'crisis' of difference. In E. St. Pierre and W. Pillow (Eds). *Working the ruins/feminist poststructural theory and methods in education*. New York: Routledge, 237–57.

Moss, P. A. (2005) Toward 'Epistemic Reflexivity' in Educational Research: A Response to Scientific Research in Education, *Teachers College Record*, 107(I): 19–29.

National Research Council (NRC) (2002) *Scientific research in education* (R. J. Shavelson and Lisa Towne, Eds), Washington, DC: National Academy Press.

Oakley, A. (1981) Interviewing women: A contradiction in terms? In H. Roberts (Ed.). *Doing feminist research*. New York: Routledge, 30–61.

Parker, L., Dehyle, D. and Villenas, S. (Eds) (1999) *Race is … race isn't: Critical race theory and qualitative studies in education*. Boulder, CO: Westview Press.

Patai, D. (1994) (Response) When method becomes power. In A. Gitlen (Ed.). *Power and method*. New York: Routledge, pp. 61–73.

Pillow, W. (2000) Exposed methodology: The body as a deconstructive practice. In E. St. Pierre and W. Pillow (Eds). *Working the ruins/feminist poststructural theory and methods in education*. New York: Routledge, pp. 199–219.

Pillow, W. S. (2003) Confession, catharsis, or cure: The use of reflexivity as methodological power in qualitative research, *International Journal of Qualitative Studies in Education*, 16(2): 175–96.

Pillow, W. S. and Mayo, C. (2006) Toward Understandings of Feminist Ethnography. In S. N. Hesse-Biber (Ed.). *Handbook of Feminist Research: Theory and Praxis*. New York: Sage, 155–71.

Presser, L. (2005) Negotiating Power and Narrative in Research: Implications for Feminist Methodology, *Signs: Journal of Women in Culture and Society*, 30(4): 2067–90.

Rabinow, P (1977) *Reflections on fieldwork in Morocco.* Berkeley, CA: University of California Press.

Riach, K. (2009) Exploring Participant-centred Reflexivity in the Research Interview, *Sociology*, 43(2): 356–70.

Rice, C. (2009) Women's Embodied Lives Imagining the Other? Ethical Challenges of Researching and Writing, *Feminism Psychology*, 19(2): 245–66.

Richardson, L. (1994) Writing: a method of inquiry. In N. Denzin and Y. Lincoln (Eds). *Handbook of qualitative research.* Thousand Oaks, CA: Sage, 516–29.

——(2000) Skirting a pleated text: De-disciplining an academic life. In E. St. Pierre and W. Pillow (Eds). *Working the ruins/feminist poststructural theory and methods in education.* New York: Routledge, 153–63.

Sampson, H., Bloor, M. and Fincham, B. (2008) A Price Worth Paying? Considering the 'Cost' of Reflexive Research Methods and the Influence of Feminist Ways of 'Doing', *Sociology*, 42(5): 919–33.

Sanders, J. (1999) Dissertation as performance [Art Script] (Take Three), *International Journal of Qualitative Studies in Education*, 12(5): 541–162.

St. Pierre, E. (1997) Methodology in the fold and the irruption of transgressive data, *International Journal of Qualitative Studies in Education*, 10(2): 175–89.

Taylor, V. and Rupp, L. J. (2005) When girls are men: Negotiating gender and sexual dynamics in a study of drag queens, *Signs: Journal of Women in Culture and Society*, 30(4): 2115–39.

Threadgold, S. and Nilan, P. (2009) Reflexivity of Contemporary Youth, Risk and Cultural Capital, *Current Sociology*, 57(1): 47–68.

Van Maanen, J. (1989) *Tales of the field: On writing ethnography.* Chicago, IL: University of Chicago Press.

Varadharajan, A. (1995) *Exotic parodies/subjectivity in Adorno, Said, and Spivak.* Minneapolis, MN: University of Minnesota Press.

Villenas, S. (1996) The colonizer/colonized Chicana ethnographer: Identity marginalization, and cooptation in the field, *Harvard Educational Review*, 66: 711–31.

——(2000) This ethnography called my back: Writings of the exotic gaze, 'othering' Latina, and recuperating Xicanisma. In E. St. Pierre and W. Pillow (Eds). *Working the ruins/feminist poststructural theory and methods in education.* New York: Routledge, 74–95.

Visweswaran, K. (1994) *Fictions of feminist ethnography.* Minneapolis, MN: University of Minnesota Press.

Wasserfall, R. (1997) Reflexivity, feminism, and difference. In R. Hertz (Ed.). *Reflexivity and voice.* Thousand Oaks, CA: Sage, 150–68.

Williams, A. (1990) Reading feminism in fieldnotes. In L. Stanley (Ed.). *Feminist Praxis: Research, Theory, & Epistemology in Feminist Sociology.* New York: Routledge, 253–61.

23

Emotions and being a doctoral student

C. Herman

Most researchers seldom admit to the emotional aspects in doing and writing research; therefore, the accumulated body of knowledge in this area, although expanding, is still limited. Moreover, researchers tend to under report their negative feelings and to over report their good feelings and enjoyment of the fieldwork (Van Maanen *et al.* 1993). This reflective account of my own doctoral research journey engages the debate by identifying a host of emotions that were generated during the various stages of my own research and demonstrates the impact they had on the process, the research participants and myself. The chapter demonstrates that the attempt to ignore or separate one's emotions from the research process may reduce the researcher's ability to engage with the process and limit the data that could be collected. It proposes that researchers' emotions need to be acknowledged and managed throughout the research process, not only to provide them with emotional relief but also to encourage self-understanding, making researchers aware of how their emotions influence the research process. Though I am aware of the distinction some scholars make between feelings and emotions (Damasio 1999; Solomon 2003), for the purpose of this chapter these terms will be used interchangeably.

It is now widely acknowledged that the researcher's values, feelings, culture and history shape and define the enquiry, and that research is often a personal matter (Wilkins 1993). This is even more so when research is undertaken by doctoral students, as it involves the students' personal development and is sometimes motivated by the students' need to take stock and make sense of their life and experiences so far (Reason and Marshall 1987; Boucher and Smyth 2004). Despite these developments, doctoral studies still tend to emphasise the rational and technical competencies of producing research and neglect the emotional aspects of doctoral learning. The role of emotions is mostly ignored in the standard literature on research methodology (see, for example, Bell 1993; Cohen *et al.* 2000; Silverman 2005). There is an implicit expectation that researchers will separate what Peshkin (1984) describes as the two general categories of selves that they bring into the field: the human-participant and the research-participant. Some researchers explain this approach by referring to what Hochschild (1983) describes as 'feeling rules' – that is, how we are supposed to feel in different situations, and 'display rules' – how we are supposed to express our feelings (Kleinman and Copp 1993; Young and Lee 1996). As members of a research fraternity, researchers share a culture dominated by systematic methodology and an ideology of professional distance. In this interpretation of professionalism, emotions are suspect as they are assumed to contaminate research by impeding objectivity. Consequently, researchers try to control or suppress their emotions by wearing a mask of objectivity. Even those who abandoned this positivist goal of objectivity still argue that researchers need to maintain 'social distance' from the case to allow analytical work to be accomplished (Gilbert 2001: 18).

A growing body of literature, however, is beginning to challenge the polarisation between the rational and emotional in the research journey (e.g. Hallowell *et al.* 2005). There is a view that denying the emotions of research means also ignoring the relation between emotions and reason, in other words, the emotional nature of learning. McLaughlin (2003) maintains that the research process is deeply entwined with feelings and perceptual processes. Therefore, the researcher's self-understanding and self-reflection strengthen the research. Feelings should be used as data, helping to tease out the researcher's assumptions that are taken for granted (Kleinman and Copp 1993; Cylwik 2001).

My doctoral research journey

The issues discussed in this chapter emerged during my own experience as a doctoral student, researching a controversial process of restructuring in the Jewish community schools in Johannesburg, South Africa. The schools were under the auspices of the South African Jewish Board of Education (the Board), with which I had been associated for two decades (Herman 2004). I was investigating the restructuring in real time, as it evolved, in order to explain why it happened, how, with what impact and how the different stakeholders understood and experienced this process of change. The production of this qualitative case study relied heavily on interviews with various stakeholder groups (namely teachers, parents, managers, lay leaders of the schools and community leaders), observations (participant and non-participant), document analysis and informal conversations with members of the community. The research spanned three-and-a-half years, two of which were dedicated to fieldwork. During this time I was immersed in the study as both an insider (community member as well as a professional officer at the Board) and outsider (researcher) to the change process. As a result, I was thrown into a maelstrom of emotions: those of the participants (Marshak 1996) as well as my own.

As a doctoral student and a new member of the research fraternity, I was desperately trying to prove that I could separate the emotional and personal from the professional. In hindsight, as the following sections will clearly demonstrate, this was a pointless attempt that actually impeded my research. In what follows, I first set the context of my doctoral studies and discuss my position as both insider and outsider to the case and the emotions it induced. Second, I identify the range of emotions that impacted on and shaped my choices around the research processes. And last, I discuss how, as a novice researcher, I dealt (or rather did not deal) with these emotions and contrast it with the way in which other researchers manage their emotions in similar circumstances.

The context of the research and its emotions

The restructuring at the Jewish schools took place during the first few years of the new millennium as a result of financial and leadership crises. Initially, the process was perceived as a managerial restructuring that aimed at reducing debts by introducing market-based practices, such as efficiency, decentralisation and accountability, into the management of the community schools. However, as the process unfolded, it became apparent that the managerial restructuring was masking a religious restructuring whereby the secular/traditional majority was losing its dominance to the ultra-Orthodox minority.

The restructuring created turmoil in the community, especially as selected lay leaders, with the support of the Chief Rabbi and the community's financial elite, secretly appointed a new chief executive officer (CEO), giving him a free hand to manage the schools and to replace the professional officers of the Board. Suspicions grew as the CEO himself was an ultra-Orthodox Jew, and his remuneration was directly linked to the debt reduction achieved. Feelings of betrayal and doubt polarised the school community and ignited heated debates as stakeholders positioned themselves on opposite sides of the process.

The process of the change itself was experienced by the school community as too broad, autocratic and incoherent. During the interviews my respondents exhibited various emotions, mostly negative, such as denial ('nothing really changed'), fear of the future and despondent dependency ('it could be worse if the CEO left'), defeat and disempowerment ('what can I do?'), isolation and withdrawal ('who can you talk to?'), and division and suspicion ('they are all looking after themselves').

This emotional process of change was coupled with the insecurities experienced by this Jewish community as a result of shifting local, national and global conditions. Locally, a profound despondency had overtaken a once fairly privileged community due to emigration, crime and economic hardship in South Africa. Internationally, events and processes, such as the second *Intifada* in the Middle East, the rise of anti-Semitism worldwide and the South African government's pro-Palestinian stance further intensified feelings of insecurity and frustration in the South African Jewish community at the time of the restructuring of its schools.

The restructuring of the Jewish community schools, therefore, produced strong emotions in my research respondents and it was not possible for any Jewish researcher (like myself) to observe the process from a position of detachment. Various emotions were generated by my dual position as both insider and outsider to the research.

The emotions of the researcher as insider (community member)

The research affected me personally, ideologically and professionally; each level inducing myriad emotions. My retrenchment from my position as a professional officer at the Board at the early stage of the restructuring process presented me with both losses and opportunities. On the one hand, it provided me with a research topic worth pursuing, and the opportunity to focus on my doctoral studies, which I had begun a year earlier. On the other hand, I experienced the loss of community, position and income. Furthermore, as an educationalist who has been socialised in the discourse of 'teachers as professionals' and who has been adversely affected by managerialist reform, I found it difficult to applaud the top-down managerial process of change.

The religious aspect of the restructuring carried intense emotions for the respondents who were aware of it, and especially for me. As a traditional/secular Jew with liberal views, I was deeply disturbed when I observed the permeation of certain ultra-Orthodox practices into the schools, such as when girls over 12 were not allowed to perform in public, or when sex education was curtailed. I could not follow Peshkin's (1988) advice to separate my private-self from my research-self: what happened to the schools was happening to me, my family, colleagues and friends. My distress with these changes was accompanied by shame, concern and immense sadness.

The emotions of the researcher as an outsider (academic)

At the same time, my doctoral studies were presenting me with theoretical and conceptual challenges unparalleled to any other learning experience. I had to transform from being a practitioner to becoming a researcher. I struggled to grasp the complexities of the research journey (Jansen *et al.* 2004), such as finding a focus, formulating the research questions, critically engaging with the literature, finding a conceptual framework and mastering the competencies required for conducting research. Yet a focus on the anxieties involved with the technical competence of research learning, rather than on emotions generated by the case itself, does have some advantages. This view is articulated by Hockey (1996), who, as an ex-soldier, encountered an avalanche of emotions when he confronted military life again as a researcher. He maintained that a focus on his technical ability to conduct research helped him to disguise the emotional baggage he carried from his military experience.

My position as insider–outsider also produced frustration and guilt as I had to negotiate what Labaree (2003) identifies as transformation from the normative culture of the teaching profession and its effort to produce valued outcomes, to the analytical perspective of research and its effort to produce a valid explanation of an educational phenomenon. I had to fight my urge to intervene and resist the process in order not to jeopardise the integrity of my research. I was concerned that if I made known what I discovered or disclosed my views and emotions, this might block my access to certain stakeholders and information and could direct the interviews in a particular way.

As both insider and outsider I had real difficulty in clarifying my role to the members of the community whom I observed at different meetings, and probably also to myself. The CEO was reluctant to allow me an access as an academic (outsider), but could not deny me access as a parent and community member (insider). Subsequently, I was very hesitant when I requested interviews and sometimes had to wait a few days before I gathered up enough courage to approach certain stakeholders, especially those who support the new management. As I became more confident in my role as a researcher, I followed the CEO to every public meeting and openly took minutes of the proceedings. I was never refused entry but always felt an uninvited guest.

Emotions generated by the fieldwork

On the other hand, my emotional investment in the study acted as a positive force that motivated and sustained me throughout my research journey. Most of my respondents were also deeply involved in the restructuring process and used the space provided by the interviews or informal conversations to reconstruct their experiences and deal with their emotions. This benefited the study as I had eager-to-talk respondents. Some interviewees even found it therapeutic to speak to a researcher who seldom interrupted them and assured confidentiality and anonymity. The following excerpts from interviews demonstrate this point:

> Manager: But he [the CEO] didn't acknowledge me in any way – nothing.
> *Researcher: How does that make you feel?*

Manager: Angry. I do feel angry.

Researcher: Yes.

Manager: It's nice to talk about it – there's nobody to talk to about it … It's lonely and you're isolated and there isn't really anybody to share anything with.

Parent: That's why I quite enjoy … talking to you. [This is] not a conversation I can have with just anybody. You know, it's not something everybody can relate to – I will lose them somewhere along [the way].

This experience resonates with increasing demands on researchers to attend to the emotional needs of their respondents. Female researchers in particular stress the researchers' responsibility to care for their respondents and to use the interview as a therapeutic opportunity (Finch 1984; Owen 1996; Birch and Miller 2000; DeMarrais and Tisdale 2002; Mauthner *et al.* 2002). My role as a 'therapist' generated mixed feelings, mostly because I was not always a willing therapist. While listening and recording my respondents' experiences I harboured various feelings towards them, especially towards those informants whose values and perceptions clashed with mine. At times I felt anger at those stakeholders who seemed to comply with the restructuring in order not to jeopardise their personal advancement; I felt boredom ('I have heard this story before'), self-doubt ('How am I managing the interview? Am I probing enough? Am I biased?'), depression, frustration, irritation ('Don't they see what is going on?') and sometimes pity or sadness as I realised that many of my respondents were trapped in a 'Catch-22' situation. I did not articulate these feelings to my respondents, and even to myself they were not always clear. Like Wincup (2001), I was reluctant to be honest about negative feelings toward my interviewees. According to the researcher's 'display rule', I felt that I should act as if I empathised with the participants and agreed with their interpretations, or at least refrain from displaying disagreement. My research, therefore, involved 'emotional labour' (Hochschild 1983): not only acting out feelings such as surprise and confusion, but also hiding my own emotions and producing the necessary feeling that would encourage respondents to reveal their inner thoughts and trust me.

In hindsight, the denial or suppression of emotions created an unauthentic interview situation that limited the data I was able to collect. It was also energy-depleting and detrimental to my health – as manifested by severe headaches and sleepless nights during the research journey. A fitting example is the following extract from an interview, whereby a lay leader who was involved in bringing in the CEO and dismissing the previous management, articulated his discomfort in speaking to me about the process. Instead of acknowledging my discomfort and maybe using this moment of truth to start a real dialogue, I chose to pretend that I was unemotional about the process. Consequently, I missed an opportunity to engage in meaningful dialogue about the previous management:

Lay leader: Yes. And he [the previous director] didn't address the running of the system.

Researcher: What do you mean by that?

Lay leader: The Board itself was – I'm getting into sensitive territory. You were affected.

Researcher: Personally I'm very happy, so you don't have to worry about that (laugh).

Lay leader: I mean the Board was top heavy in the structure. The schools were also top heavy.

Kleinman and Copp (1993) rightly argue that researchers who ignore their negative feelings cannot use them to generate questions about the process. Gordon (1987) similarly discovered that arguing with interviewees aided the research. He suggests that expressing disagreement and saying what one thinks can be an engaging experience, constituting closeness rather than distance.

It was easier for me to feel a strong bond with interviewees who experienced the restructuring in a similar way to me. However, as I was emotionally attuned with them I was not always able to pick up disconfirming evidence. I also believe that in some cases I transferred my feelings into the interview; a process referred to by psychotherapists as counter transference. These slips and missed opportunities became apparent during the data analysis phase. For example, many respondents argued that 'nothing ha[d] changed' in the schools. I viewed this response as their defence mechanism or as an attempt to delude me, and thus I did not take cognisance of what they were really saying. It was only later that I realised that some community members were not aware of the ideological transformation that was so obvious to me. This prompted me to look for other explanations for their perceptions, such as hegemony. I therefore concur with Delagado-Gaitan (1993) that sharing the same background and positionality as the participants does not necessarily mean that the researcher is more informed about participants' feelings, values and practices.

An additional emotional source was my niggling feeling of guilt that I was taking advantage of my participants' distressing experiences to generate data for my research and that this made me a 'spy' in my community. Admittedly, I used my connections with community members to facilitate access to information, and, as a result, have struggled with the notion of deception. A number of researchers (Peshkin 1984; Griffiths 1998) are of the view that fieldwork is always associated with deception. The punishment for this deception, Peshkin correctly concedes, is self-inflicted guilt and anxiety that accompany researchers' consciousness as they strip off their mask.

Observation, whether as a non-participant or participant, was a distressful experience for me. I observed numerous annual general meetings (AGM) and parent–teacher association (PTA) meetings, conferences, and public and private meetings, either as an employee, a parent or a researcher. As I became more knowledgeable about the restructuring process and the 'behind the scene' micropolitics, I often wanted to shout out at meetings that what the information speakers were giving was simply a manipulation of the facts. On one occasion I could not tell a friend that a lay leader was deceiving her. I was often frustrated by my self-imposed silence, especially when I realised that by the time my findings would appear most of the processes would be completed, and most of those in charge would have achieved their immediate goals. A similar feeling of frustration was experienced by Hodkinson and Sparks (1993), more so when they realised that withholding important information from stakeholders contradicted their claim of empowering the participants.

During the advanced stage of the research – after the first data analysis phase and with my growing understanding of the process – I began to understand my personal loss as part of the community's shift to the 'right', became more confident as a researcher and more aware of my emotions. My interviews then became a dialogue between equals, negotiating meanings and testing hypotheses. It was at this stage that I experienced real learning and profound growth: the mask had been taken off and I was able to become a whole person again – the human and the research practitioner became one, both an emotional and a rational human being.

Emotions of data analysis

Some of the emotions that I had attempted to control during the interviews resurfaced in the data analysis phase. As this phase involved shifting of attitudes and values, it was often loaded with emotions generated by new learning and new understandings. Hochschild (1998: 6) makes this point when she argues that emotions emerge as a result of a newly grasped reality as it clashes with the template of prior expectation. McLaughlin (2003) adds that it is vital for researchers at this stage to be aware of their emotions in order to fight the temptation to alter or ignore data that challenges their understanding of the process.

I meticulously coded line-by-line 1,700 pages of interviews, 150 pages of my research journal and three files of documents using Atlas.ti. (computer-assisted qualitative data analysis software). Reading and analysing my research diary made me aware of my emotions, my hopes and fears, as well as my struggles to control them. Halfway through the decoding process I began to notice the synergies between the managerial and the ideological/religious restructuring, thus forming the conceptual framework of the study (Herman 2006b), and I had to recode all the text again. This rather mechanical task provided me with some emotional distance from the field and allowed me to put a semblance of order to my thoughts and emotions. Barr (1998), in her reflection on this stage of the research, similarly described how she read, reread, coded and recoded her transcripts 'until the anger and the pain began to subside and [she] began to see some patterns emerging' (p. 99).

The analysis process itself was a lone pursuit, imbued with feelings of missed opportunities as well as the excitement of new insights. As I read through the transcripts I realised, like Kanuha (2000), that there were many examples where I had overlooked some information, along with many of my taken-for-granted assumptions. I became aware of the moments when I did not allow my respondents to complete sentences or thoughts because I thought that I knew to what they were referring. I realised that my perception is one perspective of the situation along other ways of seeing. I began to voice my own emerging political, ideological and epistemological stances. I spent hours searching the internet and the libraries for literature that would help me make sense of my new reality. I neglected all my other 'normal' social obligations as mother, wife, daughter and friend – but felt no guilt. I was completely self-absorbed and incapable of focusing on anything other than my own learning and the emotions it generated.

The emotions of writing

The writing phase provided me with the first opportunity to let go of my emotions, yet it produced its own set of feelings. At the beginning, the huge volume of material that I had obsessively collected and coded overwhelmed me – I was stuck. How was I going to reduce this mountain of information into some 100,000 words of coherent text? Which data should I include and which information should I leave out? I had difficulty cutting out some data that I thought was important but which disclosed the identity of the interviewees. I occasionally felt that I deliberately wanted to give away the identity of some respondents and to use the knowledge I had gained to settle some scores; to reveal the manipulation and deception. At the same time I had to remind myself constantly of my ethical role as a researcher and of my commitment to ensure confidentiality and anonymity.

I began by writing a personal story of my experience and understanding of the restructuring process. I ignored the theoretical framework and just 'poured' it all out. In a way I was an interviewee putting on paper my side of the story. The result was a 100-page emotional, non-academic manuscript that had great therapeutic value for me. This manuscript was then put aside and I began to reconstruct another text in which I was able to bring the different perceptions and experiences together. Occasionally, my personal story filtered through and my writing slipped from the social to the personal and emotional. De-personalising the text was a long and difficult process that required repeated editing in order to detach myself from the data, to let go of emotions and to view the process from a social and theoretical perspective. My supervisors' input in this progression was vital as they constantly made me aware of examples where my emotions took over my academic writing.

The emotions of wrapping-up

After I completed the last line of my dissertation, I wept; my sense of relief and achievement was tinged with sadness and emptiness. My doctoral supervisor compares this period to antenatal depression experienced by some new mothers.

An added unexpected emotion was a feeling of alienation from my community. As the research questioned the Jewish community's ethos and narrative, I had lost my innocence and the uncritical manner in which I had viewed my surroundings, and became aware of the power relations and politics within the community. Carter and Delamont (1996) are right when they argue that fieldwork in any setting where either the researcher or the respondent is emotionally engaged changes the researcher forever. Bauman (2001) maintains that the biblical story of Adam and Eve describes a similar phenomenon. Adam and Eve's penalty for eating from the tree of knowledge was their banishment from the safety of the Garden of Eden, from paradise. A community (real or imagined) provides a sense of paradise and is a safe haven for those who accept and submit to its narrative. In another context, Peshkin (1984) also reports the feelings of estrangement and alienation from the field study, of being 'the odd man out'. For me, the feeling of estrangement from the field study meant alienation from my community. This also brought tensions into my home as my family did not go through the same process of transformation. Although they on the whole supported me, they also wanted me to tone down some of my criticism so as to not jeopardise their position in the community. It seems that researching one's own community should come with a warning: do so at your peril!

Interestingly, although I felt like the 'odd woman out', certain stakeholders did not perceive me as such. As mentioned before, during the study I became a confidant and a sounding board for many school members who eagerly unburdened themselves in the space provided by the research. As a result, by the end of the process I was emotionally exhausted and even resentful. I constantly had to remind myself that I had volunteered to take on this role for my own ambitions – to understand a process that could have an irrevocable impact on the community and to obtain a doctorate. This posed another ethical and emotional predicament: was it fair for me to stop being a sounding board once my fieldwork was complete and I no longer required the information? When I eventually detached myself from my respondents I felt guilty at having abandoned them.

It seems that exiting fieldwork is an emotional endeavour seldom mentioned in the research literature. Williamson (1996: 30) makes this point when he argues that 'despite the wisdom of research methods textbooks, it is often much harder to get out of the door than to get into it in the first place'.

The emotions of publication

The dissemination of data and publication of the study generated conflicting feelings. I struggled with a perennial problem affecting Jewish researchers: that is, the extent to which we would like to expose the 'inside' stories of our community to outsiders, especially as I was not indifferent to the community's feeling of isolation and depression in the post-1994 democratic South Africa. I constantly debated whether uncovering processes in the community and disseminating the research findings would mean that I was being disloyal to the community, and whether those who have a less favourable view of the community could exploit these findings.

Even though I have now published my dissertation as a book (Herman 2006a), I still wrestle with conflicting emotions. It is exhilarating seeing one's first book in print, yet there is constant uneasiness as to whether the book will have the desired impact. It seems that some emotional issues cannot be fully resolved, and that emotional turmoil is the price researchers have to pay when engaging in emotionally loaded and controversial study.

Reflection – dealing with the emotions of research

When I began my research I did not anticipate the vortex of emotions that would engulf my respondents and me, and I had no means of dealing with them. As demonstrated in this chapter I wasted vital energy controlling my emotions for the sake of objectivity and validity. At the same time I gained a deeper understanding of the process when I was able to acknowledge my emotions. It is evident that researchers need to manage their emotions not only in order to ease the emotional burden (which is important by itself), but also in order to explore who they are and what they believe or feel when they undertake research. Without this self-understanding researchers might not see or understand reflexively how they shape the story.

In my postdoctoral studies I reflected on my research journey and engaged with the literature on qualitative research in depth. It was comforting to me that other researchers, in their reflective accounts on qualitative studies, articulated similar errors of perception and lack of preparedness to deal with emotions that surfaced during the research process (see, for example, Kleinman 1991; Wilkins 1993; Sutton and Schurman 1988; Wincup 2001; DeMarrais and Tisdale 2002; Mauthner and Doucet 2003; Rager 2005). There is an argument that one can never prepare students for the research experience and that the only way to learn it is to actually do it (Ball 1990). In many aspects it is a rite of passage, and a high degree of understanding of the factors that impacted on the research is mostly achieved with hindsight (Mauthner and Doucet 2003). Although I fully agree with these statements, there are ways in which this emotional passage can be managed and supported. I do not imply that by managing emotions researchers could or should avoid the pain and ambiguities of the research process. I merely suggest that being aware of the emotions would enhance the quality of the research and facilitate the journey.

This reflective account underscores the role of writing as an emotional release. This includes the research diary, the writing of a personal account, the writing and rewriting of text, as well as the writing of this reflective account. The literature suggests other

291

means by which novice researchers manage their emotions, such as group support (Kleinman and Copp 1993; Sutton and Schurman 1988; DeMarrais and Tisdale 2002; McLaughlin 2003), anticipating the emotional level of the research (Sutton and Schurman 1988), enlisting the supervisor's support (Reason and Marshall 1987; McLaughlin 2003; Boucher and Smyth 2004) or even the support of a clinical psychologist (Sutton and Schurman 1988; Rager 2005).

The main problem is that doctoral students are often not aware of the emotional aspect of the research journey. Rager (2005) revealed that she did not discuss the personal or emotional impact of her research even with the sympathetic chair of the research committee because she had not encountered writing on the emotional facets of qualitative research, and she therefore felt that what was she experiencing 'was unique and best kept within [her] private circle of support'. Like Rager, I perceived my emotions as a personal matter that I had to overcome alone. I therefore support her call for more 'formal safeguards' during the research process and propose that doctoral students may be better prepared to manage their emotions if they would be exposed to researchers' reflective accounts (such as this one) on the role of emotions in research.

Concluding remark

Research learning is a complex process strewn with obstacles, anxieties and frustration as well as excitement and satisfaction. Many doctoral students never complete their journey. Perhaps the emotional price that they have to pay is just too high. This reflective account provides a glimpse into a relatively neglected, yet important, area and should be read together with other researchers' accounts. Even though each case study is unique and produces a distinctive set of emotions, there is some commonality. Further study of the emotions of research learning is needed in order to add conceptual substance to this notion, to gain a better understanding of the ways that researchers not only manage their emotions, but also integrate them into their research processes, and to provide practical suggestions to those responsible for designing and supervising doctoral studies.

References

Ball, S. (1990) Self-doubt and soft data: Social and technical trajectories in ethnographic fieldwork, *Qualitative Studies in Education*, 3(2): 157–71.

Barr, J. (1998) Theoretical voices and women's own voices: the stories of mature women students. In J. Ribbens and R. Edwards (Eds). *Feminist dilemmas in qualitative research: public knowledge and private lives*. London: Sage Publications, 87–102.

Bauman, Z. (2001) *Community: seeking safety in an insecure world*. Cambridge: Polity Press.

Bell, J. (1993) *Doing your research project: a guide for first-time researchers in education and social science*. 2nd edn. Milton Keynes: Open University Press.

Birch, M. and Miller, T. (2000) Inviting intimacy: the interview as therapeutic opportunity, *International Journal of Social Research Methodology*, 3(3): 189–202.

Boucher, C. and Smyth, A. (2004) Up close and personal: reflections on our experience of supervising research candidates who are using personal reflective techniques, *Reflective Practice*, 5(3): 345–56.

Carter, K. and Delamont, S. (Eds) (1996) *Qualitative research – The emotional dimension*. Aldershot: Ashgate Publishing Limited.

Cohen, L., Manion, L. and Morrison, K. (2000) *Research methods in education.* 5th edn. London and New York: Routledge Falmer.

Cylwik, H. (2001) Notes from the field: emotions of place in the production and interpretation of text, *International Journal of Social Research Methodology*, 4(3): 243–50.

Damasio, A. (1999) *The feeling of what happens: body and emotion in the making of consciousness.* New York: Harcourt Brace.

Delagado-Gaitan, C. (1993) Researching change and changing the researcher, *Harvard Educational Review*, 63(7): 389–411.

DeMarrais, K. and Tisdale, K. (2002) What happens when researchers inquire into difficult emotions? Reflection on studying women's anger through qualitative interviews, *Educational Psychology*, 37(2): 115–23.

Finch, J. (1984) It's great to have someone to talk to: the ethics and politics of interviewing women. In C. Bell and H. Roberts (Eds). *Social researching: politics, problems, practice.* London: Routledge and Kegan Paul, 70–87.

Gilbert, K. R. (Ed.) (2001) *The emotional nature of qualitative research.* Boca Raton, FL: CRC Press.

Gordon, D. F. (1987) Getting close by staying distance: fieldwork with proselytising groups, *Qualitative Sociology*, 10: 267–87.

Griffiths, M. (1998) Educational research for social justice – getting off the fence. Buckingham: Open University Press.

Hallowell, N., Lawton, J. and Gregory, S. (2005) *Reflections on research. The realties of doing research in the social sciences.* Maidenhead: Open University Press.

Herman, C. (2004) *Prophets and profits – Managerialism, fundamentalism and the restructuring of Jewish community schools in South Africa*, PhD Dissertation, University of Pretoria.

——(2006a) *Prophets and Profits – Managerialism and the restructuring of Jewish schools in South Africa.* Cape Town: HSRC Press.

——(2006b) Managerialism, fundamentalism, and the restructuring of faith-based community schools, *Educational Theory*, 56(2): 137–58.

Hochschild, A. R. (1983) *The managed heart, commercialization of human feeling.* Berkeley, CA: University of California.

——(1998) Sociology of emotion as a way of seeing. In G. Bendelow and S. J. Williams (Eds). *Emotions in social life, critical themes and contemporary issues.* London: Routledge Publishers, 3–15.

Hockey, J. (1996) Putting down smoke: emotion and engagement in participant observation. In K. Carter and S. Delamont (Eds). *Qualitative research – the emotional dimension.* Aldershot: Avebury, 12–27.

Hodkinson, P. and Sparks, A. C. (1993) To tell or not to tell? Reflecting on ethical dilemmas in stakeholder research, *Evaluation and Research in Education*, 7(3): 117–29.

Jansen, J. D., Herman, C. and Pillay, V. (2004) Research learning, *Journal of Education*, 34: 79–102.

Kanuha, V. K. (2000) Being native versus 'going native', *Social Work*, 45(5): 439–47.

Kleinman, S. (1991) Field-worker's feelings: what we feel, who we are, how we analyze. In W. B. Shaffir and R. A. Stebbins (Eds). *Experiencing fieldwork, an inside view of qualitative research.* Newbury Park, CA: Sage Publications, 184–95.

Kleinman, S. and Copp, M. A. (1993) *Emotions and fieldwork.* London: Sage Publications.

Labaree, D. F. (2003) The peculiar problems of preparing educational researchers, *Educational Researcher*, 32(4): 13–22.

Marshak, D. (1996) The emotional experience of school change: resistance, loss, and grief, *NASSP Bulletin*, 80(577): 72–8.

Mauthner, M., Birch, M., Jessop, J. and Miller, T. (Eds) (2002) *Ethics in Qualitative Research.* London: Sage Publications.

Mauthner, S. N. and Doucet, A. (2003) Reflexive accounts and accounts of reflexivity in qualitative data analysis, *Sociology*, 37(3): 413–31.

McLaughlin, C. (2003) The feeling of finding out: the role of emotions in research, *Educational Action Research*, 11(1): 65–79.

Owen, D. (1996) Men, emotions and the research process: the role of interviews in sensitive areas. In K. Carter and S. Delamont (Eds). *Qualitative research – the emotional dimension*. Aldershot: Avebury, 56–67.

Peshkin, A. (1984) Odd man out: the participant observer in an absolutist setting, *Sociology of Education*, 57: 254–64.

——(1988) Virtuous subjectivity: In the participant-observer's I's. In D. N. Berg and K. K. Smith (Eds). *The self in social inquiry*. Newbury Park, CA: Sage Publications, 267–81.

Rager, B. K. (2005) Self care and the qualitative researcher: when collecting data can break your heart, *Educational Researcher*. Online. (Available at www.aera.net/uploadedFiles/Publications/Journals/Educational_Researcher/3404/3404%20Rager%20PDF.pdf Accessed 5 November 2007).

Reason, P. and Marshall, J. (1987) Research as personal process. In D. Boud and V. Griffin (Eds). *Appreciating adult learning: from the learner's perspectives*. London: Kogan Page Publishers, 112–26.

Silverman, D. (2005) *Doing qualitative research: a practical handbook*. 2nd edn. London: Sage Publications.

Solomon, R. C. (2003) *What is an emotion? Classic and contemporary readings*. 2nd edn. New York: Oxford University Press.

Sutton, R. I. and Schurman, S. J. (1988) On studying emotional hot topics: lessons from an investigation of organizational death. In D. N. Berg and K. K. Smith (Eds). *The self in social inquiry*. Newbury Park, CA: Sage Publications, 333–49.

Van Maanen, J., Manning, P. K. and Miller, M. L. (1993) Editors' introduction. In S. Kleinman and M. A. Copp (Eds). *Emotions and fieldwork*. London: Sage Publications, vii-viii.

Wilkins, R. (1993) Taking it personally: a note on emotion and autobiography, *Sociology*, 27(1): 93–100.

Williamson, H. (1996) Systematic or sentimental? The place of feelings in social research. In K. Carter and S. Delamont (Eds). *Qualitative research – the emotional dimension*. Aldershot: Avebury, 28–41.

Wincup, E. (2001) Feminist research with women awaiting trial: the effects on participants in the qualitative research process. In K.R. Gilbert (Ed.). *The emotional nature of qualitative research*. Boca Raton, FL: CRC Press, 17–35.

Young, E. H. and Lee, R. M. (1996) Fieldworker feelings as data: 'emotion work' and 'feeling rules' in first person accounts of sociological fieldwork. In V. James and J. Gabe (Eds). *Health and the sociology of emotions*. Oxford: Blackwell Publishers, 97–113.

Part 4

Making a contribution to knowledge

P. Thomson and M. Walker

We take making a contribution to knowledge as multi-faceted and overlapping. This section is nested within the other sections of the book but the particular issues that we take up here concern the situated quality of doctoral work and what it can and cannot do.

Students and supervisors both need to make judgements about whether work is good enough to meet what counts as the standards of doctoral scholarship. We suggest that making a contribution to knowledge requires thinking about whose and what knowledge made available to whom, as well as the research communities within which such knowledge is produced. These practices take place within particular communities of practice, which are sometimes tightly framed and possibly in need of change. We also consider the relationships between doctoral research and policy in the light of increasing requirements for researchers to not just make a contribution to knowledge, but also to have effects on policy and practice.

i) Quality agendas

Lyn Yates considers two key aspects of quality agendas: the understandings of the disciplinary field and the changes currently affecting universities (discussed also in Part 1), changes that shape the experience of doctoral work by both supervisors and students. For example, an emphasis on targets for completion and efficiency shapes what kind of study a doctoral student might undertake. Yates discusses the importance of understanding that doctorate standards will be judged by the norms of the field (see also, for example, Piantanida and Garman, Volume 1, Chapter 20). Norms of writing, the staging of arguments, for example, will differ across fields and students need to show they have mastered these. If they work across disciplinary fields they will also need to justify their approach. Increasing concerns with ranking and reputation and with producing high-level economically productive knowledge workers (see Szkudlarek, Chapter 29) mean that governments and universities want more regulatory control over doctoral programmes and closer monitoring of supervision and supervisors. But this move to regulation also helps to make expectations of doctoral students explicit rather than being left to chance and the individual supervisor. Recent developments may risk emphasising the instrumental over the intrinsic – for example, what project will yield the most benefits in terms of publications. In all this, the question that student and supervisor need to ask is – is the work good enough? Yates shows that this is not only a hard question, but also one that is helped by a self-conscious understanding of context and criteria. The point is to know where you are going, as well as how to get there.

ii) Knowledges

This section returns to the site of knowledge-making also explored in Part 2 but focuses on different kinds of knowledges, challenging us to think more and more insightfully about knowledges and their production and reproduction.

Gary Anderson and Kathryn Herr focus on the dearth of knowledge produced by practitioners, as opposed to knowledge about practice and practitioners produced and disseminated by the academy. They argue that systematic, disciplined practitioner enquiry (in particular practitioner action research – PAR) can not only transform practice, but also build grounded theory; it is also transferable to other practice settings. They pursue their argument for PAR around four themes: that it is political; has its own rigour; there are many valid approaches; and that it produces knowledge uniquely suited to the realties and contexts of practitioners. They suggest that when knowledge is produced by practitioners that it is accorded respect or formal academic recognition as a contribution to professional knowledge and not only to professional development.

Peter Cole and Pat O'Riley also take up the knowledge 'cause', that of indigenous knowledges and epistemologies marginalised and othered in the academy, presented in the form of conversation and gathering infused with rich metaphors and deliberative exchanges. They explore what doctoral students might need to know about such marginalised knowledge (some, of course, will be from those marginalised communities and bearers of marginalised epistemologies). Cole and O'Riley ('Coyote' and 'Raven') resist dominant and patronising ways towards other knowledges and set themselves against narrow scholarship in favour of respectful research. They highlight problematic research practices that feed off the lives of communities – 'siphoning out of indigenous intellectual property' – for royalties and doctoral degrees. They address how it is that highly sensitive issues can be taken up as research topics because 'no subject matter is off limits' to academia. They suggest that researchers need to be people first; they have to learn to form 'real' relationships and they need to learn patience. Cole and O'Riley emphasise the richness of the knowledge held in communities so that at stake is a more inclusive approach to producing knowledge and a more generous and expansive view of different knowledges, and the possibilities also of hybrid knowledge construction.

Qing Gu emphasises the changing conditions and contexts of knowledge production within which doctoral students now work. Research students need to come to terms with their situatedness in an interconnected globalised world. Globalisation has been accompanied by the increasing mobility both of knowledge and of students, while information and communication technologies have transformed the way knowledge is produced, assessed and disseminated. What then does it mean, she asks, to be a research student in a time of change, in knowledge societies? She then explores the conditions shaping students' experiences in globalised times, pointing to the increasing emphasis on translating research into policy and impact, and that universities no longer have monopoly on knowledge production, which is now more widely socially distributed. This context and these conditions of the knowledge society and the knowledge economy have magnified the importance of knowledge, while also creating rich learning environments for students. Expanding knowledge within and across contexts further opens up blind and opaque spots in our knowledge.

The first three chapters emphasised knowledge and contexts of its production. Robert Lucas and John Willinsky explore who gets access to this scholarly knowledge; how widely is it disseminated? How open is access? These are not simply technical matters, nor matters only for academia. As Lucas and Willinsky explain, it is a matter of public good and public value to make research as accessible as possible to all who might find it useful so that rigorous, shared research can increase its contribution to the public good and do so globally. They first sketch the development of the Open Access Movement in the face of the soaring costs of journals to academic libraries across the world, and the beginnings of publication on the internet by scholars. Open access online journals soon followed. At stake are efforts to open science to review and critique and to innovation and development, and by opening publishing to enable new knowledge to be verified, legitimised and incorporated into larger bodies of work. They further suggest that this is an ethical matter where much research is publicly funded and ought to make its way back into public domains. They describe two routes to open access – archiving and open access journals – and suggest strategies for finding materials online and briefly describe open data as parallel development. For doctoral students the issue is that publishing scholarly work is changing and being transformed; doctoral students are positioned to influence such changes in different ways. Importantly, open access is a matter of equity enabling countries and communities far from metropolitan centres of academic power to 'join the conversations'.

iii) Making and participating in knowledge communities

The next section considers making a contribution to knowledge from the perspective of participation in knowledge communities. Continuing the theme of perspectives on knowledge, Szkudlarek opens up the debate about knowledge economies to which doctoral graduates as high-level knowledge workers are increasingly important in driving further economic growth. Whether overtly conscious of this policy climate in which advanced human capital is instrumental in policy terms, it shapes in one way and another experiences of undertaking doctoral education – why universities value it, how it is funded, how it is institutionally supported, why student mobility is such a key feature, why completion rates are much to the fore, and so on. Szkudlarek's chapter therefore invites doctoral students to reflect critically on the times in which they find themselves studying for a doctorate and through this understanding have the opportunity to exercise greater or more knowing agency with regard to their own doctoral training and the formation of their own scholarly identities framed by processes of knowledge production, institutional contexts and policy discourses. Szkudlarek brings all this together in his small-scale situated study in one Polish university where he asks doctoral students: What happens to knowledge in the context of being a doctoral student? From what the students say, it seems they are located both inside and outside the gates of academe, there but not quite in, struggling with the formation of new identities. Inclusion, exclusion, alienation, ambivalence, critical autonomy all work to co-create these emergent scholars. The chapter works to encourage thinking about this 'within–without' positioning and the mechanisms of power that underpin university and doctoral education structures and processes.

The next chapter is by Ian Menter, Joanna da Silviera Duarte and Radhika Gorur. They also argue the importance of doctoral researchers forming international networks. They describe the work of the European Education Research Association doctoral network as one example of the ways in which learned societies can support doctofical researchers to form new associations and globalised sensibilities. The Universitas 21 FINE network follows as an example of the ways in which formal coalitions of universities can also provide occasions and support for global doctoral and early career networking. Both examples cited do actively engage doctoral researchers in the formation of their network as well as in the design and organisation of its face to face and virtual operations. The authors note that one of the benefits of organisational mediation of international networking can be that inequalities of wealth and power can be addressed and alleviated so that all can participate equally.

iv) Policy linkages, impacts and effects

In this section we see the relationship between doctoral research and policy as flexible, and research influences on policy to be quite diverse and indirect and incremental for the most part, but not necessarily impossible. We do assume that the knowledge produced by doctoral students has the potential to influence policy, writ large or small, in some way and that it is important for doctoral students to give some thought to possible impact and influence of their own work and implications for social improvement and justice.

Bob Lingard's chapter considers more explicitly the impact of doctoral research on policy making in education. He first defines his understanding of educational research, which he takes to involve a concern with improving policy and practice in education (this is what makes it *educational*), as well as contributing to knowledge. What then of the connectivity between research and policy? For Lingard, research is only ever a contributing factor in education policy, given that policy making is a political activity in which policy makers will look for 'certain and replicated knowledge', or look to research that legitimates policy directions that have already been decided. Policy makers are more concerned with problem solving than complex knowledge. But doctoral researchers seek to make an original contribution to a field, to produce better conceptual understanding of an issue, to enhance understanding and to contribute to theory building. Thus, Lingard argues, research cultures and policy cultures are different and educational research and education policy making operate as 'contested terrains of competing interests and competing approaches'. Closely aligning educational research and policy may narrow what counts as evidence and knowledge and restrict critical approaches and ways of doing research. For Lingard, the slow percolation of research into policy and the generation of knowledge and critical understanding is arguably the most profound impact of doctoral research.

24
Quality agendas and doctoral work
The tacit, the new agendas, the changing contexts

L. Yates

There is a plethora of manuals and regulations on the subject of what counts as quality work, or even as good enough work in the doctorate. But the rules themselves are never the whole story; playing a game well is different from just knowing the formal rules of the game. In this chapter, I want to discuss some of the institutional and academic cultural arrangements that shape the judgements that will be made about whether the doctoral work is good enough. In particular, I want to talk about two things: the tacit elements of understanding a particular disciplinary field, and the wave of changes affecting universities today – the benchmarking and league tables, the concerns about productivity, research assessment exercises, the Bologna process, and the like. These are beginning to filter quite markedly how supervisors think about their work, and the kinds of pressures as well as supports doctoral students will encounter. They are also beginning to expand the ways in which success in doctoral work is being measured, no longer as just about the quality of the thesis itself, but extending to activities and outputs during and beyond the process of study.

Doctoral studies and expectations are not identical across different countries and fields and times. This chapter speaks less to doctoral studies in the USA, which continues to be a relatively self-contained system in which a solid array of coursework has always been part of the doctoral journey, than to changes that are being widely experienced in other parts of the world. Over the past decade governments have been increasingly taking some interest in doctoral studies and seeking to influence, measure and regulate what happens in doctoral education. At the same time, universities are themselves demonstrating a growing awareness of global student mobility and of international and competitive contexts in the ways they approach their own doctoral provision.

In Australia, as in much of Europe, it is only recently that doctoral studies have begun to be widely referred to as 'research *training*'. Especially in the humanities and social sciences, a doctorate was thought of rather as an opportunity offered to talented and already well-qualified individuals to produce something of worth, something that would be their own distinctive contribution to knowledge. 'Training' was something associated with vocational trades, not something that happened in universities; it was associated with learning an already defined activity rather than producing a new contribution to knowledge. Even now in my university, whereas bachelors and masters graduates are acknowledged at graduation ceremonies only by their name and a handshake, for doctoral graduates a short account is read out of the new contribution to knowledge that each has made and the chancellor stands and tips his hat as well as shaking hands with each new graduate. The sense that completing a doctorate is an individual achievement and a special achievement is strong.

But over the past decade doctoral studies have also very much become part of a *research training* agenda, both within universities and in the policies of governments and external agencies (Quality Assurance Agency for Higher Education 2004; University of Oxford 2009). More and more work is taking place to ensure that doctoral students have received proper training as part of their studies. New scrutiny is set up to ensure that those who 'supervise' them are sufficiently expert; that the environments they study in expose them sufficiently to what good quality research looks like; that they have been taught and assessed in courses that ensure they have mastered the principles of research in their particular fields. What is at issue here is not the individual and what they have achieved, but the process and its collective output to the university or to national research productivity.

This is a changing environment for many universities and supervisors. In this chapter I want to consider some of the paradoxes of doctoral work and some of these changes that have been taking place in the management and expectations of doctoral studies.

I begin by looking at the doctoral task and the importance of understanding that the doctorate is about being judged by norms of a field. In judging whether a sufficient/ good/doctoral-level contribution to knowledge has been made, examiners apply their *substantive* understandings about the state of play in the field of the doctoral endeavour: what is already known and what marks an advance. Methodology textbooks and doctoral regulations proliferate, but ultimately can never alone spell out this particular substantive standard. So 'norms of a field' is not a static set of criteria, and examiners' judgements, too, are also being influenced by changes, changes in the global arena of knowledge production, and in the way they themselves are being assessed.

The chapter then considers how today 'quality' has now also become a descriptor that can refer to the *conditions and activities* through which doctoral students study, not just the work they produce. It has become something that is seen as amenable to technical definition and benchmarking and measurement; something that is associated with national research assessment exercises, that is part of the research 'productivity' of universities. It might seem that these moves are not ones that need directly concern doctoral students, but in fact they are beginning to impact on the experience and pressures and ways doctoral students will be judged, and this is a second ongoing theme of this chapter.

The doctoral task, fields of knowledge and 'quality': why does it seem so hard?

Doctoral studies are surrounded by tightly specified university regulations and an industry of guides and self-help books. And yet for many students, getting a confident grasp of standards or criteria they should be working towards remains difficult. When the thesis is to be submitted, especially with non-quantitative studies, the question of whether it is 'good enough' remains troubling, often to supervisors as well as to students. The doctorate is the apex of the university system of qualifications, and the criteria for achieving it involves both a mastery element and a creative element: students must demonstrate that they have approached their topic in ways that meet the standards for doing research in that particular field, and they must make 'an original contribution to knowledge'. How do you achieve mastery? What counts as an original contribution? What are the actual standards? Studies of doctoral students suggest that they experience these demands differently from their previous, often successful, experiences as a student and as a professional in fields such as education or social work. Many doctoral students in social science and humanities go through periods of great anxiety and self-doubt during their studies (Holbrook and Johnston 1999).

A few years ago, a study of academics that asked them to recall their memories of doing their PhD brought forth what Lee and Williams (1999) called 'narratives of trauma'. Lee and Williams (1999) suggested in that study that the process of undertaking a doctorate brings forward not just the issue 'is it good enough?' but the question 'who am I?' In some cases, especially in fields where students do not proceed directly from undergraduate studies, this is about the difficulty of seeing oneself as a researcher rather than a teacher, or a social worker or a lawyer or a mother. But Lee and Williams (1999) were talking about a deeper level of doubt: 'Am I the autonomous expert, the self-actualising individual that the examination seeks to expose?'. The transitions involved are not easy ones for many students (especially women) to master.

When I did my own PhD I was struck by how different my experience was from that of friends who had undertaken PhDs in science. They had usually been part of a laboratory group before even beginning their doctorate; had been sent to conferences and co-published research papers while they were still completing honours degrees; embarked on their PhD as full-time (and young) students directly following completion of their honours year. They were used to working as part of a team in which a programme of investigation was already well established, and in which their own project was already defined within that broader programme of work. They had to develop and demonstrate mastery and creativity within their own project, but they were already working in their daily activities quite extensively with others in their field.

I embarked on my own PhD some years after I had completed my own honours year. I had gone into a professional field and worked for a few years in that, and had also broadened my background by undertaking two further masters degrees. When I did decide to take on a PhD it was as a part-time activity alongside my full-time employment. The first year of my study consisted of trying to create and develop a topic for the thesis. I had not been to an academic conference during my earlier studies, and the project I embarked on was one in which most of my time would be spent working by myself on the project. I would have periodic sessions with my supervisor, but I was not part of a joint programme of work that was identified as such. If I wanted the equivalent of the laboratory discussions along the way, it would be up to me or my supervisor to find or set up relevant contexts. These were not part of the day-to-day activity of how this field worked.

The issues about quality implicit in these contrasting experiences are in part about forms of knowledge and in part about the development of the person who undertakes doctoral work. Different disciplines and fields have developed different forms of knowledge making; different modes of what it means to demonstrate 'mastery' or 'a substantive original contribution to knowledge' in different fields. (Biglan 1973a; 1973b; Becher 1989; Parry 2007; Muller 2008). Some fields (or parts of fields) work with a strong and agreed paradigm from which the particular enquiry will begin. Here, students encounter a clear programme of work that has already marked out different problems for investigation. In other fields the conceptualisation of an object for study, and the assembling of what will be the theories as well as methods to be brought to bear on the study, is itself part of the task and achievement. Writers on disciplinarity often associate the first of these fields (the agreed paradigm and programme of work, what Biglan and Becher call the 'hards') with the physical sciences, and the second kind (the 'softs') with the humanities. But in many social science departments examples of both kinds of work, and both kinds of supervision arrangements, can be found.

Of course the metaphors 'hard' and 'soft' are problematic and misleading to the extent that they suggest a hierarchy of degrees of difficulty, and they under estimate the kind of complexity and scrutiny that is part of the testing in the so-called soft approaches. But they do point to some relevant differences in the *experiences* of the researcher and research students in different kinds of research environment. For example, in the department where I undertook my own study, many students were working on issues related to English as a Second Language or English as a Foreign Language. They often drew on a broadly common set of existing theories, and then designed a project that would test out and refine an aspect of a theory by focusing in more detail on a particular group, or a particular setting, or a particular element of pedagogy or language. My own thesis was on 'Curriculum theory and non-sexist education': it was about putting together some new questions for a field as well as working out ways to provide argument and evidence about this.

Different kinds of disciplinary approach have implications for how supervisors work, and for how recognition is achieved by students. In fields that are more discursive and fluid in their boundaries, and in many professional fields such as education, supervision can be a greater chore for supervisors than in fields where they are directly contributing to the supervisor's own programme of research, because supervisors often supervise outside their own specific research focus area (Neumann *et al.* 2002). In these cases, supervisors need to put more time into reading and understanding the work students are doing, and the kind of project they are putting together, and they will not be experts on all parts of the study. In areas of this kind, supervisors' lack of expertise across the whole project may be experienced by students as a personal failing of the supervisor, when it is a reflection of the kind of knowledge being built or project being undertaken, a result of the fluid and changing and interdisciplinary forms of investigation, and also in many cases a result of the conditions (such as growing and unrealistic university workload) of the supervisor(s). Nevertheless this kind of experience, which many students in humanities and social sciences experienced in the past, is beginning to be seen as unacceptable as authorities take a closer scrutiny of completions and 'quality' supervision. Students may now experience less freedom to design a study themselves, and more pressure to tie their work to explicit 'research strengths' of a supervisor or department. The pressure is to move PhD studies in other fields to more closely approximate those that characterised science.

In work that is at the humanities end of the social sciences some supervisors may see it as inappropriate to give too much direction into the work being created. Their image of the successful student is of one whose work is clearly 'their own' distinctive contribution. Supervisors are often influenced by the experience they themselves had as doctoral students, and many of those who supervise today experienced some form of that tradition of expecting considerable autonomy and initiative on the part of the student (Lee and Williams 1999). However, with the national 'quality supervision' agendas, this older view is now under some process of enforced modification as the move to see all doctoral work as 'training' becomes more embedded.

Different conceptions of good research are evident in traditions of authorship of publications emerging from doctoral studies. In fields with traditions of multiple authors, there is an implicit understanding that the research is only possible because of a programme of research in which resources are available (both financial and human), and related work is happening; and supervisors and others are acknowledged for their contributions to the work of the main researcher on a particular project. In fields where single authors have been the norm, there has been more emphasis on the idea of a doctorate or of research as an individual's own creative production. Because in the case of the paradigm-focused fields there is more clarity and consensus about what a particular project has added, some writers see the task of achieving recognition in the sole-authored 'creative' fields as more difficult than in the laboratory forms of research:

> Because of higher agreement and interdependence, innovative work by young scholars in [hard paradigm, science] disciplines is more easily recognised than in [soft paradigm, lacking consensus] disciplines, where it is easier to be overlooked [...] Young scholars find it difficult to break into [the latter] disciplines. One consequence is that there are age differences in discovery patterns, summed up [in Merton's ironic comment] 'This sort of thing can thus foster the illusion that good mathematicians die young, but that, say, good sociologists linger on forever'.
>
> Muller 2008

Against this, one could consider my own experience as a judge on a national 'best thesis' committee for a number of years. In the three years (2002–4) I was on this committee, at least half of the Education theses universities had submitted as their 'best' for the previous year were praised by examiners as having broken conventions in some way (Yates 2004). This may have reflected a particular time-specific period, a time in which poststructural theories were becoming conventional in the field, and in which being seen to break rules was part of a new convention of the field (and this may again be changing as 'evidence-based' discourse takes hold). But it may also reflect a broader criterion for judging quality in doctoral research: that rule-following (training) may allow a thesis to be seen as adequate, but to be recognised as prize-winning or as a high level of achievement, a thesis is expected to have done something that more clearly goes beyond the rules with which it has begun. Achieving some creative output is not necessarily a mysterious inspiration-dependent activity. One classic way of constructing a thesis, in hard paradigm fields as well as in what Muller (2008) and others call 'soft' ones, is to bring to a topic or question some different theories or strands of work that have not previously been brought together in that context.

Publication and authorship: some changing pressures and norms

The different cultures and traditions of disciplinary fields are themselves changing as greater government scrutiny and regulation enters universities, and as common measures of benchmarking research achievement begin to spread across fields and across the world. This can be seen concretely in relation to protocols of authorship. In fields where multiple authorship has been a norm (psychology for example), past practices of automatically including the professor of the department even if they had played no direct role in the research are now seen as inappropriate (the 'Vancouver Protocol', uniformly mandated by all editors of biomedical journals www.icmje.org/, requires direct involvement in conception and design, drafting of the article and approval of the final version for authorship credit to be given). Conversely, in fields where single authorship has been the norm, that practice is coming under pressure within universities, as supervisors have to account for their own productivity (that is, the number of their publications are literally counted each year, and can affect the funding that flows to the department and to the university), and as national bodies begin to see co-authored publication as a sign of good supervision practices.

Today in the social sciences, students are likely to encounter much earlier than they once would have some pressure to write and submit a publication prior to finishing the thesis. Today, quality is measured not just by examiners' reports on the thesis itself, but by what is produced during the candidature and signs of external 'impact' of the work beyond the thesis. Just recently a colleague told me that she was coming under pressure to change a longstanding conference policy because of new pressures on supervisors to be able to co-author and count their work with students. The conference in question had always limited the number of submissions on which a person could be named as an author and most doctoral students had previously submitted single-authored papers, given that supervisors would have multiple students presenting. But at least one university had now apparently decreed that supervisors must be named co-authors on all their students' publications. For the university, that rule would ensure that the maximum count is made of that university's research productivity, but it would also even the playing field for supervisors, where previously some had normally had co-author credit and others had not. On the other hand, it is probable that a blanket rule such as this would be in breach of the Vancouver Protocol on authorship. Clearly, issues of ethics and of recognition are involved in these changing practices. The worry for the student is whether their own contribution will be diminished by naming their supervisor as co-author; the concern for the supervisor is that their work and contribution is made invisible when they are not named. And each may have different views of the extent of the contribution that has actually been made by the supervisor.

The tacit elements of standards

Demonstrating quality in doctoral work involves some induction into the culture of the field of study and some ability to speak as a member rather than an outsider to the culture, an ability to identify the way in which the new work connects with, changes, adds to the field. This placing of work involves voice, not just knowledge about the research literature; and understandings about what to emphasise or elide (Kamler and Thomson 2006).

Attendance at conferences and seminars may be even more important to those working on more individualised projects and kinds of theses than those where the paradigm, questions and methods are more explicitly agreed within the field, and where the student is working as part of a group. Demonstrating adequate understanding of where a field is, and that the new thesis has made a good creative contribution to it in these individualised projects is much more a product of the writing itself, of style and voice and editorial judgement. It is about quite subtle abilities to place the discussion: to know how much to say about particular areas of the literature, and what kind of criticism of other theories sounds informed and expert rather than merely brash. The issue of tone is one that is caught as much as taught, and it matters.

The issue of language and tone for thesis writing has become more problematic in recent times, in part because of the increasing numbers of students writing in a language (usually English) that is not their first language; and in part because of the growing number of interdisciplinary theses. Universities have been very eager to draw international fee-paying students, but in many of them this has led to considerable debate about the standards of language required for admission to doctoral studies, and also the level of editing assistance that is proper.

- A thesis must express the candidate's voice
- The integrity of the work relies on the thesis as demonstrably the candidate's work and must indicate that the candidate has the ability to write and argue with clarity
- Only in rare and exceptional circumstances and with the knowledge and support of supervisors, should students use paid editorial assistance from an outside source. The use of third party editorial assistance, either paid or voluntary, must be acknowledged in the preface and is limited to the guidelines adopted by the University.

Decisions on these issues continue to be difficult ones for examining bodies, because they recognise that often the writing (tone, choice of words, emphasis and the like) *is* the research or the research contribution (Lee 1998). It is not that the language is merely a vehicle for some research achievement that is separable from it. And even in fields that have findings that can be expressed in numbers or graphs, demonstrating a level of facility with language is seen as one expectation of achieving a doctorate. So regulations commonly try to spell out what forms of editorial help are legitimate and what are illegitimate. Given international student mobility as well as a growing development of co-badged PhDs (such as the co-tutelle agreements between France and designated institutions in other countries), these practices are likely to be under some continuing review. But for the present, the expectation remains strong that the doctorate must make apparent 'the voice' of the student themselves, must demonstrate their own ability to express themselves.

Norms of writing also differ between fields: first person reflexive narrative is not just acceptable but methodologically necessary in some kinds of enquiry; 'objective' distance is methodologically intrinsic in others. But even more subtly, the staging of arguments differs in different fields. A social science-oriented study on identity and young people with a particular kind of illness may need to meet different norms if it is being undertaken within a university medical faculty, than within a faculty of social science, even if similar theories are being drawn on. Given changing flows of knowledge, and calls to cross-disciplinarity, many students now have to confront quite explicitly the question of how they intend to write and for whom (for which traditions or kinds of departments and journals) they should write. My own university recommends that this be a discussion students and supervisors should take up explicitly at the beginning of the candidature – and in the case of interdisciplinary theses, that both supervisors need to be clear and in agreement about the approach that is to be taken.

Changing times, changing fields of knowledge

One of the characteristics of knowledge in the late twentieth and twenty-first centuries is its rate of change and its interconnectedness. This raises one of the paradoxes of doctoral work. To succeed, students will have to show they have mastered the norms of what it is to do good research in their field, but to do good or interesting work they need to be open to ideas and theories and interests from areas that may lie outside their field at the time they begin their project.

One of the reasons many universities now are arranging cross-disciplinary seminars for graduate students; or are wanting students to be closely tied to good research groups who themselves are likely to be interacting with new ideas and connections from other areas, is to help support this immersion in fields of enquiry, which at the top levels, the apex of the discipline, are constantly changing and reinventing themselves (Bernstein 1971). Inspirations and possibilities for original projects or for potentially new kinds of interpretations often come from putting previously separate strands of thinking together.

But at the same time, a doctorate, especially in its 'research training' persona, is a certification of mastery, a demonstration that the candidate is a qualified researcher. The problem for students and supervisors is how this is to be done when the project draws on lines of enquiry that have some different histories and norms for what good research looks like. Some element of this problem is inherent in constructing most doctoral projects. But it is more acute when the project wants to draw on traditions that might be seen as at odds with each other in terms of how they approach the world. Here, students need to be able to explain and justify the logic of their own study overall, which is a quite different task from being able to understand and defend particular methods within it and is one of the aspects of the project building that students find most difficult (Yates 2004). A common example of this is that often feminist theses or theses in fields such as education or social work want to work with a commitment of collaboration and non-hierarchy in relation to their research subjects, and to making central the voice of the people they study; but they also have often been influenced by critical or poststructural theories (of Foucault and the like), which do not set up a humanist relationship between researcher and research. Here, the thesis needs to be able to defend not only why these different commitments and ways of doing research are both of interest in relation to the proposed topic, but also concretely and in terms of the design and organisation of the thesis, how the contending assumptions are to be put together and enacted.

Although some task of putting together different traditions and arguments about research is common in most theses, it becomes more difficult as universities encourage cross-disciplinary proposals and as universities themselves restructure and faculties take on new forms. Nisselle and Duncan (2008) discuss a range of epistemological, academic and practical challenges and strategies for students who want to engage in trans-disciplinary projects with supervisors in more than one department. They warn of the need to find supervisors who can be complementary rather than unfeasibly disparate in their expectations, and caution students

- Be clear who will drive decisions about how to disseminate the research and how this might change across the course of the candidature. Will this be driven by impact factors of journals, the intended audiences or both?
- Engage in open discussions about authorship [...] Different disciplines have different traditions regarding what constitutes an original contribution and how this is recognised in the order of authors.
- Make an explicit decision about what discipline the examiners of the thesis will work within. This will influence the style, structure and format of the thesis.

Nisselle and Duncan 2008: 151

Nisselle and Duncan (2008) argue that students who are working across different departments need to think about where they are located physically, as different departments have different expectations of workload, supervision practices and the like. These issues are particularly acute if students want to combine studies that envisage a strong professional audience as the intended arena of impact of a study and disciplines with departments that recognise only 'academic' arenas of productivity.

Quality: the external environment

Thanks to the OECD and the EU and the growth of international rankings and ratings of various kinds, governments now want to measure and compare and steer what takes place in doctoral programmes. Doctorates are seen as part of economic productivity, as training, so it matters that they be efficient (thus the Bologna Process moves to limit the length of doctorates), that they be working on problems that governments consider significant (hence moves to tie doctoral scholarships to grants to supervisors, which themselves are shaped by declarations of national research priorities), that they have consistent standards in the product that they give rise to (the doctoral graduate). These moves impact on doctoral students both directly and indirectly.

Some positives: induction becomes an explicit norm rather than a hidden curriculum

The moves to regulate the doctoral experience through the UK Quality Assurance Agency and like bodies have the value of not leaving the student's induction to the vagaries of their different supervisors. The new regulations are intended to make sure that students have a defined minimum of taught foundations for the work in terms of methodology courses, and that their supervisors or advisers are themselves competent researchers and able to give good advice – this has not always been the case in the past. Expectations about publications, about criteria in the examining process, and discussion about what is going to make a difference in making a career beyond the thesis are now all likely to be included in the doctoral programme, not left to chance. And there is less chance that students will be left unnoticed when they are struggling or slipping away: regular monitoring, progress reports and hurdles are set in place to act as early warning systems. As well, there is a greater understanding of the need to connect students to an international research community. Institutions are likely to encourage and support travel to conferences or other universities. So these new regulations provide some safety-nets, some foundations and some opportunities.

Some new pressures: efficiencies and moves to a standard template

The Bologna process, the greater benchmarking between countries, the greater auditing of universities in general brings with it a higher degree of monitoring of the progress of each doctoral student. Students will experience more pressure and surveillance to move through their programmes at a regular rate (just as in undergraduate studies the US-based 'GPA' has begun to infiltrate many systems in which previously the first degree was accepted as an opportunity for students to do a range of things, not just apply themselves to getting the best possible grade in every subject). A decade ago, Leonard (1997) wrote about this pressure that was just beginning to be felt:

> In the current debates, the dominant – government – discourse concerns the need to make the PhD a training for high quality generic researchers [...] relevant to the needs of employment and the nation's economic growth and competitiveness. The PhD is apprenticeship work which should be completed promptly.
>
> Against this, debate is finally being joined more systematically by those who take an 'education' stance: who say a PhD is about personal development, growth and satisfaction; and that unlike a PhD in science or engineering, a social science or humanities thesis produces important original work, which takes time.
>
> Leonard 1997

But a decade later, the debate Leonard (1997) talks about has largely been lost. There is a broad consensus, at least in regulations and monitoring, that doctoral studies should be held to a common template, held to efficiency targets with sanctions for those who do not complete in a limited time, monitored for evidence of regular progression and milestones. From the point of view of external bodies, it is the apprenticeship and economic productivity model of the PhD that now dominates.

Quality as proxies and an enhanced attention to what can be measured

A good deal of benchmarking and accounting by external agencies uses quantification and proxies: time to complete; numbers of students; numbers of publications, and the like. There is a much more emphasis on indicators outside the judgement of the quality of the thesis itself by a very small number of examiners: evidence of published papers, impact and commercialisation during and beyond the thesis. In some ways this is helpful for students in the non-sciences. Traditionally, science students in the laboratory learnt very early about applying for grants, and what counted in terms of achievement (hierarchies of journals, etc.), whereas for many non-science students this was seen as something they might think about after their doctorate, if they went on to academic employment. Now this is on the agenda from the beginning. But the price is a potential distortion of the enterprise: less emphasis on the open invitation to think deeply about what is worth studying; and more emphasis on what kind of project will produce good publication opportunities and indicators in the time available. Of course, this is not necessarily a binary situation in which only one or the other emphasis can be in play. The danger of moving too far towards a pragmatic and instrumental focus is to lose the interest that sustains the work on the thesis. The danger of worrying too little about the pragmatics is not completing the study, losing the scholarship, not getting a job beyond the thesis.

Doctoral studies and the changing environment: summary and conclusion

The basis from which I've reflected on current changes and agendas for doctoral work in this chapter reflects three of my own ongoing interests in this area: an interest in knowledge and disciplinarity and changing forms of that (Yates and Collins forthcoming 2010; Mauthner and Doucet 2008); an interest in government steering of universities and research agendas, and effects that is having on the substance of the work being done (Yates 2005; 2009); and an interest in subjectivity and identity, and how students and supervisors are likely to experience the changing environment (Yates 2004). The changes for doctoral studies in education and social science I have been talking about in the chapter relate to all three.

The change that is likely to be most obvious to supervisors, and to some extent to students, will be the regulatory regime that now more closely monitors the work they do, and requires that a range of practices that were once unevenly present across departments and universities (explicit guidelines about the doctoral progress; courses and seminars to provide adequate foundations and peer support; some monitoring of supervisor adequacy) are now routine. As I have discussed in the later parts of the chapter, these practices may be experienced as new forms of intrusion and restriction, but to some extent they do try to extend to all students the forms of induction and support that only some students received previously.

But what is also happening within these changes is a changing approach to knowledge building itself, one that may lead to more fundamental changes in the nature of disciplinary fields. The case of authorship practices discussed earlier in the chapter is a good example of changes that are happening, and whose eventual outcome is as yet undetermined. As governments, not just universities, insist on regulating and finding indicators to measure the quality and impact of the work universities do, we are moving towards a single template for doctoral work and for assessing research itself. The direction of change is towards having all research and all doctoral study take on characteristics traditionally associated with the physical sciences (knowledge building as an enterprise of research teams not individuals; outputs evident in quantity of publications; emphasis on training and standards), and away from accepting characteristics associated with some parts of the professional and social sciences (mature students who themselves want to decide on the project, and who do not necessarily want to move on to work in universities rather than their professional field; or a valuing of the iconoclastic and creative and autonomous brilliant mind, which sees guidance rather than critical feedback from a supervisor as a sign of weakness).

But the regulatory and funding context is just one contributor to changing forms of knowledge production and a changing context for the doctorate. As knowledge building and transformations in fundamentals become more rapid in many areas (especially in the physical and technological sciences); as universities reorganise faculties and departments and no longer name them according to traditional disciplinary fields; as new forms of cross-disciplinary and academic/professional collaborations are encouraged, the tasks for doctoral work too must change. Understanding this broader context, and being able to explain where a particular thesis project is coming in to it, becomes a new essential and self-conscious task of the doctoral study.

References

Becher, A. (1989) *Academic Tribes and Territories*. Milton Keynes: Open University Press.
Bernstein, B. (1971) On the classification and framing of educational knowledge. In M. F. D. Young (Ed.). *Knowledge and Control: new directions for the sociology of education*. London: MacMillan.

Biglan, A. (1973a) The characteristics of subject matter in different academic areas, *Journal of Applied Psychology*, 53(3): 195–203.

——(1973b) Relationships between subject matter characteristics and the structure and output of university departments, *Journal of Applied Psychology*, 53(3): 204–13.

Holbrook, A. and Johnston, S. (Eds) (1999) *Supervision of Postgraduate Research in Education*. Coldstream: Australian Association for Research in Education.

Kamler, B. and Thomson, P. (2006) *Helping Doctoral Students Write: Pedagogies for supervision*. London: Routledge.

Lee, A. (1998) Doctoral research as writing. In J. Higgs (Ed.). *Writing Qualitative Research*. Sydney: Hampden Press.

Lee, A. and Williams, C. (1999) Forged in fire: Narratives of trauma in PhD Pedagogy, *Southern Review*, 32(1): 119–27.

Leonard, D. (1997) Gender and doctoral studies. In N. Graves and V. Varma (Eds). *Working for a Doctorate: A guide for the humanities and social sciences*. London: Routledge.

Mauthner, N. and Doucet, A. (2008) 'Knowledge once divided can be hard to put together again': An epistemological critique of collaborative and team-based research practices, *Sociology*, 42(5): 971–85.

Muller, J. (2008) *What good is knowledge? Specialisation and genericism in a global world*. Paper presented at the ECER 2008, From Teaching to Learning? Conference, Gothenberg.

Neumann, R., Parry, S. and Becher, A. (2002) Teaching and learning in their disciplinary contexts: A conceptual analysis, *Studies in Higher Education*, 27(4): 406–17.

Nisselle, A. E. and Duncan, R. E. (2008) Multiple supervisors from multiple disciplines: Lessons from the past as multidisciplinary supervision becomes the way of the future, *Traffic*, 10: 143–65.

Parry, S. (2007) *Disciplines and Doctorates*. Dordrecht: Springer.

Quality Assurance Agency for Higher Education (UK) (2004) *Code of Practice for the Assurance of Academic Quality and Standards in Higher Education*. Mansfield: QAA.

University of Oxford (2009) *Trends in Doctoral Education*. (Available at www.learning.ox.ac.uk/rsv.php?page=325 Accessed 24 April 2009).

University of Melbourne (2009) *PhD Handbook*. (Available at www.gradresearch.unimelb.edu.au/current/phdhbk/thesis.html Accessed 24 April 2009).

Yates, L. (2004) *What does good education research look like? Situating a field and its practices*. Maidenhead: Open University Press.

——(2005) Is impact a measure of quality? Some reflections on the research 'quality and impact' assessment agendas, *European Education Research Journal* 4(4): 391–403.

——(2009) The quality and impact agenda in Australia, in T. Besley (Ed.). *Assessing the Quality of Research in Higher Education*, Rotterdam: Sense Publishers.

Yates, L. and Collins, C. (2010) The absence of knowledge in Australian curriculum reformulations? *European Journal of Education*, 45(1).

25

Generating practitioner knowledge through practitioner action research

Moving from local to public knowledge

G. L. Anderson and K. Herr

In most applied fields, whether education, nursing, social work or business, knowledge is generated not by practitioners in those fields, but rather by university researchers. The education of practitioners does not often include much in the way of preparation of them as producers of research; if research coursework is included, it is commonly approached with the idea of practitioners being critical consumers of research that someone else, often an academic, produces. When practitioner action research is taught, it is taught with the goal of producing local knowledge to be fed back into one's own practice, rather than producing public knowledge to be consumed by other practitioners and/or researchers. Beyond the lack of useful preparation to produce research, the organisations in which practitioners work do not often provide incentives for the production of original research. And, although many dissertations in applied fields are done by part-time doctoral students who are working as teachers, social workers, managers, and nurses, they are often dissuaded from conducting research in the settings in which they work for a variety of epistemological, political or ethical reasons.

The dearth of practitioner knowledge produced and disseminated by practitioners trained in research methodology leaves universities and research institutes with a monopoly on producing knowledge about practice. This has traditionally led to a single model of research generation, dissemination and implementation in which practitioners are often pathologised for not faithfully implementing 'evidence-based' practices developed by researchers located at universities and research institutes. For example, teachers are expected to faithfully implement curricula step-by-step with little or no deviation, as the curriculum has been 'debugged' though experimental research designs. Faithful implementation of these research vetted teaching practices is ensured through high stakes testing, instructional 'coaches' and administrative 'walk throughs'.

Research done in universities can reinforce these disciplinary practices. As Schon (1995) noted, schools of education have agreed to view professional practice as though it consisted of the application of science or systematic knowledge to the instrumental problems of practice. Under girded by the adoption of technical rationality, this view of professional knowledge frames practice as 'instrumental, consisting in adjusting technical means to ends that are clear, fixed, and internally consistent, and that instrumental practice becomes professional when it is based on the science or systematic knowledge produced by the schools of higher learning' (Schon 1995: 29). A subsequent body of research succeeded in legitimating knowledge generated via critical and feminist researchers, often utilising qualitative methods of enquiry. Unfortunately, a more recent and sustained call to return to 'scientifically based' and 'evidence-based' practices, has undermined even these now well-established modes of enquiry. If qualitative research has been rendered suspect, practitioner action research is located somewhere out beyond the pale.

Although practitioners are encouraged to do action research studies in their organisations that produce local knowledge to be recycled back into their daily practice, such knowledge is not viewed as formal knowledge, nor is it viewed as making a contribution to a professional knowledge base to be widely shared. This chapter will discuss implications for practitioners doing dissertation research aimed at contributing to both practitioner as well as the wider knowledge base. We will focus on the use of practitioner action research as a methodology well suited to making such a contribution. As an exemplar, we will locate the conversation within the field of Education, but we believe that these tensions between practitioner and formal knowledge, as well as the possibilities of practitioner action research, become apparent in many applied fields.

Practitioner knowledges

Although most professions have a knowledge base that is taught in university programmes, such programmes are often criticised for being out of touch with the realities of practice. One intractable dilemma evident in nearly all professions is the question of why some excel in their chosen field and why others remain merely competent or even mediocre. The Federal No Child Left Behind legislation passed in 2001 in the USA called for a 'highly qualified teacher' in every classroom, but beyond making sure teachers are appropriately certified in the field in which they are teaching, there is limited discussion of what constitutes 'highly qualified'. Several authors have attempted to look across various professions for an understanding of the nature of professional knowledge and how it is acquired and utilised. Schon (1983) explored through case studies how reflective practitioners acquired and refined their knowledge over time. Sternberg and Horvath (1999) gathered together researchers in various fields of practice to explore the role of tacit knowledge in professional practice.

Most agree that practitioner knowledge is a combination of tacit knowledge acquired through years of practice and more formal knowledge acquired though university coursework, internships, workshops and professional reading. In Education, there is a move to create programmes that are more practice-based, in which new teachers or administrators apprentice with a veteran practitioner. Alternative certification programmes often require less university coursework and recruit candidates from other areas of work. However, although many support practitioner action research and greater respect for the knowledge practitioners have acquired though years of practice, most also recognise that practitioner knowledge is also full of myths and prejudices that require some form of problematisation and interrogation (Tripp 1994). Raw practitioner narratives and anecdotes too often contain unexamined theories-in-use (Argyris and Schon 1974), unsystematic observations and personal prejudice. It would be a mistake to naïvely enthrone practitioner knowledge as superior to other sources of knowledge. In fact, without processes of interrogation and enquiry, commonly held beliefs and practices can reproduce views antithetical to the production of new knowledge. But it is worth asking how both new and experienced practitioners can continue to add to their knowledge domains and how practitioner action research can encourage the refinement of everyday practices while adding to this overall knowledge base.

Although we do not advocate in this chapter the abandonment of a traditional model of knowledge use and generation, we do advocate the exploration of alternative ways of thinking about how knowledge of professional practices can be produced and used. Our thinking is that when practitioners begin to see themselves as generators of knowledge, they are more likely, not less, to seek out and use research done by 'outsiders'. But neither do we advocate the dissemination of mere anecdotal narratives and war stories as constituting a new practitioner knowledge base. We do believe, however, that intentional, systematic, and disciplined enquiry on educational practice by insiders or insider–outsider teams, has great potential for challenging, confirming and extending current theory, and for identifying new dimensions of practice for study.

Unfortunately, practitioner knowledge, even when it represents disciplined enquiry, is often relegated to categories such as practical knowledge and is not seen as measuring up to the rigour of formal knowledge production (Fenstermacher 1994; Huberman 1996; Richardson 1994). This gives academics permission to ignore action research, because it is not viewed as a serious partner in the generation of formal knowledge. These status tensions are often played out in practitioner-oriented doctoral programmes that abandon rigour in their curricula because students do not do 'real' research. Or, practitioner action research is seen as appropriate for practice-oriented EdD programmes but not those conferring the more research oriented PhD. We argue instead that action-oriented, insider research forces a redefinition of *rigour* in research and that it has both local and external validity in that its results can be used for the immediate transformation of practice, the building of grounded theory and the transference of knowledge to other settings (Anderson *et al.* 2007; Anderson and Jones 2000).

What is practitioner action research?

A hallmark of much traditional research is the 'objective' stance of the researcher who attempts to study social reality via decontextualised variables or observations conducted in such a way that the researcher does not disturb the natural setting. Practitioner action researchers define their work differently in that their research is all about delving deeply into areas and sites in which they are already involved with the intent to disturb the settings they investigate. They conduct research with an eye toward greater understanding, change and improvement in their local sites and themselves, as well as contributing to the larger knowledge base in their field. Although objectivity is not the goal, practitioner action researchers undertake deliberate, systematic enquiry to generate understanding based on evidence. Their tacit knowledge of the site may be how an issue for study is chosen initially, but the collection of data is expected to challenge these previous understandings, deepening them in unexpected ways.

Practitioner action research is oriented to action or cycles of action to address an issue of concern and curiosity. It can be thought of as a series of cycles that involve planning actions, acting, assessing the effects of these actions via data gathering, and making meaning or reflecting upon one's observations. These cycles form a spiral that results in refinements of research questions, resolution or deeper understanding of issues and

313

transformations in the perspectives of the researcher and other participants. The research is pursued until the researcher is satisfied that a complex understanding has been arrived at and actions pursued based on this understanding. Although the actions are local, the complex understanding may have implications for other settings and practitioners. This is similar to the way qualitative researchers utilise the concept of transferability (Lincoln and Guba 1985).

Working assumptions about practitioner action research and their implications for dissertation research

In the rest of this chapter, we will take up what we consider important working assumptions about practitioner action research that doctoral students should consider for dissertation work: (i) practitioner action research is carried out within unique micro- and macro-political contexts; (ii) practitioner action research has a different, but equally rigorous, set of quality criteria; (iii) there is no one best way to do practitioner action research – there are multiple approaches; and (iv) practitioner action research produces knowledge that is uniquely suited to the realities and contexts of practitioners.

Practitioner action research is political

Any research that makes knowledge claims is necessarily political but practitioner action researchers face political challenges in at least two dimensions. Practitioner action research takes place in local contexts at given points in time amid various vested interests. Critical questioning threatens the equilibrium of the status quo and whoever is privileged by it. Even if a researcher's questioning is focused on one's own practices, the enquiry is taking place in a larger institutional context. Once the action research spiral is set in motion, researchers should not assume its spiralling is totally under their control. It is impossible to completely anticipate the directions the enquiry will take or the kinds of interests it will attract or threaten. If we as researchers have set these possible changes in motion, we may welcome the insights that come with the data-gathering process and even happily anticipate changes. Others in the site may feel differently and may see the enquiry as a threat or an imposition, something done to them rather than chosen (Noffke 1997).

Practitioner action research though also faces the politics of the academy. Generating knowledge from the field can be seen as a challenge to the knowledge-generating systems of research located within most universities. It can threaten the sense of university faculty as the creators and gatekeepers of knowledge generation.

> One of the strengths of practitioner action research is its link with reconceptualizing the work of school practitioners as intimately linked to ongoing inquiry (Duckworth 1986) and the restructuring of schools as a collective process of inquiry-oriented professional and organizational learning.
>
> Anderson and Herr 1999: 14

This ultimately could lead to a rethinking of schools as centres of critical enquiry, places where educators produce knowledge as they intervene in complex and challenging educational situations. This potentially challenges the system currently in place of practitioners applying the expert knowledge of those outside their sites, often located in university and governmental positions, and increasingly in corporate boardrooms. Ideally, this could result in collaborative partnerships between academics and practitioners. But it also challenges and potentially dismantles the hierarchies under which we currently operate, in which the expertise of academics is seen as the only path to knowledge generation. And, although university faculty see themselves as mentors to doctoral students, interested in preparing the next generation of scholars, their views and expertise in research may not necessarily fit with the pathways of practitioner action researchers.

As we have written elsewhere (Anderson and Herr 1999), knowledge generated by practitioner action researchers may be seen as threatening both in the academy as well as in the practitioner's own site of enquiry. Academics struggle with preserving traditional turf, whilst redefining possibilities and partnerships. Academic institutional structures often reflect these struggles, with commonplace practices not necessarily well serving these emergent forms of research. For example, it is not uncommon that institutional review boards are not equipped to consider the unique ethical, political and methodological puzzles presented by practitioner action research (for an in-depth discussion of some of these issues see Herr and Anderson 2005). They seldom have faculty with expertise in action research on the review board. It is not uncommon that solutions to minimise risks, although perhaps helpful to one form of research, are nonsensical for insiders practising action research. Rethinking how to guide ethical action research with the input and approval of the IRB often lags behind the realities faced in the field. Practitioner action researchers and institutional review boards are often mutually frustrated with trying to work through these gate keeping functions in a timely and satisfactory manner. Similarly, doctoral advisers, well trained in research but not necessarily experienced in action research, may be challenged to offer helpful advice and guidance to those undertaking this process (Herr and Anderson 2005).

Beyond these institutional challenges, we name one more in terms of the politics of practitioner action research for dissertation work. Dissertations are typically the culminating experience in a lengthy programme of study. The dissertation establishes the doctoral student as an expert in an area of research as well as a methodology; it is an announcement of sorts of one's professional expertise and identity. There is a sense of vulnerability in the experience of a doctoral student conducting what is often one's first extensive research project culminating in a dissertation. This vulnerability is magnified with practitioner action research as the researcher documents changes in herself via the process, as well as the experience of threading through what can be a politically charged research process. The document lays bare the decisions made, the negotiations undertaken, the alliances built and tested. The researcher is not a dispassionate observer but rather an actress front and centre, now documented as a main character in a written document.

Documenting change from the perspective of one experiencing and to some degree orchestrating, it is a valuable contribution to our larger understanding of institutional change. It can present the messier, authentic side of this kind of undertaking. At the same time, the very complexity of both working for change while documenting it, recording both the 'successes' and 'failures', the bafflement and the breakthroughs, is a daunting task both to keep track of as well as write up.

Practitioner action research has its own rigour

As with more traditional research, some practitioner action research is more rigorous than others. As we have insisted earlier, there is a difference between anecdotal, unexamined narratives and systematic enquiry. Although practitioner action research is a departure from other forms of research, it is not without criteria for conducting trustworthy, rigorous research. There is some concern that as action research is increasingly popularised, this sense of systematic enquiry, ironically, gets left behind. For this type of research to be seen as an equal contribution to other, more well-established forms of enquiry, it is important that standards of rigour appropriate to the form of research be maintained. Practitioner action research is already vulnerable to being considered a 'lesser than' type of enquiry. Therefore, the onus is on us as action researchers to challenge ourselves to maintaining research design and implementation that results in a rigorous process leading to valid outcomes (Herr and Anderson 2005).

Having said that, it is also apparent that some of the criteria designed for other types of research are not necessarily useful standards here. Early naturalistic researchers (Lincoln and Guba 1985) insisted on their validity criteria separate from that of Campbell and Stanley (1963), because they felt their work would be unfairly evaluated by others' criteria. In keeping with this line of thought, we would suggest that practitioner action research should not be judged by the same validity criteria with which we judge other forms of research. We have found that the insider status and action-orientation of this type of research create conditions that require serious rethinking of traditional notions of research and establishment of trustworthiness or validity. The question then becomes one of holding ourselves to criteria that push us as practitioner action researchers and uphold the integrity of the process.

How then do we conduct 'good' practitioner action research and evaluate against what criteria? These issues have been taken up by a number of authors (see, for example, Greenwood and Levin 1998; Reason and Bradbury 2001), ourselves included (Anderson and Herr 1999; Herr and Anderson 2005). We based our own validity criteria (outcome, process, democratic, catalytic, and dialogic) on the goals of action research that seem to be generally agreed upon: the generation of new knowledge; the achievement of action-oriented outcomes; the education of both researcher and participants; results relevant to the setting that generated them; and a sound and appropriate methodology (Herr and Anderson 2005). Although our understanding is that practitioner action research is an iterative, emergent, ongoing process of planning and implementing, this does not mean that researchers head into the process without a plan. In addition, the initial and ongoing planning is done in conjunction with criteria designed to establish its validity.

It is not uncommon in dissertation research for researchers to lay out their research design for insider action research but then revert to criteria established for other research traditions to establish validity. It is a force fit that does not really work, as the tasks are different. For example:

> Academic researchers (outsiders) want to understand what it is like to be an insider without 'going native' and losing the outsider's perspective. Practitioners (insiders) already know what it is like to be an insider, but because they are 'native' to the setting, they must work to see the taken-for-granted aspects of their practice from an outsider's perspective.
>
> Anderson *et al.* 2007: 37

Although practitioner action research may share some data gathering methods and techniques with other research approaches, both quantitative and qualitative, that does not imply that we also borrow wholesale the validity criteria or techniques used to establish them from either one. While there may be overlap, there are also points of departure. For example, one common technique used to establish trustworthiness in naturalistic forms of research is prolonged engagement (Lincoln and Guba 1985), which is the idea of investing sufficient time to learning the culture of a site. As mentioned above, the work for a practitioner action researcher is to question what it is they already 'know' via their lengthy involvement in a site and there is nothing in unexamined 'prolonged engagement' that necessarily leads to that kind of questioning of one's tacit knowledge and familiarity of one's site. At the same time, it is unlikely that an ethnographer could ever really gain the same depth of knowledge of a site that an insider accrues by virtue of being an employee there, but the key then is to not assume that insider status and the familiarity it brings is an asset if left unexamined. Again, our point here is that our locations and intentions as practitioner action researchers require different tasks of us to establish rigour. This is particularly important for those utilising this methodology for dissertation research as the contribution envisioned is beyond that of the local site to the larger body of disciplinary knowledge.

There are many valid approaches to practitioner action research

Although our own work has appropriated qualitative data gathering methods, adapting and altering them for action research, we do not wish to imply by this that action research is inherently more compatible with qualitative methods. Our stance is the question driving the action research and the context in which the question is derived will necessarily guide the approach to data gathering. Furthermore, while we have emphasised here the role of organisational insiders doing research in their own setting, there is a growing interest in more participatory forms of action research that can involve various combinations of insiders and outsiders doing collaborative research. There is also concern that much practitioner action research leaves out the perspectives of some stakeholders, such as community members and students. As organised communities demand greater participation in schools and other organisations, community-based, participatory forms of research will become increasingly popular (Cammarota and Fine 2008; Minkler and Wallerstein 2003).

Data gathering is prevalent in many institutions, for a variety of purposes. We encourage any practitioner action researcher to both build on existing data that is available and also question its utility and limits. For example, in education there is currently a move toward 'data-driven decision making', typically drawing on quantitative, statistical scores on a variety of instruments such as aggregate scores on standardised tests for students. This kind of data can perhaps point out areas for improvement or concern, but it is not likely that it can explain why this area of concern has emerged. Practitioners in the setting typically make meaning or informally hypothesise as to what the scores mean, and it is not uncommon that whole programmes of intervention are put in place based on someone's best guess as to what has occurred to cause, for example, the dip in students' scores (Herr and Anderson 2008). This kind of jump from statistical scores to solutions, without some further data gathering to unpack what caused the issue, is not, in our opinion, practitioner action research. It could be the beginning of the process, but only if practitioners ask what other data are needed to understand the phenomenon and work out a research design that furthers complex understanding. This kind of complex understanding is necessary to illustrate and meet criteria for validity in practitioner action research (Anderson *et al.* 2007).

Many of us went through our graduate coursework without much, if any, instruction in action research. Our models of research are more likely to involve quantitative or qualitative approaches, leaving practitioner action research more to the imagination. In addition, methodologies for this approach are still being hashed out, with work still needed to design data gathering techniques that are 'friendly' to practitioners in terms of implementation in the face of the constraints of job demands. Add to this the realities of the action research spiral, where data gathering evolves throughout the process, based on the assessment of interventions and actions, and it is easy to see that we need to be well-versed in as many research tools as possible. We need to be positioned to take advantage of data in our sites that are routinely gathered as well as be able to design methods to interrogate it. This necessarily requires a familiarity with multiple approaches to data gathering.

For many of us, practitioner action research is the most complex, and perhaps the most exhilarating, research we will undertake. To utilise this approach for a dissertation study is not for the faint of heart. We say this not to dissuade any scholar from this direction, but rather to encourage them to put in place the supports necessary for the success of the project. Among these necessary ingredients is a solid acquaintance with a variety of research methodologies that would allow researchers to creatively meet the demands that practitioner action research requires.

Practitioner action research produces knowledge that is uniquely suited to the realities and contexts of practitioners

Like many other forms of knowledge, practitioner knowledge is what feminists and post-modernists call subjugated knowledge in the sense that in formal academic settings it is not viewed as legitimate (Anderson and Grinberg 1998). For many academics, the acceptance of practitioner action research is given only on the condition that a separate category of knowledge be created for it. This is usually expressed as some variation on 'formal (created in universities) knowledge' versus 'practical (created in schools) knowledge' and a strict separation of research from practice (Fenstermacher 1994; Huberman 1996; Richardson 1994). For example, Richardson (1994) defines action research as 'practical enquiry', which focuses on the 'improvement of practice' and then uses her own definition to relegate it to secondary status vis-à-vis formal (read 'real' research). Fenstermacher (1994) declares that practical knowledge results from participating in and reflecting on action and experience, is bounded by the situation or context in which it arises, may or may not be capable of immediate expression in speech or writing, and deals with 'how to do things, the right place and time to do them, or how to see and interpret events related to one's actions' (p.12).

In response, Cochran-Smith and Lytle reject the formal/practical knowledge dualism as unhelpful and see it as greatly limiting the very nature of teaching and teacher research, which they claim is more about,

> [H]ow teachers' actions are infused with complex and multi-layered understandings of learners, culture, class, gender, literacy, social issues, institutions, communities, materials, texts, and curricula. It is about how teachers work together to develop and alter their questions and interpretive frameworks informed not only by thoughtful consideration of the immediate situation and the particular students they teach and have taught but also by the multiple contexts – social, political, historical, and cultural – within which they work.
>
> Cochran-Smith and Lytle 1998: 24

Clandinin and Connelly (1995), drawing on Schwab (1962), have further argued that outsider knowledge is often experienced by teachers as a 'rhetoric of conclusions'. Using a funneling metaphor, they argue that this rhetoric of conclusions funnels propositional and theoretical knowledge to practitioners without understanding that their landscape is personal, contextual, subjective, temporal, historical and relational among people. This suggests that the formal/practical knowledge debate is about more than research epistemology and methodology; it is about the very nature of educational practice itself.

It is not necessary to create a hierarchy of knowledge to recognise that knowledge produced by practitioners is well positioned to have an impact on practice. Our own experience is that our students who are teachers and administrators read practitioner research with more enthusiasm than traditional research. However, they also read traditional research enthusiastically when the knowledge responds to a problem that they are trying to resolve. We are not recommending the abandonment of the quest for a knowledge base through academic research. Practitioners respond not only to knowledge constructed by other practitioners in the crucible of their own practice, but also to academic research when they seek it out in the process of doing their own enquiry.

Nor are we suggesting that the public knowledge that practitioner action research generates is only useful for school practitioners. We support the idea that knowledge produced by practitioners should also inform educational policy, the practitioner knowledge base, as well as university-based research agendas. However, in applied fields, having an impact on professional practice is a major goal of most research agendas.

Because the practitioner's world is personal, contextual, subjective, temporal, historical, and relational, practitioner research, which tends to be communicated though narrative findings, communicates practitioner knowledge in a vicarious manner. There are many ways to approach the question of how results of action research are 'generalised' or transferred to other settings (often referred to as external validity), but we will suggest one taken from the work of Stake (1986) on *naturalistic generalisation*. Although Stake developed this approach to generalisation in the context of qualitative, responsive, evaluation research, we feel it has powerful implications for action researchers. Stake's concept of naturalistic generalisation is similar in many ways to Lincoln and Guba's (1985) notion of 'transferability', in which findings are not generalised in a statistical sense, but rather transferred from a sending context to a receiving context.

Although similar to the notion of 'transferability', Stake's elaboration of naturalistic generalisation is more closely tied to *action* and therefore will serve our purposes here better. After years of well-documented failure by outside experts to bring about planned change in schools, Stake argues that it is time to rediscover the lessons about change that John Dewey taught us:

> Almost absent from mention in the 'change literature' is the common way in which improvement is accomplished, a way followed intuitively by the greatest, and the least, of our thinkers. It is the experiential way, an evolutionary way, recognized particularly by John Dewey. One may change practice when *new experience* causes re-examination of problems: Intuitively we start thinking of alternative solutions.
>
> Stake 1986: 90

Besides Dewey, Stake cites the work of Polanyi (1958) and Schon (1983), who argue that practice is guided less by formal knowledge than by personal knowledge based on personal or vicarious experience.

319

Stake's argument stipulates that action or changes in practice usually occur as a result of either some kind of external demand or coercion or the conviction on the part of practitioners that an action or change is necessary. We have seen time and again how coercion is successfully resisted by practitioners, and how most lasting change takes place through *internal conviction*, or to use a more popular term 'ownership'.

A further premise is that a practitioner's internal conviction is influenced by deeper understanding, which is arrived at through dialogue and reflection drawing on two kinds of knowledge: experiential and propositional. These two kinds of knowledge, according to Stake, are tied to two kinds of generalisation: formalistic and naturalistic. 'Continuing the analysis, we might say that theory and codified data are the main constituents of our formal, verbalized generalizations – whereas experience, real and vicarious, is the main constituent of the naturalistic generalizations' (p. 97).

Stake describes how naturalistic generalisation is different from more traditional, formalistic generalisation:

> The intention of most educational research is to provide formalistic generalization. A typical research report might highlight the correlation between time spent on team projects *and* gain in scores on an achievement test. The report might identify personality, affective and demographic variables. Even with little emphasis on causation this report is part of the grand explanation of student learning. It provides one way of knowing about educational practice.
>
> A more naturalistic research report might deal with the same topic, perhaps with the same teachers and pupils, yet reflecting a different epistemology. The naturalistic data would describe the actual interactions within student teams. The report would probably report project work – conveying style, context, and evolution. A person would be described as an individual, with uniqueness not just in deviance scores, but as a key to understanding the interactions. A reader senses the experience of teamwork in this particular situation. It is a *unique* situation in some respects, but ordinary in other respects. Readers recognize similarities with situations of their own. Perhaps they are stimulated to think of old problems in a new way.
>
> Stake 1986: 98–9

This type of research fits well with current practitioner culture where, although less systematic, stories are shared daily among practitioners as part of an oral craft tradition. This notion of naturalistic generalisation does not preclude the potential for practitioner action research to generate, test or extend social theory. But perhaps its greatest potential is in contributing to the knowledge landscape of practitioners.

Conclusion

We have chosen to discuss in this chapter several key issues that arise for doctoral students who choose to produce practitioner knowledge though the use of practitioner action research. We have only scratched the surface of the many dilemmas that practitioner action research raises for doctoral students. Luckily, there is now a considerable body of work to guide doctoral students along this journey, and these resources should be consulted along the way. We will continue to learn more about practitioner knowledge though traditional research methodologies, but we hope that practitioners themselves – armed with knowledge of research methods and action research approaches – will also make significant contributions to this knowledge base.

References

Anderson, G. L. and Herr, K. (1999) The new paradigm wars: Is there room for rigorous practitioner knowledge in schools and universities? *Educational Researchers*, 28(5): 12–21, 40.

Anderson, G. L., Herr, K. and Nihlen, A. S. (2007) *Studying your own school: An educator's guide to practitioner action research*. 2nd edn. Thousand Oaks, CA: Corwin Press.

Anderson, G. L. and Grinberg, J. (1998) Educational administration as a disciplinary practice: Appropriating Foucault's view of power, discourse, and method, *Educational Administration Quarterly*, 34(3): 329–53.

Anderson, G. L. and Jones, F. (2000) Knowledge generation in educational administration from the inside-out: The promise and perils of site-based, administrator research, *Educational Administration Quarterly*, 36(3): 428–64.

Argyris, C. and Schon, D. (1974) *Theory in practice: Increasing professional effectiveness*. San Francisco, CA: Jossey Bass.

Cammarota, J. and Fine, M. (Eds) (2008) *Revolutionizing education: Youth participatory action research in motion*. New York: Routledge.

Campbell, D. T. and Stanley, J. C. (1963) *Experimental and quasi-experimental designs for research*. Dallas, TX: Houghton Mifflin.

Clandinin, J. and Connelly, M. (1995) *Teachers' professional knowledge landscapes*. New York: Teachers College Press.

Cochran-Smith, M. and Lytle, S. (1998) Teacher research: The question that persists, *International Journal of Leadership in Education*, 1(1): 19–36.

Fenstermacher, G. (1994) The knower and the known: The nature of knowledge in research on teaching In L. Darling-Hammond (Ed.). *Review of research in Education*, 20: 3–56.

Greenwood, D. and Levin, M. (1998) *Introduction to action research: Social research for social change*. Thousand Oaks, CA: Sage.

Herr, K. and Anderson, G. L. (2005) *The action research dissertation: A guide for students and faculty*. Thousand Oaks, CA: Sage.

——(2008) Teacher research and learning communities: A failure to theorize power relations? *Language Arts*, 85(5): 382–91.

Huberman, M. (1996) Focus on research moving mainstream: Taking a closer look at teacher research, *Language Arts*, 73(2): 124–40.

Lincoln, Y. and Guba, E. (1985) *Naturalistic inquiry*. Thousand Oaks, CA: Sage.

Minkler, M. and Wallerstein, N. (Eds) (2003) *Community-based participatory research for health*. San Francisco, CA: Jossey Bass.

Noffke, S. (1997) Professional, personal, and political dimensions of action research, *Review of Research in Education*, 22: 305–43.

Polanyi, M. (1958) *Personal knowledge*. Chicago, IL: University of Chicago Press.

Reason, P. and Bradbury, H. (Eds) (2001) *Handbook of action research: Participative inquiry and practice*. Thousand Oaks, CA: Sage.

Richardson, V. (1994) Conducting research on practice, *Educational Researcher*, 23(5): 5–10.

Schon, D. (1983) *The reflective practitioner: How professionals think in action*. New York: Basic Books.

——(1995) The new scholarship requires a new epistemology, *Change: The Magazine of Higher Learning*, 27(6): 27–34.

Schwab, J. J. (1962) The teaching of science as inquiry. In J. J. Schwab and P. F. Brandwein (Eds). *The teaching of science*. Cambridge, MA: Harvard University Press.

Stake, R. (1986) An evolutionary view of educational improvement. In E.R. House (Ed.). *New directions in educational evaluation*. London: Falmer Press, 89–102.

Sternberg, R. and Horvath, J. (1999) *Tacit Knowledge in Professional Practice: Researcher and Practitioner Perspectives*. Mahwah, NJ: Lawrence Erlbaum.

Tripp, D. (1994) *Critical incidents in teaching: Developing professional judgement*. London: Routledge.

26

Coyote and Raven talk about equivalency of other/ed knowledges in research

P. Cole and P. O'Riley

Coyote and Raven were sitting in the library with piles of books and journals and notebooks and bookmarks and sticky flags and laptops all around them, they had taken up a whole huge table – and they were eating food and getting crumbs everywhere!

So Coyote, what are your thoughts on this companion piece for graduate students?

(chompchomp) Well Raven, first off from what I'm reading here *companion* comes from middle English, via old high German, Germanic Anglo–Saxon, old French, a soupçon of Romany, a smidgen of Gothic and a dash of Protobasque, and it basically means someone (or in this case 'something') you eat bread with. They don't say if it's a loaf of bread or a bun or a sandwich, though they do mix in *Xlaib zaXlaibaz* and *gahlaiba* indicating loaf.

So it's a noun! Otherwise I guess that pretty much leaves it wide open eh? What about the 'graduate student' part, what does your etymology book say about that?

It's not so straightforward Raven. I had to use online sources because the goat ate all of my reference books and I'm banned from the local library until I pay for the goat's lunch, besides which I had to look up 'graduate' and 'student' separately in an etymological sense so there is a dissembling multi-furcation. It gets a bit complicated: on the one paw it depends on whether you're talking about a person, a human being or if you're talking about a flask or tube or other container marked with a progressive series of degrees (lines or numbers or both) for measuring liquids or solids.

I'd go with the first one: it's less complicated or perhaps less 'implicated' (Bohm 1980).

Okay, it seems 'graduate' *ipse* comes from Latin via middle Latin and relates to either 'taking a degree' or a step or grade presumably in that process, so I guess we could still be talking about a flask jar or tube depending on which syllable the accent is on.

In the context of what we're supposed to be doing as 'others' [alterrific] it relates also to postgraduate, in other words to taking an after degree or a degree after, though it could also refer to an interpenetrating enfolding (Deleuze 1988) time-fulness after the graduations or gradations are worn off and you can't measure accurately with it anymore except to say 'a flask of' or 'a tube of' or 'a student of', though that might be quite useful in particular recipes and instances.

'Student' comes from Latin, the noun comes from a second type conjugation verb through middle English and means 'to direct one's zeal at'.

Zeal? Verb? Hmmm, perhaps we might encourage graduate students to work more in the verb category – at least the active verb not passive voice.

Raven, but we can't just stop at Latin in our search for roots or 'rhizomes' (Deleuze and Guattari 1987). From what I've heard, Latin didn't come to the Italian peninsula until around 900 BC and it was influenced by Greek and Celtic and probably Etruscan, too, and the sounds of the natural world. I'm not sure where the derivative nature of knowledge is going to get us other than playing around with the journey of words describing that to which they are referring. How far back do we go to discover context? Scratches on rock cave art, archaeografitti petronyms? You and I both know that there are no beginnings, just continuations of muddles.

Hmmm, we seem to be getting stuck in a linguistic magquire. Well, let's slog through it, eh Coyote? Do you remember way back, *quando quando*, we took a trip to protoindoeurope and had to learn Venetic Raetic Ligurian and Liburnian and that was just in the cis-Alps and proto-Adriatic? We hadn't even gotten as far south as the Etruscans and were already multiply linguistically challenged. Ah, but the grapes, the wine, the sun.

I remember we decided to go somewhere where there was less linguistic variation. Yes, our archaeonordic trip in a leaky sea raft. Pass the bread, please.

Librarian: This is a library. Please confine your eating to the vestibule or the out-of-doors. We don't want pests consuming the books! Hmphh!

Coyote, to get back to thinking about how we can share some of our discoveries with graduate students, so far we're looking at directing zeal and eating bread with now we're getting somewhere! We'll probably need to drink something, too, one cannot live on bread and loans.

What is it basically that these graduate students are needing to know? Shouldn't they already know all this stuff after 16 or more years of schooling of directing their zeal? Sharing bread with?

Where is the talk of 'equivalency' (Rengifo 1998) of 'others', 'othered' epistemologies and methodologies? Do normalised knowledges and practices have an origin or did they just pop out of the ether fully writ?

Well, equivalency can be complicated for those brought up on reason. It seems to have joined with a lot of other terms in its journey, making up compound terms as permutational equivalence inversional transpositional improper rotation equivalence logical moral dynamic probabilistic equivalence bioequivalence.

But the root, the rhizome, whatever botanical metamorphosis we're working with?

Well, one place equivalence seems to have carnated for a time was Latin via middle and late Latin *aequus* being equal, and *valere* meaning to be well or to be worth.

So Coyote, all things being equal taken within a situated postprotoeurocontext …

Ah, but who is to judge? Who determines the worth the quality? The words do not evolve themselves outside of human power relations and connotations.

But stitching together these words and expressions, companion graduate student equivalency can be counter productive, and even eating bread with those with degrees or marks around them at regular intervals who direct their zeal within a system of equal value in a contextually laden axiopraxic multifurcative powered domain can come to naught, or even less if meaning's primary residence is reason then woe to Alteric the Unready.

A bit cumbersome Raven, but I think you've captured it quite well.

Le nom du jeu is going with the lowest common denominator we have to prepare a *prandium* that suits all tastes. It could be bland and safe, both/and piquant and risqué, though feel free to add ors where you will.

We could search in the realm of mathematics for an algorithm to determine if there is a proof or even risk assessment for our dilemma before we begin.

I say divide and conquer? 'Survivance' (Vizenor 1994) of the fittest! The *entscheidungsproblemarbeit* is not the angle I would look at dealing with this, and please don't throw an *incompleteness theorem* at me. It's not how we deal with relationality in a peopled environment: it might work if we were numbers but *cogito ergo* compute is not ...

Librarian: Ssshhhhhhhhh!

Everybody: Sshhhhhhhhh!

But we have to look after all and everybody, and yet keep up a kind of intellectual momentum that fits the community rather than bulldozing through. Today, students are not so homogeneous as they used to be. They come from different cultural gendered abled stabled labelled spaces.

Taking into account othernesses as a dominant way of patronising those who have been disposed of in accusative spaces and verbless unsubjected phrases, I would say that we're running the risk of alienating anyone whose idea of scholarship is narrowly focused.

However, there is a growing acknowledgement that one dominant or dominating cultural point of view as the norm and everything else as abnorm is on its way out over!

To the trashbin?

No, the 'main stream' is never so drastic. It may be rash and unrealistic and insensitive, but it does often stick to a strategic plan. It will go to the recycling centre for retro-repackaging. They'll find a way of reintroducing it in another guise, it's as plain as the face around your nose putting racism genderism ableism anthropocentrism into different stages of dormancy refurbishment hibernation estivation and renaissance. It's not so much a step backward as the temporal diameter of your circle whose centre is 'same', and who is in charge of the constants as well as the variations on the theme of validity and authority.

Raven, are you assuming that there is a last or lasting solution? Maybe we should have a Coyote and Raven weekend heist session – hold a workshop, get everyone loosened up.

Touchy feely, no thanks. Encounter sessions are best left to real life. Unfortunately, though, as long as someone is perceived to be different or 'other', they will be targeted by someone who has a bias to promulgate.

Are you saying that one particular gendered abled cultured space is not the only way? That there are acceptable alternatives?

No no no, Coyote, not alternatives. It is the citing of those who do not fit into the mainstream as exhibiting altericness *andere*-icity that is problematic – the naming is troublesome.

325

I agree, Raven, we need to 'minorize' (Deleuze and Guattari 1987) the majority language that positions those of non-European heritage as 'alternatives' or 'minorities'. We are all part of a/the main stream, which as every creature of the 'wild' who has encountered a riverine system, a spring, a leaf holding rainwater, knows is made up of countless tributaries, rain melting glaciers, groundwater, spontaneous generation dew, transpiration fog and mist.

Most graduate students seem to want to graduate from their university with an understanding of how to do research in a respectful way, including with people who are not perceived as being within the normalcy pool.

Many professors I've encountered have no idea of how to do respectful research with Aboriginal people. They assume that they have 'the right to know'. Sometimes you just end up as a nosy stranger who is minding somebody else's business and just generally causing trouble. They think they can just come and ask the Indians and they will be enlightened *fiat lux ab origine*, just open the cedar box the bitten birch basket.

But Coyote, in a consumer-centric society you research by consuming, by naming, claiming. Research in such an environment is about taking ownership of the knowledges of those upon whom the research is enacted.

Perhaps we could teach graduate students *Indian whispering* as a successful strategy, so that they don't continue with the siphoning out of Indigenous intellectual property so that the co-researchers who are the sources of the knowings and practices can copyright them themselves (or not) and turn them into royalties, PhDs and PBS documentaries, rather than the party of the first part appearing as acknowledgements or footnotes on a manuscript of the second party?

Yes, learning to do research without hurting the people whose lives they're interfering with, doing the least harm I'm just hoping we can keep the colonisers from creating strife by their investigation of sensitive issues like suicide or sexual abuse among Aboriginal people and similar issues.

Raven, unfortunately in academia there is no subject matter that is off limits. Academia is a subset of capitalist hegemony not just in an economic sense but as a politicised colonialist continuum; so, too, is Western ethics a contagion that subsumes and infects.

Under the Western flag students are to engage curiosity, Lacanian desire messianic pretense, the subduction of innocence.

Innocence is not so much a state of being as a presumptive state of hegemonic imputation. How might the research be used and by whom can research be harmless? Does helping really help?

Coyote, are you saying that studying how imaginary, or perhaps I should say speculative, protolanguages operated in the past could cause harm today?

When does speculation become research and of whose rigor do we speak and how long has the corpus been moribund? Dead sheep, coyote DNA, therefore *canis latrans* did it in the conservatory with the candlestick; or *canis latrans* found the dead sheep and sniffed around, discovered whiffs of prionic residue and skedaddled leaving behind genetic residue; or coyote hater X disposed of said ovine, spread coyote DNA around to incriminate the accused, knowing that CSI Hooterville would equate suspicion with guilt – *les cous rouges un peu partout*, you're with us or you're with the coyotes.

Enter spirit of chief Dan George with the sound of hand drums.

Chief Dan George: Snikeeyap spaal 'li tseep 'o"eli"ul? hwlyuneem'tseep. Hello my sisters and brothers.
Ah *tes-wah-no.*
Slaholt ama7 sqit.
Chief Dan George: Since we are between stanzas I thought that I would share something I learned from walking on this Earth and from these many years hanging around in the spirit world watching the earthbound people of my nation struggling with the blackrobes. This is where part of the problem lies: 'When the white man came, we had the land and they had the bibles. Now they have the land and we have the bibles' (George and Hirnschall 2004: 8). *(poof!)*
Mmm Raven, he's got a point there though. With respect to evangelism, there are many people of the land who have taken up the settler religions. Some see these as new traditions, some believe that if they translate the Christian scriptures into their Indigenous language they become Indigenous scriptures.
Well Coyote, some of the settlers still think we're the lost tribes.
But we're being rediscovered, we're found/lings *objets trouvés.*
Since we are in charge of constructing this narrative, let's ask Musqueam Elder Vince Stogan if he might share his thoughts with us.

Spot on Vince as he appears.

Vince: [M]y Elders taught us that all our people who have passed on are still around us. We can still keep our beliefs even though we are now in a modern world. Once we go the Western way we are lost (Kulchyski *et al.* 1999: 456).

Elder Stogan moves downstage left but remains on stage. Light fades. More and more Elders begin to appear in the library and when they speak a spotlight or less intense light illumines them. Some sit at tables or desks or in chairs, browse the bookshelves or sit with their eyes closed or knit. Others work on baskets and hides, cutting up salmon, making kindling. The librarian frowns at this activity.

Raven I had better make some tea as we have so many visitors. I wonder if the librarian would let me use the staff lunchroom?
Let it go for now. I don't think this is a social visit, maybe just light some medicines and that will do. They have come to help us with our task. Some are visiting from the other world, others are doing work in the here and now.

Spot on elder Molly Chisaakay from Dene Tha' quietly playing a drum.

Molly, you're looking smart today. You've always stood up for your people, maybe you could help us figure out how to help these graduate students who want to learn to do respectful research? They need some direction before they continue on their journeys.
Molly: The drum represents the circle of life. It's made of an animal skin and wood, the Creator's gifts to us, and you have to heat it up near fire for it to sound good (Meili 1991: 6).

What can the drum do?

Molly: There's a real power behind it. The drum brings people together and awakens something. When you hear it and dance, it's a way of expressing yourself, rejoicing. You realise you have this powerful connection between yourself, the Creator, and everyone else. [M]y grandfather. ... [w]hen I would talk and talk about my problems, he would tell me to take time to be quiet and listen (Meili 1991: 6).

Stoney Elder Nancy Potts how can students learn to do their work in a good way?

Nancy: The best things in life must be earned (Meili 1991: 15).

Mm, so we have to work hard for our answers is that it? Not just expect them to be given?

Nancy: Cities block your energy. They're made of things that shouldn't be there. If you believe in spiritual things, you have to be in open spaces like this, amongst the trees, not in the city (Meili 1991: 15).

I think that a lot of students would agree but many of them are trapped in the city and many of them love the city and can find inspiration there, a sense of belonging.

Sooo, *George Kehewin respected Cree Elder*, we're talking about the importance of being in nature and about spirituality and tradition. How do you ground yourself?

George: I talk to little children. They are the most powerful little things, you know ... make you happy ... make your life come back to normal. ... If you still can't find anyone, take a walk. Or talk to a tree. You don't have to move your lips, talk from your mind. Try to communicate with creation (Meili 1991: 152).

I'm wondering if these ideas will be useful for students in deciding on what research to do and how to do it? A lot of them these days need concrete ideas.

Cement more like. Fixed and unmoving people need to become more flexible and also disciplined in different ways, hey Raven?

Coyote, it sounds like the Elders aren't talking that much about how they think researchers should act. They're talking more about how they should live themselves and how they should act.

Well it makes sense. People who are researchers have to be people first and they have to know how to act as people, then they'll know how to act as researchers. It's about having good manners, it might keep them from looking at research as being about capturing the essence of an exotic species.

Elder Albert Lightning Cree Ermineskin reserve: People must not look for physical or material results from everything they do. Instead, they should pay attention to their dreams and develop their spirits, feeling good about helping others and putting themselves last (Meili 1991: 82).

Paskwaw mostos awasis Albert, how can people get ahead if they put themselves last? Some of the young ones aren't that keen to help the Elders like they used to be they're in such a hurry.

Elder Rick Lightning: It's called *ohpikihakan* in Cree. It's where an old man takes a son into his family to act as his helper, to look after him and do things that are too difficult for him to do. In turn, he shows the young man his secrets for him to carry on (Meili 1991: 85).

We're putting together some words about researchers doing things in good ways.

Albert: Even though some people think cameras and tape-recorders shouldn't be taken near spiritual ceremonies. I think differently. It's a way of communicating the traditional ways to others who can't read about them or be fortunate to take part in such ceremonies. It's time we stop being secretive about our beliefs and experiences and share them with the world, because the world needs it (Meili 1991: 82–3).

Light on Albert fades.

Raven, that's a big step to take to trust those newcomers with vital knowledges including our traditional deep rapport with nature. *Caveat vendor* Raven, Do you think that our ideas about nature can reach university researchers at an indigenous level?

I don't know if they can see nature as we do Coyote. I'm not sure that their languages allow them to or if they can make their minds silent for long enough.

What about the First Nations children who don't speak their language?

Being brought up in the culture, I think, makes the difference. There is something that you get from being brought up in your culture in whatever language, whatever knowledge of traditional ways that also comes across.

You mean that being brought up say with a coloniser culture and the English language can still put across Aboriginal values to Aboriginal children?

Even those who have attended residential school and were forced to become almost non-aboriginal were enacting aboriginality. It seeps back into you as your relationships are nurtured. Perhaps some changed, but at base there is some essence that is aboriginal.

Could learning to speak *Siksika* work to sensitise a non-Aboriginal person to the Blackfoot idea of the natural world?

You can't separate the person from the language from the culture. We are the language and we are the culture.

So how does that work for non-Aboriginal people?

It depends on the effort the people make and how they enact their culture. They cannot enact a First Nations culture if they are not of the culture. We are not simulacra to be copied, despite the cultural appropriation of our knowings and practices by the new wage movement.

Russell Wright Siksika Blackfoot reserve: What always comes back to me is the way my grandparents taught me. They were always telling me stories, always explaining things to me. They didn't say, 'This is bad, this is good.' They didn't differentiate between the two, everything was nice to them – nature, other people, animals – they were all nice (Meili 1991: 55).

I'm wondering how comfortable you might be with people coming in and just making themselves comfortable and starting to ask questions?

Russell points his lips at Diane.

Dianne Meili: Russell teaches young people. … to, 'Make enquiries of old people, instead of asking questions, because traditionally, to question was to challenge' (Meili 1991: 55).

I guess that making an enquiry as differentiated from asking questions is being indirect or non-confrontational in your dialogue getting around to it when it happens rather than being direct and getting instant results.

Russell: It has something to do with face-to-face conflict – if you question me, you are doubting me. You're not open to what I might tell you if you're already thinking of questions. But if you make an inquiry and ask, 'Can you tell me a good, honest answer?' (Meili 1991: 55).

So, collecting data is not collecting data, it is making relationships that are real and not just for the convenience of one person. It's not question answer question answer.

Elder Rose Auger Cree Driftpile reserve: Most people, especially young people want knowledge right away, but it doesn't happen like that (Meili 1991: 23).

Raven, one thing that's hard for lots of researchers is to actually go into an Elder's kitchen or tent or lean-to, like Christine Horseman's up in the Cree reserve of Horse Lake, and eat what they're offered. What do you do if you're offered boiled moose nose or stuffed intestines or roast hooves, roast horns or eyes, ears, tongue or moose brain, whether you're a mixed eater or a vegan? How you respond determines your level of commitment and readiness.

Imagine getting a researcher to do without, to go away from the conveniences of electricity, TV and Wi Fi, iTunes and cellphones, and toilet paper.

I think that researchers need to know something about the shifting authorities on First Nations reserves and how to understand the differing stories they will hear.

And some of them don't understand about how the gaze works in aboriginal cultures – it is important in terms of body language.

Charlie Noskiye Cree Chipewyan Lake settlement: If you looked directly at someone, it was a sign of disrespect. There was a man here who would look at you from a distance, but when he got close to you he'd always put his head down. Women used to wear scarves to cover the sides of their faces so they couldn't look at anyone (Meili 1991: 214).

Sioux scholar Vine Deloria Jr, you've had experience within Western belief systems and Western academic spaces, you've seen how the people of the land are treated.

Vine: [T]ribal peoples are placed at the very bottom of the imaginary cultural evolutionary scale (Deloria 1997: 49).

You say that Western religions and philosophies have a lot of strange assumptions when it comes to non-Western peoples. Can you give an example?

Vine: [A]ll peoples *began as primitives* and *inevitably* moved toward Western forms of organization (Deloria 1997: 51).

But so many Aboriginal people live in fear, they live with the idea that they are colonised and therefore powerless.

Taiaiake Alfred Onkwehonwe scholar: Colonization is a lie. It is built on flat-out propaganda and the manipulation of innate human fears to force the acceptance of the false claim of Settler authority over our people and the land. ... If colonial authority is an artifice built on lies, then the way to confront and defeat it is with truths (Alfred 2005: 149).

Chief Dan George appears again smiling.

Dan: Of all the teachings we receive this one is the most important: Nothing belongs to you of what there is, of what you take, you must share (George and Hirnschall 2004: 27).

That's a tough one. Sharing with those who refuse to share. Sharing with those who refuse to acknowledge our aboriginal rights as deriving from ourselves and not from them, yet it is they who have the power, the firepower.

Raven, genocide is not just something that happens during warfare in Canada, it has been government policy for more than a hundred years. 'Other' is to be eliminated one way or another.

Othering is part of the societal fabric, the majoritarian political will. It's embedded in the language and research enacted on other/ed peoples that engages Eurocentric norms is simply another form of genocide.

For Maori scholar Linda Smith, Western research has been about an encounter between the West and the other (Smith 1999). The West defined as good right knowledgeable, whereas other reflects barbaric and backward.

Yes, National Geographic all the way, ghastly business!

But so much of our traditional methodologies have been replaced by European ideas of what counts as appropriate research protocols. Our voices and traditions are being drowned out by mainstream university rules and regulations.

Robina Thomas lyackson of the Coast Salish: Most First Nations peoples traditionally come from an oral society. A storytelling methodology honours that tradition and the Ancestors. ... we are compelled to listen and document stories in the spirit of the Ancestors (Thomas 2005: 242).

Librarian (voiceover): The noise level in the library is increasing. Please refrain from speaking so as not to disturb others. This is your librarian speaking.

Raven we need to examine both how some peoples/civilisations are othered and how some peoples/civilisations are normalised and privileged through dominating ideologies and political–social systems/structures reducing the complexities of difference to sameness.

Grimaldo Vasques Rengifo, my *Andean* friend, what about research for you and your community?

Grimaldo: If a world, like the Andean one, is constituted of persons and not of subjects or objects, its members are not interested in 'knowing' the other, because they do not see the other as an object or a thing and also because they are not interested in acting upon or transforming the other (Rengifo 1998: 177).

Coyote, do you remember Frédérique Apffel-Marglin (1998)? She began as an anthropologist and became a friend of the Andean people over many years.

Yes Raven, I remember Frédérique speaking at a conference with Julio Valladolid from the PRATEC (Proyecto Andino de Tecnologias Campesinas) community about knowledge making in the Andean context not being about accumulation of knowledge knowing more but an ongoing dynamic dialogue with all life forms. They refer to this form of knowing as 'nurturance', a reciprocal relationship of knowing how to nurture and allowing oneself to be nurtured.

Imagine teaching graduate students research methodologies of nurturance reciprocity, giving back—not just taking.

Coyote, you have been a critic of knowledge being treated as a monoculture by the occupier society and talk about equivalency of epistemologies.

That's right Raven. Indigenous peoples have been marginalised on their own homelands by white settler societies, their intricate and complex spiritual philosophical epistemological and ontological contributions are mocked as primitive and inconsequential to contemporary global societies and economies because they are not mechanistic and linear but interconnected living systems.

Yup. Western society has a long way to go to catch up to the sophistication and sustainability of the philosophies, ethics and knowledge systems of those they so easily dismiss. What might be some examples of this knowledge that graduate students and other researchers might consider?

Dismissed as myths or legends or superstitions is astounding knowledge of astronomy and surgery (Incas) architecture engineering art (Incas, Mayans, Stl'atl'imx, Haida) irrigation, bronze tools (Incas) agriculture (Incas, Ongwehonwe) intricate social structures (Ongwehonwe, Incas) living sustainably ocean navigation (all coastal First Peoples).

We can't miss out on speaking with Gerald Vizenor, White Earth Chippewa 'postindian warrior' originator of 'survivance' (Vizenor 1994), which goes beyond resistance theories. Oops, just when I thought he was going to speak he turned into a rabbit and took off. Well, maybe there's a message in there somewhere.

Maybe he was suggesting that we use shapeshifting as a methodology?

Sounds good to me, though it might trouble the Western concept of identity and the foundation of scholarship. What is the true shape of that which constantly shifts and how can you build on something that is itself constantly changing?

Yes, change is the essence of tradition to become other subject object verb pre position positron electron antiuniverse ity quarks is us are we. What's your strangeness number? What colour is your angular momentum?

Gloria Ladson-Billings, you've come up to visit us. You must have something to say about research as an African American scholar of many years practice?

Gloria: Scholars must be challenged to ask not only about whom is the research, but also for whom is the research (Ladson–Billings 2003: 414).

Pat O'Riley (2005) and Peter Cole (2006) also suggest that if the asymmetry of power relations of the other/not-other researched/researcher is to change we need to ask *with* whom?

And, Coyote, how the *withness* is negotiated, becoming one of the most crucial aspects of the research project.

More people start to come in to the library in the low light, and as they speak the lights come up on them and then fade after they have spoken. Some people are playing cards, some are playing the bone game. The librarian seems to be a bit flustered by it all, she starts to make tea and is constantly washing dishes.

Coyote, this Eurocentric epistemological arrogance dismisses tens of thousands of years of interconnected cosmologies, philosophies, epistemologies and practices in use today by non-Western civilisations worldwide, in favour of only a few hundred years of Western mechanistic, linear, rationalist knowledge systems.

Imagine being considered other, your knowledge as other, your culture as other, supplementary, extra, less who has the effrontery to empower themselves as makers and markers of epistemological embodied and territorial spaces of other/ed and not-other/ed. How has it come to be that Western knowledges and knowledge making have become privileged over the majority of the world's civilisations and knowledges, which have been around many thousands of years longer than Western knowledge, some since time immemorial?

That's right, before the coming of churches, residential schools, prisons before we knew how we knew we knew (Cole 2006).

The idea of other has always been part of the status quo of the colonisers, especially the English and the French the so-called founding peoples of Canada. How did it get founded if it was never lost? Tell me more about this 'methodology of difference'. You talk about a methodology that is about both generating and regenerating knowledge (O'Riley 2003).

It has to do with listening, leaving space, being attentive and receptive. This offers a way to opening ourselves to the else/where and other/wise of the world, to prepare for and participate with(in) weather/whether blurring and humbling our assumptions so that we can hear the silence/silents. This requires coming out of the *co*-closet and planting our diverse knowings together rather than engaging the usual monocropping accepted as research.

It's okay to talk about it in a theoretical space, but how might this be made operative on the ground?

You have to have a balance between theory and practice and cultural sensitivity. Some researchers need Western rhetoric or Westernised rhetoric. They need to be reassured in a space that is comfortable. For them you can't decolonise, 'post'-colonise, Aboriginalise something for someone else. They have to do it, they have to do the work, the self-empowering. They have to have and enact the vision.

Raven this might dissolve the relentless forces of sameness and engaging sustained negotiation in more creative kinds of subversion and more humble and joyous kinds of struggle enacting research so that '"*others*" become *actors*, active subjects, rather than objects of the Western gaze' (O'Riley 2003: 90).

If we want a more equitable, socially just peaceful and ecologically healthy world, we need to start learning how to live in spirit attuned to our place(s) and relationships, so that we can 'know' our responsibilities in the world. There is much research to be done Raven!

Aaah! But by whom and with whom? And for whose benefit?

Time! That's it! Library Closed.

References

Alfred, T. (2005). *Wasàse: Indigenous pathways to action and freedom*. Peterborough, ON: Broadview Press.

Apffel-Marglin, F. (Ed.) (1998) *The spirit of regeneration: Andean culture confronting Western notions of development*. London and New York: St. Martin's Press.

Bohm, D. (1980) *Wholeness and the Implicate Order*. London: Routledge.

Cole, P. (2006) *Coyote and Raven go canoeing: Coming home to the village*. Montréal, QC: McGill–Queen's University Press (Native and Northern Series).

Deleuze, G. and Guattari, F. (1987) *A thousand plateaus: Capitalism and schizophrenia*. Trans. B. Massumi, Minneapolis, MN: University of Minnesota Press.

Deleuze, G. (1988) *Le pli: Liebniz et le baroque*. Paris: Minuit.

Deloria, V. Jr. (1997) *Red earth, white lies: Native Americans and the myth of scientific fact*. Golden, CO: Fulcrum Publishing.

George, Chief D. and Hirnschall, H. (2004) *The best of Chief Dan George*. Surrey, BC: Hancock House Publishers.

Kulchyski, P., McCaskill, D. and Newhouse, D. (Eds) (1999) *In the words of Elders: Aboriginal cultures in transition*. Toronto: University of Toronto Press.

Ladson–Billings, G. (2003) Racialized discourses and ethnic epistemologies. In N. K. Denzin and Y. S. Lincoln (Eds). *The landscape of qualitative research: Theories and issues*. Thousand Oaks, CA: Sage Publications.

Meili, D. (1991) *Those who know: Profiles of Alberta's Native Elders*. Edmonton, AB: NeWest Press.

O'Riley, P. (2005) Research and Aboriginal Peoples: Toward self-determination, *Native Studies Review*, 15(2): 77–96.

——(2003) *Technology, culture, and socioeconomics: A rhizoanalysis of educational discourses*. New York: Peter Lang Publishing, Inc.

Rengifo, G. V. (1998) The Allyu. In F. Apffel-Marglin (Ed.). *The spirit of regeneration: Andean culture confronting Western notions of development*. London: St. Martin's Press.

Smith, L. T. (1999) *Decolonizing methodologies: Research and Indigenous Peoples*. Dunedin, NZ: University of Otago Press.

Thomas, R. (2005) Honouring the oral traditions of my ancestors through storytelling. In L. Brown and S. Strega (Eds). *Research as resistance: Critical, Indigenous and anti-oppressive approaches*. Toronto, ON: Canadian Scholars' Press.

Vizenor, G. (1994). *Manifest manners: Postindian warriors of survivance*. Hanover, NH: Wesleyan University Press.

27

Knowledge in context

Whose knowledge and for what context?

Q. Gu

The purpose of this chapter is to contribute to doctoral students' understandings of the dialectic relationship between knowledge and context. The chapter will discuss, within the contemporary context of globalisation and the internationalisation of higher education, the personal and contextual nature of knowledge and through this, key issues with regard to the ownership of knowledge and its implication for knowledge production, exchange and utilisation.

Globalisation and internationalisation: the contemporary context for research students

Global flows of knowledge and skills

The international exchange of markets, skills and cultures has been occurring for millennia (Little and Green 2009). Globalisation is, therefore, not a new phenomenon. However, as Little and Green (2009) rightly remind us, 'the latest phase of globalization is qualitatively distinct' (2009: 166). The unprecedented information and communications technology revolution has transformed the ways that knowledge is produced, assessed and disseminated (Coolahan 2002). Moreover, the sheer rapidity of change and its accumulated effects have also altered the character of work and many features of contemporary living in a fundamental way (Held *et al.* 1999; Coolahan 2002; Little and Green 2009). Friedman (2005) pronounces that the world is now flat in the third wave of globalisation and that the 'flat–world platform' is 'enabling, empowering, and enjoining individuals and small groups to go global so easily and so seamlessly':

> Globalization 3.0 [phase3] makes it possible for so many more people to plug in and play, and you are going to see every colour of the human rainbow take part.
>
> Friedman 2005: 11

However, this phenomenon of global flows of knowledge and skills is nowhere better represented than in the dramatic rise of the internationalisation of universities across the world, fuelled by the process of economic, social and cultural globalisation and localisation (Rizvi 2006). Statistics show that in 2004 more than 2.5 million tertiary students studied outside their home countries compared to 1.75 million in 1999 – a 41 per cent increase (UNESCO 2006). The Global Student Mobility 2025 report (Böhm et al. 2002) foresees that the demand for international education will increase to 7.2 million in 2025.

Concomitantly, since the 1990s, migration flows of highly skilled workers have also expanded dramatically (OECD 2008). Many students have remained in the country in which they study. In the USA the average stay rate for Chinese doctorate recipients skyrocketed to 96 per cent from 65 per cent between 1992 and 2001 and from 72 per cent to 85 per cent for Indians. OECD (2008) data show that of the 113 countries for which information is available, 27 have expatriation rates of their tertiary educated people to the OECD area of over 20 per cent, including nine countries where the rate is over 50 per cent.

The significant increase in East–West and South–North student mobility and the skewed expansion of internationalised higher education are most likely to witness a continued increase in the scale of the international migration of skills in the world of work. Thanks to the continuing advancement of science and technology, the mobility of people and skills has already made possible for everyone – including those who travel and those who do not – to consume cultural products and knowledge and ideas that are globally produced and distributed; and through this, transformed the nature of work and social life in the wider world (Rizvi 2008). Rizvi, in agreement with Appadurai (1996), argues that global imagination

> [N]ow plays a crucial role in how people engage with their everyday activities, consider their options and make decisions within the new configuration of social relations that are no longer confined to local communities but potentially span, either directly or indirectly, national boundaries.
>
> Rizvi 2008: 18–19

The trend of skills mobility is likely to see continued change in the ways that knowledge is produced, displayed and exchanged and utilised in the 'flattening and shrinking' world (Friedman 2005: 11), driven by unevenly distributed economic, political and ideological forces, as well as the forces of cultural (and local) diversity and forces of global interconnectivity.

What it means to be a research student in times of change

Current changes in the process of globalisation pose profound implications for today's research students, relating to the changing role of research, and subsequently, the changing nature of higher education, the changing environment for their study and purposes of their research.

First and foremost, the role of research is substantially changed by the profound and accelerating changes that society is undergoing. Knowledge and skills have become the most valuable commodities for economic development as countries compete internationally in knowledge-based goods and services (Little and Green 2009). The research itself, as Gibbons et al. (1994) observe, 'is likely to be part of a national programme directed to some socio-technical goal', 'be sensitive to its commercial possibilities, and may be initiated or carried forward out of a sense of these possibilities' (1994: 75). The tradition of theory-oriented free enquiry is under growing threat of being replaced with problem-oriented, interdisciplinary research (Gibbons *et al.* 1994). Knowledge transfer, as a means and an end of ensuring products of research can best influence and benefit the development of policy and practice for all parts of society, has become high on the national agenda in many nation states. For example, in the UK, the Economic and Social Research Council (ESRC) pronounces that 'if we [the UK] are to compete in the global marketplace, we need to increase our knowledge transfer and collaboration to get our research into policy and practice'. The UK government has identified knowledge exchange and transfer as a priority for the future and increased funding to ensure that research is translated into policy and practice at national, regional and local levels (Economic and Social Research Council 2009).

Associated with the changing role of research is the transformation of higher education in the process of knowledge production, dissemination and utilisation. As the emerging knowledge economy is establishing itself in society it has become increasingly difficult for universities to have the monopoly on knowledge production. Neither can academic researchers remain self-confined or isolated in ivory towers enjoying the legislation and diffusion of knowledge and ideas. Gibbons *et al.* (1994) observe that the production and utilisation of knowledge is by default diffused throughout society. Facing the emergence of 'a multi-billion dollar knowledge industry', traditional research-focused institutions are under pressure to transform their role in the business of knowledge transfer by forming and becoming 'part of a larger and denser network of knowledge institutions', which extend into industry, government and the media (Gibbons *et al.* 1994: 71). The UK ESRC (Economic and Social Research Council 2009) argues that 'academic researchers collaborating with business, the public sector and/or the third sector on projects of mutual interest is one of the most effective mechanisms for knowledge exchange and transfer'. Within such policy contexts, universities are expected to extend their services to adjacent communities through outreach programmes which aim at creating opportunities for dialogue, knowledge application and ideas sharing between the research community and its targeted users.

Universities are, also, expected to respond to the wider context of internationalisation, which is perceived as a proactive response to globalisation (Knight 2004) and vital for today's tertiary institutions to survive and thrive in times of change (OECD 2007; 2008). The internalisation of higher education places universities on a platform where the process of knowledge transfer transcends disciplinary as well as cultural, societal and national boundaries. The mobility of ideas and knowledge has to be created on the basis of mutual interests between all stakeholders involved and disseminated through continuous negotiations concerned with differences in systems, values, purposes, practices and the nature of the contexts in which the knowledge is to be produced and to be applied. Nonetheless, the benefits of collaborating with researchers, institutions, business and public sectors beyond these boundaries may significantly outweigh potential challenges in that universities could draw on a broader range of resources and expertise in the production, exchange and utilisation of knowledge, and through this, sustain their leading role in the changing knowledge industries.

Taken together, fundamental changes in the role of research and the role of higher education have created an intellectually stimulating and culturally rich learning environment for research students. With greater and easier access to global flows of technology, skills, images and knowledge, it is no longer an option that research students do not connect up with ideas, cultures and research results generated in the rest of the world. As Rizvi (2008) observes, sources of learning in today's cosmopolitan

337

environment are 'more diverse and extensive, and can no longer be contained within the borders of the nation-state' (p. 29). In addition, research students find themselves increasingly exposed to multiple cultural and social relations with their peers, tutors and supervisors. Gardiner (2006) rightly asserts that the global age requires students to develop cognitively flexible and culturally sophisticated qualities and skills so that they can analyse issues and solve problems from multiple perspectives. Moreover, completion of their doctoral studies is not an end but a beginning of their learning to conduct scientific enquiries in the world of research because, in part, university researchers are no longer 'in a strong enough position, either scientifically, economically or politically, to determine what shall count as excellent in teaching or research' (Gibbons *et al.* 1994: 8):

> Many graduates continue to develop their specialist skills outside the walls of the university and are now in the position not only to understand what university researchers are doing but are able to pass judgement on this quality and significance.
>
> Gibbons *et al.* 1994: 8

To summarise, the emerging knowledge society in the contemporary era has magnified the importance of knowledge and ideas in production and services (Little and Green 2009). Global interconnectivity and the increasingly intensified relationships between the global and the local contexts create new possibilities as well as challenges for knowledge to be integrated, exchanged and utilised across the boundaries of diverse locations, cultures, societies and nation states. In addition, the tradition of higher education universities as the primary site of knowledge production has begun to wane. Knowledge transfer has led to profound changes in ways in which research is conducted and disseminated and these changes expose universities and academic researchers, as well as research students, to a whole new phase of knowledge economy in which knowledge production and knowledge dissemination and utilisation are not two processes but one single process. Critical understandings of not only the contexts in which knowledge is produced, but also the nature of the contexts in which the same knowledge is to be utilised, are not only important, but vital in promoting and facilitating the process of knowledge transfer. To achieve such understandings, one has to understand the nature of knowledge.

The nature of knowledge: social, contextual and personal

The question of what knowledge is remains the current focus of philosophical debate (Fernie *et al.* 2003). Fernie *et al.* (2003) posit that this question has 'plagued philosophical debate since the beginning of philosophy itself', most notably revolving around attempts to distinguish the source of knowledge and the method of acquiring knowledge. It is not within the scope of this chapter to participate in the continuing debate and find answers. Rather, the following discussions will be developed to focus our attention upon the social, contextual and personal nature of knowledge, and through this, address an important question which underscores the process of knowledge acquisition, production and dissemination and which many doctoral students would need to think through in their endeavour to make an original contribution in today's knowledge economy: Whose is knowledge and for what context?

The *Compact Oxford English Dictionary* (2005) defines knowledge as '1. information and skills acquired through experience or education. 2. the sum of what is known. 3.

awareness or familiarity gained by experience of a fact or situation'. Essentially, this definition suggests an underlying association between experience (of individuals, institutions and research communities) and the formulation of information, facts and theoretical and practical understanding of a particular field or subject. The assumption is broadly in line with Dewey's views on knowledge and education, which has a primary concern over learning through problem solving and the mastery of ways of testing one's own hypothesis and procedures by using material from prior experience to guide present enquiry (Noddings 2007). Experience in this pragmatic sense is learned and acquired through human interactions with the reality and is a result of cognitive reasoning, critical thinking and emotional discernment. It follows that knowledge that is constructed through human experience may bear strong social, contextual and personal characteristics.

Knowledge as socially constructed

Arguing from a social constructivist perspective, Blum argued that

> [I]f objective knowledge is taken to mean knowledge of a reality independent of language, or presuppositionless knowledge, or knowledge of the world which is independent of the observer's procedures for finding and producing the knowledge, then there is no such thing as objective knowledge.
>
> Blum 1971: 129

Blum's argument suggests that reality is socially constructed and that it has 'to be continually interpreted' (Esland 1971: 75). Writing earlier, Berger and Luckmann (1966) proposed the notion of the social stock of knowledge and made a useful distinction between subjective reality and objective reality – that is, 'reality as apprehended in individual consciousness' as opposed to 'reality as institutionally defined' (1966: 167).

> Since socialization is never complete and the contents it internalizes face continuing threats to their subjective reality, every viable society must develop procedures of reality-maintenance to safeguard a measure of symmetry between objective and subjective reality. ... the reality of everyday life maintains itself by being embodied in routines, which is the essence of institutionalization. Beyond this, however, the reality of everyday life is ongoingly reaffirmed in the individual's interaction with others. Just as reality is originally internalized by a social process, so it is maintained in consciousness by social processes.
>
> Berger and Luckmann 1966: 166–67, 169

Thus, an absolutely objective view of knowledge tends to deny the active role of human beings in the process of knowledge creation. Esland (1971) sees this denial as 'fundamentally dehumanizing' as it 'ignores the intentionality and expressivity of human action and the entire complex process of intersubjective negotiation of meanings' (1971: 75). In agreement, Bruner (1990) argues that the process of meaning making is inherently *situated* in cultural and social realities (p. 105). He takes the view that the process of 'assigning meanings to things in different settings on particular occasions' involves 'situating encounters with the world in their appropriate cultural contexts' (Bruner 1996: 3). Bruner (1996) further postulates that the nature of knowledge and knowing (i.e. coming to know something) is both situated and distributed in social realities.

Writing in the discourse of organisational studies, Lam (1997) observed that many of the problems of collaboration and knowledge transfer in global co-operative ventures 'lie not in structural barriers but in the nature of knowledge itself and its social embeddedness' (p. 974). Following Lanzara and Patriotta (2001), Fernie *et al.* (2003) also criticise the epistemological orientation of the project management discipline for its tendency to 'conceptualize knowledge as an objective, transferable commodity' (p. 178). They challenge the underlying assumption of this orientation for its lack of scrutiny on the context-bound nature of meaning and knowledge, arguing that knowledge derived from experience cannot easily be codified and transferred across organisational structures or systems. It can be further argued that a large part of human and professional knowledge can hardly retain its original meaning when it is divorced from the contexts in which it is constructed and produced (see also Polanyi 1962; 1966; Nelson and Winter 1982).

Writing in the field of international and comparative education, Gu (2007) observes that the history of educational development projects in developing countries is predominantly featured, with conflicts and problems caused by dilemmas of difference and challenges of appropriating knowledge into a contextually, socially and culturally sensitive form (Gu 2007). It has long been a challenge for educational development projects to ensure that their advocated knowledge on teaching and learning effectiveness is communicated to local practitioners and incorporated into day-to-day practices in a sustainable way. The reality of cross-cultural educational development programmes begs the question of whether their advocated practice of teaching and learning is, in fact, 'more effective' irrespective of the educational contexts in which it is practised. Whilst the good intentions of western agencies to improve the quality of education in less developed countries have seldom been questioned, it has been a concern for donors and expatriate specialists that such good intentions are not always well received. One of the key challenges in transferring knowledge remains the ownership of knowledge and the expertise.

Knowledge and expertise: a personal entity

If we accept the notion that knowledge is socially constructed through human interactions, individuals' personal stock of knowledge can then be perceived as developing in breadth and strength through their actions and endeavours to explore, discover and familiarise themselves with new territories of the changing reality. It will, also, be nourished by their improved understandings of the reality. The fast changing nature of the modern society has moulded a dynamic context in which individuals' personal stock of knowledge, which at the very least mirrors Berger and Luckmann's social stock of knowledge, is destined never to be complete. John Dewey's (1997) assertion that knowledge is strictly relative to human interaction with the world continues to offer an insightful framework for understanding the spiral development of individualised professional knowledge.

> [E]very extension of knowledge makes us aware of blind and opaque spots, where with less knowledge all had seemed obvious and natural. ... Increase of the store of meanings makes us conscious of new problems, while only through translation of the new perplexities into what is already familiar and plain do we understand or solve these problems. This is the constant spiral movement of knowledge. ... Our intellectual progress consists, as has been said, in a rhythm of direct understanding –

technically called *ap*prehension – with indirect, mediated understanding – technically called *com*prehension.

Dewey 1997: 119–20

Eraut provides a complementary viewpoint on the construction and development of personal knowledge. In his attempt to explain the problem of 'how theory gets to influence practice' and the problem of 'how people use the knowledge they have already acquired', he argued that

> The key to unlocking these problems was my realization that learning knowledge and using knowledge are not separate processes but the same process. The process of using knowledge transforms that knowledge so that it is no longer the same knowledge. But people are so accustomed to using the word 'knowledge' to refer only to 'book knowledge' which is publicly available in codified form, that they have developed only limited awareness of the nature and extent of their personal knowledge.

Eraut 1994: 25

The essential point is that as a result of the process of 'learning knowledge' and 'using knowledge', theoretical images, formulas and structures held by individuals will no longer be the same as the images presented in theorists' publications, but will be modified by personalised knowledge arising from practical experiences. Furthermore, even the theorists' knowledge may vary from publication to publication over time. Thus, we would not be surprised to find that individual experts and researchers may hold varied interpretations of a body of knowledge and make differentiated assumptions about its application in the contexts of dissemination and utilisation.

Bereiter and Scardamalia (1993) argue that every kind of knowledge has a part in expertise – from the most obvious kinds, such as procedural knowledge (skill) and formal knowledge (as in 'book learning'), to the least obvious kinds such as informal knowledge and impressionistic knowledge. The traditional view of expertise sees it as knowledge (Smith and Tiberius 2006). However, the difference between experts and non-experts does not necessarily lie in the kinds of knowledge that they have. Rather, it lies in 'how much [knowledge] they have, how well integrated it is, and how effectively it is geared to performance' (Bereiter and Scardamalia 1993: 74).

The growth of expertise is situation-specific and is a personal entity. It builds on experiences and is embedded in a continual process of problem solving in a critical and self-reflective manner. Experts 'carry their learning in different settings and continue in complex ways' (Evans *et al.* 2006: 17). However, the effectiveness of expertise can be relative, particularly when it is tested in the global knowledge society. Success in solving problems within a particular context contributes to the repertoire of professional experiences, in that it feeds into not only the experts' understanding of the problems but also their understanding of the context within which the problems have been diagnosed. Key to the development of expertise is the building of a capability to identify appropriate and responsive ways that can best resolve embedded problems and more importantly, lead to further improvement. It is thus important that research students are aware that their professional knowledge and expertise are not only context-dependent, but also are a personalised entity. In the process of learning and research, their knowledge and expertise evolve and carry with them values embedded in a range of structures, systems

341

and contexts in which their enquiries are located. Their intellectual development is interwoven in the fabric of their lives.

Conclusion

To summarise, the third wave of globalisation has created a whole new learning and research environment for today's doctoral students. They are working on a 'flat-world platform' where different values, systems, cultures and knowledges and ideas interact and interconnect and create a complex and rich resource for their enquiries into the world. At the same time, they are also experiencing a changing context of knowledge sharing and transfer, which has seen knowledge production become increasingly a socially distributed process across society (Gibbons *et al.* 1994).

Within such research and policy contexts, a university needs to 'enlarge its view of its role in knowledge production from that of being a monopoly supplier to becoming a partner in both national and international contexts' (Gibbons *et al.* 1994: 156). Creating a dialogue between the research community and the user community is no longer an option but a necessity, to ensure that knowledge production and knowledge utilisation are not conducted in separate and isolated contexts and that knowledge and ideas produced by research can make a real difference to policy and practices in society.

For students, and doctoral students in particular, it has become increasingly important that they 'learn how to find, appropriate and use knowledge that might have been produced almost anywhere in the world' (Gibbons *et al.* 1994: 156). Rizvi (2008) also emphasises the importance of helping students come to terms with 'their *situatedness* in the world':

> [S]ituatedness of their knowledge and of their cultural practices, as well as their positionality in relation to the social networks, political institutions and social relations that are no longer confined to particular communities and nations, but potentially connect up with the rest of the world.
>
> Said 1983, quoted in Rizvi 2008: 30

It follows that it has become an increasingly relevant challenge for research students to be able to identify the location of their research in the interconnected global knowledge society and exercise their wisdom to capture, acquire and appropriate their knowledge and expertise in the business of knowledge production and dissemination.

References

Appadurai, A. (1996) *Modernity at Large: Cultural Dimensions of Globalization*. Minneapolis, MN and London: University of Minnesota Press.

Bereiter, C. and Scardamalia, M. (1993) *Surpassing Ourselves: An Inquiry into the Nature and Implications of Expertise*. La Salle, IL: Open Court.

Berger, P. and Luckmann, T. (1966) *The Social Construction of Reality*. New York: Penguin.

Blum, A. F. (1971) The corpus of knowledge as a normative order. In M. Young (Ed.) *Knowledge and Control: New Directions for the Sociology of Education*. London: Collier Macmillan, 117–32.

Böhm, A., Davis, D., Meares, D. and Pearce, D. (2002) *Global Student Mobility 2025: Analysis of Global Competition and Market Share*. Australia: IDP.

Bruner, J. (1990) *Acts of Meaning*. Cambridge, MA: Harvard University Press.

——(1996) *The Culture of Education*. Cambridge, MA: Harvard University Press.

Compact Oxford English Dictionary (2005) 3rd edn. Online. (Available at www.askoxford.com/concise_oed/ knowledge?view=uk Accessed 15 March 2009).

Coolahan, J. (2002) Teacher education and the teaching career in an era of lifelong learning, *OECD Education Working Papers*, No.2, Paris: OECD. Online. (Available at www.oecd.org/edu/workingpapers Accessed 28 July 2006.

Dewey, J. (1997) *How we think*, Mineola, NY: Dover Publications.

Eraut, M. (1994) *Developing Professional Knowledge and Competence*. London: The Falmer Press.

Esland, G. M. (1971) Teaching and learning as the organization of knowledge. In M. Young (Ed.). *Knowledge and Control: New Directions for the Sociology of Education*. London: Collier Macmillan, 70–115.

Economic and Social Research Council (2009) *Knowledge Transfer*. Online. (Available at www.esrcsociety today.ac.uk/ESRCInfoCentre/Support/knowledgetransfer/ Accessed 20 March 2009).

Evans, K., Hodkinson, P., Rainbird, H. and Unwin, L. (2006) *Improving Workplace Learning*. London: Routledge.

Fernie, S., Green, S., Weller, S. and Newcombe, R. (2003) Knowledge sharing: context, confusion and controversy, *International Journal of Project Management*, 21: 177–87.

Friedman, T. L. (2005) *The World is Flat*. London: Penguin Books.

Gardiner, H. (2006) How education changes: considerations of history, science and values. In M. Suarez-Orozeo and Qin-Hiliard (Eds). *Globalization: Culture and Education in the New Millennium*. Berkeley, CA: University of California Press.

Gibbons, M., Limoges, C., Nowotny, H., Schwartzman, S., Scott, P. and Trow, M. (1994) *New Production of Knowledge*. London: Sage Publications.

Gu, Q. (2007) *Teacher Development: Knowledge and Context*. London: Continuum.

Held, D., McGrew, A., Goldblatt, D. and Parraton, J. (1999) *Global Transformation: Politics, Economics and Culture*. Palo Alto, CA: Stanford University Press.

Knight, J. (2004) Internationalization remodelled: definition, approaches, and rationales, *Journal of Studies in International Education*, 8: 5–31.

Lam, A. (1997) Embedded firms, embedded knowledge: problems of collaboration and knowledge transfer in global cooperative ventures, *Organization Studies*, 18(6): 973–96.

Lanzara, G. F. and Patriotta, G. (2001) Technology and the courtroom: an inquiry into knowledge making in organizations, *Journal of Management Studies, Special Issue: Knowledge management: Concepts and Controversies*, 38(7): 943–72.

Little, A. and Green, A. (2009) Successful globalization, education and sustainable development, *International Journal of Educational Development*, 29: 166–74.

Nelson R. R. and Winter, S. G. (1982) *An Evolutionary Theory of Economic Change*. Cambridge, MA: Belknap Press of Harvard University Press.

Noddings, N. (2007) *Philosophy of Education*. 2nd edn. Cambridge, MA: Westview Press.

OECD (with the World Bank) (2007) *Cross-border Tertiary Education: A Way towards Capacity Development*. Paris: OECD.

OECD (2008) *Policy brief: Cross-border higher education and development*. Paris: OECD.

Polanyi, M. (1962) *Personal Knowledge*. Chicago, IL: University of Chicago Press.

——(1966) *The tacit dimension*. London: Routledge and Kegan Paul.

Rizvi, F. (2006) Postcolonialism and globalization in education. In *Cultural Studies Critical Methodologies*, unpublished manuscript.

——(2008) Epistemic virtues and cosmopolitan learning, *The Australian Educational Researcher*, 35(1): 17–35.

Smith, R. A. and Tiberius, R. G. (2006) *The nature of expertise: implication for teachers and teaching*. Online. (Available at www.lcc.edu/cte/resources/teachingexcellence/packets/packet4/nature_of_expertise.html Accessed 20 November 2006.

UNESCO (2006) *Global education digest. Comparing statistics across the world*, Paris: UNESCO

28

Open access and the ongoing transformation of scholarly publishing

A guide for doctoral students

R. Lucas and J. Willinsky

'The chorus of "yeas" was thunderous', Harvard University librarian Robert Darnton told *The New York Times* on 12 February 2008. 'I hope this marks a turning point in the way communications operate in the world of scholarship' (Cohen 2008). Harvard's Faculty of Arts and Sciences had just passed a resolution declaring that because it was 'committed to disseminating the fruits of its research and scholarship as widely as possible', the faculty would grant the university a broad, non-exclusive license to distribute its scholarly articles, and specifically to 'make the article available to the public in an open-access repository' (FAS 2008). Harvard's action is a particularly dramatic instance of a broader transformation, intent on increasing access to knowledge within scholarly communication, which has been facilitated by developments in information technology. Harvard was not the first institution to pass such an open access mandate, but it was an especially significant milestone for what has become known as the open access (OA) movement in scholarly publishing.

The OA movement was officially named in 2002, but it built on a decade of momentum for internet-enabled distribution of scholarship and on a centuries-old tradition of open science (David 1998). Numerous OA mandates like that of Harvard have been passed, with some funding agencies, such as the U.S. National Institutes of Health, creating open access mandates for all publications resulting from funded research. In addition, thousands of journals have adopted OA policies, of varying strength, that result in published work being made free to readers on, and for some time after, publication. As of 2006, an estimated 19.4 per cent of all published articles were available under OA, that is, free to readers online (Björk *et al.* 2008). This expansion of access is a defining characteristic of research in the early twenty-first century and holds the potential to enhance both its public and scholarly value.

In this chapter, we first provide an overview of these changes in the principles and practices of scholarly publishing. In the second half of the chapter, we provide practical information to help new and not-so-new scholars with a way to navigate this environment. What intellectual property rights do you have over your writings? How do those rights differ in different forms of publishing? How can you ensure that your research sees as wide of an audience as possible, does the most good and – to set aside for a moment the pretence of complete altruism – brings you the greatest reputation-building exposure? We also point readers toward noteworthy and interesting projects in networked scholarly communication. Beyond merely negotiating the new information landscape, opportunities are now available to reshape that environment on the side of greater openness, greater public impact and a greater global scale to the exchange of knowledge. This can happen through innovation, new initiatives, and through decisions made by voting members of faculties, scholarly societies, research groups and other organisations engaged in forms of scholarly communication.

Development of the OA movement

Technological changes may have made OA possible for scholarly work, but the stage was set by a crisis of journal subscription rates during the 1980s and 1990s. As OA maven Peter Suber puts it (2004), during that period journal prices rose at a rate 'four times faster than inflation for nearly two decades'. And the increase was not evenly distributed. The journal eco-system includes several types of publications. Some are put out independently, others by scholarly associations, and the majority – approximately 60% – by commercial publishers. The increasing subscription rates were mainly driven by this last group. In economics, for example, after adjusting for inflation, these profit-maximising commercial publishers raised rates by 300 per cent between 1985 and 2004. By comparison, non-profit journals in the field increased rates by 50 per cent (Bergstrom and Bergstrom 2004). At the upper extreme, *Brain Research*, published by Elsevier, costs a library well over $20,000 a year.

This crisis hit university libraries hard, even well-funded ones. The leading North American libraries, represented by the Association of Research Libraries, increased their journal spending by 260 per cent between 1986 and 2003 (Association of Research Libraries 2004). Eventually, though, libraries were forced to begin cutting subscriptions and scaling back their book purchases (Suber 2004). Given that the subscription crisis strained budgets at even the Harvards, Dukes, and MITs of the world, it should not be difficult to imagine its decimating effects on less well-endowed libraries in North America and especially in the developing world.[1]

As subscription rates skyrocketed, the internet was simultaneously enabling wider, cheaper dissemination of knowledge than ever before. Scholars began to post pre-publication copies of articles on their personal homepages, and the more ambitious amongst them experimented with new forms of publishing. In 1993 Arizona State University education professor Gene V. Glass founded the peer-reviewed journal *Education Policy Analysis Archives* (*EPAA*). Glass's journal harnessed the power of email and the web to publish on zero budget – not a widely replicable model perhaps, but one that would have been unfathomable only a few years before. And its daily viewership – by researchers, but also by teachers, parents, and other interested observers – dwarfed the number of print subscriptions typical for a journal in the field (Glass 2003). Just ask Colorado professor emeritus Robert L. Linn, whose 2003 critique of the performance standards in the No Child Left Behind Act was cited, a mere two weeks after its *EPAA* publication, in Malcolm Gladwell's 'Talk of the Town' *New Yorker* column (Linn 2003; Gladwell 2003). Linn's article had been posted with little fanfare. No press release was issued as, say, *The New England Journal of Medicine* might do to publicise a striking study. One can only assume that Gladwell was able to search for and then read the article because it was available in OA (Willinsky 2005). As of this writing, *EPAA* has published

561 articles in its 17 years of existence. Current traffic information is unavailable, but as of 2003, *EPAA* drew approximately 2,500 visitors a day from 70–80 countries (Glass 2003).

Although most OA journals employ traditional forms of double-blind peer-review (without author or reviewer knowing each other's identities) and publish on the same periodical basis as print editions, online publishing has allowed publishers to experiment with previously taken-for-granted aspects of the publishing system, such as regular publication cycles and the particulars of peer review. This mixture of innovations is perhaps best exemplified by the Public Library of Science (PLoS), and although they have yet to become commonplace in educational journals, these developments suggest the type of changes young scholars can expect to see – and effect – in the coming decades.[2] The interdisciplinary journal *PLoS ONE* publishes hundreds of studies a year as soon as they 'are judged to be technically sound', while providing tools for a more thorough assessment of the article's significance and contribution through what might be called a post-publication open review ('*PLoS ONE* Journal Information'). This policy allows for the publication of more studies with negative results or those that replicate earlier findings – two important categories of studies that often go unpublished due to a publication bias toward novelty and positive findings (Dickersin 1990). As in research, not all of these experiments have been successful, but it seems likely that these tools will proliferate, and that OA journals will be better positioned than closed ones to become part of an annotated, interlinked web of scholarship.[3]

In December 2001, the Open Society Institute brought together in Budapest a small group of professors from various fields to discuss the challenges and opportunities facing academic publishing. Together, they drafted and signed what would become known as the Budapest Open Access Initiative, which set out the terms of this new approach:

> By 'open access' to this literature, we mean its free availability on the public internet, permitting any users to read, download, copy, distribute, print, search, or link to the full texts of these articles, crawl them for indexing, pass them as data to software, or use them for any other lawful purpose, without financial, legal, or technical barriers other than those inseparable from gaining access to the internet itself.
>
> Chan *et al.* 2002

In late 2007, two months prior to the passage of the Harvard's Faculty of Arts and Sciences Mandate, the National Institutes of Health declared that final, peer-reviewed versions of the research that it funds be deposited at its archive, PubMed Central, within 12 months after publication. In the wake of Harvard FAS's Open Access mandate, numerous other institutions started similar initiatives. Other faculties at the famously decentralised Harvard have adopted similar policies – the Law School and the Kennedy School of Government in March 2009, with mandates pending in the university's other faculties (Lauerman 2009). Stanford's School of Education mandated OA in June 2008, as did MIT for the entire institution in March 2009 (Viadero 2008; Abelson 2009).

Although OA is a relatively recent development, its roots lie in a long tradition of efforts to open science, that is, open to review and critique, as well as innovation and development, that dates back to early modern Europe and the Enlightenment. With the Scientific Revolution came a shift from the closed knowledge of guilds, alchemists, astrologers, and others trafficking in 'nature's secrets', to a regime in which scientists' prestige came from their claim to first discovery, which could only be established through publication (Eamon 1994). Along with these self-interested motives, publication allowed scientists to verify each other's discoveries, discard ones that could not be replicated, avoid duplication of effort and integrate various lines of research (David 1998). In the *Philosophical Transactions*, widely considered the first scientific journal in English, Henry Oldenburg published letters from among members of London's Royal Society. It was in those pages, on 3 January 1671, that Sir Isaac Newton first published his groundbreaking research on optics. And it was there that he spent the next four years responding to critics and providing details of research design – establishing a norm that findings, methods, and sources should be made public so that readers may replicate and challenge them (Kuhn 1978; Willinsky 2005a: 234–44). Publication, then, is a matter of epistemological implications. It is only by publishing – describing research thoroughly and circulating the write-up as widely as possible (given current technologies and other means of distribution) – that knowledge is verified, legitimised, and accepted into a larger body of work.

It is also an ethical matter. Most research is funded, in one way or another, from public coffers. It is our responsibility to make the fruits of that research as public as possible. And especially so with educational research, given that work on this topic is intended to contribute to the improvement of learning in so many ways among so many people. Mounting evidence suggests that such openness in the circulation of this knowledge has practical consequences. It makes research available to policy makers (Willinsky 2003) and professionals (Willinsky and Quint-Rapoport 2007). Open access articles improve the quality of Wikipedia (Willinsky 2008). Academic libraries in the developing world are especially hamstrung by journal subscription prices, and reducing barriers to access can help scholars worldwide read the latest research and enter the global academic conversation (Willinsky 2005a, chapter 6). Open access publishing tools (such as Open Journal Systems, described below) lower the cost of producing a journal and allow groups of scholars to do so that otherwise could not, which in turn provides an outlet for publications and legitimises lines of research that are important in particular contexts but may be neglected by current gatekeepers, such as scholarly societies or commercial publishers (Willinsky and Mendis 2007).

As we have seen, though, the push for opening science was brought about for reasons of prestige and primacy (claim of invention and discovery), as well as altruism and the dispassionate pursuit of knowledge. So may today's scholars be altruistic as well. Fortunately, OA appeals to *vanity* as well as *valour*. Open access to research has been shown to increase its readership (Davis *et al.* 2008), and although the evidence is somewhat murkier, to increase its citation rates (Hitchcock 2009). This 'open access advantage' may be transitory; in a world of universal access, there is no advantage to be gained. But in the interim, there may be reputational rewards for academics that take advantage of opportunities to make their work OA, whether through OA archiving of their published work or through publishing in OA journals, which represent the two most prominent routes to OA.

Two routes to open access

The OA landscape is heterogeneous enough to require some explanation. Articles can become OA in several different ways, and policies vary from journal to journal. The first step in untangling this web is to distinguish between two types of OA: OA archiving and OA journals. Below, we describe each and explain how they affect you as an author.

Archiving

In the archiving route to OA, an author deposits her published journal articles in a publicly viewable web-based archive, either on her own website or her university's or funder's. Archiving requires the permission of the publisher but is done without their active assistance. Most publishers grant authors the right to archive, to one degree or another, but OA mandates like Harvard's see university faculties asserting their right to archive regardless of journal policy. In the writing and archiving process, intellectual property rights work as follows.

As an academic, you own the rights to the words you write (which is not the case if you write software, for example, for a corporation; McSherry 2001). But don't let yourself become too attached. When your work is accepted for publication in the typical journal, you will be asked to sign a publication agreement in which you sign over all intellectual property rights to the journal or its publisher. They, in turn, licence back to you the right to use the work in certain ways – for example, in classes that you teach. However, until your paper is accepted and the publication agreement signed, you have the right to archive your copy on a personal website, in your university or funder's archive, or however you like. This applies up to the final draft of the paper, that is, the version that is accepted for publication after peer review. This is the version that the publishers typically allow you to post to an archive – and it differs from the published version as a result of layout, copyediting and proofreading – sometimes with restrictions although journals commonly impose a delay of 6, 12 or 24 months before archiving is allowed – a so-called embargo.[4]

Of the four major corporate academic publishers with a substantial number of journals in the social sciences – Sage, Taylor & Francis, Elsevier, and Wiley-Blackwell – the first two are most important in the field of education. Sage, which began, for example, in 2007 to publish the prestigious journals of the American Educational Research Association, allows all authors to archive preprints, or the version prior to peer-review. Postprints, the authors' versions that reflect peer-review, may be deposited in personal or institutional archives after a 12-month embargo (while the final, published versions may never be archived). Similarly, Taylor & Francis allows archiving of preprints without restriction. However, a postprint embargo of 12 months is imposed for science and technology journals and 18 months in the social sciences and humanities. Elsevier's relatively permissive archiving policy is provided in Appendix A.

Each journal's terms will be specified in your publication agreement, but if you would like to know about a journal's policies beforehand – for example, when you are deciding where to submit – the SHERPA/RoMEO database (www.sherpa.ac.uk/romeo/) is an invaluable resource. Administered by SHERPA, a consortium of universities in the United Kingdom, RoMEO is a collection of archiving policies searchable by either journal name or publisher. SHERPA also provides similar directories of funder OA mandates, institutional archives, and more. It will also be useful for verifying whether the publisher policies described above are still valid – not a certainty in this rapidly changing and consolidating industry.

The recent wave of OA mandates represents a form of archiving that generally pays little regard to the distinctions between journal policies. Rather, these mandates use the leverage of the university or the funding institution to require a journal to grant immediate archiving rights. These mandates generally function in similar ways: When an article has been accepted and the author is asked to sign an author's agreement, he or she submits along with it an 'author addendum' specifying that the university claims a non-exclusive (and non-commercial) right to archive a pre-publication version. Faculty or staff then deposit the article into the university's online archive. If a publisher objects, the author can request a waiver from their mandating institution, but the OA policy is opt-out rather than opt-in. Mandates vary in their specific policies and in the rights they claim, and you can view the Stanford University School of Education's archive, with which we have been involved, at openarchive.stanford.edu. Supporting documents such as the Stanford mandate and policies can also be found there.

Open access journals

If posting copies of published work in an open access archive represents an indirect route to increased access, a more direct, if not as widely available path is found with journals that have an OA or free-to-read policy. This OA sometimes takes effect immediately, but other journals impose a delay (of six months, in the case of *The New England Journal of Medicine*) in order to keep some incentive for subscribers to continue with the journal. The *Directory of Open Access Journals*, established by the University of Lund, currently lists 4,000 titles and provides the most complete listing of journals that offer readers immediate OA on publication (www.doaj.org). In the area of education, the Communication of Research group within the American Educational Research Association maintains a list of titles that currently runs to 247 OA journals (aera-cr.asu.edu/ejournals/).

Compared to self-archiving, OA journals have the advantage of providing free access to the definitive copies of articles. Several publishers are now experimenting with ways of providing access to their journals, while recouping the same revenue they have received from subscriptions by using article processing fees (running as high at this point as US$3,000). Hindawi and BioMed Central, for example, are commercial publishers that publish only OA journals, largely in the life sciences, funded by article processing fees. However, the majority of OA journals do not charge such fees to authors, but rather rely on other revenue models that include institutional or scholarly society support, as well as grants, while in some cases they are supported by subscriptions fees for their print editions. While the Public Library of Science publishes the open access *PLoS Biology*, which has the highest impact factor in its field (meaning that it is cited more often than other titles), education's leading general journals are not OA at this point, although there are certainly a good number of more specialised titles in education that are OA.

To help new and existing journals consider publishing with an OA policy, the Public Knowledge Project, founded in 1998 by one of the authors of this chapter, John Willinsky, has developed Open Journal Systems, free and open source software for managing journals' submission, peer-review, and editing processes and for publishing articles to the open web (Willinsky 2005). This software, which helps journals reduce their costs with online management and publishing, is being used by close to 3,000 journals, 85 per cent of which are OA.[5]

Many OA journals publish their contents under Creative Commons (CC) licences, which allow for the reuse of the published work in teaching, public forums, or other non-commercial settings, while protecting the claims of authorship (Lessig 2005). Creative Commons licensing, which is used by millions and millions of items on the web, well beyond scholarly work, draws inspiration from the free and open source software movement, and both might be considered cousins of OA and open science (Willinsky

349

2005). Just as open source software is published under a licence that permits users to view, modify, and redistribute software's source code, the basic CC licence allows users of cultural content to modify and redistribute it, on the condition that they attribute the work to its original creator. Much content on video-sharing websites such as YouTube and photo-sharing sites like Flickr.com is licensed under Creative Commons, as are text and images from the collaboratively written website Wikipedia. The Creative Commons licence has become a widely recognised symbol, reflecting a broader cultural interest in allowing others to share one's work as a way of increasing its value to others, rather than diminishing its potential for commercialisation.

Finding articles

This chapter is not the place for a full course in research strategies, but a few significant information sources for those working in the area of education bear mentioning. ERIC, the Education Resources Information Centre, is the U.S. federal government's directory of articles and other materials related to education (eric.ed.gov). ERIC itself is not a new development, having existed since 1964 (Hoover and Brandhorst 1982), and during that time served the cause of access through its search and document reprint services and its popular research digests for scholars and policy makers. A controversial 2003 privatisation eliminated many ERIC programmes, such as the research digests and the topical, university-based clearinghouses that published them, and reoriented the service toward online search. After a rocky transition, ERIC has developed a sophisticated set of search tools, prominently displayed indication of peer-reviewed articles, and links to OA versions of a number of the indexed articles. Efforts are underway to digitise and provide access to 340,000 resources from ERIC's microfiche archive, beginning in 1992 and working back to 1966. ERIC has not, however, incorporated the sort of participatory tools that are typical of modern web applications. One can imagine Amazon.com-style user-curated lists of related articles.

Google Scholar (scholar.google.com) is the search tool of first resort for many academics, as well as students, and it has recently begun to provide greater assistance for those interested in finding OA materials. Although Google Scholar has, since its origins in 2004, linked to publishers' versions of articles, these articles are usually only available with a subscription. For members of the public (or even scholars working from off-campus) accessing these articles can be inconvenient, expensive or impossible. Google Scholar now also links prominently to OA versions of articles, when available, whether from archives, websites or journals. Such links are marked with a green arrow – we like to think in a nod to the symbolic significance of 'green'. Google Scholar is also an effort that brings Google back to its roots. The PageRank algorithm used in general Google searches was famously inspired by citation analyses of academic publications. Webpages that receive more inbound links, from more other highly linked-to sites, are displayed more prominently in search results (Battelle 2006). Similarly, in Google Scholar, articles with the most citations are favoured, and searchers can conveniently click to see what articles have cited a given article – the opposite of the time-honoured process of following bibliography citations backward. Although still crudely executed at times within Google Scholar (with multiple entries, for example, for a single item), this feature suggests how the web is also open to more sophisticated citation analysis methods and visualisation tools, such as inferring the *types* of citations (extension, rebuttal or citation of a methodological classic) and mapping the relationships among bodies of work and the development of research lines (Moya-Anegón *et al.* 2007).

Open data as a parallel development

Open access to research and scholarship is but one element in this new spirit of openness to academic work. Just as vital a development is open data, which enables readers and researchers to access the complete data sets, source documents, and other resources drawn on by a given study (King 2007; Kühne and Liehr 2009). This access adds greater to the quality of research, as it enables a more thorough review, as well as facilitating replication studies and reanalysis (which also improves the economic efficiency of research in some cases). When articles are published online, supplementary files can be published alongside them – videos, image collections, datasets, etc. This is an extension of the open science imperative to specify the grounds on which claims are made. There are competing interests, such as the effort required to clean up a dataset for public consumption and the researcher's interest in protecting them for further analysis. Despite this, a movement is afoot to raise specification requirements. Drexel's Jean-Claude Bradley writes in support of what he calls Open Notebook Science: '[I]t is essential that all of the information available to the researchers to make their conclusions is equally available to the rest of the world. Basically, no insider information' (Bradley 2006). Cambridge chemist Peter Murray-Rust advocates for the Open Data movement on the grounds that 'much important data is under-analyzed and contains huge amounts of undiscovered science' (Murray-Rust 2007). The non-profit Science Commons has released a legal framework for data sharing, the 'Protocol for Implementing Open Access Data' (sciencecommons. org/projects/publishing/open-access-data-protocol/) and Harvard's Dataverse Network Project produces open source software for publicly archiving datasets for others to analyse (thedata.org).

Conclusion

Because the opening transformation of scholarly publishing that we describe is gaining momentum, many of the facts in this article will have changed by the time you read it. Publisher webpages and academic search engines will have added new features. Further OA mandates will have been adopted, we hope, and a higher percentage of articles will be freely available. Commercial publishers are exploring new models for offering OA, in response to those mandates. But we expect that even the narrow issue of how to ensure universal access to published journal articles will remain contested for much of the next decade. Considering OA more broadly, it is easy to imagine some of the next issues that will come into focus, among them book publishing, open data, and innovations in open commenting and possibly peer review. And of course if the past is any guide, the future will present possibilities of which we cannot currently conceive.

You, the readers of this chapter, will have the opportunity to participate in and influence these developments. You will make decisions about where and how to publish and for which journals you are willing to review and serve on the editorial boards. You will have the opportunity to archive your own published work as fully as policies allow. As future journal editors and editorial board members, you may be in a position to influence these policies. As future faculty members and scholarly society members, you may be asked to vote on OA mandates and may even feel moved to introduce one, as well as to support OA journals. Some of you will have the opportunity to shape scholarly communication technologies, as users, testers and perhaps designers. Some of you may even make these issues of access to knowledge an object of study within the field of education and the social sciences. After all, OA is a matter of public education, broadly conceived, as faculty and students, as well as professionals and the public at large come to see greater advantages in having research and scholarship more widely available. We look forward to seeing the relevance and implications of this new standard for public access become clear, for epistemology, deliberative democracy, the sociologies of science and knowledge, social dimensions of technology design, and networks of knowledge diffusion – to name just a few areas of potential impact.

In this time of transformation for scholarly publishing, we ask you to keep a few considerations in mind. Publishing is a matter of equity, as it allows those far from the centres of academic power to join in the conversation and to define research agendas meaningful in their contexts. Publishing is also a matter of scholarly value. Along the lines just mentioned, it can help to uncover research talent, disseminate methodological advances, and drive research in productive new directions. It also allows researchers to efficiently and effectively verify each others' work, build on it, and integrate it into meaningful bodies of work. Finally, scholarly publishing is a matter of public value and public good. In education and the social sciences especially, much research is clearly relevant to the concerns of parents, teachers, administrators, school board members, curriculum developers, legislators, policy makers, and citizens. The internet opens possibilities for access to these particular forms of knowledge, forming a natural but still exciting extension of what has been achieved since the early years of open science or the postwar years of journal expansion. By taking care to make work as accessible as possible in an age of internet-enabled knowledge sharing, rigorous research can increase its contribution, as a public good, on a global scale.

Acknowledgement

This chapter draws on previously published material from Willinsky (2005a; 2005b; 2009) and on Lucas and Willinsky (2009) – work that has been supported by the Pacific Press Endowment at the University of British Columbia and the Khosla Family Professorship at Stanford University.

Appendix A: example of a publisher's policy enabling authors to post a copy of their work online

Elsevier is liberal with respect to authors and electronic preprints. Unlike some publishers, we do not consider that a preprint of an article (including a prior version as a thesis) prior to its submission to Elsevier for consideration amounts to prior publication, which would disqualify the work from consideration for re-publication in a journal. We also do not require authors to remove electronic preprints from publicly accessible servers (including the author's own home page) once an article has been accepted for publication. Further, we have announced in May 2004 a change in policy that facilitates institutional repositories by permitting authors to revise their personal versions of their papers to reflect changes made in the peer review process. This new policy permits authors to post such revised personal versions on their own web sites and the sites of their institutions, provided a link to the journal is included. Our policy however is that the final published version of the article as it appears in the journal will continue to be available only on an Elsevier site.

www.elsevier.com/wps/find/authorshome.authors/preprints (27 April 2009)

Notes

1 Scholarly monographs and edited collections did not experience the same increase in prices over this period, and have not, to date, taken to the web, which has meant that within scholarly publishing open access has been almost entirely focused on journals. Library scanning projects such as Google Books and devices such as the Amazon Kindle or Sony E-Reader portend changes in book publishing, but it remains to be seen whether these changes will be characterised by an increasingly open form of access or by a more privatised arrangement.

2 Stanford biochemist Patrick Brown and Berkeley computational biologist Michael Eisen took the first steps toward PLoS in early 2001, when they launched a petition in which scientists pledged only to submit their work to journals that made full articles viewable by all. Two years later, Brown and Eisen partnered with Nobel Laureate and NIH director Harold Varmus to launch the Public Library of Science and its first journal, *PLoS Biology* ('About PLoS'). In the six years since, PLoS's slate has grown to include eight online journals, with the innovative *PLoS ONE* among them. PLoS is funded through foundation grants and by charging a fee of $1,300 to the authors or the funding agency that sponsored the research ('PLoS ONE Journal Information'). Such an arrangement is not uncommon in the sciences, especially those with ample funding, and fees typically range from $1,000–$3,000. However, it would be a mistake to assume that OA necessarily involves author fees. We know of no journals in the field of educational research that require them.

3 Publishers do have varying policies with regard to the version of an article that may be archived. A minority allow no archiving. Some allow authors to archive their submitted, uncorrected versions, also called *preprints*, but not their peer-reviewed, proofread *postprints*. *The majority of* publishers allow archiving of postprints (in a few cases the actual published version, but more often the final draft), but not preprints. This is considered preferable for authors because the archived version is identical to the published one in text, if not in layout and pagination. A journal might choose blue access to keep substantively different versions of its articles out of circulation. Finally, *some* publishers allow archiving of either pre- or postprints (www.sherpa.ac.uk/documents/sherpaplusdocs/Nottingham-colour-guide.pdf).

4 OJS provides indexing metadata to ensure maximum find-ability by searchers. It also attempts to augment the reading experience by providing, for example, searches of related scholarly and news articles. A set of annotation tools, currently under development, will allow readers to highlight text, make comments, and engage in discussion with other readers. The Public Knowledge Project also produces Open Conference Systems, for running conferences and making conference papers OA, while Open Monograph Press, software for writing scholarly books, is under development, both seeking to extend access to research and scholarship.

5 Publishers can easily add several restrictions to the basic CC licence that will be of interest to scholars, including provisions that the work not be modified or used for commercial purposes. It is important to note that Creative Commons does not entail the cession of copyright but rather the granting of a licence. All the same, a CC licence is permanent and irrevocable (Lessig, 2005; CC website creativecommons.org).

References

Abelson, H. (2009) MIT Adopts an Open-Access Policy, *Blown to Bits*. Online. (Available at www.bitsbook.com/2009/03/mit-adopts-an-open-access-policy/ Accessed 27 April 2009).

Association of Research Libraries (ARL) (2004) Monograph and serial costs in ARL libraries, 1986–2003, *ARL Statistics 2002–2003*.

Battelle, J. (2006) *The Search: How Google and Its Rivals Rewrote the Rules of Business and Transformed Our Culture*. New York: Portfolio Trade.

Bergstrom, C.T. and Bergstrom, T.C. (2004) The costs and benefits of library site licenses to academic journals, *Proceedings of the National Academy of Sciences*, 101(3): 897–902.

Björk, B. C., Roosr, A. and Lauri, M. (2008) Global annual volume of peer reviewed scholarly articles and the share available via different Open Access options, *Proceedings ELPUB2008*, Toronto, Canada. Online. (Available at www.oacs.shh.fi/publications/elpub-2008.pdf Accessed 29 March 2009).

Bradley, J. (2006) Drexel CoAS E-Learning: Open Notebook Science, *Drexel CoAS E-Learning*. Online. (Available at drexel-coas-elearning.blogspot.com/2006/09/open-notebook-science.html Accessed 13 April 2009).

Chan, L., Cuplinskas, D., Eisen, M., Friend, F., Genova, Y., Guédon, J., Hagemann, M., Harnad, S., Johnson, R., Kupryte, R., La Manna, M., Rév, I., Segbert, M., de Souza, S., Suber, P., Velterop, J. (2002) *Budapest Open Access Initiative*. Online. (Available at www.soros.org/openaccess/read.shtml Accessed 13 April 2009).

Cohen, P. (2008) Harvard Research to Be Free Online, *The New York Times*. Online. (Available at www.nytimes.com/2008/02/14/books/14arts-HARVARDRESEA_BRF.html Accessed 30 March 2009).

David, P. A. (1998) Common agency contracting and the emergence of 'Open Science' institutions, *The American Economic Review*, 88(2): 15–21.

Davis, P. M., Lewenstein, B. V., Simon, D. H., Booth, J. G., Connolly, M. J. L. (2008) Open access publishing, article downloads, and citations: randomized controlled trial, *BMJ*, 337 (jul31_1), a568.

Dickersin, K. (1990) The existence of publication bias and risk factors for its occurrence, *JAMA*, 263(10): 1385–89.

Eamon, W. (1994) *Science and the Secrets of Nature*. Princeton, NJ: Princeton University Press.

Faculty of Arts and Sciences (FAS) (12 February 2008) *Regular Meeting Agenda*. Cambridge, MA: Harvard University. Online. (Available at www.fas.harvard.edu/~secfas/February_2008_Agenda.pdf Accessed 29 March 2009).

Gladwell, M. (2003) Making the grade, *New Yorker*, 31: 34.

Glass, G. (2003) Education Policy Analysis Archives activity. Paper presented at the annual meeting of the American Educational Research Association in Chicago, IL.

Hitchcock, S. (2009) The effect of open access and downloads ('hits') on citation impact: a bibliography of studies, *OpCit project*. Online. (Available at opcit.eprints.org/oacitation-biblio.html Accessed 29 March 2009).

Hoover, C. and Brandhorst, T. (1982) *Development and current status of the Educational Resources Information Center (ERIC)*. In International Meeting on Educational Documentation: Present and Future. Florence, Italy, June 1982.

King, G. (2007) An Introduction to the Dataverse Network as an Infrastructure for Data Sharing, *Sociological Methods Research*, 36: 173–99.

Kuhn, T.S. (1978) Newton's optical papers. In I. B. Cohen (Ed.). *Isaac Newton's papers and letters on natural philosophy and related documents*. Cambridge, MA: Cambridge University Press, 27–45.

Kühne, M. and Liehr, A. W. (2009) Improving the traditional information management in natural sciences, *Data Science Journal*, 8: 8–26.

Lauerman, J. (2009) Harvard Government School to Offer Access to Faculty Papers, *Bloomberg.com*. Online. (Available at www.bloomberg.com/apps/news?pid=20601103&sid=aIeYW.08YTsk&refer=us Accessed 18 March 2009).

Lessig, L. (2005) *Free culture: The nature and future of creativity*. New York: Penguin.

Linn, R. L. (2003) Performance standards: Utility for different uses of assessments, *Education Policy Analysis Archives*, 11(31). Online. (Available at epaa.asu.edu/epaa/v11n31/Accessed 13 April 2009).

Lucas, R. and Willinsky, J. (2009) Open Access to E-Research In N. Jankowski (Ed.). *e-Research: Transformations in Scholarly Practice*. New York: Routledge.

McSherry, C. (2001) *Who Owns Academic Work?: Battling for Control of Intellectual Property*. Cambridge, MA: Harvard University Press.

Moya-Anegón, F., Vargas-Quesada, B., Chinchilla-Rodríguez, Z., Corera-Álvarez, E., Munoz-Fernández, F. J. and Herrero-Solana, V. (2007) Visualizing the marrow of science, *Journal of the American Society for Information Science and Technology*, 58(14): 2167–79.

Murray-Rust, P. (2007) Data-driven science – A scientist's view, *Phoenix, AZ*. Online. (Available at www.sis.pitt.edu/%7Erepwkshop/papers/murray.html Accessed 13 April 2009).

PLoS ONE. Journal Information. Online. (Available at www.plosone.org/static/information.action Accessed 13 April 2009).

Public Library of Science: *About*. Online. (Available at www.plos.org/about/index.html Accessed 13 April 2009).

Suber, P. (2004) Who should control access to research literature? *SPARC Open Access Newsletter*. Online. (Available at www.earlham.edu/~peters/fos/newsletter/11-02-04.htm#control Accessed 31 March 2009).

Viadero, D. (2008) Stanford to Offer Scholarly Articles on Education for Free, *Education Week*. Online. (Available at www.edweek.org/ew/articles/2008/07/30/44stanford.h27.html?tmp=1759990956 Accessed 18 March 2009).

Willinsky, J. (2003) Policymakers' Online Use of Academic Research, *Education Policy Analysis Archives*, 11(2). Online. (Available at epaa.asu.edu/epaa/v11n2 Accessed 13 April 2009).

——(2005) Open Journal Systems: An example of Open Source Software for journal management and publishing, *Library Hi Tech*, (23)4: 504–19.

——(2005a) *The access principle: The case for Open Access to research and scholarship*. Cambridge, MA: MIT Press.

——(2005b) The unacknowledged convergence of open source, open access, and open science, *First Monday*, 10(8). Online. (Available at firstmonday.org/htbin/cgiwrap/bin/ojs/index.php/fm/article/view/1265/1185 Accessed 28 April 2009).

——(2008) Socrates Back on the Street: Wikipedia's Citing of the Stanford Encyclopedia of Philosophy, *International Journal of Communication*, 2: 1269–88.

——(2009) The Stratified Economics of Open Access, *Economic Analysis & Policy*, 39(1): 53–70.

Willinsky, J. and Mendis, R. (2007) Open Access on a Zero Budget: A Case Study of Postcolonial Text, *Information Research*, 12(3). Online. (Available at informationr.net/ir/12–13/paper308.html Accessed 13 April 2009).

Willinsky, J. and Quint-Rapoport, M. (2007) How Complementary and Alternative Medicine Practitioners Use PubMed, *Journal of Medical Internet Research*, 9(2). Online. (Available at www.jmir.org/2007/2/e19 Accessed 13 April 2009).

29
Inner university, knowledge workers and liminality

T. Szkudlarek

Higher education and knowledge capitalism

In Poland, it was only a few years ago that doctoral studies became the dominant mode of advanced academic education. As in other EU countries, this development is part of the Bologna Process and it is strictly linked to the political strategy of building knowledge-based societies. This political vision connects vague concepts and metaphors that form an ideological structure, which implies that: a knowledge economy builds a knowledge society composed of life-long learning individuals and learning communities; people are valuable assets of such societies, and the best way of providing for welfare is investing in people; so the human capital that is created brings quick and certain return. In addition, human capital is balanced by social capital – it is not only individuals, but also their communities, families and cultures that 'count'.

The policies that are involved in this ideology combine antagonistic ideas of *investing* in people and their knowledges on the one hand, and *cost reductions* on the other. As Western economies usually compete with cheaper states with lower wages and limited social provisions, it is cost-efficiency rather than growing investment that, in fact, becomes the chief aim of reforms of the public sector. The dominant and globally promoted solution of this conflict is *private investment* that has to supplement deficiencies in public expenditure. When it comes to learning, more and more often those who are supposed to invest in it are the learners themselves. In Poland, more than 50 per cent of tertiary education students have to pay tuition fees nowadays.

The policies directed to a knowledge economy are the background for many developments in research and higher education. There is a constant and growing pressure on the universities to become 'practical' in training professionals and to provide research-based solutions to problems defined by people in business and politics. To put it briefly, those who claim to have 'invested' in higher education, including politicians, business people and students themselves, demand 'return'. Higher education becomes a mass phenomenon, with enrolments running at around 50 per cent of the population of 20-year-olds in many countries. Therefore, HE must become cheaper, shorter BA studies are meant to practically train the cohorts of youngsters and quickly throw them into unstable job markets. Of course, the large numbers of those students *do not* come to the university for traditionally understood 'knowledge' (usually described as *dry*); what they need is *skills* that make them employable. In this context, the categories of 'knowledge' and 'skills' are sometimes difficult to differentiate, as the following fragment of an interview with a German graduate illustrates:

> Q.: What *knowledge* do you consider significant from the point of view of your present employment?
>
> A.: When I look back on my studies, there are some significant key *qualifications* I have acquired at the university: First, oral and writing *skills*, they are important for teaching in order to be able to develop useful methods and contents of learning in very short time [...], and to know how to socialise with others, e.g., for exchanging materials, experiences and for making friendships.
>
> Hult *et al.* 2004: 48–49, italics added

As the authors of the report notice, 'Forms of knowledge are often seen as secondary compared to social skills and a manifold repertoire of acting' (Hult *et al.* 2004: 49). I would add that this primacy of skill over knowledge is a product of a powerful politico-economical discourse rather than the mere mistake of a single student. If contemporary economies are to *produce knowledge*, they do not have to expect it from graduates. What employers need from their newly hired staff is *skills in knowledge making*. We may say that the university has become an institution that is expected to train *a new working class* for knowledge economies (Szkudlarek 2006; 2009). In the classic analysis by Marx (1999), the development of capitalism in England was conditioned by two mutually related factors: concentration of capital and creation of a class of people dispossessed of anything but their hands to work. The latter was a result of evictions of peasants following the concentration of land and parcellation of the commons (Marx 1999). The potential workers created were willing to be employed, but they also lost the ability to sustain themselves and had no other means of subsistence but the skills ('hands') needed by employers. The present situation in higher education seems to resemble that described by Marx (1999) in several ways. In knowledge-based societies, knowledge becomes subject to parcellations (e.g. an offensive on intellectual property rights) and expropriation (e.g. transfer of research results from publicly funded universities to private business). At the same time, the mass of enrolled students seem to realise that the industries that may employ them need their *skills to produce knowledge* rather than their knowledge itself. Higher education strengthens its formal character, which means that knowledge is but a material through which proper skills and capabilities are meant to be 'trained'. Therefore, it does not have to be up-to-date knowledge. State of the art knowledge, if produced at the university, and if that university acts 'rationally' in the knowledge-based economy, should be capitalised: it will not be freely available to the mass of enrolled undergraduates. The broad discourse of *academic capitalism* provides for many examples of restricted access to those areas of knowledge where private capital is involved in its production, or which have been sold to private owners (Slaughter and Leslie 1997; Muzzin 2005).

Doctoral studies: politics and ambivalence

Regulations concerning doctoral studies in Poland create flexible possibilities for the universities to organise the process of advanced research education, and they do not pose strict demands as to the provisions for doctoral students. The students, for instance, *can* obtain scholarships, and the law declares that those *must* be at least 60 per cent of the salary of a junior researcher. What is regulated here is the bottom line of the subsidy, but not the fact that it has to be paid. As a result, actual provision depends on the financial standing of the faculty. Universities *can* oblige doctoral students to teach 90 unpaid hours a year in the form of internships. Doctoral programmes *can* be paid (part-time) or free (full-time) – but if the students do not get scholarships, they have to work elsewhere, therefore free programmes become in fact part-time as well.

We may look at such uncertainties through the lens of the rules of discourse analysis and see them as traces of power games played outside the academic world, as an outcome of contradictions in the politics that stand behind the adoption of present regulations. To make it brief, there is a conflict between the rhetoric of knowledge-based societies that pushes the states towards the gargantuan growth of higher education institutions on the one hand, and the ideological context of neoliberalism, with its stress on deregulation and private investment, in which that discourse is rooted. Put simply, state budgets do not support state policies and as a result it is the students themselves who have to pay, at least partially, for the political fantasy of a knowledge economy.

To sum up, the present pressure on higher education and the demand that it produces a mass of highly skilled workers for economies aspiring to be based on knowledge, results in a highly ambivalent form of institutional organisation of research training that can be simultaneously understood in terms of: (i) broadening the accessibility of higher education and of providing low-paid labour for the knowledge industry; (ii) enhancing the knowledge potential of the universities and of colonising their resources; and (iii) achieving a quality education while also wasting the time of students in classes that distract them from research. And this is just the beginning of the list of ambiguities. In this context, the position of a doctoral student is very likely to be ambivalent and signified by contradictory semioses of ambition and disappointment, of elitist claims to the status of professionals or intellectuals and of radicalism traditionally ascribed to working class; of creativity in research and boredom of menial work paying the possibility of the former. This ambiguity is imposed on something that is ambivalent by its very nature, on the *liminality* of educational experience as such. Being a student of whatever degree is marked by a logic of transition, or in-betweenness. This is a phase in life when one is *not* expected to participate in 'normal' social settings, when normality is suspended, and when some temporary location 'in the corridor' towards something else is offered as a sphere of change (Mendel 2009).

I would like to illustrate this ambivalence with some data from incidental research conducted at the University of Gdańsk, where I am heading the doctoral programme in education and political science at the Faculty of Social Sciences. The programme has been running for three years, and in many respects it is still under construction. The number of unsolved problems and the degree of uncertainty is, therefore, higher than in other doctoral schools, also at the same university. I collected the data electronically through the distance learning platform that is also used for communication between the administration and the students. The platform has also become an open forum for the students where I have witnessed several heated discussions on their daily problems. One day I joined the forum asking the students to express their ideas about what is happening to their knowledge in the course of their studies. The context of previous debates, often addressing problems and difficulties the students experience at the university, certainly influenced the responses. However, I do not consider this to diminish the value of the interview. Thus, the question of knowledge has been situated in the context of broader social conditions, inviting critical reflection on power/knowledge regimes operating within and around the university. There were eight students taking part in the interview, and six of them engaged more than once in the conversation. Most of them chose education as the discipline of their dissertation, some are known to me as social activists. As the students could mutually read their responses and engage in discussion, the research took the form of a focused group interview. In the report below, I am not identifying particular individuals; I just give the positions in the transcript and the sex of the informant. What I am interested in here is not so much individually expressed ideas but the presentation of the *discourse* that circulates in the group of doctoral students and forms a framework of their possible identification. Coding and analysis of the data was performed with RQDA software for Linux (Huang 2008).

The question 'What happens to knowledge in the context of "being a doctoral student"?' elicited a fairly broad scope of ideas that can be grouped into the following themes:

Educational policies (economisation and marketisation of higher education and research) and their results experienced within the university, including those personally felt as insecurity and poverty

Identity (positioning within the university and in the outside world, inclusion/exclusion, barriers and independence)

Critical distance and alienation.

The overall image is fairly consistent, probably as a result of the dialogical process of data collection. In spite of the incidental character of the research, it seems to reflect some important aspects of power/knowledge regimes informing the contemporary landscape of advanced academic education.

What are doctoral studies?

The first issue that should be reported here is the very *idea of doctoral studies*. The relative novelty of doctoral studies in their present form, with limited time and obligatory courses, means that they are still seen as a kind of peculiarity, and their legal basis is subject to frequent changes. The students do not always accept that in order to earn their degree they have to attend regular classes. A fairly often expressed opinion is that advanced learning, not to mention research, is not necessarily related to organised forms of education.

> As it is possible to do a doctorate without being a doctoral student, and as it is possible to gain knowledge more extensive than that we get in the courses, it means that the studies are not crucial for an average MA holder to learn. I do not think that they make independent search for knowledge easier, either [9753:10069]. I therefore think that the relation between the studies and knowledge is none. Studying and acquiring knowledge are vessels totally unconnected. One does not harm the other, but does it help? [10656:10847; male]

Such resistance relates to the conviction that organised learning takes the time that could otherwise be devoted to doctoral research. The exception is peer learning in group discussions.

Moreover, when I have time, it is taken by reading for the classes and writing essays more than by the pursuit of knowledge related to my project. And as I have heard this is not only my problem [4681: 4877, female].

I have not come here for concrete knowledge. I can use the library or internet myself, I can watch online lectures that I want and when I want. This does not mean I do not want to take part in the classes; it is important that we meet and discuss rather than sit alone at our projects or screens. I just don't like the form of lecture or writing exam papers [13228:13598, female].

This unenthusiastic attitude to formal learning is exacerbated by the fact that the informants have to earn a living outside the university. Most of them do not get regular scholarships, and if they get some kind of academic job, it is usually part-time and low-paid.

What seems to be the most significant context of understanding knowledge in doctoral studies is defined in terms of the mass character of the studies and their rationality informed by economy. It has strong implications for several aspects of studying: freedom of choosing a research topic, quality of studies, and career opportunities. As one student says:

There are masses of doctoral students, many theses are written for the sole interest of supervisors or indeed they are part of their research. That perhaps is normal in biochemistry, where they work in teams, but in the humanities? Doctoral studies have become just another kind of studies [1282: 1552, female].

'Just another kind of studies' does not necessarily have to be completed with a doctorate. Present regulations make it possible to graduate with a certificate, and in fact the proportion of students at my university who manage to defend their theses within four years of studies is below 5 per cent. The number of students enrolled on the programmes vastly outnumbers the availability of academic positions, which sums up to a suggestion that some students must not consider the programme as a path into the academe. This creates a kind of disorientation:

If the university is not considering doctoral studies as a way of training its own resources, if it maintains that the studies do not necessarily have to be completed with the thesis, that they are merely important as a step in our professional teacher's careers, and that hardly anybody is able to make a valid proposal for the faculty to register a thesis anyway, how can we feel that we make science and that what we do here is important? We get a clear message: do it for fun. It is not important [12302:12830, female].

Identity: positioning

A highly dramatised aspect of this situation relates to the position doctoral students occupy within the university. The ambivalent meaning of 'doctoral' studies that do not need to produce 'doctorates' positions the students in a border zone from where the university looks like a closed and repulsive system, as a place that apparently invites newcomers, but in fact keeps them at the gate. This shifts the meaning of liminality. Anthropologically speaking, liminality is a phase in the process of transition, it leads towards a new social status (Turner 1975; McLaren 1986). The outcome of being in transition here, however, is not predictable. It is not obvious that it will lead to the desired identity. In many respects, it resembles the status of the marginalised, identified by Maria Mendel in her research on homelessness (Mendel 2007). This is a kind of liminality that turns back to itself, that *revolves* around its own limits and *bends* the moment it touches the border of inclusion; a liminality that feels like a threat of permanent alienation, a *rite de marge* that reaffirms itself in a premonition of permanent marginalisation:

> We keep revolving around a system in which we are needed, we generate some profit on the one hand, and on the other the same system makes it impossible for us to get inside. We are too many, there is no money for us, we must earn our living [...], we therefore cannot engage in science. Finally we prove to be not good enough, the circle closes. The massive nature of those studies will only feed this machine, and the university [...] will become more and more closed, much more than when doctorate was something meant for individuals really prepared for academic work [7775: 8446, female].

This ambiguous 'strategy' of the university (inverted commas mean that I do not believe it is a conscious policy) may sound suicidal:

> I remember myself arguing two years ago, like the others did, that the third cycle of studies in the Bologna system is not a privilege. I would not say that now, I had to see the system from within to see that this is how you undermine science [1843: 2096, female].

'Undermining science' is illustrated by several traits that refer to trivialisation of knowledge and to contrast between the pressure of commercial application and quality of research:

> This is a broader issue connected to the marketization of the university. On the one hand, simplified science for the masses. On the other, the hermetic 'true' science [2903: 3157, female]; Commodification of science excludes originality and quality [2376: 2436, female].

Even if those issues are 'in the air' rather than result from personal experience of the students (the ideas expressed here are circulated in numerous texts on contemporary education that the students read, and I do not think they might have had a chance to experience *how* and *if* 'commodification excludes originality' personally), they say something about the composition of the discourse that forms the framework of self-understanding for doctoral students.

The structural exclusion mentioned above can be understood as less suicidal, however, if we look at it from the perspective of governance of social marginalisation. What comes to mind first is the Marxist notion of 'reserve army' of the unemployed that serves the needs of the labour market. The crowds of doctoral students at the gates of the academe form a reservoir of low-paid or unpaid teaching and technical work; they also lower the wage pressure from those employed full-time. Their positioning is expressed in clearly *spatial* terms (they 'revolve around' and 'cannot get inside'), and its presentation evokes

361

the medieval urban space. The university resembles a closed, walled city surrounded by populous suburbs where unstable mobs wait for their chance to make their living on what gets 'in' or 'out' of the city, on supplies and waste products. They can be dangerous people (like heretics, outlaws or peasants on the run), but they can also be creative, like craftsmen unrecognised by city guilds, producing goods cheaper than those behind the walls. The image evoked by the students in the above passages speaks of a kind of *inner university* that, like a walled city, attracts students and remains closed, tells them how to 'do science' and keeps them at bay, needs them and makes it 'impossible to get inside'.

This phenomenon is strictly connected to the corporate model of educational management. Under the labels of professionalism and strengthening the links between the university and the economy, we are witnessing large reductions in the levels of full-time employment, and hence the limiting of academic autonomy. Doctoral students arrive like migrant workers ready to do the job for half the wage, and are welcome by 'academic entrepreneurs' solely concerned with economic efficiency. Giroux (2005) puts it this way:

> As full-time labor is outscored to temporary or contract labor, the intellectual culture of the university declines as overworked graduate students and part-time faculty assume the role of undergraduate teaching. Undergraduate teaching in many universities is now largely being done by graduate students and contingent faculty who have no role in university governance process, are detached from the intellectual life of the university, rarely have time to engage in sustained scholarship, and appear largely as interchangeable instructors acting more like temporary visitors than faculty committed to full-time and secure positions. Power now resides in the hands of a new cadre of corporate-oriented trustees and administrators who actually define themselves largely as academic entrepreneurs and CEOs than as educational leaders.
>
> Giroux 2005: 6

Identity: exclusions

Let us look at the composition of alienation in the interviews. It seems to be strictly related to the *transition* that doctoral studies present in the biographies of young people: they mark the liminal phase of 'becoming a researcher'. Liminality is construed by *exclusions* from the spheres of life where the students used to live, and by *denials of inclusion* into where they aspire. Marginality, or liminality thus created, has to be ritualised to be maintained. We may, therefore, speak here of *institutionalisation of not belonging* to the academe. The students are 'there' but not 'in', their status shifts between that of 'just another kind of a student' and a member of the faculty. When they arrive in the building they feel insecure in its spaces, occasionally they are refused access to certain rooms or meetings, and they happily find refuge in a separate, clearly marked space of the 'doctoral students' room'. So positioned physically, they learn their status of trainee, of someone practising skills and languages that mark the status of 'full' insiders. As one of the students puts it, referring to the extensive use of philosophy in the programme:

> We experience the language of the disciplines in which we should feel comfortable as a minefield full of 'hi-diggers[1]'. And when we finally start using it, it must be something inhuman. People without education like ours no longer understand us [5155:5404, male].

This linguistic dimension connects to a broader layer of knowledge that plays a double-edged, critical role. On the one hand, theoretical education, when one gets through its linguistic barriers, provides for critical distance necessary to understand social issues and to take up the role of intellectual:

We are packed with theories. I think it is very important in the process of becoming a doctor in the humanities that we learn how to see things and use theoretical knowledge [11564:11823, female].

On the other, and this is where 'hi-diggers' continue their undermining work, the acquisition and internalisation of knowledge creates identity problems, sometimes expressed in fairly dramatic ways. A female student, and an experienced teacher, describes it as *excluding* her from her professional community:

I must have read too much of exclusion, and I am beginning to think that my knowledge excludes me from my workplace. What I know slowly makes it difficult for me to work in the system in which I have been for over 15 years. The knowledge made me see things so sharp, [...] and so many things make me uneasy ... And I have an impression that the others want to discuss with me less and less eagerly. That [for them] I am a misfit, that I doubt things that have been legally regulated for years, that theories match no practices [...]. The less I know the easier it is to come to terms with reality. If knowledge makes me free, it also makes me painfully realise the nature of the trap I have put myself in [6298:7116, female].

Another student comments on this:

Exclusion through doctorate? Possibly, [...] nobody will want to talk to us. From the flock of normal [...] people we will be excluded by the doctorate, and into the club of university elite they will not take us because of our low activity (costly conferences and publications, and simply the lack of time to learn) [19210:19527, male].

The student quoted before (6298:7116) is well on the way to distancing herself from the world of everyday practice that 'does not like' making things overcomplicated by critical reflection, and could probably appreciate changing her position into a more academic one where her criticism would not (hopefully) exclude her. In the light of the research presented by Jones (2007), this is, however, dubious: academic teachers who consider criticism an important task of education feel nowadays 'ontologically insecure' in the system that under the guise of 'quality management' reduces education to consumerism (Jones 2007).

Fantasies of inclusion, practices of ambivalence

Those fragments speak of clearly negative experiences. However, the position the students take here is not 'simply radical'. In the background, those ideas evoke strong concepts of traditional, liberal education. They are simultaneously radical and conservative in the way they refer to academic work as distanced from reality, or indeed as opposed to practice. Distance is *radical*, because it conditions critique and change; it is *conservative*, because it speaks to the Promethean myth that positions academics in a lofty sphere of intellectualism. Presently, this combination has a paradoxical expression in the discourse of new managerialism. As Jones (2007) notices, in the context of present changes in educational policy, the stress on critical thinking in academic education may be understood as conservative rather than radical. Unlike complaints typical of lay people, distancing takes place here not through some alleged 'lacks' in theory that is 'too abstract' to grasp reality, or 'too esoteric', Heideggerian or whatever curiosity we apply here, but through the very *strength* and effectiveness of theory that, although making people free, at the same time positions them at distance to the vernacular. It implies a *difficult privilege* of work that is challenging and fulfils one's interests, and a privilege of self-creation strongly motivated by the traditional academic *fantasy of autonomy* (Johnson *et al.* 2000).

> The most interesting moment in becoming a doctor is when we realise that we are somehow independent. Or, in other words that we want to be independent because we want to make science rather than simply recycle it … I mean independence in acquiring knowledge, in researching, a 'scientific pilgrimage' and the right to it. Scientific independence as the interface between the academic system […] and our individuality [549: 1001, female].

It is fuelled by joy ('I am still happy that I do not have to but want to do it' [14183:14241, female]). It is seen as a seductive opportunity of personal growth:

> I am here mainly because science fascinates me. I just want to contribute to its creation. Besides, the university is a special place for me, in progress and not allowing for stagnation, at least when you are active yourself, and it is hard for me to quit [3604: 3859, female].

As Johnson *et al.* (2000) notice, the fantasy of being in the academe as an independent scholar, often visualised through sensual, corporal icons (leather-bound tomes in the library, walking through the campus, tweed jackets, etc), strongly influences academic identities and sustains traditional pedagogies that ignore the fact that, for instance, doctoral *supervision* is a mechanism of power that hides the pedagogical *construction* of the self behind expectations of independence and maturity. Referring to the case of an Oxford professor who told the students that he would never read more than one-half of their work, Johnson *et al.* (2000) say about so implied ability to work independently that the students:

> [W]ere to find in themselves the capacity to be autonomous, and they were to demonstrate that they could work on their own without supervision [...] Recognising themselves as 'always-already' able to be independent scholar such students clearly were expected to be members of an elite whose previous training had produced in them the capacities and the sense of themselves that would secure their entry into this academic world.
>
> Johnson *et al.* 2000: 138

One of the students interviewed in Gdańsk speaks of the same implication of elitism from a reversed perspective:

> More and more I am convinced that becoming a doctor, writing a thesis and creating a space in the world of science, relates not so much to knowledge as to technical and organisational skills [...] and time. The studies do not offer us the development of those skills at any level, nor do they give time for research, or means to buy the time [22328:22675, female].

It seems that the university applies here a hidden curriculum that selects the students on the basis of economic and cultural capital that they 'have to have' as their personal cultural heritage. Those who think that they miss it already seem to fear that theirs is liminality that will *never conclude in inclusion* and that will, in fact, turn into permanent marginalisation or a journey back to where they came from. The poverty trap many of them have found themselves in makes it a fairly realistic assessment. As a result, what we can see here is *alienation* – an institutional production of estrangement, detachment and solitude. As I have mentioned, apart from its marginalising effect, it is in a way a very *traditional* function of liberal education. In order to be *critical* you need *autonomy*. And the *autos* here detaches you from the others, from commonsensical knowledges and stereotypes, and turns you into a stranger: someone capable of changing societies from within, be it in the form of managerial or revolutionary leadership, a 'positive deviant' as Znaniecki (1934; 2001) used to call such figure.

Thus poverty, exclusion, and the impenetrability of the walls of the 'inner university' paradoxically co-create the curriculum of becoming elite, free or detached, intellectuals. Or conversely: the ambition of becoming critical intellectual may turn the students into aliens incapable of finding for themselves room in the social system. The fantasy of 'being academic' is thus eventually *radicalised* by redundancy, feared as a trap of the ambivalent positioning at the gates of the university, in poor suburbs of the inner circle of the 'real' academe. Interestingly, this radicalism cannot express itself in a clear manner. The students oscillate between revolutionary radicalism, complicity and conservative elitism. One of my students defines himself as militant and keeps speaking of the conflict with 'the establishment' of the university; he set up a forum solely devoted to 'manifestations, demonstrations and riots' described as 'internships' for social science students. At the same time, in exchanges taking place on the same platform, the students complain about doctoral studies becoming 'just another kind of studies', speak of 'undermining science' through mass education, and bitterly feel excluded from the 'inner university'. This complexity has been perfectly captured by one student:

> We either join the assembly line of doctoral theses, or we start fighting for our jobs, which de facto means that *we oppose the system into which we at the same time want to get*. Our fight for material issues, for stipends, hostels, teaching hours, is nothing but the fight for a place in the system, for recognition of our work [15074:15410, female, italics added].

That fight *for* decent conditions of doctoral work in order to pave a secure way into the 'inner university' is experienced as a fight *against* the system that maintains that inner university as such. However bitter or cynical it sounds, this may be considered an educational experience per se, and it seems to foretell the strange position of social researchers, even if some of the students will never become ones. It is precisely this *ambivalent relation to 'the system'* that seems to characterise the social scientist. In a broad sense, we are critics of the system employed and paid by the system itself, agents of change on commission, strangers inside, aliens within. Thus, the failure to be smoothly accepted within the academe becomes an uneasy practicum in ambivalence for those who will eventually succeed, and a school of coping with disillusionment for those who will not. It seems that it is those who manage to understand that peculiar position of 'within–without', of being strangers inside, that stand a chance of coping with the demands of the academe. It seems that the awareness of those tensions and impossibilities that make the system both open and restricted, and thus disclose the very mechanism of power that informs its structures, may become the first condition of finding oneself in the revolving motion around its inner walls.

Radicalism and aspiration

The metaphor of 'knowledge workers', borrowed from literature they read for the classes, is occasionally and perhaps provocatively used by the students in self-identification. Thus, pronounced radicalism is moderated by clearly expressed dreams of inclusion and the nostalgia for a more elitist university. It seems that *both* those dimensions are of phantasmatic nature. The dreams of 'being academic' are obvious; and the aura of radicalism – however justified in the materialities of being doctoral students – sometimes resembles a graffiti I remember from Lindsay Andersson's film *The Lucky Man: Revolution is Opium for Intellectuals*. Becoming social scientists, be it in education or political science, almost automatically implies *some* radicalism. But this radicalism is broken by *aspiration* to move upward, just as well as motivation to become academic is broken by the radical experience of exclusion from the 'inner university'. The constitutive phantasms (in Žižek's terms, Žižek 1989) collide and mutually displace the subjects from each other's respective dreams. The liminality of being a doctoral student is thus a *double liminality*.

And perhaps this is not just the case of doctoral studies. Rancière (1988), in his account on the histories of XIX-century working class activists, noticed that the leaders of the movement did not identify strongly with their position. 'Quite the contrary' – says Hewlett (2007) – 'many […] were primarily preoccupied with planning or at least dreaming about an escape from their own trades and ways of life and were hankering after the lifestyles and cultures of the bourgeoisie' (Hewlett 2007: 87). And *aspiration to another world*, a fantasy of 'being different', is at the core of motivation of growth and becoming. And the experience of being marginalised *within the university* may give the students imagined legitimacy in their future attempts at being leaders to otherwise marginalised social groups for – with – against whom, as social scientists, they may have to work.

Notes

1 The sentence, as all other utterances, was originally in Polish and is provided in my translation. 'Hi-diggers' here is my invention that aims at representing the way the author ironically referred to Martin Heidegger.

References

Giroux, H. (2005) Academic Entrepreneurs: The Corporate Takeover of Higher Education, *Tikkun*, March/April, 20(2): 18–28. Online. (Available at web.ebscohost.com Accessed 3 March 2009).

Hewlett N. (2007) *Badiou, Balibar, Ranciere, Re-thinking emancipation*. London, New York: Continuum.

Huang R. (2008) *RQDA: R-based Qualitative Data Analysis. R package version 0.1.6*. Online. (Available at rqda.r-forge.r-project.org/ Accessed 3 March 2009).

Hult, H., Handal, G., Lababidi, T. and Cackowska, M. (Eds) (2004) Understanding the transition from Higher education to Work life'. Unpublished report of Project 'Journeymen, Deliverable 15, European Commission, May 2004.

Johnson, L., Lee, A. and Green, B. (2000) The PhD and the Autonomous Self: gender, rationality and postgraduate pedagogy, *Studies in Higher Education* 25(2): 135–47.

Jones, A. (2007) Looking over our shoulders: critical thinking and ontological insecurity in higher education, *London Review of Education* 5(3) : 209–22.

Marx, K., (1999) In F. Engles (Ed.). *Capital*, vol 1. Trans. S. Moore and E. Aveling. Online. (Available at www.marxists.org/archive/marx/works/1867-c1/index.htm Accessed 5 March 2009).

McLaren, P. (1986) *Schooling as Ritual Performance. Towards a Political Economy of Educational Symbols and Gestures*. London, Boston, MA: Routledge and Kegan Paul.

Mendel M. (2007) *Społeczeństwo i rytuał. Heterotopia bezdomności*. Toruń: Wydawnictwo Adam Marszałek.

——(2009), University as a Place. In M. Cackowska (Ed.). *Learning in the Academia. Socio-Cultural and Political Perspectives. Ars Educandi Monographs* Vol. 1. Gdańsk: Wydawnictwo Uniwersytetu Gdańskiego.

Muzzin L. (2005) Academic Capitalism, Inequality, and Knowledge Construction in University-Based Professional Schools, *International Journal of Applied Semiotics*, 4(2): 49–66.

Rancière J. (1988) Good Times or Pleasure at the Barricades. In A. Rifkin and R. Thomas (Eds). *Voices of the People: The Politics and Life of 'La Sociale' at the End of the Second Empire*. Trans. J. Moore. London: Routledge, 246–52.

Slaughter S., and Leslie L. (1997) *Academic Capitalism. Politics, Policies, and the Entrepreneurial University*. Baltimore, MD and London: The Johns Hopkins University Press.

Szkudlarek, T. (2006) Parcelacje. Topografie społeczeństwa wiedzy. In M. Mendel (Ed.). *Pedagogika miejsca*. Toruń: Adam Marszałek.

——(2009) Knowledge society and knowledge exclusion. In M. Cackowska (Ed.). *Learning in Academia. Socio-Cultural and Political Perspectives. Ars Educandi Monographs* Vol. 1. Gdańsk: Wydawnictwo Uniwersytetu Gdańskiego.

Turner, V. (1975) *Dramas, Fields, and Metaphors: Symbolic Action in Human Society*. New York: Cornell University Press.

Žižek, S (1989) *The sublime object of ideology*. London: Verso.

Znaniecki, F (1934; 2nd edn 2001) *Ludzie teraźniejsi a cywilizacja przyszłości*. Warszawa: PWN.

30
Global students for global education research?

I. Menter, J. Da Silveira Duarte and R. Gorur

In this chapter we discuss the importance of 'internationalising' the experience of education research students. First, we look at some features of the increasingly globalised landscape of education and education research and consider three main reasons for urging students to join international networks during their period of study. We then take two examples of contemporary developments in international networking, one at a European level and one at a global level, before concluding by suggesting a number of steps that supervisors and students might take to ensure that they engage effectively with the global education research community.

Education research in a globalised world

Formal education around the world is largely provided through national systems. Indeed, state education systems play a key role in sustaining the very polity of the globe, the arrangements that have been dominant in political organisation for varying lengths of time around the world, but which now prevail in all but the remotest regions. That is not to suggest that these arrangements are stable in all parts of the world, indeed very much the reverse is true. There is instability, whether visible or incipient, within and between nations in all regions of the world. In this unstable world, nationbuilding and the creation of national identity among citizens are key functions for education systems. As Green (1990) has eloquently demonstrated, education systems have played a central role in the very formation of the state, at least since modern times, alongside legal and political systems.

There is a fairly long tradition of comparative education research (Crossley and Broadfoot 1992). Early work tended to be very descriptive, setting out to capture the key organisational features of schooling, curricula and pedagogical approaches (e.g. King 1967; Grant 1968). But during much of the twentieth century, there had also been a significant 'trade' in educational approaches, which at times had a deeply colonial aspect. For example, curricula and examination systems from Britain were exported to many of the former colonies in the Caribbean, Africa and Asia. But more recently we have seen if not the opposite phenomenon, nevertheless a kind of reverse process of importing practices from other countries deemed in some ways to be more successful than those of the home nation. This 'policy borrowing', which, for example, so much influenced approaches to numeracy teaching in England during the 1990s, following visits to Korea and other 'Far Eastern' countries by researchers and inspectors, is now somewhat discredited.

The background to such policy borrowing was largely the growing anxiety amongst politicians concerning global competitiveness, a particularly economically oriented ideology, which was emerging strongly as part of the neoliberal globalisation processes of the late twentieth century (Olssen *et al.* 2004). The increasing influence of international studies of educational performance – both in schools and in higher education – is very much a late twentieth century phenomenon that is certainly observable not only in education but also in other fields of practice. It has led to the notion of 'governing by numbers', a theme developed by Ozga and others in relation to education (Ozga and Lingard 2007). In school education the influence of reviews such as PISA, TIMMS and PIRLS has been very clear, especially in 'advanced countries'. In relation to universities, league tables created by the media appear to have had undue influence, especially given the somewhat arbitrary nature of much of the 'data' on which they are based. The grip of accountability and performativity has itself become global (Ball 2007).

To return to the notion of 'policy borrowing' in state education systems, the main reason such an approach became discredited was that it was frequently found that policies appearing to be successful in one context did not seem to have the same effect in another context. This may not come as a surprise now, in hindsight, as comparative education has developed a much more nuanced and subtle awareness of the significance of cultural, historical and social factors. The concept of 'context sensitivity' has indeed become a touchstone in comparative education study over the past 20 years or so (Crossley and Watson 2003).

The effects of such developments on education research have been interesting. Global influences on education policy and practice have themselves become a subject of study, for example with work that seeks to identify the influence of transnational organisations, whether intergovernmental (such as the OECD, see Rizvi and Lingard 2006) or commercial (such as the IBM or Mott Macdonald corporations, see Ball 2008 or Mahony *et al.* 2004).

Somewhat paradoxically, however, in the light of these developments, there is still considerable ethnocentricity in much educational research. This can be very apparent for Europeans attending American conferences or for Scots attending 'British' conferences. In the field of teacher education, for example, there is a very strong tendency for much work to refer only to previous work carried out within the same nation as the researcher is working in. Comparative work is relatively rare (though what there is can be very fruitful), and even the opportunities for drawing on methods or theories derived in other contexts are rarely taken.

Some of this ethnocentrism can undoubtedly be attributed to the dominance of the English language in much educational research. International citation indices for journals include an overwhelming number of English language journals. This must be deeply frustrating for the majority of Europeans, not to mention education researchers in China, other parts of Asia, South America and Africa, for example (see Ozga *et al.* 2006). However, this cannot account for the way in which North Americans tend to ignore research from the UK, Australia, New Zealand, etc., nor for the way in which English and Scots frequently ignore the others' work.

369

These issues become deeply political when education research plays a part in the international development agenda. How may it be possible to develop education research that is not imbued with a colonial and/or western cultural legacy? How can education research that is fit for a global society that respects diversity and accords parity – at least economically and intellectually – to researchers and scholars across the world be developed? Our argument is that a key element in this agenda must be the way in which education researchers experience the early stages of their careers and that is our main concern in what follows.

If research methodologies in education have been influenced by poststructural and postmodern social theory (Edwards and Usher 2007), is it not time we sought to develop a political economy of educational research that is positively postcolonial, one that would celebrate diversity and interculturalism as well as reject inequality and injustice? As long as some western universities continue to see 'developing nations' as a market for research students that is exploited for financial gain, then there is a deep asymmetry in the relationship. Until we see genuine reciprocity involving two way movements of staff and students – as well as ideas – we cannot be confident that our research is based on a just footing.

Next, we summarise three key elements of the rationale for developing a global community of education researchers, before giving two examples of networks that may play some part in these sorts of developments.

The significance of an international dimension for education research students

(i) Education is increasingly subject to global influences

There is almost general consensus that educational research is growingly subject to the influences brought about by globalisation (Stromquist and Monkman 2000; Burbules and Torres 2000; Zajda 2005). According to Zajda (2005), most changes in education over the last three decades are to be found in policy making and comparative education. Three main trends in educational research caused by global influences can thus be found. First of all, a general change of the dominant research paradigms could already be felt in the 1980s; the dichotomy between positivism (empiricist quantitative research) and anti-positivism (non-empiricist qualitative research) were gradually replaced by post-structuralist and postmodernist education and policy approaches (Zajda 2005). Mitter (1997) termed this paradigm shift the 'postmodernist revolt', and it mostly influenced the educational and policy meta-narratives by attempting to empower the learner by restating its central role in the curriculum and highlighting the diversity of learners' needs (Zajda 2002). The second major change happened at the level of educational reforms and planning. Williams (2000) states that after the 1980s the focus was on a more holistic, global perspective, focused on integrative aspects of policy making, whereas before educational planning was more based on the idea of human capital and the investment that education had to make to turn each student into a potentially productive individual. The third change happened at a content level, as the focus of much educational research turned towards global humanistic and egalitarian themes, such as education for democracy, inclusive education, language diversity, education and poverty, gender, equity, minorities and human rights. As stated by Zajda,

[K]ey policy issues as reflected in education and policy reforms during the last three decades could be described as the restatement of an egalitarian-inspired imperative – the equality objective – ensuring that equality and quality of educational opportunities enjoyed only by the best-served few are available to all.

Zajda 2005: 2

(ii) Education research is increasingly focused on global themes

Universities recruit students from every corner of the world. Many students base their research in their home countries whilst gaining their degrees from some distant university. Theses completed in the last few years at the University of Glasgow, for instance, include such titles as 'Attitudes and Difficulties in Upper School Physics in Libya', 'Evaluative Study of Science Education Programme in Colleges of Education in Oman' and 'Popular Education and Social Change in Latin America'.

Notions such as 'the knowledge era' and 'world's best practice' have become universal concepts. Several factors have contributed to the ability to imagine these concepts in abstract, decontextualised terms. The development of the World Education Indicators and the growing popularity of large-scale international tests such as the Programme for International Student Assessment (PISA) have made international education databases available for research. In recent years, particularly in the USA, the emphasis has been on statistical and quantitative research exploiting national and international databases. Research themes are consequently increasingly comparative and/or abstract and 'global'. Many major education conferences encourage submissions with international themes. A survey of recent thesis submissions at the University of Melbourne yields such global titles as 'Factors that promote effective teaching practices in a thinking curriculum', 'Meaning making with real-time images of Earth in Space', and 'Evaluating Capacity Development'.

International acceptance appears to add a certain reassuring legitimacy to policy and research claims. Moreover, 'good' education research findings are often seen as being valid everywhere. This increased reliance on the international community to validate research has led to a profusion of journals in the field. The University of Melbourne's electronic journal subscription list yielded 77 entries to a search with the keywords 'international AND education'.

(iii) The career landscape for educational researchers is an international one

There are clearly major implications for educational researchers deriving from the two propositions outlined above. Although it is certainly not a requirement that all education research is directly focused on policy, it is nevertheless the case that all education research requires contextualisation. Educational interactions and processes that may be the subject of research all happen at specific times and in specific places and although some theorists – especially those of a philosophical bent – may be seeking some form of universalism in their work, one of the key tests of this must be the ability to demonstrate that a phenomenon is indeed consistent at different times and places. Or if we consider the work of great learning theorists, whether Piaget or Vygotsky, we can see that account must be taken of the time and place, the conditions and environments in which their research takes place. So, although organised education still is mainly organised through national or federal systems, educational researchers do need to be able to compare and contrast, to understand the influence of specific contexts, in order to interact with each other in culturally sensitive and democratic discourses. As we have noted above, there are huge inequalities in power and wealth that create the conditions under which education researchers in different parts of the world operate, but it is in the interests of education research that the movement of ideas and indeed of the researchers themselves is unimpeded. Electronic communication has greatly enhanced the facility with which global interaction may take place, but it will remain very important that researchers have direct experience of education processes in locations other than that with which they are familiar. The depth of insight that can be derived from empirical research in different settings around the world is nowhere better demonstrated than in Alexander's major work *Culture and Pedagogy* (Alexander 2000).

One way of providing early career education researchers with opportunities to begin to be aware of the significance of these matters is through organised networks. Before concluding this chapter, we provide two examples of such networks, each of which has the potential to be highly influential in the formation of a new cadre of globally aware education researchers.

A European approach: the EERA Postgraduate Network

The European Educational Research Association (EERA) was founded in 1994 mainly due to the need felt by institutes and individual researchers, as well as national associations to exchange ideas amongst European researchers, to promote a more global collaboration in research and improve international research quality. Its aims are thus consistent with a more global perspective in educational research: encouraging collaboration, promoting and improving communication, as well as disseminating findings and results through a journal and an annual conference. The academic work is now organised in 27 thematic networks, and this number has increased significantly over the years. However, due to the need for developing research training in Europe a postgraduate network for students was also founded within the EERA, although its work is not of a thematic nature. Its main aim is to support new educational researchers in Europe by constructing a space in which organisational issues such as mobility, contract work and new initiatives, and postgraduate training can be discussed. Thus, its main strength lies in the support it offers to emerging researchers in providing a space for discussion and collaboration with peers across Europe.

The network includes students from all over the world and due to its fluctuating population (students are only members until they finish their PhD projects) it does not have a fixed number of members. However, students have the opportunity to fill an online form with their main research interests and thus engage in networking with peers from all over the world. The network is also responsible for a two-day conference for postgraduates within the EERA's annual meeting, the ECER (European Conference on Educational Research). In order to provide optimal support for students, a mentorship programme has been developed whereby every contribution is given feedback by a professor. The network also has a Senior Mentor and Senior Fellows who advise and orient its work and activities.

In addition, and in keeping with one of the EERA's current aims, the network offers two scholarships for excellent postgraduates from Eastern European universities for participation in the annual conference. The aim is to involve larger numbers of Eastern European students. Moreover, the best postgraduate paper presented at the ECER is selected for publication within the EERA's Journal *EERJ* (*European Educational Research Journal*).

Almost immediately after its establishment, two trends became evident within the postgraduate network. The first trend is an enormous demand for clarity in its rationale and for the expansion of its activities. The number of active members, as well as their direct involvement in the networks' activities, has increased significantly over the past five years, so that the postgraduate network is now the biggest network within the EERA. Additionally, it is the only network with a direct representative on Council and with its own conference, held prior to the main conference. In 2009 the network will also have its own publication – a journal for and from postgraduates, intending to publish papers of emerging researchers related to European research themes, on the one side, and addressing topics of an educational nature at a European level, on the other. The second trend of the network is even more related to the influence of globalisation on educational research – the number of participants from non-European countries has been increasing greatly over the last three years. In the 2008 conference of the network, in Gothenburg, Sweden, almost 20 per cent of the postgraduates came from Asia, Australia, North and South America, and Africa. The future of the network thus probably involves a more global perspective on European educational research.

A global approach: FINE and Universitas 21

Universitas 21 (U21) was established in 1971 to harness the collective potential of a group of research-intensive universities, which, between them, 'enrol over 650,000 students, employ over 130,000 staff and have over 2 million alumni' (Universitas 21 2009) and have an annual research grant income of US$3 billion. With a ceiling at 25, U21 currently has 21 enrolled members who believe that, although every member need not participate in every venture, the network makes possible better use of the collective resources than individual universities or bilateral arrangements could accomplish.

U21 aims to engage in globally significant issues that are of interest to its members and to facilitate innovation through collaboration between them. To promote this interest in collaborative research in areas of global significance, U21 offers encouragement to staff and students in member universities to establish links with other members through travel scholarships, fellowships and other bursaries, and support for networking at major international conferences.

The annual American Educational Research Association (AERA) affords an ideal opportunity for students from U21 universities to meet each other, explore issues of mutual interest and pave the way for possible research collaboration in the future. The Forum for International Networking in Education (FINE) was started in 2007, when eight doctoral students in education from such universities as McGill, the University of British Columbia, the University of Virginia and the University of Melbourne met in Chicago the day before the start of the annual AERA conference to explore how participating students could benefit from such networking, and in a more immediate sense, how they could be supported at the conference itself. The meeting was coordinated by two U21 academics. This exploratory meeting revealed that few students within U21 universities knew very much about the potential and the activities and goals of U21. The importance of engaging the co-operation of Associate Deans with responsibility for research students, and of better publicity and communication to publish U21 forums and activities was established. Two student representatives from this meeting attended a meeting of the Deans of Education to present a report of their meeting and to request support for further networking.

A major highlight of the FINE forum was the opportunity it provided for social networking. U21 academics and students could socialise and network over sponsored dinner and breakfast events, which, it is hoped, could lead to greater ties and collaboration opportunities between universities in the long run.

The interest in the Forum grew, with 20 students in attendance in 2008 in New York. The meeting this time included a representative from the U21 Secretariat, who made a presentation about the ways in which student initiatives could be supported by U21. Presentations and discussions led by U21 academics gave advice with regard to managing the PhD process and tips on publishing. Furthermore, it was decided that an online discussion forum and database of U21 students would be started as initial activities. Both initiatives were implemented during 2008.

The FINE forum has made a modest start, and although the forum and database are now operational, few students are actively using these facilities. Proposed future plans include a newsletter advertising upcoming regional events and conferences; enhancing possibilities for more U21 meetings; an online, peer-reviewed, student-run publication to give students an opportunity to publish their work; and regional networking opportunities and video conferences.

There are many differences between the EERA student network and the FINE group. Unlike the EERA student network and its equivalent, the AERA Graduate Student Council, membership of the FINE group is limited to U21 students. Unlike the EERA group, the FINE group aims to be relevant beyond and outside any particular conference; whilst annual meetings have been organised to coincide with AERA, the hope is that eventually there will be bilateral and regional events throughout the year.

One of the biggest challenges facing the FINE group is one of identity. Whereas there is a strong 'European identity' within the EERA group, an equivalent 'Universitas 21 identity' has so far not been achieved. Technological advances make it possible for groups to gather around common interests using video conferencing, wikis or blogs. Often these groups are a loose affiliation, without formal bodies such as U21, or long-term commitment to remaining a 'body'.

The ability of the FINE forum to make itself relevant and to realise the aims of U21 are largely dependent on the initiative the students take, and on the support they receive from advocates within universities.

Conclusion: ways forward

The two examples of student networks described above take somewhat different approaches. What they have in common, however, are at least two points. First, they share a belief in the value of international dialogues between early career education researchers. Second, they share a view that such dialogue is best located within a wider framework of dialogue and co-operation between more experienced researchers. As co-authors of this chapter we represent that range of experience among ourselves and would certainly urge other experienced researchers, as well as research students, to endeavour to make links of the kind described here. Of course, other smaller scale activity can be just as fruitful, such as, for example, research student involvement in multi-national research projects or through topic- or subject-based networks and conferences. We would encourage all students to be seeking to present their work as it develops, at national and international gatherings where there are appropriate opportunities.

The potential for international networking has been enormously increased through communications developments over recent years. Certainly in these times of growing concern about the global environment, it is not always necessary to travel in order to have such engagement across national boundaries. However, we would suggest that firsthand experience of different education systems and different research cultures is a very powerful experience in itself, especially for those who are early in their career.

Over the period 2007–9, discussions have been taking place between national and regional educational research associations about developing a 'global association of associations'. The World Educational Research Association (WERA) is likely to be formally established during 2009/10 and one of its key aims will be to encourage the development of international educational research capacity through the support of early career researchers.

As international networking develops, it will be crucial that those involved take due cognisance of inequalities of power and wealth and ensure that relationships are based on mutuality and parity of esteem. Equally, it will be important to ensure that language issues are not ignored and that every effort is made to facilitate intercultural and inter-linguistic communication within such developments. The process of interaction is itself a deeply educational one and if such principles are followed then the potential for international networking to contribute to the development of high-quality research and to educational improvements across the globe are enormous.

References

Alexander, R. (2000) *Culture and Pedagogy: International Comparisons in Primary Education*. Oxford: Blackwell.

Ball, S. (2007) Big policies/small world: an introduction to international perspectives in education policy. In B. Lingard and J. Ozga (Eds). *The Routledge/Falmer Reader in Education Policy and Politics*. London: Routledge/Falmer.

——(2008) *Education plc*. London: Routledge.

Burbules, N. C. and Torres, C. A. (Eds) (2000) *Globalization and Education: Critical Perspectives*. Routledge: New York.

Crossley, M. and Broadfoot, P. (1992) Comparative and international research in education: scope, problems, potential, *British Educational Research Journal*, 18(2): 99–112.

Crossley, M. and Watson, K. (2003) *Comparative and International Research in Education: Globalization, context and difference*. London: Routledge/Falmer.

Edwards, R. and Usher, R. (2007) *Globalization and Pedagogy: Space, place and Identity*. 2nd edn. London: Routledge.

Grant, N. (1968) *Soviet Education*. Revised edn. Harmondsworth: Penguin.

Green, A. (1990) *Education and State Formation: The Rise of Education Systems in England, France and the USA*. London: Macmillan.

King, E. (1967) *Other Schools and Ours*. 3rd edn. London: Holt, Rinehart and Winston.

Mahony P., Menter I. and Hextall I. (2004) Building dams in Jordan, assessing teachers in England: a case-study in edu-business, *Globalization, Societies and Education*, 2(2): 277–96.

Mitter, W. (1997) Challenges to comparative education: Between Retrospect and Expectation, *International Review of Education*, 43(5–6): 401–12.

Olssen, M., Codd, J. and O'Neill, A. M. (2004) *Education Policy – Globalization, Citizenship and Democracy*. London: Sage.

Ozga, J. and Lingard, B. (2007) Globalization, education policy and politics. In Lingard, B. and Ozga, J. (Eds). *The Routledge/Falmer Reader in Education Policy and Politics*. London: Routledge/Falmer.

Ozga, J., Seddon, T. and Popkewitz, T. (Eds) (2006) *Education Research and Policy: Steering the knowledge-based economy, World yearbook of Education 2006*. London: Routledge.

Rizvi, F. and Lingard, B. (2006) Globalization and the changing nature of the OECD's educational work. In H. Lauder, P. Brown, J. Dillabough and A. Halsey (Eds). *Education, Globalization and Social Change*. Oxford: Oxford University Press.

Stromquist, N. and Monkman, K. (Eds) (2000) *Globalization and Education: Integration and Contestation Across Cultures*. Lanham, MD: Rowman & Littlefield Publishing.

Universitas 21 (2009) *About Universitas 21*. Online. (Available at universitas21.com/about.html Accessed 20 March 2009).

Williams, G. (2000) Changes in Government Policy and the Development of Higher Education in Wales. In R. Daugherty, R. Phillips and G. Rees (Eds). *Education Policy-Making in Wales*. Cardiff: University of Wales Press.

Zajda, J. (2002) Reinventing the Past to Create the Future: the Rewriting of School History Textbooks in Post-Communist Russia. In M. Schwesfurth, C. Harber and L. Davies (Eds). *Learning, Democracy and Citizenship: International Experience*. Oxford: Symposium books, pp. 211–24.

——(Ed.) (2005) *International Handbook on Globalization, Education and Policy Research, Global Pedagogies and Policies*. Dordrecht, The Netherlands: Springer.

31

The impact of research on education policy

The relevance for doctoral researchers

B. Lingard

This chapter is concerned with the impact of doctoral research on policy making in education. Doctoral research is regarded as having as a central purpose a contribution to knowledge and understanding, a purpose similar to that of academic research in education, while the impact on education policy also works in similar ways. We can also distinguish between doctoral research in education generally and that explicitly focused on education policy. There are also professional doctorates in education, which seek a more direct policy and practice impact, but which also have an outcome criterion of contribution to knowledge. The distinction between research *of/for* policy is a useful analytic here (Gordon *et al.* 1977), with the former the more academically oriented education policy research and the latter more akin to commissioned research. This binary will be utilised in this chapter and will assist in assessing the impact of research upon policy, which it is argued is always heavily mediated and indirect.

In the next section, some preliminary considerations are traversed, including how we might usefully define education research, how we might define impact, and how we need to reconceptualise what we take as education policy today, given the effects and workings of globalisation. Following these definitional preliminaries, the complexity of the relationship between education research and education policy will be considered. The subsequent section will seek to elaborate and understand this relationship through an account of the 'distinctive and misaligned cultures' of education research and policy (Orland 2009: 117). Finally, the conclusion will summarise the argument proffered regarding the complex connections and disconnections between education research and policy and offer an evaluative view of this state of play.

Preliminaries

There are a number of factors that have to be accounted for when considering the impact of education research on education policy. These include a definition of education research. They also include an understanding of the concept of 'impact' and its varying meanings and targets, as well as understanding of education policy today and the processes associated with its production. In this chapter, the place of doctoral research in relation to this range of matters will be regarded as part of academic research in education, as opposed for example to government commissioned research, and can thus be subsumed under broader considerations of the impact of research on policy. We also need to make a distinction between how education policy research is positioned in relation to actual policy and research focused explicitly on understanding this relationship. The latter research seeks to understand the actual manner and multiple pathways of dissemination of research into policy, as well as how it affects policy in the short term and also has longer term impact in relation to changing the broad assumptive worlds of policy makers. I would note here also that the chapter is interested in the relationships between research and policy and not concerned with policy implementation, nor the impact of research on school-based practitioners. We know that the impact of research on practitioners works in multifarious, mediated and non-linear ways (Figgis *et al.* 2000; McMeniman *et al.* 2000), and as such there are some parallels with the research/policy relationship in education, as will be illustrated throughout this chapter.

Defining education research

Education research can probably be defined through consideration of two bundles of things: first, its focus or topic and second, the intellectual resources, both theoretical and methodological, brought to bear on an understanding through research of the topic. In a sense then, education research might be seen as the application of social science theories and methodologies to education, assuming agreement on education. Indeed, this is one way of considering a definition of education research, seeing it as defined by its focus or topic. We might see this as research *on* rather than *for* education (Carr 1997). However, I would argue, following Bernstein (2001) and Thomson (2006), given contemporary social changes associated within the emergent 'totally pedagogised society' and with the pedagogisation of everyday/everynight life, that we have seen a de-differentiation of educational institutions (Young 1998). De-differentiation has widened the definition of what we might see as an educational institution and as pedagogical practices. In the knowledge society, learning is everywhere and directed through policies, both direct and indirect, around pedagogies. Bernstein (2001) suggests what we have witnessed is 'pedagogical inflation'. The potential topic of education research is thus expanding. So the topic or focus of education research is more problematic than it might at first appear. Thus, we might see education research as the application of social science theories and methodologies to a topic, education, which is changing and expanding with the move towards learning and knowledge societies.

Given the centrality now of education to national economic competitiveness and of pedagogies to learning across the life span and to both cultural and social reproduction, it also might be the case that theorising about such 'educational matters' might move towards centre stage within the social sciences. Furthermore, all of the myriad changes associated with globalisation have also offered challenges to the social sciences, particularly to the now erroneous assumption of a homology between society and nation-state and associated 'methodological nationalism' (Beck 2000; Appadurai 2001).

Returning to considerations of how we ought to define education research today: I would argue that it might be more appropriate to speak of *educational* research to define our topic and that the distinction from the nomenclature of *education* research carries important meaning (Bartlett 1987/2009; Griffiths 1998). The educational/education distinction is somewhat akin to the research *for/on* education binary. When we use the descriptor 'educational' attached to research, it seems to me that we are arguing that such research has educational or educative purposes, that is, such research is progressive in the sense of seeking and desiring to improve both education policy and professional practice in education (Lingard and Gale 2009). This is an additional purpose to the contribution to knowledge and understanding purposes of mainstream social science research. Elsewhere, I have argued that this means that educational researchers ought to have a 'pedagogical disposition' and as the converse that practitioners (policy makers and teachers) ought to have a 'researcherly disposition' (Lingard and Renshaw 2010). In terms of this researcherly disposition, practitioners (both policy makers in education and teachers) need to be both research-informed and research-informing. At the same time, the pedagogical disposition for educational researchers has implications for how we define education policy research and its relationship to actual policy making in education. My position is that any education policy research of any type ought to have at the broadest level a desire to make things better in education, explicitly in the case of our concerns here, to improve education policy. We thus need to ask, 'How does this commitment to improvement have impact on actual education policy?'.

Defining impact

Impact in relation to research is also a complex concept. Crudely, we can see research as having impact directly through its effects as measured through citations and the like in the academic literature, as well as in journal impact measures. This might be seen as academic impact and is that which is usually most highly respected amongst academic researchers and within high-status universities. This is the most likely impact of top-quality doctoral research. However, impact in a field such as educational research can also be taken to refer to impact on policy and practice. This construction of impact is often signified in talk of the 'end-users' of educational research and their involvement in the assessment of research grant applications in education. End-users, for example, were members of the Review Panels of the UK's Research Assessment Exercise. It is necessary to point out, however, that this form of policy and practice impact comes from research that seeks explicitly to do this, as well as in more mediated and often more long-term ways by research that seeks ostensibly to enhance knowledge and understanding. In talk of educational research, as I have indicated above, even this type of research driven by researcher curiosity would need to have a pedagogical disposition in terms of a desire to improve and thus have impact upon policy.

Defining education policy

Education policy has been used in a somewhat non-problematic way to this point. The classic public policy definition developed from the work of the US political scientist David Easton (1953) who defined policy as 'the authoritative allocation of values'. This remains a useful definition, but needs some elaboration and extension in the context of the impact of globalisation on education policy. We need to understand how globalisation has destabilised each element of this definition (Rizvi and Lingard 2010). Political authority in the present post-Westphalian reality has seen the sovereignty of national polities challenged by agencies, organisations, fields and discourses from beyond the nation.[1] This means that political authority – the legitimate right to exercise power in a Weberian sense – now is exercised beyond the nation as well as within the nation. This

379

does not mean a weakened nation–state, but rather one that works in very different ways from older Westphalian practices. What we see here is the new educational governance, the 'rescaling' of politics and policy and its 'pluri-scalar' character (Dale 2005; Rizvi and Lingard 2010). Processes of allocation in policy have thus also been affected. The state itself at the national level has been restructured under new public management and now steers at a distance though outcome accountability measures, including international comparative measures of student performance. The values now allocated in and through education policy are also linked to globalised education policy discourses. Thus, when we are thinking of the impact of research on education policy, we need to be aware of this rescaling of policy and also be aware of relevant related changes. We thus need to understand that impact today applies to institutions and sources beyond the nation, as well as within the nation. This is the emergent postnationalism that theorists such as Appadurai (1996) have spoken about. As noted earlier, it is this range of matters associated with the rescaling of education policy that has also challenged theories and methodologies in the social sciences.

Research/policy relationships

Research only ever a contributing factor in education policy

This section will consider the connectivity between research and policy in respect of both actual and desired relationships. Suffice to say at the outset, that research is only ever one 'determining', perhaps 'contributing', factor in both education policy content and processes, as well as in professional practice. Even today with much talk about evidence-based policy, this remains the case. As Head (2008) has shown, policy is always a varying mix of values/ideology, professional knowledge and research evidence. The mix for any given policy is dependent on a range of factors. In terms of values and ideology, policy is linked to politics and framed by the political intentions of governments, politicians and ministers and thus is linked to ideology, but always mediated by other factors, including at times research evidence. Policy can be seen to be the rearticulation of political intentions through the logics of practice of the state and policy makers. If we accept Easton's (1953) definition, referred to above, that public policy is the 'authoritative allocation of values', we can also see that research is and perhaps can only ever be a contributing factor to policy. As Orland (2009: 115) notes:

> Even the most compelling and relevant research findings may fail to penetrate the policymaking process and, where research influences are manifest, their contributions are likely to be both indirect and incremental.

Policy making is a political activity, mediated by state structures and production rules, by professional norms, and informed by research. The allocation of values through policy mobilises the distribution of capitals (human, material, symbolic) of various kinds across the education system seeking to reconstitute some imagined future. Power/knowledge imbrications are involved here in particular ways, and are manifestations of the different universes of discourse of policy and academic research, including doctoral research. At the most abstract levels, the two are located within different epistemic communities. These are matters that will be traversed in the next section of the chapter on the disjunctive cultures between research and policy, between the research community and the policy community.

We also need to recognise that policy makers (and practitioners) can also be researchers, as well as utilisers of research. It would be wrong simply to see both as inert recipients and translators of research. The first point, though, that we need to acknowledge is that research is only one contributing factor to education policy processes and policy content and intentions. So research, including doctoral research, can and will only ever be one contributing factor to education policy and changes to it. Of course, there is still the question of which research contributes to policy, which research is utilised by policy makers. Here, it also might be useful to speak of policy-based evidence (as the obverse of evidence-based policy), that is, research implicit and used in the policy production process. Research here can be used in multiple ways, including as both rationale and justification. As Orland argues:

> To the extent it is relied on at all, educational research is much more likely to be paid attention to by educational policy leaders when it buttresses arguments about particular policy directions or prescriptions *already* being advocated, thus furthering a particular political/policy position. It is research as ammunition not as knowledge discovery.
>
> Orland 2009: 118

Research of/for policy

As already alluded to, there has been a classic distinction in education policy studies between research *of/for* policy (Gordon *et al.* 1977), which picks up on the intent of the policy research, who is defining it and who is doing it and for what purposes. Research *of* policy is the more academic pursuit, research for research's sake, with new knowledge and understanding as the desired outcome – what we might call here an 'enlightenment' purpose of policy research (Trowler 2003). Doctoral research on education policy as a genre of research is clearly situated within this enlightenment frame. Research *for* policy refers to that research commissioned by policy makers to assist in the production of actual policy. Here, the policy problem is taken as given and any research is framed by the interests and intentions of the policy makers. Following Trowler (2003), we might see this as an 'engineering' relationship between research and policy. However, we need to note that this research *for* policy is not usually conducted by doctoral students, apart perhaps from the intentions of professional doctoral students. Rather, the participants in this kind of research are usually seasoned policy researchers of a particular kind. Some-times this research is conducted by researchers whom Ball (2006) has called 'policy entrepreneurs', those who make a living doing research *for* policy within agendas set by governments or international organisations.

Problem-solving versus critical research

We can see here the distinction between 'problem-solving research' and a more critical academic approach (Cox 1996: 88–89). Commissioned research most often tends to be of the former type and is to be utilised within the actual policy process. Even though, even here, we need to acknowledge that this research will still be filtered through the 'preconceptions, values and attitudes' of policy makers (Trowler 2003: 183). Trowler says in this way there is some similarity between policy research even of this kind and policy implementation: both can be seen as palimpsest, being re-read through new lenses in policy practice. This filtering, of course, applies to both research *for* and *of* policy, if the latter does come to the attention of policy makers. We need to acknowledge that research *of* policy can also have policy effects, particularly in relation to policy activists involved in all stages of the policy process (agenda setting, development, formulation, implementation, delivery, evaluation and monitoring) (Yeatman 1998: 11).

In a sense, it might be better to see research *of/for* policy sitting on a continuum as suggested by Cibulka (1994), rather than as a clearly defined, tight binary distinction. Activists utilise all types of research in their political activity seeking to affect all stages of the policy process. Pressure groups also work in this way in their utilisation of policy research. This research utilisation, however, will be filtered through their particular political lenses, as with policy makers. We see here the complexity of issues to do with research impact in respect of policy and the always indirect, non-linear, mediated relationship between the two.

The *problem-solving/critical research* binary is, of course, not perfectly homologous with the research *of/for* binary, when applied to education policy research. The problem-solving and critical approaches speak to different epistemologies and ontologies and very different politics and political intentions. But we need to acknowledge that both approaches can apply in the *for/of* binary, but noting that research *for* policy is nearly always problem-solving in orientation, whereas research *of* policy can be of either orientation. As Robert Cox (1996: 88) observes, the problem-solving approach accepts the world as it finds it, including existing power relations, inequalities and oppressions, and thus accepts the status quo as the framework for action. This positioning allows for a focus on the specific problem, a tinkering and targeted approach, as it were. In contrast, as Cox (1996) notes, critical theory does not take for granted these realities, rather it challenges them. Indeed, what is taken for granted within problem-solving approaches is open to full appraisal by critical theorists. The relational approach of critical theory also links particular institutional practices with overall social structures. The critical approach is more theoretical in orientation and more political in a capital 'P' sense, thus making it less attractive to most policy makers. However, policy makers inside the state are often aware of this research, as are policy activists both inside and outside the state, who use it in their critiques and politicking around particular policy agendas. Academic education policy research (including doctoral research) is often of this critical kind. Thus, its influence on the policy process works in vastly different ways from that of policy research set within a problem-solving paradigm.

Engineering versus enlightenment models of research/ policy relationships

For heuristic purposes, Trowler (2003: 177) constructs a binary between engineering and enlightenment models of the relationships between research and policy. The engineering approach can be seen as akin to research *for* policy of a problem-solving bent, whereas the enlightenment approach can be seen as similar to research *of* policy and of a more critical theory bent. Trowler (p. 177) suggests that within the engineering research/ policy relationship, that data tend to be quantitative, the ontology is foundationalist, the epistemology positivist/absolutist, and the relationship to policy that of 'informing policy makers about the "facts"' and 'proposing solutions to "problems"'. In contrast, he sees the enlightenment model as tending towards qualitative methods of data collection and analysis, adopting a relativist ontology, and working with a relativist/intrepretivist epistemology. The explicit relationship to policy of the enlightenment model is about enlightening policy makers and 'challenging the accepted definitions of "educational problems" and reframing what is problematic in education' (Trowler 2003: 177).

Trowler's is a useful heuristic, but as with many binaries overstates distinctions between the two models. Thus, for example, enlightenment research might tend towards qualitative approaches to data collection and analysis (e.g. semi-structured interviews and textual analysis), but there is no necessity for this to be the case. Indeed, it would be very foolish to see quantitative approaches as not having a place in education policy research of this kind (Fitz *et al.* 2006), and even more foolish to see qualitative approaches as somehow inextricably linked to progressive politics and quantitative approaches as inevitably not.

We know that policy constructs the problem, to which it is the putative solution, in a given way. McLaughlin (2006) has called this 'the problem of the problem'. The first step of critical education policy analysis demands a deconstruction of the problem-construction work of a given policy. In stark contrast, research *for* policy, commissioned policy research, takes the policy problem construction as a given and frames research within that as taken-for-granted. We can see here a distinction made by Seeley (1966) between the 'making' and 'taking' of social problems. Research *of* policy, particularly within a critical framework, sees the deconstruction of the problem-construction work of policy as a necessary step in policy analysis, whereas research *for* policy takes the policy problem as a given. The result is vastly different relationships and connectivity to actual policy.

Research on the policy impact of research

There is another body of research that focuses explicitly on understanding the real impact of research on actual policy making (e.g. Weiss 1979; 1989; Vickers 1994; Watson 2008; Orland 2009). Utilising Weiss's well-known work on 'the politics of knowledge utilization' in policy processes, Vickers (1994), for example, outlines four types of connections and utilisations by policy makers and politicians of research knowledge: research as *warning* of problems; as *guidance* for possible policy options; as *enlightenment*, which can lead to the reframing of policy problems and approaches; and as *mobilisation* of support for a politically desired policy option. These are connections between research *of* policy and the actual politics of policy making. Weiss's (1979) classic account of the impact of social science research on public policy outlined seven types of research utilisation in public policy: knowledge-driven (research *for* policy – more applicable in science-related domains than in the social sciences), problem-solving (research *for* policy), interactive approaches (involving researchers on relevant committees or as part of consultation in the policy process), political (research used as legitimation for policy option adopted), tactical (used to delay policy action due to lack of research evidence or research still being conducted), enlightenment or 'percolation' (referring to the complex dissemination of research knowledge over time, changing the assumptive worlds of policy makers), and intellectual enterprise (both policy research and policy development are affected by the dominant ideas of the period). Weiss argues that the most profound impact of research on policy, and I would include education research here, is through her notions of enlightenment and percolation. Here, 'research-based knowledge affects policy gradually by shaping how decision makers understand and frame a problem and decide on potential solutions' (Orland 2009: 115). Percolation thus attempts to pick up on the longer time frame of this type of research impact upon policy. Thus enlightenment can take time and policy makers most often will not even be aware of the way such research over time has reframed and constituted their assumptive worlds, their policy dispositions and habitus, which come to bear in the policy process.

Orland (2009) has suggested that the proclivity of policy makers to utilise education research and which type of research, will be filtered through external influences (public opinion, opinion leaders, political party beliefs), organisational culture and procedures and personal values and dispositions. Thus, research can reach and affect the policy process through impact on opinion leaders, interest groups and activists and political leaders, as well as through more direct influence in the policy process (Orland 2009: 115).

There is today also a way in which policy affects research. This occurs in a number of ways. The most macro of these relates to the ways in which policy makers today have sought to (re)define what good education research is. This was most evident in the USA during the Bush period, when experimental studies using randomised controls were constituted as the 'gold standard' of education research. Jenny Ozga and her colleagues (Ozga *et al.* 2006) have also demonstrated the multiple ways in which public policy today also seeks to set research agendas. Just as research can impact on policy through agenda setting, policy about research has sought to affect research agendas. Luke and Hogan (2006: 170) have argued in this context that 'current debates over what counts as evidence in state policy formation are indeed debates over what counts as educational research'.[2] As they note, currently there are attempts around the globe to wind back gains in critical theory and methodologies as applied to education research and to tame educational research in the direction of state policy requirements and problem-solving epistemologies and ontologies. In relation to these matters, we see attempts to redefine research agendas, priorities and methodologies through state policy making. The starkest example of this politics occurred in relation to Bush's *No Child Left Behind* agenda in the USA, which demanded that research evaluations in relation to it be of the randomised control trials variety and articulated the need for 'scientifically based research' in education, a signifier of opposition to critical theory and qualitative methodologies. These changes were also a policy attempt to ensure a greater and more direct research contribution to education policy making (Orland 2009). More broadly, this might be seen as an attempt to align research and policy making cultures and communities, a matter that is the focus of the next section of the chapter.

The disjunctive cultures of academic research and policy making in education

Disjunctive cultures between social science research and public policy making

Some indication has been given to this point of the disjunctive cultures extant between research and policy, including specifically between doctoral research and policy. There is a general literature about these cultural disjunctions (e.g. Weimer and Vining 2005; Lauen and Tyson 2009; Orland 2009). Lauen and Tyson (2009), drawing on Weimer and Vining (2005), have written about the misalignment between academic research and research done in the policy process, what we have classified as research *for* policy. They outline distinctions in respect of academic research and research *for* policy, in relation to: objectives – theory building and understanding versus understanding of impact of variables open to policy manipulation; clients – 'truth' versus policy actors; style – rigorous methods and theorising versus applied approach; time constraints – limited external time constraints versus deadline pressures; and weaknesses in respect of policy – irrelevant to policy makers versus difficulty translating findings into policy action. We can see these misalignments between types of research as indicative of the cultural disjunctions between research and policy and their respective communities.

Orland (2009) has also written about these broad disjunctive cultures, drawing on the general literature on the research/policy relationship. Additionally, he comments specifically on the idiosyncratic features of education as a public endeavour, which he argues also limit the usage of research in education policy production. Orland (2009: 117) documents five general factors that contribute to the research/policy cultural disjunctions. These are: 'original contribution versus replication/refinement', 'understanding versus fixing problems', different 'communication conventions', disciplinary versus 'interdisciplinary', and collaborative approaches and differing time horizons.

In terms of the original contribution focus of research as opposed to the need for replication and refinement of research knowledges for the policy process, Orland makes the point that there are different reward structures in each culture. Researchers are rewarded for original contributions to a field, whereas policy makers need more certain and replicated knowledge so as to be able to recontextualise research findings to policy contexts. Academic research, including doctoral research and explicit education policy research, all stress the creation of a 'better conceptual understanding of the broad issue' (p.117), whereas policy makers are more focused on problem-solving. I would note though, that knowledge and understanding should be a precursor to action, including policy action. However, the differing time pressures of researchers and policy makers mean that policy making is often about 'sufficing' and incremental change. Nonetheless, as Weiss (1979) demonstrated, over time research can have an enlightenment effect through its percolation into the habitus of policy makers and politicians.

Academic researchers are rewarded for publishing their research in high-status academic journals with an implied readership of other academics, rather than a readership of policy professionals. As Orland (2009: 117) observes, 'The emphasis in the academe on research method explication, developing well-justified theoretical constructs, and preparing complex narratives with tightly woven and carefully nuanced arguments are endemic to high quality research scholarship'. These are also the features of doctoral research. These conventions inhibit the communication of research to policy professionals, thus limiting its impact. I would also note that there is a tentative character to research findings, which sits in contrast to the need for action in policy making. Orland also notes that most academic research tends to be based in a single discipline, whereas the complex character of problems that policy seeks to 'solve' require interdisciplinary understandings, another feature of the disjunctive cultures between research and policy. Finally, in terms of Orland's account of these cultural disjunctions, he notes the differing time frames or horizons of the researchers and the policy makers, with the policy maker usually functioning within shorter time frames and with 'time-sensitive information needs' (p.117). I would also suggest that the policy cycle is framed by the political cycle, that is, the effluxion of time between elections. This temporal frame is asynchronous with the temporal frame within research cultures and indeed with the accumulation of research-based knowledge and understanding over time. Unfortunately, in terms of policy implementation, there is also a dysfunctional misalignment between political temporalities and imperatives and those necessary for real educational change.

Education, educational research and education policy

To these differing cultures, which help us understand the complex and indirect effects of research on policy, Orland (2009: 118) adds three factors specific to the nature of educational institutions and practices. The first factor here is the public and political character of education and its contested nature. The cumulative effect is, according to Orland (2009), that 'the general culture around educational decision-making revolves much more around the public allocation of individual and societal values than studies of objective fact or truth' (p. 119). Public policy is always about the allocation of values. Orland suggests, and I agree with him, that this observation applies even more profoundly in the domain of education policy. Thus, we see another factor limiting the impact of research on education policy. The second factor addressed by Orland in relation to research/education policy relationships is the 'conditional nature of salient explanations for nearly all educational phenomena' (p. 118). The nature of educational institutions and educational practices do not readily lend themselves to 'the technology of scientifically rigorous research' (p. 119). In contrasting the research/policy relationship in medicine with that in education, Orland notes:

> It is only to say that given the inherently social and co-dependent nature of educational service delivery, the number of variables for educational policy makers to consider in deciding on approaches or interventions likely to work in achieving particular outcomes is much larger than it is in medicine.
>
> Orland 2009: 119

The final idiosyncratic factor about education and educational research considered by Orland is a specifically USA one, namely the limited amount of government monies actually invested in educational research, say, as compared with medical research. This specific point probably applies in most countries around the globe.

Orland also sees developments in respect of policy on educational research during the Bush era in the USA as an attempt to focus educational research and potentially make it more policy-relevant. As noted earlier, this attempt worked via the constitution of randomised control trials and 'scientifically based' research as the 'gold standard' for such research. I would regard these developments as ideologically driven and actually misaligned with the need for multiple methods and theoretical approaches in education research, given the complexity of educational problems and the necessity of a diversity of approaches to knowledge production within a democratic society. There needs to be the opportunity, in my view, for education researchers generally and specifically in relation to research on education policy, to 'make' their research problems and to choose the appropriate methodological and theoretical framework. Instead of the attempt to create and establish one gold standard, what is required is the productive development of concepts of quality applicable to the broad range of research approaches in education (Lingard and Gale 2009).

Conclusion

In this chapter I have argued that both educational research and education policy making are contested terrains consisting of competing interests and competing approaches. I have also argued that research is only ever one contributing factor to education policy, despite contemporary calls for evidence-based policy. This will always be the case in my view, given that policy is the authoritative allocation of values. It has also been demonstrated how research and policy are located within different orbits (Orland 2009), within different cultures and epistemic communities and within variant temporalities, thus offering one explanation for the complex, mediated, indirect and non-linear effects of research on policy, including doctoral research. The nature of this relationship holds if we are talking of education research generally and to specific education policy research, including doctoral research of both kinds. I am also wary of attempts to more closely align the two as pursued by the Bush administration in the USA, as these political attempts most often seek to narrow and redefine research approaches and methodologies, to establish a single 'gold standard' for research, and in so doing, deny the importance of critical approaches, alternative methodologies and research agendas established by researchers. A plurality of approaches would seem to be necessary within a liberal democracy and demands a broad calculus of quality across varying types of research. Doctoral research on education policy has an important role to play here, as does the broader range of doctoral research in education, which can also have policy effects. Jill Blackmore (2003: 1) has asked in relation to the role of educational research: is it as 'policy service, policy critique, technical expert or public intellectual?'. Doctoral research, I would aver, ought to be about policy critique and enhancing understanding and as such is a central component of a democratic and open society. Any more direct role and impact in relation to education policy would demand that the doctoral researcher take a more activist political role. That would be a function of political activity and the utilisation of research knowledge. I am not arguing for a 'de-politicisation of policy scholarship' (Thomson 2006), but rather recognising that doctoral research is about enhancing understanding and contributing to theory building. Such theoretical elaboration can contribute to more effective political activism in the longer term.

Research that has the most direct and immediate effect on policy is that commissioned by policy makers for a purpose and framed by a problem-solving disposition. This is research *for* policy. Interest groups often sponsor this type of research as well. However, the more academic exercise, research *of* policy, including most doctoral research on education policy and on education more broadly, fits within a critical framework and seeks to deconstruct the problem as constructed by policy and to deconstruct many of the 'taken-for-granteds' of the contemporary world. This research is about enhancing human understanding, about enlightenment in the broadest 'post' construction of that concept. As such, this type of policy research has much less immediate impact and effect on education policy, which is not to say that it might not have policy effects. However, as Carol Weiss (1979) argued, such research often percolates into the education policy process in the longer term through understanding and enlightenment, which it produces and which reframes the assumptive worlds of policy makers. This is a profound policy effect, but one which is most often not recognised as such, given its long time frame and its asynchronous relationship to the temporal frame of political and policy cycles. Doctoral research, as with other academic research in education, can add to this through its contribution along with other academic research to enhanced understanding. Such research is also often utilised by policy activists both inside and outside the state and can be a contributing factor to the heteroglossic nature of most policy documents, which sees a suturing over competing discourses and interests.

Research on the research/policy relationship, traversed in this chapter, demonstrates the complexity of the relationship. Trowler's enlightenment/engineering relationship of research to policy is one example, as is Vickers account of policy utilisation as a warning, guidance, enlightenment and mobilisation. As Orland noted, research is most often mobilised in the policy process as a legitimation of already decided policy directions. This is research knowledge as ammunition. Doctoral research on education, as with all other academic education policy research can be used in this way, but it is through longer term enlightenment and the percolation of this research into policy processes that potentially such research has its most profound effects.

Notes

1 International relations until the current era of globalisation have worked within a Westphalian frame, which recognised the political sovereignty of nation-states and which saw international relations as bi- and multi-lateral relations between sovereign nations. Under globalisation, there have been some challenges to national sovereignty with the nation-state now functioning in different ways. Politics have been rescaled so that now we see global and regional agreements, supra-national (e.g. the EU) and multi-lateral politics and a related reworking of national politics.

2 Luke and Hogan (2006) seek to reconstitute an approach to evidence-based policy drawing upon both qualitative and quantitative research data and the insights from critical educational research and theory. In so doing, they describe an approach to the research/policy relationship being put in place in contemporary Singapore.

References

Appadurai, A. (1996) *Modernity at Large: Cultural Dimensions of Globalization*. Minneapolis, MN: The University of Minnesota Press.

——(2001) Grass roots globalization and the research imagination. In A. Appadurai (Ed.) *Globalization*. Durham, NC: Duke University Press.

Ball, S. J. (2006) *Education Policy and Social Class: the selected works of Stephen J. Ball*. London: Routledge.

Bartlett, L. (1987/2009) New and Old Testaments of Alliance in Educational Research. In T. Gale and B. Lingard (Eds). *Educational Research by Association: AARE Presidential Addresses and the Field of Educational Research*. Rotterdam: Sense Publishers.

Beck, U. (2000) The cosmopolitan perspective, *British Journal of Sociology*, 51(1): 79–105.

Bernstein, B. (2001) From pedagogies to knowledge. In A. Marais *et al.* (Eds). *Towards a Sociology of Pedagogy: The contribution of Basil Bernstein to research*. New York: Peter Lang.

Blackmore, J. (2003) Tracking the nomadic life of the educational researcher: what future for feminist public intellectuals and the performative university? *Australian Educational Researcher*, 30(3): 1–24.

Carr, W. (1997) Professing education in a postmodern age, *Journal of Philosophy of Education*, 31: 309–27.

Cibulka, J. G. (1994) Policy analysis and the study of education, *Journal of Education Policy*, 9(5/6): 105–25.

Cox, R. (1996) *Approaches to World Order*. Cambridge: Cambridge University Press.

Dale, R. (2005) Globalization, knowledge economy and comparative education. *Comparative Education*, 41(2): 117–49.

Easton, D. (1953) *The Political System*. New York: Knopf.

Figgis, J., Zubrick, A., Butorac, A. and Alderson, A. (2000) Backtracking practice and policies to research. In Department of Education, Training & Youth Affairs (Ed.). *The Impact of Educational Research*. Canberra: Commonwealth of Australia, 279–373.

Fitz, J., Davies, B. and Evans, J. (2006) *Educational Policy and Social Reproduction*. London: Routledge.

Gordon, I., Lewis, J. and Young, R. (1977) Perspectives on policy analysis. *Public Administration Bulletin*, 25: 26–35.

Griffiths, M. (1998) *Educational Research for Social Justice Getting off the fence*. Buckingham: Open University Press.

Head, B. (2008) Three lenses of evidence-based policy. *Australian Journal of Public Administration*, 67(1): 1–11.

Lauen, D. L and Tyson, K. (2009) Perspectives from the Disciplines: Sociological Contributions to Education Policy Research and Debates. In G. Sykes, B. Schneider, D. N. Plank and T. G. Ford (Eds). *Handbook of Education Policy Research*. New York: Routledge, pp. 71–82.

Lingard, B and Gale, T. (2009) Presidential Address as Pedagogy: Representing and Constituting the Field of Educational Research. In T. Gale and B. Lingard (Eds). *Educational Research by Association: AARE Presidential Addresses and the Field of Educational Research*. Rotterdam: Sense Publishers.

Lingard, B. and Renshaw, P. (2010) Teaching as a research-informed and research-informing profession. In A. Campbell and S. Groundwater-Smith (Eds). *Connecting Inquiry and Professional Learning in Education*. London: Routledge.

Luke, A. and Hogan, D. (2006) Redesigning what counts as evidence in educational policy: the Singapore model. In J. Ozga, T. Seddon and T. Popkewitz (Eds). *World Yearbook of Education 2006: Education Research and Policy: Steering the Knowledge-Based Economy*. London: Routledge.

McLaughlin, M. (2006) Implementation research in education: lessons learnt, lingering questions and new opportunities. In M. Honig (Ed.). *New Directions in Education Policy Implementation: confronting complexity*. New York: State University of New York Press.

McMeniman, M., Cumming, J., Wilson, J., Stevenson, J. and Sim, C. (2000) Teacher knowledge in action. In Department of Education, Training & Youth Affairs (Ed.). *The Impact of Educational Research*. Canberra: Commonwealth of Australia, 375–549.

Orland, M. (2009) Separate Orbits: The distinctive worlds of educational research and policymaking. In G. Sykes, B. Schneider, D. Plank and T. Ford (Eds). *Handbook of Education Policy Research*. New York: Routledge, 113–28.

Ozga, J., Seddon, T. and Popkewitz, T. S. (2006) Introduction Education Research and Policy – Steering the Knowledge-Based Economy. In J. Ozga, T. Seddon and T. S. Popkewitz (Eds). *Education Research and Policy Steering the Knowledge-Based Economy, 2006 World Yearbook of Education*. London: Routledge, 1–14.

Rizvi, F. and Lingard, B. (2010) *Globalizing Education Policy*. London: Routledge.

Seeley, J. (1966) The 'making' and 'taking' of social problems, *Social Problems*, 14.

Thomson, P. (2006) Policy scholarship against depoliticization. In J. Ozga, T. Seddon and T. Popkewitz (Eds). *World Yearbook of Education 2006: Education Research and Policy: Steering the Knowledge-Based Economy*. London: Routledge.

Trowler, P. (2003) *Education Policy*. 2nd edn. London: Routledge.

Vickers, M. (1994) Cross-national exchange, the OECD, and Australian education policy, *Knowledge and Policy*, 7(1): 25–47.

Watson, L. (2008) Developing indicators for a new ERA: Should we measure the policy impact of education research? *Australian Journal of Education*, 52(2): 117–28.

Weimer, D. L. and Vining, A. R. (2005) *Policy Analysis: Concepts and Practice*. 4th edn. New Jersey: Prentice Hall.

Weiss, C. (1979) The many meanings of research utilization, *Public Administration Review*, 39(5): 426–31.

——(1989) Congressional committees as users of analysis, *Journal of Policy Analysis and Management*, 8(3): 411–31.

Yeatman, A. (Ed.) (1998) *Activism and the Policy Process*. Sydney: Allen & Unwin.

Young, M. F. D. (1998) *The Curriculum of the Future – From the 'New Sociology of Education' to a Critical Theory of Learning*. London: Falmer.

32
Last words

Why doctoral study?

P. Thomson and M. Walker

As the conclusion to this weighty *Doctoral Companion*, we want to reconsider the purposes of doctoral studies. Readers may think that it is odd that we have placed these comments at the end, but we have done so precisely because this is what we want readers to remember as they close the book. Many of today's doctoral students, we think, are faced with three myths during their study – that methodology is a matter of technique, the point of the thesis is to add new knowledge, and the task of the researcher is to disseminate knowledge in both scholarly and public fora. We will address these three myths and offer some alternative ways of thinking about what it means to do scholarly work.

Myth one: learning to do research is about the acquisition of a set of tools and techniques

All major social science publishers carry burgeoning lists of research methods texts – general encyclopaedic volumes that address major traditions of enquiry, and more specialised volumes that give details and examples of modes of generating and analysing data. There are also some philosophical texts that focus on questions of epistemology and methodology, the basis on which we claim to know things and thus establish an approach to methods. If we were to go on sheer quantity, the plethora of books about methods might suggest that this is the most important aspect of research. However, many research methods texts do gesture at questions of knowledge, although these are often again rhetorically attached to methods. Thus, we have the quantitative and qualitative wars, with the new orthodoxy of 'mixed methods' as the means of maintaining peace between them.

Doctoral students, when seeing these texts, and perhaps also influenced by research training provisions and the default thesis structure, generally address these questions in a specific chapter called methodology. Such chapters in our experience too often gesture at – or worse still – labour through a discussion of quantitative and qualitative methods, before going on to outline the specific techniques that have been used. Too rarely do they justify their methodological (rather than a methods) choice – for example, action research rather than ethnography. Students may include a short discussion about episte-mology, but many hesitate to take a categorical stance, unless they have opted for something oppositional such as feminist poststructuralism (Gallagher 2008; Jackson and Mazzei 2009; Lather 2007), or a decolonising position (Bishop and Glynn 1999; Jaya 2001; Smith 1999), which begins from the premise that knowledge is cultural (see Connell 2007 for an explicit working out of this position). In their reluctance to position themselves, many of these hesitant writers, we suggest, leave aside some more basic questions about the purposes of doctoral study.

Some years ago Thomas Popkewitz (1984) wrote a book about research methodology that contained no discussion of research methods. We work with his particular text in some detail here because we think it succinctly deconstructs the singular focus on pro-cesses that is now found in many doctoral 'programmes'. Ironically, this book preceded the fetishisation of methods 'training'. Popkewitz argued in his introduction that

[R]esearch is often thought of as a series of techniques in statistics, testing or observation that are practiced independently of questions, assumptions or concepts. Labels such as qualitative or quantitative research, for example, ignore the under-lying values and commitments of science that give variation to the use of statistics or field study.

Popkewitz 1984: ix

Popkewitz argues that, rather than being about the dispassionate application of pro-cesses and instruments, research exists within specific discourse communities of practice in which there are explicit and tacit agreements about shared ways of working and of 'seeing the world' (p. 3). All data generation and its analysis 'emerge from some theory about what the world is like and about how the phenomena of that world ... are to be given coherence' (p. 8). The job of enquiry, he suggests, is to 'search for new metaphors for thinking about everyday affairs', which 'enable people to rethink and give coherence to daily events that before seemed incomprehensible or troubling' (p. 7). And even though different communities of researchers, or sciences, address different kinds of questions and contain their own rationalities and conflicts, disagreements about methods within and between disciplines Popkewitz reasons, are generally about underlying con-ceptions of the world and its possibilities – that is they are political as well as methodo-logical and epistemological. Some research seeks implicitly or explicitly to uphold the status quo or to revise it just a little, whereas other research works with subjugated knowledges and/or seeks to provide alternative understandings and ways of seeing, acting on and being in the world.

Popkewitz notes that a focus on techniques and procedures produces three limitations in research, namely:

- It produces 'knowledge that is often trivial and socially conservative' because of the lack of connection with specific social and philosophical contexts
- It obscures the varying competing traditions of enquiry, which either form the basis of differing approaches or constitute different ways of using the same techniques, and
- It works to 'mystify social arrangements' because social science not only attempts to describe what happens in the world, but also provides people with an orienting set of possibilities (p. ix).

He concludes that it is thus not only important to understand the rituals and routines of technique that are held to be valid within specific research communities, but also to examine the ways in which research functions to:

- Provide a rationale for changing social and economic conditions, making these changes seem reasonable
- Provide a mechanism to legitimate institutional interests, and
- Give direction to alternative social arrangements (p. 12).

We agree with Popkewitz.

We think it is important that doctoral researchers are exposed to debates about the social and cultural production of knowledge. Research is not simply a question of taking a question from extant literatures or policy settings, applying a set of standard operating procedures to collecting data that already exists in a world external to the research endeavour, and simply writing it up, as if writing were not a creative and culturally specific process of producing meanings. We hope that all doctoral researchers are encouraged to ask unsettling questions about their research, namely

- Where did the question and categories of understanding that are used in this enquiry come from? What were the underpinning assumptions about the world? To what ends were they directed? In whose interests did they work?
- What kinds of knowledges are being produced through this enquiry? To what ends are they directed? In whose interests does this enquiry work?

Myth two: the test of a doctorate is whether it produces new knowledge

Doctoral students are nearly always told that their task is to add something to knowledge – something new. This often creates mild panic, as what counts as new, original and innovative, particularly in a knowledge economy, is a moot point. However, underpinning this anxiety-producing notion is a particular conception of knowledge.

In the additive model, knowledge is conceptualised as if it were a thing and the process of research one of finding the thing and adding to an existing pile of other things. Perhaps it is a stone, and what is being built is a dry stone wall. Perhaps it is a seed and what is being grown is a thick forest. Or perhaps it is dirt and we are adding to a large heap that is deposited layer on layer, year after year like so much landfill. We hesitate to keep adding similes but they serve to make the point. As we have already suggested, not all knowledge is the same; it works in particular interests and in particular ways. What's more, the knowledge produced in doctoral, or indeed any, research only makes meaning because of the ways in which we theorise it. Simply reporting a set of findings is insufficient. We need to elaborate what the findings mean, asking questions such as 'why is this so?' and 'How did it get to be this way?'. In order to do this researchers often have to draw on various forms of theory to help make the argument that the findings are significant (see Anyon 2009; Dressman 2008; Thomas 2007). But there is no getting away from the fact that some knowledges are just more important than others because they have a broader sweep, allow us to make more sense of the world, and/or disrupt taken-for-granted ways of thinking about things. Although it may be an ambition to generate such knowledge from research, it rarely occurs. More humble definitions of contribution are required – a new voice in the conversation, a different angle and slant on something that many are concerned about.

In a chapter reflecting on the role of academics as public intellectuals, Craig Calhoun (2008) argues for social science for public knowledge. He addresses the question we posed in the previous section – In whose interest does this research work? – and argues that the research topics we choose to address, as well as the technique and the outcome, are vitally important. He suggests that current research policies, which argue for public 'engagement' of researchers, obscure the relationships between scholarly agendas, the public interest and public policy agendas (p. 299). Calhoun proposes that simply reaching a broader public audience ignores the importance of social science that addresses pressing public issues. This is not to ignore the importance of blue skies research nor debates about the maintenance of standards of research, he suggests, but rather to argue for more of what he calls 'real time social science'.

'Real time social science'

- Is directly responsive to public issues that are already subject to public debate/policy making
- Brings knowledge into public discussion in policy making time scales
- Is dependent on longer term scholarship already under way about rapidly changing social circumstances (p. 300).

According to Calhoun, academic researchers ought not to understand 'real time' as the task of simply bringing techniques to problems identified by policy makers. Instead, researchers should choose topics for enquiry that emerge from an analysis of what is important in the world around them, and part of their endeavour ought to involve asking why problems are posed in particular ways and with what implications. The development of better theory and more robust methods are important, Calhoun asserts, in order to strengthen the capacities to perform well when called on to address public debates or policy. He cautions that the point is not that all social science should be harnessed to the immediate task of addressing public debates of public policy. Some division of labour is appropriate along with a diversity of task. But it is a crucial point that social science demonstrates its usefulness by informing public knowledge, not simply accumulating esoteric knowledge inside disciplines (p. 301).

This was an argument made most vehemently by the late French social scientist Pierre Bourdieu, whose corpus of work includes detailed analyses of the ways in which the academy functioned to promote self-serving scholarship rather than address issues that arose from material social conditions (e.g. Bourdieu 1988; 1990; Bourdieu et al. 1991; Bourdieu et al. 1995; Bourdieu and Wacquant 1992). Bourdieu also undertook studies that addressed key social issues, inter alia, the production of privilege in and through education (e.g. Bourdieu and Passeron 1977; 1979), the housing market (Bourdieu 2005), the impact of changing industrial and economic conditions on ordinary people (Bourdieu et al. 1999) and the ways in which the arts and lifestyle were implicated in the production of social and political privilege (e.g. Bourdieu 1984; 1991; 2000). In his later years he also became more politically engaged outside the academy, engaging in public debates by mobilising the body of scholarship he had built up (see Bourdieu 1996; 1998; 2003). Bourdieu is a tangible example of Calhoun's thesis, that is, that 'real time social science' is addressed to issues of public concern and is able to literally 'speak' at appropriate times in important public debates.[1] Importantly, this speaking mobilises the 'weight' of specialist expertise in the service of expanding democratic, public deliberation.

'Real time social science' is thus not the same as applied social science, Calhoun suggests, and does not need to come at the expense of basic social science knowledge, which: provides the basis for further scholarship 'like good theory, a useful research technique or an exemplary research study'; 'articulates a pattern in social life, a casual relationship' or a new explanation; or is of 'widespread significance' (p. 303). Such work is not the lot of most scholars, let alone doctoral researchers. Nevertheless, all of us can aspire to research that is not only authoritative, well reasoned and well produced, but which is also directed to issues that are not just of interest to a small academic elite. This is not the same as an aspiration to generate 'new knowledge'. It is instead a commitment to addressing issues that are not arcane, trivial, elitist or self-serving, but which might form part of an endeavour to clarify understandings and inform social activities, relations and agendas. And the question of technique, therefore, becomes one of ensuring that the knowledge that we produce is not high risk, but as reliable as we can make it, given the uncertain times in which we live.

Myth three: the task of researchers is to pass on their knowledge to the public

It may seem from the previous section that we are advocating that all doctoral researchers ought to aspire to become active in public debates, but this is not the case. We do, however, want to pursue further the question of what it might mean to bring social science about matters of pressing public concern into public debate.

Many countries now have research policy agendas that suggest that research must engage with national concerns. This is a matter of knowledge 'transfer' or knowledge 'mobilisation' or 'research impact'. In the UK, for example, competitive research funds are now only to be given to bids that can demonstrate some likely social or economic impact or an impact on the field of knowledge production itself. Research quality is also to be judged on the capacities of various institutions and disciplines to have 'impact'. In such policy agendas, knowledge is again understood as a thing that is generated in one place (the university) and then shifted to another (business, government, civic structures). Research is also understood as either being foundational or somehow to be applied, rather than being part of a 'real time social science'.

Such research policies play out in disciplinary communities, where debates about 'impact' are both noisy and worried. One key agreement among those who work in higher education is the assertion that university teaching constitutes an important 'impact' and 'transfer' activity, which ought not to be ignored. The promotion of teaching as an important function and the potential contribution of research foregrounds a key social role for a liberal higher education – that of educating ever greater numbers of the population to ensure the generational (re)production of common cultural and scientific understandings and endeavour (Nussbaum 1997). Doctoral researchers who are considering how their research might make a difference need to consider the ways in which their findings might inform their own teaching and that of others. Research-led teaching is a goal not to be passed over in the search for 'contribution'.

It is, of course, important to make the point that university-based researchers are not the only public intellectuals and to suggest that this is or could be the case is a conceit.

Indeed arguably, many public intellectuals now sit well outside of higher education in 'quality newspapers' for example. However, this book and this chapter are directed towards doctoral and other researchers and so we confine our remarks to higher education in this instance.

We want to examine examples of four disciplinary discussions before offering an alternative developed by philosopher Linda Alcoff. The four come from geography, social work, education and sociology.

Geography

In an extended book review, Noel Castree (2006) argues for geography as a public intellectual activity. He notes that the notion of a public intellectual is a difficult one in contemporary times. It raises a spectre of elitism and arrogance because

> [T]o lay claim to the signifier public intellectual runs the risk of sounding insufferably pompous while opening oneself to unfavourable comparisons with the 'real' public intellectuals of yesteryear, like George Orwell or Jean-Paul Sartre.
>
> Castree 2006: 396

The texts Castree examined are not of interest here, rather it is his analysis of why they exemplify public intellectual activity in geography. He claims, resonating with the arguments made by Calhoun (2008) that we reported in the previous section, that the authors under discussion 'apply years of academic training to issues of broad public concern' (p. 397). Furthermore, they:

- Address the current globalised political situation
- Offer analyses of live political issues
- Try to identify leverage points for progressive change
- Present readers with grand analyses
- See themselves as speaking truth to power (p. 399)
- Make few attempts to relate arguments to extant academic debates
- Are highly accessible, make light use of references and are written in essayistic style (p. 400)
- Offer compelling narratives
- Are addressed to a defined audience (p. 401) identified as a numerically significant sub and counter public.

In short, they deploy intellectual capital built up during a successful academic career to inform a literate and not necessarily academic audience (p. 403)

Castree notes that publics are also in part created by public intellectuals and he reiterates the arguments made by Edward Said (1994) in his Reith lecture series that the value of public intellectuals is collective, and that their/our task is one of proliferating the voices of criticism (p. 405). Castree suggests that geographers must not only respond to events and provide answers, but must also take issue with the significant questions of the day (p. 406).

In a critical engagement with Castree's text, Ulrich Oslender (2007) observes that those who are most commonly cited as public intellectuals are male and white, and very often from the French traditions of public intellectual life. This indeed was the example that we gave above, that of Pierre Bourdieu; Castree listed many more. However, Oslender suggests, this French tradition of public debate and commentary is now subject to and the subject of a mediatised celebrity culture, in which most French intellectuals have not only 'become self satisfied with their role in society as commentators on themes constructed and diffused by the mass media' but also indifferent to questions of social injustice (p. 103). Despite his concerns about dead white men, Oslender, however, does take up the Bourdieuian notion of 'the collective intellectual' – networks of critical scholars not celebrity individuals – who oppose conservatism and offer political alternatives. Oslender reasons that geographers in particular ought to adopt their own theorisations about public space – that it is now multiple and diffuse and networked – in order to take up this collective public intellectual activity.

Social work

Social work has a long tradition of public intellectual activity. In the UK, for example, the work of social work pioneers such as Joseph Rowntree is etched into public policy memories. However, it is difficult to find the equivalent today. In an article analysing the retreat of social workers from public debates, Howard Karger and Marie Hernandez (2004) offer three reasons:

> *The institutional conditions under which social workers are employed*. Karger and Hernandez note that contemporary public and not-for-profit corporatised social welfare organisations actively discourage employees from public engagement with debates about controversial issues. Furthermore, working conditions mitigate against involvements outside of paid employment.
>
> *Narrow ideas about professionalism*. The adoption of 'micro practice and hyper-professionalism' now valued in social work creates the conditions for a 'partial withdrawal from its earlier social justice mission' (p. 54). Social work has now transformed, Karger and Hernandez argue, 'into a marketplace commodity as skill-building replaced intellectual training' and 'a narrow preoccupation with methods and skills' has replaced 'a utopian vision' (p. 58).
>
> *The insularity of academic life*. A preoccupation with the academic discipline, its acceptance and status have created impermeable disciplinary and professional boundaries. Because it lacks a 'clear body of discipline-specific knowledge', they advocate a reconnection with 'the sociological, philosophical, economic and social theories that informed social work pioneers' (p. 61). They urge the profession to eschew a view of social work as 'technical/vocational rather than academic' (p. 62), and to develop research that 'find(s) a sub-specialisation, stake(s) a claim to it, and then mine(s) it relentlessly' (p. 63).

In sum, the two authors suggest that the discipline needs to re-find itself and re-establish its intellectual traditions in order to build the basis for new forms of public engagement, which work in the interests of the client groups it claims to serve.

Education

Education, too, demonstrates a nostalgia for an era of public intellectual activity that once was.

396

Ivor Goodson (1999) harks back to the UK tradition of school-based research in which teachers were promoted as agents of curriculum and school reform. Goodson argues that there is now a crisis of positionality in which the teaching profession is detached from its histories of collective action for social justice and divorced from visions of alternative futures. He suggests that when educators spoke of practitioners and the value of practice in times when the relatively benevolent welfare state governed, this was a progressive stance. However, in the Thatcher regime the arguments were translated by policy makers as a technicist orientation. Ironically, the promotion, through the actions of education public intellectuals such as Lawrence Stenhouse, of the importance of schooling as a site of development in education backfired under conservative policy regimes. It actively assisted the shift of teacher education into schools and out of universities, while at the same time the focus in universities become much more about status as former teachers' colleges became absorbed into mainstream higher education.

The result Goodson argues is that now 'faculties of education and school practitioners talk past each other'. The 'paradox of progressivism', Goodson notes, is that 'the focus on applied research stripped the field of its capacity to critique' (p. 287). Goodson suggests that educators need to 'move beyond piecemeal pragmatism to envisioning a new moral order' (p. 290), and that this re-visioning will form the basis for new forms of public engagement.

In a similar vein William Pinar (2001) suggests that in the USA politically conservative policies have commodified the disciplines and separated curriculum from that of teaching. Debates about knowledge and pedagogy have largely been separated and suspended. He suggests that curriculum theory demands hybrid disciplinary relationships, and thus it needs to be reconnected with other disciplines within and outside the education field and that this is a precursor to curriculum theorising that recreates a public sphere about what it is important to know.

There are clear resonances here with the situation in social work and it is important to note that in higher education both social work and education are directly involved in the education of professionals, unlike the discipline of geography, or sociology, as we will demonstrate in a moment. The analysis of the problem of public intellectual work is different in each case, but there are also some broad similarities in the purposes of the disciplinary areas.

However, the debates about 'real work science' also appear in education. Henry Giroux will serve as one example of this strand of argument. Giroux (2003) suggests that in order to become public intellectuals academics must 'betray the legacy of professionalism and specialism' (p. 277). He, too, takes up Bourdieu's notion of the collective intellectual, but not he hastens to add, at the expense of scholarly rigour and artistry. 'Nor is it an excuse', he says, 'to substitute a celebrity-like, public-relations posturing for the important work of collective struggle and intervention' (p. 277). He argues that under marketised neoliberal policies, it is difficult for citizens to challenge the myth that they are merely consumers. Nevertheless, he suggests that there is a critical role for education and other social science intellectuals to focus on what is happening to children and young people. How a society views its children is, he proposes, a key to democratic health.

He asserts that neoliberalism wages war on children.

As the social contract between adult society and children disappears, the old ideology of public investment and social renewal has given way increasingly to repression. For instance children, especially children of colour, are increasingly portrayed as a danger to society.

Giroux 2003: 179

Therefore, he suggests, researchers and others concerned about this situation have a moral obligation to use children as the referent for broader discussions. He notes that there is almost no mention of children in debates about globalisation and wars on terror He proposes, in line with Calhoun's case (2008) for the prime importance of the choice of research topic, that

[Y]outh provide faculty and administrators with a political and moral referent for addressing the relationship between knowledge and power, learning and social change, and values and classroom social relations as they bridge the gap between the diverse public spheres that youth inhabit and the university as a site of socialization and public engagement.

Giroux 2003: 182

Sociology

Sociology has perhaps not suffered quite the same level of nostalgia as social work and education. Boasting influential public figures, such as 'Third Way' proponent Anthony Giddens in the UK, the internal disciplinary debates are more about the different kinds of public intellectual activity that are possible, desirable and morally defensible.

Bryan Turner's 2005 presidential address to the British Sociology Association (Turner 2006a) offered a mapping of the national history of public intellectual activity within sociology. He argued that British sociology had been heavily dependent on the migration of postwar Jewish refugees whose intellectual activity was forged in turbulent conditions, which not only required, but also produced critical opposition. Nevertheless, there was he argued, a distinctive British sociological tradition that focused on questions of class, gender, social citizenship and race. Scholars did engage in the postwar period in vigorous public debates on these topics. However, when Britain became much more affluent and consumerist, sociology followed this trend and many become absorbed in studies of markets, cultures and consumption. This then formed the basis for their public engagement. What was missing, he argued, were studies that focused on the broader implications of Britain's decline as an imperial power and the subsequent silences in public debates as the effects of those shifts and changes become more apparent.

Sitting at the heart of this argument were two important assumptions − (i) that public intellectual activity is produced from its social context, but that it can also intervene in it, and (ii) sociologists did not choose the topics to research that were to be of significance in the future. In Calhoun's (2008) terms, sociology had not lived up to its possibilities to engage in 'real time social science'.

Turner's article provoked debate, as it was intended to do, and two responses appeared to accompany the text of his address in the *British Journal of Sociology*. One was from Neil Smelser (2006), who queried Turner's casual explanation of crisis and critique. This was acknowledged and accepted later by Turner. Smelser also suggested that attributing a blanket sociological lethargy to (studies of) the effects of consumerism also dodged more specific explanations. He proposed that it was important to also focus on 'the close relationship between sociology and the Labour party', the 'continuing assault' from the right on sociologists as 'socialists' as well as a less-than-respectful press (p. 216), paradigm competitions within the discipline and the effects of Thatcherist policies on higher education, and 'the government imposition of weighty productivity and accountability measures on the universities that clearly affected academic's morale' (p. 217). The other commentary was from George Ritzer (2006), famous for his 'McDonaldisation' thesis of contemporary consumerist life (e.g. Ritzer 1993; 1998). Ritzer offered an 'if you think Britain's bad you ought to try living in the USA' narrative, sprinkled with anecdotes about comparative lack of media attention and commercial publisher interest combined with a defence of sociological studies of consumerism.

Turner's response (2006b) recalled other contributions to the debates in sociology, explaining that his intention had been primarily concerned with the question of whether anything could be learnt from the postwar history of sociology that might help rebuild it. Recognising the difficulties with some of his analyses, he undertook a further critique, but held to the ambition for the discipline on the grounds that 'it is important to have a convincing large scale vision of where a society should be going and some plausible and detailed prescriptions for how to get there' (p. 347). He provocatively noted that 'we cannot blame journalists or their publishers for the fact that we do not have an audience'; it was not simply the lack of a public sphere or public intellectuals that were at issue, he argued, but 'the absence of a plausible message' (p. 248) that addressed pressing social, political and economic concerns.

Towards an alternative framing

Philosopher Linda Alcoff (2002) offers a comprehensive way of understanding the public obligations of scholarship. She notes that, whereas in countries such as the USA and the UK public intellectual work can be at expense of career/tenure, this is not the case in all countries – for example, Latin America has an expectation of scholarly engagement in public life. She argues that public work is devalued in the academy because it is seen as lacking rigor and challenge and often as compromised. The term public intellectual is equated with elitism and with celebrity intellectuals who have made it onto primetime TV and newspaper columns. She proposes instead the notion of the 'publically engaged intellectual ... who spends a significant portion of his or her time engaged with the nonacademic public' (p. 524) in more local contexts (p. 525).

She proposes that there are three ways in which a publically engaged intellectual can be conceived:

1. As a permanent critic. But, she says, there are dangers here. Advocacy is not only seen as compromised but is also often worthy of derision. The feminist social critic, for example, is almost always cast as a moral prude or a closet authoritarian. Therefore, the permanent critic may be ineffective. Furthermore, the so-called independence of the university-based critic is not necessarily any more intellectually autonomous than those who offer defence of organisations or specific agendas from 'inside'. 'Pure neutrality', she argues, 'is an illusion that excuses the refusal to engage in self-reflexivity' (p. 527). And the 'fear of cooption that is expressed through the advocacy of independence assumes that one can devise a politics free from potential cooptation' (p. 528). Everyone argues from somewhere, she suggests, and it behoves all who claim to speak on behalf of, or to, the public to consider where that is and what it stands for.

2. As a populariser. Alcoff is more approving of this category of action. A populariser is someone who has taken ideas from the academy and translates them for a wider public. Critics of popularising activities assert that this 'sacrifices nuance and rigour in favour of clear examples and unambiguous claims' (p. 528). This idea, Alcoff notes, is based in a normative idea of the academy as a pure monastery cut off from the world. Although popularisers are seen as unoriginal and antitheoretical, Alcoff argues that the aim is valuable and need not sacrifice all nuance.

3. As a public theorist. This is Alcoff's preferred position – and also our own. Alcoff comments that theoretical development and creativity do not just happen back at the monastery (p. 530) but happen in most walks of life (see also McLaughlin 1996). She argues for a notion of 'doing theory in public' (p. 531). 'The public arena can be a space where intellectual work is done, where problems emerge to be addressed, and where knowledge and experience are gained that can address a variety of issues, such as speaking for others, labor/academic alliances, public and democratic deliberation, the nature of white or male supremacy and heterosexual ... one can receive vital feedback' (p. 530).

This is public activity in which one is simultaneously teaching and learning (p. 533) and contra to the view that what happens in public is the corruption of academic rigour, Alcoff suggests the reverse.

> [P]ublicly engaged work is actually one of the BEST sites from which to engage in at least certain kinds of intellectual work, not because one is merely applying and testing theory developed in the academy to the public domain nor because one can simply gather raw data from which to build theory, but rather because the public domain is sometimes the best or only place in which to alter one's thoughts ... and thus to engage in intellectual work.
>
> Alcoff 2002: 533

Alcoff conceives of knowledge 'transfer' or 'mobilisation not as transmission, but as the testing of metaphors, beliefs and theories in and with the public. She sees the public domain as more than a sphere 'for gathering data, proselytizing or popularizing' (p. 534), but as a site where there can be reciprocity, conversations, debates and mutual respect.

In sum

We are aware that, in addressing what we understand as three myths about research in general and doctoral research in particular, we have outlined an ambitious agenda. We hope it is not a terrifying one. We do not see that any of this can be simply accomplished or can be achieved through the one agenda of doctoral research. We want rather to offer a way of thinking about the work of research, its value and its conduct, that might be more ethical and truncated than that which is generally presented in doctoral training workshops and courses.

In the spirit of this chapter, we are interested in your feedback on our argument here, and on the text as a whole. We do sincerely believe research is dialogic, and we invite you to continue the conversation with us, your peers and your scholarly colleagues.

Notes

1 See Swartz (2003) and Wacquant (2005) for further explication of Bourdieu as a public intellectual.

References

Alcoff, L. M. (2002) Does the public intellectual have intellectual integrity? *Metaphilosophy*, 33(5), 521–34.

Anyon, J. (2009) *Theory and educational research. Towards critical social explanation.* New York: Routledge.

Bishop, R. and Glynn, T. (1999) *Culture counts: Changing power relations in education.* Palmerston North: Dunmore Press.

Bourdieu, P. (1984) *Distinction. A social critique of the judgment of taste.* Trans. R. Nice. Boston, MA: Harvard University Press.

——(1988) *Homo academicus.* Trans. P. Collier. Stanford, CA: Stanford University Press.

——(1990) *In other words. Essays towards a reflexive sociology.* Stanford, CA: Stanford University Press.

——(1991) *The love of art: European art museums and their public.* Trans. C. Beattie and N. Merriman. Cambridge: Polity Press.

——(1996) *On television.* Trans. P. P. Ferguson. New York: The New Press.

——(1998) *Acts of resistance. Against the new myths of our time.* Cambridge, Oxford: Polity Press.

——(2000) *Pascalian meditations.* Trans. R. Nice. Oxford: Polity Press.

——(2003) *Firing back. Against the tyranny of the market 2.* Trans. L. Wacquant. New York: The New Press.

——(2005) *The social structures of the economy.* Cambridge: Polity.

Bourdieu, P., Chamberon, J.-C. and Passeron, J. C. (1991) *The craft of sociology.* Berlin: de Gruyter.

Bourdieu, P., *et al.* (1999) *The weight of the world. Social suffering in contemporary societies.* Trans. P. P. Ferguson. Stanford, CA: Stanford University Press.

Bourdieu, P. and Passeron, J. C. (1977) *Reproduction in society, education and culture.* London: Sage.

——(1979) *The inheritors, French students and their relation to culture.* Chicago, IL: The University of Chicago Press.

Bourdieu, P., Passeron, J.-C. and de Saint Martin, M. (1995) *Academic discourse.* Trans. R. Teese, ed. 1965. Stanford, CA: Stanford University Press.

Bourdieu, P. and Wacquant, L. (1992) *An invitation to reflexive sociology.* Chicago, IL and London: University of Chicago Press.

Calhoun, C. (2008) Social science as public knowledge. In S. Eliaeson and R. Kalleberg (Eds). *Academics as public intellectuals.* Newcastle: Cambridge Scholars Press.

Castree, N. (2006) Geography's new public intellectuals? *Antipode*, 38(2): 396–412.

Connell, R. (2007) *Southern theory. The global dynamics of knowledge in social science.* Cambridge: Polity.

Dressman, M. (2008) *Using social theory in educational research. A practical guide.* New York: Routledge.

Gallagher, K. (Ed.) (2008) *The methodological dilemma. Creative, critical and collaborative approaches to qualitative research.* New York: Routledge.

Giroux, H. (2003) Betraying the intellectual tradition: public intellectuals and the crisis of youth, *Language and intercultural communication*, 3(3): 172–86.

Goodson, I. (1999) The educational researcher as public intellectual. *British Educational Research Journal*, 25(3): 277–97.

Jackson, A. Y. and Mazzei, L. A. (Eds) (2009) *Voice in qualitative inquiry. Challenging conventional, interpretative and critical conceptions in qualitative research.* London: Routledge.

Jaya, P. (2001) Do we really 'know' and 'profess'? Decolonising management knowledge. *Organisation Speaking Out*, 8(2): 227–33.

Karger, H. J. and Hernandez, M. T. (2004) The decline of the public intellectual in social work. *Journal of Sociology and Social Welfare*, XXXI(3): 51–68.

Lather, P. (2007) *Getting lost. Feminist efforts toward a double(d) science.* New York: State University of New York Press.

McLaughlin, T. (1996) *Street smarts and critical theory. Listening to the vernacular.* Madison, WI: University of Wisconsin Press.

Nussbaum, M. C. (1997) *Cultivating humanity. A classical defense of reform in liberal education.* Cambridge, MA: Harvard University Press.

Oslender, U. (2007) The resurfacing of the public intellectual: towards the proliferation of public spaces. *Acme: An International E-Journal for Critical Geographies*, 6(1): 98–123 (Available at www.acme-journal.org/vol116/UO116.pdf. Accessed 12 June 2009).

Pinar, W. (2001) The researcher as bricoleur: the teacher as public intellectual. *Qualitative Inquiry*, 7 (December): 696–700.

Popkewitz, T. (1984) *Paradigm and ideology in educational research. The social functions of the intellectual.* Lewes: Falmer Press.

Ritzer, G. (1993) *The McDonaldisation of society.* Thousand Oaks, CA: Pine Forge Press.

——(1998) *The McDonaldisation thesis.* Thousand Oaks, CA: Sage.

——(2006) Who's a public intellectual? *British Journal of Sociology*, 57(2): 209–13.

Said, E. W. (1994) *Representations of the Intellectual. The 1993 Reith Lectures.* London: Vintage.

Smelser, N. (2006) Comment on Bryan S Turner's 'British sociology and public intellectuals: consumer society and imperial decline'. *British Journal of Sociology*, 57(2): 215–17.

Smith, L. T. (1999) *Decolonising methodologies. Research and indigenous peoples.* London: Zed Books.

Swartz, D. (2003) From critical sociology to public intellectual: Pierre Bourdieu and politics. *Theory and Society*, 32, 791–823.

Thomas, G. (2007) *Education and theory. Strangers in paradigms.* Maidenhead: Open University Press.

Turner, B. (2006a) British sociology and public intellectuals: consumer society and imperial decline. *British Journal of Sociology*, 57(2): 169–88.

——(2006b) Public intellectuals, globalisation and the sociological calling: a reply to critics. *British Journal of Sociology*, 57(3), 345–51.

Wacquant, L. (Ed.) (2005) *Pierre Bourdieu and democratic politics.* Cambridge: Polity.

Index

worldviews and writing research 247–49
worthwhileness of research questions 172,
176–77, 177–78, 179, 180–81
wrapping-up, emotions of 290–91
Wright, R. 329, 330
writing: analytic process, writing about 210–11;
authoritatively about knowledge production
155–56; distancing and 99; emotions of
289–90; norms of writing, differences
between fields 305; style and argumentation
239–41; thinking and 109–10; writing
analytically 203–5, 206–9; writing review
sessions 108
Writing for Social Scientists (Becker, H.) 38–40
writing research 149–59, 244–54; aesthetics 253;
Carnegie Foundation for the Advancement of
Teaching 244–45; criteria for 253; deliberative
process of 245; diffidence 154, 157;
disconnection, problem of 158–59; electronic
dissertations 246–47; emotional attachment
151; ethical sensibility 253; experience and
stories 246; field of knowledge production,
engagement with 152, 155–56; grammar
police and 247; identity devaluation 151;
identity reconstitution 151; identity work,
research writing as 150–52; integrity 253;
interconnections of reading and thinking with
245; knowledge production, writing about
152, 155–56; language an approximate
medium 150; language and 246–47;
literatures, working with 152; literatures,
writing about 153–55; multimodality 157;
New London Group (NLG) 157, 158;
ontological relationship with language and
246–47, 252–53; *Oxford English Dictionary*

245; personalisation 151; positivism,
epistemological assumptions of 248;
reading and 245; reading scholarly texts 151;
research and writing, textual separation
of 149; research genres and 249–52; research
methods books 149; research practice 146–47;
research without writing, impossibility of 150;
research writing 150–52; rhetorical
conventions 248; rigour 253; self-conscious
method 253; sources 250; text work,
research writing as 150–52; textual scholarly
identity, ongoing process of development
156–58; thinking and 245; transformative
nature of 244–45; truth 253; utility 253;
verbal language and 246–47; verisimilitude
253; visual imagery and 246; vitality 253;
worldviews and 247–49; writerly decisions,
examples of 249–52; writing authoritatively
about knowledge production 155–56; writing
research proposal 132–33; and writing the
researcher 151

Yates, L. 3, 11, 295, 303, 306, 309
Yates, L. and Collins, C. 309
Yeatman, A. 382
Yeo, E. 104
Yin, R.K. 201
Young, E.H. and Lee, R.M. 283
Young, M.F.D. 378
Yu, K. 260

Zajda, J. 370, 371
Zeller, N. 191
Zeni, J. 260
Znaniecki, F 365